First Published by Sandie and Doug Webb 2017

Text Copyright Sandie and Doug Webb

Written and researched by Sandie and Doug Webb

British Library Cataloguing in Publication Data.

A catalogue record for this book is available from the British Library.

Cover designed and printed by Corsham Print.

Insert pages typeset and printed by Corsham Print.

IBSN 978-1-78808-800-8

FOREWORD

By Neil Carroll

Toolstation Director Marketing 2008 – 2016

In the Spring of 2005 I first met with the then Chairman of the Western League, Cliff Ashton, and I had little idea of what sponsorship was about. Toolstation was a small company and I had a correspondingly small marketing budget; the proportion that would be employed in sponsoring the League was substantial, and I had to decide whether it would provide enough publicity, compared with other options at the time. I recalled being at Screwfix the previous year when the decision was delivered from 'on high' that League sponsorship was no longer appropriate. Having only just moved to join the entrepreneurial team that had got Toolstation under way, it seemed to me that the opportunity to replace 'our competitor' was too good to miss. What a great decision it has turned out to be!

My personal sentiments about the Western League are now well established and do not revolve entirely around football. What has impressed me has been witnessing the small army of voluntary workers at club level – maintaining grounds and buildings, providing refreshments, working behind bars, coaching children, organising fixtures, booking (and providing) transport, and so on. All this because of – yes – a love of the game, but more in fact to do with an instinct to provide others with facilities, recreation, friendship and a sense of community.

This perspective was brought into focus when, in 2011, I noted that one club had made a point of displaying a 'mission statement' on its website. Was their primary objective to win the FA Vase, or to get into a higher league in the Pyramid? No. Under the heading, 'Our Purpose', they simply stated that – 'Our club exists to enable children to play football in a safe, enjoyable and encouraging way'.

Since then, this one phrase has shaped my attitude and outlook regarding the immense value that individual clubs, and the Western League, have brought to us all.

Over many years I, and Toolstation colleagues, have been welcomed wholeheartedly by Cliff Ashton, and later by his successor John Pool, as well as Board and Club officials alike. Several years on, I have learned a great deal about the commitment that sponsorship entails, and maybe a little about the world of grass-roots football.

First and foremost, sponsorship at this level is not about commerciality, it is about serving the community. It was a revelation in our early years of sponsorship to appreciate that, although the public focus for most clubs was on their 'first team', the majority ran multiple youth teams, events in other sports, fundraising events for all sorts of charitable endeavours, and social evenings of all kinds. Many Western League clubs are at the heart of their neighbourhood; indeed, the football clubhouse has become the sole 'community centre' in many small towns and villages.

Many club representatives continue to tell me that without Toolstation's support, they could not keep things going. I am inclined to believe that even without League sponsorship, the energy and commitment shown by so many of the people running their local club would prevail – however it is most gratifying to have a real sense that we are helping.

So, for Toolstation, sponsorship of the Western League has become less about publicity and more about 'doing our bit'. We live in a world where schools are having to sell off sports grounds just to keep going, and yet at the same time, unimaginable amounts of money are paid by broadcasters and advertisers into the top levels of sport. In this climate, it is simply the moral and responsible thing to do, to help balance that equation without trying to measure any 'advertising' benefit.

At the beginning of our term of sponsorship, our designers came up with the 'Toolstation League' shield, which was immediately adopted by the League, and within a very short space of time the League became widely referenced in that way. At the time of this 125-year anniversary, we happen to be the current 'borrowers' of the League's reputation. We are privileged to have the continued opportunity so to do, but we have the humility to recognise that – to paraphrase an advertising campaign for valuable watches – it is not the 'Toolstation League', we are merely helping to keep the Western League going for future generations.

It is a great pleasure to consider that once we complete the 2017/18 season, Toolstation will have sponsored the Western League for 13 years of its marvellous history. All at Toolstation hope to be involved for many more years to come, and wish the Western League another 125 vibrant seasons!

Neil Carroll

Summer 2017

Since the beginning of the 2005/2006 season as a league, and as members of that league, many have been delighted to get to know both Neil and his wife Pauline. Together with Adam Keates and his wife Jane, who have attended every Convention Weekend, and have become an integral part of the Western League family.

In recent times, they have been joined by John Meaden who is now the company's Marketing Director, and we look forward to seeing both John and his wife with the hope that they too enjoy the welcome that is given by clubs throughout the season and at our yearly weekend together.

THE WESTERN
FOOTBALL LEAGUE

THE STORY

INTRODUCTION

How it all began

It took vision and fortitude for our ancestors in Bristol to initiate the formation of a league to organise football in the West Country. With the English League barely four years old, and concentrated in the north of the country, the only southern example that our men of vision had to follow was that of the Birmingham and District League, who in their first three years had experienced all sorts of problems.

To put the span of one hundred and twenty-five years of the Western League into perspective, and to understand its history, it is important to take events within the social context of the time, and to look at what was initially happening in Bristol and the surrounding towns that facilitated its formation. It is also interesting to look at how Association Rules of the game changed throughout the period, which gives a deeper understanding of the nature of the sport as we know it today.

From the birth of the Football Association in 1863, both the social conditions and the attitudes of the working man changed the class consciousness of the country. That, combined with the alterations in work and leisure activities, and of course two World Wars, were also to effect changes in the game. The original rules were somewhat different throughout that time than they are now, and all of that, together with other factors, came together and resulted in football as we know it today; a national obsession and an international bond.

Many years prior to the introduction of football to the West Country, the Industrial Revolution had been in full swing, and with that there was a dramatic movement of the rural population into the towns and cities. Bristol's population increased so rapidly that in 1866, when a cholera epidemic killed 444 people in the City, there were as many as 60,000 people living in the Clifton area alone, the largest population mass for the area that had ever been seen.

A distinct divide between work and leisure had also occurred with the movement to industrialisation, which meant that families moving into Bristol from the countryside had to adapt, not only to new surroundings, but also to a loss of the leisure activities that had once been an integral part of their working lives.

It took until the middle of the 19th century for the working week to allow time for any leisure activity that was separate from working life conditions. It occurred when, after a long series of Factory Acts which were instigated by the Earl of Shaftsbury in 1871, that some semi-skilled workers were given a half-day off on a Saturday, enabling those hard -pressed Victorian workers a newly found, albeit limited, leisure time.

Until that point both men and women had been expected to work long hours, six days a week, allowing little time for enjoyment. With the only day-off being a Sunday, there was no time to enjoy sport, as all were expected to

"DRIBBLING" IN THE ASSOCIATION GAME

honour the Sabbath. The hard-working population eventually got its reward with the introduction of that half-day, allowing the workers to finish at 2pm and hurry off to catch the kick-off at their local ground.

Cricket was the nation's game up until the 1880s, but, of course, the summer game took all day to complete, which put it out of the reach of most working-class men and boys who had to utilise their meagre time-off to the maximum. The limited time at leisure, therefore, favoured the game of football, both as a participant and spectator sport. Such was the growth in its popularity that the first ever International match was held on 30th November 1872 between Scotland and England at Hamilton Crescent, Partick, when over 4000 spectators watched the match. It was reported as 'a dull affair that failed to produce a goal'.

In the Bristol area until the late 1870s, rugby, boxing and cricket were the main sports, even though Association football had been popular in the North of England from the mid-1860s, and it was as late as the 1880s that Association teams began to appear locally and play matches on a friendly basis.

Many of those games saw the rules of the day decided by the players and officials in accordance with the type of players who turned up and the physical size of the team, with rugby rules chosen for the more robust and larger turn-outs. The length of each half was agreed prior to kick-off which made for a chaotic and often frustrating day's sport for both the players and supporters alike.

While the sport was gaining in popularity locally, a movement toward the health of the nation was also growing. A national cholera epidemic had decimated large numbers of the work force in the late 1860s and that, combined with other factors, led the Government to realise that the country could not be defended efficiently, or continue as a world leader, if the nation's working men were unhealthy.

With those areas of influence came an involvement by both the church and factory owners in sport, the former of which spawned a movement called the 'Muscular Christians' who firmly believed that games such as soccer promoted Christianity among the poorer sections of the communities, focusing mind and body away from beer and women, and countering the vices that were reported in villages, towns and cities throughout the country.

It may seem surprising to learn that the 1884 Reform Act, which gave the mass male electorate the vote, also influenced the rise of the game, but it was through this that many prominent politicians and other members of the upper-classes found a sudden love for the game of soccer as it grew in popularity, with the working man's vote all important at election times.

It became a trend, by the late 19th century, for many important members of society to be seen backing the sport by contributing time in attending matches, together with presenting trophies and medals to local teams; something that was demonstrated by the MP for Bristol, Mr Edward Colston, who had the distinction of purchasing and presenting the first Cup to the League in 1893.

The Reform Act had been partly forced by the spread of a more literate population thanks to the various education reforms of the century, which also meant that from the 1880s local newspapers began to give more coverage to the workers game and often posted results of the local soccer matches in their company office windows.

The introduction of postal and telegraphic services also contributed to the growth of soccer to convey results, but communications were often a problem in the early days, and it will be shown later how some Western League clubs occasionally used ingenious way to communicate half-time scores to their villages.

It is a widespread belief reported in the press nowadays that the bad behavior associated with football is a recent phenomenon. As you read this tribute to the Western League, however, you will realise that the over-zealous behaviour of some fans, players and officials, in the very early years of the game, continually formed and reformed the rules of the sport. Despite many eminent studies in recent years attempting to explain our 'modern disease', clubs and crowds are, in fact, better behaved today than on many occasions during our League's early life.

The concept of organising football into a league system, in which teams played on a home and away basis, was only introduced to the west with the birth of the Bristol and District League, which widened its net to become the Western Football League after its first three years of existence.

League systems then grew in popularity, partly in recognition that professionalism was permitted in 1888, money had to be generated to pay players wages and make profits for the companies that owned the larger football clubs. That, in turn, meant that spectators who paid to watch had to be guaranteed not just that two teams would turn up, but also that within reason the game would take place at the specified time published, something that did not always happen when the sport was played on a friendly, casual basis.

The year 1892 also saw the English FA introduce an Amateur Cup competition, thus emphasizing further the distinction between amateur and professional clubs, and while the Western League remained amateur until 1897, when the concept of professionalism was eventually incorporated, it was to signal the demise of some of the more successful founder member clubs, who discovered that the cost of maintaining their status was too much to cope with. Even in those heady days, when gates could often be more than 1,000, some clubs still struggled with their finances; demonstrating that some things really don't change much.

A final factor that goes to explain the growth in the popularity of soccer in Bristol, both as a spectator and a participant sport, is the transportation system of the time. The introduction of the safety bicycle by John Kemp in 1885 had produced a form of transport that could be enjoyed by the masses, making visits to nearby towns and villages possible for many teams throughout the west. The city also had the extra advantage of an extensive horse-drawn tram-system, enabling comparative ease of travel within its boundaries. That in turn opened-up the possibility of teams travelling to opponent's grounds together, and of spectator's congregating to watch the games with ease. The main Brunel rail network passed through Temple Meads station and made access easier to clubs from towns a greater distance away who were then able, with considerable effort, to test their skills against the City sides.

It is also interesting to note that, when the League began, there was already a growing industry for football kits, but, at first, some Bristol and District clubs would turn out wearing non-standard kits and even ordinary footwear. Of course, the compulsory numbering of player's shirts did not come into operation until as late as 1939, and so it must have been very difficult to referee a game under those circumstances, until the eventual rule to standardize the playing kit was agreed.

The ball of the day was heavy, especially compared to the ones kicked around the parks all over the world today, making injuries to the feet all too common if attacked without the correct large and cumbersome boots. It did not take long, therefore, for pharmaceutical companies to realise that there was money to be made in extending their range to include specialist medicines and liniment to treat the injured footballer.

With all those conditions in place, in a country that was rapidly changing, the story begins. It is a story that now spans 125 years, and one that involves countless thousands of men and women who have devoted themselves to keeping football alive in their villages, towns and cities.

Many well-known names are associated with the vision that was needed throughout the decades - with many more still to come. While in the previous 'View from the Terraces' specific reference was made to such individuals as Mr 'Personality-Plus' Les Phillips, whose introduction of the Annual

Convention at which we all meet as friends without the encumbrance of the rivalry on the field of play, over such a long span of time the names are too numerous to list. It is, however, both those present and future members of the Western Football League who work relentlessly for their clubs, that are the reason to believe the best is yet to come.

An organisation such as the Western League is stronger than its composite clubs, and will continue to flourish long after its great administrators and participants have gone. While this book is a small tribute to record 125 years of soccer in the West Country, it records just a moment in time, and while the human body is frail with no-one alive today who was born in the year 1892, the body of the Western League continues to grow in strength with the passing years.

For the Centenary celebrations, the story of the Western Football League was told in *'A View from the Terraces'* through the experiences of a football veteran, Tom, who reflected life as he lived it, with the good times always remaining fresh in his mind.   With Tom gone, the story goes on in a world that continues to offer up its own challenges and, while using references to his enduring memories, the story is now taken up to give 'Another View…'

CHAPTER 1

The Bristol and District League

Tom opened the story in the centenary book with these words; *'To me there was something very special about 24ᵗʰ September 1892; it was the day that I came into the world. I didn't take long to learn that the day was also special for another event that took place, as my father was Association football mad, and one of the Victorian pioneers of the game in the West Country. Because of this he missed my birth as he was out watching one of the first games to be played in the new Bristol and District League. I was told later that I was named Thomas after the best footballer that he saw that day who played for the Wiltshire club of Trowbridge Town'.*

As Tom's words demonstrated, football was already popular and had been gaining support through the 1880s in Bristol, but there were problems for supporters and players alike because each game was on a casual friendly basis. One snag about playing such unstructured football was that the time of kick-off was usually left on a very loose basis, which would often mean a long cold wait for supporters and players alike before both teams turned up to play; and of course, sometimes the visiting team did not arrive at all if a more attractive fixture was found with another club.

Because of that it was soon found that the Association game was beginning to lose popularity in the west, and by the start of 1892 the game was at its lowest ebb, with many prominent proponents of the sport expressing real concern about the future. Those concerns were soon addressed by Percy Stout of Gloucester, who suggested that the introduction of a League system would solve indiscipline, and add structure; which seemed to appeal to many of the men present at that meeting who were anxious to see a solution to the decline.

After many discussions, it was then decided to adopt the English League system, in which teams played on a home and away basis, with two points for a win and one for a draw, and a league table then drawn up from those results to determine the winning club; a solution that was seen to be the way to go to satisfy both players and supporters alike. The implementation of such a solution did not come without its own problems, however, as the very system it was based on was the first of its kind in the world, and the English League seemed to be dealing with all sorts of growing pains.

Around the same time, in February 1892 a meeting was called by Woolwich Arsenal to discuss a similar proposal to introduce a Southern Football League along the same lines, but the idea was not adopted, and it would be two more years before Millwall resurrected the proposal and their league was formed.

From that early suggestion by Mr Stout, it was only a matter of months before the first recorded meeting took place on the 30ᵗʰ March 1892 at the Russell Hotel, Lawrence Weston, where the Victorian men from both the city and surrounding towns and villages unanimously agreed that the new venture would be called the 'Bristol and District League'. A committee was then elected to organise affairs that comprised of: Messrs. A Lacey-Sweet, J R Riddell, AW Francis – who presided over the meeting, TB Summers, WA Deakin, FW Yates, CT Bryant and EA Young. Mr Summers was appointed the Hon. Secretary and the clubs present were: Bedminster, Clifton, Eastville Rovers, Mangotsfield, St George and Warmley.

The news of the venture was not universally welcomed, with the cricket fraternity as wary as ever about anything that might accommodate a rise in the sport taking popular support away from them. Their initial objections were overcome, however, by agreeing not to start the season until after the summer game had finished; which would also suit many clubs in the years to come who shared facilities on local cricket grounds.

There were also objections from some of the local County Football Associations, ironically with Gloucester particularly vocal about the possibility of the new league taking support from their highly popular Senior Cup competition, but as many of the prominent proponents of the Bristol and District League were also members of those organisations, the objections were soon overcome.

That summer the committee continued in their quest to formalise football in the area, and a further meeting took place on 31st August 1892 at which all nine founder member clubs were present. Bristol based clubs, Bristol St George, Warmley, Bedminster, Eastville Rovers, Clifton Association and Mangotsfield were joined by Wells City, Clevedon Town and Trowbridge Town whose mainline railway afforded the opportunity to travel to the city for games. With just sixteen matches to be played in the League, it was agreed that clubs could continue playing friendly games along with their league commitments, to keep both players and supporters happy, and of course, to bring in extra revenue.

In the Chair for that meeting, where the rules were discussed at length, was Mr Snailum of Trowbridge Town FC, who was also Secretary of the Wiltshire Football Association. His appointment was not permanent, however, and as time progressed some of the decisions made that day would be changed, because it was a very experimental time in the game with even the local and national Associations learning 'on the job'.

One problem faced by the committee was the appointment of referees. In the very early years of the sport it had been assumed that the game was played by gentlemen, and that any disputes could be settled by the two club captains, but in 1872 as the game progressed, it had become the practice to appoint one umpire from each side who were then positioned on the side-lines to receive appeals, if necessary.

As time progressed, games were increasingly being decided by this method, or by consultation with the nearest newspaper reporter, whose judgement could also determine the result. When the concept of a referee in the middle of the park was finally introduced to the game in 1891-92, his powers were similar to those of today and, the umpires took on the role of linesmen. Of course, the whistle (the 'Acme Thunderer') then became an integral part of the game.

A problem faced in this area by the Bristol and District committee was that there were no Referee's Associations to facilitate appointments, and the only qualification for the man in the middle was that he should think he knew the rules. Typical of the time, the solution was found that initial year by appointing the new league committee members to fill the role. Messrs. Snailum, Millard and Stancome, who were all from Trowbridge Town, were elected to referee the first Bristol and District League games, along with the Reverend W Wheeler, from Bradford on Avon.

It was also agreed that the committee would consist of two representatives from each club, but that the post of chairman and secretary would only be held by those who were not directly involved with a member club.

Because of that ruling Mr Snailum was happy to step down from his temporary position of chairman, and gave way to the first official man in the post, Mr J R Riddell, who had been one of the main men in setting up St George football club shortly after his arrival in Bristol in 1882. He was also headmaster of Easton Road Boarding School, and had captained St George before giving up his place on the field to become Chairman of the Gloucester Football Association.

The new Chairman was voted in unanimously and was joined by Mr Francis of Clifton, who became both the Treasurer and a joint Vice-Chairman alongside Mr Snailum. The important post of secretary was left in abeyance for talks to take place with a popular local footballer, Mr A J Stevens, and club delegates were: Messrs. Summers and Nettle from Warmley; Snailum and Millard from Trowbridge; Dekin and Clevendon from Bedminster; Francis and Lacey-Sweet from Clifton; Bryant and Hemmings from Mangotsfield.

With the business side of the league set-up, the first games were eloquently recalled by Tom who wrote: *'As I said earlier, the first game took place on the day that I chose to take my first kick at the world, but not all clubs had a fixture that day and Clifton, Bedminster and Eastville did not kick-off until a later date'.*

'Bristol was, of course, a different city in those days form the one we know today with Bedminster and Eastville people mainly involved in heavy manufacturing while Mangotsfield, St George and Warmley were mining villages on its outskirts. The game that my father watched involved Trowbridge Town travelling to Warmley and although this would be a local derby today, that journey would have taken far more planning and effort than our modern footballers would realise as although there were good rail networks, the trains were slow and billowed smoke all the way. Because of that the Wiltshire players would have set out early in the morning and would have changed trains on their way, at least once, at Bath Spa, to transfer to the Midland railway for their remaining journey'.

'That day the Trowbridge players were rewarded for their efforts with a fine 4-1 win against the eventual first League Champions, who were to go on to dominate the sport in the West for most of the 1890s. I was told in later years that the game was extremely rough and threatened to get out of control on more than one occasion. It was generally agreed by most who watched the spectacle that Mr Dekin of Bedminster failed to show sufficient firmness in his task as referee, and the point was amply demonstrated by Mackie from Warmley, who openly kicked his opposite opponent Everett, on the shins, and got away with it unpunished!'

'Now, my father was quite a fan of Warmley, but even he thought that their constant appeals for hand-ball were out of order and that the result was justified with the backs for Trowbridge rarely bothered by the three home forwards. Watching football now I find it quite strange to remember the earlier versions of the rules. For instance, the off-side law stated that there had to be three players between the advancing forward and the goal. This meant that the ball was held on to by the player in possession for as long as possible, and when any structured football was attempted it was centered around heavy stoppers at the back. Alongside that it was also perfectly legal to charge a player to stop him in his tracks, which was a hangover from the rugby rules.'

By the turn of the 20th century that law was adjusted with only shoulder charges allowed, but until that time it was not unusual for a player to be charged to the ground, with or without the ball. The rule also applied to the goalkeeper even when he was in full flight attempting to catch the ball, which caused constant injuries. From that position on the field, the rules of the time showed just how much the game played today has changed, with the keeper allowed to handle the ball all the way up to the half-way line, providing he did not take more than two steps when carrying it, without throwing it up and catching it.

Alongside that, another rule allowed for any member of the team to take up the goal-keepers position during the game providing he told the referee that he had assumed the position. With the keepers' jumper still not adopted by many teams to distinguish the player in a packed goalmouth, the men of the Bristol and District league who took to the field in the middle must have had their work cut out to arbitrate, given the vagaries of the rules at the time.

Because of the style of football played, strikers were not as revered as they are today, and the industrious Wells City player who was the first to score in the new league, was left unnamed in local newspaper reports as his team went on to beat Mangotsfield, 2-0, and record their only win of the season.

The only other game on that first day saw St George fulfil their promise of earlier years by beating Clevedon at the 'Dragons' ground behind the Lord Rodney Public House on Two Mile Hill. It was common then for teams to be attached to pubs because changing rooms were a rare English League luxury, and some inns would provide a room for that purpose. If a team was very lucky they would also provide food after the match, but that was usually the exception rather than the rule.

Stories abound of the problems such close associations between teams and public houses, not least those where players prepared for the task ahead by drinking several pints of ale prior to kick-off; but that is a story to be told later.

The second committee meeting was held just four days later, on September 28th when Mr AJ Stevens took-up the vacant position as Secretary and quickly attempted to organise proceedings by suggesting that all players should be registered with the League, and that notification of the registration should be in writing. It was also agreed to issue a booklet containing the League rules and fixtures, together with the addresses of member club grounds. The booklet was then published and sold for 6d, with all profits going to League funds.

As the season progressed it became clear that a large amount of interest had been created, and clubs were attracting better gates at games than had been anticipated. Soccer may have been late in coming to Victorian Bristol, but it was soon to gain momentum with the large mass of working-class people in the area. Interest in League football was growing nationally and 'the peoples game' was beginning to bring about mass crowd movements along with a greater participation in the sport.

That progression was made possible because, unlike today of course, there was neither television or radio to entertain the population during their few hours of leisure time, and there were no English League soccer clubs in the area.

Travelling any great distance was at the time, and for some years to come, also not an option. As Tom summed up when he referred to the difficulty of getting to games during his long life that *even in later years, I can still remember having to plan journeys to away grounds many days before I set off rather than just get up and go as we do now'*. And so, especially in those early days, the popularity of the game was focused on Bristol and District League clubs.

It was clear as the first year of organised games progressed, that there was a notable increase in interest in the Association rules game all-round, and with that upturn local newspapers began to report matches more widely. However, while some, like Tom's father, *'was always convinced that what he read in print had to be true,'* it is obvious that many of those early reports contained more personal opinions about the teams and officials than is usual today. In fact, Arthur Budd, writing in 1892 observed that *'To this day, even though the evidence of science has removed some of the coarseness of the primeval game and reduced to a minimum the risks that attend it, the horrors of football still remain a favourite theme with journalists and correspondents.'* Thus demonstrating, that actually little changes over the years with many daily publications still focusing to this day on the negative side of the game; but given the rules as they stood, maybe the Victorian press had more cause to comment.

Within a couple of months of that first season some matches had fallen prey to travelling difficulties, while others had been ended early due to kicking-off late and bad light. On several occasions when that happened the League committee resolved clubs involved should play the five or ten minutes of short-time on another date, or have the odd minutes tagged onto return encounters. While it must seem strange to read that teams were expected, at times, to travel long and cumbersome journeys to play such short games, those were the type of decisions that were often arrived at in the infancy of the League; and it did not stop there.

The first attempt to organise a game in aid of funds took place just before Christmas 1892, but unfortunately ended in disaster when many players let the League down at the last moment. The game was played at Kingswood in front of 1,500 disgruntled spectators, who were unhappy to be rewarded for their time and money by what was described as 'a farce.'

To add insult to injury there were tickets on sale after the game for the next 'Big League Match;' with the crowd responding accordingly to the offer. The problem with the match lay with the expectation that players would turn up to games if selected regardless of other offers, as there were no rules to prevent free-agent movement. Added to that, of course, it was also the case that while an opportunity to play a game to represent a County FA held some kudos, the Bristol and District League was yet to achieve that status.

Following the game, the final months of that first season did not get off to a good start with two out of three matches due to be played on Saturday 7th January 1893 postponed due to frost; and that despite a willingness to play on pitches that would today be considered as dangerous. There was just one game that seemed to escape the winter weather conditions, but that was also called-off because Clevedon were unable to field a side for their journey to Bedminster, and with three inches of snow falling the following Saturday, it was not until the end of the month that League football took-off again.

A difficult train journey by Clevedon to Wiltshire for a match against Trowbridge Town on 18th February was then another disaster for the seasider's, who found themselves a man short when one of their players missed the train at Temple Meads. Prior to Mr Stevens new rule that players had to be registered in writing with the League, Clevedon would simply have called on a supporter to make up the numbers, which had been common practice prior to the new rule coming into force. As it was, Clevedon then became the first League club to play with ten men and inevitably lost the encounter 4-1, despite putting on a good display for the large crowd that had gathered.

It was not always the visitors who arrived short of men, however, as was demonstrated when several supporters turned up to watch a friendly game around that time between St George and Chippenham Town at the Dragon's ground. After a long journey, the Wiltshire side arrived to find the gates still locked and no-one around, and after 30 minutes the small crowd, together with the Chippenham players, had no option but to leave. To the dismay of some supporters the reason for the no-show became apparent when they called in on a County Cup game being played nearby, only to find the crowd boosted by the inclusion of the whole St George team watching the match in preference to taking to the field themselves!

TROWBRIDGE TOWN FC 1892

The men of the Bristol and District League did not have an easy ride in that first season, and continually came under fire from the press. A Gloucester Senior Cup match at the end of January had given further fuel to the media men when it attracted a very large crowd and rewarded the spectators with a good display of football and an organised match. Those facts were, of course, quickly seized on by the local press who compared that game with the League's Christmas disaster and highlighted just how much was still to be learned.

By the end of the season the question of refereeing standards had come to such a pitch, both in the press and on the field of play, that a meeting on the 8th April 1893 was devoted almost entirely to the subject. Many suggestions were made to improve the standard of decision making, but Mr Stevens solutions to the problem, that officials should be chosen from prominent members of the home teams committee, was not received favorably, and brought strong and loud claims that a 'bias' would inevitably be added to results. Without an agreed solution, the subject was then simply left unresolved for another day.

After that lively meeting, the first League Dinner was also discussed, but it was finally decided that it would be impossible to arrange the occasion by the seasons end date of April 29th and the decision was also shelved. It was agreed, however, that medals would be awarded to the Warmley players for winning the League and that a Trophy, donated by Mr Edward Colston, the MP for Bristol, would also be presented. The Cup which is still in existence today, was made of silver, and was extremely lavish (especially given that the League had such few competitors), standing 19 inches high with a wonderful silver footballer on its lid.

The men of the Bristol and District League did not have an easy ride in that first season, and continually came under fire from the press. A Gloucester

Senior Cup match at the end of January had given further fuel to the media men when it attracted a very large crowd and rewarded the spectators with a good display of football and an organised match. Those facts were, of course, quickly seized on by the local press who compared that game with the League's Christmas disaster and highlighted just how much was still to be learned.

By the end of the season the question of refereeing standards had come to such a pitch, both in the press and on the field of play, that a meeting on the 8th April 1893 was devoted almost entirely to the subject. Many suggestions were made to improve the standard of decision making, but Mr Stevens solutions to the problem, that officials should be chosen from prominent members of the home teams committee, was not received favorably, and brought strong and loud claims that a 'bias' would inevitably be added to results. Without an agreed solution, the subject was then simply left unresolved for another day.

After that lively meeting, the first League Dinner was also discussed, but it was finally decided that it would be impossible to arrange the occasion by the seasons end date of April 29th and the decision was also shelved. It was agreed, however, that medals would be awarded to the Warmley players for winning the League and that a Trophy, donated by Mr Edward Colston, the MP for Bristol, would also be presented. The Cup which is still in existence today, was made of silver, and was extremely lavish (especially given that the League had such few competitors), standing 19 inches high with a wonderful silver footballer on its lid.

As would be expected, money was tight, and at the first AGM held on 26th April, Mr Francis, the Treasurer, reported that income for the season had amounted to £34-16s-9d with expenditure at £33-16s-9d, leaving a working surplus of just over £1. While that was all that could be expected with such a new venture, news of the withdrawal of Wells City after winning just one game, was hoped to be tempered by new club Southbroom (now Devizes Town), joining. However, the club found that rail connections to Bristol were not good enough to get to and from in one day, and had no option but to withdraw their application at the last minute.

And so, the first season of League football in the West Country ended, with a certain amount of success both on and off the field, but with a lot of public criticism and unresolved problems to unravel. Many games had attracted gates of over 1,000, and with the three top teams, Warmley, Trowbridge Town and St George in predictable positions, the future was seen to be one to embrace.

The competition was heading for an expansion in popularity that would bring with it more problems to solve in a country that was working hard. Economic output per head of population had increased by some 500%, improving living standards and demanding more quality in the working man's leisure hours in return; something that the Association clubs from the Bristol and District League aspired to provide.

CHAPTER 2

An accident happened today.

In early September 1893, the committee attempted to resolve the problems associated with refereeing, prior to the new League season kicking-off. This action was even more pressing because the league had expanded to two divisions so that reserve teams could be accommodated. It was therefore decided that all referees would come from the committee rather than leave the task to the individual home clubs, and to show commitment to that decision, both the Chairman and Secretary agreed to combine their duties with a spell in the middle of the park.

The Constitution of the League was then amended to allow for the second division to be added and it was agreed to administer it following the guidelines set by the English League, who had also implemented a new division the previous season. Along with those reserve teams from the Division One clubs, St Paul's, Barton Hill and Waverley were voted in, while Gloucester AFC and Staple Hill joined to replace Wells City, thus expanding the League to twenty clubs.

A series of friendly matches took place on 9th September, just prior to the season proper, with a large crowd turning up to watch Warmley score a 3-0 victory over Radstock. It was always assured that the meeting of two tough mining community sides would result in a very hard-fought contest with a lively crowd of supporters. The game was no exception, with both vocal and physical exchanges contributing to an exceptionally menacing, but somehow carnival-like, atmosphere.

After the game, the long awaited first League Dinner was held at which Mr Colston presented Warmley with the League Challenge Cup, and each of their players with a gold centered silver medal.

Later, Warmley, was one of a few League clubs to take up the challenge of the English Cup, with just four entering, and none progressed further than the first stage. The Cup games saw Warmley travel to the Calvesham ground of Reading, only to be shown a lesson, in front of over 2,000 spectators, losing by six goals without reply.

In the same competition, Clifton fared a little better when, in front of 1,500, they managed a credible draw with Newbury Town, leading to a replay the following Monday at Kingswood, which was refereed by League Chairman, Mr Riddell. At half-time the game was still in the balance with the visitors 2-1 ahead, but the following forty-five minutes told a different tale, and the subsequent 5-1 drubbing highlighted the inexperience of the Bristol side. The report that appeared in the Bristol Times and Mirror the next day gave a fine reflection of the game, with several references to the Newbury team carrying more weight, and of their ability to push a player to the ground before the ball was played; which showed the evident cross-over still in Rugby and Association rules of the time.

The local press was, indeed, increasing both coverage and criticism of the League and its clubs, typified by the following observation that appeared in the above paper regarding a St George match in late October, that had been watched by a large crowd. The reporter wrote, *'Football has been played in Bristol quite long enough now for the public to have become thoroughly acquainted with the rules which govern the sport. It is therefore disgusting, Saturday after Saturday, to find on many a ground a section of the spectators prepared to create an unseemly demonstration directly a decision is given averse to their favourites. Every excuse can be made for the patrons being enthusiastic over the doings of the teams whose headquarters it may happen to be, and accordingly little applause to the visitors. But all ideas of fairness and honesty in sport are outraged when first the referee, and then the side whom he may have awarded a just penalty, are hooted and yelled at as they were a set of knaves'.*

The paper further suggested that they and other Bristol and District League clubs should be warned of this *'dangerous practice'*. Of course, one thing that can be said throughout history, is that the passion of spectators will always remain high, no matter what conditions surround the game.

As the season progressed the rain seemed relentless and by November 4th very few matches had been played, but Bedminster were winning the popularity stakes for providing a certain amount of shelter for the press and supporters, which was a rarity indeed.

Such was the topic of weather conditions for the sport that a classic opening line in one of the local papers read *'An accident happened on Saturday, it didn't rain!'* Ironic though the line was, it was not, however, the only accident to happened during that season, with many young men injured while playing what was fast becoming the nations favourite sport.

Trowbridge Town had played four games by that time, but then went through a very unlucky spell with four of their players side-lined with serious injuries, in just three weeks. One of the players broke his collar bone on a frozen pitch that was described as little short of an ice-rink, a second broke an arm, and in a game against Bedminster on 9th December, one broke a leg and another crushed a knee bone in a match that was lost 3-1, in front of some rowdy home support of more than 1,000.

While those two clubs were in action their reserve elevens were also doing battle at Bedminster at a match in which the referee, Mr Greenbough, failed to turn up, which meant that Mr Snailum had to step in. There were, of course, two problems with that appointment, he was not the officially appointed man in the middle, and from the Bedminster point of view, he was an official of the home club, which they alleged contributed to the subsequent defeat of 1-0. At a committee meeting later it was agreed that the game should be replayed, but strangely also that the match should take place at the Trowbridge ground. Such were the anomalies of the time, and after many heated discussions on the venue, the encounter was scratched with the points awarded to Bedminster reserves.

In those Victorian days that saw most of the working population engaged in long hard hours of work, the prospect of playing professional football as a full-time, well paid occupation, that could often also bring with it a house, was a remote dream for most men and boys. In common with many of the new League's springing up throughout the South and West of England, players in the Bristol and District League were classified as amateur. However, the first charge of professionalism raised its head following an emergency meeting just before Christmas on 23rd December 1893, when a Warmley player called Phillips was brought to the attention of the committee.

It was alleged that he had signed professional forms for Lincoln at the start of the season, before returning to Bristol to play in a game for his home club. Prior to the game, he had appealed to the Football Association to be released from his professional commitments, but that appeal was not accepted, and the ruling had been that he would not be able to revert to amateur status until September 1894; a ruling that he clearly ignored.

While today the worst that would have happened to players and clubs in that situation would be a fine and/or point deductions, such was the law at the time that in the same month as Warmley fell foul to allegations of professionalism, a player called Beharrell was convicted at the Central Criminal Court to fourteen days in prison for entering himself as an amateur for Hackney Athletic under an assumed name when he wasn't entitled to claim that status; a ruling that sent shock waves through the body of Association football.

Fortunately for Warmley, they escaped being penalised for their transgression. They did not learn their lesson however, and were in trouble with the league again later when a complaint was again lodged by St George alleging the inclusion of another professional player, after Warmley had won 2-1 at the Dragon's ground. This time the League declared that the game should be replayed, and that two points should be deducted from the Champions; which brought a huge cry of protest, but to no avail, and became the first time that there was a deduction of points for such a transgression. They also ordered that the Warmley books should be presented for inspection to prove that nothing over and above the hotel bill and expenses of a player, James Lynne of Plymouth, had been paid, suspecting that there were further shortcomings that might come to light.

All the profits from the gate of the first game were then taken for League funds, which further intensified the atmosphere at the replay which was said to have a great deal of bad feeling all round. The subsequent draw, 1-1, further punished the Champions who dropped yet another point in their battle to retain the title.

The question of bringing in outside players to strengthen a team for vital matches had become a talking point, and was obviously on the mind of Mr Williams of Staple Hill FC when he attempted to push through a rule that all clubs should prove a ten-mile residential qualification for their players, thus ensuring that only local talent could determine the result of a game. The motion was, however, defeated as the open registration system that had been introduced by the Secretary was felt to be sufficient to prevent the practice of borrowing players from teams such as Aldershot and Plymouth for vital games.

The season was shaping up to be one fraught with problems, and Warmley were top of the list of errant clubs, both on and off the pitch. The mining community worked and played hard, and while referee, Mr Bloor, had managed to keep a lid on passions throughout the game he officiated against Clifton, bad light had given him no option but to call the game to a halt with ten minutes remaining, with the home side well on top. An action that infuriated the Warmley faithful.

The subsequent 'crowd disturbance' was reported to the committee, who were again called on to meter out the punishment. It was made quite clear to the club's officials that the men of the Bristol and District League committee had decided that firm action was needed, and Warmley were ordered to issue hand-bills at the following home game warning their spectators that if there was any more crowd trouble the club would not be allowed to play in the competition again; an action that obviously helped to quell the volatile miners at the St George game shortly afterward that went off without the predicted riots, despite a highly charged atmosphere.

Although it was a turbulent time, Warmley scored a double victory at the end of the season with both of their teams winning their respective divisions. At the League's AGM, the reserves were presented with the new Division Two Trophy that had been donated by Mr John Durran of Bedminster, and the Warmley first team received the Colston Cup for the second time.

The League positions at season's end showed a marked consistency, with the Champions closely followed by St George and Trowbridge Town in both divisions. While Eastville Rovers, who were later to become Bristol Rovers, and their reserve team failed to display the talent expected of them, and ended the term just above bottom place.

A six-a-side competition was held at seasons end on 21st April between all the League's clubs, which proved extremely popular with over 3,000 people attending. The competition saw one point scored for each corner and four points for a goal, with Warmley again taking the honours in the final, winning, 9-7, over Clifton AFC.

While the mining community of Warmley celebrated, at their AGM the price of success was clear for all to see. A £5 surplus from the previous season had turned into a £29-2s-3d shortfall, which was more surprising given that the average gates had been more than 1,000.

During that second year, the Management Committee had come in for some bitter criticism from many quarters. They were continuing to go through a learning process, with little guidance from people with experience to solve the problems that were attached to such a venture. They had managed to introduce some successful initiatives, especially with the formation of an Emergency Committee, which was set up to consider the conditions of a playing surface the evening before a game, to avoid unnecessary travelling and inter-club disputes, but their popularity among local journalists was still at a very low ebb.

Despite that, the League's popularity, where it mattered with its clubs and the public, was growing, but there were still many difficulties to be resolved concerning refereeing standards, registrations, and rowdy supporters, together with the general problems associated with rough play.

Contrary to Warmley's financial problems, the League's balance sheet just prior to the start of the 1894/95 season showed a healthy profit of £25-3s-3d after the 25 guineas honorarium for the Secretary had been deducted. To add to the good news, the Management Committee were also getting to terms with some of the problems it faced, and issued a sound dictate that all games should last a full ninety minutes or the whole game would have to be replayed; a decision that was well received, but that would, later in the year, have its own consequences.

Questions regarding the problems of the refereeing system were also partly solved following the formation of the Bristol and District Referees Association, which aimed to ensure that all potential referees passed an elementary examination on the rules of the game. Further to that they also decided to appoint all referees at their monthly meeting, rather than leave the task to the clubs to resolve.

Just prior to the season kicking-off, a request was received from Bristol South End for permission to enter two teams into the competition, one in each division. The request was, however, turned down because they were not an established club, having been formed only a few months previously in April 1894. Their formation had followed the demise of Bristol South, a club that had won both the newly established Junior League, and the South Bristol and District League in its initial season. They were to eventually gain admission a few seasons later, just before changing their name to Bristol City Football Club.

New clubs, Hereford Thistle and Swindon Wanderers, joined Division One, while Willsbridge were admitted to Division Two, bringing a total of 23 clubs to the Competition. However, Wanderers initially withdrew without kicking a ball after many of their players moved their allegiance to Swindon Town following objections by them to playing Bristol and District League football. The club were also deep in debt and had to give up their County Ground site to the Town side. They did, however, eventually reform and rejoined the Western League in October 1894.

Although the Football Association were continuing to consider rules to the game in the light of injuries to players, a meeting in November confirmed that a player could still be physically charged if he was within striking distance of the ball. That decision was made even though injuries to players had become so frequent, that local papers often carried a special column to summarise the catalogue of casualties from the previous Saturday's matches.

It wasn't only the rules of the game that were at fault, however, as medical skills were not as refined as they are today, and some young men died because of a lack of medical supervision and knowledge. For many years in the early stages of the Association game the cost of medical treatment was out of reach for most amateur footballers, with no National Health Service established until after the Second World War. But there were also other associated problems due to the lack of real medical knowledge. Unfortunately, it was not uncommon for people to die after being given blood transfusions as it was not until November 1900 that different blood groups were identified and established. It was also the time when the use of the X-Ray machine to determine the location and extent of broken bones was very much in its infancy. Even when that machine was initially introduced in Glasgow in 1896, it took 90 minutes to produce an image, and it would be many years before West Country footballers would have instant access to that diagnostic tool.

While the early rules in the game did nothing to protect players from injury, and administrators were attempting to get tough on dangerous play, there were other aspects of the game that also needed to be addressed; as demonstrated after a particularly tense game at Mangotsfield on 23rd February 1895. Such was the nature of the match that the referee, Mr Somerton, still had problems after the final whistle and reported no less than ten of the home players and an official for insulting him in his changing room after the game.

Although the attack was not of a physical nature, the League committee got tough, and after the subsequent enquiry into the incident, nine of the players were suspended for three weeks, and the other fellow suspended until the end of the season, which left Mangotsfield with a crisis on their hands, unable to field a whole team.

Because of that it was widely expected the next scheduled game would be cancelled. However, the errant club's officials had other ideas, and decided to field their only two players who were not under suspension, and rely on the off-side trap, because the law stated that three players had to be in front of the ball when a goal was scored. Those tactics seemed to be working until Bedminster were awarded a corner from which they scored a perfectly legal goal; at which stage the two brave Mangotsfield lads decided that it was a game too far, and immediately left the pitch.

Such were the early years and rules of the sport.

During the season, there were a couple of friendly matches against English League clubs in aid of League funds, with Aston Villa the first to show their talent against a selected Bristol and District League side, who were easily overcome, 8-0, in front of over 6,000 spectators. The gate encouraged the League Committee to stage another money spinning game, which saw Stoke City slot in five goals without reply; further demonstrating the huge gap that existed in playing standards between amateur and professional players.

Many of the representative side came from the St George club, who were in action soon afterwards when Wolverhampton Wanderers sent a team to celebrate the opening of their new ground, on Easter Monday. Although it was a well-attended prestigious game, most of the true supporters were more intent on the game a few days later when the 'Dragons' were due to meet Trowbridge Town in the game which would determine the League Championship.

It was not unchartered territory for the St George players, as the previous season they had entertained Warmley in a similar game to determine the title, but with minutes remaining and a goal up, Warmley scored with the final kick to take the Championship by that one point. Those memories would have been sufficient to spur the home players on, but there was an added twist to the game as this was the replay of a game that had been called off in less than happy circumstances; which contributed to a large vociferous crowd who travelled to Wiltshire to contribute to a victory.

The initial game between the clubs had been marred when the Trowbridge team declared the ground unfit to play on just prior to kick-off, and walked off the pitch. The referee, however, decided that the pitch was playable and blew his whistle to start the game. From the kick-off, St George simply dribbled the ball up the pitch into the undefended half, and scored, which led the Wiltshire team to quickly resume their place.

After seventy-five minutes, however, Trowbridge Town's initial analysis of the pitch proved correct, and the game was abandoned, with St George leading 2-0. Obscurely, at a meeting later, it was deemed that the Bristol club should be awarded the points but not the game, which had the effect of giving them a replay, and an extra game to fit in; a game that fate determined would decide the title.

With Hereford Thistle one point ahead of St George, but having completed all their games, the half-time score-line on the day saw the Bristol club leading, 2-1, with every indication that they would snatch the title, but in the end the eventual score-line of 3-3, handed the honours to Hereford, with runners-up medals for the 'Dragons', once again.

It had been widely expected that Warmley would be in the mix for honours, but it was a case of the club taking on too much, and a fixture backlog put paid to their ambition. By the middle of February, they had only completed six of their fixtures compared to an average of thirteen played by other clubs in Division One.In fact, Mangotsfield were ahead of the game at that stage having completed fifteen, and had gained eight of their eventual twelve points. Although they then faced the problem of the nine players suspended, they still somehow managed to win two of their remaining seven fixtures.

There was compensation for Warmley when their reserves won Division Two for the second time, but they could not be promoted, an honour that went to new club, St Paul's, who had performed well and ended the term just two points behind them.

During the year Hereford Thistle had lost just one game, and decided to move on to test their progress in the Birmingham and District League, which they won at the first attempt, thus demonstrating the talent and ambition that they would become known for over the years to come.

The face of football was changing dramatically. Locally the South Bristol League had kicked-off in 1893/94, followed by the East Bristol League a year later, and there had also been similar movements in the surrounding counties of Gloucester, Wiltshire and Somerset. The Southern League had also been formed following a meeting of senior clubs, called by Millwall, and had joined forces with the Birmingham and District league to push on for greater status within the ever-changing English football system. The initial season of the Southern League had been very successful, and was undoubtedly both a threat to the Bristol and District League, and a source of inspiration.

Times were changing.

Along with the rise of the league system and changes within the game, consideration was also being given to the changing lives of the communities in and around Bristol, with general economic output growing at a rate of 50%, contributing to a more affluent community who worked hard and expected more from their leisure time pursuits.

Those were, therefore, challenging times that called on the committee to introduce measures to safeguard the ground that had been gained during the initial years of the League, and ensure the continuing success of football in the West Country.

CHAPTER 3

Spreading the Net

With the changes taking place, the spring and summer of 1895 was a busy one for the men of the committee. They were fully aware of the challenges that were being thrown up, and with a view to the progress made during the initial years of football, several meetings were held after the season to address those matters.

Eventually, at a meeting in the Earl Russell Hotel on Thursday 12th June 1895, it was announced that the league would in future be known as the Western Football League, something that Tom pointed out in the centenary book would be 'a name that would live with the League throughout my spectating career;' and it would not be just the longevity of the title that would remain.

The meeting also decided that a 50-mile radius of the city would be imposed to attract more clubs and ensure that the league would compete from a stronger position with a wider area on offer attracting more ambitious clubs. Despite the optimism, however, the fresh initiative only drew in three more clubs to enter for the new season, Cardiff, Fishponds and Cumberland; none of whom lasted past their first year.

The team from Cardiff was, of course, somewhat of a challenge for the clubs competing, as travelling to and from Wales was quite problematic. The convenience of the Severn Bridge was well into the future, and did not replace the Aust Ferry until 1966, and so access to Wales was either via the ferry, which operated close to where the bridge is today and was subject to tidal variations, or by train via the Severn tunnel that had been built between 1874-1886 by the Great Western Railway.

The inspiration for the Welsh club's move to an English league may well have been the lure of the railway. But Cardiff's membership was short-lived, lasting only until January 1896, when they were expelled by the committee for non-payment of a variety of fines. Their officials and players were subsequently reported to the English FA, who imposed heavy penalties regarding their continuing future in football.

With their expulsion, the committee had to face yet another new problem, as they needed to determine how to address the points gained by Cardiff in the league table. It was a dilemma which prompted Bristol South End, who had been refused entry the previous season, to offer to take on all the Cardiff fixtures and results; which was an indication of their desire to join the league. It was, however, not received well by everyone, and in the end the proposal was defeated, by nine votes to seven by member clubs, who agreed that instead they should be invited to apply again for membership the following season.

The difficulty was eventually solved when it was decided that all points gained or lost in the process of playing Cardiff would be deducted, which saw top of the table Warmley most effected, having scored a total of nine goals against the Welsh club in their two victories, while third placed Staple Hill, who had lost their one game, then gained ground on the leaders. And it did not stop there. Shortly afterwards fellow newcomers, Frenchay, put in their resignation, after a whole raft of rule infringements were mounting up against them, and again all points won were deducted from the league table.

It was turning out to be a very troublesome season, indeed, with financial problems beginning to face some clubs, and rumours that many were close to collapse; and discipline was, as always, a problem.

Warmley were the focus of the Management Committee's scrutiny after a Cup match between the miners and Clifton turned nasty, with the crowd attempting to attack the referee at half-time. Even with the intervention of the home players, and with officials appealing for calm, the Clifton players and committee were called on to protect the hapless fellow. It took 15 minutes for order to be restored, and the game was eventually allowed to play out to its conclusion, but on the final whistle, the referee, Mr Somerton, had to be accompanied off the pitch. A subsequent enquiry saw Warmley heavily censured and the game ordered to be replayed. With this severe incident coming after the poor man's experiences at Mangotsfield the previous season, it is surprising that he continued in the middle, but continue he did.

Revised rules were filtering down from the Football League to cut down on injuries on the pitch, but even with those in place, they were not good enough to prevent the death of a young Western League player, Herbert Smith, when, in a game on 2nd April 1896 between Bedminster and Eastville, the young lad was injured after colliding with an opposition player. He left the field and went home to bed complaining of a headache, but by the morning he was sadly found dead. And tragedy in football did not stop there. Shortly afterwards a Bristol player, Joseph Powell, who played for Arsenal, simply broke his arm in a match, but subsequently died through tetanus and blood poisoning at the age of just 26 years, despite doctors amputating his arm to save his life.

Such were the dangers of playing the much-loved sport in those Victorian days, when progress in medicine and revisions of rules would eventually put paid to the needless loss of young lives.

In general, the first season of Western League football was plagued with problems. Clifton had been experiencing all sorts of troubles and at one stage threatened to resign over an issue, but were eventually persuaded to stay and did complete their games, albeit losing a point on the way for playing an ineligible player. However, their reserve side didn't manage to pick up a single point and withdrew, leaving with the reserves from St George, Bedminster and Warmley. And the problems did not stop there.

At the end of the season all un-played games were declared drawn by the committee so that the League tables could be completed, which resulted in yet another decision to be taken when Eastville Rovers and Staple Hill ended the term on the same amount of points, just behind Warmley. In line with English League rules, a test match was then ordered to establish the runners-up spot, which was held at the St George ground. Predictably the game resulted in a draw, 2-2, and failed to resolve the matter. Eventually the men in charge decided that the honours should be shared, and that the teams would be placed on the league table in alphabetical order; which meant that Rovers were placed above Staple Hill.

One of the highlights during the year was a game in aid of League funds which saw Aston Villa come to Bristol again. To the surprise of many and despite the English League side enjoying 95% of the play, it was game that was won 2-1 by the League X1, in front of 5,380 spectators. The hero of the day was 'Soldier' George of Trowbridge Town, who put on a wonderful display in goal. His heroics were later rewarded when Villa signed him on, and later still George gained international honours. In recognition of their prestigious win the players were presented with mementos of the occasion, and it was decided that the claret and blue strip of Villa would be adopted for all future League representative matches to commemorate what was a high note amid the gloom of running a league in the infancy of the sport.

There was also another very successful annual six-a-side competition at season's end, which went ahead despite moves by the English FA to outlaw that form of the sport. With over 500 attending both semi-final games at Bedminster, and the final game at St George, it was declared a success by everyone involved, with Eastville Rovers winning 14-7 over Staple Hill.

The season had seen three clubs from outside the city competing, with Gloucester City and Swindon Wanderers joining Trowbridge Town. But with the increase in financial problems being experienced, it was no surprise to see both Gloucester City, who reported a deficit at their AGM of £5-3s-9d, and Swindon Wanderers, who had experienced all sorts of problems from the start, withdraw from the Competition.

While the first 'Western Football League' season had seen the committee improve their relationship with the media, and come to terms with some of the more difficult aspects of running a football league, change was again in the wings with only nine teams entering the Division One and seven in Division Two for the 1895/96 season, but behind the scenes, change was on its way.

Despite financial problems, or perhaps because of them, it was generally accepted that the adoption of professionalism by the League would eventually be inevitable, and when Secretary, Mr Stephens, declared his support for embracing the challenge, seven of the nine clubs competing in the top division declared their intent to turn professional when the time came.

Bristol South End settled straight away into the League and were soon enjoying their first season, after having so many attempts to join rebuffed, but soon found a problem. In their first game on 19th September 1896, that saw them convincingly beat Staple Hill, 3-1, they discovered many canny locals watching the game without paying an entry fee by standing on a nearby hill. Very soon the problem was solved, however, when the wise directors ordered the erection of canvas sheets, which were eventually used by local companies to advertise their wares, as well as obstructing the free-loaders view.

As the season progressed, Mr Francis the Hon Treasurer, revealed that creditors were pressing for payment, and that the League was £120 in debt. Ironically, to solve the problem, an appeal was made to the Member clubs for donations, with a proposal from Mr Bryant that South Bristol, Eastville Rovers and Bedminster, should donate £10 each, Staple Hill and Clifton £7 each, and Trowbridge Town and St Paul's £7 each. Junior clubs were then asked to contribute either £2-10s-0d or £1-10s-0d in accordance with their means. The proposal was accepted, and clubs somehow stepped up to the plate, and were joined by Gloucester FA and several individuals all putting in money. Those donations managed to stave off the real threat of bankruptcy.

With the impending financial crisis resolved it was apparent that there was a need to increase income, which prompted the proposal to launch a new competition whose proceeds would also help the local community. Mr Flook of Bedminster donated the Trophy for the Western League Charity Cup Competition which was based on the established Birmingham Charity Cup. All monies generated from the Final were to be donated to a charity fund that had already been set-up, after expenses had been deducted, with a sixth of the gate money given to good causes, and the rest divided between the League and the finalists. It was also agreed to deduct 5/- from the income to off-set league expenses, and a rule was introduced that no player could take part for more than one club; hence the first of the 'cup-tied' players in the League. With all rules in place, the first game in the competition took place during the Christmas holiday in front of a large and appreciative crowd who were entertained with a 2-2 draw between Eastville and Barton Hill.

One way that the clubs attempted to abate the ever-present burden of debt was to capitalise on gate money, but as the New Year came in Eastville Rovers went a little too far with this when they charged both the Fishponds players, officials and the match referee admission to their ground. After reporting the unusual fund-raising activity to the committee, the club were rightly ordered to refund the money. Shortly afterwards they were again in trouble when a spectator at one of their games attempted to assault the referee (not Mr Somerton for a change). In response, Rovers were ordered to find a room close to the ground for the referee to change in, and to provide protection for visiting teams and officials, a rule that was later extended to all clubs.

For Rovers, the problems did not stop there, and they were soon up in front of the committee again answering a charge over the inclusion of a player named John McClean, who had played as a professional for Port Vale. Amid a rather heated hearing, in which statements were made and rescinded, it was established that McClean had received 15/- a week from a gentleman named Mr Hunt, to work on the new Rovers ground.

The charge had originally been brought by Bristol South End, and so it was with a certain amount of disbelief that it was eventually revealed that the same player had been offered 25/- a week by South End to do similar work, providing he transferred to their club. Despite the revelation, the case was still found proven, and Rovers had two points deducted and were ordered to pay a £1 fine.

Following that decision several clubs lodged appeals concerning the same player, and the upheld protests added to fixture backlogs as the committee ordered games that McClean had appeared in to be replayed. While Eastville managed to avoid any other point deductions, they did not let the matter rest there, maintaining that the League did not have the power to order the replay of one game, the one in which they beat South End 3-1, a protest that was upheld by the English FA. The ensuing chaos caused by that decision added further fuel to the call for professionalism to be allowed by the League, and for the committee's powers to be more clearly defined.

The English FA were, of course, constantly looking at the rules of the game, and were questioning whether to change the off-side law from the three-player rule. They were also considering whether to abolish one of the only compulsory lines on the pitch, the six-yard line, which formed a half-circle around the goal-posts to define the extent of the goalkeeper's area, in favour of a twelve-yard radius line, and whether to introduce a penalty kick for some infringements. There was also a radical suggestion that corners should decide any game that ended in a draw after 90 minutes of play; a discussion that has been exercised on many occasions since without being adopted.

CLEVEDON TOWN 1897-98

G Rich (Treasurer), F Down, H Taylor, G Stephenson, F J Brindling, T C Nunnerley, G Tripp, J Taylor, M Reed (Trainer) M J Hand (Hon. Sec.)

Once again, many games throughout the season ended less than the full 90 minutes for various reasons, and, in general, the short-time was still ordered to be played at a future date, or tagged onto the return encounter, despite the earlier directives of the committee.

As the Charity Cup continued its progress, the question of what to do in the event of a drawn semi-final tie came to the fore, when Eastville met Mangotsfield on Tuesday 27th April 1997. The agreed resolution was to order a replay on a neutral ground, after first allowing 30 minutes of extra time to be played. As the Final was set for Friday 30th April 1897, that solution would give the prospects of a replay on the 28th, and again on the 29th if no result was forthcoming. The prospects of playing four games in four days, combined with full-time jobs, must have been a daunting task indeed for the players of the two clubs concerned. As luck had it, that scenario was avoided with Eastville going through to the Final without recourse to additional games.

To continue the quest of freeing the League from its financial problems, a friendly game was arranged for Easter Tuesday 1897 against a team from Nottingham Forest. The English League club had agreed to play providing they were guaranteed £30 plus half of the gate over £60. With Warmley engaged in Southern League duties that day, the team was selected from the remaining clubs, but some of the players refused to turn out and Forest won handsomely. The gate netted a 'declared' £60-18s-9d giving the visitors £30-9s-3d for their trouble, and served its purpose by boosting the coffers of the League.

At the end of the season a meeting on the 26th May saw Mr Stevens formally propose, which Mr Tozer seconded, that the Western Football League should adopt professionalism from the following season and in all future competitions. After a short, detailed discussion, the motion was carried unanimously; a decision that would change the direction of the League and begin a period of intense activity throughout the summer.

Because of the problems encountered during the year the season finished late, which meant that the play-off game to determine promotion and relegation, a style adopted from English League rules, could not be arranged. Eventually the committee agreed to the suggestion by Mr Jarrett of Eastville Rovers to hold the game just prior to the start of the new season. However, it was then discovered that the existing League rules stated the match had to be played within the same season, and that the earlier vote to embracing professionalism had triggered a need to decide the issue of league structure as soon as possible.

The member for Eastville Rovers was neither happy nor convinced that his suggestion should be overturned, and demonstrated, once again, that his passions could easily boil over. Earlier in the season Mr Jarrett had been hauled in front of his peers to answer charges of abusing a referee at a game, and, to say the least, he was hardly pleased for his proposal to be opposed by those same members. In fact, he complained so vociferously that he was ordered to leave the meeting by Chairman, Mr Riddell. But he was not about to climb down and when he refused to leave the room, the atmosphere became charged. Eventually the meeting was abandoned, without a resolution. Within weeks the re-arrangement of Divisions caused by the vote made the debate insignificant, both clubs were placed into Amateur Division One.

The news of the League adopting professionalism went around the footballing community like wild-fire and caused a great deal of excitement. It was not long before the men of the league realised the enormity of their decision, and a sub-committee was formed to go into the rules to modify certain aspects to accommodate new clubs.

With Warmley Champions, once again, the last season as an amateur league came to an end. South End, who had worked so hard to gain entry to the League, had proved no match for the Champions, but had obviously learned from the failed applications for membership in earlier years, and were accepted into the Southern League at the first attempt under their new name of Bristol City.

The modern age of the Western Football League was heralded by a 'Smoking Concert' arranged at the Grand Hotel, Bristol, to present the medals and trophies, and with everything that had gone before, it was with a tentative air that the League entered the 1897/98 season, with a degree of optimism that would be tempered by lessons still to be learned.

CHAPTER 4

The challenge of professionalism

With professionalism incorporated into the very heart of the League for the start of the 1897/98 season, the Western League took on a new personality. Taking tentative steps at first, the men in charge tip-toed into an area of problems that the professional/amateur divide would inevitably bring.

It was not just the face of football that was changing during those final years of the 19th Century. The city of Bristol was expanding rapidly leaving many clubs under threat of losing their grounds to developers to make way for new housing and for manufacturing premises. Unlike today, when rules and regulations are in place to preserve green spaces, many established clubs found themselves homeless, and had no choice but to go out of existence.

With those developments, however, there were positive moves, including developing the transportation system within the city, which was made much easier after the electrification of the tram system. The social conditions of the working population had also undergone improvements and it was a time when the working man began to realise his own economic strength, through the spread of Trade Unions and the power of the ballot box.

The great leisure activity of football was widely recognised and encouraged by all political parties as a healthy way of spending time, when not helping maintain the economic power of Great Britain throughout the world. The threat of war, however, was always around the corner in those late Victorian days, with the British Empire both a source of pride for Britain, and a challenge to the other great Countries of the world.

Before the start of the new season, seventeen clubs were represented to hear a strong speech from the Chairman of the League in favour of creating separate Professional and Amateur divisions. The optimism of the committee for this move saw no boundaries, with talk of the Western League achieving the same status as both the Birmingham & District League and the Southern League in a short space of time. It was, however, to be something of a naïve aim that would prove more difficult to achieve than anticipated.

The meeting agreed, after a great deal of discussion, that there would be two Amateur sections, with the Professional section made up of: Bristol City, Swindon Town, Reading, Trowbridge Town, Eastleigh (Southampton), Bristol St George, Bristol Eastville Rovers and Warmley.

A target of twenty clubs was placed on the table as the aim for the Amateur sections, but in the end, it was not achieved. Bedminster, Clifton, Barton Hill, Radstock, St Pauls, Eastville Wanderers, Mangotsfield, Staple Hill, Midsomer Norton and Fishponds were all placed in Division One, leaving Cotham, Hanham, the Royal Artillery, Horfield and reserve teams from St Pauls, Fishponds, Bedminster and Eastville Wanderers in Division Two.

To accommodate the new structure, the League had to introduce a new rule that exempted the professional club's books from inspection, as they were affiliated to the English League who routinely performed that task. Immunity from election each year was also insisted upon.

A monthly list of referees was ordered to comply with the English League rule, and registration of professional players was required seven days before playing for a club, whereas for the Amateur clubs it was fourteen days. It was also necessary to introduce the concept of a 'close season' to the West with clubs only allowed to directly approach players during the months of May, June and July.

The reaction of the press to the new venture was mixed, with many expressing concerns at the number of fixtures the Professional clubs were committing themselves to, because each of the new clubs were also members of another league. Another doubt expressed by many was that the clubs would not take the new competition seriously, given the Western League's status; a charge that would be constantly voiced throughout the years amid allegations of weak sides being fielded.

Those reservations, however, were not shared by the general footballing public who were enlivened by the prospect of being able to watch a good standard of soccer locally. Warmley, who were, once again, also playing in the Division Two of the Southern League, proved particularly well supported; winning all eleven of their games in that competition, scoring 72 goals without conceding. In contrast, however, they did not field such strong teams in their Western League games and only won six of fourteen games, giving justification to the critics of the new venture.

St George, who were also playing in the Birmingham and District League, had scraped through a crisis at the end of the previous season when their landlord, the cricket club, attempted to get them evicted to enable housing on part of their ground, but, despite those underlying uncertainties they still elected to turn professional. While they were performing well in both leagues, as were Bristol City and Eastville Rovers, fears were soon growing about the sheer number of Professional clubs in the area, despite there being good crowds at every game.

Those fears seemed to justify the decision by both Clifton and Bedminster to stay as Amateur clubs. However, the reason for Clifton's decision was soon to play out, when a defeat in the FA Cup, 9-1, by Bristol City was followed by seven league games in which they won just five points, which led to dwindling gates, and the revelation that they were deeply in debt. Soon after, the club had to face the inevitable, and after providing such entertainment for the public since their formation in 1883, the club had no choice but to fold.

With that, there was the usual points deductions from the league table, but with many of the ex-players anxious to sign on for Bedminster instead, the fourteen-day rule was applied and transfers of allegiance was eventually permitted. That action, however, then raised the question of whether those players would be able to take part in the Charity Cup, having already played in a game for Clifton. After much debate, the committee decided to apply the rules as adopted, and all were declared to be cup-tied and not eligible to take part in that year.

As the season progressed, the Professional clubs enjoyed large gates; with every ticket sold needed to cover the cost of their venture, but one club took it too far and were reported for refusing entry to a Western League committee member. Thus, badges were ordered for those members, giving the right to entry to any game free of charge; a practice that is still in force today.

It was initially anticipated that the Amateur Division Two might suffer problems during the season, and that fear was founded with many crowd disturbances, countless appeals against results due to un-roped off grounds, and, in one incident, a problem where seven minutes of short-time was played due to the teams having to wait until a ball was found.

At one stage in early February 1898, Bedminster reserves were having such a poor season that they applied to pull-out of the League, a request that was denied by the committee. However, shortly afterwards they had no choice but to permit the Royal Artillery, who were stationed at Horfield, to withdraw after most of their players were posted to the North-West Frontier of India.

And it did not stop there. Eastville Wanderers reserves put in their resignation with only two months of the season to go, and although the request was initially refused, after learning details of their financial situation the committee had no option but to accept losing them as well.

The rule determining how many times a reserve team player could turn out in the Western League Professional section was not easy to apply, and when the committee discovered that a Fishponds reserve team player had turned out for his club no less than thirteen times in the Professional section, the two- point deduction for contravention of rules was contested as too harsh by the club in question; a protest that was lost, eventually leaving them with just three points. The difficulty of running a reserve team in that section was apparent and was reflected when none appeared the following season.

In the Professional section, the first real problems arose half way through the season concerning refereeing. It had been agreed that the clubs could arrange the official for their matches by mutual consent, but it had not been stipulated where they should choose the man from, and some clubs had selected men who were not members of the Western Referees Association; an organisation formed to insure standards. The solution was found by getting consent that all referees would become members of that group, and that their appointment to a game would be notified and confirmed by that body.

As the season came toward an end the question of trophies became the latest topic to occupy the men in charge of the new venture. At first it was proposed that, with the permission of Edward Colston, the existing Cup would be awarded to the winner of the Professional section, and new one's purchased for the winners of the Amateur sections, but that brought about howls of objections from those participating. Eventually, Bristol City, who had only lost two games all season and won the League four points clear of Swindon Town, agreed to accept a new Trophy, providing it was of the same value as the Colston Cup. A magnificent new Cup was then purchased at a value of £32-10s-0d, and donated by the Messrs. Chilcott.

Bristol City were truly setting the pace, and in their first season in the Southern League had finished as runners-up, in the Division One, four points behind Southampton, and five points ahead of Tottenham Hotspur. They had not, in fact, suffered a defeat in that competition until New Year's Day, when they were beaten by the eventual league champions, and while City were achieving those amazing results, Warmley were setting the pace in the Southern League Division Two, winning 19 games and remaining unbeaten all year, with three matches drawn. They were also to be the first club in that league to notch up over 100 goals in one season, with 108 scored for, and 15 against, truly demonstrating the pedigree of football on offer in the West Country.

Throughout the year, the national press had been questioning how Bristol could support so many professional clubs, with more in the city than anywhere outside London. It had led to many strong rumours that Bedminster and Bristol City in the south, and Warmley and St George in the east, would merge. Old rivalries, however, would not allow that logical scenario, no matter how sensible the move was perceived to be.

The cost of running a professional club was enormous. The average price charged for policing games was 9/-. Travelling costs, on either winding roads or by public transport, were around 1/- for every 50 miles travelled. At a time when Tom noted that his father *'would have thought a few shillings a week very good,'* it was clear why local clubs were getting even deeper into debt, especially as there were four Professional clubs in the City and two in nearby Wiltshire, all competing for large home gates to make the books balance.

Storm clouds had been gathering over many of the well-established clubs for some time, which made it very difficult for the men of the Western League to collect subscriptions, leaving the League in a perilous financial state, once more.

The experiment to change the structure of the League had only partially worked, and although a lot of lessons had been learned by the administrators, while the amateurs had tested their patience, it was the professional clubs who were constantly challenging. Many rules were changed time and time again, showing just how much there was still to be learned, but overall it was still widely felt that with a few adjustments the League was going in the right direction.

In the Amateur division, Bedminster, who had benefitted from the transfer of Clifton players into an already strong side, were runaway winners, and with that success they then applied, and gained, professional status for the following season - adding yet another club into the mix.

Mangotsfield disappeared from the League after struggling all season following trouble over the general state of their ground, their finances, and their conduct, both on and off the field. Despite that loss, it was, however, assumed that there would be sufficient clubs in the competition to ensure optimism for the coming season, and at the Annual Dinner, which took place in late April at the White Hart Hotel, Old Market, those sentiments were foremost in the mind of Chairman, Mr Riddell when he addressed the assembled crowd looking to the future.

The summer break, however, told a different story.

Both Bristol City and Reading withdrew from the Western League to try their luck instead in the United League, leaving only seven teams in the Professional section, which was renamed Division One. The number of amateur clubs taking part was also reduced by the resignation of all the reserve teams, leaving numbers considerably reduced.

There were, in fact, insufficient clubs to form two lower divisions, but with Paulton Rovers, Radstock, Bristol Amateur and Mount Hill all set to become members of the Amateur Section, Division Two, the League was still in an apparently healthy state, as the committee made the final preparations for the 1898/99 season.

Despite the declaration by Paulton Rovers and Radstock that they intended to join, before the season kicked-off Radstock withdrew without being entered onto the fixture list, and as such did not incur a fine. In contrast Paulton Rovers were still in the mix when the fixtures were arranged, but then subsequently failed to fulfil them. That, of course, did contravene the rules and a fine was imposed, which was ignored, and so the matter was referred to the GFA and the Somerset FA, but it took many months to resolve.

It was turning out to be an extremely problematic time. In November, the committee was forced to accept the resignation of Trowbridge Town because financial problems had forced them to shut their doors for a while. The club did eventually reform and re-entered the Western League in 1901 as an amateur club.

Another founder member club, and Champions for many years, Warmley, were in deep trouble as well; both on and off the pitch. Their playing strength of former years totally eluded them in the higher division of the Southern League, and with the extra competition for players in the area making it difficult to raise and pay for a team with sufficient strength, it did not improve. It took until 10th December to gain their first win of the season, by which time they were losing over £20 a week, with reduced gates and inflated wages reflecting the theory that the area could not sustain the number of professional clubs it had. Warmley were also £900 in debt, and had found that the move from their ground at the bottom of Warmley Hill behind the Tennis Court Inn, to Ingleside Road a few months before, was a costly mistake.

Warmley supporters, of course, were never known for their lack of passion, and the frustrations of the season boiled over in January when they entertained Millwall Athletic in a Southern League game that ended in a crushing 5-1 defeat. During the match, the referee had incensed a part of the crowd when two appeals for penalties were turned down, and as the poor man left the pitch, objects were hurled at him. He was said to have only just made it to the safety of the changing rooms in time, with a swelling crowd threatening to attack him still further.

That incident, plus the dour financial situation of the once fashionable club, was discussed at a meeting of shareholders a few days later, who decided that in the circumstances, the club should fold. Some of the supporters and players, however, vowed to carry on, and despite an impending FA inquiry into the Millwall incident, they managed to play two more games; albeit losing both. When the FA ruled that the ground should be closed for four weeks as a punishment for the transgression, it proved to be the final 'nail in the coffin' for the club, and even the hardiest of their supporters were forced to cede defeat.

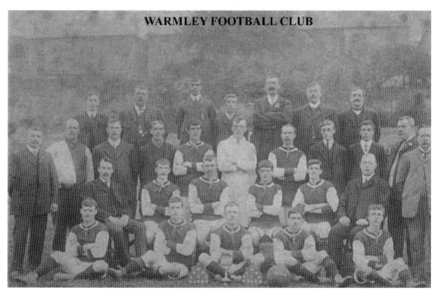

WARMLEY FOOTBALL CLUB

Their official resignation was received by the Western League committee on 8th February 1899 and was, at first, refused because they owed subscription money, but in the end, there was no option but to write off the debt. It was, however, agreed that the players from the club would not be allowed to register for any other league club until the debt was paid in full.

In early March 1899, the committee was also called on to make judgment following a complaint from Fishponds that the supporters of Midsomer Norton had encroached onto the pitch, interfering with players and throwing objects at them after they had won the game 2-1. There was also another allegation, that the Somerset club had fielded an ineligible player, Harry Hyman, who was a former Trowbridge Town player. Surprisingly the encroachment allegation was dropped, but it was proved that Hyman was not signed on, and two points were subsequently deducted.

To add to the administration problems, the thorny issue of the Charities Cup came to the fore when it was pointed out that the rules stated the competition was only open to member clubs; excluding the possibility that Bristol City could take part.

Such was the desirability of City participate, it was decided to simply change the rules, and an invitation was then sent to them. To the annoyance of the committee men, however, City declined the invitation due to their heavy fixture load; an action that infuriated the members. In response, a resolution was passed and sent to the press that simply stated; '*The committee deeply regret that Bristol City, after being given a cordial invitation, should have refused to accept the same and so assist local charities in the said Bristol Charities Cup'*.

After that sledge-hammer of diplomacy, the once cordial relationship that had existed between the Western League and the club, became somewhat strained for a while.

Eventually, after much discussion, the relationship was restored, and by season's end the Charity Cup Competition was held at the Bristol City ground, free of charge. That day, the 24th April 1899, a huge crowd watched what was generally agreed to be a thrilling encounter, in which Bedminster beat Reading, 3-2, at St Johns Lane; a great tribute to both the players and the officials involved, as well as being a demonstration of the way that football had become a favourite pastime in the West Country.

But all was not well, once again, with the League.

With the points deducted from the tables during the season, the final placings had little reflection of playing strengths and weaknesses, but more an indication of those clubs who had managed to survive a torrid year of debt and controversy.

Of the nine clubs taking part in the inaugural year in 1892, only two remained in business, Bedminster and Eastville Rovers, and the League was struggling to keep going with only four professional and five amateur clubs entering for the following season.

During the summer, it came to the notice of the committee that there was a proposal on the table to form a Southern Counties League; a move that could well have provided the last straw for the continuation of the Western League. In response to the proposal, a letter and petition was sent to the Football Association pointing out the effect that the additional Southern section of the Southern League had already placed on the membership from Professional clubs. Alongside that, on the Amateur front, the East Bristol and District League had re-launched itself as the 'Bristol and District League' and had begun a recruitment drive.

Few people realised the true position that the Western League now found itself in, with incomplete financial accounts for the previous two seasons allowing little confidence to invest money into a growing financial crisis -

which had been caused in the main by the loss of income from both the defunct and the financially unstable clubs.

Eventually the Treasurer, Mr Francis, loaned to league £25 to stave off the ever-growing number of creditors who were pressing for payment, with repayment of that loan to be from a proposed 'English Players v Scottish Players' match which was due to take place early in the season at St John's Lane.

Players for that important game were selected from Bristol City, Bristol Rovers (formerly Eastville), Bedminster and Swindon Town, and the prospects caused huge interest. However, despite a vast amount of advertising, a disappointing gate of 1911 watched a good display of football, which the English League players won by the odd goal in three.

The financial return from the game, after the Swindon players had been given their agreed expenses plus 1/6d for tea, which amounted to 6/- each, saw the £42-13s-6d passed on to Mr Francis toward the Leagues debt. While the Treasurer did not ask for the return of his loan, that receipt, together with a £10 donation from the Bristol and District League, enabled normal business to resume, and for the time being staved off the spectre of bankruptcy.

Away from football, the country found itself at war when troops were sent to fight the Boers in South Africa, which began on 11th October 1899. Despite initial predictions that it would be over in a few months, soon an appeal was being made for donations to the Transvaal War Fund; which despite perilous financial troubles close to home, the League pledged to contribute to.

With so few clubs taking part in the League during the 1899/1900 season, the administrators turned their minds to the prospects for future progress, which seemed to lay with attracting professional clubs, and so it was a positive step to find that Bristol City had agreed to re-enter the Charity Cup Competition.

An exciting semi-final game between Bedminster and Bristol City ended in a draw, 1-1, with Bedminster then progressing through to face Bristol Rovers in a game at the City ground. It then took three committee meetings to decide a date for the Cup Final, but in the end a well-attended game took place on Saturday 24th March 1900 with Bedminster picking up the Cup by the only goal of the game.

It was one of the few successful ventures in a difficult season with the gate grossing £172-11s-7d, and after a deduction of 18/- for the Bristol Rovers players and 5% working expenses, £75-13s-07 was distributed to various charities in the City, and the rest gratefully received to keep the League afloat.

With only four clubs in the Professional section, Bristol City, Bristol Rovers, Bedminster and Swindon Town, the news that came out of a meeting at The Temperance Hall, Bedminster on 10th April 1900, came as a surprise to many.

In previous years, the competition between Bristol City and Bedminster had been so fierce that even friendly matches had been refused, and when Mr

Hollis, the manager who had taken City into the Southern League, moved his allegiance to Bedminster, the rivalries within such a small area of the City were intensified. That was then made worse when he led Bedminster to finish the term runners-up in the Western League and three places above City in the Southern League.

The announcement that the two clubs were to merge was greeted with an enormous amount of disbelief both by the press and public alike. In the event, although it was supposed to be an amalgamation, Bedminster seemed to gain little for the move except a seat on the Board and a share of the debts, while City agreed to play half of the following seasons' games at St John's Lane, and the other half at Ashton Gate, to appease both sets of supporters. They did, however, manage to do so under the Bristol City banner, and five seasons later made the permanent move to play all games at Ashton Gate.

With those events occupying the minds of many football supporters in the area, the committee was trying to tackle a variety of administrative problems beside turning their minds firmly to the survival of the League; with a real fear that within a few months, the venture that had been so innovative at its inception, could have little option but to fold.

For such a small division, the Amateur section threw up a lot of extra work, which was partially caused by the team from Weston (Bath), who failed to answer correspondence and had many complaints filed against them by visiting teams over the state of their ground. Combined with that, Cotham, who had suffered from being turned off their pitch for houses to be built, earned a sever rebuke for submitting false team sheets. Despite Cotham having such problems and ending the term in bottom place for the second season, they retained their place and seemed also to learn a lesson or two in the process.

During the season, a letter had been sent to all Southern League clubs inviting them to join a new Western League Professional section for the first season of the new century, which was backed by existing members, together with Reading FC. The work put in by the committee seemed to yield results when a meeting, held on 16th June 1900, was attended by eight professional clubs, Portsmouth, Millwall, Queens Park Rangers, Bristol City, Reading, Swindon, Southampton and Bristol Rovers. Tottenham Hotspur also expressed an interest in the proposition.

A long discussion took place that day to formulate acceptable rules, and it was eventually decided to recommend to the Western League AGM that:

1. Each division would manage its own affairs, with Division One committee meetings to be held at Reading for the convenience of its members.

2. The committee should consist of the League Chairman and Secretary, together with one representative from each competing club.

3. A quorum of five would be required per meeting with other rules to be agreed to establish what would happen in the absence of the chairman.

4. That each club must field its strongest team available with a £10 fine for non-compliance.

The new format also allowed that the bottom club would, each season, should apply to retain its membership alongside any other new applicants. While some of the rules would prove difficult to administer, not least number four, progress had, indeed, been made toward a more stable future.

The news was greeted with great anticipation by the footballing mad public of the West, and even the press seemed to agree that the future was bright. With the finances of the League on the up and an improved balance sheet that was considered satisfactory, the new century was greeted with the optimism that had once been the trademark of the Western Football League.

CHAPTER 5

A whole new ball game

The first season of the 20th century was a whole new ball game for the Western League, and while the football mad public looked forward to watching an array of professional clubs, technical problems delayed the new venture kicking-off.

Through the adoption of forms and rules from established leagues and with guidance from the Football Association, most of the initial problems had been overcome, but the governing body was slow to validate the competition, and the start of the season came, and went, without progress being made.

Much to everyone's dismay, it took until a meeting with the FA on 12th November 1900 to sort out the bureaucratic dogma. All the First Division committee travelled to Chancery Lane that day, such was the urgency of the decision, and with the clubs speaking in unison for a quick solution to the problem, it was clearly a sign that the venture was one that everyone involved was backing.

By allowing a certain amount of flexibility, the committee had identified a gap in the footballing week for clubs, who had to generate as much money through the gates as possible. The directors of those clubs were more than happy to sign up and commit their talented players to two or even three game a week against fellow professionals, with spectators more than willing to hand over money at the turnstiles; no matter what the name of the competition was.

Very soon the Management Committee of the Western League was reporting a far healthier financial position than had been seen for years, with a working profit of £52-3s-1d. That offset some of the debt that had accrued though the dying years of the 19th century which at one time had stood at £102-6s-0d. Although a 'big' match in aid of the League funds was firmly anticipated, it would be well into the following season before it materialised, with the clubs concerned certainly overstretched in playing time.

In the Amateur Division, the admission of Weston-super-Mare, Paulton Rovers and Warmley Tower Rovers made up the required number to eight, but the withdrawal of Warmley before a ball was kicked because they were unable to establish a ground, reduced the number of games on offer. That was then compounded by the withdrawal of Weston (Bath) after not being able to raise a sufficiently strong side for their first scheduled game on 15th September 1900.

Despite those problems, however, such was the optimism and increased status for the League that a Press Officer was appointed, a task that fell to the ebullient Mr Sawyer of Reading.

His appointment was particularly opportune, as shortly afterwards a comment appeared in the Bristol Evening News containing a personal attack on the League Secretary, Mr Stevens, suggesting that the delay in sanctioning the Professional section had been due to his ineptitude. In response, a letter was sent and published, exonerating the Hon. Secretary, and for a while the relationship between league and press became cordial.

After the long wait, the first game in the new section took place on 14th November 1900, which saw Bristol City beat Southampton, 4-1, in front of over 5,000 paying spectators. The success of that was obvious, and despite the delay in the division kicking-off, by the end of December, Tottenham Hotspur were heading the table having averaged a game a week, and most of the other clubs were not far behind.

Off the field, the sheer increase in the amount of administration the new set-up had brought with it, claimed its first casualty when, on 13th December the Chairman, Mr Riddell, resigned. He had not been able to attend all the meetings that were an intrinsic part of the new set-up, and offered to stand aside to allow the position to be taken-up by someone without the amount of outside obligations he was signed up to.

Surprisingly, his resignation was immediately accepted despite the longevity of Mr Riddell's reign at the helm, in fact, since the formation of the League. His place was taken by Mr Stevens, with Mr Sawyer as vice-chairman, the former, however, had been a little reticent to agree to the appointment initially.

The letter of resignation was read out at a meeting of the Division Two committee later that month, where it was pointed out that constitutionally neither committee had the power to accept the resignation. Mr Stevens was asked to report that at the next meeting of the Professional Committee at Reading. They further suggested that the resolutions that had been passed referring to the matter, should be withdrawn.

After much acrid debate, that was just what happened, and Mr Riddell remained as Chairman.

Trouble abounded in Amateur Division Two and, despite beginning the season much earlier, most were not fulfilling their fixtures as well as the Professional teams. Fishponds, who were new to the League, had the only two points to their credit deducted in December for fielding an ineligible player, and it did not stop there. Shortly afterwards it was revealed that their Secretary had put in false returns in each of their four matches played. He was reported to the Gloucester FA who, at a subsequent enquiry into the club, suspended the Chairman and all the Committee members for a month. The Secretary was then also dealt with separately and banned from all football for a year on the various charges.

Despite the problems, St Francis, who joined the League later, changed their name to Bedminster St Francis shortly after and seemed to settle in. They had been in business for five years, and that season was proving to be a successful one with a good run in the Amateur Cup. To celebrate, they held a dinner at which Mr Robert Campbell, of Bristol City, gave a very revealing speech on behalf of the Western League.

In it he said that it had, in recent times, appeared quite possible that the League would go out of existence, adding that without the success of the recent restructure, it would probably have been the most likely outcome. The success of lobbying for prominent clubs in the south of England to become members had, however, now abated the crisis. Significantly he ended the speech by stating that if the weaker clubs in the Southern League were curtailed, then Saturday's could be given over to Western League games, and that in turn would then result in the League becoming as important as ever.

There really had been a great deal of work done to ensure the future of the League, and by allowing clubs to play on a mid-week basis a compromise had been found that suited all parties. However, the success was built on a flexibility that would truly test the men in charge in the years to come.

At the end of January 1901, there was a long period of mourning when Queen Victoria died at the age of 81. She had ruled the Country and Commonwealth for over sixty-three years, and the following message was sent to Buckingham Palace; '*That this meeting of the Western Football League desire respectfully to express their condolence with His Majesty the King on the death of Her Most Gracious Majesty, Queen Victoria, and to assure His Majesty of their unswerving loyalty and devotion to His Majesty on his accession to the Imperial Throne of the Realm'.*

The long period of mourning which precluded any games of football taking place, contributed to the general inability of the Amateur clubs to fulfill their fixtures. The re-arrangement of postponed games was not made easier by most clubs taking part in two, or even three leagues, and when Bedminster stated that their Bristol and District League games took precedence over Western League games, the committee did not accept that as a fair reason. In the end, Bedminster withdrew from the competition with six games un-played, and were fined a total of £1-11s-6d together with the following season's subscription of £1-1s-0d. With other games also not completed at seasons end, it was then decided to just let the table stand incomplete.

While the Professional clubs were fulfilling their fixtures, they were constantly under fire from allegations that they were failing to field their strongest sides, with the Daily Express quoting an official from one of the clubs purported to have said that the players do not take Western League games seriously. The Hon. Secretary quickly attempted to get that statement retracted, which he did with admirable speed.

There was, however, a very good reason why one of the clubs was fielding weaker teams. Tottenham Hotspur were working their way through the Qualifying Rounds of the English Cup and were about to give the North a shake-up by becoming the first southern based club to win the treasured Trophy.

Tottenham beat Sheffield United, 3-1, in a replay of the Final having been held, 2-2, in the first game, on a pitch that was marked out differently than those of today. Although the penalty shot had been introduced several years before,

TOTTENHAM HOTSPUR V SHEFFIELD UNITED

the spot was about to be added in 1902, and the goalkeeping area greatly redefined to afford more protection to the goalie. It was, however, to be many more years before the modern day lay-out of a pitch would be standard, which would then affect great changes to the game of Association football.

After that memorable victory, Tottenham agreed to contribute £5-10s-0d toward the cost of the championship medals, partly in recognition of the leniency that had been shown them for not fielding their strongest teams in each game, but also as a token to celebrate winning the English Cup. The demands of that involvement naturally caused a strain on their squad of players, but despite that, they still managed to complete their obligations and ended the season in third place behind Champions, Millwall, and runners-up, Portsmouth.

The AGM, which was held on 10th June 1901 again at the White Hart Hotel in Old Market, was well attended with Bristol Rovers, Swindon Town, Southampton, Reading, Tottenham Hotspur, QPR, Bristol East, Paulton Rovers, Weston-super-Mare, Trowbridge Town, Cotham and Bristol St George all in attendance.

For the first time in many years there was happier news regarding the League's financial position, with the audited accounts showing a reverse in the outstanding debt of £70 to one of a credit balance of £17-9s-11d, which was quite an achievement, not least because the Treasurer, Mr Francis, had sadly died during the season and a settlement of the money owed to him had been requested from his Trustees. Although this took £25 from the account, the remainder of the full amount of £38-18s-8d was waved.

It was further anticipated that, with two league Benefit Matches planned for the following season, and a bank account opened for the first time, a continued improvement would be seen. Mr Wilkinson took over the post of Treasurer together with Mr Stevens, who resigned as Hon Secretary; a post that he had held since the League's inauguration.

The AGM ended on a somber note with the announcement regarding the disaster that had befallen football on 5th April at Ibrox Park, Glasgow, when during an England v Scotland game, twenty spectators had died, and two hundred badly injured, following the collapse of a section of the stadium. There were 70,000 people in the ground that day, and many did not know the extent of the disaster until long after they had left. On hearing the sad news, it was unanimously agreed to donate five guineas to the FA's Disaster Fund.

Although there had been the usual murmurings about refereeing throughout the season, overall the problems of previous years did not arise. The Western Referees Association continued to raise the standards of officials and ensure that the man in the middle knew how to interpret the ever-changing rules of the game. The appointment of match officials was conducted at the monthly divisional meetings, but there was still a clause in the rules that enabled clubs to object to those selected, if necessary. As the season progressed a more sophisticated sub-committee sat each month to make the appointments, with committee officials often taking turns, as well, to run the line.

The Football Association passed a rule at its AGM that year, setting the maximum wage a professional footballer playing in the Football League could be paid at £4 a week. Although the payment was double what a skilled tradesman received for his work at the time, the FA also outlawed match bonuses, unless the player had been with the same club for five years. That was the first time such a ruling had been made, which caused problems as some players had been earning as much as £10 a week. The dictate then prompted some players to join Southern League clubs where no such restrictions on wages existed.

A reflection of just how this affected clubs could be seen by the amount of player recruitment advertisements placed in sections of the press. One such article was posted by Bristol Rovers in the Athletic News, which was generally the most read paper on the professional game, and which appeared just below a similar one for Liverpool Football Club, specifying; 'Bristol Rovers FC Ltd require First Class Players for next season. Full particulars as the height, weight, age and lowest terms to, AG Holmer, Black Swan Hotel, Eastville, Bristol'.

That reflected the criteria of professional clubs of the time with the main information for recruitment being height, weight and the lowest wages the players would accept!

The players often did their own washing and most of the Rovers players went off for a pint with the supporters at the Black Swan. Alf Homer, would pull on his black managerial bowler hat and proudly tell anyone within earshot *'Don't forget we have got a few internationals around here at the moment.'* The clubs trouble was that there was never enough money to pay the summer wages, they lost a lot of players that way, in fact, it was often a packet of Woodbines as the going price at Eastville in the early years of the 20th century.

In general, Tom summed up the way the League was growing when he wrote in the original 'A View From' - *'Our lives were all changing, and both myself, and my beloved Western League had grown up fast over the years. The*

League was now showing signs of maturing into a prestigious competition serving professional clubs well, and I was growing quickly into a well-read youth who still enjoyed childhood pleasures.'

He continued; *'I remember how delighted we all were when we heard that Bristol City had been elected to the Second Division of the English Football League. Although this was sad for the Western League as the club was forced to give up membership, we felt that, at last, the national game was becoming national, both for the North and the South to enjoy'.*

West Ham United took the place of Bristol City for the new season, and although Fishponds withdrew from Division Two, Trowbridge Town returned as an Amateur club, as did St George, and together with the existing members, they were also joined by the reserve sides from Swindon Town and Bristol Rovers.

The 1901/02 season heralded the start of a general period that saw the conditions of the working man change rapidly, with many Northerners moving to the south and west of the country in search of work, and with that the game of football rapidly gained in popularity.

The long-awaited League Benefit Game predictably took an inordinate amount of time to arrange, and even when the date of 16th October 1901 was agreed, it created a problem as it coincided with a similar Southern League game. With some of the Portsmouth players due to be involved in London against a Tottenham Hotspur eleven, compromise was needed; which to most people's surprise was exactly what happened.

The problem was resolved with two players from the Western League game released to play in London, while in return three were sent to other way to compete at Portsmouth against a team billed as 'The Rest of the League'.

The venue had caused a certain number of hard negotiations, as it was originally due to take place in Bristol, but in their wisdom the committee putting the game together had decided that the gate would be larger if it was to take place at either Southampton or Portsmouth; a decision that then saw both of those clubs arguing who would stage it.

At the end of the day the Western League Champions drew the short straw, and eventually handed over a net profit of £36-6s-5d toward League funds, after all the players had been given a third-class rail fare and 10/- in expenses. After such success, a 'London Club's v Provincial Club's' game was attempted, but eventually dropped amidst an administrative nightmare.

As expected, the Amateur Division, once again, threw up problems. Although the transportation system had improved tremendously over the years, both Swindon Town reserves and Staple Hill were reported to the League for playing a man short at Cotham and Paulton. Both defended the charge, explaining that they had a player who missed the train.

With registration rules at the time preventing the old practice of calling on a member of the public to step in and make up the numbers on the pitch, and the luxury of squad football as we know it today not an option, simple slip-up like these were no exception, and as Tom wrote; '*It took very careful planning to get to certain grounds in time for kick-off, as we found to our peril when we went to watch Paulton Rovers play Champions, Bristol East, one dismal Saturday. When we arrived at Midsomer Norton station after what seemed like a lifetime on the Midland Railway steam train, we found that we had missed our connection. It meant a mile walk to the ground in pouring rain, which was not rewarded by a good match, and the walk back along dark narrow lanes holding my father's hand found us in low spirits by the time we reached the station again. Such was the lot of the football spectator in the early years of our League!*'

On the professional front, Bristol Rovers suggested that the League should hold a game at the end of the 1901/02 season at their Stapleton Road ground, with a team consisting of past Western League players; a game that went ahead on 29th March. It was entitled Western League Crocks v Bristol Rovers with an admission of 3d standing and 6d in the enclosure, and the eventual profit of 30/- was shared between the League funds and Bristol Charities Cup.

For the second year, Portsmouth were declared Champions ahead of Spurs, who were a close second. There was, however, a contrast in the clubs in the division with Swindon Town, who didn't win a game all season, giving weight to allegations that they were fielding weakened sides all season, which was confirmed when they resigned in June. Their place was taken by Brentford, who won a ballot of member clubs by six votes to two over New Brompton. The second from bottom club, QPR, were successful in applying for re-election.

The Champions of the Second Division were Bristol East, for the third successive season, who had been truly formidable throughout, scoring 127 goals with just 22 against. In contrast bottom club, Cotham Amateurs had struggled in their first season, but could take heart when reflecting on previous league records. The accolade for worst club to date fell to Clevedon Town who, in 1894/95 had conceded 136 goals whilst scoring 23. This was followed closely by Clifton reserves who, in 1895/96 had failed to gain a point. That gave Cotham, with statistics of 23 goals for, with 71 against, and three points, enough hope to continue for another year.

At the AGM held in mid-June, Mr Riddell was not in the Chair as his youngest son had been involved in an accident, but there was heartening news that the accounts showed a surplus of £72-6s-5d; quite a contrast to the earlier years of deficits. At the same meeting, a discussion ensued following a claim by Staple Hill that the £7-10s-0d that they had paid during an appeal for funds to keep the League going, had been a loan not a donation, and as such should be repaid. After much discussion, the claim was dismissed, but when it was then revealed just how much of a financial crisis the club was facing, the committee agreed to donate £5-5s-0d to keep them going.

As the AGM ended, the meeting was reminded that the Boer War had just ended, on 31st May, and that, although celebrations were in order, none should forget that it had sadly cost the lives of well over 11,000 young men, some of whom had played Western League football.

After the meeting Mr Stevens was presented with an Illuminated Address that had been signed by all the League's leading players, along with a cheque for £25, with £7 of that having been donated by clubs in acknowledgement of the work the he had done for the League since its inauguration.

During the close season, a lot of work went into ensuring the continuity of the new look league structure, and so it was disappointing for all concerned to see an article appear in the press suggesting that Southampton were reviewing their membership; adding that the club feared that even if they decided to stay, their players would treat the games as make-weight and not take it seriously. That had followed reports of Swindon Town withdrawing due to a lack of gate receipts, which they said was due to the competition being run mid-week with an afternoon kick-off.

In response, and after several meetings, the men from the Dell issued a statement avowing their intent not just to stay in the competition, but also signaled their intent to aim for the Western League Championship in the season to come, which, unfortunately, did not stem speculation about the status of the competition; and it did not stop there.

While the season kicked-off with great demand for League handbooks, with 37 alone from national and local newspapers, the seemingly positive enthusiasm was quelled, when yet another article appeared in the Daily Express on 31st October 1902, purporting to quote Mr Matthews, Secretary of Reading FC saying that '*The Reading players do not take the Western League games seriously*'. A statement that was more seriously viewed given his prominent involvement within the League committee.

The comment was widely commented on in other newspapers, which resulted in Mr Riddell ordering an inquiry into the harsh words. In defence of Mr Matthews, Mr Harding of Brentford FC, protested that he had been present when the interview was given, and that he did not hear any such statement. That defence was then seen as sufficient evidence for a letter to be written to the paper on behalf of the League demanding that the inaccurate quote was rescinded. A statement to that effect was duly published, but the damage was done.

Behind the scenes there were also problems with QPR, whose spokesman had been particularly vocal about a new rule that had been introduced concerning new or re-elected clubs. The rule in question required a £25 guarantee, which was to be backed by the secretary and four Directors of a club prior to Western League entry being confirmed.

The issue was so contentious that it took until November to solve, when the committee discussed it at length during the monthly meeting at Reading, where the rule was amended to read that new or re-elected clubs should deposit £25 into the Western League's bank in the name of both the League and the club prior to the start of the season.

In the Amateur section, it was to be a memorable season for Paulton Rovers who began so well, but ended with problems. The Amateur Cup proved good hunting ground for the Somerset club with a short run culminating in a well-supported game on New Year's Day, 1903, where they held Oxford City to a 2-2 draw. The replay was lost to the eventual Amateur Cup finalists, but only after a determined show of character that was viewed as a credit to the Western League.

Unfortunately, following those games, their season took a turn for the worse, with a report that they had fielded an ineligible player in a game, and had then covered up the misdemeanor by simply omitting to name the player on the team sheet. When the League Secretary became suspicious that only ten names had been included, confirmation by both the referee and a committee member who had been present at the game, that eleven men had been on the field of play, put paid to the deceit, and the club was fined 5/-. Their secretary was also censured and cautioned as to his future conduct.

Paulton then failed to turn up shortly afterwards at a scheduled game against Bristol Rovers reserves, because they found that they could not raise a team. As they had only cabled Rovers three hours before the game was due to kick-off, the Bristol club's claim for compensation of £1-18s-3d was granted. On appeal against the fine, Mr Hall of Paulton said that several players were sick and had not withdrawn until late on, which left the team with seven players to take to the pitch; a reason that he maintained was good enough to scratch the game without punishment.

The appeal did not wash with the committee as it was noted that the club was guilty of failing to communicate with players, notifying them of their selection by simply posting a notice on the headquarters gate the Tuesday before a game. The fine stood, and it was further suggested that Paulton took steps to correct the practice. However, it was a credit to them that with all the communication, travel and administrative problems being faced by the Somerset miners, they continued in membership and completed all their games that season.

Despite the speculation earlier about low gates at Division One games and questions about players' commitment, Portsmouth let it be known that they were delighted with the gate achieved on 30th November 1902 when they entertained Tottenham Hotspur, which yielded £280. In contrast to that Millwall caused the League all sorts of problems, not least by failing to reply to correspondence regarding money owed.

As the New Year of 1903 came in, details began to emerge about the possibility of an application for membership being forthcoming from the newly formed Plymouth Argyle Football Club, on provision that they could also gain admission to the Southern League.

The following extract, relayed by historian, Roger Walters, demonstrates the club's serious intent to join the Western League, as opposed to the 'make-weight' allegations that had been circulating.

He wrote; *'On 12th March 1903, the Western League Chairman and Secretary met with Lieutenant Frederick Hugh Windrum and Clarence Newby Spooner to discuss the proposal of Plymouth Argyle Football Company Ltd to join the League, if they could gain admission into the Southern League. Windrum and Spooner had already given the Plymouth Argyle details to Western League officials to assist in their discussion at the 12th March meeting. Probably, that initial meeting was on the day of the International at Portsmouth on the 2nd March'.*

'The Western League was advised that the Club's capital, not including Home Park (owned by Argyle Athletic Club Limited) was £3,000. The ground was fully equipped; it had dressing rooms for (perplexingly) five teams, with hot and cold baths. The stand accommodated 2,000; the only further expense was for three more turnstiles. The lease stood for 12½ years at £100 per year (the freehold had been in the hands of the British Electric Traction Company from 1900). Trams from all parts passed the ground. The team would be the best they could obtain, practically the whole of the capital would be spent on securing first-class men, and they would not lure players away from fellow Western and Southern League clubs'.

PLYMOUTH ARGYLE FC EARLY 1900's

'As further endorsement, Windrum and Spooner told the officials that although rugby was strong, the new club would use every endeavour to gain a large share of the patronage of the football public. They speculated that many dockyard workers patronised rugby because there were only small local teams in the district playing association football. There was no evidence for this belief; on 7th March 1903, a crowd of 16,000 packed into The Rectory to see Albion versus Newport'.

It is interesting to note that at the time, Lieutenant Windrum was standing for Chairman of the Devon FA, but when his name was put forward, there was no seconder because most of the members believed that the post should be held by a person who favoured amateurism, and he was obviously committed to the professional game.

The subsequent successful candidate for the post, Dr George Meadows said in his acceptance speech that he *'would rather see a thousand boys kicking about a football badly than twenty-two men doing it well'* and it was notable that all the anti-Argyle remarks were greeted by 'hear, hear' from the small assembled attendance; an indication that the professional game was still a long way from the hearts of many Association men of the day.

At the AGM of 1903, the suitability of Plymouth Argyle joining the League was in no doubt, and they were voted in by eleven to four, with New Brompton, once again losing out. They replaced the errant Millwall club, who moved on owing £12-6s-1d to the League, a debt that took many months, and a good deal of correspondence, to resolve.

While Mr Sawyer was not at the AGM as he had been injured in a serious accident, members of the press were there for the first time, and heard that the financial position was still positive, with an income of £129-10s-0d and expenses of £94-1s-0d, leaving the League in a healthy position with no liabilities.

There were a couple of rule changes on the table with the rule that QPR had disliked regarding the £25 deposit prior to the season beginning, amended to read 'if required,' a move that was popular with all the other professional clubs. An attempt to solve the problem caused by games ending with short-time being played was not as popular, however, and the clubs turned down the suggestion that all games should be played to the full duration or automatically replayed. Which still left any time short still to be tagged on to the return encounter.

Portsmouth were, once again, Champions for the third year running, and a special championship flag was purchased to celebrate the achievement, along with gold medals, worth 30/-, which had the Western League Arms on one side.

Bristol Rovers won their first honours as Professional section runners-up, and their reserve side won the Division Two Championship, albeit with a little help from the strong squad within the club. The committee had, in fact, been quite lenient on Rovers over the matter of senior players taking part in the Amateur section, with the rules stating that a player could only take part in five senior games, but the committee were given discretion over the application of the rule if they deemed it necessary!

Division Two had been strengthened by the inclusion of the reserve teams, together with Bristol St George, and that reflected on the performance of Bristol East who ended the term in the unaccustomed position of half-way. In contrast, Cotham who had struggled for several seasons and had only won five of the 41 games played throughout their Western League career, ended the term bottom again, and withdrew.

During the first ten years, the League had lost the services of both Mr Francis and Mr Lacy Sweet, but had been well led by Mr Riddell, despite the difficulties that he had faced both in his private and public life. Those men who had introduced the concept of league football to the West of England had struggled throughout the period to come to terms with the intricacies of such a venture. The feat was nonetheless remarkable given the huge competition that they quickly faced from the growth of League football, and the threat of financial ruin that had loomed very close to home throughout the period.

The Western League had not only changed its name, but also its direction, with a greater emphasis from the start of the new century placed on the well-being of professional clubs, and a little of the original objectives lost in the process. The press had not been kind throughout the period, but even that relationship was gradually improving.

With an ever-quickening pace, the country was in the middle of change as well, with the working man of the 20th Century demanding a higher standard of living and more from the little leisure time that work allowed. The lessons of those demands were soon to be learned. As Tom put it; '*So there we were, the league and I, ten years old and a lot wiser. We had both matured greatly over the years and as I looked toward the prospects of going down the mines with my father, the League looked to grow by eventually enlarging the professional section to increase both income and status*'.

A statement that was so true Tom, but little did you know what lay ahead ....

CHAPTER 6

Running the new line

After a difficult initial ten-year period, the new structure of both professional and amateur clubs had brought a stability to the League. While a decline in the popularity of the amateur game had seen a reduction in gates, the professional clubs were doing well, attracting the attention of the press and increasing a strong and loyal supporter base.

The prospect of visiting the grounds of Swindon Town, Bristol Rovers and Bristol City to play against their reserve teams did, however, attract new applications in the Amateur section from both Welton Rovers and Radstock Town, with both clubs completing the mining triangle, by joining Paulton Rovers in the League, for the start of the 1903/04 season.

While there were still a few glitches in the Professional section, the most notable of which was a game between QPR and West Ham on 11th November, in which the former fielded twelve men, the competition ran quite smoothly and continued to attract spectators through the gates. In fact, in February 1904, it was reported that two games had attracted 10,000 supporters within a few days of each other, and considering that these were mid-week fixtures, it was, indeed, an amazing commendation for the competition.

The relationship between the committee and the media had also improved with one commentator observing that; '*A matter of five years ago, the Western League appeared to be tottering to its fall, but now it is the strongest mid-week league in this part of the country. Indeed, many of its members have found that Western League matches pay particularly well*'!

Because of the new interest, the committee decided to increase the League fees from £5-5s-0d to £10-10s-0d; an increase that did not deter new clubs from expressing an interest to join, therefore an application was made to the FA for an extension of the First Division from nine to eleven clubs; a request that was successful.

In Division Two, Bristol City reserves lost only one game all season, and won both their division, the Gloucester Senior Cup and the Bristol Charities Cup. To commemorate their remarkable treble a special dinner was held at the Bedminster Hotel at which many local footballing dignitaries were present.

The success of Staple Hill, who came in as runners-up and split the total domination of the reserve clubs, was noted, but although the League had funds to award a special medal to the club to reward such an achievement, they were unable to use that money without also striking medals for the runners-up in Division One. It was decided, therefore, to hold a special match to raise sufficient money, which was later achieved.

Taking part in two leagues, combined with weather problems, took its toll on Paulton Rovers during the season, and resulted in a backlog of fixtures. To solve the predicament, they decided to play both a Somerset and a Western

League fixture back-to-back. On the day, the spectators were treated to the same players competing in both games in a three-hour spectacular, with just a short break between each match. Regrettably Paulton's problems saw them withdraw from the League shortly afterwards, having completed all their fixtures.

Spurs, won the competition with some quite breathtaking displays of football, and were full of praise for the Western League, having recorded larger crowds at some games than for several of their Southern League fixtures. On receiving the First Division Cup at the AGM, their representative, Mr Hawley, said '*I can assure you all, there is money in the Western League and it pays for Spurs to be a member. Clubs must give of their best in matches or they will lose support*'.

In contrast, West Ham continued in their wooden spoon position, fueling, once again, the accusation that they were fielding weakened teams and treating the games as make-weight. They were called in front of the First Division committee to answer the accusations, and after a great deal of discussion managed to convince those present that they would be emulating their London neighbours the following year and attempting to win the League. In the event, they were to prove their point by then attaining their best league position to date; that of fifth.

At the AGM in June the Hon Sec. Mr Wilkinson congratulated clubs on getting through the year, financially or otherwise, and noted that the leading clubs in the First Division had amassed a good percentage of points. There had been 736 players registered during the season, of which 497 had taken to the pitch and just five were called in to answer charges by the FA or County Associations. Commenting on third placed Plymouth Argyle, the League Secretary added, '*the club more than justified the confidence that we placed in them*'.

The Second Division was hailed as a success that afforded those who wanted to follow the genuine amateur game an opportunity to watch top teams from Gloucester, Somerset and Wiltshire, with most featuring bona fide amateur players.

Mr Wilkinson concluded his view of the season by hailing the 'experiment' in Division One of appointing neutral linesmen, a 'triumph', even though the motion to make the move compulsory was defeated by member clubs. He pointed out that, although the move involved a slight increase in expense, it avoided the problems that appointing club linesmen threw up, and was, he concluded, an 'innovation' well worth the cost.

From the formation of the League back in 1892, Chippenham Town had been flirting with the idea of embracing the wider stage and join the League, but had resisted the temptation to step up, until circumstances forced a change of policy.

Football in the Wiltshire town had reflected challenges that were being faced by many, with the sheer number of clubs in a small area appearing to be unsustainable. And so, when the main employer, Saxby and Farmer, made it publicly known that a successful application had been lodged for a factory team to enter the Wiltshire League before the start of the 1903/04 season, alarm bells began to sound.

As most of the players for the two main senior sides, United and Town, were working for that company, it was rumored that one or both clubs could go out of existence if, under those circumstances, the men transferred loyalty to their main employer. However, with passionate vocal presentation's, Saxby and Farmer officials listened to the arguments, and instead entered a team into the Chippenham and District League; but the story did not end there.

During the summer of 1904, it was made plain that an application was about to go in for the factory side to play at Western League level, which would have presented a real threat to the seniority that the Chippenham Town club had enjoyed so far throughout its history.

Because of the threat such a move would carry, it was decided that entry to the Western League would be the only solution to retain both players, seniority and supporters. Within weeks, however, the threat by Saxby and Farmer, once again, did not materialise, but by then it was too late to withdraw from the Western League without penalties. In the end officials from Town agreed to retain membership of the Wiltshire League alongside the new demands; a safeguard if the journey into the West did not work out. It was to be an expensive decision by all accounts, but as results would show, a wise one.

Chippenham Town's initial four fixtures of the year in the Western League were all away from home, and from the start the difference in playing standards was clear. In the first game at Bristol Rovers reserves the home side slotted in three goals in the first ten minutes, and to make matters worse one of the Town players retired ill just before the interval leaving a ten man Wiltshire team at the mercy of the well journeyed Bristol club. Given the circumstances it was agreed that the 7-0 defeat was, under the circumstances, not as bad as it could have been. The result, however, was followed by two more defeats at the hands of Professional reserve teams, 7-1 at Bristol City, and 6-2 at Swindon Town.

After what had been a baptism of fire, it was no surprise that the Town's first home fixture in the Western League at their Malmesbury Road ground against Warmley, resulted in a 4-2 defeat. In the event the result did not affect the final table as the Bristol club folded after playing ten games, due to both financial problems and allegations of violence by some of their supporters.

Gates continued to rise at the Professional clubs and on 27th December a crowd of over 6,000 watched as Brentford beat Millwall, 2-0, while shortly afterwards a 4-0 drubbing of Fulham over QPR was watched by over 12,000. It seemed that the Western League had truly found the niche that it needed to continue to improve, both on and off the pitch.

At seasons end Plymouth Argyle won the First Division with 30 points from the twenty games played, two points in front of Brentford, with Reading in third place. Their show of form contrasted with Bristol Rovers, who shared bottom slot with QPR, but won both the Gloucestershire Senior Cup and the Southern League; the latter achievement bringing that huge Shield to the West Country for the first time.

Rovers reserves ended the season on equal points with Bristol City reserves, and picked up the Colston Cup undefeated, with just three drawn games, scoring a massive 76 goals and conceding just 5. They also won the Bristol Charity Cup fielding a team of 'mainly' Amateurs, who all re-register with the FA as such for the following season with the intent to emulate the success.

While there was a stability within the playing structure of the League, the committee was bidding farewell to Chairman, Mr Riddell, who had been at the helm for all the 13 years since inception, but who was now leaving the area. In recognition of all that he had done in those years he was presented with an Illuminated Address and a travelling bag, together with a letter of thanks signed by all the clubs.

Swindon Town withdrew from the Second Division to join the Second Division of the Southern League, with their place taken by Salisbury City and, once again, Paulton Rovers.

Around that time many changes were taking place within the game, both nationally and locally. The FA were in the process of altering some rules, and that, coupled with an extension of the English League to forty clubs, was soon to influence football in the West.

While those changes were in the pipe-line, there had been continual rumours that the extension would involve a merger between the English League and the Southern League. Although that was not the immediate outcome, the move would soon call for adjustments to the League, and call on a degree of lateral thinking to ensure its continuity; but that was in the future.

Some of the rule changes were quite radical, and would cause a good deal of confusion initially. Although it would not be until 1936 that the rules of the game came under greater scrutiny and were, in effect, re-written, in 1905 the FA stipulated the following alterations:

- *For the first-time the weight of the football was specified as having to be between 13-15oz at the start of the game. This was known as 'ball science' because it had been noted that the skillful player could be hampered by a hard ball, especially if the pitch was also hard.*

- *Also for the first time, the existing rule that ends were changed each time a goal was scored was deleted and thereafter teams would only change ends at half-time.*

- *The penalty kick was refined to stop players dribbling the ball all the way into the net, or passing it back to a player who was deemed in a better position to score. It was not until 1929, however, that the goalkeeper was forced not to move; in those early days, he was perfectly entitled to race out at the player or move along his line.*

- *From a throw-in, both feet had to be touching the bye-line and the ball had to be in both hands.*

- *Although goal nets were still not compulsory, the crossbar was now deemed an essential part of the game.*

Other rules were also slightly amended, with Rule 9, '*The Penalty Code*', summing up the game:

- '*Charging a fellow player in a good honest way and not amounting to rough play is allowed. The charge to be delivered with the shoulder, not below the belt, and not from behind unless he is intentionally obstructing you. You can charge to rid an opponent of the ball, stop him from getting past to take a pass, or interfere with someone else getting a pass*'.

Yes, it was a tough old game in those days!

There were also adjustments being made in the composition of the League, once again, following the expansion of the Southern League to twenty clubs. That, in effect, was viewed as putting even greater pressure on the professionals with the number of games they committed to about to increase significantly. While the easy option would have been to withdraw from the mid-week Western League, most clubs were happy with the way it was being run, and with the additional income it generated.

The problem occupied the committee at the June AGM where the Secretary. Mr Wilkinson opened proceedings reflecting that the season had been '*One of the most eventful in the career of the League, and one that has produced much discussion*'. A clear statement preceding the changes that were about to be put forward.

The solution proposed to the increase in games, and one that was agreed on by all the First Division clubs, was to divide their section into two, A & B, with six teams in each, and change the existing rule that '*Each club must play its best team in all league matches*' to '*Each club must play its best available team in all matches; with every match to include most the players who took part in the preceding Saturday.*' Although some objected to the second amendment, the majority agreed, and it was carried.

The running of the two smaller sections was then addressed with the decision that '*The clubs in Division One shall be divided by ballot into two sections of six clubs in each. Each club shall, before the end of January in each season, play home and away matches alternately with the other sides in its section. The Management Committee may, however, give permission to play matches on holidays and Saturdays after that date. The winners of each section shall play a deciding or final match for the Championship of Division One on a neutral ground, the gate being decided under English Cup rules. In the event of two or more clubs being equal in points, goal average will decide the winner of the section. The bottom club in each section shall retire at the end of each season. The travelling expenses of 12 men in these matches shall be pooled and borne equally by the whole of the clubs in Division One at the end of the season.'*

While all those rules and amendments were carried by the clubs a suggestion by the Secretary that 5% of the gross gate at the deciding matches should go to the League, was not entertained; a decision that did not go down well with some of the longer established Management Committee members.

The Hon Treasurer, Mr Stephens, resigned straight after the rule amendments, and then spoke saying that it upset him very much indeed that he had to leave the old Western League. He protested most strongly against the League being made what he termed as, '*a different organisation from any other league that held such importance in England*'. The Hon. Sec also put his resignation in, but after much discussion both were put forward to stay, with the roles they were responsible for reversed!

It was clear that the professionals had taken over the League and reshaped it to suit their requirements, and the agreement of the founder members of the League was more in accord to ensure its continuation, than an endorsement.

At seasons end QPR won Division One, a point clear of Southampton, and in Division Two, Bristol Rovers reserves were, once again, the pick of the bunch, losing just one game. The table ended incomplete, however, when Bristol East failed to turn up at Trowbridge Town on 17th March due to the numerous problems they were experiencing. With both clubs in the bottom two positions it did not affect the other club's standings and so the results stood. Unfortunately, that would be the last time that Bristol East, who had promised so much, would compete in the League.

While Staple Hill fell short of their usual standards and failed to challenge for honours, they had, however, enjoyed a run in the English Cup, welcoming Manchester United to their Bank Street ground; losing the encounter, 7-1, in front of 7,560 spectators. To celebrate the feat, a dinner was held that featured some very upbeat speeches, with one referring to the, 5-1, loss that Bristol City had suffered at the hands of Staple Hill. In the concluding speech it was suggested that, aside from the two professional clubs in Bristol, Staple Hill, was, indeed, the best around the area; a boast that was about to be tested in a stronger Second Division competition for the 1906/07 season.

Salisbury resigned during the summer to take their place in Division Two of the Southern League, and Chippenham Town decided to withdraw and concentrate on the Wiltshire League, English Cup, Amateur Cup and the Wiltshire Cup; which only demonstrated the wide variety of competitions that were on offer. In their place both Newport and Treharris joined from across the Bristol Channel, together with the 121st RFA, who were stationed in Trowbridge.

The inclusion of the Welsh clubs averted the departure of Bristol City reserves, who had been debating a move to the Birmingham and District League in search of more competitive games, and added a certain degree of kudos to the competition. Treharris had been a founder member of the Welsh

League and came into the Western League as reigning Champions of their league. They were also the holders of the Welsh Cup.

Soccer had been very slow to take off in Wales, where, of course, rugby was, and still is, very popular. After the committee's previous problems with the team from Cardiff, and all the problems that were generated during their membership, it had been with a certain reticence that the new Welsh clubs were accepted. In the event, however, both teams gave tremendous displays, fielding strong sides, and attracting a huge amount of travelling support at all their games.

By January, Treharris had experienced only one defeat, and that was to champions, Bristol Rovers, and the figures for attendances at games were at an all-time high. The City/Rovers games saw over 5,000 each match, and a similar gate was achieved for the Welsh team's meetings. In all, those four clubs were averaging 3,000+, but it was not the same for some of the less well supported members.

Paulton Rovers were again in trouble, and when they were forced to close their ground due to misbehavior later in the season, their gates were already so low that it was of no hardship to reverse the game to the Wiltshire ground of the Trowbridge Artillery; albeit losing the encounter, 4-1.

In the First Division, the sections were made up of:

Division A - *Brentford, Bristol Rovers, Chelsea, Fulham, Queens Park Rangers and Reading.*

Division B; - *Millwall, Plymouth Argyle, Portsmouth, Southampton, Tottenham Hotspur, and West Ham* United.

This format seemed to work to the satisfaction of the clubs, the League and the supporters.

The first Championship game, an all London affair, was held at Stamford Bridge on 15th April 1907, and drew a huge crowd which saw West Ham pick-up the Trophy for the first time, with a win, 1-0, over Fulham.

 West Ham had, in fact, been lucky to end the season on such a high note, after a violent match against Millwall early in September had almost resulted in the FA closing Upton Park. One of their players, Len Jarvis, was found guilty of violent play, even though he had not been dismissed during the game. Beside his suspension for fourteen days, both clubs were censured and ordered to place warning notices around the ground concerning their future behavior. Such was the severe nature of the disorder that the referee, Mr E Case, was also disciplined for failing to maintain order, and was suspended for the rest of the season.

In the Second Division, Staple Hill fulfilled those promising words spoken before the start of the season, picking up the championship a point clear of second placed Newport, and two points ahead of Bristol City reserves.

At the other end of the table Trowbridge Town picked up two points in the season, and resigned to play in the Wiltshire League.

While the competition was proving popular with supporters, who could enjoy a good standard of football at both the professional and amateur levels, there were more changes before the start of the 1907/08 season. While Division One was extended to accommodate the inclusion of Leyton Orient and Brighton and Hove Albion, Division Two saw 121 RFA follow Trowbridge out of the League, followed by Newport. They were replaced by Weymouth reserves and Kingswood Rovers.

Rumours had been rife for many months that the English League was about to extend again, and become a true National League, incorporating the whole of the Southern League First Division clubs. Up until that point there had only been four clubs in the two divisions representing the south and west of the country, with Bristol City the only one outside of London.

However, although that prompted the Southern League to protect its interests and expand, a move that had an effect eventually on the Western League, it would be many years before the hoped for National League status would be achieved by the English FA.

Tottenham Hotspur withdrew at the end of the season after successfully being voted into the English League. They were replaced by Croydon Common, a club formed in 1897 as an amateur church side, but who had just turned professional and were competing in the Southern League Second Division where they had ended their first year in third place. After suffering a fire at their Crescent ground, the club had just moved into the 'Nest' - a ground that was to become the future home of Crystal Palace - and appeared to be well-supported and forward thinking.

The Professional Section Championship game was again well attended, this time at Spurs ground, on 13th April 1908, and resulted in a single goal win by Millwall over Southampton. It was a fitting result given that Millwall had now settled into the League after all their initial teething problems, and had lost only one game throughout the season.

In the Second Division, Bristol City reserves ended the year on the same points as Bristol Rovers reserves, but were awarded the championship on a goal average of plus 13 ahead. Two points behind in third place were Treharris, showing just how strong Welsh football was becoming. Their success, coupled with the large gates they were enjoying, both home and away, seemed to encourage other Welsh teams to look at the Western League. Applications for entry were received and accepted from both Barry District and Aberdare, who had won the Welsh League in its inaugural season in 1905/06.

Also new to the League was Bath City, who had been formed in 1889 as Bath AFC. They joined to play competitive league format football, but the division that they went into was strong, boasting seven mining communities vying for honours, and the men in those clubs certainly knew how to both work and play hard.

When a special meeting was called by the Football Association on 8th March 1909, it was widely expected that the whole of the Southern League would amalgamate into the English League, and although that did not materialise, all the professional clubs resigned from the Western League after finding that fitting in 40+ games a season in the extended Southern League, combined with Cup competitions, left no spare capacity for a mid-week league.

In what was to be the final play-off game, Millwall beat Brighton and Hove Albion, 2-1, and ended the era that had seen so many professional club's as members of the Western League.

THE WESTERN FOOTBALL LEAGUE CHAMPIONSHIP MEDAL

AWARDED TO MILLWALL PLAYER, JOE BLYTHE
FOR WINNING THE WESTERN LEAUGE CHAMPIONSHIP 1907-08

Once again, it was the two reserve elevens of the Bristol clubs that fought out a close competition, with City lifting the Colston Cup, while Aberdare and Treharris flew the Welsh flag in third and fourth place.

In general, the gentlemen of the Press were all united that the changes taking place in the Western League structure was not a bad turn of affairs, with Division Two proving to be strong and well supported. While they had been sceptical about the commitment of professionals throughout the years, with the constant allegations of those clubs taking the competition as 'make-weight', it seemed to them that the lure of the Welsh clubs taking part, with profiles that seemed to fit better with the Western League, offered a better prospect. Which was good, because that was the area that the Management Committee was focused on to increase the size of the remaining Division, prior to kicking-off the 1909/10 season.

The recruitment drive resulted in both Methyr Town and Ton Pentre joining the League along with Mardy, bringing the membership to twelve clubs; with both clubs also taking part in the Southern League Division Two.

The newly constituted league covered an area from Bath to Bristol and South Wales, and had, once again, re-formed and realigned. It was the time when, both throughout the country and in football, there was a state of instability. Strikes, insolvent clubs and general unrest lay ahead, together with weather conditions that would see mother nature add her own penalties; all of which combined to challenge the reserve and determination of the men of the League, who were determined not to lose the battle for continuity.

CHAPTER 7

New Challenges to Face

The Western League AGM was held on 21st June 1909 at the Crown and Dove Hotel in Bridewell Street, with Millwall, Reading, Weymouth, Barry, Treharris, Bristol Rovers, Bath, Welton, Paulton, Radstock, Kingswood, Aberdare and Staple Hill, all present.

Mr E J Locke from Bristol City took the chair initially, and said that it had been *'a good League of late'* adding that the Welsh clubs had added both interest and keen competition, which had led to a substantially improved Division Two. He then thanked the First Division clubs who, he felt, had left the League having raised its standard, tone and financial position; putting in that both the extension in the Southern League and the attraction of the London Charity Cup were good reasons for them moving on.

Hon Sec. Mr Foster, then gave an account of the season, after which he resigned due to increased work commitments. In response, it was agreed that a medal would be presented to him prior to the start of the season to commemorate all the work that he had put in during his time with the League.

Mr G T Bryant was then voted in as Chairman, Mr J A Taylor as President, Mr Pratten and Mr Wilkinson as Vice-Presidents and Mr J S Long as Treasurer, with an honorarium of £30. After a ballot Mr Long was also elected as Hon Secretary, but did not continue in that post after his first season; handing the post over to Mr George Jenkins of Bristol City, who would then continue as an official of the League until ill-health forced his retirement from the post of President in 1951, after 42 years of dedication and service.

A ballot was then conducted to decide on the composition of the League for the coming season that saw entry granted to Methyr (12), Ton Pentre (10) and Mardy (7), with the former two clubs also set to compete in the Southern League. That left both Salisbury City, who got six votes and who were also members of the Southern League, and Bournemouth with just one vote, unsuccessful. An application for membership by the Gas Works was withdrawn.

Finally, at the meeting, Mr Skeggs of Millwall was presented with the medals for his club, and Mr Lock of Bristol City received the same for their reserve team's championship of Division Two.

Shortly after the start of the new season, in September 1909, the committee received a letter from Staple Hill asking for financial support, with the rider that if it was not forth coming they would have no choice but to withdraw through lack of funds. With the prospect of losing yet another club from the reduced competition, the committee agreed to grant them £3-3s-0d, with the provision that all their fixtures were completed. They also asked the Welsh clubs to consider giving donations to aid the ailing club, but eventually all the goodwill and actions were to no avail, and Staple Hill withdrew before a ball was kicked.

New participants, Mardy, were allowed entry to the League on the provision that they found an appropriate new site for their club, with the old facilities not up to standard. That directive was not adhered to, however, and an almighty row broke out following the visit of Paulton Rovers on the first game of the season; a game that Mardy won, 8-0.

The Paulton Secretary officially complained that several of their players had come off the pitch with severe lacerations to their legs, and Mardy were called in front of the committee to answer the allegation. Their Secretary, Mr Maltby, told the assembled trio that his club had already spent £60, a princely sum at the time, on improvements, and that a third of the old pitch had been turfed with plans to complete the job later in the season. The explanation was, of course, not accepted as the pitch was clearly both dangerous and unplayable, and so the club was expelled, reducing still further that amount of games on offer. Ironically, despite the facilities at the club, Mardy had an extremely talented team of players, and shortly after they were expelled, one of the team, Evan Jones, moved to Chelsea where he became a very successful centre-forward. The following season the club was accepted into the Southern League having completed the work on the pitch as promised.

TON PENTRE FC

The arrival of the Welsh clubs on the scene caused some unexpected problems, not least because the comparative ease of travelling had tempted some Bristol based players to move their allegiances across the water with offers of money. Although the rules stated that only professional players could accept wages for playing their favourite game, many were ignoring the rule. In fact, Mardy, in their one and only League game, had taken to the pitch sporting two players from the Bristol City line-up.

The Kingswood manager was particularly vocal on this issue, and stated in the press that he knew Aberdare were offering a half-a-sovereign per game as well as expenses; adding that, *'As soon as we have done the groundwork and got a decent team together along comes a spy and captures one, or perhaps even two, of our best men; the team then gets disorganised, and we have to do all the work over again'*.

It is still a sentiment that is still heard from Western League managers to this day, and despite rules to prevent such actions; some things do not change.

It was, of course, even more difficult to balance some players need for a financial income with their love of the game. As the League's composition stood, some men had to travel increasingly long distances to get to a game in time for kick-off. With little free time, and intransigent employers who did not see the need to balance leisure and occupation, the lure of payment to compensate for lost working hours must have been great.

Quite often a player would have to leave work before noon on a Saturday to make kick-off, an action that would result in losing money from his weekly wage packet. Then because of tiredness after toiling hard and travelling, the will to win would also not be as strong; which were the reasons often put about to explain team's poor away form.

As Tom put it in the earlier book; '*I remember well the case of two neighbours of mine who were employed by the Relief Committee, and who asked for time off to play in a game. The response of that committee was promptly to sack them on the spot. People today might think that decision harsh, but we lived in a time of high unemployment where there were always people queuing up to fill any vacancy, and so men and women were expected to fulfil every hour of work that was owed to the employer*'.

The problems that season did not stop there, and in October Bristol Rovers contacted the League with accusations against Bath City implying that they had played a man who was signed on professional forms; a charge that was accepted by their Secretary. After an extensive internal enquiry, the manager of Bath City admitted that it was, in fact, his own sister who had signed the players name on the registration form, and not the player. The matter was then referred to the FA with a recommendation that the manager should be severely dealt with, and the League then deducted a point from the club and fined them £3.

It was not proving a good season for Kingswood either, and after an incident in which the club was reported for putting nine players on the pitch, and only declaring six on the team sheet, it went from bad to worse. They eventually admitted having played three unregistered players; the trainer, a spectator who had travelled with the team, and a man they just met at Radstock before the game.

And it did not stop there. By March the club was well behind with fixtures, deep in debt, and despite signing a declaration guaranteeing the League that they would honour the remaining fixtures, failed to go to Barry on 27th April 1910. That was the last season they would compete in the League.

Aberdare were also culpable - failing to go to Weymouth, and while those two games remained unplayed, they did not have any bearing on the championship, which went outside of England for the first time in the League's short history. Treharris had done it in style, three points ahead of Bristol City reserves, and a full nine points clear of third placed Bristol Rovers reserves.

It was initially thought that the success of Treharris would encourage even more Welsh clubs to apply, but a remark by a prominent member of the committee, suggesting that the standard of football produced by the Welsh clubs, and the way they tackled games, fell some way below standard, was reported in a local paper. Added to that there were also criticisms of the five Welsh clubs' administrative skills, and when no argument was given to counter that by the League, the clubs from across the Bristol Channel were not happy.

While those remarks were being debated, the Southern League made it clear that they were looking at the possibility of running with just one division, to increase games for existing members. That proposition was attractive to Ton Pentre, Aberdare and Methyr Town, who were all members of that league, and it made the prospect of those clubs withdrawing from the Western League look inevitable.

With uncertainty, all-round, it took some time to arrange the AGM that year, but at the third time of trying, on 1st July 1910, it went ahead. Mr A G Homer, acting as Secretary reported the resignations from Treharris, Aberdare, Ton Pentre and Radstock, but he said that, while Methyr Town had also withdrawn, that resignation should, not be accepted because it had failed to conform to League rules. His protestations led to nothing though, and the Welsh miners went their way, heading toward far higher aspirations.

Both Paulton and Weymouth applied for re-election, with the former explaining the frustrations of a season where many of their players could only compete in home games as their employment would not allow for the long journeys to Wales. Both were accepted.

Bristol City reserves were in their second season as members of the South-Eastern League, a league in which many other prominent southern clubs also enjoyed membership with second teams. As they still had a few Saturday's free, it was suggested that they could remain in the League if fixtures were played mid-week, a proposition that was accepted, given the status of the English League club.

CAMERTON FOOTBALL CLUB
1910-11 SEASON

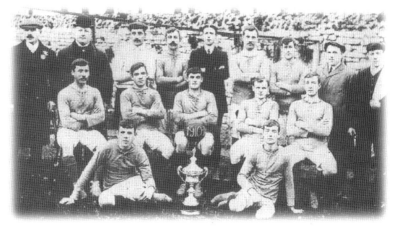

Given the general state of the country financially, and the uncertainty of a rumour that there would be recruitment soon by the Welsh League, there were a surprising number of applications for league membership to consider. With the decision that only three would be accepted, however, a ballot took place that saw Clevedon, Weston-super-Mare and Camerton all successful. Among the unsuccessful applications was one from Mardy together with Gwn Albion, Tredegar and Coombe Park.

Away from football it had been a dour season with a good deal of industrial unrest, and the nation also had to deal with losing King Edward VII who had died of pneumonia on 21st May 1910. The League President, Mr Taylor, paid an emotional tribute to the King in which he said; '*The Western League regrets the loss the football world has sustained through the decease of its patron the late King Edward VII. A good sportsman, a good husband and father, a man who had endeared himself to every nation by his amiable disposition and who, by his diplomatic capabilities, had done more to secure peace than any man for centuries past. The loss the world has sustained is clearly shown by the manifestations of regret that are pouring in continually to the bereaved family, and it calls upon us to tender our deepest sympathy to the Queen Mother and to every member of the Royal Family*'.

It was a melancholy note on which to end the season in a general time of unrest for the population of the West Country. The League had taken on a new face with the introduction of the Welsh clubs, and the committee had found themselves fully occupied dealing with problems that were peculiar to that time,

Tensions at dock yards nationwide came to a head as the new season approached, and as Tom (whose father had died earlier in the year leaving him as the provider for his family) recollected; '*We were all shocked to find that we were issued with 24 hours' notice of 'The National Lock-out of Workers' by employers throughout the country. For my family, this meant an instant cut-from the small wage I received that kept us at survival level*'.

With just ten clubs competing in the League, and 18 games to fit in, given the conditions throughout the country it was opportune that the competition was so reduced. Generally, there was little money to watch matches, and when the Welsh Miners went out on strike in sympathy with the Dock workers, the state of the nation just got worse.

Although some good football was being played, especially by Bristol City reserves who did not lose a game all season, scoring 58 goals and conceding just 14, the League competitions lacked the impact of previous years. Those statistics confirmed the fears that had been expressed by the City Directors that the league was simply not strong enough to bring the youngsters through to English League standards.

Paulton Rovers ended the term at the foot of the table for the third season in succession, but demonstrated their steely miners' resolve, and again vowed allegiance to continue in membership; which they did right up until the outbreak of the First World War.

At seasons end the weather was warm and sunny, and the forthcoming coronation of George V created, briefly, a fleeting national air of optimism. The new King was ruler of over 400 million subjects across the Empire, and Britain held a leading place in science, engineering, exploration, but all was not well.

In contrast to that optimism, during the long hot summer of 1911 there were riots in Bristol and most major cities, due to the Governments' treatment of the striking dock workers and the miners. Those workers were fighting for what they knew was a fair wage of 30/- a week, together with improvements in working conditions, and those demands were in stark contrast to the increased salaries that had just been awarded to the MP's of £400 a year; a job that also ensured security and the pleasure of very good working conditions.

On bone-dry pitches, the 1911/12 season kicked-off with eleven teams, which included Street and Peasedown St John, but without the challenge of the City reserves. What the League lacked in numbers, however, was more than made-up by the passion that accompanied amateur football, and is best told in the word of old Tom, who wrote; '*I hold very fond memories of hard fought games by the mining communities, and was to become a close friend of Reg Jones, who was the Welton Rovers Groundsman for many seasons, and who spend 25 years with the club. A game that particularly sticks in my memory around that time was one that I went to see at Camerton. It was a long, long, trek to that small village of about twenty inhabitants; of which four were relatives of mine. It is remarkable to remember that, despite the small population, the crowd that day must have been in the region of 300. I will never forget the pigeons of Peasedown who, at both half and full-time, went on their way to take the news of the score-line to the supporters left at home. I cannot recall whether Camerton or Peasedown won that encounter, only that the game was played in the usual full-blooded way that we expected in those times, with an equally avid crowd watching*'.

'*Being related to some of the Camerton team, I was lucky enough to be invited to the Camerton Inn after the match, and was delighted when the landlady, Ann Nicholls, came out with a huge joint of ham which she carved straight off the bone and served with some fresh crusty bread she had baked that very day. That was the best meal I had experienced for quite some time and, as such, was the highlight of the season*'.

Such were the simple pleasures and delights of those days so long ago when food was at a premium, but at a time when the difficulties of life were made up for by devouring those ninety minutes of football, during which time day-to-day problems could be forgotten.

Welton Rovers were truly a club in ascendance, and had the League all but won when they entertained Weston-super-Mare on Good Friday, 5th April 1912. With two games remaining, the resulting victory, 3-1, in front of a huge crowd was enough to put the championship out of the grasp of Barry District, who ended the term four points behind, and just one ahead of third placed Weymouth.

Welton Rovers FC

Western League Champions 1911/12

With just twenty games to fit in that season, it had become clear from an early stage that there was a distinct divide in the playing standards on offer, between those with professional pedigree behind them and the true amateurs, and with some still ambitious clubs in contention, the expansion of the League to twenty-two games was a generally welcome development.

While the summer of 1911 had been one of the warmest on record with the driest July and August in a hundred years, in marked contrast, 1912 saw the wettest summer in over two hundred years, and the coolest and wettest August on record, which had resulted in food rotting in the fields. Those conditions did not help improve the nations mood, at a time that saw a rigid, class-based society in place, with real pockets of poverty throughout the country; even in the comparatively affluent city of Bristol.

The floods and cold of that summer exacerbated the social and political tensions of the time, and under those adverse conditions the 1912/13 season kicked-off with little anticipation of any promise for the future that lay ahead.

Cardiff City reserves, who added strength to the League, were in contention with Bristol Rovers reserves all season to take the honours, but when they travelled to Camerton for an evening kick-off later in the season with just two games remaining, the hostility of the Welsh miners was no match for Somerset passions, and the defeat, 3-1, spelled the end of their championship ambitions.

While the top places in the table went to the two reserve elevens, Rovers and Cardiff, they were followed closely by Bath City, while Barry District were a poor fourth, 13 points adrift of the top. That failure to perform prompted Barry to leave the League after five promising years of membership, but they were replaced by the return of Trowbridge Town after a seven-year absence.

The diversity of the League was notable, with the talented Cardiff reserves side in magnificent form. They took the Western League Trophy outside of

England for the second time in its history, and in the process scored 88 goals and conceded just 10.

Along the way they managed to pick up admirers for their style of play and destiny had it, that they also managed to score 10 of those 88 goals in just one game against Camerton, who they punished for the previous season's defeat to the delight of the local press who featured a cartoon showing Bert Rudduck in the Camerton goal diving all over the place with sweat all over him, while at the other end the Cardiff keeper was seated in his goal covered with cobwebs!

Despite that unfortunate game, Rudduck was something of a local hero throughout the club's time in the League, and regularly played in goal for Somerset, attracting a good deal of interest from professional clubs for his displays. He was also, however, very laid back, to the extent that Tom wrote 'I *will always remember seeing him casually light up his clay pipe when life was a bit quiet at his end'.* Not something that occurred against Cardiff reserves that day though!

Bath City won the runners-up spot, splitting the two reserve teams, and Camerton surprised everyone by ending the term in fifth place, ahead of big spending Welton Rovers by two points.

At the AGM in June 1914, it was business as usual, and in the absence of a representative from Cardiff reserves, who had resigned to play in the South-Eastern League, Bath were awarded their medals, and several rule changes were agreed. Newport, Yeovil and Glastonbury applied for election and were in the ballot along with Weston and Clevedon, who had ended the term at the foot of the table. Only Glastonbury failed to gain admission, and with the League, once again, increased to 13 teams, all appeared normal. But storm clouds were gathering, both nationally and internationally.

When war was declared on 4th August 1914, it was widely accepted that it would be over by Christmas; despite an intense campaign being launched to recruit every available young fit adult male to fight the war in France.

In late September Bristol Rovers reserves entertained Paulton Rovers at Eastville, and were 3-1 up at half-time, but the resulting 9-1 victory told the real story of what was happening to the amateur game throughout the country. That same day Chippenham Town had been forced to pull out of their Amateur Cup game against Staple Hill, as they had been left without a side due to the number of players who had signed up to join the army; which was a sign that the intense campaign was succeeding in luring young male volunteers 'for King and Country'.

The message, that is was unpatriotic to take part in games when there was a war to fight, had come home to those men who had played football as a sport, and whose living was not dependent on the game. The Football Association, however, was mindful of the financial commitments of clubs, and insisted that the professional games should continue, leaving the professional players with no choice but to play on, and resist the taunts that they were being unpatriotic. With all the war activity, gates were down by about 50%, and both Bristol City and Bristol Rovers were left to recruit players, as and when they could.

The results of a meeting at the Crown and Dove Hotel on 9th September 1914, saw the Western League attempt to go against the wave of opinion and continue with the competition. The committee had, however, agreed not to issue any medals or trophies at the end of the season; an interim decision intended to stave off allegations of frivolity in the face of war.

In the Western Daily Press on 18th September, it was made quite clear what the official-line was in response to that decision, when it was written that *'there may be many good reasons why a man prohibited by domestic or other reasons from paying a visit to the Colston Hall should play football if he so desires, but it is not a pleasant position. The player on his way to the football ground cannot stop to explain his reasons for not enlisting to a passer-by and the latter are apt to jump to conclusions'.*

The government propaganda machine then went into overdrive, pushing the message out that if a young man did not sign up to the war effort, then he was a coward. In the face of mounting public patriotism, and as a subsequent of the reductions in gates, Western League football closed its doors; and as Tom put it *'By the time that our 22nd year together came around on the 24th September, both the League and I were tasting new experiences - I was in France, and the League was in limbo!'*

CHAPTER 8

The results of war

Although the Great War ended on 11th November 1918, for many reasons life was slow to get back to normal for those who were lucky enough to have returned.

It had been the bloodiest of wars in which three-quarters of a million young men died, but in a dreadful twist of fate, those returning from the trenches had not just brought back with them physical and psychological scars. Many also carried the influenza virus; which then quickly spread throughout our cities, towns and villages.

The world-wide 'Spanish Flu' epidemic which, by the time it was quelled had killed more people than had fallen victim to war, was responsible for 197 deaths in the city of Bristol in just one week at the end of October 1918, and was particularly virulent among the 20 to 40-year-old age group; exactly those young men whom the Western League looked to recommence football in the West Country.

During those war years, while the male population had been thrown into the chaos in far-off France, the women left at home had adapted to take on what had been a man's world of work and leisure, but despite their efforts, the cost of conflict had left the country with a huge amount of debt to contend with, along with all those other circumstances.

Despite those challenges to the return to normality, however, the English League began to implement an expansion in its structure, incorporating the whole of the First Division of the Southern League into a national Third Division South. That in turn had a knock-on effect on all non-league football, but it was a challenge that the Western League was quick to position itself to benefit from.

At a meeting to discuss the re-introduction of football to the West, which was held on 18th May 1919 at the Crown and Dove Hotel, in Rupert Street, League President, Mr G T Bryant, told those present that while Yeovil, Horfield United, Street, Welton Rovers, Bath City, Peasedown St. John, Bristol Rovers, Douglas and Newport County had agreed to take part for the following season. Cardiff City, Barry, Bristol City, Swindon Town, Trowbridge Town and Clevedon had been unable to give a definitive answer.

A letter from Mr Sam Allen of Swindon Town was read out in which he explained why his club could not commit at the time of writing, which said, *'Our position is somewhat akin to Bristol City. We are both members of the South-Eastern League, and have no desire to leave it, but the London clubs (so I am unofficially informed) are resigning 'on-bloc' so to all appearances, that would mean the breaking up of the South-Eastern League. In the event of this happening, we should have to look elsewhere for our reserve teams, and the Western League appeals to me personally. We cannot move the matter until we have it officially from the South-Eastern League'.*

While it was then agreed that the last day for receiving applications would be 24th May 1919, it was clear that the inclusion of those undecided clubs would be desirable.

Three weeks later another meeting took place to confirm participant clubs for the inaugural post-war season, with the First Division made-up of teams from Barry, Bristol City, Douglas, Horfield United, Newport County, Bath City, Swansea, Swindon Town, Cardiff City and Welton Rovers.

Division Two comprised of Frome Town, Paulton Rovers, Peasedown St John, Street, Trowbridge, Yeovil and Petters United, Glastonbury and Timsbury. Clevedon had been forced to withdraw their application due to the state of their club. Weymouth were also unable to proceed, but their problem was the infrequency of train services, which were said to be so poor compared to the pre-war years, they would not complete some of the journeys required.

Thus, the scene was set, many months after the cessation of hostilities, when normal life in the West would kick-off once again. The first game in the new era was at the Abbey Park ground of Glastonbury. It was a well-attended affair, where the vocal partisan crowd cheered their favourites on to a 2-1 victory over neighbours, Yeovil and Petters United; a result that prompted the club Secretary to grab a big drum from a member of the Town band and beat it all the way to the dressing rooms, some 400 yards away.

Those first few games heralded a particularly memorable season for many, which was even more so for Tom, who wrote in 'A View from the Terraces' that; *'Although there were very large crowds at most games around that time it was unusual to see the fair sex at football matches, and even more unlikely for them to understand the sport. It was, therefore, amazing that during the 1919/20 season I met a lady who was to become my wife, Mary. A lovely lass, two years my junior, whose interest in football stemmed back to her father's devotion to his club, Paulton Rovers'.*

While his observations about women and football were correct in part, in general the role of women had changed with the war years, which saw them becoming more involved in the game, at local level as spectators, and at national level as participants. Women's football had become popular on a large scale during those war years when employment of women in heavy industry had spurred the growth of the game; as it had done for men all those years before.

The most successful team of the era was Dick Kerr's 'Ladies of Preston', England. The team played in the first women's international match in 1920 against a team from Paris, and made-up most of the England Ladies XI against the Scottish Ladies XI that same year, winning 22-0. Those years of progress were unusual, however, and even at the time of writing today, there has never been a Ladies' section of the Western Football League.

While all was going well with the re-introduction of football, the country was being blighted again with strikes brought on by discontented workers, who had given so much for their Country and who were walking out in protest at the reward that was being shown for their efforts.

The railway and iron foundry industries that so effected the lives of people in Bristol and the West were particularly hit, and nationally over 50,000 workers went on strike in the foundry trade alone. As it was, the discontent did not stop there, and they were soon joined by teachers demanding a 100% rise on their pre-war salaries.

Eventually at the end of October 1919, the government revealed that the national debt was £473 million, a figure that most could not comprehend, and not something to calm the rising storm.

As the actions took hold, Western League games were soon being postponed due to rail strikes: an action by the workers that Prime Minister, Lloyd George, called 'an anarchist conspiracy', but somehow despite the odds, games were eventually resumed, and afforded some wonderful entertainment amid the financial gloom and a particularly wet winter.

Because of those problems there was a late finish to the season that saw the Douglas works-side kick well above their status; beating the strong reserve sides of Division One, and taking the Western League title on goal average (the number of goals scored, divided by the number conceded) from Swansea Town reserves. In contrast to that Horfield United struggled all year and won just one game, ending the term with six points from eighteen outings.

In Division Two, newcomers Frome Town won the title four points clear of both Trowbridge Town and Peasedown St John, while Glastonbury did not live up to the support they received on the terraces, winning only two games and ending the term in bottom place.

During the close season, the national re-organisation of football continued, and at the start of the 1920/21 season the Third Division North was introduced; nationalising the game and moving its focus away from the traditional natural local base.

The men of the Western League were quick to respond to those changes, and revealed an increase in participants to accommodate more teams from Wales. It gave the year an exciting fixture list with sixteen strong professional sides that included six whose First Teams were competing in the Football League. There was, however, still a strict professional divide to the divisions with only Welton fielding both a professional and an amateur team.

The year lived up to its promise as an entertaining competition, albeit one that brought with it the usual tribulations found when pitting strong mining communities against each other. It was also a year that had its fair share of travel problems, but at season's end, the extremely strong reserves from Bristol City and Cardiff fought out a run-in that saw the Bristol club just edge the League title; which was again decided on goal average.

In Division Two, Peasedown beat fellow miners, Radstock, to the title by five points; a considerable margin considering that there were only eighteen games to play, while at the foot of the table Welton Amateurs won just two games. Such was the importance of the game to those hard-working folk, that despite the results, which also saw their professional team struggle, they vowed to remain in the League.

The AGM, which was held on 17th June 1921, was dominated by the report of mass resignations by all the Professional reserve teams and most of the Welsh clubs. It was caused because of the recruitment drive by the Southern League after they had lost so many clubs to the National League's expansion.

Alongside those defections, Bath City applied to join National League South directly from the Western League (the only club to do so), but were defeated when both Aberdare and Charlton Athletic took most of the votes. They then opted to follow the other professional clubs and move into the Southern League, applying again to become a National club at the end of that season, only to be rejected again with just one vote in their favour.

Although the 1921/22 season saw only eight clubs competing in Division One and nine in Division Two, it began on an optimistic note with the country in a less volatile state, and the health of the population improving However, the huge crowds that were a feature of yesteryear had all but dissipated amid an increase in unemployment and a decrease in family income.

The Football League had also suffered a reduction in spectators through the gates. At the end of the previous season an all-time low had been recorded at Old Trafford, when Leicester took on Stockport in front of thirteen spectators! That was, of course, an exception, but the reality was that the years of war, coupled with the fear of spreading disease, had taken its toll. While the flu epidemic was contained, there had still been 804 deaths recorded nationally that had been attributed to the disease, and unemployment seemed to be rising at a totally unacceptable rate.

As the New Year came and went, the Western League was again in a state of crisis with many clubs indicating that they had problems. The situation was then made more difficult when a miner's strike at the end of March caused the government to declare a state of emergency, as coal supplies began to dramatically decrease.

On the pitch, it was Yeovil and Petters United who claimed the League title, losing only two games and heading the table from Trowbridge Town by five clear points, while in Division Two, Clandown won, two points clear of Coleford Athletic.

Radstock Town came in third, which was a disappointment to their supporters, as until losing the game on Good Friday to Frome by the only goal of the game, they had looked the most likely club to lift the honours, because they had been undefeated at that stage. Following that game, however, they failed to record another victory.

CLANDOWN AFC

1921-22

Champions of Western League, Second Division.

Committee: A Millard, J Plummer, P Matthews, A Ashman, A Cottle, D Parfitt, R Ashman, J Sparey, B Maggs, A James, R Young, A Ashman, G Ashman, R Smith
Players: G Barter, E Fear, A Young, C Fear, G Reed, G Ashmon E Barter,
J Smith (Trainer), C Witcombe, J Mansfield, A Millard, T Dallimore, C Chivers

At season's end, the initial AGM arrangements were forced to be rearranged due to the state of emergency that existed, and by the time the committee met in late June 1922, it was to announce the departure of the entire Amateur Division Two section, whose clubs had been tempted by the promise of less travelling by County League Associations.

The exception to that mass movement was Radstock Town, but although the League ran an active recruitment drive, it failed to attract any new members, which resulted in a single division competition for 1922/23 with just nine clubs taking part.

Although it was a source of great disappointment for all those concerned to see the Western League in numerical decline, once again, the games played during the season were competitive and comparatively trouble free.

Christmas Day saw traditional crowds gather to cheer on their favourite football teams, and the hard working Welton Rovers faithful were rewarded with three games at their Midsomer Norton ground, which were all won; 3-0, against Peasedown, 1-0, in front of a huge crowd against near neighbours, Radstock Town, and then a few days later, 5-2, over Cardiff Corinthians.

Despite those victories, however, they were unable to topple Weymouth, who won the title in a season that saw the Dorset club successful in every competition they entered, with the exception of course, of the FA Cup. Alongside their first ever Western League Championship, they also beat Yeovil and Petters and future league members, Portland United, to lift the top spot in the Dorset League.

The effect that the Miner's strike had on the community, combined with the financial drain of fielding a professional side, saw Welton Rovers in all sorts of trouble, and shortly after the season ended, they had no choice but to go into administration; but all was not lost.

The ground was eventually sold to the Miners Welfare Association, with local men contributing out of their own meager wages to enable the club to remain in existence, and after a break of just one year they returned to West Clewes, and to the Western League.

WEYMOUTH FOOTBALL CLUB
1922-23

Champions of the Western Football League, the Dorset League and winning every competition entered during the 1922-23 season.

On 7th June 1923 at the League's AGM, Radstock Town, Peasedown Athletic and Trowbridge Town withdrew their intention to move on. There were, however, resignations from both Hanham Athletic and Welton Rovers. Whereas Minehead and Paulton Rovers were accepted into the League, and both Cardiff Corinthians and Bath City reserves were successful in re-elections after finishing the year in basement spots. There was still the possibility of a few more applications for membership, and so the final constitution for the division was delayed until a meeting on 5th July.

Problems of attracting clubs had taken a turn for the worse with a change in direction from the Southern League, who introduced a Western and Eastern division to replace the English and Welsh sections, in response to the expansion of the English and Welsh Leagues. The move had attracted a good deal of enthusiasm from both clubs and supporters, resulting in an increase in their membership.

The move attracted reserve elevens from National League clubs, together with some Welsh clubs, but of course, it increased travel costs for participant members; a fact that did not escape those who were attempting to increase the Western League's appeal.

The 1923/24 season kicked-off with a slight increase in membership which saw the late applications from both Poole Town and Lovell's Athletic, and the

700+ crowd that turned up to watch Radstock and Weymouth fight out an entertaining 2-2 draw, was testament that Western League football was still alive and kicking.

The inclusion of the 'Toffee Men' of Wales, Lovell's Athletic, to the League was to be one of significance for some supporters, and particularly Tom, who wrote; *'The interesting thing about Lovell's Athletic was that it grew out of George Lovell's pure love of the game. George was the owner of a family sweet business in Newport, and with his son, Harold in mind, he started the factory team in 1918 as an amateur affair. Unfortunately, Harold's career ended very quickly following an injury in the first game that he played. Unbeknown to me, George was to alter the direction of my life following our chance meeting at their first Western League game at Peasedown St John'.*

'We began to talk about work, or a lack of it and the upshot of the conversation was that he suggested I should contact a friend of his, who went by the unlikely name of Edward Edwards, who ran a factory in Bristol, suggesting that I not only mention his name, but also that I was an avid follower of the Western League, as he was sure that it would go in my favour. I took his advice and the resulting job saw me in a position with good wages and rapid promotion that ensured both my future and that of my family'.

Tom was, indeed, extremely fortunate to have experienced that sort of luck from the terraces, as nationally and locally, dour circumstances were soon to produce very difficult times indeed. Unemployment had reached two million and despite the government raising benefits from 15/- to 18/- week, strikes continued to increase. In an already shrinking economy, an eight-day Rail and Iron Foundry strike in January 1924, was then followed by a crippling Dockers strike that paralysed all ports.

There was also turmoil in the country politically, with Ramsey McDonald leading the first every Labour administration in a minority Government, after the Tory government had been defeated in a vote of confidence by just one vote. His Government lasted a few months before another General Election was called.

Given all the problems being faced, it was fortunate, therefore, that there were only twenty games to put on in the Western League. Somehow, and not without difficulty, the season's fixtures were completed on time with Lovell's Athletic lifting the title at their first attempt, six points ahead of Radstock Town.

While there was another recruitment push prior to the AGM in June 1924, and although Cardiff Corinthians decided to withdraw in the face of increased travel problems, they were replaced by the return of both Welton Rovers and Frome Town.

Also, new to the League was Swindon Victoria, a club that had attracted a good deal of fame by their Amateur Cup progress in 1921, when they progressed through the rounds beating Bromley 1-0, Willington, 2-1, and Leytonstone, 3-1, to reach the Final at Ayersome Park, Middlesbrough. That day they lost, 4-2, to the 'Kings' of non-league soccer, Bishop Auckland, in front of 25,000 spectators, but they put on a good display of football and certainly inspired many involved in the non-league game in the process. To have the Wiltshire club in membership, therefore, added kudos to a League that was looking to bounce back from the many recent knocks.

Throughout history, the effect of day-to-day problems produce changes at football clubs, but for once the downturn in the economy benefitted the Western League, with reductions in gates combining with increases in both the cost and difficulties of travel, to make the Southern League less attractive.

There were many meetings throughout the season, and when the professional clubs in the Southern League, Western section, threatened to resign because most of the remaining Welsh clubs were about to leave, there was a proposal for Bristol Rovers, Bristol City, Exeter, Plymouth Argyle, Swindon Town, Taunton United, Torquay United, Weymouth, Yeovil and Petters United, and possibly Bath City, to form their own competition, which would be played on a cup-tie principal.

In response, the Southern League did all they could to accommodate the needs of those clubs, while the Western League did all they could to tempt them over to a new Professional division of their own – and their efforts were a resounding success.

The season's honours went to the wire, and were eventually decided when Yeovil and Petters United travelled to Radstock on the 2nd May 1925, needing either a draw, or a win, to beat Weymouth to the championship, but all did not go immediately to plan. As the game progressed they found the Somerset miners in no mood to cede the game. Meanwhile, at Bath City, Weymouth were capitalising on the Roman's unlucky run.

Until the last 30 minutes Bath held out, but injuries to defenders, Jack Hulbert and Adie Clarke, put them out of the game, and with no substitutes, allowed the weakened side to lose to four quick goals. While that scenario was playing out, Radstock were eventually defeated by the only goal of the game, and the championship went to Yeovil and Petters United by the two points won on that day.

At a Western League meeting twelve days later, both Yeovil and Weymouth were congratulated, and there was good news that ten clubs had applied to join the proposed Professional section. The news, however, created something of a problem because Poole, who were existing members, had put in a late application for a place; a request that was turned down.

There was also a potential glitch with the Bath City application, when a representative from the club said that their future was unsure until after a meeting of its shareholders; adding that it may or may not still be in existence by the next season. He then added that if the club agreed to continue, they would want Western League football. In the circumstances the committee decided that, should they survive, then an application would be looked at, but only as a new club.

Later, the ten clubs that had proposed a subsidiary competition of their own to the Southern League in February, made up the new Western League Division One, including Bath City. Division Two consisted of all the existing amateur members of the League, except for Peasedown St John who move into the Somerset League.

Some of the biggest changes to the laws of football took place prior to the start of the 1925/26 season, that would reshape the game. The violent shoulder charge, which had been allowed at any time during the game, with or without the ball, was redefined, and more significantly, there were changes to the off-side rule. Until that stage the off-side law had stated that three players must be in front of play, but following a proposal by the Scottish FA it was changed to allow two opponents between the advancing player and the goal-line.

The result of those changes was to encourage a more skilful game that favoured team work, plus the talent of strikers, and while it took time to get used to, those changes proved popular with spectators and players alike, as they encouraged better coached sides who could score more goals.

While the scene was set for what seemed to be an exciting Western League programme, the season played out amid a back drop of chaos both nationally and locally. The political and economic situation was deep-rooted with difficulties, and there seemed to be few solutions available. The government introduced subsidies for the Coal Mine owners to avert more strike action against looming wage cuts, and with continuing high unemployment, some clubs in the Western League were struggling to make ends meet.

It was clear as the season progressed, that while some were riding the storm, with 1,000+ crowds turning out to watch Bristol Rovers reserve games, other smaller clubs were suffering from reduced gate money. To negate the effect, clubs such as Trowbridge Town had over committed their small squad of players, and in March 1926 their action saw them hauled in front of the committee charged with fielding weakened teams.

In answer to the charge the official from the Wiltshire club pointed out that as of that date, they still had 21 games to complete, 16 of which were at home; adding that they were putting out the best teams available to them. Although the committee had sympathy with their case, they were still fined money they did not have. The case was proved with the example used of a game against Yeovil & Petters when they only put out ten men from the start. When the chips were down, it was the Western League games that took second place to the Southern League games or the more well attended County Cup games; an age-old problem that was difficult to condemn given the conditions.

The League men also had to deal with many allegations of players who had already played multiple-times in the professional division. taking part in amateur games. Bath City was one such club, and in answer to that charge they had no choice but admit that players, Pocock and Grayson, had turned out nine times for their professional side, before being included in one against Frome Town. Considering the circumstances and the conditions that prevailed, they were fined 5/-, which was the smallest amount that could be levied, with a comment from the committee that, 'We do not wish to kick a club when it is down'. Which is exactly what they were doing.

Later at a crisis meeting in Bath on 12th July1926, it was revealed that the danger of the club becoming extinct had never been greater. Problems were attributed to small gates in the middle of the season, and a lack of local support. With debts of £30, and a bank overdraft, they also suffered from a lack of man power as most of their committee had walked away.

While Bath City eventually managed to remain in both the Southern and Western leagues with their professional side, they withdrew their reserves from Division Two to stabilise the situation. That action, however, did nothing to help playing standards, and when the first game of the new season saw them defeated by Ebbw Vale, 5-0, after a long and expensive journey to Wales, it did not bode well for the coming months. At the end of the season they were at the foot of the Western League, having won just one game, and ended their Southern League season in the same position.

In contrast to that club's fate, both Bristol City and Bristol Rovers reserves put in strong performances throughout, and ended the term as champions and runners-up respectively. Poole Town picked up the Division Two title, a point clear of a newly revitalised Welton Rovers, and immediately turned professional. The club then entered a reserve team into Division Two, while their senior side were accepted into the Southern League to play alongside their acceptance into Western League Division One.

Just after the completion of the season, on 1st May 1926, the Government Commission for Miners called for wages to be cut to 1924 levels to save the subsidies that had been paid to avoid such an action, and that inevitably meant yet another strike. Two days later, a General Strike was called that effectively brought the country to a standstill. Such was the effect of the actions, that the Government immediately declared 'Martial Law', with its imposition of direct military control of normally civilian functions, which was to last for seven months, until 2nd December 1926.

While the General Strike ended months later, on the 12th May 1927, 250,000 miners held out until 12th October 1927, but such was the devastation throughout that time, that the army and volunteers were drafted in to do essential work. Food had to be imported to feed the nation.

In a country blighted with such problems, the start of the 1926/27 season held less importance, but it was to be one of success in the light of the troubled background.

While it was Poole Town's first season as a professional organisation, their league performances were not consistent, and certainly did not reflect the success that they had enjoyed in the FA Cup where they had beaten Newport County in the Second Round. That surprise victory had then resulted in a trip to Goodison Park to meet Everton, a team that boasted four Internationals.

The Everton forward-line that day included the famous 'Dixie' Dean, who was to later score over 60 goals in one season for the club. With odds stacked against them, Poole performed well, with a great 'Croker' Drew goal giving their supporters the hope of achieving a draw. At the final whistle, however, they went out of the competition 3-1.

As for the front runners, Lovell's Athletic, who had entered a reserve team in Division Two, had a superb unbeaten run between 14th October and 16th March with their professional side, but as the season progressed they were faced with two charges of failing to fulfil fixtures, against Poole and Bristol Rovers. The charges were proved, which led to a heavy fine and points awarded against them, which explained their fourth-place finish. Bristol City reserves won the Division seven points clear of Lovell's, with Torquay United in runners-up position. The League title was decided on the last game of the season, when City reserves beat Swindon Town reserves, 3-1, to take the honours by those two points.

It had been a season that saw most professional outfits addressing their lack of cash, which was caused by reduced gates, by taking on more and more games. Bristol Rovers reserves completed 52 games in all, which was only achieved by putting out trial sides for the last few Western League games. That did not put the supporters off, however, and the game in which they entertained Taunton United in wall-to-wall sunshine, saw both sides sporting unfamiliar players on the pitch in front of the 1,000+ supporters, and was more reminiscent of a pre-season trial match than a competitive game.

At the 31st Annual General Meeting of the Western League, which was held at the Bristol Sports club in Colston Street, the season was declared both a financial and numerical success by League President, Mr J Taylor. After elections, George Bryant, once again, took the position of Chairman, having served the League through all the seasons since inception. His first task was to offer congratulations to Torquay United, who had been elected as members of the 3rd Division National league, and to Welton Rovers who during the season had reached the First Round of the Amateur Cup.

Resignations had been received from Bristol City reserves and Swindon Town reserves, and from Poole Town whose reserves had won Division Two. At the meeting, however, Bristol City asked to withdraw their resignation, and a motion to accept that request was successfully placed by Mr A G Homer, from Bristol Rovers. Salisbury City successfully applied for admission from the Hampshire League, and joined Taunton and Weymouth in the top flight; both of which were re-elected.

In Division Two it was no surprise to see the resignation of Lovell's reserves, and they were joined by Frome Town who had decided to go back into the Somerset League. In contrast, Weymouth reserves and Minehead were successful in retaining thier League members after a poor season had seen them in bottom place.

Contrary to the early summer conditions that had been enjoyed in May, the summer of 1927 was the wettest on record, with up to 80% more rain than usual making pitches very difficult to play on as the season began, and it did not improve. Blizzards swept the country around Christmas time, followed by gales in February, and then yet more of the same in March, with temperatures reaching minus 9 degrees, even in the city centres.

Despite that, the League was in good shape, with twelve strong clubs in Division One, and the reserve teams from the professional clubs recording gates of between 2-3,000 spectators at many of their games. It was, however, certainly a time in which the less well supported clubs were unable to compete on the same level.

That point was amply demonstrated on 12th March 1928, when Rovers reserves entertained Bath City at Eastville on the back of a winning run that had seen them accumulate 23 points from the 15 games played, and were heading the table with Plymouth Argyle reserves. That day Bath could only field a team that included eight reserve team players, and they suffered a 7-1 defeat; which could so easily have been double that score-line.

Eventually the League was won by Argyle reserves on 25th April when they beat Rovers reserves, 2-1, at Eastville, while across the City at Ashton Gate fellow championship pretenders, Exeter City, who needed to win by a considerable score-line, were 2-0 down at half-time and eventually succumbed 3-0 in front of what could only be described as a sparse attendance by City's standards.

At the AGM on 16th June 1928, Plymouth Argyle were congratulated on being the only Devon club ever to have won the Western League championship, the previous time being during the 1904/05 season when their professional side picked up the honours. It was also a time to congratulate Trowbridge Town, an original member of the League 32 years previously, who took the Division

Two championship as the only Wiltshire club to have won that honour.

After enjoying three seasons of expansion and financial stability, prospects of a reduction in League membership was discussed. Lovell's Athletic, who had been successful in winning the Amateur Cup for a third season, but who had not performed well in their Western League games, losing their last two league matches, 6-3, to Bath City and, 6-1, to Weymouth, withdrew to concentrate on the Southern League. Poole Town followed their example. At the foot of the League, Minehead, who had found competing extremely costly with many problems associated with travelling, also withdrew.

Salisbury's bottom place in the Professional division at the end of the season with just three wins to their name, demonstrated how difficult they had found life back in West Country football, and requested that they be allowed to take part in Division Two for a couple of seasons until their financial situation improved; a request that was granted. They were joined by newcomers, Bristol St George and the reserve eleven from Bath City, a club that was setting a good example by having apparently come through a few years when they could well have gone out of existence.

Away from football there had been significant medical progress that did not escape the eye of Tom, who summed it up; *'Generally that season is remembered by me as one dominated by world and national events. Although I personally did not realise what Alexander Fleming's discovery of Penicillin would mean for medicine, Fred Parlant, a local football man (and intellectual!), spent the whole of one game telling me how he saw it help treat injuries to footballer's and contributing to our general well-being. He pointed out to me that, together with the x-ray machine, identification of blood groups and the refinements in the laws of the game, the risk to players in the 20th century was greatly reduced compared to those encountered when our league was first formed; and none could argue with that!'*

The 1928/29 season kicked off with just seventeen clubs in total, eight in Division One and nine in Division Two, but the numerical shortfall was more than made up by the quality of the clubs taking part; or so it was thought before a ball was kicked.

The truth of the matter was, however, that many clubs were still suffering, with the country struggling throughout the 1920s to pay for the First World War, and the resulting reductions in gate money meant that they were taking on still more games to combat those increasing financial problems.

For the Western League, it resulted in weakened teams being fielded for games, despite rules in place to prevent this. The practice was more than amply demonstrated when a very honest representative of Bristol Rovers Football Club was presented with the League Cup and medals for winning Division One at the AGM in June 1929, and who in response said that his club had experienced a very poor season; adding that he hoped they would do better in the next campaign.

The runners-up were Plymouth Argyle, who ended the term on the same points, but with a superior goal average to Bath City. Taunton Town, who had changed their name from United that season, were also on the same points total, but had scored just one goal less than their Somerset counterparts.

In Division Two, Bath City demonstrated that they had truly sorted out their financial and domestic issues, with their reserves winning the Division by a single point over a very strong Portland United set-up, leaving Trowbridge Town back in third-spot, five points adrift.

Resignations were received from Salisbury, who even in Division Two had failed to meet the expectations of life in the Western League, and Yeovil and Petters reserves, who were replaced by Wells City and Paulton Rovers.

There was also an application from Bristol City to enter an 'A' Colts side, which George Jenkins, representing the club, said would play at Douglas Brothers Athletic Ground at Kingswood, a ground that had laid dormant for seven years since the demise of their club. Despite reservations about the condition of the ground, the application was accepted following assurances of its potential.

With a positive financial report showing an excess of income over expenditure of £12-13s-0d at the AGM, all appeared well, but the talk of the non-league football world was a proposal by the London Combination League to introduce a second division. That move was expected to be attractive to Bristol Rovers and City, along with Exeter City, Plymouth Argyle and Torquay United if, as expected, a league featuring a total of 18 clubs could be put together.

While the Western League seemed to be surviving the turmoil that was all around them with a reasonably settled structure, the country was in turmoil. The hung parliament that was in charge during that summer following the May General Election, was unable to make progress and it was not until just before the start of the 1929/30 season that a new minority Liberal Government took charge, with the promise of change by Ramsey MacDonald's newly founded Labour Party who won the popular vote. Good news, but very soon more challenging conditions were to arise.

As Tom put it; '*It took a while for me to take in the implications of the Wall Street Crash in America on 24th October 1929, as I did not realise that this would send our country into yet another deep recession that would eventually see millions of people employed in public work with the intention of stimulating the economy and prevent the country from becoming bankrupt*'. It certainly was a difficult time, but that was not the only challenge that would face the men of the League during that season.

On 21st November, the Western League committee met to consider what could be done to minimise the effect of the proposed new London Combination League, with many existing Division One clubs being attracted to the new initiative. In response, it was decided to invite various West Country clubs to a meeting in December with a view to joining the League.

At the meeting, which was held just before Christmas, there was a poor response with less than a dozen in attendance, and after three quarters of an hour it was decided that there should be an 'Emergency' meeting called in January, to consider 'ways and means of continuing the League.' It was also agreed to insist that resignations from the League should be received by 31st December 1930, after which time they would not be acceptable!

At the later meeting, Mr Bryant said; *'When the Western League started there was an understanding that they could not have more than a certain number of clubs in it else those clubs who were agreeable would have been unable to compete. As time went on that 'unwritten guarantee' was transgressed, and that was where the first mistake was made, as they should have carried on as they intended to, and now those clubs are intent on leaving the Western League to go into another, composed of more or less, the same clubs but with more fixtures'.*

There then followed a flurry of correspondence, and of the clubs contacted, Swindon Town, Cardiff City, Portsmouth, Swansea and Southampton all said that they would not be interested in playing Western League football the following season. And while there was no response from Barry, Bournemouth, Poole and Newport, Bristol City representative, George Jenkins said that they had to wait and see what Exeter City, Torquay United and Portsmouth were going to do, while the Bristol Rovers representative, David McLean, stated that unless the Western League could supply them with a programme of games, they could not commit.

It was not good news, and when both Bath City and Exeter City said they thought they would have to resign, and Torquay United wrote to ask if they could put in a provisional resignation, the writing was on the wall. Something needed to be done very quickly to ensure the continuation, once again, of the League.

For all the promises made by champions Bristol Rovers that they would attempt to put on some good displays of football during the season, they did not come through with their pledge, ending the year in bottom spot with eight points, having won just three games. In contrast the wooden spoon professionals from the previous season, Yeovil and Petters United, picked up the 1929/30 Championship, seven points clear of runners-up, Exeter City.

In Division Two, Trowbridge Town took the title, just a point clear of Portland United, who were runners-up for the second year, while Wells City proved themselves worthy of their return, coming two points behind in third place.

The ten years since the League was put back together after the First World War had been a time of adaptation, both for the League and for the Nation, with the consequences of such a bloody and long campaign impacting on every area of life. The sport of football had changed, with circumstances calling on some innovative thinking for the men in charge to find the natural place for football in the West Country.

As the population said farewell to the trying 1920s the future that lay ahead was unpredictable, but with experience and an undiminished energy, the League looked to the 1930s confident that nothing could be more difficult than the conditions that had already been conquered.

Another day older, but wiser.

CHAPTER 9

More changes in the air

The proposed formation of the London Combination League had prompted a great deal of concern in many areas, but only Bath City withdrew from the Western League, and the new venture triggered far wider consequences for the Southern League, which saw eleven clubs resign, along with Poole, who had been forced to withdraw with four games unplayed due to financial problems.

Recalling the effect of League reorganisations previously, there was a huge recruitment campaign by the Western League committee with a view to increasing the number of clubs taking part in Division Two. And it was a huge success. Salisbury City, Warminster Town, Chippenham Town, Petters Westland, Street and Coleford Athletic, all took-up the challenge, alongside Poole who reformed as an amateur club.

CHIPPENHAM TOWN FC
Wiltshire League Champions

There were, of course, local reasons for some of the clubs to re-join, with Chippenham Town moving over after a decision by the Wiltshire League to deduct points from them for a misdemeanour. At their 1930 AGM Chairman, Mr Bulman, was said to have expressed fury at what was described as a severe punishment for a technical infringement to the rules. It was said that after showing such loyalty to the league from its inception, the ruling was one not to be endured, and Chippenham resigned, to start what would then be a long relationship with the Western League that would not diminish over the years.

With only seven teams in Division One, the championship appeared a close call for much of the season, and when Exeter City travelled to Eastville at the end of February, both clubs were neck and neck in the challenge, but Rovers were expected to make up for the poor showing of the previous season with a result to take them into pole position. The no-score draw, however, did little to decide the honours, and in the end Exeter reserves put some good results together to claim the League title, three points clear of Yeovil and Petters United. It was a great season for the club as they also won the Southern League, Western Division.

During the season Taunton Town reached the First-Round Proper of the FA Cup, and were rewarded with a match at Selhurst Park on 29th November 1930, which was played-out in front of 15,000, who paid 8d a time to watch the spectacle. On the day, Taunton matched the might of Crystal Palace until half-time, but then the quality of the English League side came to the fore, and the Third Division side progressed with six well-taken goals without reply.

Played at Selhurst Park on November 29th, 1930.

CRYSTAL PALACE v TAUNTON TOWN
English Cup November 1930

High scoring games were a mark of the Western League Division Two competition that season, with Portland United picking up the handsome Colston Cup; slotting in a record 111 goals in the process. Alongside that, Welton Rovers, Bristol City 'A', and Bath City reserves also scored over 100 goals, which was attributed to both the disparity in playing standards in the new extended division, and the change five years earlier in the off-side rule. There was also, of course, also the little matter of an increase in team managers using something called 'tactics' to win games as well.

It was to be the beginning of some good seasons in the League with entertaining games, which attracted, more people passing through the gates. And that despite severe problems throughout the country that were reaching a critical phase, once again.

Unemployment was rampant, and as a result an historic and far-reaching reduction in State expenditure was proposed, with recommendations to cut the salaries of police, teachers and the armed forces, together with imposing lower unemployment payments and substantial tax increases. Such was the severity, that even King George V agreed to take a pay-cut while the economic crisis lasted.

With that as a backdrop, the 1931/32 season began with the return of Lovell's Athletic to Division One, while Westland Petters, withdrew after just one season. Frome Town and Glastonbury both re-joined Division Two.

Lovell's Athletic had left the Southern League the previous season to join the London Combination, a move that was a disaster, with poor results and even worse gates, leaving them on the brink of disaster. It was a move which Tom summed up well, writing; *'Now, I knew that Lovell's were competing with Newport County, who were in the English League, for gates, and such a bad geographical move could not, I thought, increase the number of supporters needed; even if it did attract the likes of Northampton and Aldershot to their ground'*. Wise words indeed, reflecting the need for clubs to consider their supporter base, even in those days.

It was, yet again, a very diverse Division Two whose 32 games involved clubs that spanned from Bristol to Wiltshire, Somerset and Dorset. Many of the matches were, once again, high scoring, and as each month went by, records were being broken. Eight teams managed to score 839 goals between them, and a further eight at the other end conceded 912 in total.

But times were difficult, which was again summed up by Tom, who wrote; *'I remember one occasion around that time when I went to watch a game in Somerset during winter. On a cold, wet day I arrived in the village just minutes before the 2.15pm kick-off and saw eight miners, black as soot from their morning's toil, run past me on their way to the ground ready to don their football kit in time for the whistle. That image still lives with me today and sums up their dedication to the sport, and the severe conditions we lived under during those years of austerity'*.

In a way those men were lucky, because they still had jobs, but as the season progressed the national crisis did not abate, leading to widespread riots throughout the country over unemployment. There was even a mutiny at sea when seamen on fifteen ships in the Atlantic Fleet staged a protest at their new pay-rate which was to have left many men with only 25/- a week, and in Bristol, widespread 'bloody' demonstrations saw men and women from the area, side by side, protesting about the high rates of unemployment.

As Tom again put it; *'I had once imagined that life would never be hard again, but with two young mouths to feed and my wife in ill-health, day to day living was not easy. However, I still followed the fortunes of my league and its member clubs, but could not totally indulge my passion, as family came first'*.

'I did, however, manage to get to see Glastonbury in their first season back when they entertained Chippenham Town on 29th August 1931. It was an entertaining ninety minutes, in which I could escape from my problems. I felt that the home team deserved to come out winners by the odd goal in a

nine-goal thriller. That season Glastonbury also reached the semi-final of the Somerset Senior Cup, but went out by three goals without reply'.

And never one to miss a football opportunity, he continued; '*Although we rarely went to the cinema, my wife's birthday treat was to be in a packed audience to watch the British Movietone News that happened to feature the highlights of the 1932 Cup Final. After watching the game, we all realised how lucky Newcastle had been to beat Arsenal, 2-1 on the day. The film revealed for the first time on a big screen that the northerners first goal had been slammed in after the ball had gone out of play. That was the first time that we had ever seen an 'action replay' and when I thought about it later, I realised just how difficult life in the middle of the park is for the referee who has to make such boarder-line decisions'.*

GEORGE BRYANT

Amid the local and national conditions, there was further bad news when George Bryant died in mid-February 1931. The Western Daily Press broke the news, writing; '*Bristol sporting circles have sustained a great loss in the death of Mr George T Bryant of St George who passed away at the St Mary's Nursing Home, Clifton yesterday. He had been in failing health for some months. Mr Bryant was a well-known and esteemed sportsman. He was one of the founders of the Western Football League and had been the chairman for many years. He was also Chairman of the Gloucester Football Association and the Bristol Charity Cup Competition, and President of the Bristol Downs and Wednesday League'*

George, aged 68, was, indeed a well know figure in Bristol and beyond with his very successful shoe manufacturing enterprise, Messrs George Bryant and Sons Ltd, and in his influence on the sporting life of the area. He died leaving the grand sum of £6,662.12s.8d, which today would translate to almost £1m. He left the heritage of a League to be proud of, and one which seemed to have, once again, risen to the challenge of the age and adapted its structure to accommodate change.

Portland United proved just how strong they were by lifting the Division Two Championship for the second year running, by four points over Salisbury City. In the time that they had been members of the League they had only once been out of the top three, and for an amateur operation with a population of less than 12,000 to call on for support, that was no mean feat.

Nearby the story was not the same, with neighbours, Poole Town, suffering the added problem of where they were to play along with their financial problems. Eventually the Borough Council came to their rescue, and granted permission to use a part of the Wimborne Road Recreation Ground, which enabled them to complete the season, and end the year in a respectable mid-table position.

In contrast to the upturn in fortune for Poole, Coleford Athletic found the League far too strong, and withdrew after ending both years in wooden spoon position. Their only win all season had been at Glastonbury, 3-1, on the 3rd October; after which they went on to amass just six points and let in a total of 156 goals.

In Division One, Plymouth Argyle reserves, who picked up the Championship by two points over Yeovil and Petters United, resigned, and it would be another thirty-five years before the League would welcome another Plymouth reserve side into membership. They were replaced by Cardiff City reserves and Bath City; which ironically strengthened the division at a time when other leagues were again losing members.

In Division Two, Coleford were replaced by Swindon reserves who had elected to play in the amateur division after leaving the Southern League. One of the considerations for that decision was the inclusion of Salisbury City, Chippenham Town, Trowbridge Town and Warminster Town, in that division from Wiltshire, which increased the possibility of more supporters coming through the gates to see the local sides play each other.

The 1932/33 season kicked-off with some entertaining games. Bristol City 'A' scored a win, 7-1, at the Douglas ground over Welton Rovers in front of a very large crowd, while Bath City reserves beat Paulton Rovers, 2-0, with a last-minute goal, and Chippenham Town, who were fielding the same squad that had won the Wiltshire Cup the season before, went down, 5-4, at Glastonbury.

Later in the season, on 18th April 1933, there was a game that was more notable because of the actions of one of the players, rather than the style of play or score-line. Glastonbury were in a mid-table position, when they went to Twerton Park, the new ground of Bath City FC. With just thirty minutes played, and already two goals down, there was an injury to one of their players, Alvin Pople, who was taken by car to the Royal United Hospital, where a badly sprained wrist was diagnosed. At the time, of course, there were no substitutions allowed, which left Glastonbury with ten men. Such was the dedication of Alvin, that after the diagnosis, he immediately made it back, returning to the pitch to prevent his club from falling to more than the eventual loss, 5-0. An action that some would say was over and above his line of duty!

In general, the season was dominated again by the diversity in playing strengths in both divisions. There was, of course, a certain amount of duplication in play for some of the professional clubs, who not only met twice during the year in the Western League, but also faced each other in the Southern League west games as well. In fact, when Bristol City colts met Yeovil and Petters United on 11th February, additional Cup games had meant that it was to be the eleventh meeting between the two sides in those few footballing months.

At seasons end, Exeter City reserves just pipped Torquay United reserves to pick up the First Division Cup, by just one point. The result was achieved after a long period where both clubs had been neck-and-neck. Exeter had also accumulated a superior goal average, thanks partially to a victory, 10-0, over a weakened Taunton Town side on New Year Day.

In Division Two, Swindon Town picked up the Colston Cup a clear eight points ahead of a surprisingly strong Street side, who had not to show form in either of the previous seasons. In their final game of the season, Swindon had the added incentive of being watched by the new club manager, Ted Vizard, who was a former Welsh International with 22 Caps to his name. Having been in the job for only a couple of weeks, it was encouraging for him to see the club's up and coming players perform so well, especially as the senior squad were in the process of applying for re-election to National League Three after a disappointing season.

Around that time, a public meeting was being called by Bristol City to establish how they could continue and go forward; with an appeal for financial assistance crucial to that decision. It probably explained the withdrawal of their reserves from Division One, which along with Cardiff City reserves, who had only competed for one year, which left just twelve games to play the following season. Division Two, however, remained unchanged.

Despite the problems being dealt with at City, in general the economic state of the United Kingdom was improving at last, and by July 1933 unemployment had dropped to 2.44 million, and a more optimistic outlook was prevalent. Although a drought swept the Country during the summer, by the time the season began again that situation had changed, and torrential rain fell on rock-hard pitches. While that put out the forest fires that had raged over the boarders in Hampshire and Dorset, it created its own problems in the process.

On the playing front, Bath City proved just how far they had come from those days not long before, when they were fighting for survival, when they won the Division One championship from Yeovil and Petters United by three points. They were the only two clubs who committed themselves to over 50 games during the season by also entering a team in the Southern sections of the Southern League.

Taunton Town, in contrast, had a dreadful season, not gaining a point, and in the process letting in 57 goals while managing to score just 10. It was sad to see the demise of a club who, just three seasons earlier, had met Crystal Palace at Selhurst Park. They continued for just one more season in the Southern League, but then went out of existence, and sold their ground at Priory Park to the rugby club (who still play there today) to balance the books. Their place in the Western League was taken by the return of Cardiff City reserves.

In Division Two, Weymouth ended the seasons on 47 points, the same as Bath City reserves, and a deciding game was ordered to settle the matter. While the Dorset side came out victors, it was considered an injustice by some, because Bath had let in one less goal. Had the criteria 'goal difference' been applied, the reserves would have picked up the Trophy.

Both clubs had scored 101 goals, with the 'Terras' success due, in the main, to one of their players who was a legend in non-league circles. Wyndem 'Farmer' Giles, who originally played for Frome Town, was renowned for his playing style where he would run up and down the wing screaming '*Give I the ball and I'll put ee in*', and true to his word that is exactly what he did; scoring 51 of those goals, including six hat-tricks, in the season. The champions biggest victory came against Warminster, where they scored fourteen without reply, ending the term undefeated at home and giving their supporters a taste of just what was to come.

Rooted firmly at the foot of the table was Bristol St George, who were just one point behind Warminster Town, conceding 50 more goals, but in contrast, scoring nineteen more that the Wiltshire club.

Off the field of play life continued to improve, and the country was out of recession with the cost of living quickly reducing. The basics in life were becoming more affordable, with butter the cheapest it had been for years, and eggs costing less that they did in 1914, at 6d a dozen. Combined with that, a reduction in Income Tax by 6d in the £, meant that money began to become available to the working man once again, resulting in an increase in the numbers coming through the gates.

The World Cup that summer held very little interest, with the FA deciding not to enter the competition, however, the Final proved a talking point. For some time, the propagandists had warned about the perils of Fascism, and when the hosts, Italy, beat Czechoslovakia in extra time, 2-1, the newspapers the following day heralded it the 'Fascist' occasion, and dismissed our European neighbours achievement without more ado. Little did the population realise the true state-of-affairs, where behind the scenes and in far off lands events were stacking-up that would eventually have such an impact on the Western League and the population's everyday existence.

Ambitious club, Portland United, were spurred-on by the growing success of their neighbours, Weymouth, and strengthened their squad accordingly before the start of the 1934/35 season, with both clubs aiming for the top spot. It was, however, Swindon Town reserves who dented their ambitions when they visited both the notoriously difficult ground at Portland, and then Weymouth in successive weeks, and came away undefeated.

Under their new manager, Swindon Town had certainly benefitted, with the First team achieving an eighth place in the Third Division of the National

League, a change from the wooden spoon position that they had occupied previously. Vizard's ambitions for the club meant that the third place secured by the reserves the previous season, was not good enough, with another championship medal the order of the day for the Wiltshire club; an aim that was delivered at the end of the term, by a margin of seven points over the Division Two runners-up, Salisbury City. In the process, the Swindon youngsters had scored 108 goals and conceded just 33, conclusively showing the Dorset pretenders that they still had work to do.

In Division One, Yeovil and Petters United won the title by three points over Bath City, which mirrored their success in the Western Division of the Southern League. At the other end, Exeter City reserves finished the term one point ahead of Lovell's Athletic, and while the Welsh club elected to stay for one more season, the Devon club withdrew from the League, leaving six clubs to compete in the ten Western League games throughout the season.

At the foot of the table, Bristol St George withdrew having earned only eight points, letting in a massive 173 goals in the process, and scoring just 43. They were replaced, once again, by Poole Town who had overcome their previous problems, and were testing the strength of football outside of the Dorset County League. While Chippenham Town were ten points ahead and second from bottom, they told the AGM that the club would continue in membership and had already taken measures to improve their playing strength, by use men from outside of the town; adding that three quality players were already being pursued.

Another Wiltshire club that was in a period of change was Westbury United who, during the summer of 1935, debated a proposition to apply for membership of the Western League at their AGM. Discussion at the meeting highlighted the problem of playing in the Wiltshire League which had a small membership, with the most pertinent point made that the previous season had seen the club play numerous times against the likes of Melksham Town and Spencer Moulton, which did nothing to encourage people through its gates. The variety of visiting clubs was a positive aspect of Western League football, which was highlighted, along with both the standard of play, and the fact that the furthest away games would be at Weymouth and Portland, both of which were accessible by train from the town's station by leaving at mid-day.

It was a discussion that was aired by many clubs over time, but like the majority who considered the move, Westbury were swayed by the argument, put forward in this case by the club Captain, that although the style of play was superior, it was rougher and could not be competed in with just local town players. The argument won the day by ten votes to five, and it would be many years before Westbury United would take the step into a wider net of football.

The 1935/36 season was to be one that, once again, saw a superb standard of football played in Division Two with Swindon Town reserves putting their name on the Colston Cup for the second year. There was no need for an abacus to determine that championship either, as they won the division at a canter, a full twelve points clear of Weymouth, while Street were only one point behind.

Although it was clear for all to see that the Wiltshire club was far too strong for the League, scoring140 goals and conceding just 40, Weymouth were certainly the team to watch, with Wyndem Haines alone slotting in 62 goals in the 45 games he appeared in. He had been around for a while and before his move to the Dorset club, had been with Portsmouth in the English League; setting a record there too as the highest scoring player in a season. Aside from his remarkable form in front of goal and distinctive playing line, he was also famous in the west for his 'stand-still' penalty kick, which seemed to fool keepers no matter what level he was playing at.

At seasons end the Southern League continued to look for a solution to the problem of accommodating the professional clubs in their structure, with the spectre of reduced numbers always a threat. Although not as decimated in numbers as the Western League, their committee met to address this issue on 9th June 1936, and decided to disband the regional divisions in favour of a single competition that would allow clubs to play both on a Saturday and during the week, with the added introduction of a mid-week League for those clubs who were committed elsewhere on a Saturday.

While the new move appealed to some clubs and prompted Bath City to withdraw from the Western League along with Cardiff City reserves, Bristol Rovers reserves decided to continue; a decision that was helped by winning the Division championship that year by two points from Lovell's Athletic. They were joined by Bristol City reserves, along with three other clubs, Torquay United reserves, Yeovil and Petters United and Lovell's Athletic.

Away from football, the summer saw a black cloud hanging over the country, with rumours that talks were progressing between Adolf Hitler, who had declared himself Fuhrer (Ultimate Leader) several years before, and Benito Mussolini. Those were talks that would give rise to the real possibility of another World War. In the previous League history book, Tom noted 'After what I had experienced in the last war I was not one of the exponents of the have-a-go school of thought, and was slightly alarmed when, in July, my factory switched its production to the manufacturing of gas masks'.

Although Tom then noted that despite such omens, his leisure time was still filled with watching Western League football from the terraces, what he failed to note was that his support was for the vibrant and competitive amateur Division Two games, not the small professional Division One section.

And what a season that was to be.

The second division remained remarkably stable, with the same clubs happy to compete in what was fast becoming a hard and even contest. A fact which was graphically demonstrated when the year ended with all the clubs, excluding those in the top three and bottom four, separated in the final table by only nine points. There was also a glut of goal-scoring, which made the statistics even more remarkable, with the eventual champions, Weymouth and runners-up, Swindon Town netting a total of 283 between them, and conceding a total of only 87 goals.

This time, however, there was no run-away winner, and the championship had to be decided using goal average calculations, with both clubs earning 58 points, having run neck-and-neck all season. After the success of the past few seasons, Swindon Town then withdrew their reserves side, and were replaced by Bath City reserves; a team that was clearly not up to the challenge, and who went on to win just three of the thirty-four games played in the season.

During the summer of 1937, a new recruitment drive was launched nationally by the RAF, which saw 1,000+ enquiries a day from fit young men eager to go to war. That was to shape the rest of the decade, which would eventually see a depletion in the strength at most local football clubs, who were again losing players to the increasing build-up to war.

The surprise of the 1937/38 season was to see Radstock Town on the road to Wembley when they got through to the fourth Qualifying Round of the FA Cup, and were rewarded with a plum home tie against Yeovil and Petters United; a game that promised a huge gate and some long overdue income for the small mining club.

The match is best summed up by Tom who attended the game and wrote: *'That was a game which no-one in the area wanted to miss, and I travelled to the small Somerset ground on 13th November 1937 to witness the promised 'David and Goliath' struggle. In the souvenir programme (that I still treasure even to this day) an acquaintance of mine, Ernie Vrance, wrote, welcoming the visitors and asked them to remember that they (Radstock) were a poor club set in a district largely dependent on mining and farm work, with changing rooms that would not quite live up to the Yeovil standard. He qualified that by adding that the visitors would find the Radstock players good sportsmen and the crowd fair although enthusiastic and possibly unpolished; a statement that was truly borne out during the game'!*

He continued *'The two teams could not have been from more different backgrounds, with Yeovil parading a side of ex-League players who had gained experience with the likes of Manchester United, Newcastle and Luton, while Radstock included an 18-year-old in goal, John Aitken, and an equally young full-back, Charlie Curtis'.*

'During the game, I managed to get Ernie reminiscing about the past, and I remember the affable clubman saying that those were the days when Tom Beard was groundman, and that the half-time interval would be spent on the field sucking an orange which he or his sons, Alf, George and Walt, used to throw out to the players. Once he started this line of thought he went on, and on, and on, up to and through half-time. At one time, he was in the middle of telling me about the Somerset Cup Final between their reserve eleven and Welton Rovers, when an old supporter, Harry Bray, interrupted and in his very broad accent said 'thay cam out and jumped awver the wires like raece hosses and ourn lot comed out and got down under tawpes like a lot of auld men'.

It appeared that Radstock won the day he was talking about 4-1, unlike the encounter we were watching in which Yeovil triumphed quite easily'.

Tom finished his reminiscences; *'As I was about to leave the sagacious Ernie returned to the subject of the past, and said that what we have to remember is that, like all days, they pass, and bring in other days that to the people of the time are equally as good. Writing this so many years on I must agree, it is all well and good to remember the past, but you cannot live in it, and so we have to grow along with it, and hope that the best is yet to come'.*

Such are the friendships and memories made at Western League games, both then and now. Those two old men were, indeed, expressing sentiments that are not always heeded.

Although for some clubs the best was still quite a few years away, Weymouth were experiencing their third season without a home defeat, and walked away with the Western League Division Two title, a clear twelve points ahead of Street. Apart from those two clubs, however, the division was again generally close, with no less than five clubs with 40 points, including Chippenham Town, who, with the introduction of men from outside of the Town, had progressively improved over the seasons from the unhappy place of having to apply for re-election on several occasions.

The 1938/39 season began with a total of twenty-four clubs taking part amid a general fear throughout the country that war was soon to bring a halt to the way of life that had been achieved by hard work and sacrifice over the past 20 years. When Prime Minister, Neville Chamberlain, returned from Munich on 30th September 1938 declaring *'I believe it is peace for our time',* people wanted it to be true, but as the season progressed, news from abroad made that claim seem less a reality, and more a moment of hope.

Lovell's Athletic followed up their dismal display of the previous season by winning the championship, two points clear of Yeovil and Petters United, whose reserves also ended as runners-up in Division Two, and had just one defeat to their name.

Ahead of Yeovil's reserve side by nine points, was Trowbridge Town, who scored 166 goals and conceded just 49. The other Wiltshire clubs did not fare as well, however, with Warminster the top of the bunch in 14th place on twenty-three points, while Salisbury City and Chippenham Town ended the term at the foot of the table.

At the AGM on 24th June 1939, which was held once again at the County Sports Club in Colston Street, resignations by both Warminster and Bristol Rovers reserves were accepted, and applications by Bristol Aerospace Company, Minehead and Peasedown Miners Welfare accepted. An application from Aberaman AFC was also considered, but left on the table, only to be agreed a few weeks later.

Despite all the predictions that war with Germany was inevitable, handbooks were published and circulated, the League programme rolled out, and initial games played.

Division One was to be composed of Aberaman, Bath City, Bristol City reserves, Bristol Rovers reserves, Lovell's Athletic and Yeovil and Petters United. In Division Two it had been anticipated that all the previous members would take part, along with the newcomers, but when war was declared on the 3rd September 1939, many clubs immediately closed-down, leaving the season in doubt.

By mid-September Football League officials were in talks with the Home Office because its member clubs were already financially committed to the new season. They all had squads of professional players who were costing money, and without the games to generate the income to pay them, their clubs were quickly becoming unviable.

By the 18th September the Government instructed them to keep the players on stand-by, and shortly afterward agreed, in principal, that a war-time league could be set-up with the provisions that the clubs avoided large crowds, did not advertise games, that there was a limited travel radius (which was 50 miles; eventually amended to read 'providing the game could be played and return travel completed in the same day) and, most importantly, that it did not interfere with National Service or the National good. Those initial provisos were, or course, later revised down to a more workable level, which included a rule that all men from the Services should be allowed into the grounds at half-price.

There was then a meeting of the Western League called on 28th September 1939, to release the details of the war-time league, which was made possible by the agreement of the local Referees Associations' for its members to officiate at those games; which they did after approving the payment of 7/6d per game, plus expenses. The clubs who agreed to take part were; Bristol Aerospace, Bristol City reserves, Bristol Rovers reserves, Peasedown Miners Welfare, Paulton Rovers, Welton Rovers, Radstock Town, Street, Frome Town, Trowbridge Town, Glastonbury, Wells City and Chippenham Town.

The following day Frome Town met, however, and decided not to enter amid fears of transport problems, together with the inability to raise a sufficiently strong team due to their players leaving for foreign lands on National Service.

As an explanation of the decision to reform the League, Chairman, Mr A C Chapelle, said that they had decided to run a competition so that players and the public could play in or watch a game of competitive football, and to keep the game on the map.

On the 18th October, an article appeared in the Bristol Evening Post that gave the appearance that life had returned to normal conditions, which said *'The Western League have commenced their war-time activities, the opening games in their new competition were keenly contested. Bristol City reserves and Radstock were successful on the ground of their opponents, Paulton Rovers and Chippenham Town respectively, but Trowbridge Town at home proved too strong for newcomers, Bristol Aerospace Company.*

Although life was far from returning to normal, in general the season did produce some entertaining football. Bristol Aerospace benefited from the loan of keeper, Ted Dawson from Bristol City, and recorded some surprising victories, most notable of which was a 4-1 win over Chippenham Town at Hardenhuish Park, and 7-0 at home to Bath City reserves. At seasons end, however, they were no match for Trowbridge Town who won the championship six points ahead, with Radstock in third place, eleven points behind.

With the intensity of World War Two taking hold, and shortages of even basic items beginning to cause problems, there was no end to the hostilities in the foreseeable future, and so all competitive football ceased at season's end. It was then that daily life became more difficult than anyone could have imagined, and for once, football was far from most people's minds.

CHAPTER 10

Post war passions

The war years were especially hard in for the cities of Bath and Bristol, but while they suffered extensive bombing, some in the area were considerably more fortunate.

Chippenham was one such case, where there was very little bombing, and during that period the football club grew throughout those depressing days of air raids and restrictions. Hardenhuish Park hosted several high-profile matches to raise money for the war effort, as well as drawing on the rich vein of servicemen who were stationed nearby, to produce an entertaining football team.

CHIPPENHAM TOWN v WEST INDIAN XI

Saturday 18th November 1944

It was also the case at Twerton Park, Bath, and although they did suffer some dreadful bomb damage, the still managed to play games in which they put out teams that included servicemen from the area such as Archie McPherson, who had played 133 times for Liverpool, and centre forward (and brother of Bill), Bob Shankley, who played for Falkirk.

While the League continued during the hostilities, it was in very much a reduced form, and with resignations from Chippenham Town, Radstock, Wells City and Glastonbury early in August 1940, either because of their inability to raise a team or problems with travelling, there were only half-a-dozen clubs taking part at any one time.

It was, indeed, difficult to continue with football amid the chaos that impacted on daily life, as recalled by Tom when he wrote; '*I spent the war years on Home Guard duty in Bristol and witnessed the dreadful bombing of innocent civilian areas. The devastation caused at Ashton Gate, that began on 10th February 1941, highlighted the task we were to face on the home front. That evening while on duty 'Lemmo' Southway, who was trainer to the City war team, found all the gates locked at Ashton Gate when he went to the ground to get a couple of footballs that were needed for training, and as he attempted to climb through the window to get in, we apprehended him. We told him that there were two or three unexploded bombs in the area and that he had better move away from the ground. Later that night half of the stand was destroyed when one of the bombs went off. The following evening, he thought that the danger was past and parked his transport in the area, but it was not his week. A second bomb exploded that night destroying both his vehicle and the rest of the main stand'.*

Bristol, Bath and other surrounding areas continued to suffer damage throughout that period, and Ashton Gate was hit, yet again, when a bomb exploded on the far side of the pitch during one of many night-raids by the Luftwaffe, leaving a 20ft crater.

When the hostilities finally ceased, Tom recalled; '*Eventually, in 1945, the day we had waited for arrived and we celebrated the end of the war. Thousands of people went wild in the centre of Bristol, shaking hands at first, then kissing and hugging strangers and forming impromptu parades. Uniformed servicemen were carried shoulder high through the mass of revellers. Throughout the country there were similar scenes of unrestrained joy'.*

He continued; '*After living through those 52 years of recession, depression and war, and several spells when our mere existence was threatened, the League and I now hoped that the days ahead would be easier, and after what seemed like forever, we resumed almost normal life in the West Country when Western League football returned'.*

The 1945/46 season saw the return of most of the clubs who had taken part before the war, apart from Bath City reserves, Wells City and Glastonbury. Additions to the competition included Yeovil Town reserves, who had change their name from Yeovil and Petters United, Soundwell and Bristol Rovers. There was also, again, a team from the Douglas factory in Kingswood.

Not surprisingly, the year was to prove problematic. Throughout the country life was particularly difficult, because despite the promises of the new Labour Government, who at the time of gaining an election landslide victory had declared, 'Labour can deliver the goods', they simply couldn't.

Food and petrol rationing were re-introduced in February 1946, and that combined with clothing rationing, meant that putting a team on the pitch to play a competitive game of football had become even more difficult. The rationing of clothes, that had initially been put in place in 1941, called on some imaginative actions; with some ladies even knitting socks for players, and sometimes dyeing the wool themselves.

The amenities at most grounds were also quite basic, with some clubs forced to seek alternative sites because of war damage, but most teams had minimum standards available to them, even if a few had to rebuild their clubs from scratch at a time when building materials were at a premium.

Amid all of that, however, attendances at local games were good; partially due to the travel restrictions still in place ensuring that people supported their local clubs, but also because people were determined to enjoy themselves to the full after those years of austerity and gloom.

The problem of returning to a ground that had been neglected during the war was highlighted by events at an FA Cup tie at Bolton Wanderers that ended in tragedy on 9th March 1946. A steel barrier collapsed that day under the weight of a surging crowd, sadly leaving thirty-three supporters dead. Such were the dangers of returning to neglected grounds after the six-year break.

Easter saw a full programme of Western League games that had been greeted by large and enthusiastic supporters, epitomised by the 2,000+ who crowded into the Paulton Rovers ground on Good Friday. That was followed three days later when Paulton took on fellow Western League side, Clandown, in the Somerset Cup final, at Wells, where almost 5,000 spectators took up any position they could, and watched a full-blooded game in which Clandown came out the victors, 3-0.

At the end of that first season back after the war, Bristol Rovers reserves took the honours six points clear of three clubs who all finished the term with 34 points, Peasedown Miners Welfare, Trowbridge Town and Chippenham Town. On goal-average, Chippenham were declared runners-up, but had goal-difference been applied as it would today, Trowbridge Town would have been awarded the second place.

At the Western League AGM on 30th May 1946, there were a glut of clubs applying for membership of the League, and Lovell's Athletic proposed that a professional Division One should be formed, but that was defeated by the other professional club's present; Torquay United, Yeovil Town and Bristol Rovers.

A motion was then put forward that the existing and applicant clubs should be allocated to two Division's; a motion that was carried, and one that was to shape the future of the Western League.

The existing members of the League were allocated to Division One, alongside returning members, Portland, Wells and Glastonbury. However, Clandown, Soundwell and Douglas all elected to enter the smaller Division Two, alongside reserve teams from Trowbridge Town, Swindon Town, BAC, and Chippenham Town. That division was then completed with entries from RAF teams who were stationed at the Locking, Melksham and Colerne camps, along with Hoffman Athletic, Cinderford Town and Thorney Pitts Hostel, near Corsham.

While the first season after the war had been hard, the 1946/47 season reflected the conditions that prevailed in day-to-day life. The worse winter on record was combined with an increase in both petrol and food rationing, which saw games curtailed. Mother Nature then stepped in and a big freeze began in February, and the following month gave way to a horrific thaw that heralded widespread flooding.

A government ban on mid-week games also meant that when all the games had not been completed in June, there was no alternative but to end the season with games unplayed. Of the thirty-one clubs taking part, only two managed to compete all fixtures, but such was daily life, that completing League tables was the least of most people's worries. Two versions of the Leagues records for that year still exist, with the official one not reflecting the additional games played after the official end of the season.

Trowbridge Town won the championship with just one game unplayed, a massive ten points clear of Poole who had played two less games. Their achievement was, however, not diminished by those unplayed games, with Bristol Rovers reserves coming in third, having played the same number of matches, but with thirteen points less.

Trowbridge played on a magnificent ground at Frome Road, which sported a pavilion that had been built in the memory of Major Allen Llewellyn Palmer of the Royal Wiltshire Yeomanry, who was killed at Amiens on 15th November 1916, at the age of thirty-four.

Trowbridge had a squad of players assembled by the manager, Ted Long, that included a couple of talented German footballers, Bert Schrader and Alous (Alec) Eisenstrager, who had been interned at the Ladyfield prisoner of war camp off Kingsley Road in Chippenham. Alec eventually went on to play as a professional for many years with Bristol City, and later supported the Western League and Clevedon Town. Bert stayed in Chippenham and married a local girl. He played for Chippenham United for many a year.

In Division Two, Clandown took the honours by five points over runners-up, Soundwell, having played a game less, with Douglas Kingswood in third place, 12 points behind. In the process, Clandown had scored an average of five goals a game, and conceded only 33 times in their 23 starts.

Thorney Pitts Hostel, a team made-up of refugees from Latvia and Estonia, who were billeted at a camp at Hawthorn, near Corsham, were totally out of their depth. All season they had one win. Their defence was abysmal, letting in 158 goals in their 18 games, an average of nine a game, and they scored just 24 goals; a heartening fact for any struggling club today to ponder on!

A combination of high-scoring entertaining football, and a desire to enjoy every minute available after those war years, promoted not just good attendances at games, but also encouraged supporters to get behind their clubs. Travel, when possible, was expensive, and combined with the work needed on most grounds, meant that their Supporters Clubs were having to work hard to keep the standard of football on offer.

Salisbury, who returned to play in Division Two, were typical of a Western League club who had generated the goodwill of the local population and like many in the League were forging ahead; in their case thanks to the 750 members who did everything from raising money, mowing the pitch, and producing half-time teas. With most grounds in need of some sort of improvement, repair, or indeed upgrade, the voluntary efforts of local men and women was vital especially if a club wanted to move on to a higher level that required the provision of seating and covered accommodation.

The League continued to expand with conditions favouring local football over the national game, and there was no shortage of ambition within some of the member clubs, which saw many toying with the idea of professionalism. With no specific division for the professionals, however, the amateurs of Division Two had to pit their wits against those who could offer a higher standard of football; often because of the ingenious ways they employed to raise money,

Glastonbury were one such club, who along with gates of between 1,500 and 2,000, capitalised on their popularity by attracting no less than 178 Vice-Presidents to the club; all of whom contributed financially - to a greater or lesser extent.

For the 1947/48 season, Salisbury, Weymouth and Dorchester all joined relegated Welton Rovers and Frome Town in Division Two, along with Cheltenham Town reserves, Stonehouse, and a team from the National Smelting Company.

Those were, indeed, halcyon days in the history of the League, where the Management Committee must have been content with the progress being made. Remarkable consistency had been shown in the administration over the season's straddling the war. Mr George Jenkins, the ex-official of Bristol City, had taken over as President from the long serving Mr J Taylor after his death, and remained as such after the War. Mr Chappelle was the able Chairman, and Leonard Kennedy served the dual roles of Secretary and Treasurer. Those men worked hand-in hand with Vice-Presidents, Alan Young, George Jenkins and Charlie Webb, ensuring that the administration of the League was in capable and secure hands.

The League title went, once again, to Trowbridge Town, this time by six points over Glastonbury, with Radstock Town and Bristol Aeroplane Company relegated; with the system of promotions and relegations giving the competition the bite that it had lacked in previous years.

In Division Two, newcomers Salisbury, Weymouth and Cheltenham reserves dominated throughout, while the RAF sides playing form reflected that the country was getting back to normality, with the professional players that had contributed to their strength now plying their trade back at their National League clubs; a move that lead to the resignations of both RAF Colerne and RAF Locking.

Bristol Aeroplane Company teams were both in bottom positions in their respective divisions, which meant that their reserves had to find another league to play in to make way for their relegated senior side. The BAC's Secretary was Jack Veale, whose address at 5 Everest Road, Fishponds, Bristol, all member club Secretaries would become familiar with in future years, when he took up the post as the pedantic Hon Secretary of the Western League. The strength of the division was also diluted somewhat when Bristol City and Bristol Rovers replaced their reserve teams with young Colts sides.

Trowbridge Town Captain, Bill Lovesay, receiving the Cup from Secretary, Jack Veale and Alan Young

During the summer the 1948, the Olympic Games took place in London, with competitors based in military camps, colleges and schools. The athletes were given Category 'A' meal allowances, the same as awarded to coal miners and dock workers, with the addition of two pints of milk a day, together with a 1/2lb chocolate and sweets a week. The event was dubbed 'The Austerity Games', with the medals made from Oxidized Silver; but circumstances aside, it really did seem to lift the mood of the country, and was to be a gateway for better times ahead.

Optimism, indeed, reigned, and the new Labour Government pushed through its welfare reforms on the 5th July 1948, with the promise of 'Cradle to the Grave' cover, along with other measures. Some rationing was also eased, with footwear and furnishing fabrics taken off the books, and the prospect that clothes rationing would disappear within months.

Those were glorious days in the game, and at all playing levels gates were passing expectations, as the desire for leisure activities and entertainment increased; which meant that the 'beautiful game' was perfectly poised to capitalise to the full.

The increase in popularity was epitomised by events that had taken place in the market town of Chippenham, where during the war years the club had flourished under the able management of its Secretary, Fed Evans; a man who firmly believed that Chippenham Town FC should be playing at a higher standard. As a measure of his ambition, it was revealed at a committee meeting on 22nd July 1946, that he had been working with prominent business man and Supporters Club Chairman, Emmanuel Harris, to buy Hardenhuish Park, with a view to the club turning professional; a statement which produced heated negative discussions, and which ultimately resulted in both men walking away from the club.

A year later the two men attempted a hostile take-over at its AGM on 15th July 1947, and when that failed they immediately formed the semi-professional club, Chippenham United, which played its first game in the Wiltshire League a few weeks later.

CHIPPENHAM UNITED FC

Not content with that, Fred Evans spent the 1947/48 season lobbying prominent football officials, and applied to enter both the Welsh League and the Western League. He was then in attendance to see the fruits of his work when the Welsh League voted, by the Chairman's casting vote, not to increase its size to allow them entry, despite all his efforts.

The Western League was equally nonplussed about the prospect of taking on a second club from Chippenham, and initially voted against allowing United membership, but Fred Evans was not one to allow NO to mean NEVER, and he pursued the League with photos of how the ground had been improved over its first year, together with plans for the coming seasons.

At a meeting of Division Two that had been called to discuss the composition for the following season, the Portland United representative was particularly vocal in support of Chippenham United, and protested that the League would be stronger for their inclusion. Despite that, however, Leonard Kennedy, who was in the Chair, concluded that the club had been given a fair hearing, and that the application should go forward to the AGM in July1948, with the recommendation that Chippenham United's application would NOT be accepted.

In the event, and after much lobbying by Fred Evans, the AGM went against the recommendation, and accepted Chippenham United's application, who were admitted into Division Two, along with Weston-super-Mare and newcomers Barnstaple Town.

The rapid rise of Chippenham United both enlivened its home town and divided households; with Chippenham buzzing about the Western League games to come between the new club and the Hardenhuish Park reserve eleven, who had only avoided relegation from the League because of the RAF Colerne and Thorney Pitts Hostel resignations.

The entry of Barnstable afforded some epic journeys to North Devon along the winding roads, without the benefit of the superb Devon Link, that makes journeys so quick today. Tom recalled just one of those when he wrote; '*On these jaunts you could be sure that if one thing went wrong other problems would quickly follow. The most memorable was the time when, in the middle of a snow-storm, the windscreen wipers on our motor-coach decided to pack up. The game that day had been abandoned after a short time, and we were stuck in some cold dark Devon lane miles from home and unable to cure the problem*'.

'*The only solution that we could think of was to take it in turns to wrap up in several overcoats and sit astride the bonnet of the coach to clear the snow from the windscreen with well protected hands. Thankfully, no one suffered frost bite and we eventually reached Weston-super-Mare where a sleepy, and not very happy, garage mechanic, who we had met earlier in the season following his team after they re-entered the league, repaired the fault. We arrived home at 2am, vowing never to use that bus company again*'!

The competition between the clubs in both divisions was fierce and fast, and it was tremendous from a supporter's point of view to see so many ex-football League players turning out in Western League Division One games. In many cases the more affluent clubs were signing players in their prime because, without being hampered by the wage 'cap,' they could offer good money, jobs and even houses to attract the young men away from the national competition.

CHIPPENHAM UNITED FC

After winning Division One Championship

The rise of Chippenham United was a spectacle to watch, as they swept through Division Two, dropping just seven points all season, scoring 145 goals and conceding 35. In the photograph above, the gentleman in the suit and tie on the right of the group enjoying the presentation is Harold Clarke, father of Ken Clarke, well known to us all in the Western League family. United's promotion to Division One gave rise to a battle with Chippenham Town, the like of which would never be seen again. The Hardenhuish Park men responded by encompassing the professional status that they had fought so hard to resist, and in a small market town in the middle of Wiltshire, combat was about to commence.

Glastonbury improved their runners-up position, and reversed the Championship of the previous season, four points clear of Trowbridge Town. Third placed Weymouth left and joined the Southern League, but were permitted to put their reserves into Division One in their place.

The League Committee had been kept busy during the season with a huge amount of interest generated in the competition. In response to requests for entry, it was decided and voted through at the AGM of 1949, to run three divisions. A Cup was then generously donated by Mr G R Cooper of Weston-super-Mare, and eight reserve teams from existing member clubs were accepted in. Along with those teams, Bideford Town, Ilfracombe Town and Minehead became members, after seeing just how successful neighbours, Barnstaple, had been in their first year of membership.

With the increased number of clubs taking part, the Committee put forward a motion to the AGM that only two clubs should be relegated from Division One and four promoted, a move to achieve a numerical balance between the two higher sections. It was, however, a motion that was challenged by Salisbury City, who argued successfully that it contravened the rules of the constitution. It was an argument which could not be won and so the two up, two down, system was retained.

During the season, Mr Kennedy attended a meeting at Taunton at which all the County Football Association's in the West Country were present. The Counties had formed a Federation with the aim of obtaining the fullest co-operation throughout the area, and to further both their organisations and the sport. With a view to those sentiments, an application was then lodged for the League to get a seat at the table. Subsequently, Mr Chappelle attended the next meeting, which was held in Exeter, in his capacity as a member of the Gloucester FA, and reported back to the next Western League meeting that the application had been unsuccessful because the wording of the new constitution did not allow membership from league organisations.

As the season came to an end in May 1950, some of the problems associated with travel eased with the end of petrol rationing. It had been a season of change, introducing a new initiative for clubs to grade the man in the middle, with several retired referees forming a panel to watch and report on any official who did not come up to standard. The intention was that they could then offer suggestions on how their performances could be improved. This was to be the very early precursor to other initiatives that were to follow in later years.

Wells City and Poole Town ended the year on equal points at the top of Division One. They had both won 22, drawn 7 and lost 5 games, producing some spectacular displays of football along the way. Wells City picked up the magnificent Cup by the narrowest of decisions having scored 87 goals and conceded 43, compared to the runners-up tally of 88 scored and 45 conceded.

WELLS CITY FC

Champions 1949/50

The rise of Wells had followed on from a meeting that was held on 17th January 1948 when, with Arthur Coles in the chair, it had been decided that the club would become professional. The decision had led to the appointment of Ernie Jones from Bristol City; a man who, in his eight years in charge, was to oversee one of the most successful periods in the club's history by combining local talent with many Bristol based players.

In Division Two, Barnstaple continued their progress, powering their way to promotion in their second season, and were to remain in the top flight for many, many years to come. The two bottom clubs in that division had found the new competitive league too challenging, and both BAC and Douglas withdrew, causing Jack Veale to then become the representative for Portland, thus enabling him to remain in the role of Hon Secretary.

The experiment of running with a third division was disbanded at the end of that first season, with champions Bideford Town and runners-up, Ilfracombe Town, both promoted into Division Two along with Minehead, and newcomers, Chipping Sodbury. Clubs had found that running a reserve team in the League an expensive venture, and all other competitors withdrew.

At the AGM, held 24th June 1950, Charlie Webb, who was both a Life Member and a Vice-President, was awarded a Long Service medal for his 21 years of involvement. He was also congratulated on his appointment as Secretary of the Somerset FA. Charlie was, of course, the ebullient father of long serving League referee, Lew Webb, and between the two of them were to devote over 60 years to football in the West Country.

As the 1950/51 season began, a problem arose on the 23rd August when the match official decided to travel to a game at Street in the Paulton Rovers' coach. Apart from the obvious claims of bias that emanated from the terraces and committee room alike, the unlucky man also faced being censured by the Management Committee when the coach broke down on the way to the game and he arrived forty minutes late. To add insult to injury, he also later tried to charge the home club for a third-class railway ticket! The whole incident brought up several unclear areas in the rules regarding paying the officials, especially as the man's defence was that he intended to give the payment to Paulton Rovers for the bus ride. Paulton were fined 20/- for arriving late to the game, but the Committee found that they were unable to sanction the errant referee and so they inserted a new rule into their constitution enabling them to censure a referee, when it was necessary.

In general, there were some major developments occurring at some of the member clubs, with many attempting to improve their grounds to accommodate the ever-increasing number of supporters. Most were lucky to have washing facilities available at the ground for players after the game, as well as some form of toilet for supporters. That was especially fortunate given that one in three households in the country still had no fixed bath, with the only facility available to them being a tin bath hung up on the wall in the outside toilet, which was then brought in front of the fire and used, maybe, once a week for the whole family. One in twenty households were also still waiting for piped water; which all goes to show just what good facilities are available to both supporters and players at our grounds today!

Together with that, communication was a problem, with very few people afforded the luxury of a telephone, and the 'Peasedown Pigeon' system of employing racing birds still sometimes in operation. However, most families enjoyed a wireless set in the house, so the weekly trip to the cinema, with Pathe News reports between the feature films, was becoming less important to a nation previously starved of the news of the day.

During the season, the FA Cup provided some exceptional games for Western League clubs, with Glastonbury playing extremely well. After beating Street by the only goal in the Third Round, a win, 4-1, away at Dorchester led to a hugely inspiring First-Round Proper game at home to Exeter City. The match showed the strength of team that the Somerset club had put together, and although they went out of the Competition, 2-1, the impetus that it created helped spur them on to the Western League championship, which they won by a clear five points ahead of Wells City.

Despite expectations, the administration of the League had not run smoothly during the season, and when Yeovil Town reserves found themselves relegated, they complained at length about the way that the competition had been administered, arguing the they had no idea that they were at the foot of the division until the time that they were informed of their relegation.

The basis of the complaint was that, had they known the statistics, which eventually put them in the second relegation spot on goal-average from Portland United, with both clubs ending the season with 19 points, they could have attempted to curtail the deficit. Using todays calculations, Yeovil would, indeed, not have been relegated with a goal-difference of -41 compared to Portland's -56, but in the event, their protest was in vain, and they were relegated along with Peasedown Miners Welfare, who had won just one match and conceded 123 goals in the process.

In Division Two, Stonehouse took the title by four points over Bath City reserves, amassing 133 goals in the process. That division had, in fact, seen seven clubs scoring over one hundred goals each, with Bideford setting the pace on 158, a feat that was achieved after scoring sixteen without reply in one game against Soundwell, with Denny Miller putting in six, Glyn White four, and Tommy Robinson three.

Bideford Town were certainly becoming the talk of the League, and not only for their prowess on the pitch, but because of the amazing devotion of supporter, Tom Prentice. Tom would attend every game, both home and away, a feat made more difficult because he was paralysed from the neck down.

Accompanied by his nurse, who later became his wife, he was driven in a specially adapted van, and throughout the game would watch the action through a looking-glass pole. On the return journeys from away games, it became a normal practice to stop at the Jubilee Inn near South Mouton, where the players would carry Tom on his stretcher and lay him on the snooker table, from which advantage point he could then take part in their celebrations and often, the sing-song.

TOM PRENTICE, BIDEFORD TOWN FC

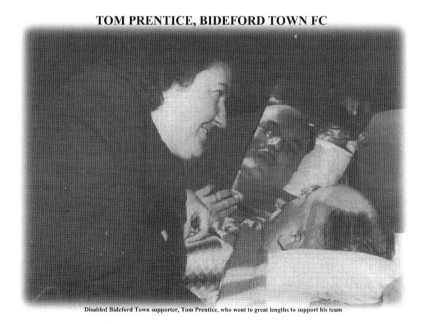

Disabled Bideford Town supporter, Tom Prentice, who went to great lengths to support his team

After the problems experience by the League administration during the season there was a very lively AGM held in July 1951, where the exchanges were as hot as the weather. The Hon Secretary, Mr Kennedy, was advised by the Chairman, Mr Chappelle, that it would be best for him to resign from the heavy roles that he held. A discussion then ensued at which time Mr George Jenkins stood down from the role of President in favour of Mr Alan Young, and the duties of the Secretary were split into that of General Secretary/ Treasurer and one of Registrations, Referees Appointments, and Fixtures Secretary. The new role was taken on by Lew Webb and Jack Veale filled the position of Trustee from Mr Kennedy, along with the General Secretary/ Treasurer role.

One of the new measures that Jack immediately took on, was to issue weekly League Tables to every club; albeit that the new initiative that was soon a monthly event to save money. There were also many other areas to sort-out, and activity went on behind the scenes right up to the start of the season; at which time the only matter not solved was the whereabouts of the Bristol Charites Cup and some other Trophies. Many years later it was found the Charities Cup had been loaned to the Bristol Church of England League, and it was handed back by Pete McPherson of the Gloucester County Football Association in November 1991, just months before the Leagues Centenary Celebrations.

As the new season settled in, the FA Cup was again the focus of many non-league supporters with Glastonbury hoping to repeat the previous seasons run. The First-Qualifying round draw, however, saw them go out in a replay at Twerton Park, 3-1, after initially holding Bath City to an entertaining 2-2 draw in the well-attended first game. The competition did, however, afford two of the League's clubs good progress through to the Fourth Qualifying round.

Bideford Town defeated Taunton Town, 8-2, in a replay; St Austell, 5-0, also in a replay and Dartmouth, 7-0, and were then drawn to play neighbours, Barnstaple Town. The fiercely competed game was played in front of 5,188, attracting receipts of £294, at 5d a time, and saw Barnstaple run out the winners 2-1. Barnstaple then went on to beat Lymington, 3-1, in a replay after holding them on their own ground, leading to a First-Round Proper game away at Folkstone, which was lost, 5-2.

In the meantime, Chippenham Town was also progressing though, beating Welton Rovers, 5-1; Salisbury City, 2-1, in a replay at Hardenhuish Park, and Newport IOW, 3-1. Their reward was a game away in London at non-league Leyton, a game they lost, 3-0.

Chippenham had experienced mixed fortunes since embracing professionalism to compete with the new United club in their town, and had appointed Tommy Dawson, a well-known and experienced League footballer as manager, to combat the opposition club's continuing success. His appointment had seen a huge number of professional players brought in on a full-time basis, but results did not justify the huge expense. By the time the 'Cup run' came around, the team was being run by the Chairman and ex-player, George Flower, a man that had the championship of the Western League firmly in his sight.

At seasons end, George Flower got just that, with Chippenham winning what was to be their only League Championship, four points clear of runners-up, Glastonbury, and eight ahead of Barnstaple Town. At the other end of the division, Bristol Rovers Colts and Poole Town were suffering a dreadful run and were relegated, having ended the year in the bottom two positions.

CHIPPENHAM TOWN FOOTBALL CLUB

Western Football League Champions 1952-32
The only time this honour was won in their 64 years of competing

In Division Two, Bideford topped the table, slotting in 179 goals, a number that is still a record after all these years, and on the way, had run into double figures in four games; beating Welton, 10-0, both Yeovil reserves and Weston-super-Mare, 11-0, and Radstock, 11-1. Ironically, their goal average/ difference could have been even greater were it not for a thrashing at home in the final game of the season, 10-0, by Bristol City reserves.

Crowds were still very good at most games, but Easter Saturday 1952 had seen a disproportionate amount of football fever in the town of Ilfracombe, when fifteen coach-loads of supporters from Bridgwater Town descended on the town. Although the Devon club registered a victory, 2-1, that day, a fall-off in form prevented them from taking the runners-up position, with Bridgwater taking that spot three points ahead, and winning promotion.

Trowbridge Town reserves were saved from leaving the League when they ended the term just above bottom placed Chipping Sodbury. That club left the League, together with both Swindon Town Colts and Cheltenham Town reserves, which meant that the reserves remained in the league.

One result of the administrative reorganisation during the season, was that Lew Webb began to tackle the age-old question of refereeing standards.

The original list that Lew had inherited was extremely large and could not guarantee that a referee would get the minimum number of three games a month; a number needed to ensure fitness and experience. He therefore produced a carefully selected reduced list with the remaining men ensured of a fee for the season to come of 30/- for the man in the middle of a Division One game, and 15/- for each linesman, together with 21/- for a Division Two referee and 12/6 for each linesman. All officials were entitled to claim the equivalent of a third-class railway ticket but, unlike today, none were allowed on the list if they were attached to any other senior league, except for the Football League.

The changes that had taken place since the resumption of football after the Second World War, had, indeed, reshaped the League, and as it moved into its 60th year, both the game and the organisation could reflect well on the thirty-eight clubs that were now in membership. Those clubs came from five counties, and represented thousands of West Country men, women, boys and girls who looked to the simple Association game to fill their precious hours of leisure.

CHAPTER 11

Never had it so good

With a certain amount of optimism, the Western League kicked-off its 60th season, but all the changes that had been taking place in the administration of the League meant that Jack Veale did not informed the FA of the significant anniversary until July. Because of that they were unable to immediately respond to his request for a representative Football Association XI to play against a selected Western League XI. Although it was understandable, given the late notification, negotiations were to continue throughout the year without a concluding date agreed.

Almost from the first game of the season the weather turned, and torrential rain battered the West Country, causing many matches to be postponed. But that was nothing compared to the severity of the conditions that prevailed in some coastal towns.

The most severely affected by those conditions was Lynmouth in Devon, whose sea defences collapsed, sadly killing thirty-four people, devastating both the lives and infrastructure of the town. When the weather improved and games resumed, many Western League clubs joined in the fund-raising efforts for the devastated town with half-time collections to add to the already considerable financial support from the country.

Tea rationing was lifted on 5th October 1952, enabling the hard-working volunteers at clubs to serve the nations favourite brew without restrictions. It was those wonderful people, combined with huge crowds, that were affording many clubs a time of growth that was almost unprecedented in the modern non-league game. Gates had continued to grow and ambitions seemed always to mirror that expansion.

In the divided town of Chippenham, for example, the long hot summer months has been taken up with officials discussing the conditions needed to merge the Town and United clubs, which had been prompted by the Southern League's proposal to increase its size, once again.

The Southern League was of high significance at the time, positioned just one step below the National League, with its member's ambitious to progress, and it was recruiting, once again from within the Western League net. In the case of Chippenham, however, no common ground for a merger between United and Town could be found to facilitate such a move, and Western League membership was set to continue.

Barnstable Town were eventual worthy League Champions, but the run-in at the end of the season could not have been any closer, and was probably the narrowest ever witnessed. After a whole campaign, the final Saturday saw the club on level points with Street, with the task ahead to win the game by a large margin to take the title, and on the day, they achieved just that, beating Dorchester Town, 6-1, in front of a crowd of over 3,000.

Unlike today, however, where every minute of every game can be followed in real-time, communications were slow, and there was a huge wait for players, officials and fans before the news was relayed that Street had also won their game, 2-1. There was then another delay while the League officials reached for the abacus to find out who had the best goal-average, and with both clubs on 44 points, the eventual calculations gave the Devon club an average of 2.081 compared to Street achieving 2.069; awarding the Western League Championship to Barnstaple Town by just 0.012 of a goal. Ironically, using the simpler calculation of goal-difference that is used to today, Street would have won the t itle with a margin of +6 goals.

There were none-such calculations needed at the other end of the table, with Paulton Rovers relegated after gaining 17 points, after losing 21 of the 32 games played. Dorchester Town, who ended the term one place above, were not relegated due to the decision that numerical parity was more important than playing strength; this time with rules in the constitution that allowed for such a judgement.

In Division Two, the position at the top was less of a problem with Chippenham Town reserves heading the table from Ilfracombe. The reserves were, of course, not able to be promoted and so the third placed club, Poole Town, took their place.

The Jubilee year came, and went, without a decision on the planned Representative Game, although at one stage it seemed possible that it would be staged at Twerton Park, on either the 9th or 16th September 1953, one year after the historic original date. However, for all sorts of reasons that was a non-starter, and eventually, after a huge amount of correspondence with the Football Association, a date was agreed for 23rd March 1954, at Ashton Gate.

Newly promoted Ilfracombe Town performed well throughout their first year in the higher Division, and were the only Western League club to progress to the Fourth Qualifying Round of the FA Cup, where they were drawn away to Welsh club, Llanelli. Although they eventually lost the tie by the only goal of the game in front of 8,500 supporters, they represented the League well with a tremendous display of football.

The next day an article appeared in the local paper which referred to a young man by the name of Les Phillips, who was involved with Ilfracombe while serving with an RAPC unit in Taunton. Even then Les had an eye for talent, and was roundly praised in the newspaper report for recommending a player to the Ilfracombe manager, who had gone on to play an integral part in that game. It was to be many years before the League would know the name of Les Philips, but there was one thing for sure; his early love of football was already apparent.

The weather at years end was dreadful, and until early March few games were played due to snow, winds and a big freeze, that made day-to-day conditions extremely difficult. However, by the time the planned Jubilee Celebration match was due to be played, the weather had eased. The game took place under floodlights at Ashton Gate, with a representative Western League XI against an FA XI which included Bristol City favourite, John Atyeo; a player who had begun his career at Westbury United. The Western League side was managed by Reg Broom with 'Lemmo' Southway as trainer, but in front of 5,809 supporters it was halted in the second-half by yet another blizzard, with the FA team winning, 4-0.

Despite not completing the game, the Celebration Dinner went ahead at the Grand Hotel in Bristol, with a five-course dinner. The principal speaker was JP and Secretary of the Football Association, Sir Stanley Rous CBE, who responded on behalf of the guests with a flurry of compliments about the League's history, and its importance in the life on non-league football nationally. He ended the speech with the promise that another representative game would be arranged for the following season, to compensate for the abandoned match.

The season had seen some tremendous displays of football in both divisions, with Bristol Rovers and Bristol City both returning to form in Division Two, with their young up-and-coming youth teams gaining promotion. Their places were filled by relegated Clandown and Stonehouse, with the latter club then having to withdraw their reserves to make-way. That then gave the League a spare place in the division, which was taken by Taunton Town, who had been interviewed in respect of an application for membership by a sub-committee earlier in the season.

During the summer the Chairman, Mr A C Chappelle, stepped down to make way for Mr John Gummow, and ex-officio of Bristol Rovers. He did not leave the committee, however, and became Vice-Chairman alongside Mr A W Hand, Mr D Hawkins and Mr A Mortimer. In recognition of the loyalty that Mr Chappelle had shown to the League, he was presented with a Long Service Medal recording 40 years of involvement.

Since the dawn of the 1950s, lives had been gradually getting better, and rationing had been completely eradicated. In general, the villages, towns and cities had begun to reflect the new normality, and some clubs were indeed, at times, spending a disproportionate amount of money in the attempt to bring footballing honours to their club.

Once again, in the town of Chippenham, its two Western League clubs were experiencing opposite fortunes, with United struggling to retain their place in the League, while Town were reported to be investing heavily to attract quality players. Such was their spending that, at the CTFC 1954

AGM, it was reported that the previous season's wages bill had amounted to £3,462, together with travelling expenses of £348. In comparison to 'real' money, that was only just shy of the tender put in by builders Smith and Lacey Ltd of Chippenham to build a pair of semi-detached police houses in the town; a tidy sum in anyone's calculations. Income, however, was good and saw gate receipts at £2,141, season tickets £350, Supporters Club donations £1,400 and over £1,000 given in other contributions. How some of the present-day clubs would wish for accounts that read like that!

Life was improving throughout the Country, and It was with a certain amount of optimism that the 1954/55 season kicked-off with the prospect of a new competition to add interest; that of the Western Football League Professional Challenge Cup. The League's amateur clubs would have to wait another two seasons before the introduction of an additional competition for them, but with a superb new Trophy to covet, which had cost the League £45-9s-0d, there was a buzz of anticipation amongst the professional clubs.

The early stages of the competition were drawn on a geographical basis, with the aggregated goals from those qualifying home and away games, resulting in a table based on goal average (keep up, there is more to come!). The top sixteen clubs then went through to the competition proper. Players were only deemed cup-tied from the semi-final onward, with the two-legged final then decided on a goal average basis. The entry fee was a Guinea (£1-1s-0d) with no opt-out option unless 'special circumstances' prevented participation.

With all those rules, it was anticipated that the competition should run smoothly, but in the event the first Professional Cup Final resulted in a draw, and it was not until much later in the season that Frome Town were ordered to go to Poole Town to play the game under floodlights and bring the competition to a conclusion; which resulted in the Dorset club becoming the first to engrave its name on the new prestigious Trophy.

In Division Two, Frome Town were enjoying a good season, both in Cup competitions and the League. Under new manager, Jock Fairweather, they had progressed well in the FA Cup, and after producing a surprise win in the final Qualifying Round against Weymouth, they were given a plum home draw to high riding Leyton Orient. A staggering record crowd of over 8,000 squeezed into Badgers Hill on the afternoon of the 20th November 1954, but despite producing a brave battle, Frome lost the encounter, 3-0.

During the season the promised representative match, between a Football Association XI and a Western League XI took place under floodlights, again at Ashton Gate on Tuesday 22nd March 1955. The captain of the FA side was also an England 'B' team member, and had been transferred only a few weeks previously from the eventual Football Association Champions, Chelsea, to Fulham. Ron Greenwood was on the cusp of his career, and would later become the manager of West Ham, before taking up his post with the National side after Don Revie left. Other International's that evening included, goalkeeper, Ten Ditchburn from Spurs and full-back, Lionel Smith - a former player on the books of Arsenal.

While it was a memorable evening, it preluded a period of frosty relationships between the administrators of the two sides, after the Western League were sent a bill for what they considered excessive expenses, and decided to refer the matter to the FA's International Committee to arbitrate. The decision did nothing to quell the bad feeling from the FA's point of view, as the committee found in favour of the League and ruled that the FA should shoulder its own expenses.

First Division League honours went right to the wire, with Bath City reserves, Dorchester and Chippenham Town in contention throughout. In the end, Dorchester picked up the historic Trophy, winning 23 games and drawing 5, compared to Chippenham Town's record of 21 games won and 7 drawn. Bath City reserves were in third place a point behind, a good six points clear of Salisbury, Portland United and Bideford, who all ended the term on 42 points.

Frome came in as runners-up in the Second Division, equal on points with Yeovil Town reserves who were crowned Champions, but with less goals scored. The promoted clubs replaced Street and Ilfracombe, while Bath City reserves, once again, resigned at seasons end.

The summer of 1955 was long and hot, resulting in a drought in some areas, and causing problems with club's who relied on the period to reseed and repair pitches. There was, however, good news generally, with the country's economy performing well and unemployment declared at under 1% for the first time in living memory.

The 'feel-good' factor did not, however, transfer to some of the League's members, and during the summer, there was talk again of financial problems at many clubs, particularly Chippenham United, who seemed perilously close to closure. While those problems were not new to the club, concerns were also being expressed about funding problems down the road at Hardenhuish Park, where only the year before accounts had been looking healthy. With gates receding and leisure options expanding, it was a period when many of our clubs would need to re-assess their set-ups, once again.

The 1955/56 season began with Trowbridge Town celebrating their Golden Jubilee by staging a game against a Western League XI on 22nd August 1955. On the day, a good crowd of over 2,000 turned out to enjoy a spirited game which resulted in a win, 2-1, for the League. The club were in a rebuilding phase with new manager, Harry Haddon, promising much, and he was not about to disappoint the football mad Wiltshire County town. By seasons end the potential of the club had been fulfilled, and Trowbridge won the League three points clear of Poole Town to pick up their first Western

League title since the 1947/48 season; a season that had seen so much suffering compared with life in the mid-1950s.

The improvement in living standards did not translate into form on the field of play for every club, with Glastonbury filling the bottom spot in the division. After the war, and into the 1950s, the Somerset side had shown great potential each season, but of late their form had dwindled, winning just three games during the season, while Chippenham United and Bridgwater Town had fared little better, ending the year three points ahead.

All three clubs were fortunate indeed to maintain their positions. The numerical strength and the equality of divisions meant there were no relegations, and both newcomers, Torquay reserves and Taunton Town, were promoted into Division One. Poole Town renewed their application to join the Southern League, but were again unsuccessful, as was the application by Torquay United to join the Football Combination.

In Division Two, Frome Town and Chippenham Town reserves left to join the new Wiltshire Combination League, and were replaced by reserve teams from Dorchester and Bath City. Bottom clubs, Paulton Rovers, Radstock and Hoffman Athletic all pledged allegiance to the League and remained as members.

The second season of the Professional Cup had seen Wiltshire clubs, Salisbury City and Chippenham Town compete for the honours; a game that saw City engrave their name on the magnificent Trophy, and at the Western League AGM in June 1956, another new competition was unveiled, that of the Merit Cup, which was to be awarded to the highest finishing amateur club in the League each season. The Trophy was purchased by Arthur Mortimer with the first name engraved, that of Welton Rovers. The Trophy is still in existence today, and rewarded to the Best Conducted club.

The FA decided just prior to the start of the new season that only two of the teams in Division Two would be able to enter the FA Cup because of their policy to promote the competition for professional clubs, thus excluding amateurs who had enjoyed competing for many seasons. It was not a popular move and one that caused a good deal of discontent.

In the event, the season saw yet another encounter between Clandown and Bath City in the Fourth and final Qualifying Round. It was a rematch from the same game the season before where the Southern League team had run out easy winners, 4-0. The well attended game, therefore, drew a huge crowd to Twerton Park that were entertained by a sterling effort from Welton Rovers, who after a superb display of equally polished football, eventually succumbed to the superior skills of the professionals, losing the encounter, 2-0.

For many years, the League had held its meetings at the Crown and Dove in Bridewell Street, Bristol, but the new relationship that had been built up with the Grand Hotel during the Jubilee Celebrations produced a move before the start of the 1956/57 season. At the AGM, it was proposed and accepted that the hotel would be used for all future meetings. By the October Management Committee meeting, however, that decision was put in doubt, when it was agreed that special or sub-committee meetings would be held at Eastville, courtesy of the Bristol Rovers Board, with a strong recommendation from the League Chairman, Mr Gummow that the proposal should be accepted.

That meeting opened with the presentation of a barometer to Lew Webb; a gift to mark his marriage to Gwen. It was to be a union that would continue for many years, with the lenience of Gwen indulging Lew's total dedication to his obligations to admin in football.

Later that evening an application was considered by Trowbridge Town who were seeking permission to put on a match-day collection to provide wedding presents for three of its players; a request that was turned down because protocol dictated that it was the FA who should rule on the matter as Trowbridge was a 'Full Member' club.

They had also put in an application for a grant from the Benevolent Fund toward the cost of contact lenses for one of their players; a request that was also refused with the reason given that it did not come within the limits of hardship, (despite those being made at the time being of hard and very unwearable plastic!).

It was not an easy season for the administrators of the League, and in December a situation came up that left them at odds with the powers of the Football Association. The incident in question arose after Radstock Town called off their Boxing Day game because they deemed the ground unfit. As they did not inform the League Secretary of this, they were fined £10-10s-0d as per rule 11. The club refused to accept the judgement, however, and went to the FA's Board of Appeal to argue their case, which they did successfully.

When they learned of the judgement, the Western League Committee men felt that their authority had been totally undermined, and called for a vote of confidence from the Western League Member Clubs. The result of that request was an overwhelming expression of confidence, which was then conveyed to the FA, together with several points about the verbal observations made by the Chairman of the Appeals Committee.

While the whole incident eventually calmed down, later Rule 11 was amended to read 'written notification' and a new paragraph inserted which read; 'Grounds suspected of prevailing weather conditions shall be inspected on the day of the match by a match official attached to the League who shall be solely responsible for any decisions in respect of possibilities of play or otherwise'. With that clarity, normal conditions between the two bodies resumed.

While there were those administrative problems to deal with, the significance of those difficulties paled into insignificance with news of several deaths that occurred to men who were well known on the Western League circuit.

Colin Reed, had been a young well-regarded player with Bristol City as a youngster, and then with Portland United. He was on National Service during the hostilities in Cyprus when he was killed, and Chippenham lad, David Tapliss, received life-changing and horrific injuries, when he was blown up by a hand-grenade in the same conflict. He then spent many months in Frenchay Hospital, before he could begin enjoying supporting his favourite club again.

Both incidents were to highlight the reality that many young men were still risking lives and limbs for Queen and Country; and the sadness did not stop there. During the season, Alan Young, who had been the League's President and a Life Member for many years, also died. During his time with the League he had also been President of Trowbridge Town and spent all his leisure time involved with non-league football.

Poole Town 1956/57: (L-R): Ron Oosthuizen, Bill Gillett, Harold Atkinson, Jack Hobbs, Horace Cumner, Frank McCourt, Dennis Martin, Jimmy Drinkwater, Bobby Barker, Stan Rickaby (P/M), Chris Conway

Alan was replaced as the League's President by Charlie Webb, who filled the position with style and with support from his son, Lew.

At season's end, Poole Town won the Championship, nine points ahead of Trowbridge Town. On the back of a successful season, they had applied for Southern League membership, but it was not confirmed until after the Western League AGM in June. Meanwhile, Cinderford Town topped the Second Division and won promotion, but because the next two clubs, Trowbridge Town reserves and Poole Town reserves, still both technically had their senior clubs in the First Division, fourth placed Minehead, were given the second promotion spot.

The result of Poole's late acceptance in the Southern League saw an appeal for their reserves to be promoted in their place. When that request was denied, they withdrew the team late, and so the Committee decided to fine them £100 as per rule; a decision that was then appealed to the FA by Poole Town. On that occasion, it was found that the League had acted within its rules, and the club was ordered to pay the fine along with the expenses of the enquiry. Following that, Poole then left the reserves in the League, thus avoiding the fine. But the controversy did not stop there.

Frome Town, who ended the term ten points ahead of bottom club, Wells City, were saved from relegation due to Poole moving on, Wells then challenged that decision with the possibility of also being saved relegation. As a part of their challenge, the club put forward the case that, with the reserve teams from Trowbridge Town and Poole Town not entitled to move up, a precedence had been set many times before that to maintain numerical parity, none were relegated. An argument that was lost.

While the Management Committee had been dealing with those issues, during the summer of 1957, Prime Minister, Harold Macmillan, said *'Let's be frank about it, most of our people have never had it so good',* a bold statement indeed, and one that would not have been universally endorsed by some people involved in non-league football; especially for those families with sons, fathers and husbands abroad on National Service in unstable situations. There was also the fact to face that, with the increase in general prosperity and new ways to spend leisure time, came a reduction in gate money for many non-league clubs.

As living conditions began to improve, the number of households owning a television set had continued to grow, as did the signal coverage. Although still in its infancy, technology had afforded the spread of transmission from London and the Home Counties, and commercial television was beginning to expand, with millions of people able to receive BBC and ITV programmes albeit in black and white.

With that development, the Committee was aware of how important it was for the Western League to get coverage on the new medium, and so Chairman, Mr Gummow, spoke at length to the BBC attempting to persuade them that more coverage of the League would benefit both the company, its viewers and, more importantly, the potential audience to come.

Within months of the meeting, however, member clubs did not hold that view, and were voicing concerns over the amount of coverage that television was giving to football, including the results of local games, which they saw might encourage supporters to stay at home. In the background alongside this, there was also the threat of live matches being shown on a Saturday afternoon. In response, Jack Veale was instructed to write to the FA suggesting that a conference of leagues should be called to discuss the effect of the media on attendances, and the subsequent financial position that would result for non-league football.

Replying to the letter, Sir Stanley Rous assured the Western League that meetings had already taken place, and that it had been agreed to limit live transmissions of International and other matches at such a level that would avoid too much soccer in any one week. He also reported that no more than ten minutes of a match would be shown after 10pm on a Saturday, and the same in mid-week.

It was to be the beginning of many discussions about the newly blossoming media that would eventually touch the social lives of every member of the population. In fact, much later in 1961, 'Television Wales and West' suggested that some Western League games could be shown in part, with revenue implications for those clubs who were lucky enough to be chosen; an offer that was, much to the disappointment of cash-hungry clubs, never to materialise.

The season was one of change all-round for some clubs, with the Southern League, once again, extending its horizons by introducing both of a South-Eastern and a North-Western area. Although League champions, Salisbury, and runners-up, Bridgwater Town, did not apply to move on fifth placed, Trowbridge Town, who had won the League seven times, and been runners-up on six occasions, followed in Poole Town's footsteps and were accepted into the Southern League. As with Poole, Trowbridge then asked to withdraw their second eleven during the summer, but rescinded the request when they were informed that they would be fined £100 for the late withdrawal.

Only one club was relegated into Division Two, Chippenham United; a club hanging on to existence by a thread, having ended the term eleven points adrift of Portland United, and in real trouble with severe financial problems.

The League also lost Clevedon Town, who had ended the year one from bottom and were also cash strapped. The seaside town club was an example of a superbly run organisation and typically sent a vote of thanks to the League for the help and hospitality that they had received during their years of membership, and went on to take part in the Bristol and District League for many years.

At the AGM in June 1958, it was confirmed that reserve teams from both Poole Town and Gloucester City had been promoted to Division One, and Bridgwater reserves accepted into Division Two. At the same meeting, Mr Gummow did not offer himself for re-election after two years at the helm, and Arthur Mortimer also stood down as he was soon to become the Mayor of the City of Bath, at the start of the following semester. The position of Chairman was then taken by Reg Broom from Salisbury, and George 'Temp' Templeman, became Vice-Chairman. There were also new Vice-President's with Mr Hand and Mr Hawkins joining Mr Chappelle.

The first meeting prior to the start of the new season then saw another resignation from the Management Committee, that of James Ladd, who had been the representative for Trowbridge Town. Few realised at the time what significance his replacement would be to the League, when the young man by the name of Les Phillips, stepped into the vacant seat as the representative of Ilfracombe Town; a man who would eventually make his mark on the League using a combination of vision and a huge personality to step-up to the mark when needed.

Generally, as the 1950s progressed, the League had grown and settled well, and together with the new rules that the committee had introduced, was generally seen as a well-run outfit. The new rules that had been adopted concerning refereeing had been praised by the FA, with the men in the middle able to progress to a higher standard of football; if they were good enough. There were, however, still pockets of problems that were not easily addressed.

In the Centenary book, Tom recalled '*With everything so ordered, it was with some amazement that I watched a game between my friends from Welton Rovers and Clandown as they battled out a Division Two match on the 17th January 1959. To say that Clandown were outclassed would be something of an understatement, but as a neutral observer I was enjoying the game despite the rain and the cold. To the astonishment of most of us, several players from Clandown decided that they had endured enough when they found themselves 5-1 down with some time yet to play, and just walked off the pitch. Now, after a bit of head scratching, we thought that the referee would let the game continue as this was the normal procedure adopted in such circumstances, but he called the game to a halt. At the subsequent enquiry by the League, it was decided to allow the score-line when the play was called off to stand, but they then censured the referee and reported Clandown players to the Somerset FA, who dealt with the offences harshly*'.

There were also problems in North Devon, where Ilfracombe Town were struggling to put any results together throughout, and as most clubs will know even today, when the chips are down nothing seems to go right! One such example was when they travelled to Trowbridge in the desperate search of even a point in early March 1959, only to find that the senior side did not have a Southern League game, and their reserve players were rested in favour of the seniors in order for them to get in some match practice.

To make matter worse, on the way to the game one of their cars was involved in an accident near Shepton Mallet, and although none of the players were injured, the car was too damaged to drive. After some time, replacement transport was found, and they managed to complete the journey in a borrowed car. On arrival, however, they were thirty minutes late at the ground with the game underway, and the seven-man Devon team in all sorts of problems. The game was lost by a large margin, contributing to the 108 goals they eventually let in during the season.

At their June AGM, the Ilfracombe faithful were informed that there were serious financial difficulties to deal with, and it was eventually agreed that the club would 'go into abeyance for twelve months' to sort affairs out and pay off some of their outstanding debts. That prompted an FA investigation into the club, and when that was concluded, it was agreed that their punishment would be just a £10 fine; which was covered by their guarantee fee being forfeited.

It was a mixed season for Welton Rovers who went on to win the Amateur Trophy for the third time, but did not gain the promotion that they so desired, finishing the year in fifth place, nine points adrift of Second Division champions, Bath City reserves, and six behind runners-up, Trowbridge Town reserves.

WELTON ROVERS 1958-59 SEASON
Winners of the Amateur Cup for the third time

Cindeford Town put in a late resignation from Division One, which was won by Yeovil reserves, four points clear of Salisbury, who also picked up the Professional Cup. While Frome Town ended the term bottom on just twelve points, and were relegated. Minehead, who were seven points clear of them, retained their place due to the withdrawal of Hoffman Athletic, and Wells City; although Wells got a special resolution passed at the AGM which allowed them to continue in membership because they had reverted to amateur status.

The AGM also heard of the resignation of Les Phillips, who had no choice but to leave after the demise of Ilfracombe Town. He was not lost to the

League for long, however, and returned the following year to represent the administration of Bideford Town. As the saying goes '*you can't keep a good man down* '.

The start of the 1959/60 season saw the fourteen clubs in Division Two unhappy that there were just twenty-six games to be played throughout the year. As the months went by, that discontent became the subject of much discussion, and so on 26th November a Special Meeting was called to discuss setting up a subsidiary competition to increase the number of games on offer.

Ten clubs attended the meeting, who were told that both Welton and Radstock were against the proposal, while Wells and Street were not at the meeting, which was interpreted that all four would not be taking any part in the proposed games. That then left the ten clubs in contention, with a suggestion that they would play in two sub-leagues with Chippenham United, Frome Town, Paulton Rovers, Peasedown Miners Welfare and Stonehouse in the North; Bridgwater Town reserves, Clandown, Dorchester Town reserves, Taunton Town reserves and Weston-super-Mare in the South.

The competition was played under League rules on a home and away basis, with a Final between the winners of each division. The FA then moved remarkably quickly to sanction the competition, and when Chippenham United offered to supply the Trophy, it seemed that an impending crisis had been averted. The first to inscribe the club name on the new Trophy was Frome Town; but it would be many seasons later that saw another club's name inscribed.

At seasons end another problem occurred when Torquay United reserves won Division One, sixteen points ahead of runners-up, once again, Salisbury, with Chippenham Town a long way back in third place - twenty-one points adrift. They also won the Professional Cup. That posed a problem because the new Alan Young Trophy game, which replaced the yearly League Benefit match that was played in aid of League funds, matched the champions of Division One with the winners of the Professional Cup, and with the same club winning both, no rules existed to solve such a problem.

After much debate, it was decided that the first and second placed clubs in Division One should play for the privilege of being the first club to have its name inscribed on the ex-Presidents Memorial Cup. The games were played on a home and away basis with Salisbury City the eventual winners. The declared gates from those games, however, demonstrated just how reduced the numbers were coming through the turnstiles, even at such prestigious games, with the League's funds boosted by just £15-1s-0d from Salisbury City, and £26-14s-0d from Torquay United.

There was certainly concern on several levels at what was happening in non-league football, and during the summer the FA was in correspondence with the Western League on the subject. The exchanges made clear that there had been almost a 50% reduction in revenue through gate receipts during the latter half of the decade, and that was threatening the very existence of some clubs.

By 1960 half the nation was sitting in front of the TV at peak times. The selected highlights of the top football matches in the country, which were shown every Saturday night, educated supporters into thinking that ninety minutes of football at local level should be of that same high standard.

Another factor working toward that decline, was the increase in ownership of cars, which had afforded supporters comparative ease of travel to English League club games within their area. The novelty of car ownership had also brought with it changes to leisure habits, with many traditional male supporter's 'under orders' to stay at home on a Saturday, save the money they had been spending at the local soccer ground, and instead, prepare for the Sunday outing with the family; and strange though it may sound now, Tom recalled *'Even I missed a game or two when I was driven with the family to visit the first supermarket in the area. The youngsters of today would not believe the fascination we held at being able to help ourselves to goods directly from the shelves of those new-fangled stores'.*

Alongside the reductions in attendances, other leagues began aggressive campaigns to test club's allegiances, and to that end a letter was received from the FA's Sanctioning Committee during the 1959/60 season in which Sir Stanley Rous made it clear that the practice was endangering grass-roots football. He indicated that at least two major leagues in the country were in the process of folding; advising caution and discussion to address the potential disaster that was presenting itself at the very heart of the game.

With the changes that were taking place throughout the game, the Western League was only too aware of the problem with inter-league relationships which were put under strain following approaches to members from County League officials, who were also looking to expand their membership. The temptation of reduced travelling costs for already hard-up clubs, made the offers by those Associations especially attractive at a time when the status of a league was totally in the eye of the beholder.

One approach, caused an outcry from the Western League Management Committee, who quickly blew the whistle on the culprits. The Dorset Combination League had proposed to rename itself as the Wessex Counties Combination League, and although that may not appear such a problem today, it was viewed then as an attempt to allow the Dorset men to encroach on the area covered by the Western League. Although the passing of time changes views, with the Wessex Football League, formed in 1986 from the Premier Division of the Hampshire County League now playing at Step Five in the Pyramid, in those days of non-regulation, such a threat was taken very seriously indeed.

With the decline in membership, and all the other challenges that were facing the League as the new decade began, a Special General Meeting was called on 26th May 1960, at which all clubs except Barnstaple Town and Torquay United were present, (they did, however, send their apologies). The single item business of the meeting was to vote on the proposal from the men of the Management Committee, that the Western League would consist of just one division for the 1960/61 season, to increase both the amount of games on offer, and the strength of the teams competing.

The meeting followed on from the fact that, given those clubs who had declared an interest in taking part in the following season, the League could consist of just nineteen clubs in Division One and a maximum of fourteen in Division Two. While that was just about acceptable to most member clubs, both Bridgwater Town and Dorchester Town indicated that they would withdraw under those circumstances, and Taunton Town indicated that their reserve team was probably going to fold, because their First Eleven was about to reform with mainly amateur players, and just four professionals on the books.

Those three clubs had teams in both divisions, and with the precarious state of other clubs also rumoured, the Chairman told the special meeting, that the clubs should look to their own finances when voting on the proposal to decide on the composition of the League. He added that although Devizes Town had expressed a desire to join, they had not yet voted on the proposal to join Division Two; leaving yet more uncertainty in the eventual outcome.

There was a very lively and full discussion over the dilemma in which each club had its say, but in the end a ballot to support the inclusion of Division Two was defeated, with only five of the fourteen clubs taking part willing to commit. Each club was then asked if they wanted their name to be included in the ballot for membership of the single division, and seven clubs then put their names forward. To the bitter disappointment of those not successful, Trowbridge Town reserves, Exeter City reserves and Weston-super-Mare, were the three elected.

That spelt the end for Chippenham United, who were already under pressure to fold under the burden of increasing debt, and the prospect of junior soccer for the following season was the final straw. Their ground was eventually sold back to the local council for a relatively huge amount of money, enabling the shareholders to recoup their investment. It later became a housing estate with a street, named The Firs, after the field of dreams that had promised so much, but which ultimately failed.

Frome Town and Clandown were also unsuccessful in the ballot, and went into the Wiltshire League, while Street opted for life in the Somerset League. The other club to figure in the rejigging of the League, of course, was Amateur Cup winner for the fourth season, Welton Rovers, who would have been promoted into Division One as champions, and so became automatic members of the single division.

The 1950s had seen enormous change throughout the country and a slow move to the conditions that had once been both promised and fought for, but which were unattainable in a country that had been left almost bankrupt after the long and bloody Second World War. Rationing had given way to the rebuilding of a different way of life, with jobs, TV's, cars and improved life-styles more readily available to everyone, but that had not translated into good news for all non-league football.

As the Western League moved into yet another decade of uncertainty the task ahead looked difficult, but if history was anything to go by, the men of football in the west had faced it all before, and in front lay a challenge to be conquered, not a problem to be solved.

CHAPTER 12

(not) The swinging sixties

The 1st September 1960 saw the return of Les Phillips to the Western League Management Committee as the duly elected member for Bideford. It was a time of change that greeted his return with just one division consisting of twenty-one clubs that covered the counties of Devon, Dorset, Somerset and Wiltshire, together with young Colts teams from Bristol City and Bristol Rovers.

Although there was only a single division to administer, the men of the League were kept busy with its administration. As early as November there had been complaints over the state of the Bristol Rovers ground at Frenchay, with both Portland United and Bideford emphasising the urgency of the problem before winter conditions set in. After thorough investigation, it was agreed that Rovers should be asked to obtain, or provide, a better ground for the following season; and that meanwhile the coming games would have to be played in the mud.

Almost as soon as that problem was solved, another followed. This time it concerned the roles that Jack Veale was performing. As General Secretary, Jack was also responsible for all financial aspects of the League, but in January 1961 a few problems came to light with the accounts that indicated the combined role was not working as efficiently as it should have been. A solution was then put in place shortly afterwards, by re-introducing the independent post of Treasurer; a role that was then taken up by Len Brown, the Chairman of Salisbury City. Those actions were then confirmed later at the AGM in June.

As the season progressed Torquay United indicated that they were looking to put a reserve team into the League. The news was greeted positively by the Member clubs, and a suggestion was then made that a Premier Division could be formed to accommodate such teams, but in the event, only one of the English League clubs who were contacted showed an interest in the proposition, and the idea was left on the table for further discussions.

A couple of months later another proposal was received, this time from the Cornish club, St Blazey, who had been founder-members of the East Cornwall League, which had been formed just one year before. At a time when many clubs were looking to reduce overheads and travelling expenses, St Blazey were seriously considering an application to take the Western League into the heart of Cornwall with membership; a move that could open the possibility of expanding the League's horizons.

In the end, the prospect of long and winding roads to travel to every game ruled out their application, and they withdrew just prior to the AGM. There was, however, a most welcomed new addition with Dorset club, Bridport, joining the ranks of the League and gaining a hearty approval of their action by the existing Member clubs.

Nationally, 1961 was probably one of the most influential periods in football for many a year, with one event about to impact on all aspects of the game at both league and non-league level. It concerned a court case that had been brought by a player, George Eastham, against Newcastle United, who he claimed had blocked his transfer from the club. For many years, the 'maximum wage' had been linked inexplicably with the accepted practice that a player was beholden to the club that paid him until that club wished to transfer him. The latter premise only existed, however, because no-one had ever challenged it; which was not because it was lawful, because as it turned out it wasn't.

Although Eastham was not challenging the maximum wage, both protocols stood in law together, and so when the 'Retain and Transfer' rule eventually fell, so did the wage ceiling. While the Eastham case dragged on until 1963, the maximum wage went almost at once, and immediately had a huge effect throughout the game.

The basis of that change affected the order which had gone back to the late 1940s and early 1950s, where many good professional players would sign lucrative deals with non-league clubs simply because there was no lid on either the perks or wages that they could receive at that level; unlike at Football League level, where the maximum wage existed. That, in turn, gave many Western League players a higher standard of living and their clubs a more skillful standard of play. It was a state of affairs which was especially attractive to those professionals who had peaked at the top of their game, and looked to a comfortable home, future, and family comforts, rather than ambition.

Of course, the abolition of the wage ceiling also combined with a general increase in the commercial activity of many English League clubs which increased their income, and saw an immediate movement the other way for those players; especially because the general fall in attendance at football games had begun to threaten the income that afforded their non-league life styles.

While the national events were going on, the League was being won by Salisbury City with an unassailable total of sixty-six points, eight ahead of runners-up, Dorchester Town. They also picked up the Alan Young Cup. At the foot of the table, fifty points below that total, Taunton Town had struggled all season, with Barnstaple faring only a little better. Both clubs vowed to continue and were re-elected, unlike Professional Cup winners, Exeter City reserves, who withdrew after just one season. Trowbridge Town reserves also pulled-out, leaving it clear that the single division system was not going to be a temporary measure.

Champions Salisbury, had a further reason to celebrate when Bill Grist retired in November 1961 at the grand age of 76 years, with 60 of those years being spent in service to the club. In recognition, the League awarded him a grant of £5-5s-0d; which enabled him to spend a shilling or two in celebration of the event in the upstairs bar at Victoria Park.

In the FA Cup, Welton Rovers had a great run, diametrically opposite to the fate down the road in Taunton, where the club was struggling to keep going. One of the measures put in place to survive was the termination of their player/manager, Ernie Peacock's, contract; an action that was then reported to the League who ruled in his favour, which did not help the situation.

The age-old subject of improving refereeing standards reared its head around this time, when the FA made a sensible suggestion that the men in the middle of Western League games could be more gainfully employed on their blank Saturday's in the middle at local league level. Together with that, there was also more refinement in the grading system which had been put into place in the 1950s. It was a system that had seen many officials progressing on to the Football League and, although unsophisticated compared to today's banding, it was equally effective, with a scoring system of zero for an unsatisfactory game, 1 for a weak display, 2 for fair to moderate, 3 for good and 4 for excellent. Sometimes simplicity brings with it, its own rewards!

At the end of the season, a referee's sub-committee was held at Lew and Gwen Webb's home in Midsomer Norton, with Jack Veale and Len Brown also in attendance. One of the Linesmen promoted to the Western League middle that evening was Maurice Washer, who at the age of 31 years had begun his career in the Church of England League, and then with the Bristol and District League. Joining Maurice on the list were Don Milverton and Bill Summerhayes; ironically, all three would go on to serve the League in the ensuing decades, with Don also going on to show his administrative skills as Section Secretary at the Association of Football League Referees and Linesmen.

Whereas the standards in the middle were rising, many of the Member clubs were finding it increasingly difficult to make ends meet with low gates detracting from the status that Western League clubs had once attracted. There were, of course, exceptions to that, with Bristol City reserves and Salisbury City attracting a large following as they battled for the League title for 1961/62. In the end, the Bristol club won the campaign by seven points, ending the term with a huge goal-scoring surplice of 132 goals scored and with just 36 conceded. It had been twenty-four years since they had won the Championship, which was at a time when just four other clubs competed in the section. To complete a superb season, they also won the newly named Challenge Cup, which had replaced the Professional Cup.

At the 1962 AGM, which was held at the '51 Club' room at Ashton Gate, Dorchester were presented with the Alan Young Cup, and both Andover and Exeter City reserves were welcomed into membership. The re-admission by Exeter had followed assurances given to the meeting by Mr C H Speirs, their representative, that the move was not a temporary measure and that a repeat of their previous sortie into the League, which only lasted one season, would not be repeated. In view of the division being extended to forty-two games, the Challenge Cup was suspended until such a date when clubs were happy that they could fit the extra games in.

During the summer months those who were fortunate to have access to a television set enjoyed brief references to the World Cup finals that took place in Chile, with Brazil conquering Czechoslovakia in Santiago to retain the magnificent Jules Rimet Trophy. They did that without Pele who had pulled a muscle in the group stages, while England, who were the only one of the UK teams to qualify, made heavy weather of reaching the Quarter Final stage where they went out losing, 3-1, to the eventual Champions; possibly due to a young lad called, Bobby Charlton, playing magnificently, but in an unfamiliar left-wing position.

One of the English referees who officiated at those games was known to most football fanatics in the West as he had spent his early years playing for St Luke's College, Exeter, before sustaining a bad leg injury that meant he had to hang up his boots. Ken Aston then took up refereeing, doing his time with the Western League, and gaining the highest honours as a FIFA referee.

He officiated at the Qualifying Round stage between the host nation and Italy; a game that was filled with passion, and one in which he sent two Italians off. He later said: 'It was billed as the Battle of Santiago. I wasn't 'reffing', I was acting as an umpire in military manoeuvres'. Armed police entered the field of play on three separate occasions, before Chile won the encounter, 2-0. Ken went on to become the Chairman of the FIFA Referees Committee, and introduced the idea of the Red and Yellow cards that were first used in the 1970 World Cup in Mexico.

While that was going on, closer to home Lew Webb and Len Brown were meeting the Chairman of the Devon FA, Mr C Marsh, who was also a Vice-Chairman of the Devon Referees Association. The one-and-a-quarter hour get together was the first of its kind, and one that had been fostered by the FA ruling on the use of referees at local level. Among other issues discussed that day was the subject of higher costs that some of the less central clubs in the League were experiencing, with a solution put forward of a 'travel expenses pool' for referees, which would be shared between clubs. The idea was eventually put to the following Western League AGM and adopted.

At the start of the 1962/63 season, Welton Rovers returned to West Clewes after playing for a season at Radstock Town while their pitch was being levelled; which had been quite a task with a drop of five foot in one area. Later in the season the club cleared four feet of snow from their pitch to play Bromley in the FA Amateur Cup, during the worse winter on record; a game that they won.

Despite their success, and with the Somerset Cup in the cabinet for the third season, Welton's form was not transferred to the League, and a fourth-place finish was not deemed good enough by those in charge. In response, a decision was made to turn professional from the start of the 1963/64 season, which would see dramatic changes at West Clewes. The ex-Huddersfield and Bristol City centre-forward, Arnold Rodgers, was appointed manager, and would have a huge influence on the Somerset club; heralding the start of a new era.

Generally, the season was remarkable for its lack of incidents and the dire weather conditions. Bristol City reserves ended the term, once again, in top spot, and Salisbury City put its name on the Alan Young Cup. The only surprise was the way that Bideford had made City fight all the way for the honour, losing the challenge by just two points, and with the same goal-difference of +64.

At the foot of the table the young Colts from Bristol Rovers had struggled all season and they ended in bottom spot, six points behind a struggling Taunton Town. While Rovers withdrew, and were replaced by Frome Town, Taunton continued in membership. Their representative, Stan Priddle, was then co-opted onto the Western League Management Committee, attending his first meeting on 3rd October 1963; a membership that he would retain for many, many years to come.

While there were a few clubs in the League who were clearly in a good place where both finance and general organisation were concerned, there were many more who were just about holding onto the concept of professionalism by a thread; something that the Chippenham Town manager, Cyril Williams, deemed vital to compete at a reasonable level of football in the Western League.

At the Chippenham AGM in 10th July 1963, it had been announced that in the previous season they had lost over £300, which was a considerable sum in those days, (when a brand-new Ford Cortina cost around £650). Despite that difficult financial news however, the manager was still offered another two years on his contract, and eight professionals were then signed, signaling the inevitability of problems to come.

The first Western League game of the season for Chippenham saw a trip to the seaside down the 'A' roads of Devon against the highly fancied Bideford Town, who were the previous season's runner's-up. Under the guidance of new captain and left-back, Dick Steele, it was a game that few expected the Wiltshire side to win, and returning with a point was seen to indicate a good omen for the season to come.

Despite initial results, however, all was not well at the Town, and a protracted dispute between the club and a player, John Watkins, did not help. It revolved around a request by him to re-join Welton Rovers, which the club agreed to, but only contingent on a transfer fee of £100; and given the losses the club was sustaining, the fee would have been somewhat of a bonus.

Both Welton and the player disputed the financial tag, and took their case to the Western League Committee, who subsequently ordered that the fee should be reduced to £25, adding that unless the club were to re-sign him or transfer him before 17th September, he would be able to move on a free transfer. With that judgement, there was no other course but to let him go for a nominal payment, resulting in the loss of yet another talented player to a team that was already in transition.

The Western League, with its one division, had become a very strong and difficult one to compete in. The clubs who had the money to fully embrace professionalism vied at the top for the ultimate prize, while most teams seemed to pick-up a point where and when they could.

Welton Rovers, who boasted those many ex-Chippenham Town players, were up there with the top teams for most of the year, but for all their expenditure, there were just three clubs in true contention throughout. At season's end, Bideford took the Championship from Bristol City reserves by three points, with Bridgwater third by the same margin, while Welton Rovers were twelve points off the pace in fourth place.

After the final home game of the season against neighbours, Barnstaple Town, an out-of-shape Championship Trophy was presented to Bideford's player/manager, Ken Whitfield, by 'Temp' Templeman. The change in the shape of the historic Cup had occurred when Les Phillips was involved in an accident earlier in the day at Coombe Bissett near Salisbury, where his car was written off. Luckily Les escaped, shaken-up and bruised, but in true form continued his journey, and was still there in time for the presentation.

Bristol City reserves also won the Alan Young Cup, and so it was a surprise to many when their letter of resignation was received shortly afterwards, along with one from Poole Town. Although both resignations were later withdrawn, it proved just how delicate the balance was to run a league with just one division at a time when the face of football was changing.

At the AGM, which was held in the new stand of Yeovil Town Football Club, it was confirmed that the League would run a single division, once again, with twenty clubs, and 'Temp' Templeman made a formal presentation of a Championship Flag that would be flown with honour at the Winner's ground throughout their Championship season.

It was, indeed, a time of challenge for the men in charge of the League with clubs doing whatever they could to survive. Early in the new season the results being achieved by Bristol City reserves were surprisingly poor, which called into question the teams they were fielding. Eventually, it was revealed that they were, in fact, putting out their third team to play Western League games, while their reserve side played friendly matches. In response, the League committee wrote making it quite clear that such action was strongly disapproved of; it was, however, indicative of what was to come.

A young Les Phillips flying the Championship

In contrast to the form City showed, Bideford Town continued to outperform expectations, and during the season reached the First-Round Proper of the FA Cup after defeating St Austell, Barnstaple Town, St Blazey and Cheltenham Town in the Qualifying games. In all matches played, the boss, Ken Whitfield, had only made one change, which gave an indication of just how strong the squad was.

The important FA Cup game was away to Colchester United, and was played in front of a huge crowd which included two train loads of supporters from North Devon. To the surprise of the crowd, Bideford were ahead for most of the game, only to let the lead slip to a 3-3 draw. That was as far as Cup glory went, however, and on the 18th November 1964, Colchester made no mistake at the Sports Ground, winning the tie, 2-1.

In all, it was a season for those clubs who were on top of their game, and Welton Rovers certainly were such a club, picking up the Championship Trophy over runners-up Bideford Town by three points. That was to herald the start of one of the most successful periods in their history, and at a special celebratory dinner on 4th June 1965, they also commemorated a notable Alan Young Cup Final appearance; which despite losing to Bideford Town, had realised the sum of £57-14s-5d, a record receipt, to boost League funds.

Few supporters had realised, as they watched Chippenham Town record a victory, 2-1, over Taunton Town in the final Western League game of the year at Hardenhuish Park, that it would be their last game in the League after 30 years of competing. The size of the crowd that day, which was the best for many months, was just under 200, and made what was about to happen almost inevitable, because the money was simply not there to compete at such a high level.

At season's end, the new arrangement at Hardenhuish Park was announced that saw the First team take place of the reserve's in the Wiltshire Premier League, and Wanderers, a local Youth Team who had merged with the club, play as the new reserve team in their existing league.

Town's resignation from the Western League caused quite a stir within the town, and Ken Scammell, who had taken on the role as Treasurer, told a well-attended 1965 AGM that there had been no choice in the matter. The club's severe financial situation was such that had it not been for the money that was received, yet again, from the transfer of the ex-Town player, Alan Scarrott, to Reading, the financial problems would have been even more severe

A few days later at the Western League AGM, Bath City, Poole Town and Yeovil Town all joined Chippenham in resigning, and with no names coming forward to fill the places, it was agreed to run with just eighteen clubs; which included a Bristol City Colts team. The meeting was also informed that Arthur Chappelle had retired as President, with that position filled by George Templeman, while Lew Webb stood down as Referees Appointments Secretary, to be replaced by Don Milverton.

One explanation that was widely acknowledged as the reason for many club's dour financial situations, was the wide-ranging changes to leisure patterns that had begun way back in the md-1950s, but those were nothing compared to the effect that the ownership of a 'little black and white box' in most homes had made.

While the popularity in TV ownership had increased, the situation had been compounded with the introduction of 'Match of the Day' on BBC TV in 1964, which showed highlights of the day's professional games; accentuating skills that could not be matched at most non-league grounds, both with or without the addition of professionals on the pitch.

That in turn changed the footballing public's perception of the game. No longer did the average supporter need to hand over money at the gate, and suffer the elements to see ninety minutes of football, all they had to do was to turn-on, sit back, and watch - even if it was in black and white. Around the corner, however, there was to be the even more threatening concept of colour TV, but that was still a story to come.

In view of the reduced number of games on offer for the 1965/66 season, it was agreed to re-introduce the Western League Challenge Cup competition. That decision gave rise to a search for the trophy that had not been seen since Bristol City won it in 1962, as they had never returned it to the League.

After many enquiries, it was revealed that only the plinth and the wooden container could be found at Ashton Gate and the matter was then left between the club, their Insurance Brokers and the Insurance Company to resolve. It was not that simple, however, and with the competition well underway in September 1965, the Cup was still not forthcoming with no explanation to its whereabouts, and so the matter was put into the hands of a solicitor.

Before long the FA go involved after the Western League Chairman, Reg Broom, asked them to intervene to avoid the direct conflict of legal action; which swiftly resulted in a cheque for £49-9s-0d being received from City for the purchase of a replacement.

The new Trophy was engraved 'The Western Football League Challenge Cup', with the names of the previous winners still on the plinth. In view of what had occurred, the new Cup was sent to be valued for insurance purposes prior to being presented to the winners, Glastonbury, and a silversmith from Salisbury put a value of £72-10-0d on it, allowing for the value of the magnificent box and plinth, as well as a premium price to replace it.

Once again, Welton Rovers strolled through the League, this time without losing a game, and ended the season a clear eleven points ahead of an improving Portland United. During the year, the club had broken several League records, and in striker, Ian Henderson, had found a player who had scored 53 goals, with six hat-tricks included in that figure. Their best performance came early in September 1965, when they travelled to Dorchester and slotted in ten goals without reply; with Henderson scoring three and 'Ginger' Watts, six.

At the foot of the table Bristol City Colts only won four games all year, and ended nine points adrift of Barnstaple Town. Taunton Town, who for several seasons had occupied the foot of the table, improved their form, and for the first time since joining the League ended the term in a respectable mid-table position.

At the 1966 AGM, which was held at the Bridgwater Town Headquarters, it was announced that Yeovil Town reserves had been successful in applying to re-join the League, together with St Luke's College, Exeter and Plymouth Argyle reserves; bringing membership back up to forty games for the coming season, and so the Challenge Cup was, once again, suspended.

The summer of 1966 saw the eighth staging of the FIFA World Cup, which this time took part in England from 11th – 30th July. It was to be last time that the Competition would be televised in black and white, and attracted a huge audience transfixed during the Final game at Wembley, where England beat West Germany, 4-2. The competition featured one player who was a familiar name around the area, Roger Hunt, who had turned out for Devizes Town while he was stationed in the area.

The huge success of the World Cup was to be a catalyst for changes to some aspects of both domestic, national and international football, which would have wide-ranging consequences for the Western League. The optimism that followed the games fueled discussions about the general facilities at grounds, and where the non-league game was going; with installing floodlights a lofty aim for many clubs.

A significant rule-change, heralded the start of the 1966/67 season which allowed a substitute, just one, to sit on the bench, and come on to the field if a player was injured and deemed unable to continue. That change had been introduced successfully during the World Cup, and was soon to be relaxed to include using the extra-man as a tactical substitution. It was an action that was seen by many as a step in the right direction for the modern game, encouraging the use of skill, rather than employing tactics to gain an advantage with the sole intention of injuring a player from the opposing team to reduce the amount of opposition players on the pitch!

Prior to the start of the season, the Management Committee wrote to clubs informing them that the name of the substitute should be placed at the end of the list of players on the match return sheet, and by the start of October, fifteen substitutes had been used. It was not until over a year later, however, that the League ordered teams to inform the referee prior to the start of the game of the name of that player; something that was open to a certain amount of leeway until that date.

Flushed with their recent success, Bideford Town turned on their magnificent corner stanchion floodlights in September 1966, kicking them off with a game against a League XI which had been arranged by Reg Broom. The experience seemed to have quite an effect on Reg, and after seeing the effect of playing football under lights, he immediately began to investigate the possibility of putting on a floodlight regional mid-week competition.

Welton Rovers were League Champions, once again, but this time they did not have the luxury of a season without defeat, and were challenged all the way by Minehead, who had come to the fore under the guidance of new manager, Ron Gingell, a man best described by Tom, who wrote *'Now, Ron was a real football character the like of which is rarely seen today. Apart from the ninety minutes on a Saturday afternoon during the winter months, he was the perfect gentleman. In fact, he was an accountant with the Bristol Water Works Company, but for the duration of a game, like Dr Jekyll's Mr Hyde, he took on a whole new personality. Totally involved he cursed, cajoled, berated, belittled and screamed at his players to produce the goods. Once the game was over he would resume his normal self, and no matter what the result may have been, he would always treat the players to a drink'.*

Ron had two great ambitions, one to win the Western League, and the other to see his club reach the First-Round Proper of the FA Cup. During the year, it had seemed possible for the first ambition to be realised when Minehead had not lost a game in the first three months of the season. He was, however, up against the amazing side that had been assembled by Arnold Rogers at Welton Rovers, and eventually had to be content with the runners-up spot, five points adrift.

The FA Cup dream was also nearly fulfilled, after the team had produced an almost perfect display of football to progress to the final Qualifying Round, beating neighbours, Bideford Town, 5-0. In the final vital game, however, they were drawn against Southern League, Poole Town, and lost, 1-0.

Welton Rovers, who had become only the second Western League club to win the Championship on three successive occasions, succeeded where Minehead failed, and progressed through to the First-Round Proper with a tremendous win, 3-0, over Trowbridge Town, and a 4-1 victory over Fareham Town. The following draw then proved a game too far against National League side Bournemouth and Boscombe Athletic (who became AFC Bournemouth in 1972), and they lost the encounter, 3-0. The year was then topped off by them also winning the only other competition in the Western League, the Alan Young Cup. Although on paper that was a superb season for Welton, it was also one that began to see problems in the making.

At the1967 Western League AGM, which was held at the Antelope Hotel, Dorchester, a proposition was put to member clubs that games should be allowed on a Sunday, but it was defeated on the casting vote of the League Chairman. A full report was also given over the investigations of Mr Broom into the possibility of operating a regional competition within the League. Of the fifty-seven clubs that had been contacted, however, there had been an insufficient number of replies to warrant further work on the matter. Instead it was agreed that a Floodlit mid-week competition could be operated at short-notice, should enough clubs call for it; a proposal that was left on the table for further action when required.

There was, however, a new competition sanctioned, when Mr W Rice from St Luke's College presented the League with a new Cup, to mark his club's centenary. It was to be awarded by interclub nominations, was inscribed 'Western League Merit Cup, presented by W O Rice, 1967', and is still in circulation today.

Exeter City reserves withdrew, yet again, from the League along with Weymouth, who joined the Southern League. Those two clubs were replaced by Devizes Town and Bath City reserves, with the former club successful in its application having won the Wiltshire Senior Cup Competition on seven occasions. Both Yeovil Town reserves and Barnstaple Town were successful in being re-elected having finished adrift at the foot of the table behind St Luke's College.

The season's end had seen financial problems which had been mounting at Welton Rovers, resulting in a mass movement of players to Bath City after manager, Arnold Rogers, moved in that direction. Remembering his time in non-league football, director, Tony Salvidge, who has been the Western League's Fixtures Secretary, Director and Life Member, recalls watching Bath at Hillingdon Borough when he was living in Ruislip and being amazed to recognise almost the whole Welton team in unfamiliar colours. Only player/manager, Ted Holehouse, and player, Alan Margary, remained at Welton from the successful championship side, and yet despite such problems the club still achieved a respectable eighth position at seasons end.

On the memories, Tony has of his life in football he wrote; '*I first became interested in Football at the early age of 8 years. Dad was a follower of Paulton Rovers in those days. We often went to watch Bristol Rovers or City. I remember watching the first Floodlight match at Ashton Gate when Wolverhampton Wanderers were the guest team. My first introduction to team football was Youth Team Football. I was the Captain of Thicket Mead Youth team, I then played for Welton Arsenal until the early 60s when I had to retire from football due to ill health. Then Dad, Val and I followed Welton Rovers and from that time on I became a Welton man, going to all the away fixtures wherever possible.*

My initial working life began in 1955 as an Apprentice Electrician with the National Coal Board. Upon completion of my Apprenticeship and subsequent studies I obtained The Ordinary National Certificate in Mining Electrical Engineering, followed by IEE Ordinary National Certificate in Electrical Engineering and finally the IEE Higher National Certificate in Electrical Engineering in 1963. Following these results, the NCB promoted me to Assistant Electrical Engineer at both Kilmersdon and Writhlington Collieries.

Valerie and I were married in 1966 and have 3 daughters and seven grandchildren. Following our marriage, we moved to Ruislip Manor, in Middlesex.

I resigned from the position in 1966 to take up a position as Shift Engineer responsible for the control of all maintenance operations to the Shift General Manager during my shift. I was responsible for the operations of three maintenance tradesmen.

In 1971, we decided to return to the West Country and joined BAC at Filton as an Instrumentation Engineer. This involved conducting tests on a range of military equipment at Filton and various military sites around the Country. I remember taking over one of the first Thermal Imagers to conduct a whole range of engineering tests to prove the equipment was suitable.

This position ended in 1993 due to the reduction in the requirements for military hardware and I was made redundant. Following this change in my working life I returned to college and started the 1st year of a System Computer course. I passed this but was unable to continue with the course the following year due to taking up a position as a Test Engineer at Westinghouse Brakes in Chippenham. This position lasted for over 5 years until late 1999. My last job before retiring was again as a Test/Project

Engineer on Naval weapons system for JS Chinn Project Engineering in. Fishponds. A position I held until 2005 when I eventually retired.

On my return to Midsomer Norton I was asked to join the Board of Welton Rovers in 1971 as assistant Secretary. It was not long before I became Club Secretary, Company Secretary, Social Club Secretary and Membership Secretary all at the same time. It was during this period that Welton won the Premier Division Championship in season 1973-74 under the stewardship of Chairman Arthur Ladd and Manager Dave Stone. The following season Welton entertained Bishop Auckland in the Rothmans Interleague Cup, memory tells me that the Bishops won easily. My tenure as Club Secretary ended in about 1984, but I remained a Director and for a short time was Vice Chairman until I stood down in December 2002. Whilst a member of the Welton Board the Club won the First Division Championship in season 1987-88. During my time, many happy times were spent doing lots of different jobs helping wherever I could to ensure the club ran smoothly, with entertainment a major event on a Saturday night.

It was during my time at Welton that through speaking to Les Phillips, the then Chairman of the Western League that he was interested in someone to write software for a fixture making programme. I volunteered my services. Over the next couple of years, the programme was completed and I then gave a demonstration to Club Officials at the League's Annual Convention at The Narracott Grand Hotel in Woolacombe Bay, North Devon, the date of which escapes me. The software was produced using BBC Master, running BBC Basic software. After several years using the BBC Master computer I upgraded to an Archimedes computer which enabled me to produce the fixtures much quicker. Once all the data had been inputted into the computer the system took approximately 24 hours to produce the fixture list. The initial fixture list was produced in my Hotel room in Southend on Sea whilst I was working away with British Aerospace.

It was during this period that I joined the Western League Management Committee. During this period of some 10 years my system produced the fixtures for both division's, although I had no control over the day to day management of the fixture system, this was handled by the League Secretary, Maurice Washer, until I stood down from the Management Committee in about 1994. My last appointment in Football administration came when I was appointed League officer responsible for the production, and day to day management of the League fixture system using Mitoo as the main web based system. I have happy memories of producing the annual fixtures whilst sat in the sun in Spain at my daughter's residence. I developed a system using the Excel based spreadsheet to produce the fixtures prior to uploading to Mitoo. This system enabled me to give a well-balanced fixture list.

Welton were replaced by Salisbury City as the 'team of the moment' in the FA Cup, when the Wiltshire side showed their amazing diversity of playing strength by reaching the First-Round Proper, beating Dorchester Town, 2-1, on their own ground. The reward for such a result was an away draw to fellow Wiltshire club, Swindon Town, a game in front of a bumper crowd, which was lost, 4-0.

In the League, Bridgwater Town picked up their first Championship title by three points over Salisbury, with Glastonbury a further four points behind in third place. After such a successful season, the Wiltshire club's resignation late in June was not foreseen, following a late acceptance by the Southern League for entry, and the club was fined £100 as per rule.

The AGM of 1968 was held at Ashton Gate, where a minute's silence was held in memory of both Arthur Chappelle and Arthur Mortimer, who had both served the League well and had passed away during the season. It was not a happy meeting, with the news that Plymouth Argyle had also withdrawn their reserve side, and that there were no new applications for membership. The result was that, once again, the competition was reduced to just thirty-six games.

The debate over playing matches on a Sunday that had been lost on the Chairman's vote came to the fore again when Taunton Town were successful in obtaining permission to play Bristol City Colts in October 1968. It was something of a pioneering step, and proved to be a great success with a far higher attendance than would have been expected from a Saturday game. Because of that, both Welton Rovers and Weston-super-Mare followed the example a couple of week before Christmas, but while those also resulted in higher than expected gates, the move did not herald a widespread change in the pattern of playing League games on a Saturday.

The system of marking referees came into consideration as the season progressed, with observations that there was often a huge disparity in the marks awarded by the home and away clubs. Eventually, after much discussion, it was agreed that in the event of such incongruence, clubs should be asked for an explanation. It also heralded a change in the marking system from the formerly used 1-4, to a wider 1-10 scale.

Overall, the 1968/69 season was entertaining despite the reduced number of games on offer, with reserve teams from Bath, Torquay and Yeovil contributing to the standard, together with former Southern League clubs, Andover and Dorchester. In the event, none of these clubs won the major honours as it was to be Taunton Town's year, when they lifted the title by four clear points from Merit Cup Winners, Bideford Town.

Yeovil Town reserves ended the term at the foot of the table, for the second season, and the Alan Young Cup, which was not won outright for the first time, was shared between Bridgwater and Glastonbury. The Amateur Cup went to the previous year's runner-up in that Competition, Devizes Town.

The final AGM of the decade began with yet another minute's silence, this time to honour past President and active football enthusiast, Charlie Webb, who had given unfailing service to the game. Against this somber start, it was announced that both Weymouth and Warminster Town would be joining the League, after reassurances from members present that the Wiltshire club's ground was up to standard. With the prospects of an increase in membership, it was, therefore, with great regret, that shortly after the announcement both clubs withdrew their applications.

The only other request for membership had come from Plymouth City, but that had been turned down because the letter had turned up too later for consideration. In the event, the club was so anxious to join the League that they appealed to the FA against the decision, which was subsequently upheld. Later the club had a meeting with League officials, and after an inspection of their ground, a new request being submitted on time, they were elected to join for the 1970/71 season.

The FA introduced the new Trophy competition in 1969 for those clubs who still employed professionals and were, therefore, not entitled to enter the Amateur Trophy. They also continued to consider other aspects of the game, and wrote to all clubs in the country about funds for the launch of a National School for Association Football.

Times were indeed changing, and in February 1970 the League Committee gave their permission for Bath City reserves to use fund raising during games, providing a written request with details of any scheme they were going to run was submitted in writing prior to the event. The new age of sponsorship and self-sufficiency was coming into the game, and would in the years to come reshape many people's views of the sport.

The last season of the decade saw both Glastonbury and Minehead represent the League in the Fourth-Qualifying round of the FA Cup. For Ron Gingell it seemed that his dream of seeing the club progress through to that important First-Round game would a last come true when, after beating Trowbridge Town, Bridport, Bridgwater and Bath City on the way, they held Yeovil Town to 0-0 draws, both home and away. In the epic third game, however, the dream crumbled and five goals without reply denied the affable Ron, once again.

Included in the Minehead squad of players that day was a young lad called Tom Smith who, on 28th March 1970, was awarded with a plaque by Western League Chairman, Reg Broom, for completing 500 appearances for his club. He would go on to take the role of club Secretary when his playing days were over, and continued to be a frequent visitor to League grounds long after his club had left.

That was to be one of the last duties performed by Reg in his role as Chairman, because at the 1970 AGM, which was held at the Morlands Social Club, Glastonbury, it was announced that he had stood down with immediate effect. Replacing him, Wilf Escott paid tribute to the wonderful service Reg had paid to the League, and he was joined by new Vice-Chairman, Mr Bush, the secretary of Bristol City, and President 'Temp' Templeman, in further warm tributes to the years that Reg had spent with the League.

Hosts for that event, Glastonbury, were congratulated on winning the Championship along with their progress in the FA Cup, which had only been halted in a replay at Cheltenham Town in the Fourth round, losing 4-1, after holding the club to a 0-0 draw in front of a huge home crowd. They had ended the term ten points clear of third placed, Bridgwater Town and five points clear of Andover, scoring 100 goals in the process.

The honours were spread that season, with the Alan Yong Cup going to Bideford Town who triumphed over Taunton Town, while Bridport picked up the Merit Cup, and Devizes, once again, were worthy winners of the Amateur Cup.

As the 'Swinging Sixties' faded, the Western League was, once again, in decline. Resignation letters were received from the reserve teams of Bath City, Yeovil Town and Weymouth together with Portland United, and although Bath City reserves remained after reconsideration, the prospects of just 34 games and one division for the start of the new decade, did not bode well. While the Western League Challenge Cup was again re-introduced, it was clear that action was needed to halt the decline of one of the oldest Leagues in the country.

As Tom concluded all those years ago, '*The continuing demise in the popularity of local football throughout the 1960s sent alarm bells ringing in my mind, I had lived long enough to be aware of how easy it was to allow a situation to go beyond the stage that would afford a rescue plan. There were many rumours around the Western League of changes that were about to occur, and although I remember a general feeling of uncertainty about the direction we would take in the 1970s, even I was not prepared for the events that would gradually unfold'.*

CHAPTER 13

From decline to delight

With all that had passed in the years that had been branded the 'Swinging Sixties', the Western League was, indeed, facing probably the biggest challenge that it had seen in recent decades.

It was a time of both change and stimulation, with the Football Association aware of the problems and introducing measures to halt the decline in popularity of football at grass-roots level. Coupled with that, there was a recognition of the problems associated with the decline in the number of referees and linesmen coming into the game. In response to that, a feeder system was introduced to enable the promotion of any up-and-coming young officials at county level, for them to progress at a quicker rate.

There was also another initiative that was to prove significant in the eventual changes to the League, prompted by the officials at the Southern League who were quick off the mark to ensure that their own league continued to flourish. It came at a time when the Western League had settled into something of a routine, accepting between nineteen and twenty-one teams in a single division competition; a complacency that was shaken with strong rumours that some of the more robust clubs were about to move on.

The initial response to the threat was to call a meeting in November 1970, at which a resolution was passed to appeal for intervention from the FA. That request was crafted in the strongest of terms, but had little effect, and eventually the response received was that nothing could be done as no rules had been broken, and that it was in the hands of the League to safeguard its strength, and maintain its status as a Contributory League.

The Committee Meeting, just a month later, was devoted entirely to the subject, and when President, George Templeman, arrived late with the discussions in full flow, he was immediately asked to leave the room, as he also served on the Southern League Committee, and as such was unable to contribute to the subject, without compromising his position in the discussion.

Following on from that, progress seemed to have been made, and later a meeting took place in London on 14th January 1971, which was attended by the Southern, Western, Kent, Metropolitan, the United Counties and Eastern Leagues', to discuss the subject. Despite all the rhetoric, however, nothing came from those discussions and a further meeting a month later concluded that the only option open was to begin an aggressive co-option campaign to recruit more clubs and safeguard the future of the oldest league in the west.

The following month saw Chard Town, Cinderford Town, Chippenham Town, Hanham Athletic, Mangotsfield United, Thornbury Town, Westland Sports and Yate Town, all expressing an interest in joining. New members, Plymouth City, also prompted further optimism when they announced that they were soon to amalgamate with Bodmin Town, and would anticipate that Bodmin would be happy to accept membership as well.

With such interest, expectations were high that others would follow from Cornwall, Devon, Wiltshire and Gloucestershire, with the expectation that adding a second division could be a stepping-stone for clubs from county football level. It was also thought that by dividing the division into two regionalised sections, reduced travel costs would further attract clubs.

While all that was going on, Minehead were progressing through to the First-Round Proper of the FA Cup, at last. Although they then faced a resurgent Merthyr Tydfil, which most would have expected to win through, a firm defence and two goals late on from Derek Bryant and Tom Smith, eased them through to do battle at home against Division Three side, Shrewsbury Town.

That day, as with every home game since he was appointed, Manager, Ron Gingell stood on the same spot that he had done for every game, without moving; a ritual that he maintained throughout his time with the club. The talisman action was to no avail, however, and despite putting up a great fight, his team went down, 2-1. When he later left Minehead to take over the same position at Taunton Town, the fans urged the club to dig up the hallowed turf where he always stood, and present it to him as a memento; something that did not happen.

Despite the Cup run, Minehead only achieved fifth place at season's end behind neighbours, Bideford Town, who won the title six points clear of runners-up, Andover. Although St Luke's College were again in bottom spot, having only won two games, and were a full ten points behind Bath City reserves, they were winners of the Merit Award for the second year running.

After all the talk of increasing numbers of participant clubs, it was, indeed, a disappointment for everyone involved to learn of the resignation of Andover, Bath City reserves, Bristol City reserves and Frome Town. Alongside that, the merger between Plymouth City and Bodmin failed to come to fruition, and they were given no option but to resign when their ground at Pennycross was sold for redevelopment.

There was also an additional threat to the continuation of the League when the South-Western League gave notice, under FA Rule 26, that they would be approaching Bideford Town, Barnstaple Town and Torquay United, and although none of those clubs accepted the invitation, prospects were not looking good for the season to come with just fourteen clubs in membership. It was the smallest number of member clubs recorded since those difficult days prior to the First World War, and even the re-introduction of the Subsidiary Cup Competition, which had again been put on ice the season before, did not enhance prospects.

Hard times, of course, call for strong and brave actions, and so it was that at the AGM of 1971, Les Phillips was elected as Vice-Chairman in the place of Mr Bush, who had been forced to withdraw due to his future activities with another Association. Up until that stage, the real Les had been quietly waiting in the wings, just biding time for the opportunity to bring his own inimitable personality into action, and very soon the League was to learn that time waits for no man; especially when his name is Les Phillips.

The AGM was one of great change, with George Templeman standing down as President due to heavy commitments elsewhere, and for health reasons. Reg Broom filled the void that he left. Tony Barnes also arrived on the scene; a man whose organisational ability would prove such an asset to the League in the later years of change and re-organisation. It was, however, not quite the time for him to shine, and although he was co-opted just after the meeting, he withdrew after only a year due to his commitments at Frome Town.

On the refereeing front, a Bristol man who would eventually become a Western League official, Maurice Washer, was promoted to the Football League, while Lester Shapter was promoted to the list of Football League linesmen and Mike Bevan, who began his career as a goalkeeper for Melksham Town, was promoted to the Western League list of referees.

While the season kicked-off short of both member clubs and with scant prospects, everyone was trying to play their part in ensuring the future of non-league football in the west of England, and new President, Reg Broom, told a meeting in October, that he was in contact with County Associations about a new competition for senior clubs in the area. While it was generally agreed that it would be acceptable for him to continue pursuing the idea, the meeting emphasised that it was a future avenue to explore and not one that would solve the immediate problems being experienced by the Western Football League.

Later that month, thirteen clubs from Gloucestershire, Somerset and Wiltshire attended another meeting to discuss the formation of a regionalised Second Division, and this time agreement was reached about the running of such a competition. It was unanimously agreed that it should be open to the First teams of both senior, amateur and professional clubs within a fifty-mile radius of Bristol, with promotion optional for the Champions. Other matters were also discussed, but eventually it was agreed to leave the final details until later in the season when clubs could establish if they were going to join.

Following on from that, Les Phillips took the chair for the first time as acting Chairman at a get together of Member clubs at the Four All's Hotel, Taunton, on Sunday 21st November 1971. Les told the Members that although many clubs had expressed an interest in joining the new division, after investigation it had been established that many of their grounds did not come up to senior status, and that they would, therefore, not be able to enter. There was then, what can only be described as, a 'no-holds-barred' debate, at which Les asked each representative directly if they intended to remain loyal to the League.

Of the club's present, only Bideford Town declared an interest in joining the Southern League, while Taunton Town intimated that they would have to consider entering the Somerset League if the numbers participating dropped any lower. At the end of the discussion, which included several appeals for those present to stay loyal for at least one more season, a vote was taken, and the proposal that the Western League would carry on as it was without an increase in membership, was defeated. The clubs appeared both solidly loyal, and to hold the same ambitions as the Chairman that day; to see the League once more a vibrant and viable organisation.

While most people left the meeting with a renewed faith in the future, by January 1972, Minehead, Dorchester and Bideford had all tendered their resignations, to join the Southern League. They were replaced, however, by applications for membership from Ashtonians United, Bristol City Colts, Mangotsfield United, Avon Bradford and Exeter City reserves. There was also a letter read out to the committee from Chippenham Town, who expressed their desire to re-join the League, but were in the process of financial problems which negated their return.

In Tom's words, it was to be a very significant time in the history of the League. He wrote 'As I look back now I consider that season to be one in which we 'turned the corner' as it was the first time that I heard the word 'sponsorship' used about a competition to be operated by our League. Les Phillips was always a man who would pick up on ideas, told the committee meeting that he had already been in contact with three companies who had shown an interest in sponsoring a Subsidiary Competition'.

 Even Tom could not have anticipated the impact that the statement would eventually have on the continuation and status of the Western Football League in future years as Les pursued his vision.

The season was, of course, a low-key affair on the playing front with only fourteen teams taking part, and although the AGM, which was held at The Shires Hall, Trowbridge, congratulated Bideford on winning not just the League title, but also the Subsidiary Competition and the Challenge Cup, those words were tinged with regret, as it was known that they were off to join the Southern League. The runners-up spot was won by Minehead, while the Alan Young Cup went to Bridgwater Town.

Once again, the Amateur Cup was retained by Devizes Town and the Merit Cup went to Bridport, but in addition to those awards, the AGM also had the pleasure of awarding a 'League Meritorious Service Award' to Den Perry, who had just retired from the post of Secretary at Taunton Town, a post that he had held for many years.

The 1972/73 season kicked-off with thirty games to play, along with a general feeling that eventually the League would progress under what was becoming a determined and active Management Committee, whose aims were not restricted to the past.

With a view to that, yet another meeting took place in November at which Jack Veale revealed that he had been in contact with the FA in relation to the prospect of regionalisation, which FA Council Member, Mr LC Parker of Bridport, confirmed would be considered shortly as a special meeting convened to look at the proposals. The Meeting also held a minute's silence in the memory of Vice-President, Mr S Hawkins, and Treasurer, Len Brown, who had both recently died, after which there was a very informative speech from Eric Berry, the Chairman of Frome Town, in which he made the position clear about the newly introduced government legislation on Value Added Tax. advising that it would be of little benefit to most member clubs.

The season saw the Championship go to Wiltshire for the first time in twelve years, when Devizes Town pipped Taunton Town to the title by two points. They also won the Subsidiary Cup, 5-3, over two legs, defeating Torquay United. Under the guidance of Manager, Ken Owens, and with a team made up almost entirely of Wiltshire County Squad players, Devizes had experienced a tremendous year. It was, however, not to be the start of a period of success, when six of the squad left at season's end to join Andover, resulting in a huge rebuilding task ahead for the club.

DEVIZES TOWN FC 1972-73

Back: P Meehan, M Grubb, K Bond, B Hayward, C Roberts. Front: M Ackling, M Sanders, D Corbin, R McCombe, C Moss, R Lowe

While mid-table Bridport Town, put their name on the Challenge Cup, Torquay United won the Merit Cup for the first time, and bottom club Ashtonians United were re-elected to keep numerical parity. It was, therefore, with regret that Torquay then withdrew, along with Bristol City Colts, who had only been members for that one season. They were, however, replaced by Dawlish Town, Exmouth Town, Keynsham Town and Chippenham Town.

The AGM, which was held at the Headquarters of Bridgwater Town, was a much happier affair than of late, and Les Phillips was voted-in unanimously as the new Chairman. With a beaming smile and a booming voice, he conveyed his delight and appreciation, in a speech that was filled with promise of further progress. Wilf Escott, who had stood down in favour of Les, took over from Reg Broom as Treasurer, and Stan Priddle became the newly elected Vice-Chairman.

As the new season began under the leadership of Les and Stan, it was quick to see just how their partnership would benefit the League; Les had a full-blown style of bluster, where everything was possible and the goal was the benefit of the League and its future, while Stan would advise caution at every turn, and was sometimes listened to by his boss as well!

The new clubs in the League brought with them their full share of personalities, as Tom recalled eloquently about a conversation he had when attending one of the first games of that season between Mangotsfield United and Dawlish Town. He wrote *'That day I met a young gent who had obviously been keen to see his club, Dawlish, progress into our competition. Throughout the game, Gerry Turner entertained me with his enthusiastic tales and he spoke of the important influence that Harry Cordell, an ex-England Amateur International and secretary of the club at times, and of Jack Batten who had been a reporter for the club for almost 40 years'.*

'Gerry had succeeded Cordell as Secretary in the 1960s and later took over as First Team Manager, and said that the previous season had been the best he had known, winning every Trophy with both their First and Reserve Teams with each winning their respective leagues without dropping a point'.

He continued: *'Typical of almost every club, there were personalities who had been involved with Dawlish for years, and as the second-half began (not that I had really been aware the first-half had ended such was the flow of conversation) Gerry told me about the devoted services of Life-member, Frank Bolt, who had also served as Chairman, Vice-Chairman and an active committee member. In all, he had devoted over 50 years, and his son, Roy, was treasurer of the club and had been involved since boyhood'.*

'As the game ended, I was about to say my goodbye and ask the score-line! when Gerry remembered an amusing story with a moral touch from early club success in the 1957/58 season. It was about a Devon Senior Cup Final game against red-hot favourites, Dartmouth Town. It appears that Dawlish were such under-dogs to pick up the Trophy, that the Mayor of Dartmouth had arranged a Civic reception to receive the expected victors; only for Gerry's team to spoil the party by winning the game 4-3. The Mayor was left ruing his presumptions with the moral of the story being to never assume anything in the game of football; it is a fickle master and cannot be predicted'!

And Tom ended the tale; *'Over the years, I have kept in touch with Gerry and can assure you that he hasn't changed at all, he is still able to hold a 90-minute conversation on the topic of his club, almost without drawing breath'.*

Back at the League, Les too was also hardly drawing breath in his first few months as Chairman. At a meeting called in October he suggested to clubs that they should consider improving the general appearance of their grounds and facilities, to further both their own standards and those of the League. He also added that, despite the co-option of both Tony Barnes and Les Heal onto the Management Committee, there were still vacancies and the need for new blood.

By November Les then called another meeting; this time to announce details of the sponsorship package that had been agreed with Rothmans by the Isthmian League, and seek the agreement of those present for him to open negotiations in relation to a similar package for the Western League. Which, of course, he got.

Armed with the blessing of the member clubs, Les, Jack Veale, Don Milverton and Wilf Escott all went to London for a meeting with Carreras Rothmans on 31st January 1974, to discuss matters further. The seriousness that the company placed on the venture was clear to see when the Western League party was greeted by Tony Williams, who was Rothmans Special Events Manager for Football, and Jimmy Hill, the very well-known footballer and TV pundit.

Just a few weeks later, on 26th February, written confirmation of an offer was received by Les for the season's 1974/75 and 1975/76, with an option for 1976/77. The document emphasised that the aim of the sponsorship was to provide more sporting, attractive, and competitive football, and included the controversial condition that there should be a 'three points for a win' system to encourage attacking football.

The other details included;

- £1000 for the Champions

- £500 for the runners-up

- £300 for the third placed club

- Seasonal awards for the top three clubs who scored the most goals outside of the top three positions in the table.

- £40 for the club winning a game by three clear goals or more.

- A £2000 Sportsmanship Pool which would be decided by clubs losing four points for a sending-off; one point for a booking and a rider that any club loosing eight points or more would be excluded from taking part.

While the total package was worth £10,000 a season, the intangible benefits of being promoted by such a huge organisation were unquantifiable. Rothmans had, indeed, realised the tremendous potential of non-league football as an advertising medium, and were looking to further spread the net to other senior leagues in the country, if this expansion proved to be as cost-effective as anticipated.

Those were, indeed, exciting times, after a long period where non-league football had been on the decline, and a meeting at the Francis Hotel, Bath emphasised the success of the scheme so far, when a message was received from Barry East, Chairman of Rothmans Isthmian League, in which he sent both his congratulations to the Western League and his intention to invite officials of those leagues who accept similar deals with the company to a special meeting in London sometime in the future, at his own expense.

News of the sponsorship spread rapidly throughout the west, and amid great excitement, a General Meeting held at Taunton Town FC, learned of an almost endless list of formal applications to join the League for the following season, which included: Bodmin Town, Falmouth Town, Bristol St George, Bath City reserves, Cadbury Heath, Calne Town, Clevedon Town, Hanham Athletic, Holsworthy, Locking Villa, Melksham Town, Ottery St Mary and St Austell.

Alongside those clubs, written enquiries had been received from: Abbotonians United, Almondsbury, Bemerton Athletic, Bromham, Corsham Town, Elmore, Hambrook, Heavitree United, Poole Town reserves, Saltash United, Sanford Youth Centre, Thornbury Town, Wadebridge Town, Westland Sports, Wootton Bassett and Yeovil Town; with telephone enquiries from Trowbridge Town and Westbury United.

There was also a great deal of discussion about the format that the new season would take. Despite previous thoughts, it was unanimously agreed that two geographical sections in Division Two would not improve the standards of the clubs or the League, and that initially there should be just one division made up of twenty-two clubs. The clubs also concurred that no reserve teams would be permitted unless attached to Football League clubs.

It truly was an exciting time to be involved with football, and optimism for the future was high. Doug Ibbotson, a journalist for the London Evening News summed it up, writing; *'No-one is more familiar with the push and professionalism of modern day football than Jimmy Hill, one of the first wonder-managers of the post war game, and now the BBC's TV soccer analyst. But when we chatted this week he had taken time off to go to the Western League meeting in Taunton. It was, he told me, a jolly and chastening experience, adding there were players and officials from clubs such as Bodmin, and I was amazed at the enthusiasm for the game at that level. They really love football for its own sake, love talking about and playing it. We talk about Bill Shankly and Don Revie, about the European Cup...but its good, from time to time, to be reminded that there is another side to the game'.*

To kick-off the new association, Les received a letter, dated 26th April 1974, from Tony Williams confirming details of a tour of Zambia, a country that had been runners up to Zaire in their previous World Cup Qualifying group. The flight was to depart from London Airport on the evening of 23rd May, with the return journey on the 7th June, and the tour requirements included a valid passport and inoculations for Smallpox, Yellow Fever and Cholera.

The invitation extended to Les as Chairman, plus five selected Western League players; Brian McAuley, Marcus Scott, Tony Payne, Colin Calloway and Graeme Sommerville. They were then to combine with a similar delegation from the Northern League, to play two games against a side representing the African nations. It was intended that an Isthmian League side would also be included and play two games.

As if that was not grand enough, Les also wanted to present a cheque to the St Francis Mission for Leprosy in a township on the Zambian/Congo border. The £325 had been raised by the Round Table in Wimborne that Les was a member of, and with a view to this the MP for Taunton, Edward du Cann, was requested to arrange a meeting for the party with the President of Zambia, during the tour.

Everything was going surprisingly well with the complicated arrangements, and so it was hugely disappointing that, out of the blue on the 16th May, the tour was scrapped due to the anti-apartheid movement, which had led to the boycott of all UK sporting tours to African countries

Although it was unfortunate for those about to make the trip, the majority involved with the new era of sponsorship were still on a high, with a good deal of excitement at the prospects for the seasons to come. There was, however, one drawback to the new arrangements when Exeter City were forced to withdraw from the League because the FA refused to give them permission to take part in a sponsored competition. The national guardians of the game were said to be cautious of a club in Membership being beholden to commercialism; Oh, how times change!

At a packed and optimistic AGM, held at Wordsworth Drive on July 1974, Welton Rovers, who had been restructuring under the guidance of Dave Stone and Alan Hobbs, were congratulated on becoming League Champions by one point over runners-up, Taunton Town. Mangotsfield United, in only their second season, lifted the Challenge Cup and, once again, Devizes Town won the Amateur Cup, while Bridport won the Merit Cup for the third time.

At the bottom of the table, Chippenham Town were successful in their application to stay in the League having won only three games all season. They were to be joined the following season by Falmouth Town, Melksham Town, Paulton Rovers and Westland Yeovil in the new and exciting competition.

It was certainly a time of change and as Tom put it, *'A regeneration of life had begun for the League, with the modern era of football in the West Country, which was eventually to move on into a much-improved national structure for our beloved sport'.*

True words, but it would take both time, and continued work by the League's active Management Committee for the dream to be realised.

CHAPTER 14

Home and away with Rothmans

With the problems that had been tackled throughout the 1960s and early 1970s, it was interesting to see how the men in charge of football in the West Country progressed as the challenges of the time continued.

The 1974/75 season was, indeed, the start of a new era with the first change of name for the League since 1894. Seventy-nine years of Association Football distinctiveness, was about to be assigned to history to welcome in The Rothmans Western Football League.

With the new sponsorship came the introduction of three points for a win; a move that was intended to eliminate the defensive style of play that was often blamed for games that were dull and unattractive to supporters. And it certainly seemed to work.

In the first month, seven clubs shared a total of £400 for winning games by three or more clear goals, a clear indication that teams were adopting a more attacking and tactical approach to the game.

The system was not adopted by the Football League until 1981, with a great deal of work from Jimmy Hill's 'think-tank' on the state of the game, and was, until that date frowned on by many who sat in those hallowed halls as an unprofessional way to award points. Those reservations were also held by some on the ground as well, however, as Tom pointed out when he wrote: '*At a later AGM, I heard it suggested from the floor that is was a 'Micky Mouse' way of compiling a League Table'.*

One of the advantages of working with such a large and influential organisation such as Rothmans, was its ability to promote the League and clubs into the public eye, which they did by employing various methods. To the delight of many non-league football fans, who had been ignored in the various areas of the press since the footballing decline of the 1950s, a publication came out called 'The Rothmans Football News' which covered all the four leagues the company now sponsored.

Responsibility for the publication was within Tony Williams realm of responsibility at Rothmans, and he gained tremendous experience as Editor, and went on in later years, to produce many excellent magazines and books on non-league football; still writing for the Non-League Paper to this day.

Some clubs, however, were not as delighted by this new venture because, under the terms of the League's sponsorship deal they were obliged to support the venture with a £25 contribution to purchase a number of the magazines per edition whether they wanted them or not. The bi-monthly colour magazine is still the treasured possession of many people today, and the first edition included a forward by Ted Croker, the Secretary of the FA, (grandfather of Eric Dier), and included an article by Jimmy Hill.

Two of the main ambitions that occupied both the League Chairman and his Committee, was the aim to eventually have two divisions with twenty-two clubs in each, and to see conditions at grounds improve considerably for spectators, players and officials alike. The underlying reason for those improvements was the belief that spectators would only begin to return to non-league games if the grounds were of an acceptable standard with good basic facilities.

As the season progressed, Inter-League games were introduced, the first of which was held at Cossham Street, Mangotsfield, with the Hellenic League as the visitors.

Representative Western League Team

The Western League team selected from those who were all seen as top-class players; Colin Calloway, Paul Smith, Colin Chegwyn, Steve Millard, Tony Payne, Brian McCauley, Alun Williams, Bev Dixon, Harold Jarman, Brian Mortimer, Ron Low, Dave Corbin, Bob Baird, Vic Barney, Pete Crowley and Alan Hurford.

With such a side assembled it was widely expected that the home side would win the encounter with ease. As everyone who has been reading this book will know, however, football can be a very unpredictable game. The Hellenic League won the encounter, 2-1, with the only compensation the hosts that the goal of the game was scored Harold Jarman. The grand after-match social evening went extremely well, but did not prevent a post-mortem into the performance, which it was decided suffered from an anticipation that the victory was won before a ball had been kicked!

Les Phillips, Stan Priddle and Wilf Escott meet Arthur Clark and Gordon Nicholson of the Northern League

The performance was on the minds of Les and the Management Committee when a further representative match took place on 16th March, at Hungerford to celebrate the opening of their new changing rooms. It was a game that began in snow, and ended in bright sunshine, with an early goal by Tony Payne, after soaking up pressure for the opening minutes. By half-time, however, the score-line was all even, and that is how it stayed. Tony Payne did, however, restore pride in the final representative game of the year at Wordsworth Drive on 3rd May, when he scored the only goal of the game against the team from the Northern League.

Just before that game, the largest crowd of the season had been recorded at Wordsworth Drive, when Taunton Town entertained Falmouth Town on the final Saturday of the season in a game that would decide the Championship. The new initiatives had encouraged good attacking football throughout the year, and that game was no exception, with Falmouth scoring four goals in the first half-hour to take the coveted Trophy back to Cornwall for the first time in the League's long history.

In their first season, Falmouth had taken the League by storm, and were undefeated all year, scoring 122 goals and conceding just 26. Second placed Taunton, however, topped that with 136 goals scored, and 24 conceded; losing just that one game to the eventual Champions. Both clubs benefited from the new sponsorship deal, with Falmouth gaining £680 for the seventeen times they had won by more than three goals, £55.05 from the sportsmanship pool and £1,000 for picking-up the League title. They also won the Challenge Cup.

Taunton Town also did extremely well financially, topping the Falmouth achievement by winning 23 games by three or more goals, for which they received £920, along with £91.75 from the proceeds of the Sportsmanship Pool, and £500 as League runners-up.

The financial benefits did not, however, help those clubs who were struggling, and at the foot of the table with Exmouth awarded just £40, Clevedon £120, and both Melksham and Devizes, £131.75.

As if to emphasise that football is but a moment in time, the Final Table of those who benefited from the Rothmans sponsorship, listed non-league Wycombe Wanderers from the Isthmian League as the top recipients, with Falmouth Town in second place, just £57.70 behind. Over the years since that time, Wycombe have gone from strength to strength, and are now a well-established Football League club, while Falmouth Town eventually returned to the South-Western League and are no longer a club to evoke fear in non-league circles.

The tide of time also alters perceptions, and none was more demonstrated than at the discussion held to arrange the Presentation Dinner on 6th June 1975, when it was seriously suggested, and discussed, whether the evening should be an all-male occasion or not! How times changed, not that many years later, when the Western League was to be the trailblazer for equality when they agreed to the female referee, Wendy Toms, being taken on to their list to officiate at games; but that is a later story.

All, in all, the new union of commercialism and sport was declared a total success by everyone concerned at the end of that first year. Progress was, indeed, the order of the day. Not being one to sit back, however, Les was on a mission, and had already informed the Chairman of the Football Association, Sir Andrew Stephens, who had attended the League Dinner, that it was the intention of the League to expand the following season.

The carefully researched proposition, combined the vison and forthrightness of Les, with caution from number two, Stan Priddle, and was to produce one of the biggest expansion to the League for many years with the provision of a

Premier and a First Division. While that move was still in the future, the return of Bideford from the Southern League, and Exeter City reserves, who had obtained permission to take part in a sponsored league by the FA, increased those taking part for the 1975/76 season to twenty-three clubs.

While there was no stopping Les, there was also no stopping the expansion of the Rothmans non-league family, with the addition of the Channel Islands attracting the prospect of Inter League games across the Channel quickly becoming a reality. A Channel Island Touring Party was assembled without too much trouble which included five Western League players; Bob Perrott, Alan Hurford, Ray Shinner, John Megett and Mike Jordan.

Rothmans National X1 after arriving at Jersey Airport

They were accompanied by the Chairman, and had the time of their lives, playing in Jersey and Guernsey to commemorate the Island Leagues first season of sponsorship.

The proposed League extension was on a list of topics for discussion at a meeting on 11th December 1975, where it was suggested that reserve teams from Southern League clubs could be allowed into the First Division, but would not be eligible for promotion to the Premier Division. It was also agreed that discussions should be held with the Southern League about the future of football in the West Country, and that to enabling those from more remote areas to consider applying, a travel pool should be set-up.

Following discussions regarding refereeing, it was agreed that a panel would be established to allow assessors to comply with FA guidelines. Discussions regarding the marking system that was in operation concluded that similar scores were being given by both clubs, which was seen as an indication that the clubs both took the task of marking officials very seriously, and that their similar scores reflected the officials' performances fairly.

As a further safeguard to those standards, the meeting agreed that if an assessor found a referee to be below standard, the Referees Appointments

160

Secretary, Don Milverton, would personally make sure the he went out to judge the man-in-the-middle himself.

When implemented, Don's assessment was then handwritten, full of constructive criticism, and sent to the referee in question, so that he could act on the observations and improve his standards. However, although that scenario was how officials thought the referees would take the critique as a positive, it was not unknown for the poor man in question, on reading the observations to spend the next few hours in a state of anxiety, eventually plucking up the courage, and shaking with fear, dialling Don's number to thank him for his observations!

Beside his role on the Western League, Don was a man to be reckoned with on the Somerset FA, and often acted as a chauffeur to Lew Webb on the journeys back from meetings in Wells over the Mendip hills. On one such occasion, during the outward journey Lew's Rover car developed a rattling noise, and when they reached the City, they found that one of the wheel-caps was missing. In his usual doctrinaire way, the homeward journey then took a disproportionate amount of time, as Lew insisted in leaving no ditch un-searched in his quest for the missing piece. Such was the friendship between the two men, that even such a journey of discovery did not diminish their bond.

A further special meeting was held 5th February 1976 at Wordsworth Drive, where it was ratified that both a Premier and a First Division would be formed for the season 1976/77, containing eighteen clubs in each division, and also allow room for further expansion when needed. To fulfil that requirement, it was decided that the lowest positioned clubs at the end of the current year would be placed into the First Division together with new entrants.

A few pre-requisites had to be complied with before kicking a ball for all new entrants that:

- All grounds should have an acceptable barrier around the field of play to prevent encroachment.
- Grounds should be adequately enclosed to enable the club to have full control over spectators.
- Separate changing rooms should be provided for the home team, visiting team and match officials; each with its own washing facilities.

With that initial aim for an expansion to the League fulfilled, Les was then on a mission, with his next aim to encourage the South-Western League to merge, thereby giving a total of three divisions with twenty clubs in each. He also wanted the Champions of the Western League to be given automatic entry to the Southern League, and any club winning their County League to be given automatic entry to the Western League First Division. What he did not realise all those years ago, is that he was describing the Pyramid system of football that has come into being, and one which now enables clubs to play at as high a level, both in non-league and national level, as their ambitions and budgets would allow; given, of course, the vagaries of football where nothing is certain no-matter how much money is thrown at a dream.

At the end of what was to be an historic season, the question on most people's minds was just where the fairy-tale of Falmouth Town would end, after they finished the year a clear twenty-one points ahead of Taunton Town.

1976 FALMOUTH TOWN FC

Left to right, back row: Richard Gray, Brian Helley, Richard Francis, Geoff Freeman, Keith Etheridge, Alan Morris, Richard Davis
Front row: Dave Ferrett, Tony Kellow, Joe Scott, Keith Manely, Colin Chedwyn.

In the process, they had scored 134 goals, and conceded 43. And in Tony Kellaway, a player signed from Penzance who worked in the Falmouth docks, they had found a striker capable of scoring 46 goals in a season. They also won the Cornwall Senior Cup, and banked £1841.81 in prize money.

Clevedon Town, had also found a superb striker in Derek Robbins who later took on the role of manager, achieve a very respectable third place, while St Luke's College picked up the Amateur Trophy, and Devizes Town the Merit Cup.

During the year, Les had suggested that a League Convention Weekend could be held at the end of each season, and in his usual manner he forced his brainchild through a rather sceptical Management Committee, proceeding to work with Tony Barnes to find a venue that could hold the anticipated numbers.

It was not an easy task and in the process, they found that there were few hotels in the area that could offer the accommodation needed at a competitive enough price to make the event a success. As this was the first weekend of its kind anywhere in the UK for non-league football, Les and Tony had no guide-lines to follow, and there was an unforeseen additional problem in the sheer number of people from other League's and Associations who wished to attend.

After many hours of work and miles travelled, the two intrepid organisers did find it possible to take over a whole hotel for the Bank Holiday weekend, as it was a time when short-break holidays were still in their infancy. The first Convention Weekend took place on 13th and 14th May 1976 in Dawlish at the

Langstone Cliff Hotel, under the guidance of the owner, Geoff Rogers, and with the hands-on administration of Tony Barnes.

Few are still involved today who attended that event, but Tom summed it up well when he wrote; '*I remember, even at the age of eighty-three, being able to drink some of the young referees under the table that weekend. Lads by the names of Gale, Morgan, Bissex, Baldwin, Ashton, Hamer, Cooper, Milford, Clarke and Mitchell, all come to mind. Yes, they were all there, trying to blind me with the science of the game, but I was more than able to tell them a thing or two – without being sent off… to bed'!*

Through this innovation, the League became one of the friendliest in the country, and over the years the weekend has been adopted by many others in non-league football. It not only gained the league national recognition, but also assured a warm welcome at every meeting and ground during the cut and thrust of the competitive season.

Apparently, when Tom asked Les at the 1976 AGM where the Western League was going after recent developments, he replied in his usual forthright manner 'FORWARD'. And so it was. The newly structured Rothmans Western League came into existence for the start of the 1976/77 season with the top eighteen clubs forming a Premier Division.

LES PHILLIPS
1976

The results of the previous season had condemned five of the existing member clubs into the First Division, with Chippenham Town, Devizes Town, Exmouth Town, Keynsham Town, and Melksham Town all joining the new entrants to the League, Brixham United, Chard Town, Clandown, Heavitree United, Ilminster Town, Larkhall Athletic, Ottery St Mary, Portway Bristol, Saltash United, Shepton Mallet Town, Swanage Town and Herston, Torquay United reserves and Yeovil Town reserves, who had fulfilled the minimum ground requirements

On 26th November, Jack Veale was presented with a memento to mark 25 years as Secretary of the League. However, with the growth that had been achieved since Les had taken over as Chairman, the administration side was becoming far too large for one person. Several incidents had already pointed to this fact, and so it was agreed, with a few protestations from Jack, that an assistant was needed, and to this end Tony Barnes, once again, stepped in to deal with the Registrations side of his duties.

Although the early leaders of the new division were Shepton Mallet and Keynsham, they were overtaken by Saltash United by the end of October; a club that was to remain in that position for the rest of the season. To most followers of non-league football in the West Country, it did not come as a surprise to see such form, as the club had won the South-Western League for the two seasons prior to joining, and were made up from the manager, Mike Howard's, star-studded St Austell side of 1973/74. The club had also spent money on their ground, which included covered accommodation and new changing rooms in anticipation of further success.

As anticipated, Division One did not run smoothly, and trouble was brewing. Near the end of the term, Portway Bristol failed to put on a game against Ottery St Mary, whose officials and players had arrived at Bristol to find the pitch was not available. Because Portway was new to the League, members of the Management Committee tried to help the situation by meeting members of the Shirehampton Recreational Ground Users Committee, to prevent any repetition of the oversight, but eventually, they were to face many years of frustration and problems in the League before finally calling it a day.

The Rothman's Inter-League Cup was a well-run and well supported Competition, that saw Frome Town progress through with victories over both North Shields and Hungerford Town. It was there that the journey, and the Western League's interest in the competition ended, when after embarking on their longest trip, Blyth Spartans beat the plucky Somerset side by the only goal of the game.

The new Premier Division did not suit Taunton Town, who had been narrowly pipped to the League title for the previous four seasons, but were looking a shadow of their former selves. It was therefore, somewhat unexpected that notification was received in February 1977 informing the League that they were considering membership of the Southern League; a move partially prompted by the opening of the M5 motorway which would ease the problems of travelling. While there was no formal resignation, and when they ended the season in ninth place, it appeared by all indications that the intention was just that. Just prior to the AGM, however, they moved on and were fined £150 under Rule 14, for a late withdrawal.

Predictably, Falmouth Town were the runaway League Champions, 14 points clear of runners-up, Weston-super-Mare, who were two points clear of their neighbours, Clevedon Town. Weston did, however, pick-up both the re-introduced Challenge Cup and the Merit Cup. Dawlish Town, who finished just below Taunton Town in tenth place, were highest placed Amateur Cup winners.

After many years of running the League with just a single division, the re-introduction of promotion and relegation made end of season games more important, and although only Westland Yeovil were relegated, both Saltash United and Shepton Mallet were promoted. During the season, it had been agreed that the First Division would increase to twenty clubs, and while Heavitree were successful in their application to remain having ended the term in bottom spot, they were joined by Bristol Manor Farm and Odd Down, who beat off competition for membership from Cadbury Heath, Elmore and Wellington in the ballot of clubs.

After the end of the season, representatives from each the sponsored leagues were a part of a Rothmans squad who travelled to the Canary Islands for a series of games against under 23's teams from La Palmas, Gran Canaria, FC Artesanto, and FC Ortavio, in Tenerife.

Rothmans National Squad in Tenerife

Les Phillips was accompanied by four Western League players; Bob Perrott (complete with his lucky mascot, Dobbin the parrot), Alan Hurford, Joe Scott and Ron Dicks. It was an experience that would top even that of the Channel Islands tour. Geoff Hurst, who was then playing for Telford FC, exhibited that he had not lost his golden touch, and it was, indeed, a fine tribute to the skills and talents of non-league football that brought with it the promise of progression inspiring confidence in the future.

The 1977/78 season kicked-off with football in the west still glowing from all the progress that had been made, and with new clubs to accommodate. The sport was looking good, and in the words of Tom, fate had matched newcomers, Bristol Manor Farm with Odd Down on the opening day; a game that was as entertaining off the pitch, as on it. He wrote: '*The result was a fair 0-0 draw, but the game was memorable to me because it was the first time that I encountered the diminutive figure of the 'Farm' manager, Mike 'Minnie'*

Fisher; a man who was occasionally known to employ unusual methods to make an impact. I can remember several occasions when I saw him in later years, where his forthrightness astounded me. On one such occasion, his team were 5-2 ahead of Frome Town by half-time, and yet when they went in for tea, they were greeted with a blistering attack for not leading by a bigger margin. Later still at another game when his side were trailing by two goals at the break, I could hear 'Minnie' say, in a voice that could be heard by the passengers in the train that passed adjacent to the ground......'never mind the ******** tea', which was quickly followed by the sound of clattering cups as they were smashed on the shower walls!! Such was the passion; such are the memories'.

Tom continued; 'That was, in fact, quite a day for memories, as I also met up with my old friend Lew Hill, who had been with Odd Down since the tender age of 16 years old, and whose life since had evolved around the club, beginning with balancing the books from the age of eighteen. When I met him back in 1946 at Coombe Hay Lane, his club were about to play a team of Italian collaborators who were based at Westbury, but on the day, the visitors put up a superb display and won 7-1. It was a great game but the next planned match had to be called off because most of the team had been released to go back home to Italy'.

He then recalled; 'As we caught up on all the years since we had last met, Lew told me an amusing story about a game that his club played against Bridgwater in the 1950s when they left Bath with just ten players. While passing through Clandown, however, they noticed one of their former sponge men sitting on a bench, and stopped the coach to ask him if he would like to come along. Being game for anything, 75-year-old Charlie Meadows promptly agreed and even volunteered to play in goal. The home crowd were particularly amused by this when Charlie took to the pitch, complete with cap and fully dressed. Miraculously, Odd Down scored first and for every shot at goal the plucky pensioner would either raise a right or left arm or foot and for high balls he would use his cap to bat them away! Bridgwater won the game, but the crowd gave a standing ovation to the visitors for a truly memorable match'.

'Lew hung up his boots after 800 appearances at the age of 45, but that did not stop his association with his club, and in 1967, when he was approached by a player about the possibility of building a clubhouse, he and his happy band of volunteers, began work on the project that was eventually completed in 1972. His 59 years of devotion are mirrored by many, and are what makes non-league football a way of life'.

Sagacious words, indeed.

Overall, everything was going well, and even when some incidents of drunken fans were reported to the Management Committee, regarding a First Division club that had allowed drinking to go on pitch-side during games, it was a small problem that was dealt with by agreeing not to sell drinks until after the final whistle. The incident, of course, did not deter the campaign that Les was promoting for clubs to increase income by building clubhouses, but was a cautious note and seemed to emphasis, as we know today, that football and alcohol do not always sit well together.

Gates were improving for many clubs as the games became more entertaining with less goalless draws, and all seemed to be progressing on target, but it was not to stay that way without effort, faith and direction. The news that Rothman's would be withdrawing their sponsorship after the end of the season, prompted by new government legislation that banned tobacco companies from giving financial assistance to sport, came as both unexpected, and as a shock.

In response to the news, the ever-resourceful Chairman suggested that he would be happy to accept £15,000 worth of Rothmans products instead of the sponsorship money to get around the law, and added; '*I have told them that we could arrange for the cigarettes and cigars to be distributed among our clubs instead of the prize money*'. A suggestion that was not taken up.

Despite the setback, Les then contacted all the clubs to emphasise that in his opinion the future of both the clubs and the League was going to be through sponsorship, and that he was fully in favour of shirts and tracksuits being used for advertising purposes, providing they conformed to FA and County FA rules.

Meanwhile, all the leagues that were involve with the Rothman's sponsorship met up in Oxford to discuss what they could do next, but came away with the conclusion that they might have to look for individual sponsorship, rather than seek a large company to take them all on.

That final Rothman's year was a record-breaking season on the field, with Falmouth Town taking the title for the fourth time, as well as the Alan Young Cup. Falmouth did not have it all their own way, however, as Bideford Town pushed them all season, and only lost the Championship by goal-difference of +61 compared to +68. Bridport won the Challenge Cup for the third time, albeit over a sixteen-year period, and Weston-super-Mare won the Merit Cup for the second year-running.

There was a sad note to the end of the season when St Luke's College disappeared from the League after being absorbed into Exeter University. St Luke's FC had been in existence for 118 years, and were the fourth oldest football club in the world behind Notts County (1862), Stoke City (1863) and Nottingham Forest (1865).

With the demise of St Luke's, there was no relegation from the Premier Division, and Division One Champions, Keynsham Town, who won by nine points, were promoted with both runners-up Clandown and third placed, Ilminster Town. Three more clubs joined Division One; AFC Bournemouth reserves, Elmore and Wellington.

The Annual League Convention was held again at the Langstone Cliff Hotel in May, and was a combination of work and pleasure for many, with a series of meetings on refereeing matters, floodlight services and coaching, together with an Inter-League forum, that was chaired by Les. There was also the last of the Inter-League games, which saw the Northern League XI play a select

Western League XI on the Saturday afternoon at the Dawlish Town ground in Sandy Lane.

It was the end of an era, and the start of a new phase, and none present would ever forget the Northern League contingent's rendition of the 'Blaydon Races' in a sing-song in the early hours of the Sunday morning, at the end of a most enjoyable and memorable weekend.

One friendship that continued for many a year was that of Bob Juggins and his wife Wendy, who supported the Convention until he passed away. His son, Neil, the Secretary of the West Midlands (Regional) League spoke for the Guests at the Langston Clift, and the family continued to attend. Bob's name is still revered in the Midlands, with the Bob Juggins Hospitality Award presented each year in his honour.

Sadly, the three years of sponsorship that had broadened horizons, and brought five leagues together, had come to an end; although friendships had been made which would continue for many years to come. During that short-time the Western League had grown into an attractive competition that covered all the counties in the West Country.

Although it was impossible to predict what would happen next with Les in charge of matters, one thing could be guaranteed, the advances that had been made would not be ceded lightly.

CHAPTER 15

Self sufficiency

With a League boasting thirty-nine clubs and a strong Management Committee, the future looked good, even given the withdrawal of the main League sponsorship. Clubs and Officials were more than aware that both sponsorship and self-sufficiency was the name of the game, and most were happy to accept the challenge.

With the new era, came a suggestion from Tony Barnes that a Grand National Draw could be organised to bring in money that would be centrally organised, with the proceeds shared between League and club coffers. The fund-raising scheme was to become a yearly event, and would last until the end of the decade; at which time, it was then decided that it had ceased to serve its original functions. Lotteries were springing up in several towns, and many clubs began to take part in that activity to attract additional ways of raising funds.

Some individual clubs were busy negotiating with local companies for sponsorship, and with a view to that Mangotsfield United approached the League Management Committee for permission to change its name, after a deal they had brokered included a slight change to reflect the company's involvement. Although they only wanted to drop the term 'United' and replace it with PF, the abbreviation of the sponsors name, Park Furnishers, it took a great deal of negotiations before permission was eventually given.

On the administration side, Tony Barnes stepped down as Registration Secretary, but was willing to stay on as Assistant Secretary, and Mike Bevan, from Melksham, was invited to take up the post by Les Phillips; an invitation that he accepted. Mike then attended the Management Committee meeting at Glastonbury on 14th September 1978, but it was to be his only one, as he died tragically during the following month.

At the next Meeting, a minute's silence was held followed by a tribute conveyed by Referees Secretary, Don Milverton, in which he referred to the many years of service and help Mike had given to younger referees. As a mark of respect, a donation from the League was forwarded to the Sheila McBryan Coronary Care Unit at Bath.

Possibly shaken by this, and combined with a heavy workload, Don Milverton then asked to be released from his duties as Referees Appointments Secretary, recommending Charlie Cotham of Corsham to take his place; who duly took over the post on 1st January 1979.

In a countrywide initiative, the FA were in the process of introducing a National League system to enable grass roots football to progress. The Alliance League was the first of those changes and the subject of much speculation at non-league level, which prompted Ted Croker and Adrian Titcombe to represent the FA at a meeting in November 1978 at Ilminster, with the most obvious question to address, just what effect the move would have on the Western Football League.

The main fear expressed was the extra pulling power that it might give to the Southern League, as the Alliance was to be directly fed into by its members, together with those competing in the Northern League. Although assurances were given that it was not designed to attract the stronger clubs to move allegiance, in general those members present were not convinced, and after all the work that had been put in during the preceding decade to strengthen the Western League, ground was not about to be ceded without a fight.

In view of the geographical problems that surround the League, concern was also expressed at the prospect of increased travel for clubs who were not on a main motorway. The Chairman of Bideford, Aubrey Loze, was one of several members to state that there was already too much travelling in the Southern League; something that he had learned first-hand in his clubs' time there. The overall feeling was that more regionalisation and rationalisation of the structure was needed, not only in the west and south west, but also throughout the country. After much discussion, it was generally agreed that the League would 'go into the melting pot' with other league's if the FA was prepared to undertake the task of restructuring non-league football by taking views expressed into account, and if they could put measures in to avoid the uncertainties of clubs simply seeking pastures new.

On the playing front, Tiverton Town had survived their financial crisis of 1976/77 and were revitalised; topping the Premier Division for a short-time, and putting together an FA Cup run after beating Barnstaple Town 2-1, to reach the Final Qualifying Round. That game was played at Ladysmead against Farnborough Town, with the game recorded by TV cameras for the first time in their history. Although Tiverton lost the encounter, 2-1, their success did not go unnoticed, and their fan base increased considerably, enabling their highest position in the League at seasons end of fourth, with the Amateur Cup in the cabinet as the highest finishing amateur club.

Frome Town and Bideford Town were neck-and-neck challenging for the Championship, which from the Somerset club's perspective could not have been predicted at the start of the season, when Frome were in second from bottom place after six games. The appointment of Bob Boyd as manager, however, changed their fortunes, and they lost just one of the following thirty-two games leaving the final match of the season to decide the title challenge.

That final game was at Badger Hill against Paulton Rovers, with just a draw required on a glorious Bank Holiday; a game that attracted a crowd of over 800 spectators, who were treated to a truly nail-biting match with the visitors putting the ball in the net early in the first-half. That goal, however, was ruled off-side to the joy of the vocal Frome supporters behind the top goal, which raised such cheers that anyone present would still have ringing in their ears today. As the time ticked on slowly for some of the home supporters, some doubted that Frome would hold out, but when the final whistle blew with the score-line still at 0-0, hundreds of fans ran onto the pitch to celebrate a rare year of success.

Swanage Town and Herston also recorded one of their few successes, picking up the Merit Cup for the first time, while their neighbours, AFC Bournemouth reserves lifted the Championship Trophy, seven points clear of First Division runners-up, Portway Bristol. Both clubs were promoted and replaced Glastonbury and Shepton Mallet. Shepton were unlucky to be relegated, ending the term on equal points with both Clevedon Town and Dawlish Town, but with an inferior goal-difference.

The 1978/79 AGM was held at the headquarters of new League members, Wellington, and heard of the resignation of Charlie Cotham as Referees Secretary. While there had been a replacement lined-up, the nominee for the post declined the offer, and so it was delegated to a sub-committee to agree someone for the post. Within the month, Don Milverton, who had stepped in to fill the position on a temporary basis, handed over to Alan Wallace.

The AGM also saw some more changes with the appointment of Maurice Washer as Assistant Secretary, and after running the 'three points for a win' system, the clubs decided to return to the widely accepted two-point system. New members were welcomed into the League with Bath City reserves and Radstock Town once again returning, and Liskeard Athletic joining to become the third club from Cornwall to seek a wider sphere of competition. The addition of those club brought the membership of the League to forty-two; fulfilling yet another aim set by the Chairman.

The 1979/80 season ran extremely smoothly, even without the benefit of having a major league sponsor. There was, however, another commercial initiative that began; that of an Inter-League Competition, which was sponsored by Office Cleaning Services Ltd. It had been arranged with the help of the well-known representative of that company, referee, Clive Thomas.

The Western League Team Manager was Dave Stone, who was ably assisted by Mike Williams, and games were played on a knock-out basis against teams from the Alliance League, Southern League, Northern League, Northern Premier League and the Isthmian League, with the latter taking part in the first game held at Frome Town. The following match against the Southern League, on a sunny Sunday afternoon in Dartford, however, was lost on penalties, and denied our League a chance to progress through to the play-offs.

AFC Bournemouth reserves adapted to their place in the Premier Division with ease, and at one stage looked set to take the title in only their second season. Barnstaple, however, had other ideas, and won the Championship by one point, thus chalking up their second League title; albeit after a wait of twenty-six years. The Amateur Cup winners were Portway Bristol, who were continuing to prove all the doubters wrong, having settled successfully into life in the League after such a difficult start.

At the AGM, held on 22nd May at Ilminster, Les Phillips could not disguise his annoyance at the news that Bournemouth had withdrawn their reserve side after having received assurances just a couple of seasons earlier that they were looking to a long-term commitment, not short-term gain. His mood was not helped by the withdrawal of both Westland Yeovil and Exeter reserves as well. In view of those changes, First Division Champions, Melksham Town, runners-up, Devizes Town, and third-placed, Liskeard Athletic, were all promoted to the Premier Division, and only the host club that night, Ilminster Town, was relegated.

LISKEARD ATHLETIC FC 1980/81

It was a memorable AGM in some ways, as recalled by Tom, who wrote; '*I will never forget the way that Jack Goodenough, the Chairman of Melksham Town, reacted to his club's tremendous season that evening. I could see throughout the meeting that he was in fine spirits, and as with all of us through the years, the pride in his club shone through. Now, until that night I had always thought that Jack was a teetotaller, but when I went to find him later, I was a little taken aback, as he was precariously perched on a bar stool with a line of drinks in front of him. From the way that he was downing what looked suspiciously like double or treble brandies, I quickly realised that my view of Jack had been wrong and that he had been practising the art for many years*'!

And, God rest his soul, that is the way that Jack continued to support the club that he loved until his final breath.

Frome Town were unable to repeat their form in the League, but did pick up the Challenge Cup after they held Devizes Town to a draw in the first game of the two-legged Final, and then beat them in the return game, 3-1. It had, once again been a good season for the Badgers Hill club, and in the FA Trophy they had progressed to the First-Round Proper only to be beaten by the odd goal in three by Hastings in a very hard-fought encounter.

Just prior to the start of the new 1980/81 season a new publication appeared called 'The Western Leaguer' magazine, produced by Packet Newspapers, of Falmouth. It was an innovative publication which attempted to keep the West Country up to date with all aspects of the game. It was the only time in history, to this date, that one publication has been devoted exclusively to the League. Unfortunately, it only lasted a short-time due to the lack of advertising revenue. Communications had come a long way from the 'Peasedown Pigeons' conveying half-time scores back to the villages; communications were, however, soon to move light-years ahead, and beyond anything that the new decade could have foreseen.

Early in the season, Doug Webb introduced Les Phillips to a representative of Goldliner Ltd, who were interested in sponsorship of the League. Dave Pearce eventually took the information from that meeting back to his company, who agreed to offer both a Manager of the Month Award in the shape of a gallon of whisky, and sponsorship of the Challenge Cup. For the first-time the Challenge Cup had a change of name, to the Western League Goldliner Cup, with the sponsorship deal worth over £3,000.

As the company representative, Dave attended the Management Committee meeting on 11th September 1980 to oversee the draw for the first two rounds of the competition, and was also available to watch one of the first games which involved a trip for Odd Down to League leaders, Barnstaple Town.

What made the game even more remarkable, was that the visitors had two players injured during the game, with both taken to hospital in the same ambulance. While Roy Chandler was the worst injured of the two with a broken leg, plucky young Trevor Wade recovered after treatment and ran back through the town in his football kit to finish the last minutes of the game.

The resulting win, 1-0, for the visitors was a remarkable result, and helped them reach the Quarter-Finals, which was one stage too far and they went out to Frome Town. The first Goldliner Cup was won by Dawlish Town, who up until then had been experiencing an indifferent season, thus demonstrating that League form is no indication in a Cup competition.

It was, indeed, a season for innovation, and one that saw Les Phillips working closely with Tony Barnes to negotiate a deal with the Philips Group to bring floodlights within the financial reach of Member clubs. It was to be a unique deal that saw Tony Barnes design, advise, and watch over the installation of the do-it-yourself package for clubs, with Frome Town, Glastonbury, Clevedon Town, Paulton Rovers, Clandown, Shepton Mallet and Saltash United, the first clubs to take advantage of the package.

Tony Barnes home club, Frome Town, was the first to turn on their newly installed lights on 24th September, where some of the vociferous home spectators made their presence felt. Fittingly, the FA XI drew, 0-0, with a select Western League XI.

Frome were a very well supported club, both home and away, with coaches arranged by a gentleman of Polish extraction called Mike, who eventually became known on the Western League circuit as 'Freddie Laker'. Their supporters were sometimes not popular with away ground staff, however, as they employed a method called 'Argentina' to celebrate; a method which owed its origins to the ticker-tape welcome given to the host nation of the World Cup. The ritual saw many supporters occupied the night before a game tearing up confetti-sized pieces of newspaper and stuffing them into carrier bags ready to scatter, blizzard style, when Frome took to the field or scored a goal. The resulting debris took a huge amount of work to clear, with the small pieces evident for many weeks to come.

Western League XI

Phil Morris (Frome Town) ; Harry Thomas (Weston super Mare); Bob Perrott (Clevedon); Paul Gardiner (Frome Town); Gary Mockeridge (Clevedon); Steve Blackmore (Weston super Mare); Dave Wiltshire (Frome Town); Dave Awcock (Bideford); Steve Gregson (Frome Town); Chris Venner (Dawlish); Pete Fryer (Weston super Mare) Dave Allen (Frome Town); Craig Foley (Frome Town); Kevin Prue (Paulton Rovers); Steve Massey (Weston super Mare).

As the season progressed discussions with the Southern League and others continued concerning the fate of non-league football. The importance of those discussions was paramount, as the formation of the Alliance League was shaking up the structure of the game throughout the country. Talks took place about the type of promotion and relegation system that would best benefit both non-league clubs and their supporters; and was to be the very early days of serious considerations about the future of the game from park football to the professional game.

It took until January 1981 for the next stage of development in the national talks to emerge, when at a meeting of all Western League clubs that month it was agreed, by a majority vote of thirty-five, to accept the Southern League proposal that they would form a Premier Division with two divisions below feeding into it, and that the Western League would act as a feeder league into that new structure. To begin the process, it was approved that three clubs would be allowed to move from the end of the existing season, with Bideford

174

Town, Bridgwater Town, Clevedon Town and Frome Town all nominated as candidates for consideration.

It seemed that progress had been made, but in March a standstill was imposed on all senior football leagues entering that type of arrangement by the FA; which scuppered all the discussions and decisions that had evolved.

Later still that year, the Football Association published a communication called; 'Football Outside of the Football League,' which itself suggested an expansion of the Southern League along the very lines that had been agreed. The League sent a very strong letter in response, despite the content being so like that agreed earlier, insisting that any reorganisation by the FA should not be considered without FULL consultation between all the parties concerned.

With all that activity going on in the background, the committee also had to deal with an influx of applications for Western League Membership. At the end of March 1981, a special meeting was convened with Member clubs who voted unanimous that the League should run with just twenty clubs in each division. That decision then called for a ballot to decide who would be chosen, which resulted in Almondsbury Greenway, Backwell United, Teignmouth Town, Torrington Town, Westland United, Wimborne Town and Yate Town, all pitching for just one vacancy. In the event the successful club was Wimborne Town, home town of League Chairman, Les Phillip.

BRIGWATER TOWN

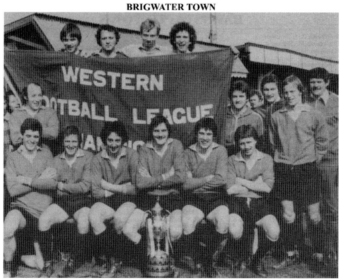

Champions 190/81

At seasons end Bridgwater won their first League honours, taking the title, six points clear of Barnstaple Town. In the First Division, Chippenham Town lifted the Championship, six points clear of the runners-up, Wellington, and both were promoted in the place of Tiverton Town and Paulton Rovers. The Merit Cup passed from Saltash to their neighbours, Liskeard Athletic, and Portway Bristol again won the Amateur Cup.

Paulton had been particularly unlucky to be relegated, gaining the same amount of points as Weston-super-Mare and Welton Rovers, but with an inferior goal difference, but off the pitch were progressing well. Just a month before seasons end, they had celebrated the switching-on of their new floodlights at Winterfield Road with a game against a Radio Bristol XI, on a day that saw them record a memorable victory, 3-1, in front of an enthusiastic crowd that included Bobby Charlton, who said later; '*Paulton Rovers club is obviously very progressive and deserves all the support it can get. I hope that in the future, the lights will shine on some very good footballers who play on this ground'.*

The social club at Paulton had raised much of the money needed for the floodlights, and had grown throughout the years. In 1969 another famous personality, Sir Stanley Rous, had been present to witness its opening when an 'All Stars' team attracted a large crowd to celebrate the first game on the new playing surface.

CHIPPENHAM TOWN FC
FIRST DIVISION CHAMPIONS 1980-81

Colin Moss, Paul Stephens, John Howell, Keith Nash, Martin Glanvill, Kevin Pattern, Chris Meech
Eamon Scully, Bob Radcliffe, Alan Gale, Ian Monnery, Rod Pratt

With the re-organisation of football in progress, it was the turn of Western League match officials to look at their structure, and as the new season kicked-off, various informal discussions were taking place. From those discussions, a steering group was set-up, with the aim of producing a consultative document to emphasise the lack of formal representation that referees and linesmen of the Contributory System had.

The initial group consisted of Ken Bissex, Ray Banham, Jeff Cox, Bob Hamer, Richard Horswell, Don Morgan and Bill Phillips, who all set about finding a solution to the problem. Eventually, after meeting with the Western League Referees subcommittee, a draft constitution and rules were prepared which were presented to the inaugural meeting of the new 'Association of Western League Referees and Linesmen,' at the Shrubbery Hotel, Ilminster, on Sunday 21st February 1982.

At the meeting, Ken Bissex was elected as Chairman, Dave James and Don Morgan, vice-chairmen, Brian Baker as Secretary and Bob Hamer as the Treasurer. The committee was made up of Jeff Cox, Ray Banham, Keith Cooper, Cliff Ashton (who was later to become League Chairman) and Ray Rowe; with Terry Mitchell later appointed as President.

OFFICIAL AND
CAPTAINS
BEFORE
THE MATCH

Captains and officials
line-up
for the
Western Leaguer
before the
January 31st 1981
match between
Odd Down
and
Torquay United
reserves.

The objectives set out by the new Association were:

1. To secure close co-operation between the officials concerned on all matters affecting the control of Western League matches.

2. To improve still further the relationship that exists between match officials and the Western League Management Committee.

3. To pass on information to members in respect of the Laws of the Game and other matters as deemed desirable.

The status and standing of referees has now moved on, but in the establishment of this Association, the seeds of those improvements were sown.

It was, indeed, both a time of great change in the game, and a pivotal season for the Western League. Old League hands, Reg Broom and Wilf Escott, who had both been an integral part of the League's survival over the years and would obviously be missed, bowed to the inevitability of age and resigned. During the preceding decade, the League had grown in strength, and was now able to face the challenges that were being presented with a stability that would ensure whatever was around the corner would not thwart the progress.

As Tom put it; *'The League and I differed now like chalk and cheese with the passing years; I had the experience of time and the frailness of age, whereas the League had the vitality of its revitalised body, and the enthusiasm of its ebullient Chairman. Midway through our 89th year together I was content indeed at the way that life was shaping up'.*

CHAPTER 16

Great Mills and beyond

It was a very busy season for the administration of the League with all that was going on in the game, but alongside that there were talks behind the scenes which were kept secret with an unusual amount of discretion. Such was the concealment, that even fellow members of the Management Committee were surprised to receive the following invitation on 19th April 1982, which read; *'Laurie McMenemy, Southampton FC Manager, in conjunction with Great Mills DIY Superstores, invite you to a press conference to announce a major sporting sponsorship award'.*

That was the first that most people had heard of the impending sponsorship, and at 11am on Tuesday 27th April at Ashton Court Mansion, Ashton Court Estate, Long Ashton, Bristol, Mike Robertshaw, the Managing Director of Great Mills, showed his enthusiasm, both for the game, and for his new association with the Western League.

Tom was there, of course, and described just what it was like that day when he wrote in the Centenary book; *'What a day that was, with Lawrie McMenemy giving a speech on the beauty of the non-league game, and happily signing autographs. Afterwards I talked to him about his son and he explained that although the lad loved the game he was not good enough to play at Football League level, but was still delighted to play amateur football with Romsey Town. Les was in his element, and although our guest of honour was, and still is, a tall man, our Chairman certainly was not dwarfed by him. Peter Bastin, the Great Mills Sales and Marketing Director, who went on to become a Vice-President of the League, outlined the proposal of the sponsorship, and explained to us all what the company expected from member clubs in return'.*

Articles appeared in all the national newspapers the following morning announcing that the League would benefit from a sponsorship deal worth £100,000 over five years, and in general the press seemed to like the suggestion that Great Mills were proposing to introduce a 'pound-for-a-goal' bonus scheme.

The deal had come about following a chance conversation in the Clandown clubhouse between Terry Gillard and Neil Montgomery. Terry, ever vigilant of a chance to help his club, asked Neil if his employers, Great Mills, might be interested in supplying a few match balls. This request, however, went further than he could ever have imagined as, back at work the following week, Neil broached the subject with his boss, Jim Dunning, who happened to be another ardent non-league follower. From those discussions, an appointment was made for Les Phillips to meet the directors of the company, and the idea of Great Mills becoming a part of the Western League family was born. Jim Dunning went on to become a very popular speaker at the Annual Convention.

The launch of the Great Mills Sponsorship April 1982.

The initial five-year deal continued for fourteen happy years, and endured during a time when both the League and the game changed dramatically. When times became tough later, with a deep recession biting throughout the country, it was the insistence of Mike Robertshaw, together with the persuasive tongue of Pete Bastin, that kept the association going when companies were withdrawing their sponsorship from other leagues.

The combination of the backing by Great Mills, and the work going on to produce a Pyramid System of Football, were two big leaps in the game locally. The idea of the Pyramid System was to give clubs the chance to progress though to English League level if they so wished, and, of course, if they had the resources that this would demand. Both initiatives combined to increase the push from the League to improve facilities at grounds, and with a view to that Stan Priddle was given the task of devising grading standards and delegated to carry out the inspections.

The national ground improvement scheme had raised a good deal of discussions within the League, and just a couple of months prior to the tremendous news about the new sponsors, officials had written to the FA suggesting that caution should be imposed before imposing too stringent a scheme. Stan was clearly aware of those concerns when devising the standards that the Western League clubs would be expected to work with.

News of the new Great Mills Western League structure increased the interest of clubs wishing to gain membership, and applications were received from Plymouth Argyle, Exeter City and Weymouth for their reserve teams to join. Those were provisionally accepted, with a rider that the teams had to play at their club stadium, and not at secondary pitches elsewhere. In accordance with the rules laid down by the FA, the side from Plymouth could enter directly into the Premier Division, because they were transferring from the Football Combination, while the other applicants were placed into the First Division along with late entries from Bristol City reserves and Newport County reserves.

By seasons end, however, some of the applications had hit the rocks. Exeter City withdrew late on, as did Torquay United reserves, who were fined £350 for their surprise exit by telephone. Newport County, however were tied up with the Welsh FA, who imposed a six-month delay; which put paid to their efforts to become the first club since Lovell's Athletic left, in 1939, to travel to England for Western League football.

At the end of what was to be the last season that the League would be unsponsored, Bideford Town beat near neighbours, Barnstaple Town to the title by three points. In contrast to the footballing fortunes in North Devon, Welton Rovers had known happier days, and were well rooted at the foot of the Premier Division, seven points below Mangotsfield United. Both clubs were relegated to be replaced by Shepton Mallet and Exmouth Town.

Third placed Bridgwater Town won the Goldliner Challenge Cup, while just one place below them, Clandown, received the Amateur Trophy in the last year that it was awarded. It was also the last year that the Merit Cup would be awarded to just one club, because the new sponsorship afforded a change of direction for the Trophy, with some new criteria which awarded the honour to one club in each division.

At the foot of the League, both Ottery St Mary and Ilminster Town were well adrift of the rest of the pack, and were forced to apply for re-election. It was, however, the first year that ground-grading came into its own, and Ilminster were refused re-admission, not because of their dreadful playing record, but rather because they had failed to implement improvements to their ground that had been instructed.

The newly established Association of Western League Referees mixed business with pleasure when they attended the Dawlish Annual Convention weekend on-mass. Those were men who could both work hard, and play hard - which played out during the weekend. At a meeting on the Saturday morning, after a rather heavy first night, one of the initial questionnaires that they were asked to fill in involved answering twenty questions in one minute. Now, that may appear to be quite a task normally, but the late night had made it even more challenging.

The initial instructions were; *'Before you commence this paper, be sure to read all the questions',* which was a simple enough instruction, but one that many of them failed to carry out as they were anxious to complete the task in the time allowed. They then went on to the initial question which was; *'what is your name,'* something that most managed to get right despite the lack of sleep. Most then continued to scribble away until they got to question twenty - which read, *'Only answer question one.'*

Of course, that was the whole point to the exercise; that an official should read and understand what is required of him *before* the game begins!

The new Great Mills Western League season opened in August 1982 amid lovely weather and great optimism. On the administration side, it was a time when Maurice Washer would step forward from his role as Assistant Secretary to hold the fort for Jack Veale who was suffering ill-health.

Maurice then picks up the story of what happened next; *'Les Phillips was an early visitor to my house, and when he called in and met my family, he asked me if there were any alterations to the methods employed by Jack, who was still processing the minutes using the Gestetner stencil method, which was messy with ink and hand rolling. I tested the water and suggested that instead we should acquire a photocopier and that we needed a separate phone line at home to ensure that clubs could contact at any time exclusively. A few days later he phoned to say that he would be getting a photo copier from a friend's company in Gloucester, and that I should go ahead and arrange the extra phone line. It was a wonderful start and I was amazed at the connections he had; realising that if you were clear on your grounds, Les was a great guy to work with'.*

While Maurice was fitting into the administration role, the 'get tough' stance that was being enforced on clubs over ground grading standards was progressing. Most clubs agreed that the new standards were desirable, and that they would initially especially affect those clubs in the First Division who were successful on the field because it was rumoured that they would not be allowed promotion if they fell short.

The clubs had known for some time about the grading, having been sent questionnaires on facilities, and had seen incoming clubs subjected to more stringent entry requirements. It was, therefore, generally agreed that the efforts being made to improve conditions by proving more toilet facilities and hard-standing could not be argued against, and that this was the way forward.

To that end, Stan Priddle, who was nicknamed by his Chairman as *'Mr Hardstanding',* spent many hours visiting grounds, then presenting the grading reports back to the Management Committee, and together with wife Mon, would make a special trip each time to inspect the toilet facilities available to both male and female supporters.

A newly formed Joint Liaison Committee met for the first time in December 1982 which had been created to bring together all non-league administrators and the FA. At that meeting it was revealed that, although everything appeared to be going well with the re-organisation of non-league football, caution was needed, and so it was no surprise when the FA announced in February that there were problems with the Contributory System which meant that the changes would not come into place until the 1984/85 season; a statement which most sceptics translated as being predicted with fingers firmly crossed behind their backs.

Jack Veale returned to full duties in March 1983, where he found a huge workload due to the increase in applications for membership from clubs who all had to be ground-graded prior to their applications being considered. Alongside Taunton Town and Minehead expressing an interest in returning from the Southern League, Avon Bradford, Backwell United, Shirehampton Sports and Warminster Town also applied.

In the event Avon Bradford 'blotted their copybook' by then withdrawing their application because they had been accepted into the Hellenic League, and Shirehampton Sports, who played at Penpole Lane, were also unable to take up a place after failing to meet the grading standards.

The potential increase in membership prompted a Special Meeting to be called, at which the possibility of splitting the First Division into east and west was again discussed; a move that was not favoured by the clubs. Those present also heard that Lew Webb had been elected as a Vice-President of the FA, a moment that Tom recalled, writing: '*I remember that the man with the big cigar just sat there, with an enigmatic smile on his face and accepted our applause, which was typical of Lew's style.*"

At the end of that first Great Mills season Bideford, once again, took the title, five points clear of Frome Town. The runners-up had experienced a superb year, winning the Merit Cup along with Chard Town in the First Division, and beating Plymouth Argyle reserves, 3-0, at Dawlish on the Saturday afternoon of the League Convention, to take the Great Mills Western League Challenge Cup. They had also picked-up the Somerset Premier Cup, and Frome's Manager, Steve D'Arcy, won the newly created 'Manager of the Year' Award.

Keynsham Town and Portway Bristol had experienced a difficult season and were relegated, to be replaced by Bristol Manor Farm and Mangotsfield. That was a real problem for Portway because they played on the same ground as Shirehampton, who had been refused admission to the League after failing ground-grading criteria, which put in doubt their chance of promotion, should playing performances allow, at any time in the future.

The AGM of 1983 was to be held at the Shrubbery Hotel, Ilminster, but for some reason the venue had double booked the night; which left Les Phillips outside the venue directing traffic toward the local Church Hall instead. Later in his speech, the Chairman said that because of the events of the evening, a quick prayer and a lesson from the New Testament, should precede the business of the meeting!

Mike Robertshaw, in his first year as President, saw the funny side of the situation, and later Peter Bastin summed up the twelve months of sponsorship in a very positive way, but emphasised how important co-operation between his Company and Member clubs was for it to continue. Following that, the constitution of the divisions for the coming season was announced, with both Minehead and Taunton Town welcomed back into membership from the Southern League, along with successful applicants, Backwell United and Warminster Town.

During the summer, Weston-super-Mare was, at last, on the move from their Langford Road ground after years of rumours and uncertainty. The move had first been proposed in 1979, and during the interim time the club had, on more than one occasion, looked to be about to go out of existence, but due to the diligence of a few die-hard members, and the intervention of the local council, they had survived.

Their re-location to Winterstoke Road, which was marked by the visit of Forest Green Rovers in the FA Trophy, initially afforded just very basic facilities, with post and rail boundaries. In a quest for a higher standard of football, and under the Chairmanship of Paul Bliss, however, eventually over £100,000 was invested to build a Clubhouse, and generally improve standards for players and supporters alike.

The 1983/84 season kicked-off with much optimism, and an early meeting in the League Cup between First Division, Odd Down, and high flying Premier Division side, Liskeard Athletic, was viewed by many as potentially a one-sided affair, but football is not a predictable sport. In the event, after 120 minutes of play the score was even, and eventually the under-dogs won through to the next round on a penalty shoot-out, 6-5. Predictably that result then heralding huge celebrations for the both the Odd Down and many non-partisan spectators, who inevitably cheer for the underdog on such occasions.

LISKEARD ATHLETIC FC

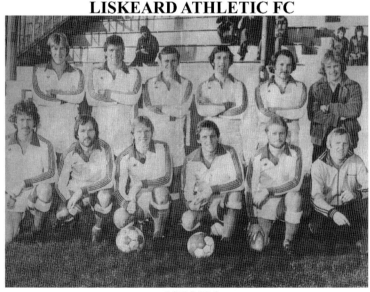

1983/84

The long and fiercely contested game left the players and officials extremely hungry, and as it was a Sunday with few places open on the long journey back, Liskeard Official's attempted to source some hot food. Eventually, the Odd Down Secretary, Mike 'Henry' Mancini, found a chip shop that was prepared to deliver a telephone order.

Mike knew the renowned sense of humour that accompanied Liskeard officials wherever they went, and when a Chinese gentleman appeared in the clubhouse doorway, complete with a large cardboard box filled to the brim with fish and chips, he was not disappointed. The visiting club Chairman, 'Ticker' Hick, and his unforgettable Secretary, Adrian 'Jethro' Wilton, both forgot the result on the field and put on a hilarious sketch to mark the event. For years to come they would always greet Mike with the enquiry 'how goes the Chinaman', a bond had been formed that would endure.

The expansion of the League to forty clubs in each division was short-lived when Bridport failed to fulfil their fourth fixture of the year at Weston-super-Mare because they were heavily in debt. They were in crisis, and when a £500 fine was then imposed for withdrawing from the League, together with an order to pay £100 for not fulfilling the fixture, and another £128 to compensate those clubs they had already played, their situation was made even worse. The October Management meeting had imposed the penalty, and insisted that the fines should be paid within seven days, but, of course, had it been within the grasp of the club to raise such funds within such a time-scale, they would not have withdrawn in the first place! In the end, it was sensibly agreed that an initial £128 would be accepted, together with a pledge to pay the rest at £100 a month; none of which helped to re-establish the club.

Nationally, progress was being made, and the Joint Liaison Committee rubber-stamped the proposal that four clubs could be promoted from feeder-leagues subject to suitable grading, and providing those clubs had ended the season in the top three of their respective leagues. That then gave the incentive to the more ambitious Western League clubs, but it also gave a clear message that excellence and expenditure on the field of play would have to be combined with improvements to their grounds, which included the installation of an approved floodlighting system.

One such ambitious club was Frome Town, who had a vocal support second to none with their own brand of wit that could match the Cornish humour. The flavour of that drollness was recalled by Tom in the Centenary book about a day he watched them take on Tiverton from the safety and warmth of his grandson's car parked conveniently near the pitch.

He wrote; *'From my vantage point I noticed that a vast number of Frome supporters were gathering behind the opponent's goal, an area they seemed to call their own. After the game a young man, by the name of Steve Jupp, recalled some of the goalkeepers that they had enjoyed a particularly special relationship with. Favourites have apparently been Richard Crabtree of Dawlish Town and Keith Nash of Chippenham Town, who apparently once shared his goalmouth with a hedgehog, and on another occasion, was showered with Mars bars because of his 'Gazza' style paunch. Steve maintained, however, that the undisputed number one was Phil Hewlett, a bearded school teacher from Saltash United who was a dead ringer for Rolf Harris and who would often be welcomed onto the field with a few bars of 'Tie me kangaroo down' along with haunting digeridoo noises! Not one to disappoint his audience, 'Rolf' or Phil, would then pretend to paint his goal-posts. On his last appearance at Badgers Hill, the start of the second-half was delayed while he was presented with a commemorative pot of paint and a brush'.*

Football is a game that is not confined to just those twenty-two players on the pitch, but a game that often brings out the entertainer in so many on the terraces as well. Colourful clubs and colourful characters has always been what the Western League is about!

At seasons end it truly was the Devon clubs who shone. Exmouth Town won the League Championship, two points clear of Saltash United, and their Manager, Bob Davis, picked up the Manager of the Year award. The Challenge Cup was won by Dawlish Town and the Merit Cup went to both Barnstaple Town and Larkhall Athletic.

In the First Division, Bristol City reserves strolled through the League and won promotion eight points clear of second placed Chard Town. They were replaced by Wellington, and with only one club relegated, Devizes Town could retain their place in the Premier Division. Tiverton Town were the bottom of the Division One and were re-elected, despite having only won five games all season. They were joined by Ilfracombe Town, Torrington Town and Westbury United, to make twenty-two clubs in each division, the largest number for ten years.

EXMOUTH FC OFFICIALS

Geoff Morris; Ray Clements and Rod Webber

At the Annual Convention weekend, there were various events scheduled including a new six-a-side competition, which was sponsored by Cuprinol thanks to Great Mills backing. In glorious sunshine on the Saturday morning a good crowd turned out to cheer on the teams, and were treated to some wonderful tactical displays, with one club, Clandown, entering a veteran's team that included young Terry Gillard, Clive Heron and the 'one-day-in-the-future' to be League Chairman, John Pool.

Eventually the final game between Chippenham Town and Saltash United was won by the Wiltshire team; a feat that was achieved by the huge number of corners that had been conceded against the Saltash player/manager, Peter Darke, to the cheers of the neutrals in the crowd who were backing the clear 'under-dogs'. Unfortunately, the competition only ran for another two years, with Saltash 'B' and Devizes Town the other names engraved on the Trophy.

Referee, Don Morgan, was always happy to take part in these competitions. He was very involved in the summer Champion of Champions six-a-side competition in Wiltshire each year. He experimented with a 'sin-bin' for errant players, but when the Wiltshire County FA learned of this he was fined £20 and banned from refereeing for a month. Ironically, in the season 2017/18, thirty-two leagues across the country will be trialing 'sin-bins' as part of a new FA initiative to try and improve respect toward referees. The Taunton Saturday Football League is one such league for the pilot scheme.

TAUNTON TESTIMONIAL MATCH

Ian Botham and Viv Richards with Tony Payne during his Testimonial Game.

186

Early in the 1984/85 season Chairman of Taunton Town, Tom Harris and his directors, put on a 'night of nights' at Wordsworth Drive to celebrate the service provided by long service players, Tony Payne and Graham Smith. Both Ian Botham and Viv Richards, who were themselves in the middle of their own Testimonial Year with Somerset Cricket Club, took to the pitch and kicked-off the celebrations, and when, with minutes to spare, 'Beefy' was awarded a penalty for a 'deliberate' foul in the area, his spot-kick made the final score-line 2-2, which heralded a party that will still be recalled by those present.

While Botham and Richards were at the height of their popularity nationally, Tony was himself a local celebrity who was moving towards the tremendous feat of 1,000 games for his club, scoring 264 goals in that wonderful loyal career. He and his wife Rose had two children who also played the game to the full, with daughter Julie turning out for Taunton Town Ladies, and after moving to Cornwall enjoying time with Truro City Ladies FC at a time when the women's game was still in its infancy.

Later in the season, Taunton were drawn away at 'in-form' Mangotsfield United in the League Cup; a game that resulted in a draw with the return leg set for two days later at Wordsworth Drive on the Monday evening. While that suited the players, there was one devoted Mangotsfield supporter who was desperate to see his side go through, but who was due on nights at the Post Office that evening. As devotees generally do, a 'logical' solution was found, and Ron decided that with the kick-off set for 7.45pm, he could still make it back to Bristol by around 10pm, just a little late for his shift. However, he did not consider what would happen if the game was again a draw and extra-time needed; which, of course, is exactly what happened.

Young Ron then had the dilemma of whether he would support his team to the end and phone in 'sick' or walk-away - a choice with an obvious answer for almost every true supporter, and the phone call was made. Despite his support, Taunton won the game 2-1, and after a couple of pints in the clubhouse and some fish and chips on the way back to the M5, he began to wonder how he was going to explain to his wife why he was returning home around midnight when he should still have been working.

There is a saying by Walter Scott that goes; '*O, what a tangled web we weave when first we practice to deceive',* which may have been something he was mulling around as he settled down in the rest area of the Brent Knoll service station with the intention of getting a few hours' sleep, before continuing the journey at 6am to arrive home in time to take his wife to work as usual, none the wiser about his night with the motorway lorry drivers.

As often in life, however, even the best laid plans sometimes do not work, and this was one of them! Although he soon fell asleep in his Fiat Estate, when he woke up he quickly grasped that something was not quite right. Apart from the fact that it was daylight, he noticed there were no lorries around, and looking at his watch found that it was 7am. Arriving home late, Ron was, of course, unable to do anything other than confess the situation to his wife, who promptly banned him from attending Cossham Street for many weeks for his night of madness.

Such is the passion and commitment of supporters at all levels of the game.

As the quest for improvement to the game continued, the FA contacted the League in November 1984 to inform them that any club taking part in FA Competitions would need to meet some stringent ground grading conditions, which included having functioning floodlights. In response, and at Chairman Les Phillips insistence, the Management Committee put forward the proposal that alongside this, all Premier Division clubs should be entering the FA Trophy, while First Division clubs would take part in the FA Vase, with the ground grading criteria adjusted accordingly. His proposal was ratified eventually at the Western League 1985 AGM, but was never put into practice because it was rejected by the FA; causing the Chairman as much annoyance as anything that happened during his time in office.

During the season, the exploits of two new clubs in the FA Vase became the talking point. Torrington made it to the last sixteen only to be drawn away from home as they had been in every previous game. Those away games were particularly significant to the older supporters from Torrington, because as legend had it, Sid Trickett, whose ashes had been buried under the top goal-mouth when he died, and who had been a prolific player for the club, once slotting in 11 times in an 18-0 win over Ilfracombe Town, was said to bide his time at the Calf Street end, and nod in any Torrington shot that looked to be going wide.

The first of those away games had been at Flight Refueling, Bournemouth, followed by games at Wellington, Clevedon Town, Shortwood United and Old Georgians from Bristol. Finally, there was an away game at Steyning in West Sussex on a cold February day. Torrington looked favourites to go through when they were a goal up with just four minutes to the final whistle. As in most Cup games, however, it's never over until the man in the middle blows the whistle, and two late goals stole the dream of an appearance at the Twin Towers for the Devon faithful, some of whom were convinced that Sid Trickett would have ensured a win for his favourites, should the game have been played at home.

Exmouth Town, however, did progress further, and captured the imagination of non-league fans by reaching the two-legged semi-final against Fleetwood. In the Final Qualifying Round, they had travelled to Hucknall Colliery, Nottingham, staying at a hotel in Leicester on-route, only to have the game called-off because the pitch was covered with snow. When the same journey was made again the following Saturday, they found strikingly similar conditions, but this time the snowfall had come in time for the home committee to work hard on the pitch all morning clearing it in time for kick-off. As fate would have it, the supporters coach from Devon broke down on their journey, and when the faithful eventually arrived at the ground they found their team a goal down. However, a late resurgence saw Exmouth progress with a 3-1 victory, taking them through to the Quarter Finals for a game that they again won, progressing into the Semi-Final for the first time in their history.

Cup fever spread through the town of Exmouth while the preparations were being made for the first of the two games which would determine who would reach Wembley. On the day of the match, the visitors, Farnham Town, were greeted by a loud and hostile crowd, and with the home side going two-goals up, all looked to be progressing well. In the second-half, however, a couple of bad defensive errors leveled the score-line, but with just five minutes to go, and to the joy of the assembled crowd, Exmouth scored again, increasing their chance of making it to the Final, with the need for just a draw in the return game. But it was not to be.

Despite many platitudes, Exmouth missed two open-goal opportunities in the first ten minutes of that crucial final game, and the last ten minutes saw the home side score twice; killing the dream that every non-league club holds at the start of each season.

In March, the Management Committee met with Member clubs with a proposal to increase the size of the League to forty-five clubs, which would allow the admission of Calne Town. The proposal was rejected, however, as it was generally felt that with both National, League and County competitions, the League programme was already heavy enough. There was also a lively discussion regarding the proposal to establish a feeder-league system saw some positive, but strong views on how the Western League could develop in the future, but a motion to divide the First Division into two geographical sections was, once again, defeated.

After the long and successful run in the FA Vase, Exmouth suffered a tremendous fixture back-log, and combined with the disappointment of not making it to Wembley, were unable to gain League honours again; ending the term in fourth place, twelve points adrift of Champions, Saltash United, and eight points below runners-up, Bideford Town.

The conditions at grounds had been a constant talking point throughout the season, and in December Portway Bristol had been informed that they would not be promoted regardless of playing strength because their ground was below the standard acceptable to the League. In the event, they went on to win the First Division under manager Dave Stone, by a point from Torrington Town, and became the first club to be held back due to ground grading requirements. With that decision, only Devizes Town were relegated, having won only two games all season and were nine points adrift of Shepton Mallet.

During the year Les Phillips had suffered ill-health and on the eve of the Annual Convention, held once again in Dawlish, he suffered another heart-attack. It was devastating news for all who knew him as over time he had always appeared to be an impermeable rock. With the constant dread of ill-health for the man who had revived the flagging League and taken it into the modern-day era, a midnight Management meeting agreed that changes were unavoidable. Stan Priddle then stepped up to take over the helm from Les, with the big man reversing roles and taking on the unfamiliar position of Vice-Chairman.

The AGM, which was held at Tiverton Town's ground in May, was a low-key affair given the news of the charismatic man's continuing ill-health. There was also another change in the administration of the League with Tony Barnes standing down as Registration Secretary; the post that was then taken-up by young Mike Crichton, a sports master from Minehead, who was also secretary of his local football club. Mike became one of the youngest officers in the history of the League, and continued in the role for many years, until a career move took him out of the area. In 2016 Mike became Chairman of the National Association of Physical Education, and was vocal during the last General Election regarding securing a positive outcome for PE in schools for all children and young people.

MIKE CHRICHTON

Registrations Secretary

Stan Priddle was about to experience the difficult task of running a progressive league that had been led by the prevailing personality of Les Phillips. It was a task that he would prove himself proficient to take on, and one that would rely on those around him being both reactive and proactive, in an era with many thought provoking initiatives being discussed at both local and national level.

CHAPTER 17

Illuminating times

With his old boss now in the unfamiliar role of 'number-two', Stan Priddle made sure that the way forward was clearly spelt out to Member clubs. From those directives, it was explicit that any club with ambitions would need to raise the money required to improve the standard at their grounds, as well as provide the cash to cover the talent needed on the pitch to progress and to cover day-to-day expenses.

Of course, floodlighting was the biggest of the essential requirements, and Tony Barnes continued to work on the excellent scheme that he had been instrumental in introducing to all the League clubs. The success was evident when, just prior to the season, he announced that Exmouth Town, Bristol Manor Farm, Ottery St Mary, Tiverton Town and Radstock Town, had all taken up the new deal offered by Thorn-EMI, and that everything was in place for them to switch-on in time for the dark evenings of the new season.

Interest in the scheme then gained momentum, and by October 1985, Dawlish Town, Mangotsfield United, Melksham Town, Taunton Town, Weston-Super-Mare, Chippenham Town, Keynsham Town, Truro City and Teignmouth Rugby, were all present to hear a presentation given by Tommy Thomas about the Thorn-EMI scheme. Rod Webber presented a report on the scheme, warning clubs present that groundwork had proved expensive for his club. Exmouth had not taken the advice of Tony Barnes to dig the stanchion holes by hand themselves, and the total cost had been £11,000 for an eight pole, twenty-four lamp installations; not an inconsiderable amount of money, and an amount that some considered incredibly hard to find.

KEYNSHAM TOWN FC

1985/86

Despite the initial fears and an increase in the basic cost of the scheme from £7,000 to £8,000 a few months later, the more ambitious Great Mills clubs were not deterred, and within a year voted in favour of making floodlighting a compulsory condition for membership of the Premier Division; the first Feeder League in the Country to do so.

It was not, however, just the problem of financing the lights, as Wellington soon found. Despite considerable efforts to raise the money needed for the project, they shared their ground with the cricket club, and had been given Special Dispensation when they joined the League to play their early matches away from home, until the cricket season closed. It meant that at the end of each football season the stanchions needed to be removed for the summer game; a practical problem that caused a good deal of discussion.

Undeterred by what some would have seen as an insurmountable problem, the plucky Wellington Committee members came up with a solution that involved erecting portable stanchions on the far side of the ground, which attracted even more problems to solve. The sheer weight of those structures made it almost impossible for easy removal and storage, and so the answer was to design them in such a way that a crane could lift them up and away at the end of the season, and that the electrical system be put in with an ease of disconnection. As if that was not enough, one more piece of the jigsaw still had to be found.

A member of the club's committee was an engineer, and he designed a specially constructed metal tray that could be placed over the holes, to lie flush with the surface, giving room for artificial turf to be place on top to disguise the offending squares. Along with that there was also the difficulty of allowing access in wet conditions when the crane needed to transverse the pitch; a problem that was overcome by boards being placed in the vehicles pathway thus avoiding heavy tire tracks, and the possibility of the vehicle getting bogged down.

Wellington proved both that even the toughest of tasks can be overcome with ingenuity, and that where there is a will there truly is a way. Long-serving Chairman, Selwyn Aspin and Secretary, Tony Brown, were rightfully very proud when the lights were switched on for the first time, after winning their fight against the odds.

Despite many clubs stretching themselves in the quest for ground improvements and progress, the season was one of financial problems for some, but Clevedon Town, who had long been rumoured to be on the brink of bankruptcy due to an accumulation of debt, seemed to be overcoming their problems with the arrival of a new Chairman at the end of November. Brian Baker was a qualified FA coach who held the distinction of being the youngest player ever to turn-out for the clubs first team at 14 years old. He was full of confidence that he could take Clevedon forward, and announced that his eventual ambition was to take them into the Southern League. Although, far into the future that ambition would be achieved, Brian and his fellow directors had a lot of troubled water to tread before they could progress toward their ambition.

While the immediate future was not in doubt for the 'Seasiders', Shepton Mallet were not in such a fortunate position, with the taxman camped out at the club, and in no mood to accept a compromise. In January 1986, they were forced to the edge of extinction when an order was issued for £18,000 of tax on expenses paid to players. The action caused many club treasurers to re-assess their own books, with the Inland Revenue officers considering figures for the past six years. In the light of those problems, and with no way to disprove the allegations, Shepton Mallet withdrew membership at the end of the season after completing all their fixtures.

The season ended late, and in a cathartic meeting during the game between Chard Town and Bristol Manor Farm, Tom was able to summarise the view of a typical old non-league supporter when he wrote of the Chard Town Secretary; *'Colin is one of those people who enjoy a good yarn, and he waxed lyrical about football in the 1960s which, he said, was more fun than today. He firmly believed that life in the Great Mills League was all about getting results with defences having to tighten up with extra men and goals at a premium. While in full flow, Colin's chairman, Brian Beer, joined us in the car and with a glint in his eye spoke enthusiastically about the time prior to Colin joining the club in 1962 as the best he had ever known. My newly found friend came back into his own, however, when his Chairman left'.*

'He then spoke of the best game he had ever watched, which was a 10-7 win in the Somerset Senior League against Winscombe in 1964/65, where Chard had struggled to field a team and had regular goalkeeper, Chris Loader, leading the attack and smashing in six goals. He continued, that then there was the worst game, a 2-0 drubbing at Bridgwater in the first match for over three months after the big freeze of 1963, when the home-side fielded their First team against a scratch Chard side. The most outstanding player he had ever seen was Dennis Nicholls, a local lad who was a top notch mid-field player. And then he continued with a description of the best moment of skill that was performed in 1971 by a Frenchman, Pierre Guivarch, who could kill a ball on his instep, and as the opposing full-back rushed towards him, flick it over his head… and so it went on.'

'Just before we parted, he said that there is a saying that goes, it is the downs that make the ups so good, so remember that the next time you are bitterly cold, your side has just lost heavily, and you face a 100 mile plus journey home'. Tom finished the memory by honestly stating that; *'I didn't have the heart to tell him that those days were gone for me'.* But it just about sums up football as we live it today, and have lived it in the past.

The end of the 1985/86 season saw Exmouth lift the title for the second time, just a point clear of Liskeard Athletic, with third placed Bideford Town seven points adrift. Their manager, Bob Davis, also won Manager of the Year; a successful season by anyone's standards, but one that Chairman, Rod Webber, could also attribute to another reason. It seemed that Rod had broken one of the golden rules of football - never, never, book a holiday during the football season - a cardinal sin that was compounded by the fact that he was due to go away on the day of a home League game that was vital to win, to keep the Cornish challenge at bay.

As almost everyone who is reading this book will know, it is not just the players on the pitch that determine the outcome of a game, or even the officials. It is also, of course, the position you stand on the terraces, that lucky pair of pants you have worn since the good run of results began, the routine that is performed every Saturday without fail…and so on, and so on.

With that in mind, Rod was unsure of what effect his absence would have. Aware of how heavy this was weighing on his mind, Rod's wife, Heather, searched for a solution to the dilemma with a trip to a local department store, from where she returned with a tailor's dummy which she dressed in the Chairman's clothes, right down to a pair of his lucky underpants. On the day of the game, with the couple in constant contact with the club from a far-off beach, the dummy was placed, first on the terraces, and then in the clubhouse against the bar, with a pint of Rod's favourite tipple in front of him. It did the trick and the points were safely banked, with the League title still firmly in sight.

The 1986 AGM was held at Dawlish on the Saturday morning of the League Convention, where the bleary-eyed representatives from the clubs were told that the composition of the League for the coming season would not be concluded until the FA had considered an appeal from Portway-Bristol against the decision not to allow them promotion, due to their shortfall in ground grading. Eventually the appeal was dismissed, which strengthened the hand of the League on ground standards. While that decision was not known until later, the withdrawal of Shepton Mallet had allowed space for one new club into the League, and at the second time of applying, Calne Town were successful over fellow applicants, Avon Bradford, Bemerton Athletic and Braunton.

There was a change in the administration of the League with Don Milverton stepping down as Treasurer, with his place taken-up by the first woman to serve on the Management Committee, Joan Ellis, the Secretary of Taunton Town. Joan stayed in the position for many years, and proved herself a most able, intelligent, and efficient member of the administration. Her work in arranging the Annual Conventions' was above and beyond the call of duty.

JOAN ELLIS

League Treasurer

Jack Veale also stood down, retiring as Hon. Secretary after 35 years of unbroken service. In all, Jack had completed 64 years of active involvement with football, and was awarded the FA Long Service Medal in recognition of the fact just a year later, in March 1987, when an FA Representative XI played at Wordsworth Drive in his honour. Taking over the post permanently from Jack was Maurice Washer, who had begun his career in football as a referee and had already served an apprenticeship as Assistant Secretary to Jack, as well as Acting Secretary when he was ill, and Referees Appointment Secretary.

The summer is generally a quiet time for the League Committee members, but a special meeting was called on 23rd July 1986 to discuss the proposed move by Bristol Rovers to Twerton Park, because they had to leave their Eastville ground. This meant that Bath City reserves would not be able to play Western League games on their own ground, and they were proposing to move instead to Hambrook Park. To facilitate the club, the Committee agreed to the move with certain stipulations. Although they were to begin the season there, the arrangement did not last, and the reserves moved on to Radstock Town, which suited all concerned perfectly.

Overall, the clubs involved in Pyramid League's were about to discover that, from the Alliance down, there was to be an increasing demand on them to provide even better facilities at their grounds. In fact, throughout the 1986/87 season the Committee worked hard to make sure that its policies on the matter were consistent, and that there were sufficient clear rules to preclude any further appeals to the FA over a refusal to promote a club due to shortcomings in their facilities.

Initially it involved agreeing to inspect all clubs during the season to make it clear where their grounds were in relation to compliance to the new standards. Where there was a need for minor improvements, it was agreed that a time limit would be set for those to be carried out. However, in the event of major work, it was proposed, and accepted, that the Committee and club would liaise to approve a fixed time-table for the alterations to be carried out. To further avoid misunderstanding, it was also agreed that all clubs would enter a written agreement to adhere to any time-table set.

The most controversial proposals, which was put to Member clubs, was the insistence that a club without floodlights would not be promoted into the Premier Division; a proposal that was voted through to be actioned from the 1988/89 season.

On the playing front, newcomers, Calne Town found the fresh challenge of Great Mills football difficult to adapt to. They had to wait 194 minutes before scoring their first goal, thanks to Colin Voulters, and at half-time went into the break ahead of their visitors, Swanage Town and Herston. Their lead, however, was short-lived, with a prolific second-half producing just one additional goal for them and six for their opponents. Their first taste of success came on 9th September1986 at Westbury, but they then had to wait a further five weeks to record their first win at Bremhill Lane, beating Elmore, 2-0.

With an active young committee, the club then settled well into the League, and achieved the accolade of Best Conducted Club in their very first year. They were also active in fund raising, and by 1988 the club switched on their new floodlights for the first time.

In the FA Vase, it was Dawlish Town who seemed to promise much, with the help of a young player, Kevin Smith, who had arrived at their Sandy Lane ground during the close season. Kevin was to become a firm favourite with the home crowd, due to both his own self-confidence, and his scoring ability. One of the first stories demonstrating his ability to impact on the club was captured in the local paper, the Dawlish Gazette, under the headline of 'Cheeky Chappie's Sheer Poetry Hat-Trick' after a local reporter had interviewed him as he stood on the pitch at Wordsworth Drive, Taunton, for a game on 11th October 1986.

It was a game that saw the home-side as favourites to win, but the reporter recalled; *'Forty-five minutes before kick-off last Saturday, the new 'cheeky chappie' of Dawlish football, Kevin Smith, strolled across the Taunton pitch, took a long look at his surroundings, and playfully suggested that he would score three goals in the match. Invited to pick which end he would inflict the damage upon, he indicated the far end where the lofty ambition of a row of popular trees may well have had their secret attraction. Smith refrained from choosing the timing of his goals after the manner of the famous heavyweight boxer, Cassius Clay, who used to predict his round of victories, but nonetheless fulfilled his promise three minutes from time with his own impression of a floating butterfly dance and bee-sting when he completed his hat-trick at the 'poplar' end. Sheer poetry at the aptly named Wordsworth Drive'.*

His scoring prowess had already been evident in the clubs Extra-Preliminary Round victory in extra-time over Ilfracombe Town, 5-2. Further victories over Tiverton Town, Yate Town, and St Blazey, saw Smith score in each match, leading to a game against Hungerford Town; and a victory that many hailed as Dawlish's finest, with goalkeeper Richard Crabtree grabbing the headlines from Smith, but with each player coming out as a hero.

The Fourth-Round tie then produced another away game, this time at Old Georgians, with the Devon side in control early on, 2-0 up, but two goals in a minute for the home side soon put the result in doubt. Once again, Smith came to the rescue with a sensational 30-yard strike, with seconds to go. The result was then followed by a very competitive game in the fifth round against Mangotsfield United, which was decided just two minutes from the end of extra-time with an Adie Harris goal, enabling Dawlish to progress through to the Quarter-Finals of the competition for the first time in their history.

The reward for their great run of results was a trip to play Emley AFC on the Yorkshire Moors. The Northern club had a much-fancied striker themselves, John Francis, who was later to join Sheffield United, and was then transferred to Burnley. By half-time Dawlish were three goals down, and without the scoring prowess of Smith, who had been suspended for a series of bookings, mainly for dissent, the manager, Adrian Chown's message to his players was 'death or glory'. Two goals by Andy Best then almost forced extra-time, but it was not to be, and the dream was shattered for another year.

As the season progressed, the football administrators were continuing to progress the specifications for improvement of facilities at grounds, and a circular was sent to all clubs in March 1987 warning that, even with new standards set, those may not be good enough to allow progress into the Southern League, should playing strength allow for an application to be lodged. Although the Pyramid of Football had been formed to technically give clubs a chance to progress, the quest for improving standards was having the effect of scattering that progress with expensive obstacles.

The question of refereeing performances and recruitment was also a subject that was demanding many hours of debate and discussion, and to that end, in the unlikely setting of Cliff Ashton's dining room, Stan Priddle sat down with Maurice Washer and Joan Ellis to discuss the subject with their counterparts from the Referee's Association, Keith Cooper, Bill Summerhayes, and, of course, the host for the night, Cliff Ashton. By the end of the evening an assessment scheme had been agreed, that would be the basis for the scheme that exists today, which has resulted in all referees being marked methodically. Later the FA took the discussions to another level by making the position of the man in the middle both a professional career, and one that encourages recruitment.

Once again, the season had seen a diversity of playing strengths, with Saltash United strolling through the League, losing only three games, and ending the term sixteen points clear of second-placed Exmouth Town. The Cornish club also won the League Cup, and their Manager, Peter Darke, picked up the Manager of the Year Award. Runners-up, Exmouth Town, and Elmore jointly won the Merit Award.

Although both Minehead and Chard Town were initially relegated from the Premier Division, only Swanage were promoted following the resignation of both Wimborne Town and Portway Bristol. A subsequent appeal to the FA by Minehead Town against relegation resulted them in retaining their Premier Division status.

The League Convention weekend saw a change from the Langstone Cliff Hotel to the Narracott Grand Hotel at Woolacombe Bay in North Devon, because the demand for rooms had outgrown Geoff Rogers Hotel; such was the popularity of the Great Mills League. The Narracott was in the hands of the receivers, but the staff did themselves and the League proud, with the finest spread of food many had ever seen.

The sun shone, and the small village of Woolacombe resounded to the laughter of the hard-working men and women of West Country football; all enjoying their 'end of year' treat to the full. Pitch and Putt challenges, walks along the vast beach, a Sunday Market, and the funny hats worn by the 'Cornish Liberation Army' of Liskeard Athletic, made the whole occasion a total success.

On the Saturday morning Tony Salvidge gave a talk on his new computerised fixtures programme, and at the Grand Dinner in the evening both Keith Cooper and Paul Durkin were congratulated on their promotion to the Football League. There were also some very reassuring and uplifting speeches from the Great Mills representatives.

On a melancholy note, Tom wrote of the weekend; '*I remember sitting in the Atlantic Lounge of the hotel with a very frail looking Jack Veale reminiscing about the 'old days' of our League. With a combined age of 184 years, we may have looked over the hill to the youngsters around us, but I doubt that they would ever know the League as well as we did. That was to be my last meeting with Jack, who sadly died just before Christmas that year'*.

As the summer progressed, there was a lot of work to do behind the scenes, both at clubs and on the administration side, and in September 1987, Paul Britton produced a paper proposing the setting-up of a Combination League for the reserve teams of existing member clubs. The idea was well received, and work then went on to enable the initiative to get off the ground for the start of the 1988/89 season.

Teams entered from Tiverton Town, who were Champions that first year, Taunton Town, Exmouth Town, Minehead, Barnstaple Town, Dawlish Town, Heavitree United, Torrington Town, Wellington and Elmore. A knock-out Cup and Subsidiary Competition were also run, with Minehead and Heavitree United putting their names on those new trophies.

On the refereeing front, the post of Referees Appointments Secretary, which Maurice Washer had filled since the resignation of Alan Wallace, was taken over by Torquay based referee, Lester Shapter, who accepted the appointment despite his busy schedule in the middle of the Football League. The League also lost two experienced referees when Ken Bissex was forced to resign due to injury, in December 1987, and Don Welch emigrated to America. With those two characters gone the cry of 'don't, me babbee', was not heard quite as often on the field to quell the actions of a strapping defender's intent on sliding tackles!

There was another departure when Maurice Down, who like his grandfather before him was Chairman of Welton Rovers, and a valuable member of the Management Committee, decided to emigrate to Canada. He went on to organise youth matches for his adopted country and never fails to visit West Clewes on his frequent journeys home to see friends and family.

It was, indeed, a time for change on the Great Mills League Management Committee, but change sometimes also heralds progress, and from Maurice Washer's office, that was exactly what was happening. Earlier we wrote of the innovative ways that people would communicate scores in the early days of the League, and progress on this front could not have been more pronounced.

On a Saturday at ten past five, the Press Association phoned Maurice for the results that were then sent nation-wide, and even appeared throughout the world in popular UK based newspapers on the Sunday morning. His telephone was, in fact, red-hot for an hour or so with local radio stations, HTV and other local media all wanting the results. By 5.30pm the Secretary would have up-to-date League Tables ready in time for the important Sunday Independent Newspaper, a media used by most non-league fans throughout the West Country. Following that he would then begin to prepare the 135 bulletins to post at Temple Meads ensuring that they would be delivered by First Class post on Monday morning. Although communications today have made this hectic schedule much more stream-lined, it still takes manual effort and dedication to ensure that the information channel works efficiently; albeit with no need to feed the Peasedown pigeons before dispensing score-lines!

As the season was coming to an end, the news that every non-league fan in the West was dreading. It was announced that Les Phillips had died. The news of anyone's death is a shock, but it was even more difficult to accept when the person was such a larger than life personality. The following League meeting was a very somber affair with Stan Priddle paying tribute to his old boss and a letter of commiseration sent to Jane Phillips and her family on behalf of the footballing family of the Western League. In his memory, it was agreed that the League Cup would be re-named as the Les Phillips Challenge Cup; even that seeming inadequate as a memorial.

In the next match-day programme at Ilfracombe, Ron Rose wrote a tribute to the man who had begun his footballing career with them, saying; '*The words of wisdom and voice of integrity, from that man of strong principals, will never be heard again. The father of the Great Mills League, Mr Les Phillips, passed away on Easter Monday, losing his long battle with the heart ailment that caused him concern for many years. For those of us who knew him, his humorous jokes, his quick wit, and his captivating orations will be forever missed. We at Ilfracombe are proud of the fact that Les began his long football administration here at Marlborough Park, before becoming the League's youngest ever Chairman. We always felt honoured when, in terms of endearment, he mentioned Ilfracombe Town Football Club at League meetings. The man who gave 32 years of loyal and respectful serviced to the West of England's Premier League, was brought back to his native West Downe, where his funeral took place last Saturday. We express our deepest sympathy to his wife and family – RIP'.*

Later, at the Memorial Service at Wimborne Minster, a packed congregation learned that Les not only performed miracles for the League, but also used his considerable talents for the good of many organisations in the area. A moving address by Ken (Digger) Morris JP, paid tribute to the work that Les had contributed to the Scout movement, his involvement with the church, and his activities in raising money for community projects.

In memory of Les, the League donated £3,120 that had been given by the clubs, which went to Holt Village Church and the Victoria Hospital in Wimborne.

At seasons end it was announced that Mangotsfield United had been the first of the Great Mills League clubs to formally apply for promotion to the Southern League under the new system in March 1988, but that their eventual third position behind Champions, Liskeard Athletic by eight points, had precluded them from being in the mix.

Later a Joint Liaison Committee was told that fourteen clubs had applied for the four places available in the Southern League, and that in the future an application would only be considered through the parent League. A further innocent enough sounding statement was that from 1992, ALL members of the Southern League would be subject to more stringent ground grading criteria. A dictum that would, once again, in future years put a strain on clubs who wished to progress in the ever-changing Pyramid system.

Bristol City reserves resigned from the Premier Division after the end of the season, and were fined £500 for their late withdrawal. Because of that, a Special Meeting was called a week prior to the AGM, which agreed that both Melksham Town and Clandown should be relegated, and Welton Rovers and Chard Town promoted, allowing 21 clubs in each division.

It was especially hard on Melksham, who had been neck-and-neck with neighbours, Chippenham Town, at the foot of the table with two games to play, and with both fighting to avoid the second relegation place. The penultimate game, however, saw the club at Ashton Gate for a mid-week game when the City Manager, Joe Jordan, decided to put out seven first-team players, resulting in a defeat, 6-0, and the inevitable relegation on goal-difference. Ironically, they won their final game to runners-up, Saltash United, while Chippenham lost the same day to Champions, Liskeard Athletic.

It certainly was a season for Cornwall to celebrate, and although Saltash United were a clear eight points behind their neighbours, they picked up both the Challenge Cup, Premier Division Merit award, and the Manager of the Year award. In the First Division, the Merit Cup was shared between Yeovil reserves and Larkhall Athletic, with the latter club stamping their name on the trophy for the fourth time.

The sun shone, once again, at Woolacombe for the League Convention weekend, and the large contingent of the Liskeard committee and supporters (some nineteen people) celebrated their achievement, the like of which had seldom been seen before. The revelries went on, not just in the wee hours of the morning, but for some, until the sun came-up over the golden sands of Woolacombe Bay as they strolled along the beach waiting for breakfast to be served.

The death of Les Phillips had ended an era, but he had left the League in a very strong position, with the continued sponsorship of Great Mills (Retail) Ltd. The new demands on the clubs that were being imposed from the top to the bottom of the Pyramid of Football, had seen many 'step up' to the challenge, with the introduction of some ingenious ways to raise new funds and facilitate ground improvements. Technically, the League no longer had the problem of other leagues attempting to 'poach' the more viable Western League clubs, which had, at one stage, sapped its strength and threatened the future.

There was also good news nationally, with low unemployment comparatively prosperous, and a housing boom in full flow. Many of the clubs were grasping the need to engage local communities in their improvement plans, with the commercial involvement of businesses an integral part of the schemes.

In general, non-league football in the West looked to be in good shape, and appeared well placed to continue into the 96th year of the Western Football League with optimism.

CHAPTER 18

Changing times

At the start of the 1988/89 season Tom wrote; *'On a warm September evening in 1988 I was sitting in my grandson's car waiting for the kick-off at Radstock Town when I began to wonder what I had to look forward to; except, of course, my message from the Queen, which was still four long years away. As you get older, the days seem endless because there is so little to occupy your time when the mind is still agile but the body frail. Looking around I could still see the faces of the miners who, in my earlier days with the League, had put up such physical performances on the pitch straight after their days' toil down the pits'.*

He continued; *'During the game a lad I had known for years, Brian Moore, introduced me to the Chairman of the visiting team, Doug Webb, and his wife, Sandie. They told me of all the plans that Les Phillips had in mind for the League Centenary celebrations that he would now so sadly miss. Les had suggested that the League could charter 'The Black Watch' cruise ship for the weekend, he had even provisionally booked it and was awaiting a quote. In opposition to this, Stan Priddle argued that the dining room would not be large enough to take the numbers at one sitting. Les lost the argument. Sandie then asked if I would be interested in reliving my time with the League by putting my memories down in the form of a Centenary book. At first the task seemed enormous as a life-time of memories are not so readily recalled. I was, however, persuaded by their enthusiasm for the project, and my doubts were soon overtaken by some wonderful journeys into the past'.*

And that is how the whole project began. A project that is now continuing to record 125 years of Western League football history; a League that lives on and is still flourishing way beyond the mortal life of its participants and supporters.

Despite conditions being favourable, the season did not get off to a totally smooth start, as the new agreement requiring all members of the Premier Division to have floodlights, was causing quite a few problems. Nevertheless, by the time the lights were needed, both Barnstaple Town and Torrington had completed their work ready to switch-on.

The need to get illuminated caused quite a problem at Welton Rovers who were in the process of constructing a new clubhouse which was, innovatively, being built around and over the existing functioning building. With the new directive, however, the process had to slow down so that funds were available for floodlights; a decision that caused their Committee all sorts of heartache and debate.

There always seemed to be a good number of clubs progressing through in the national Competitions, and it was to be Clevedon's year in the FA Vase, with the Twin Towers beckoning. Prior to the Quarter Finals they beat Southern League Corinthians at Teignmouth Road, 2-1, which brought back memories of the 1950s when the 'Seasiders' had been prolific in the FA Amateur Cup. In those days' huge crowds watched as they beat teams such as Wimbledon, Wealdstone and Methyr, whereas a crowd of just 360 watched that day.

Despite putting up a good display against Sudbury Town in the following round on 27th February 1989, Clevedon lost by two first half goals. Although it was as far as they went, it was good for both the League, and their able Managers, Dave Stone and Mike Williams, who had done so well under difficult circumstances during their time with Portway Bristol.

In the newly named, Les Phillips Challenge Cup, newcomers Bridport, reached the semi-final beating Mangotsfield United, Calne Town and Swanage and Herston in the first three rounds. Their luck ran-out, however, against the eventual winners, Exmouth Town, when they went down, 4-0, at Southern Road.

Exmouth were having an amazing season again, and at one stage looked to be odds-on for the Championship, but were pipped for the honours by Saltash, who won on a goal-difference of +55 compared to the +36 achieved by the Devon club. Saltash had, however, achieved that by notching up ten games drawn, when Exmouth had only four draws; a fact that did not escape comment. Both of those clubs were way ahead of the third and fourth clubs, Taunton Town and Liskeard Athletic

Ironically, that was the last year that a title would be decided by holding on for a single point for a draw when, at the 1989 AGM, it was agreed by Member clubs that the three points for a win system would be re-introduced for the first time since the 1979/80 season; a system that was said to encourage a more dynamic style of play that rewarded teams who competed to win the game outright.

In Division Two, Larkhall came out on top, a point clear of the 'rising stars' of Tiverton Town, but were denied promotion due to a lack of floodlighting and facilities. It was especially disappointing for their manager, Dave King, who had been with the club for many years and had put together a good squad on a shoestring budget.

Their situation was opposite to that of Tiverton Town, whose promotion was due in part to the backing of several 'men with money'. Minehead, did not escape the drop this time. Their relegation to Division Two was especially sad for Noland Elson, Jim Walder, Aubrey Copp and Les Axon, who had served the club for more years than they would wish to remember, and who said that they could still hear the crowds' cheers in those days when they were on top of their game playing in the Southern League.

Westbury was presented with their second award since joining the League at the Convention Weekend, which was held at Woolacombe Bay, once again, when they picked up the Merit Cup alongside Plymouth Argyle reserves, who were also awarded the Sportsmanship Trophy.

The Merit Award was well deserved for the Westbury club who had so many long-term dedicated voluntary members. Long serving Secretary, Ernie Barber, used to carry the kit for the club as a seven-year-old, and began his administrative career back in 1962 after he was forced to give up his place on the pitch due to injury. Like many other Western League clubs, Westbury also had a strong family tradition, with Wilf Alford, who played for them prior to the war before joining Portsmouth, providing them with the services of both his sons, and two grandsons, Phil and Geoff Back. Then there was, of course, also the well-known characters, Eli Manasseh and long serving Treasurer, Gordon Pearce.

The Narracott Grand Hotel was still in the hands of the Official Receiver, but everyone had fond memories of the previous Convention Weekend and a huge number of people turned up for the Presentation Dinner and Dance. Things had, however, taken a turn for the worse. Unbeknown to any of the guests, the chef had apparently walked out, with almost 400 guests about to turn up, just hours before the evening four-course meal was due to be served, and they were already short-staffed. It was just as well that the family of the Great Mills Western League have such a jolly time in their one weekend together, or it could so easily have been worse.

The service was not only slow on some tables, but non-existent and some of the guests resorted to sending someone down to the local fish and chip shop for sustenance. Others were kept amused by officials of fellow clubs who had already been fed supplying them with their left-overs, in jest of course, or taking the matters into their own hands and acting as waiters to serve the cheese course. Eventually, Alan Sampson raised his white handkerchief in surrender, and Terry Gillard summed up many people's thoughts when he remarked afterwards that it was probably the funniest evening he had ever experienced!

While the men and women of the League made the best of what could have been a disastrous situation, Clevedon Town, who had been in all sorts of financial problems during the season, were on the verge of closing their doors for good when at the eleventh hour, they signed a deal to sell their ground for development. The situation had, in fact, been so desperate that in July 1989, the Directors of the club lodged a petition for liquidation at Companies House.

The intervention of Ideal Homes, a division of the Trafalgar Housing Group, had secured them a very rosy future indeed. It had been made possible by the devotion of the late Bill Hand, way back in the 1930s, when he mortgaged his home to keep the club alive, and provided money for the purchase of Teignmouth Road.

It was, indeed, the line of the Hand family that had kept the club afloat throughout the years. Great grandfather Herbie Hand, had started his career with St George before moving to the Black Arabs (later to become Bristol Rovers) and then on to Clevedon, began the dynasty. Then along came Bill who became Secretary, and with his wife Rose and young son, ensured all match-day areas were serviced. Then there was Doug, who was President when the ground was sold, and must have had mixed feelings after their years of family devotion.

With the last decade of the Nineteen Hundred's about to arrive, nationally the Government was boasting that the country had never had it so good; a sentiment last put to the population back in the 1950s. The reality of the situation, however, was that the economy was in trouble. House prices were falling with some being discounted by up to 20%; dock-workers had been on strike; the GDP was 1.7%, the lowest since 1981, and some economic experts were talking about a second recession. Few realised it, but times were about to change

During the previous season, a tragedy had struck Liskeard Athletic when, in January 1989, one of their popular local players, Neil Moxam, had died in a tragic accident at work. He was just 24 years of age. In his memory, the club dedicated a Trophy, which was to be played for throughout the Premier Division on a 'Round-Robin' basis, and which began its round at the start of the 1989/90 season at Liskeard.

It then stayed with the club until Plymouth Argyle reserves beat them, and then ironically, remained in the Trophy cabinet at Home Park until Liskeard then won the return fixture. It was a touching tribute to a young lad who had loved football, and would continue to circulate for many years to come. Thanks for the tribute was conveyed to the League by their President, Ted Brown, who had just been made a Life Member for his services to football.

It was to be a time of change on the Western League Committee, when Rod Webber took up the post of Vice-Chairman from Tony Barnes, who was moving on for personal reasons. When Tony attended his last Committee Meeting in April 1990 he expressed his thanks and appreciation for the support that he had enjoyed in his many years of association with the League. Chairman, Stan Priddle, in turn paid tribute to the unstinting loyalty and work that Tony had provided, especially in the construction of floodlighting for the clubs, and reiterated just how much he would be missed for his vast experience and opinion.

Competition for the Premier Division title was close all year, with Taunton Town, Liskeard Athletic and Mangotsfield United all in the frame, and it was not until an evening game at Lux Park, on 5th May, that the position became clear, when Liskeard entertained Exmouth Town knowing that they had to win both that game and the final one of the season to depose Taunton Town from top spot.

A large crowd from throughout the West boosted the numbers at that game, and saw Liskeard miss a penalty with the score-line at one apiece, making the Western League Championship mathematically out of their grasp. Despite going on to beat Paulton Rovers 4-0, they had to settle for runners-up spot. Taunton Town lifted their first Championship title in 21 years and manager, Keith Bowker, was awarded 'Manager of the Year'.

Western League Champions

A happy Convention weekend saw the Western League family take over Woolacombe, once again, but this time it was the Woolacombe Bay Hotel who played host. The events that followed are best told by Tom, who wrote; *'The Friday evening buffet was tremendous and we all slept heartily that night and enjoyed the warmth of the May sunshine the next morning. John Hore and his wife decided to make their annual pilgrimage across the hills to Mill Road for the Cup Final at Barnstaple, and actually arrived in time for the kick-off; a game that was won by Elmore over Ilfracombe Town'.*

As usual, everyone then hurried back to the hotel to don their Sunday best for the highlight of the year, the Presentation Dinner, which was being held at the Mary Rose Centre overlooking Woolacombe Bay. The unlucky ones travelled by car for the event, whereas our top-table guest's chose to take the hotel's open-top bus, which promptly broke down half-way up the hill. Fortunately, Adrian Wilton, the very funny Secretary of Liskeard Athletic, kept the passengers in stitches with his 'Jethro' style humour, while Dave 'Ticker' Hick set to work on a running repair, and as the minutes ticked by our honoured passengers ceased to worry about being late. Eventually the bus was fixed, and they picked themselves up, dusted themselves off and started the journey all over again; arriving for dinner in a very good humour indeed'.

The subject of the Convention was discussed at a pre-AGM meeting of the Management Committee in June 1990, together with the issue of relegation and promotion. While the problems experienced were dealt with, the composition of the League for the following season was not at all clear.

An application was made by Swanage Town and Herston to be granted a side-ways move into the Wessex League to alleviate travelling costs, which was granted. Runners-up in Division Two, Backwell United, were refused promotion because their attempt to gain planning permission for floodlights had failed amid objections from the surrounding houses. As the rules stood, third placed Ilfracombe Town could not be promoted in their place.

In the end, it was decided that Ottery St Mary, who won the division by twelve points would be promoted, but no club would be relegated from the Premier

Division, to maintain numerical parity. That meant a reprieve for Welton Rovers, who had only won three games all season. At the foot of the Table, Minehead and Glastonbury were both successful in gaining re-election to the League.

There were five applications for entry to the league, Bishop Sutton, Brislington, Crediton United, Torquay United reserves and Yate Town. After a vote by clubs the two available places were awarded to Crediton and Torquay.

The campaign that Crediton had mounted to gain entry had begun early in 1990 with their officials visiting as many Western League clubs as possible to make themselves known. They also produced brochures and pamphlets that were sent to all clubs, and raised enough money to build new changing rooms to comply with ground grading.

Improvements to the club were a tribute to the determination of Committee members, that included Bill Ash, Life-member and President over the 50 years of his involvement, who had also acted as Secretary and Chairman, together with Ian Grinney, Dave Blanchford, Chris Gillard and Geoff Lee. They also ran a reserve team in the Combination League, and offered football for all abilities including youths.

Torquay reserves joined after success in their first year as members of the Combination League, which they won along with the Subsidiary Cup. Because there was no promotion from that competition to Division Two, they had to apply for election alongside other clubs; a fact that those present at the AGM were acquainted with.

In an extremely innovative move, a proposal was then put to the AGM that Wendy Toms, who had been progressing as a referee through the Contributory System, should be recruited as a linesman for the following season; a proposal that caused some of the more conventional members to argue long and hard against. Modern man won the day, however, and the Great Mills Western League became the first in the country to recognise that talent should be rewarded regardless of gender. Wendy went on a year later to officiate at the AFC Bournemouth v Reading fixture in the Third Division. She is the first female to officiate at Football League and Football Premiership level.

The long association with Great Mills was extended for the 1990/91 season to include an award in each division for the 'Best Conducted' club, which was to be decided on a vote from each club plus one from each of the committee officials. It was immediately perceived as a valuable addition, not only for the monetary reward attached to it, but also as a matter of pride for the recipient that their efforts had been acknowledged by their peers.

Early in the season it came to the committee's attention that the Wessex League had approached both the Wiltshire and Dorset County Leagues with a view to becoming a feeder league into their league; a move that crossed the boundaries in which both leagues operated. The approach was reported to the respective Associations, and a meeting was called by the Wiltshire League at Pewsey in September to discuss the proposal, at which Member clubs voted to approach the Western League with a view to becoming a feeder league under the pyramid system.

A couple of months later, Member clubs agreed to allow promotion and relegation from Division Two, which seemed to be the trigger needed. Co-operation between the Western and Hellenic Leagues increased, as first Gloucestershire and then Somerset joined the ranks of counties who recognised the benefits of a structured pyramid. When the newly formed Devon County League also expressed an interest, it looked as though Les Phillips vision of all those years before was about to come to fruition, and afford a route for clubs to progress at last.

All the while the Committee was faced with a problem to solve when Referee's Secretary, Colin Phillips, who had taken over from Lester Shapter at the start of the season, resigned due to work commitments. While the search went on to replace him, Maurice Washer stood in, once again. Eventually in November Cliff Ashton, the long serving referee with the League and Chairman of the Referees Association, stepped into the role; a position that was to be the precursor to a long and fruitful relationship with Leagues administration.

It was to be another season of change when, in April 1991, President, Lew Webb died. Lew had been an indomitable character and his life was summed up in an article in the Western Daily Press by David Foot under the headline, 'LIFE AND TIMES OF A LOVEABLE AUTOCRAT'. He wrote; *'Over the years, when this column has felt the need for Pythonesque reflections, it has turned to the more odd-ball traditions of some teams that make up the Somerset FA. We have gleefully recited a few of the more hilarious and hoary stories, the laws of libel have baulked us with the others. There have been times when meetings of the Disciplinary Committee at Wells have appeared to be transported straight from the Hammer House of Horror films'.*

'Whatever would the wing-collard predecessors of the present County officials have made of the incident of eccentric behavior, forget the violence for a moment, that come up regularly for adjudication? Only on the way home do the committee men allow themselves a sigh and a chuckle'.

'In his office at home in Midsomer Norton, the Somerset Secretary, Lew Webb, would survey a mountainous pile of forms, denoting the footballing felons of the West. His language could be ripe and he would say that it is always pretty-bad around here but now I think it's worse than ever. Don't ask me to say why'. He would, of course, then start by blaming professional footballers for the poor example they set with their open dissent and histrionics. Then he would read out one of those extraordinary confidential reports sent in by despairing village secretaries and add 'Don't you dare print a word of that, there'll be a dozen lawyers on our backs'.

'You never would DARE with Lew. He was a cigar-smoking autocrat, with a rather fearsome manner on the phone who could frighten the life out of fledgling club officials. If someone rang him with a query, his voice responded with a venom which threatened to collapse any lingering mine-shaft for miles around. He wrote in the Somerset FA handbook that he expected to receive phone calls outside of normal working hours but does not like calls at unreasonable hours, so don't take advantage of him – and who can blame him if he loses his patience'!

'Already a respected referee, he followed his father, Charlie, in the Somerset Office. They both knew the rule-book backward and in their forthright, distinctive ways were likeable characters. Charlie once danced on the bar at the London Inn, Keynsham, after the local team had won the Senior Cup, and Lew, with his beloved drams beneath his belt, could also be most convivial company'.

'He enjoyed a little boardroom hospitality at Ashton Gate, Eastville and the County Ground, as well as the grassroot rigors of touchline support on the Mendip Hills. Occasionally on the way home from Lancaster Gate, he was known to fall asleep and miss his destination. He was, for a quarter of a century a major influence in West Country Football and we are all going to miss him'.

A fitting tribute, indeed, to a large and loveable character.

The season saw Mangotsfield, once again, pressing for membership of the Southern League. During the year, the club had completed some tremendous improvements to their ground with a new three hundred seater-stand and full ground enclosure. Their most difficult problem lay with the floodlights which had failed on several occasions, but on the field, they were superb with just four games lost, scoring 113 goals, leaving them ten points clear of their nearest rivals, Torrington Town.

Western League Champions 1990/91

The footballing public in the East of Bristol had recently lost their Bristol Rovers club to Twerton Park, and took the 'Field' to their hearts, with average gates of between 450-550 supporters. Manager, Harold Jarman, ably supported by his assistant, Terry Rowles, were further rewarded with the Manager of the Year award, and so it came as something of a surprise to most people when the Southern League Grading Committee recommended their application for membership should be rejected.

The Southern League had also received application for membership from Swanage Town and Herston, who had won the Wessex League, after moving side-ways to reduce the cost of Western League travel just one year before. With more than a suspicion that the move had been made to access a less competitive route to promotion, many Western League watchers were satisfied that the application was also rejected.

Second placed Torrington Town proved all form books wrong after struggling in previous years, which demonstrated what an impact an able manager can have. John Hore had experienced a good deal of success during his management career when, after leaving Bideford to take the hot seat at Plymouth Argyle, he spurred the League side on to reach the semi-final of the FA Cup. From there he went to Torrington and worked extremely hard to build a good young squad that had flourished under his encouragement and experience. Local Barnstaple boy, Martin Nicholls, was one of his prodigies who proved himself to be a prolific goal-scorer.

In the First Division, it was a similar story when the previous term's bottom club, Minehead, powered their way to the top at a canter, some fifteen points clear of Elmore; who picked up the Merit Cup for the second time.

In the Premier Division, the Merit Cup was shared between Dawlish Town and Plymouth Argyle, the third year that the Football League club had picked it up, and was a tribute to the professional attitude that they showed toward their membership of the League. The new, 'Best Conducted Club' awards went to Taunton in the Premier Division with Chard as runners-up, and Ilfracombe in the First Division with Crediton United in second place.

It was sad that in Elmore's most successful year to date, the man who founded the club, Eric Garnsworthy (better known as Mr Eagle as his initials were EAG) passed away during the season, on 23rd February 1991 without seeing their success. Mr Eagle had played for the club as a young man, making his debut in the 'B' team. He then went on to be both Treasurer and a Trustee. Eric left a club that had an eye to the future; and one that made no secret of the fact that a higher status was their aim in future years.

The Combination Subsidiary League Final was held at Elmore with Taunton Town beating Barnstaple Town, 3-0. Taunton also went on to win the Combination Knock-Out Cup, but were denied the treble by Tiverton who won that League by eight points.

After all that had happened at Woolacombe Bay previously, the Convention Weekend saw a return to the Langstone Cliff Hotel at Dawlish for the first time in four years. Geoff Rogers and his staff did not seem to have aged at all and were working as hard as ever. Even the sun shone throughout and an almost full complement of the Western League family enjoyed the Friday evening entertainment, followed by a stroll to get over their hangovers the following morning with friends made throughout the seasons. After a lavish lunch most then made their way to the Dawlish Town ground to watch Elmore complete their season and pick up the Les Phillips Challenge Cup.

At the AGM in June 1991, Ted Brown, President of Liskeard Athletic, accepted the honour of becoming the League President, and a little later was invited to become a Vice-President of the Cornish FA. There was a return to the promotion and relegation of two clubs after many years without the movement, with Radstock and Barnstaple relegated; which was especially unfortunate for the Devon club as it was the first time that they had to face life in the lower flight since their promotion to Division One in 1950.

The resignation of Yeovil Town reserves was accepted with both Bishop Sutton and Brislington becoming members of the First Division. Brislington had followed Crediton United's example the previous season, and ran a very slick campaign to gain entry to the League. Their decision to aim for a higher standard had been made back in 1988 after the appointment of joint managers, Steve D'Arcy and Jamie Patch, both of whom had played Western League football. Under their guidance, the club had won both the Somerset Premier League and the Somerset Cup, and their young vivacious committee were working hard to improve facilities to progress further.

Backwell United was another club who were anxious to progress, even though they had been refused promotion because of the lack of floodlights. After a good deal of active lobbying, with League Chairman, Stan Priddle, speaking for the club, together with an appeal against the planning judgement which precluded the installation of floodlights, planning permission was eventually given and they swiftly went about the installation.

Throughout the 1980s, both the League and its member clubs had become more professional in their approach to the game, and many managers from higher status leagues looked toward Western League players to fill any void in their squads. In national competitions, many fared well against higher opposition, with Tiverton Town reaching the First-Round Proper of the FA Cup, only to go down, 5-1, to Aldershot. Dawlish also continued their previous success in the FA Vase, with a narrow defeat in the Third Round at the hands of Southern League Trowbridge Town, who had somehow managed to enter the 'Vase' instead of the 'Trophy' for that season.

There had also been a great deal of success in refereeing standards, with many progressing on to the Football League after earning their spurs while officiating Western League games. The contribution of the League to referee development was highlighted when Roger Milford was appointed to the middle for the 1991 FA Cup Final between Nottingham Forrest and Tottenham Hotspur. Spurs won the Final exactly ninety years after becoming the first non-league team to have their name engraved on the Trophy while they were in membership of both the Southern and the Western League.

Prior to the 1991/92 season, a recession throughout the country began to bite hard, and some Member clubs were finding it very difficult to make ends meet. As companies began to feel the squeeze, they were unable to support their local clubs, and lottery ticket sales, that had once been such a life-line, began to lose their popular appeal. Many years before Les Phillips had said that every club should have a clubhouse to generate income, but the relaxation of licensing laws, which permitted all-day opening in pubs, had also reduced that income stream.

It was not only the clubs who suffered during the latest recession, as many senior leagues throughout the country also lost the sponsorship deals that had given them such vital additional income. Great Mills, however, did not falter in their generosity toward their adopted Western League family, and with good administration, as well as the continued sponsorship, the League managed to make the books balance.

Not all clubs were affected by the dour financial problems that the country found itself in, however, and the good folk at Clevedon Town were in no doubt as to what the future held. With money in the bank from the development of Teignmouth Road, they were within months of completing the new, state of the art 'Hand Stadium', which was expected to be open by Christmas 1991. In anticipation of the development, they had appointed a new manager, Terry Rowles, who had experienced tremendous success at Mangotsfield with Harold Jarman, and who had recruited a new squad with the view of promotion.

As with most things in football, it is hard to predict outcomes, even given the seasider's favourable circumstances. When the season progressed, it became clear the they were not going to have it all their own way, with neighbours, Weston-super-Mare equally as determined to win the promotion place and move on.

Over the years, the management at Weston had quietly been building a squad of players that were equal to the task, and the committee had been working toward improvements at Winterstoke Road that conformed with Southern League grading; no-one said it had to be pretty. They were also confident that the town of Weston was growing, what's more, that the growth would see increasing commercial activities which could generate more than enough money to support a Southern League outfit.

By the time 1992 came along, the seaside towns, just seven miles apart, were neck-and-neck, and with a promotion place only open to the winners of the Western League, there was no room for slip-ups. Which is where it all went wrong for Clevedon. A couple of indifferent results let the lead slip at a vital time, and on 11th April 1992, Weston ironically beat the reigning Champions, Mangotsfield United, and their Chairman, Paul Bliss, was presented with the magnificent League Cup by Stan Priddle.

The season was not over then, however, as with two games remaining Clevedon still had to pick up a point to clinch the runners-up spot, with Tiverton Town still in contention, and on Easter Saturday they did just that. Terry Rowles men clinched a draw, 1-1, over fourth placed Bideford Town and made any other results academic.

Tiverton had, however, enjoyed a very successful season, reaching the First-Round Proper of the FA Cup yet again. It was achieved after being held to a draw in the first two rounds; 2-2, at Torrington, winning the replay, 3-2, and then, 0-0, at home to Saltash, winning the replay, 2-1.

The following round they were in Cornwall again, where they beat Liskeard, 3-1, which then yielded a very difficult match, away to Dover Athletic. After beating the Beazer Homes side by the only goal of the game, the reward for Martyn Rogers' men was an away day at Fourth Division Barnet, and although the game was lost, 5-0, they had, once again, achieved a feat that most clubs dream about at the start of each season.

In the First Division, Calne Town had begun the year as one of the favourites for promotion, after missing out on their chance the previous season by just one point, and although they began well, injuries denied them. Fellow Wiltshire club, Westbury United, however, made steady progress throughout, and were rewarded for their efforts by guaranteeing a place in the Premier Division for the first time in their history, with three games in hand.

Torquay reserves, who had tentatively given notice of withdrawing from the League at Christmas, together with Saltash, Liskeard and Bath City reserves, had until then looked the most probable to win the First Division with ease. They eventually withdrew their resignation, but failed to reclaim the ground they had lost, and came in as runners-up. Both Cornish clubs also withdrew their resignations.

The second relegation place in the Premier Division was occupied at various stages during the first four months by Frome, Welton, Chippenham and Chard, but with Chippenham hitting form after the New Year and gaining thirty points in the second half of the season, and Chard likewise, both Welton and Frome were left to fight it out in the final game of the year. That day Welton travelled to Minehead, and Frome to Saltash, and in the event Frome scored an unexpected victory, 1-0, while Dave Stone's men lost, 2-1, and were condemned to the lower flight for the Centenary Year.

Although everything was in place for clubs from the contributory County Leagues to gain a place in the Western League First Division, none had facilities that were up to the standard required and so both Heavitree United and Melksham Town escaped the drop into County football.

In the Combination League, Taunton Town gained the honours, once again, and won both the League and Subsidiary Cup, with runners-up, Chard Town denying them the treble by defeating them, 4-3, in the Knock Out Cup Final.

Torrington reached the Les Phillips Challenge Cup Final by beating the reigning League Champions, 1-0, in the semi-final, while the young squad from Plymouth had triumphed over Bath City reserves by the same score-line with their youthful squad.

 In contrast, they then fielded a much more experienced team in the final, beating Johnny Hore's North Devon side, 3-1. The Cup and Medals were presented after the game by Jane Phillips accompanied by her son, Nigel, who had inherited his father's love of the non-league game.

The evening of the Presentation Dinner saw senior Marketing Manager of Great Mills, Ian Marshall, present the major awards, with Martyn Rogers winning 'Manager of the Year'. In the Premier Division, the Merit Cup was won by Torrington with Elmore in runners-up spot, while Wellington gained the First Division honour just beating Larkhall Athletic. The Best Conducted Club award went to Chippenham Town, just ahead of Weston-super-Mare, together with Division One joint winners, Ilfracombe Town and Calne Town.

At the 1992 AGM, held at Taunton Town, Weston-super-Mare were congratulated on becoming the first club to achieve promotion to the Southern League since the Pyramid System had been introduced. Chairman, Stan Priddle, also informed clubs that Maurice Washer had attended a meeting in Walsall a few months earlier at which all twenty Leagues, from the Conference down, were present.

They had met to consider the formal development of a pyramid system of promotion and relegation which was designed to encourage progression. From that meeting agreement was reached that the group would be known as the 'Assembly,' and would meet twice a year as the voice of non-league football. The aim was to foster co-operation between Leagues and to lobby for representation on the Football Association Council; progress indeed, that would with time reap rewards.

The AGM welcomed Clyst Rovers into membership of the League and congratulated young referee, Steve Dunn, who had been promoted to the Football League middle. It was also with some pride that the meeting heard that Wendy Toms had, once again, been promoted.

As the 100th year of the Western Football League loomed, everyone involved could look with optimism at both the story that the history told, and a future for a League that had proved the nay-sayers wrong throughout its time. With strong sponsors, administrators and member clubs, there was a confidence borne of both adversity and longevity.

CHAPTER 19

A hundred years and rising

As the celebrations of the Leagues Centenary began, Tom summed up what it was to like to be a member of the Western Football League when he wrote; '*I met my young friend, Iain Anderson from Bristol Manor Farm, and his words of wisdom really summed up what the last hundred years have been about when he said; 'I recall many happy occasions associated with relating to my club. The pride felt when we played our first game under floodlights in 1985. The friendliness from fellow Great Mills League clubs and officials. Some of the committee members that I have known throughout the years, such as Mervyn 'Scrooge' Brown, treasurer for many seasons; Alex Thomas, once accurately described by Les Phillips as a flamboyant Chairman; players such as Chris Rex, a loyal servant to the club who, just once, scored a penalty; and many, many more occasions and people who make being a member of a Great Mills club so worthwhile and rewarding'.*

'*Although his club had not won a championship, up until that moment in time, like many before him, and many thousands to come, Iain has enjoyed taking part. During my life, I have known many people who have never experienced the passion, friendship and feeling of belonging that I have in my time with the League; and for that reason, if I had the choice, I would live my life the same over again'.*

'*In a few days' time, on the 19th September 1992, I will be attending the Centenary Dinner to celebrate the passing years. The last time that I sat in the Wessex Suite of the Grand Hotel in Bristol, we were toasting the League's Golden Jubilee. Little did I know then that I would still be with my league, just six days before my own celebrations. I hope that you recognise me, will stop for a while, enjoy a dram and your memories with me, and forgive an old man for lacking the vitality and strength of our league'.*

On the night of the Dinner, In the Wessex Suite of the Grand Hotel, proceedings commenced with President, Ted Brown saying Grace. Those present included: Stan Priddle, Rod Webber, Chris Willcox, Graham Kelly, Ken Aston, Peter Bastin, Don Milverton, Tony Barnes, Cliff Ashton, Paul Britton, Bill Coggins, Mike Crichton, Alan Disney, Joan Ellis, Tom Harris, Les Heal, John Pool, Tony Salvidge, Doug Webb, and Mike Williams. There were also some 340 friends and associates from the Football Association, County FA's, Neighboring Leagues' and every Western League club in Membership.

As the main course came in Stan Priddle carved the Baron of Beef, drank a strong whisky in celebration and said: '*It is a privilege to welcome you this evening to the Centenary Dinner of the Western Football League. I extend a special welcome to our honoured guests and their ladies, and to our sponsors, Great Mills DIY (Retail) Ltd, who have done so much to encourage football in the West Country over the past decade. In this our hundredth season, we can allow ourselves to reflect on the progress that has been made over the years, and to feel content indeed at the strength we find our League in. With this knowledge, we can look forward to the future with confidence'.*

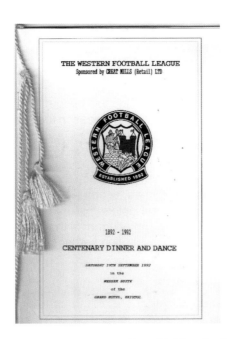

After the meal and presentations, the Ray McVay Orchestra and Singers completed a memorable evening in the Ballroom, where dancing continued late into the night, with one or two seemingly responsible persons' finding it difficult to rest against a wall that appeared to move!

Tom's last entry in the original 'View from the Terraces' was; '*Viewed from my position on the terraces, the past hundred years have been about the men and women who have devoted all those precious moments to football for the love of the game and of their clubs. I have been privileged to be a part of those years in which a great deal of progress has been made, but it is now time for me to hand over the League and its future to those of you who are involved now, and those of you who are yet to come. Enjoy it as I have and you will never regret being a member of the Great Mills Western League family*'.

From there, after enjoying a memorable Centenary Dinner, the old man signed off for good.

While there was delight in the memories of past seasons that surrounded the Centenary celebrations, the League clubs were competing in the 1992/93 season amid the backdrop of a recession throughout the country that had seen no end since it began early in 1990. During September, there had been another drop-in GDP and unemployment was at a five-year high, creeping up toward three million, with around 10% of the working population affected. To add to this, Sky Sports TV began televising Premier Division football games, seven days a week, encouraging potential supporters of non-league football to swop allegiance and enjoy the sport from their sofas.

As a demonstration of how influential Premier Division football was becoming, just prior to those dreadful financial statistics being released, Alan Shearer had become Britain's most expensive footballer, completing a transfer from Southampton to Blackburn Rovers for £3.6 million.

Closer to home, and in a different, but still enviable position, Clevedon Town were also enjoying life in the 'fast-lane' as they settled well into their new stadium, with the management working to a budget that many would be more than grateful for today. From the start the season took shape, working toward the promotion they had so coveted since completing the sale of Teignmouth Road; and miraculously escaping bankruptcy.

Clevedon won the Championship, and in the process clocked-up 106 points from their 38 League games, scoring 137 goals, conceding just 23, and losing none. It was the most points that had been amassed since the 1975/76 season, when the undisputed team of that era, Falmouth Town, had set a record of 110, but the Cornish club had amassed those points playing six games more.

Tiverton Town 1992-1993

Team Photo

Wembley Squad: Keith Simmonds (Physio) Steve Hinds Phil Everett Ian Nott Mark Saunders Jason Smith Steve Daly Mark Short and John Ower Assistant Manager Front row Peter Rogers Lee Annunziata Kevin Smith Martyn Rogers Manager Hedley Steele captain Neil Saunders and Matthew Scott

It was not only Clevedon making the headlines, however. Tiverton Town, who were themselves celebrating their own Centenary, came in runners-up, fourteen points adrift, but during the season they had experienced a phenomenal run in the FA Vase, reaching Wembley Stadium on the back of some staggering results against higher opposition. During the progression, Forest Green Rovers were hit for six, while Barton Rovers and Buckingham Town both went for four without reply.

The FA Vase had replaced the Amateur Cup, which had run for 80 years between 1893-1974, and was one in which no Western League club ever reached the Final, which made the achievement more historic. The day out at Wembley coincided with the Annual League Convention Weekend at Dawlish, and such was the excitement at the achievement, that many of the men and women who usually looked forward to a stress-free week-end, dashed up to London by car, train, and even plane, to witness the spectacle. Most still made it back in time for the Presentation Dinner in the evening; just.

CALNE TOWN FC

1994/95

Although Tiverton Town were defeated by Bridlington, 1-0, it was a amazing feat, and was to be the beginning of a period that would see them rise from the time in which they were in danger of extinction ten years before, to a remarkable period in the future.

In Division One, Odd Down were crowned Champions, ten points clear of second placed Calne Town. It was their first promotion since gaining admission to the Western League in 1977/78, and came in the wake of their hard-working steering committee providing them with a social club, to afford an income, and improving the standard of football on offer

LEAGUE CHAIRMAN STAN PRIDDLE
Presenting the Division One Championship Trophy to
Odd Down skipper, Terry Mancini

Calne Town, were similarly set-up. In 1985/86, a new young committee had been formed, with the objective of bringing a higher standard of football to Bremhill View, and the following season, in their Centenary Year, they had an application to join the Western League accepted. Ground improvements were then undertaken, and the social club extended further income with a lounge as well as bar facilities. It was the highest level that Calne Town had played at; an achievement that was also in part due to their young manager, Tommy Saunders, whose ambitions were only matched by his larger than life character.

While Calne joined their Wiltshire neighbours Chippenham Town and Westbury United in the Premier Division, down the road, Melksham Town, who had finished the season in bottom position, went in the opposite direction returning to County football after eighteen years of membership.

At the AGM, the League decided to promote three clubs into the Premier Division due to the resignations of both Plymouth Argyle and Torquay United reserves, along with the promotion of Clevedon. That decision benefited Crediton United, who had only joined the Western League in 1990, and had ended the season just a point behind Calne Town in third place.

In the Premier Division, Westbury United, who owed their origins to the amalgamation of two local sides, Westbury Old Comrades FC and Westbury Great Western Railway XI, had joined the Western League in 1984, and achieved promotion to the Premier Division 1991, while fellow Wiltshire club, Chippenham Town, had been members for some years. Despite League honours not being within either club's grasp, the competition was fierce between them, and when the new pretenders finished fifth, three points ahead, and three places above Chippenham Town, they celebrated the seasons end with an eye to progressing further as the top Western League team in the county.

A similar rivalry was seen in Cornwall, where Saltash United and Liskeard Athletic spent the season competing in each other's pocket, with both ending the term in a mid-table position on 45 points. Liskeard had won the headlines, however, having made it through to the fourth-round of the FA Vase, the furthest they had ever achieved. In the process, they defeated Wellington, Bideford Town, Cindeford Town and Tunbridge Wells (in a replay 2-0), but eventually went out, 2-0, at Lux Park to fellow Cornish side, Falmouth Town.

Unfortunately, at the end of the season both clubs left the Western League to move back into the South-Western League, but during the years that Liskeard had competed, they had made many, many, friends. Chairman, Dave 'Ticker' Hick, Secretary, Adrian 'Jethro' Wilton, Treasurer, Brian 'Big G' Glanville, and President David Rawlings, had certainly made a lasting impression, not forgetting, of course, their patient and long-suffering wives who travelled to games with them. Without question, they were to be very much missed by everyone involved.

Big G and Ticker Hicks before their Charity bike ride with President Ted Brown and friends

Likewise, Saltash United had made an impact on the League, wining Division One at their first attempt, and then going on to lift the Championship three times, coming in as runners-up twice, and winning the League Cup twice. Alongside that they had enjoyed comparative success in the FA Cup and FA Vase.

Both clubs had experienced arguably one of the most successful periods in their histories, and so it was particularly sad to see them move-on due to an increase in travelling costs, and possibly having an eye to being the top club in a more local league.

Because of the Cornish clubs' withdrawal, Frome Town and Torrington Town were saved from the drop into Division One, having ended the term in the bottom two places. Frome had experienced a particularly torrid year winning just three games and conceding 101 goals with just 12 scored.

In contrast, Division One Champions, Brislington, had gone ahead with the installation of floodlights and construction of the Park Pets Stand, which enabled them to be promoted, while runners-up Glastonbury were denied advancement as their new ground did not come up to the accepted standard.

Backwell United, who ended the term on the same number of points as Glastonbury, and who had worked so hard to meet ground grading standards, went up to the Premier Division in their place, and the composition of Division One was then completed with both Dawlish Town and Minehead surviving the drop into county football after a lack of suitable applications from clubs wanting to join the League.

There were also new entrants with Melksham Town and Bridgwater Town returning to the league and were joined in Division One by yet another club from Wiltshire, Amesbury Town.

The 1994/95 season had seen Elmore enjoy their most successful season to date, and as well as achieving the runners-up position, one point adrift of their neighbours, Tiverton, they had also put in some superb performances in the various Cup competitions.

In the FA Cup, they reached the Second Qualifying Round, and in the FA Vase progressed through to the Fourth Round, and to top that, they also picked up the Les Phillips Challenge Cup. It was a deserved reward for the hard-working Management Committee at Horsdon Park, and had been achieved after many of their traditional supporters had move to cheer-on the revolution that was going on just down the road at Ladysmead.

To test Elmore's plan still further, however, Tiverton had also progressed through in the FA Cup, and they had gone one better and reached the First-Round Proper, once again, in a game that saw them host Leyton Orient. It was a game that drew a capacity crowd of 3,000, and one where they put on a sterling performance, with the audacity to be leading at one stage by a single goal. Eventually the encounter was lost 3-1, but in the process the club had well and truly began to show just what they were capable of, and in the process, had entered the hearts of more and more local soccer supporters.

Elmore, Taunton Town and Tiverton Town, were all situated bang in the middle of the Western League map, and were producing a standard of football in the area that had not been witnessed for many, many, years. There was, however, a catch to that success, as it did not come without a very hefty price-tag attached. The hunt for suitable quality players was in the hands of the manager's, but the money to recruit them sat firmly with the club's officials; and many, if not most of those players were demanding ever increasing wage packets and expenses.

A big part of the key to success on the pitch was then, as it is now, contingent on the ability to attract sufficient income alongside a healthy gate-return. Increasingly, it had become apparent that, even at non-league level where a certain amount of commercial activity in clubs had been widespread for countless years, a new approach was needed. The employment of a full-time commercial manager with a commercial department was becoming essential, and at Tiverton, in manager, Martyn Rogers, they had found the perfect man to both raise, and spend, the money wisely.

None were more aware of the need for commercial income than the officers of the Western League. It was still clearly in many memories just what life had been like back in the early 1970s, before the involvement of Rothman's had revitalised the fortunes of non-league football in the west, not just with financial aid, but also with innovative ideas. When the relationship ended, Great Mills had joined in April 1982, and were still an integral part of the progress that was still being made, as well as making valuable financial contributions. But nothing is forever, and nothing was taken for granted.

The special relationship was acknowledged by Sales and Marketing Director, Peter Bastin, when he wrote in the forward of the Centenary book in 1992 that; *'It seems incredible that ten years have passed since Great Mills first started sponsoring what was then, the Western League. We offer you our warmest congratulations on this, the League Centenary, and our hope is that non-league football, such as we have had the privilege of sharing with you over the last decade, will continue to flourish and provide communities with the spirit of friendly rivalry. This has been a trademark of non-league football in general and the Great Mills League, but sadly it is a diminishing part of many sports. Although Great Mills is now a 92-strong chain of DIY retailers, we share our South-Western roots with the League. We wish the member clubs and their many supporters a bright and happy future'.*

While at the time those words were meant with absolute conviction it was with enormous regret and trepidation that the Officers of the League learned that the company was to withdraw its sponsorship from the end of the following season,1995/96, and during the summer a statement was issued which said; *'The League has appointed a firm of consultants to find sponsorship for next season, and are close to finalising sponsorship of the League and the Les Phillips Cup'.*

The search then continued during the long, hot summer months, and while that was a continuing process, over at Tiverton, Martin Rogers, was finding the task of persuading local companies to sponsor his club on the back of several seasons of success, getting easier. His efforts were not going un-noticed by some fellow Premier Division clubs, who were also spending more time talking to local businesses than would have been in previous decades, but while some flourished, others were finding the fight for survival a losing battle, and, down the road at Elmore, life was becoming more difficult despite their recent success.

As the season began, there was no news on new League sponsors and attention was soon turned to games in the FA Cup and FA Vase with the competitions offering increased rewards for successful clubs, and It was to be a case of so near, yet so far, for Mangotsfield United as they made their way through the various rounds FA Vase.

Their Cup run had begun with a win over Truro City, 3-0, which was then followed by a victory away at Godalming and Guildford, 5-2. Although the next game resulted in a goalless draw away at Hungerford Town, they won the replay, 5-2, and then easily dispatched Paulton Rovers in the 4th Round, 3-0.

With Taunton Town beaten away at Raunds Town, 4-1, this left all eyes on Cossham Street where, after a 2-2 draw away at Wivenhoe Town, Mangotsfield did the league proud with a decisive victory, 3-0, to progress through to the Quarter-Final stage, where they travelled to, Raunds Town.

After carving out a draw, 2-2, in a very competitive game, a huge crowd cheered on the Bristol side to a victory, 1-0, and into the first-leg of a semi-final against Clitheroe.

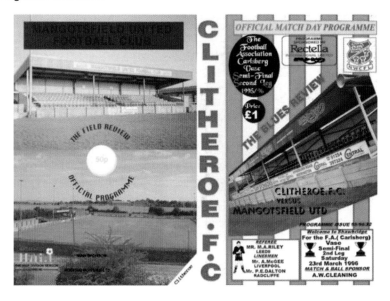

With the resulting home draw, a win, 1-0, saw the Mango's dreaming of Wembley on the back of a ten-match unbeaten run. The 11th game away in Lancashire to Clitheroe of the North-West Counties League was, however, just one game too many, and the dream was cut short with a defeat, 2-0. The dream of a Wembley appearance was lost by an aggregate score of just 2-1.

With such a run in the FA Vase, Mangotsfield United found it difficult to catch-up in the race for the League Championship, and that honour was left to two clubs, Tiverton Town and Taunton Town. After 34 games and almost nine months of competition, there was little to separate the two clubs with both having lost only two games. The coveted third Championship title that was so desired by Tiverton, eluded them however, and Taunton picked up their second Championship since re-joining from the Southern League in 1983/84, thanks to the three points earned from the games drawn.

In contrast, to the successful season of the top-flight clubs, the year had not gone well for Elmore, with results and events, both on-and-off the pitch, a real cause for concern. At season's end, the club had won 24 points, as opposed to the 86 they gained the previous season; a dire contrast. They did, however, escape relegation with the advantage of a two-point cushion over Frome Town, who had not capitalised on the advantage given the previous season when they were handed a Premier Division life-line despite ending in bottom place. Frome were joined in relegation by bottom club, Crediton United, who had experienced a truly poor year, conceding 96 goals and scoring 18.

Bridgwater Town, who had been promoted to the Western League from the Premier Division of the Somerset League just a year before, picked up the coveted First Division Trophy on goal-difference from second placed Chard Town. Both clubs were promoted while at the foot of the table Exmouth Town and Ilfracombe Town survived the drop thanks to no suitable applicants applying for membership.

The Les Phillips League Cup final was held at Crediton on the 4th May 1996, with Tiverton Town taking on Barnstaple in front of 757 spectators and a host of special guests. It was a hotly contested game which had Tiverton as firm favourites on league form, but that assumption did not reckon with the steely determination of their North Devon neighbours.

The game resulted in a draw after extra-time, and for once, it was decided not to resort to penalties to decide whose name would be engraved on the beautiful historic Cup. Instead a replay was ordered, but as it was so late after season's end, a venue was hard to find as most clubs were already working on their pitch maintenance. Fortunately, Barnstaple had not planned their close season programme and eventually a result was registered when, in front of 508 vocal spectators, Tivvy made no mistakes, slotting in four times without reply.

The league went into its summer break with much activity behind the scenes. It was the end of an era in which Great Mills had served the Western League's family well; and had benefited as a company from that sponsorship. All was still to play for…

CHAPTER 20

New sponsors, Fix the Day...

The Summer of 1996 was a particularly happy one for the hard-working officials of the Western League with the news that a new sponsorship had been secured from Screwfix Direct, who were based in Yeovil.

The company's origins had been based on selling screws through the Exchange and Mart, and had started life as The Woodscrew Supply Company in 1979, before being purchased in 1981 by Jon and Jenny Goddard-Watts. In the following years, two more companies that traded in the same area were added, both of which had acquired a reputation for selling good-value products.

The company's first mail order catalogue consisted of a single page solely dedicated to screws, and in 1987, that was increased to a four-page version that offered hardware to DIY and Trade professionals in the name of 'Handimail'. The first catalogue to be produced in the name of Screwfix Direct had appeared in 1992, and a year later, when they combined the companies under the name Screwfix Direct to create a comprehensive telephone ordering service for building supply products, turnover had reached £350,000.

When trading reached £4 million in 1994, they moved into larger premises at Pen Mill, Yeovil, and around that time Jon and Jenny's two sons arrived in the business, with one using his background in logistics software to create a distribution software package, while the other had an intuitive feel for what tradespeople wanted, and set about expanding the product range.

The rapidly expanding and successful business was being run by a family who happened to love football, and when contacted with a proposal to sponsor the Western League, they could see the benefit in the new relationship. The company also had an enthusiastic Marketing Manager, Derek Skeavington, who takes up the story and wrote of his time with the League;

'*The Screwfix sponsorship of the Western League came about in an unusual fashion. In 1995, I'd joined Screwfix in Yeovil which was a mail-order business with about 20 staff and was growing rapidly. One Monday in late 1995 the owner's son came in and said 'Great Mills were on the telly Saturday night with the West Country football results. You're supposed to be a marketing bloke, why aren't Screwfix there?' [At the time, we were a tiny £5m turnover company...] What he didn't know was that I knew the non-league football scene, and knew Great Mills were pulling out, so I called the Secretary of the League, Maurice Washer, and went to see them. I found out what they were looking for sponsorship-wise and came back to Screwfix with the deal: '£100k for a 3-year deal and your name will be on TV and in the local papers all the time'.*

'*A bit flabbergasted that there was a firm proposal, the family owners of the business discussed it, had a meeting with the League and that was that, a done deal. I recall after that meeting – with Stan Priddle, Maurice Washer,*

Rod Webber and Joan Ellis – the Chairman of Screwfix, Jon Goddard-Watts, said 'This'll be great for us. These are honourable people. They do this for the love of football not money'.

'After an official launch, which featured a bizarre 'kick about' between Mr Goddard-Watts and ex-England international Graham Roberts (then Yeovil Town's Manager), season 1996/7 began as the Screwfix Western League. Of course, the press, both local and national, had fun manipulating the words 'screw' and 'fix' into their coverage, plus it helped that the Secretary of the League sponsored by a tools and fixings company was Maurice Washer….'

'We wanted to monitor the coverage we were getting so I employed a cuttings agency to check the word Screwfix in the press. After 3 months, we were swamped with ring binders full of thousands of cuttings – this unknown West Country business was certainly getting well-known in the West and indeed nationally. And of course, we had our name on the TV every Saturday evening as the results of the Screwfix Western League were read out.'

'Some of the press coverage was phenomenal. For example, one week the Taunton Somerset Gazette gave 15 mentions of Screwfix in just one issue. I knew the League was a strong one, however even I was surprised when 'our' clubs reached the FA Vase Final 4 years consecutively during this time, Tiverton winning twice, Taunton once and Chippenham losing narrowly. In addition, Team Bath reached the First Round of the FA Cup, playing Mansfield Town in front of the TV cameras. All bonus coverage as far as we were concerned'.

'All great stuff from a professional point of view, however personally, as a football lover all my life, I was lucky to be a guest at Wembley three seasons in a row, to be involved with the Western League during a golden era of success and to be able to converse with 'true' football people be they administrators, managers or players. Past Chairman Cliff Ashton, Secretary Ken Clarke, current Chairman John Pool and their colleagues went out of their way to welcome me to their world. Not forgetting the 'old' crew mentioned above of course'.

'The managers and club officials too, greeting me at the annual conventions like an old friend. As an outsider, it was fascinating to listen in on all the talk between real football people like Martyn Rogers (Tiverton), Russell Musker and Tom Harris (Taunton), Mike Perrin (Melksham), Brian Beer (Chard), Selwyn Aspin (Wellington) and so, so, many more, including the authors of this book'.

'Some random memories…

Leaning on the barrier at Wellington with President Stan Priddle, then 80 or 81 years old. Just before the end of the match he apologised and said he had to leave early. 'My dad's in Musgrove Hospital in Taunton, so I've got to nip in and see him on the way home'.

'One evening in 2000 a Screwfix League match at Bridgwater had to be abandoned at half-time when a helicopter 'in distress' had to make an emergency landing on the pitch. Made all the nationals, that did, as well as the BBC. But they did take away my hammer after that…'

'Standing with Cliff Ashton at Willand during a cup match when an irate supporter of the opposition team walked halfway around the ground to berate Cliff about a referee's decision, wanting to know what Cliff was going to do about it. (Who'd be an administrator of a football league?)'

'Shortly after the sponsorship was announced, I was invited to lunch by John Fry, Chairman of Yeovil Town who had just put their reserve team into the Western League. He wanted to know what Screwfix was all about, and more importantly who the money-man was! I introduced him to Jon Goddard-Watts, the Chairman, who ultimately invested in Yeovil Town FC. They turned full-time professional and the rest as they say is history. It's an ongoing joke between Mr Fry and myself that 'we' really started something that lunchtime'.

'Screwfix ended up sponsoring the League for nine seasons, which at that time was one of, if not the, longest sponsorships in UK football. But all things come to an end. Screwfix had been taken over by Kingfisher plc (owners of B&Q) in 1999, and it was time to finish our sponsorship at the end of the 2005 season, to be replaced by a business whose name I can't quite recall at the moment….'

With a national economy that was thriving, and the announcement of the new League sponsors, it was a happy summer that was made more exciting by the European Championships which were being playing out in the UK. Terry Venables produced a crowd-pleasing team; albeit with Glenn Hoddle waiting in the wings to take over the England job as soon as the competition was over. After many twists and turns, both on and off the pitch, the hopes of football supporters that their England team might become European Champions for the first time were dashed in a penalty shoot-out, after a draw, 1-1, with Germany in the semi-finals.

As usual, the Western League faithful soon got over yet another 'almost there' International experience, and turned their hopes toward the season to come, with, of course, every club a possible champion, before a ball was kicked.

The 1996/97 season began amid much promise, with a settled Management Committee made up of; President Stan Priddle, Vice President Don Milverton, Chairman Rod Webber, Vice-chairman Cliff Ashton, Secretary Maurice Washer, Treasurer Joan Ellis, Registration Secretary Mike Crichton and Referees Secretary Martin Taylor. All were secure in the knowledge that the League was about to benefit from both the financial involvement of Screwfix, and from the relationship with a company that had football at its heart.

Predictably, the season belonged to Tiverton and Taunton again, who battled all year for honours. In the end, however, it was to be an easy victory for the Ladysmead club, who won the League sixteen points clear of Taunton, but despite scoring 103 goals and conceding 20 along the way, their top scorer, Phil Everett, was way down the list of the Western League top scorers, with Wellington's, Nick Woon, three goals clear at the top.

Attendances at games were variable, with Taunton Town, commanding the highest gate of the year for the second season, declaring a crowd of 1196 when they entertained Tiverton on 2nd April 1997. Of course, Tiverton Town were also well supported with six gates of over 500, but if anything, they were disappointed, because their average was only up by 28 on the previous season despite a long unbeaten run.

Although Bridgwater Town finished in a mid-table position, their first year in the Premier Division had attracted additional support, and that helped to swell the crowd at Wordsworth Drive on August Bank Holiday Monday, to 1112. They continued to attract an increase in fan base, and ended the season with an average declared gate of 331, which was considerably higher than the numbers they had achieved during their previous Championship winning season.

At the foot of the Premier Division, Elmore were in decline on the pitch and only managed 16 points from the 34 games played, but despite that, their core of support had returned, and the average gate was back up to 126, from the dismal 73 the season before.

Odd Down, who had been enjoying one of their best years for some time, reeled at the punishment that was handed out to them for fielding ineligible players. The nine-point deduction denied them a sixth-place finish, which would have been the highest they had ever achieved.

There were no such mistakes over at Melksham Town who had experienced a tremendous second season back in the League, and won the First Division a point clear of Keynsham Town. In the process, they scored 82 goals and conceded just 20, which was thanks in part to the wonderful skills of keeper, Steve Perrin, and striker, Brent Murden; who was listed as one of the top scorers in the League at seasons end.

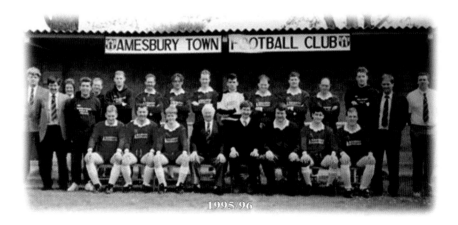

At the foot of the table, Amesbury Town had managed to win just one of their 36 league games, and although they were happy with average gates of 99, which included one crowd of 200, they had been unable to get to grips with the cost of travelling and general demands that came with the level of football. Their resignation at season's end to play in the Salisbury and District League was not totally unexpected. With the departure of Amesbury, Bitton and Street, who had both agreed to a programme of work suggested by officers were accepted into membership.

After many years of trying, Chippenham Town reached their first Les Phillips Cup Final, after beating Mangotsfield United at Cossham Street by the only goal of the game. It was the first success for Chairman, Malcolm Lyus, who had taken over the position from long-serving, Doug Webb. Their opponents in that final, however, were Tiverton Town, who had shown little mercy to newly promoted, Keynsham Town, putting four goals past them without reply in the semi-final. Tiverton did not, however, find the game as easy as form suggested, with the 'Bluebirds' putting up a solid display. However, in the end the Trophy went to Devon for the fourth time in five seasons, by the only goal of the game.

The 1997/98 season saw a new initiative that drew inspiration from the Rothmans years when the 'Screwfix Direct Scrapbook' came out in September 1997 for the first time; a monthly newsletter to clubs which was produced under the guidance of Derek Skeavington and Nigel Davis, who acted as Editor. In their first publication, Nigel, who ran the League's telephone news-line, pledged that they would be attempting to upgrade the information service by posting all results by 5.30pm on a Saturday. That pledge was quite an undertaking, given the reliance it would put on the ability of hard pressed club secretaries to phone in the results promptly. It was envisaged that the new fast service would work alongside the existing one that already gave more in-depth reports by midday on Sunday.

It was, of course, a time when few members of the population had internet access, with just 4% of the population, around 2.5 million, on-line. Ownership of mobile phones, however, was increasing, with the advent of prepaid services about to make SMS the communication method of choice among the young. That one technological advancement would eventually ease the pressures on match-days, offering huge innovation in communications between the clubs and the League.

A favourite topic for both those taking part in the sport and for the media, were the discussions taking place to improve standards at grounds, which the FA had been working on for many years through their Joint Liaison Committee.

In response to this the Western League set-up a Standards Committee, which was chaired by Cliff Ashton, and at a meeting on 1st September 1997, it was agreed that two teams of officials would set about grading and advising clubs. Maurice Washer, Bill Coggins and Alan Disney were tasked to inspect and advise those clubs in the South West of the area, while Cliff Ashton, Doug Webb and Roger Gray, were to visit and inspect those clubs in the

North or the area. The first clubs visited for full-grading were; Heavitree United, Dawlish Town, Frome Town and Westbury United, with Exmouth Town singled out for a visit to grade their changing facilities.

The meeting also agreed that the marking of technical areas and trainer's boxes would to be done according to FIFA guidelines, with a maximum of six people allowed in those areas; a decision that was needed because of several complaints about crowded areas which were causing problems for officials.

On the field, there was notable progress in the Preliminary Rounds of the FA Cup, the most remarkable of which was Tiverton Town's defeat of Weymouth, 2-0, in front of 785 spectators, and the thrashing, 5-0, that Paulton Rovers handed out to Beazer Homes hotshots, Farnham Town,

Tiverton Town then, once again, got into the First-Round Proper, and despite going behind by a goal within the first few minutes against GM Conference front-runners, Cheltenham Town, they put up such a good show that it prompted the Chairman of Cheltenham to remark that; 'No-one has come close to beating us as Whaddon Road this season, but Tiverton certainly did'. And he added; 'The better side probably lost'. Praise indeed.

The thrill of the national Cup competitions did not end there. In the FA Vase, it was to be a year like none before, with both Taunton and Tiverton progressing through, stage after stage. As luck would have it, both were kept apart in the draws right up to the semi-final two-legged stage, where just two games stood to deny an historic all Western League Vase Final at Wembley Stadium.

The prospects of such a Final had most football enthusiasts of the West Country non-league football scene on the edge of their seats, as Taunton Town travelled away to Tow Law, and Tiverton Town entertained Kidsgrove Athletic at Ladysmead. The results of those first-leg games saw Tiverton favourites to progress with a win, 2-0, but Taunton went into the final qualifying game with everything to play for after a thrilling, 4-4, draw.

As fate would have it, and after all the hard work away from home, Tow Law went into the Final, beating Taunton, 1-0, at Wordsworth Drive, and Tiverton Town just hung-on and progressed after losing the return encounter, 2-1, but winning through, 3-2, on aggregated. The dream of the Western League FA Vase final that had been so close, faded for another season.

It must have been especially hard for Taunton Town Chairman, Tom Harris, to cheer on Tiverton Town in the name of the League, but cheer he did, and when the final whistle was blown at Wembley, Tiverton became the first Western League club to put its name on the historic Trophy, winning by the only goal of the game.

In the meantime, in the League during the season, both clubs had been neck-and-neck fighting it out for honours, and in a normal year Taunton would have been successful, gaining 96 points with 107 goals scored, but it was not a normal year, and Tiverton were a different class.

Despite their other commitments, they didn't lose a game all season, scoring 154 goals and conceding just 20, which in turn amassed 110 points from the 38 games played; a Western League record that is still in place today. Despite ending the year fourteen points ahead of the runners-up, and achieving their historic Vase win, the club still resisted the temptation to move on in the growing Pyramid of Football; which was no real surprise as with four Championship's in five seasons, and exceptional results in National Cup Competitions, life was comparatively easy for both officials and spectators at Ladysmead, with no immediate need to push on.

While those top two clubs were in a predictable position, the third-placed club had outperformed all expectations. Melksham Town, had so recently bounced back after relegation into the Wiltshire League, and shown how much progress they had made since those days, gaining 73 points, just one more than fourth placed Bridgwater Town.

Both Chard Town and Torrington Town were relegated to the First Division, with Torrington recording just 14 points all year. They were replaced by Bishop Sutton, who had only lost twice during the season, and runners-up, Yeovil Town reserves, who were eight points adrift of the title in their first year back with the League.

Crediton United who had struggled all year, both financially and in terms of a reduced voluntary workforce, withdrew, returning to County football after making such progress early on. That enabled Pewsey Vale to escape the drop, and with Corsham Town joining the League in Crediton's place, numerical parity was again established.

The Les Phillips Cup had been a happy hunting ground for Crediton amid so many problems and they had progressed through to the Third Round with a win, 5-4, over Chippenham Town. That day all five Wiltshire clubs, including Devizes who had been given a bye in the previous round, were beaten, and in the Quarter Finals it was only Clyst Rovers that remained to fly the Division One flag.

As the competition progressed, the semi-final stage saw Tiverton beat Mangotsfield United, 2-1, at Ladysmead, and Taunton knock Clyst Rovers out, 3-0, which set up a game that the Somerset club were particularly keen to win given all the events of the season.

It was, of course, a wonderfully well supported Final, and one that saw passion, controversy and goals, which ended in Tiverton Town picking up the Les Phillips Cup for the fifth time in six years, to put into their overcrowded trophy cabinet, next to all the other symbols of their success.

The summer of 1998 was filled with the wonder of the World Cup which was being held in France, and where our National team, once again, failed to make it through amid rumours of problems between players and the manager. The street violence that accompanied those games brought shame on football in England, with the resulting effect even filtering down to Western League level, with everyone in the game under the microscope of media attention.

232

In response, before a ball was even kicked in the League programme, there was a call to 'clean up the game', which was not something that was generally needed at non-league level, but the perception of the national game had reflected badly on the sport in general. To a degree, that perception quickly had a negative effect on member clubs' activities, affecting both gates and commercial activities.

With that as a back-drop, the 1998/99 season kicked-off with the news that Taunton had strengthened their squad, and that Tiverton Town were looking to match the previous season's achievements; setting the scene for another 'battle royal' to come.

.Down the M4 motorway at Chippenham, the Town had plundered the squad of neighbour, Calne Town, attracting most of their previous year's players to join ex-manager, Tommy Saunders and assistant manager, Colin Bush to Hardenhuish Park; an action that left a long season ahead for Calne Town with just a skeleton squad left to keep their hard-fought Premier Division status intact.

In the FA Cup, only two Western League sides remained after the Second Qualifying Round, with the shock local result, a defeat for Tiverton at the hands of Falmouth Town by the only goal of the game. The honour of the League was then left in the hands of Barnstaple Town, who had beaten Elmore, 1-0; and Taunton Town, who had won, 3-1, at home to Cindeford Town.

The following round saw Barnstaple drop out after putting up a plucky performance against Cheltenham Town, after falling to a single killer-goal, while Taunton Town again moved on with a win, 4-3, over high riding Kettering Town.

While the exploits of the FA Cup always enthral football enthusiasts, it was the FA Vase which, once again, was the talking point of the season, when both Taunton and Tiverton progressed through to the semi-final stage again. Unlike the previous season, however, the draw this time saw the two Western League clubs pitted against each other in the semi-final, and to the despair of the Somerset club, Tiverton made no mistake in their quest for another Wembley appearance, winning the first of the deciding games, 3-0, at Ladysmead, and then going though despite losing, 2-1, at Wordsworth Drive.

The other FA Vase Finalist this time were hot-favourites, Bedlington Terriers, who produced a shock win, 4-1, in the FA Cup First-Round Proper over Division Two, National League, side, Colchester United. Martyn Rogers men were, however, not about to cede to the Northern League club, and just as Tow Law Town had fallen to a single late goal in the Wembley Final the previous season, so too did Bedlington.

With two minutes to go, it was Scott Rogers who this time wrote his name into Devon folklore. The victory, 1-0, did, indeed, well and truly put both the club and the Western League into the public spotlight.

FA VASE FINAL 1999

Bedlington Terriers v Tiverton Town –the goal goes in

While Vase victory saw Tiverton make yet another mark in history, Taunton well and truly stormed the League, winning the title eleven points clear, scoring 134 goals in their 38 games, with just 33 conceded. The club then chose against promotion to the Southern League; an option that was taken up by the League runners-up. After all those years of dominating the Western League, it was ironic that Tiverton Town went into the Southern League as runners-up in the League, and not as Champions, but with the FA Vase in the cabinet for the second year running, most people who were involved at Ladysmead knew it was well and truly time to move on.

In third place Chippenham Town were a good twelve points clear of fourth placed Melksham Town, while at the foot of the table, it was no surprise to find that Calne Town had failed to recover from the destabilising effect of losing both their managers and all their senior team, and they were relegated back into Division One, along with Keynsham Town.

Corsham Town, who were in their first year in the competition after finishing the previous season as Champions of the Wiltshire League, where they had also won the Wiltshire Senior Cup, had found the new level a challenge. They did, however, achieve a respectable mid-table position, below Minehead and Dawlish Town, who topped Division One and were promoted. In the opposite direction, both Glastonbury and Heavitree United ended the year at the foot of the table with 15 points each, and left to play County football.

LES PHILLIPS CUP FINAL 1998/99

After the game; Lifting the Cup to the Yeovil fans on the terraces

The Les Phillips Cup was played at Paulton Rovers F.C. on 8th May 1999 between Clyst Rovers and a young Yeovil Town reserve side. It was an even competition with the Clyst keeper in great form and just one goal separated the sides. Yeovil came out on top, picking up the Les Phillips Cup for the first time in 40 years.

The League had been left with an imbalance between the Divisions with 36 games in the Premier Division, and 32 in Division One, and officers worked behind the scenes to address the problem during the summer. As a part of that action, there were several meetings with County leagues, and with the

Football Association who were anxious to see the promotion and relegation system working well; providing, of course, that standards at grounds were met.

As well as those meetings, the close season also saw a flurry of activity in the transfer market as usual, with the League's Registrations Secretary, Mike Crichton, kept busy, but while there were some comparatively higher end movements of players, none could compare to the transactions that were being conducted at Premier League clubs, where new records were being set, with the largest the transfer of £10 million paid by Chelsea FC to Blackburn Rovers for the services of Chris Sutton. A record that would soon be broken.

In contrast to those exceptional amounts of money that players in the Premier Division and beyond were enjoying, the normal working fans on the terraces had just been rewarded with new government legislation guaranteeing them a 'minimum wage' of £3.60 per hour. The contrast was obvious, and was a long, long way from those days in football where the maximum wage applied, and the time when professionals often chose Western League football for an occupation over the national game.

Times had, indeed, changed.

Maurice Washer, looking back over his time in football and especially with the Western League, put pen to paper and wrote: *'My very first connection with the game began back in 1946 when sport was recovering from WW2. Like others, at 16 years old I was being chased to join a sports club but as I was not built very well and was the last to be selected in a team, I turned to the refereeing game instead. With the GLA guidance, I joined a class in Bristol, and they in turn asked the FA for guidance as someone my age was not the usual type of student.*

After passing exams I was pushed toward the Church of England League, which had just two divisions that went by the name of Town and Country. The Secretary was a man by the name of Mr Wildgoose, who sent me a Handbook and a postcard with fixtures on it. My first experience was with Failing United, a Bristol side who played near the Sea Walls area, with changing facilities at the nearby Anglesea Place school; and that is where the bubble well and truly broke.

At Failing, as I walked out proudly onto the pitch I was greeted with the home captain shouting 'Crikey, they have sent us a schoolkid to referee today' – at the end of the game, however, he came up and apologised for the remark and complimented me on my performance! Following that I moved further afield and soon found that transport to the likes of North Somerset was the key, with a bus from Bristol to the grounds of Radstock or Paulton much quicker than the rail links.

National Service followed, where I was based at West Kirby, Liverpool, and then RAF Kenley in Surrey, which was the HQ of the Battle of Britain Command, and the Eastern Group HQ. During those two years, I both lined and refereed matches, including the RAF Group Final, and was flown several times to some games with sixteen of us crammed into a Dakota twin-engine aircraft.

Returning to civilian life at Bristol Imperial Tobacco, I registered with the Bristol and District League, and was eventually promoted to the Western League where I met Lew Webb, a man I respected greatly, a great character, and any stories about him are invariably true. My first big game was the initial floodlit match at Bristol City against Wolves which featured Billy Wright and Bert Williams among other stars. Later I was promoted to the Football League line and then into the middle. During the latter years, in 1969, I was linesman at the Inter Milan v Hansa Rostock game with Norman Burtenshaw and Roy Capley, in the famous San Siro Stadium. It was a fantastic experience, not least because the East German side was accompanied by the guards of Stasi, the most hated and feared secret police agency in the world; assumedly because of the fear that they would defect to the West.

Retirement followed, and after two years on Somerset FA as the referee's representative, I had a phone call from Don Milverton inviting me to a meeting at Paulton Rovers where I was to meet the Western League officers. I think that it was an education for both me and Les Phillips as he had found someone who would stand firm where referees were concerned. Later I was appointed as Assistant to General Secretary, Jack Veale, who had held the position since the end of WW2.

Events that followed are told in the main storyline of this book, but the era of change and improvement was temporarily halted when we lost our Chairman, Les Phillips to a heart attack at such an early age. Les was a tremendous character and football, especially, was the loser. His number two, Stan Priddle, then took charge and we both intensified the issue of ground grading; including that of new member clubs. The early retirement that I took from Imperial Tobacco afforded me the chance to visit our clubs during the week, and sometimes we managed three inspections a day. The whole League was covered in just two seasons; and for once we were ahead of the FA.

When Stan Priddle lost his battle with cancer, Rod Webber assumed the reins. For me, all the years that I had worked for the League with Stan and the copious meetings together, had led to a unique partnership and friendship borne of trust and understanding, and I missed him. A final mention must be made of League Treasurer, Joan Ellis, the highly respected Taunton Town Secretary, and who for this League had maintained and ensured that it stayed financially stable.

As we reached the Millennium in 2000, I had the honour of receiving an engraved gold carriage clock, presented by Geoff Thompson, the Chairman of the FA, at a dinner that was held after the final game at Wembley. In the same week, I had also received the news that Brenda, my wife, who a lot of clubs had met over the years, had been diagnosed with Alzheimer's with a ten-year prognosis. I therefore stood down from the League with a year's notice for the transition to be made, to hand on and keep the League working safely in the hands of Ken Clarke.

I keep my eyes on the League and left with thanks and regards to all the colleagues that I had met over the years; remember, it's by your deed that you are known, but it's by your standards you will be remembered'.

MAURICE WASHER

Away from football, the summer months saw the launch of a mobile phone internet service in Japan. Although it was not something that would immediately affect changes to non-league clubs, it signalled the start of a communications revolution that would do just that. As it stood, mobile phones were becoming much more widely used, and were soon to change the relationship between managers and players where, in some cases, the ease of contact would blur the concept of an 'illegal' approach!

It was in years to come, however, and in the meantime the season that would straddle the end of one century and the beginning of another, kicked-off with Mangotsfield United declaring an intent to move on into the Southern League at seasons end, with the obstacle of Taunton Town to overcome if that ambition was to be realised.

Ken Clarke recalls his introduction to the Western League; *'Having spent many years as secretary of Chippenham and District Sunday Football League and variously as a Wiltshire FA Councillor, Secretary and Chairman of Chippenham Referees' Society, Referee Instructor and Referee Assessor, I applied for the soon to be vacant role of General Secretary of the Western Football League. The management committee called me to meet them in a hotel conference room in Taunton, and I was surprised to be confronted by eight or nine officers and management committee members in the room, but that assembly fired questions at me and then decided that I should be able to succeed Maurice Washer, who was a member of that interview panel. I assume he didn't remember our previous encounter'.*

'At the 1999 AGM, I was elected General Secretary and it was all systems go. My first task was to assist in compiling the fixtures for the coming season and my eyes were opened to one of the big differences between Non-League Football and local football; less teams but many more complications; but with the help of League Committee members and club secretaries my inauguration commenced'.

As the 1999/2000 season began, the FA Cup was, once again, the early season's headline grabber, but only Taunton Town and Chippenham Town progressed into the Third Qualifying round, and both were defeated; Taunton with a 3-0 defeat at home to Margate, while Chippenham achieved a draw at Hardenhuish Park against Worthing, only to then lose the replay, 3-1.

The FA Vase, however, was a different story, and once again proved a fascinating distraction for both loyal and neutral non-league fans. Taunton Town, once again, progressed through to Round Three, and were joined by Chippenham Town and Paulton Rovers, who both held the wild cards. In the event, all three were drawn at home, and all three went through, with Paulton Rovers, 2-0, winners over Corinthian Casuals, Chippenham Town by the same score-line over Northwood, and Taunton Town putting Tooting and Mitcham out, 4-1.

In the following round, all three clubs were drawn away from home, and although Wroxham put Paulton out, 3-2, the other two ties went into extra-time, with Chippenham progressing thanks a single goal at a cold and uninviting, Glossop North End, and Taunton likewise winning in similar conditions, 3-2, at Skelmersdale Town. Those results were then followed by victories for both clubs, with Chippenham beat Wroxham, 3-1, at Hardenhuish Park, and Taunton showing their superiority over Cowes Sport, scoring seven goals without reply.

After the success of previous seasons, there was again an anticipation that the Western League would be major players in the closing stages of the prestigious competition. Taunton Town were favourites to go through, not just because of their good form in previous seasons, but also because Chippenham Town received a home fixture against the highly-fancied finalists from the previous season, Bedlington Terriers.

At this stage of the competition there are very few easy games, and Taunton found that adage to be true as they took on what turned out to be a team in Vauxhall Motors that manager, Russell Musker was later to describe as one of the best he had ever come across; a statement borne partly out of the, 5-1, defeat they suffered at Wordsworth Drive that day.

At the same time Chippenham were putting on a sterling performance and the subsequent draw, 2-2, after extra-time at Hardenhuish Park, left them the only Western League club still in the draw a couple of days later. With the prospects of a battle to come in Northumberland, the task was non-the-less diminished when the name of Vauxhall Motors came out of the hat as the semi-final opponents awaiting the result of the replay.

Few would have taken a bet on the Wiltshire club progressing to the Final, but their manager, Tommy Saunders, however, had the camaraderie of the Western League to thank for some sound reports that he received from Russell Musker and Martyn Rogers who had already played both Bedlington and Vauxhall.

The well supported club travelled to the north with an army of enthusiasts, and after coming away from 'Terriers' ground with a 2-0 victory to reach the two-legged semi-final, the task that lay ahead was clear for all to see.

The subsequent trip to Elsmere Port, Cheshire, to the soulless ground of Vauxhall Motors, and in front of a crowd that mainly contained the travelling

Wiltshire crowd, saw a game filled with incident and passion, with a Chippenham player stretchered off, and the home side down to ten men for the last 50 minutes. The goalless score-line at the final whistle heralded loud celebrations by the home side team, knowing as they did that, not only would they be starting the final game before Wembley with eleven players on the pitch, but also that their star striker, who had been suspended for the game, would be available.

The Wiltshire town got behind its football club for that final game, and a crowd of over 3,000 packed in to see a match that would determine which club took the coveted place at Wembley. And it couldn't have been any closer. Ninety minutes came and went without a goal until, with just minutes of extra time left to play, Chippenham scored, sending the club through to play in the last FA Vase Final at the old Wembley Stadium, and the Western League to celebrate yet another interest in the Vase Final.

A steaming hot day in London on 6th May 2000, League officials joined a huge wave of West Country supporters to cheer on Chippenham Town at Wembley, as the club attempted to make it three Vase wins in a row for the Western League. Of the 23,000 crowd that day, over 15,000 were 'Bluebirds' supporters, but although the game was a well-balanced contest, a killer goal with nine minutes to go denied both the Wiltshire club and the League, the honour of lifting the Trophy.

FA VASE FINAL 2000

The Wiltshire crowd - Chippenham Town FC v Deal FC

It had been a wonderful day for the League and club and the celebrations that greeted the team in that Wiltshire town on their return the following day, belied the reality that they were not taking the historic cup back with them.

In the quest for League honours, Taunton Town made no mistake, and sailed through the season losing just two games, amassing 94 points in the process and ending the year 16 points ahead of runners-up, Mangotsfield United. While they again decided not to apply for promotion into the Southern League, runners-up, Mangotsfield United did just that, and gained admission, nine years after (unjustifiably in many peoples' opinion) being turned down for entry after winning the Western League in 1990/91.

MANGOTSFIELD UNITED

1999/00

At the foot of the Premier Division, Minehead's topsy-turvy progress continued, which saw them immediately return to Division One, together with Odd Down. They were replaced by Devizes Town, who had beaten Welton Rovers into second place by eight points, while both Corsham Town and Frome Town escaped relegation back into their respective County Leagues.

At the AGM in June, Chippenham Town were congratulated on both their appearance at Wembley, and on winning the Les Phillips Cup. The Manager of the Year Award was shared by Taunton Town and Devizes Town, while both Ilfracombe Town and Yeovil Town reserves picked up the Sportsmanship Merit Cup.

After a busy summer, five new clubs were welcomed into Division One for start of the 2000/2001 season; Cadbury Heath, Hallen, Worle St Johns, Bath City reserves and Team Bath; with the University team, the most controversial of the new entrants.

In 1999 the Sports Department at the University of Bath had established a football squad under the name of Team Bath, with the intention of not only playing within the English professional set-up, but also allow players to continue their education at the University. It was designed to help young men who had spent their formative years with professional clubs, with the aim of a full-time contract firmly in their grasp, only to be rejected.

The project was spearheaded by Ged Roddy, who had been appointed Director of Sport at the University of Bath in 1992. His vision was to realise the University's full sporting potential, and that eventually led to a significant £8 million investment in sporting facilities at the university campus.

Football was his real passion, however, having played as a semi-professional for more than ten years, and entry to the Western League allowed Ged to begin the pathway to realise his dream. To that end he appointed Paul Tisdale, a recently retired professional who had played for Southampton and Yeovil Town, (and is now the long-serving manager of Exeter City) as the team's head coach, and all was set for the next step.

Although this unconventional team was not totally accepted by all member clubs, most were willing to accede that the concept might work within the Pyramid of Football. There were also doubts about accepting Bath City reserves back into membership, but as the club's directors vowed it would be a long-term commitment, after their ten-year absence, they were welcomed in with reservations. There were none such doubts about both Cadbury Heath and Hallen entering the League, as they had earned promotion after finishing as winners and runners-up in the Gloucestershire County League.

With the first full season of the new 21st century about to begin, the Western Football League could look back on an interesting and progressive 20th century. The League had reflected life, and shadowed both national and local events, as well as surviving two World Wars, many recessions, changes in transport and leisure activities, the widespread ownership of cars, the construction of motorways, the ownership of televisions and radios in every home, the rise and rise of commercialism, the introduction of new technology, and dramatic changes to the rules of soccer.

Those years had, of course, also seen the spread of the 'people's' game that had gone from a local leisure activity, to becoming an International obsession.

It was from that very solid base that the future could be faced with confidence, assured in the knowledge that, no matter what life held in the 21st Century, there was a certainty that the game at non-league level in the west was alive and well served within the family that is the Western Football League.

CHAPTER 21

The challenge of the noughties

Taunton Town put together an instant winning run in the League, with the realistic expectation of a third Championship ahead of them, but when it came to progress in the lucrative FA Cup competition, their form went missing, and a Preliminary round defeat away in Gloucester at Tuffley Rovers, 4-1, certainly set nerves on edge.

Tuffley Rovers then went on to entertain Chippenham Town in the next round on a dull wet day, with the continual thudding of an impromptu drum setting the large contingent from Wiltshire on edge while they watched their Vase heroes scrape a draw, winning the replay with an equally uninspiring display by the only goal in 180 minutes of play. Progress was then denied, again by a replay, losing to Gloucester City, 5-3, at Hardenhuish Park.

In fact, it was not a spectacular year in the FA Cup for any of the Western League line-ups, with Devizes Town the only club to reach the Third Round and progress through with a win, 2-1, away at Saltdean United. As usual, a Fourth-round appearance by any club provokes a certain amount of anticipation, but that was as far as Devizes went, losing, 5-2 away at Kingstonians, whose progress was then halted by Bristol City after a replay.

It was a different story in the FA Vase, where Chippenham Town and Taunton Town carried the flag for football in the west, matching each success with more anticipation, once again, that a Western League Final could be on the cards. In fact, round's three, four and five all went by, with both clubs' names still in the hat, but it was then that the dream failed for one of the Western League contenders.

In the quarter game at Hardenhuish Park, and in front of the huge Wiltshire following that Chippenham had attracted since their Wembley appearance, Clitheroe walked away with a decisive win, 2-0, and into a two-legged semi-final against Taunton Town, who had defeated Tooting and Mitcham United, 3-0, at Wordsworth Drive.

TAUNTON TOWN FC

FA Vase Winners at Aston Villa 2001

Remembering the lost opportunities of days' past, Taunton then made no mistake, and defeated the Northern League outfit, 5-0, at home, and 4-3, on the road.

Because Wembley Stadium had been closed on 7th October 2000, to facilitate building the new state-of-the-art national centre, the well-attended FA Vase Final was held at Aston Villa. It was a deserved reward for their long standing and hardworking Chairman, Tom Harris, his wife Elsie and his committee, who truly deserved to see Russel Musker and his players lift the FA Vase, and put West Country football again in the minds of the nation.

Their 2-1 victory over Berkhampstead Town was only the third time that a Western League side had lifted the historic Cup since its inception in season 1974/75.

Although successful on the pitch, the year was not without its administrative problems, some of which were caused by the two clubs prolonged progress in the Vase, which once again made a backlog of fixtures inevitable. It was also not helped by near arctic conditions at the end of December which saw temperatures fall in some places to 13 degrees below zero, with a widespread gridlock to transportation on both the roads and railways.

While those two factors were not without quandaries, the task of running a league that is centered very much around rural topography, was also made that much more difficult by a virulent outbreak of Foot and Mouth Disease, which began on 10th February 2001, and with the crisis conditions set to remain for the following eleven months.

The most dramatically effected club was Clyst Rovers, whose ground was closed for a period to stop the spread of the disease. Because of that, they offered to resign from the League, but it was agreed that while they would take no further part and their results be deleted from the table, they would be permitted to remain in membership and compete again the following season.

CLYST ROVERS GROUND

The League table at seasons end told the tale of just how success in a National competition can affect lasting changes to a club, with Chippenham Town attracting all but four of the top attendances of the year. The club had gradually built success with Chairman, Malcolm Lyus, who had been able to keep those who had built the club over the years on-board, whilst adding his own people behind the scenes, to help it grow.

Although Chippenham challenged Taunton for the title, as with Tiverton and Mangotsfield United previously, it was as runners-up that they were promoted to the Southern League, having been beaten to the Championship by just two points. They went out of the League after many years of participation with few rewards, having picked up the Championship Trophy in 1951/52, and the Division One Championship in 1980/81.

Taunton Town, who were crowned as Champions for the third year running, once again did not apply for promotion, but having at last achieved the ambition of putting the FA Vase in the Trophy Cabinet, made it clear that they would be focusing in the season to come on the aim of promotion that had been previously spurned. It was the sixth time that the name of the Somerset County Town had appeared on the magnificent Western League Trophy, equaling the record set by Bristol Rovers, but still two titles behind the overall League Champion holders, Bristol City.

CHIPPENHAM TOWN FANS

Celebrating Les Phillips Cup success

With such success, it was a surprise to many that Taunton's manager, Russel Musker, did not get the 'Manager of the Year' award at the League Convention; an honour that went to the Chippenham manager, Tommy Saunders, by just one point. The factor that enabled the accolade to go Wiltshire's way was the 'Bluebirds' second successive victory in the Les Phillips Cup, which had been won at Bideford in a hard-fought contest against Division One, Exmouth Town. One Dave Bright goal in the last minute of injury time separated the two clubs.

Team Bath proved to be effective competitors in Division One and gained promotion at their first attempt, along with Keynsham Town. Both clubs were well ahead of third placed Frome Town. At the other end of the table, for the second year, Calne had not been able to overcome the raid on their playing staff by Chippenham Town, and had to apply to stay in the League, together with newcomers, Worle St Johns. Both were successful. They were joined by Shepton Mallet Town and Willand Rovers, which enabled second from bottom, Westbury United, to remain in the Premier Division. Minehead was the only club to be relegated.

Following the death of Stan Priddle during the season there were changes to the Management Committee, with Cliff Ashton stepping up to the role as Chairman from Rod Webber, who became President, and Doug Webb became Vice-Chairman.

Stan, who worked in management for Somerset County Council at County Hall, Taunton, was also on the committee of the County Town's Football Club. He joined the Western League Management Committee in 1964 because Taunton were in danger of being thrown out of the League. He worked hard for the League and when Les Phillips became Chairman in 1973, Stan worked closely and was elected Vice-Chairman a year later, until 1988 when he took over as Chairman when Les became ill.

His work on the Joint Liaison Committee with those leagues feeding into the Southern League took up a phenomenal amount of his time, and he commanded respect, trust and honesty in all his dealings for the betterment of the league, our clubs and our sponsors. He became President in 1996 until his untimely death.

STAN PRIDDLE

With little time to settle into their new roles, Cliff, Ken and Doug faced problems to tackle immediately, the most time-consuming and challenging was around a problem that had been rumbling around for some time after a 'no-win no-fee' case had been brought against the League. Recent changes to the law had taken place nationally in litigation with such cases, and it was with a good deal of help from the Football Association, that the League stepped up to defend against the allegation.

Although the case went against the League, the judge ordered such a small amount in compensation that the litigant and his lawyers went away out of pocket with reputations more than slightly tarnished in many eyes. The case had, however, highlighted how vulnerable the Western League Management Committee members were as they could have been held personally liable for all costs had the FA not stepped in.

One of the issues that it highlighted was that the League was one of a small number that was still run by a management committee, and the Football Association strongly advised that it should become a Private Company Limited by Guarantee, without share capital, with immediate effect.

Cliff Ashton, Doug Webb, and Ken Clarke, had already set-up a Steering Group to carry out the instigation of the Limited Company, and after many months of meetings, and with advice from the FA and a firm of specialist solicitors, that is just what happened.

On the 4th June 2001, 'The Western Football League Limited' was incorporated as a Limited Company, with Cliff as Chairman of the Board and Ken Clarke as the Company Secretary. The Directors of the Company were elected from the Management Committee to serve on the Board, and as with many aspects of the game in the UK, the nature of football in the oldest league in the West Country was changed forever.

Cliff Ashton, recalling his time with the League wrote; '*My early memories of the Western League were of real excitement, waiting and hoping that as a young referee officiating in the local county leagues in Gloucestershire, my promotion might come.*

To my delight I was appointed to the Western League as Linesman at the start of the season in 1978.

I remember being appointed to the Les Phillips Cup Final as a Linesman in 1981 at Dawlish. The Referee was Keith Cooper with myself and Alan Nash assisting.

Prior to the match, the sponsors Cuprinol had provided Referee and Linesman kit which didn't fit any of us. Mad panic set in and I believe that Ron Groves wife Megan stepped in and practically remade them in time for kick off!

Following my appointment to the Les Phillips Cup Final I was to have my dream come true to be appointed to the then Supplementary List of Referees and the following season to be appointed to the Full List of Referees.

I enjoyed many diverse roles, one being in the early days, the treasurer and Chairman of the Western League Referees and Linesman Association which sadly was disbanded by the Football Association during reorganisation.

I well remember a funny incident that occurred at a League Convention when we had to be bussed from the Woolacombe Bay Hotel to another venue for the Convention gala dinner. The open top buses arrived and they clearly had been left out in the open, allowing all sorts of muck, seagulls and all, to splatter!!! Watching the ladies in their finery was memorable. My refereeing career ended in 1991 due to age restraints imposed by the Football Association. The then League Referees appointment secretary Lester Shapter stepped down and I applied to become his replacement.

I well remember attending a scary meeting of the full Management Committee which lasted some hours and then being asked to leave the meeting. It was to be a few days before receiving a telephone call from Maurice Washer confirming my appointment.

Four years later the newly elected Chairman Rod Webber asked me to be his vice chairman, and this changed my close allegiance with refereeing and propelled me into a new and exciting role in supporting my Chairman.

My primary role was to be responsible for the ground grading of both existing clubs and new clubs wanting to join the league.

One of the highlights of the grading was visiting a new club with Doug Webb at Willand Rovers, in both our opinions this was a well-run club with excellent facilities which would be a great asset to the League.

However, there was a problem. The playing area was too small in one small area close to the club house. We overcame the problem by extending the measuring wheel!!! The club repaid that small favour by being one of the many great clubs to grace the League.

Chairman Rod Webber and Heather became close friends with Carol & I and remain so, asking me if I would take on the responsibility if, subject to agreement of the Management Committee in becoming League Chairman. I was elected in 2000.

One of the highlights of my time as Chairman was to Chair the complex procedures of taking the League from a Management Committee to a Limited Company and the other of course was the instigation of the Toolstation League sponsorship alongside Ken Clarke which remains to this day'.

Times truly were transforming throughout the country; not just those that would affect changes to the League, but also those that were to impact day-to-day on our clubs, with the world in the throes of the dot.com boom which would affect all communications, including the administration of every league in the country.

There was a way to go, however, with the world-wide use of the internet equivalent to just two-thirds of those using Facebook today, and the UK was lagging, not even in the top ten countries using the revolutionary tool. Times were, however, changing fast, with the League's savvy sponsors, Screwfix Direct, at the front of those changes.

With that as a background, the 2001/02 season opened in hot, summer conditions, with the promise of a healthy competition from the forty clubs competing. Behind the scenes, the FA were continuing to consult about varying the system to improve movement in the Pyramid of Football; a change that would be welcomed by many member clubs who had put in place standards that would enable such a move if, and when, results allowed.

The FA had also been busy attempting to introduce a pathway of progression for budding referees, linesmen and women, and to that end took the control of most aspects of the appointment and progression of match officials away from the Leagues who had been responsible for them.

It eventually meant the end of the '*Western League Referees and Linesman Association',* an organisation that had been set up in the mid-1980s, with, (it must be said), a fair amount of opposition from the management committee, and one that had, in fact, worked incredibly well with some notable young up and coming members over the years. Roger Milford, Paul Durkin and Steve Dunn all progressed to the highest level of the Premier Division.

The monies left in the Association's accounts when it was wound up, around £2,000, was donated to the Stan Priddle Memorial Fund, and to the regret of many, another era was about to begin.

Roger Milford, Paul Durkin and Steve Dunn

While the Premier Division was strengthened by the challenge set by the well drilled students team from Bath University, established clubs were not intimidated by the full-timers, and some had quite a few comments to make about the facilities and hospitality on offer at Claverton Down. Team Bath also learned very quickly that progress in national competitions had to be worked at, and an early exist from the FA Cup was followed by defeat in the Third round of the FA Vase at the hands of Arlesey Town.

It was not, however, to be a year for any Western League clubs in FA national competitions, with the only real surprise in the FA Cup, a 3-1 victory for Bideford at Bath City in the Second Qualifying-round. The progress stopped there, however, and the following game saw Basingstoke progress at the Devon Club's expense by the same score-line.

In the FA Vase, Taunton Town, was the only Western League side left in the draw at the Fourth-Round stage, and a well-deserved win, 3-2, in extra-time against a much-fancied West Auckland team, seemed to increase the possibility of making it through, once again, to the Final. When the following game resulted in a draw, 1-1, away at Tiptree United after extra-time, confidence was naturally high that Wordsworth Drive would hold the advantage for further progression. As everyone in football knows, however, nothing is certain in a game that pays lip service to form, and the favourites were beaten by the odd goal in three after failing to convert their chances.

Although it was a disappointment, news that Taunton Town had applied for promotion to the Southern League gave the last few months of the season interest; especially so because the Championship fight was being spearheaded in North Devon, with Bideford Town in amazing form under the watchful eye of experienced manager, Sean Joyce.

There was then true irony at season's end when Bideford took the title by eight clear points, while Taunton Town had to fight it out with Brislington for the vital runners-up place to have any chance of the promotion to the Southern League; a promotion that they now so desired. After all those years of dominating the Western League, the league table places went down to goal difference, allowing Taunton to progress, coming in as runners-up with the advantage of +21.

This was certainly a time to celebrate for Tom and Elsie Harris. Tom had been on the League Management Committee since 1985 and was made a Life-Member. One of Tom's biggest achievements was as Chairman of the Combination League, a most difficult position which called on his long experience. Tom recalls that time: *'My first association with the Western League was way back in the 1954/55 season when my club, Taunton Town, joined Division Two. We were promoted to Division One in 1956/57 and then had to wait until season 1968/69 for our first League Championship win.*

After a short spell in the Southern League, we returned to the Western League in season 1983/84 and a couple of years later while playing at Melksham Town, during the game a rather large gentleman arrived; namely Les Phillips. He invited me to stroll around the ground with him and promptly told me that I was Management Committee material and that I should fill out the relevant forms. The rest is history.

I served on the Management Committee until the League became a Limited Company and then on the Board as a Director until my club won the Championship for three years on the spin. We were then promoted to the Southern League in 2002 and I left.

I was very proud and honoured to receive my Life Membership of the Western League that year and will always remember the wonderful times we have all had together during the season and at the various Conventions'.

It was a tremendous achievement for the Bristol club to achieve third position, Brislington's highest finish since moving into the Western League in 1991/92, after they had been successful in the Somerset County League for many years.

Fellow Bristol club Bristol Manor Farm were not as fortunate, finishing the year at the bottom of the Premier Division, just above Westbury United. Both clubs were relegated, and replaced by Frome Town, who won Division One comfortably by nine points; albeit with Bath City reserves suffering a three-point deduction for fielding an ineligible player.

Frome had experienced a superb season after facing relegation from the league only two years previously, and put together a winning run that marked a post-war club record, and their crowds had swelled accordingly.

The final game was against Clyst Rovers, who had done well themselves after all the trials faced following the foot and mouth outbreak, after which the magnificent First Division Trophy was presented. There was then a reasonably long break before they could sign off a successful season at Twerton Park, where they were due to meet Bideford in the Les Phillips Cup Final.

On the day, a vivacious crowd cheered them on from behind the goal at the 'Bristol Road End', to no avail as the League Champions proved too strong and picked up the Trophy, winning the encounter, 2-1.

Yeovil Town were in the throes of change, and their reserves had, at one stage, looked unlikely to finish the year because of problems with their pitch. The solution to the problem lay with the League permitting Yeovil to complete their home fixtures at Wordsworth Drive; a permission that was given, but which did not prevent them withdrawing from the competition at seasons end.

The summer was taken up at most Western League member clubs with the usual frantic workload that is associated with running a football club. Each year, while the supporters and players rest, the huge number of volunteer officials and clubmen toil away to ensure that grounds and pitches are in pristine state for the pre-season friendlies, a workload that is, of course, still tackled by every club today.

During the break, however, there was also the distraction of watching the efforts of our England team in far-off Japan, and most were amazed with the rare victory, 1-0, over Argentina in the indoor Dome at Sapporo, thanks to a Beckham goal. The Quarter-Final defeat, 2-1 at the brilliant feet of Brazil however, ended the dream, but the competition boosted the game in the UK from the elite to the park level footballer.

Fan take over the Bristol Road End at Twerton Park at the Les Phillips Cup Final in 2002

The World Cup was then followed by the Commonwealth Games taking place in Manchester at the new magnificent City of Manchester Stadium, which was due to be re-modelled after the games to become the home of Manchester City. The Western League faithful could only dream of such a gift; with most clubs struggling to adhere to the new and stringent standards being placed on the shoulders of the non-league by the FA and League officials.

The National Competition's once again saw a mix of success during the early stages of the 2002/03 season, with Team Bath the most successful in the FA Cup, dispatching Barnstaple Town in the Preliminary Round, 4-0, followed by Backwell United, 3-1, and Wessex League Bemerton Heath Harlequins, 6-1, at the University. The Third Qualifying Round then saw them drawn away to Southern Premier League Newport County, who were also no match, as the 'Scholars' went through, 3-0. The final Qualifying Round was away to Isthmian League side, Horsham, and ended up in a scoreless draw, with the replay back at Claverton Down, where a draw, 1-1, after extra time in front of a bumper crowd of over 1,500, was followed by a penalty shoot-out that resulted in the students progressing through, 4-2.

The First-Round Proper match at Mansfield attracted a crowd of 5,469, and attracted a huge amount of publicity for the University and Ged Roddy, but Team Bath found themselves trailing, 3-0, by half-time. Despite two goals in the second-half for the Western League side, however, it was Mansfield who progressed in the end with a, 4-2, victory.

In the FA Vase, it was the exploits of Bideford Town and Devizes Town that captured local imagination, when by the Third-Round, the two clubs had progressed through thanks to victories over fellow West Country sides, Bitton and Portleven respectively. Although those games were followed by a defeat for Bideford Town at Oadby, 4-2, Devizes progressed through at home to Christchurch, 3-1. With League fixtures then not a priority, the

Wiltshire club travelled North to the much fancied, Clitheroe Town, and duly dispensed of them by the same score-line.

That was where the Wembley dream ended, however, and the Quarter-Final game at home to Maldon Town from Essex, was lost, 3-0, which heralded a quick return to the routine of league games. After all that the season had promised, the backlog of fixtures saw Devizes fail to step up to the mark, and they ended the year at the foot of the Premier Division with just six wins.

At the other end of the table, Brislington had been working hard to meet the grading standards that a promotion would demand, should the opportunity arise. During the season, they had performed well and were neck-and-neck with both Team Bath, whose own ground was well below the standard required for promotion, and Bideford Town, who did not apply to move on.

After such sterling efforts, when the Bristol club came in as runners-up, having lost only five games, it was widely expected that they would be able to progress, but due to restrictions of access to their ground, they failed to achieve the grading necessary.

Ben Foster and Ged Roddy join the Hall of Fame at Bath University

Champions, Team Bath, however, who won the title by eleven points, were accepted for Southern League membership, overcoming the problem of their inferior ground standards by moving to Twerton Park, in a ground-share approved by the Southern League. It was a win, win, situation for Bath City who not only got a good rental income, but also used them as a 'feeder' team, and with that agreement, they withdrew their reserve eleven from the Western League.

Ged Roddy had achieved his initial aim to move swiftly up the Pyramid of football and was showing his talent that sees him today the current Director of Football Development with the Premier League. He also received an MBE, and this year, with swimmer Mark Foster, who is the winner of six World titles and two Commonwealth Games gold medals, has been inducted into the University of Bath Hall of Fame for Sport. The ceremony was held at the £30million Sports Training Village on the Claverton Down campus, which was built during Roddy's tenure.

The question of ground standards was positively highlighted when Torrington Town won Division One. They were just one point clear of Exmouth Town, and as both clubs had worked hard to upgrade their facilities to meet standards required for Premier Division membership, their promotion was heralded as an example of what could be achieved with determination and hard work.

With both Team Bath and Bath City reserves leaving the League, Elmore and Devizes Town escaped relegation to maintain numerical parity. Their departure also afforded Minehead Town, who were at the foot of the First Division, continued membership of the League, and they were joined by new clubs, Clevedon United and Shrewton United.

At seasons end, there was compensation for Brislington losing that second spot, when they beat Exmouth Town in the semi-final of the Les Phillips Cup, but in the Final at Melksham Town's ground, the only goal of the game went to Bridgwater Town, who lifted the Trophy in front of a large vocal crowd on a balmy late spring day in early May.

A new Western League weekly bulletin was issued at the start of the 2003/2004 season, which was both informative and innovative in its content. An improvement in communications was foremost in the minds of the Chairman, Cliff Ashton and Company Secretary, Ken Clarke, and while the postal system was still a main aid to those communications, the world wide web was becoming a driving force both to further administration, and to generally improve the exchange of ideas.

Work in that area was contributed to by John Cuthbertson from Corsham Town FC, who was widely acknowledged for his dot. com ability. In the process, he re-organised the existing website, and demonstrated just what new technology could offer, with the promise of more enhancements to come. It was, however, not a medium that was always used with the best of intentions.

The use of the armchair forums was already way out of control in some areas, with a lawlessness in postings that often-showed scant regard for the libel laws of the written word. While this was widespread, it was something that the officers of the League were bringing to the table to address. Their task, however, would be one that even the FA's legal department was unable to get to terms with.

New additions to the Board saw Tony Stone appointed Finance Director to replace Martin Taylor, and a directorship for both Tony Alcock from Ilfracombe Town, and Colin Hudd from Corsham Town. They were welcome new faces who showed a testament to the changing times, bringing with them a wealth of experience in non-league football.

Tony Alcock was to serve on the board for thirteen years, and is now a Life-Member of the League, recalls; '*My club, Ilfracombe Town, was successful when at a special general meeting of the Western League at Taunton in March 1984 our application had been successful by a majority vote.*

I had met Les Phillips the Chairman of the League during his inspection of Marlborough Park and he impressed us all with his presence and commitment to the league, he told us what was expected of Ilfracombe Town and that he was going to recommend our application. He said to me, I don't want to see you in the league for just two or three seasons. It was 30 years later that we had to resign from the league.

Jack Veale and Maurice Washer, two Secretaries that influenced me in the early years, they were both very fair and professional and I could contact Maurice for advice, who was very approachable in those early years.

At the meeting we were elected, Jack Goodenough and Dave Phillips of Melksham Town greeted us at the bar for a celebration drink, we were the last to leave that night, Dave had to drive his Chairman home and I was driving our Chairman and President home. They were all, well and truly under the weather. Bill Coggins of Backwell was another Secretary who became a good friend, a man who was committed to his club, but good company on match-days home or away.

Brian Beer our current President is another great football man, who always made me welcome at Chard Town with a glass of whiskey on the bar.

League chairman Stan Priddle and his wife Mon, on a visit to Marlborough Park, Mon would always have a walk around the ground, you knew she was checking on a few things and keeping Stan informed later, but always fair and supportive. I first met our current chairman John Pool at Clandown where he was sponge man at the time, little did we both know what an influence the Western league would have on us both over the years, with John becoming a well-respected chairman, over the years he has been a true friend.

Tony finished his reminiscences in a way that sums up the League when he wrote '*The friends I have made over 30 years' association with the league has been an experience that I would not want to have missed'*. A sentiment that says it all.

By the time the 2003/2004 season kicked-off there was a new structure to non-league that would be in place for the following season. It entailed an additional layer at Step Two in the Pyramid between the Conference Proper, Southern, Northern and Isthmian Leagues, which would be known as Conference North and South. The knock-on effect for Western League clubs was that there would be twenty clubs promoted from the fourteen feeder leagues that made up the League's Premier Division, which was to be placed at Step 5; a key to any ambitious club that promotion in the new structure would hold a greater chance at the end of the season.

In national competitions, both the FA Cup and FA Vase held the attention of the non-league West Country footballing community, with Bideford making it through to the two-legged semi-final of the Vase by beating Billingham Town and Chertsey Town on the road. That then led to a potentially difficult quarter-final at home in front of a large crowd of vociferous local support against Gosport Borough. The subsequent victory, 3-0, showed what a good squad Sean Joyce had retained, and with the first game of the semi-final granting home advantage, the club looked favourites to progress through over Winchester City.

On the day a draw, 3-3, left it all to play for in the final game that would decide who would make the trip to Birmingham City's ground, St Andrews Park, for the FA Vase Final. However, Bideford were well beaten with Winchester City having all the play, and progressed through, thanks to four well taken goals without reply.

In the FA Cup, it was a similar story of, so near yet so far, for one of our Western League sides. Like Bideford Town, Paulton Rovers were having a tremendous season in the League after several years of top ten finishes, and progressed through the competition to the fourth-qualifying round with home victories over Bishop Sutton, 4-1, and Hampton and Richmond, 2-0. They were then drawn away to Hornchurch FC from East London in the vital game before the competition proper began. On the day, a very tight match could have gone either way, but unfortunately it was the London club whose name went into the hat, winning with the only goal of the game.

Division One was particularly competitive all season, with three Bristol clubs in contention throughout, together with a surprise challenge from Corsham Town, who had struggled the previous season, winning just 8 of the 36 games they played. In the end, however, it was Hallen who won the Championship, three points clear of Bitton, who were then two points ahead of Bristol Manor Farm.

With Biddestone joining the League for the first time, and both Radstock Town and Saltash United re-joining, the two bottom clubs, Shepton Mallet and Minehead Town, escaped relegation, giving each division a parity of thirty-eight games for the 2004/2005 season.

The Les Phillips Challenge Cup was keenly contested throughout, with the semi-final between Barnstaple and Paulton decided on penalties after a goalless draw, while the other game was won by Bideford Town, 3-2. The Devon club then went on to win the Final by the only goal of the game, and add to their Western League Championship title which had been achieved five points clear of in-form Paulton Rovers.

Once again, the new League Champions had not applied to move into the Southern League; an honour that was embraced by Paulton Rovers, who followed in the footsteps of Tiverton Town, Chippenham Town, and Taunton Town, who had all moved on after achieving the runners-up position.

Many of the clubs who expressed a reluctance to progress did so because the move would entail withdrawing from the FA Vase, and moving instead into the FA Trophy. The games in the Trophy inevitably involved clubs from higher leagues, which made progress and financial reward less likely. There was also the consideration that promotion might bring about an increase in the playing budget and travel expenses, which would not necessarily be compensated by an increase in gates. Despite measures being put in place by the FA to open-up the Pyramid of Football, the ability of a club to determine its own future was still a closely guarded key to its survival; something perhaps that is being challenged today.

Mid-May saw the Annual League Convention weekend held, once again, at the Palace Hotel, Torquay, where a new Hospitality Award appeared for the first time. It was something of an overdue recognition that clubs throughout the Western League had, for years, held a widespread reputation for the way that they treated officials and guests at their grounds. The first recipients of the award, Willand Rovers, were only in their third year with the League, but had proved themselves valuable members, both on and off the field, since joining from the Devon League.

The summer of 2004 was particularly busy with more changes to the structure of the non-league game being discussed. The Directors, however, found themselves busy dealing with what seemed to be, a huge challenge when Screwfix Direct, who had been taken over by Kingfisher PLC, gave notice that the following season would be their last.

Fortunately, both Chairman, Cliff Ashton, and Company Secretary, Ken Clarke, were on the ball (so to speak), and had noticed in a local business paper an article about a company known as Toolstation, that had been formed by the members of the family who had founded Screwfix Direct. Armed with the news, the Chairman wrote a letter to Mark Goddard-Watts, both congratulating him on his new venture, and tentatively enquiring if there was any possibility of negotiating another sponsorship deal.

Within three days, a response was received from their Marketing Director, Neil Carroll, suggesting a meeting to discuss it further, but emphasising that he would want the whole situation to be kept secret until negotiations were well advanced.

The first tentative step to forming a new partnership was very low key, and a few weeks later Cliff and Neil met at a pub in Bridgwater to explore it further. It was to be the catalyst toward more proactive discussions, and many more meetings between the Chairman, Ken Clarke and Neil, before the terms of the sponsorship could be agreed. The nature of discussions, of course, precluded any wider discussions, and the full Western League Board of Directors were not able to be informed until everything was agreed.

The new structure of non-league football had seen the Western League Premier Division placed at Step 5/6, alongside the Isthmian League's Division Two, with 13 Feeder Leagues, and as the season kicked-off it was anticipated that this would enable a more open system by encouraging clubs to enter the League and progress through the system.

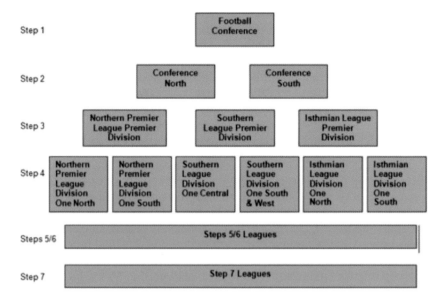

Step 1		Football Conference	

Step 2 — Conference North, Conference South

Step 3 — Northern Premier League Premier Division, Southern League Premier Division, Isthmian League Premier Division

Step 4 — Northern Premier League Division One North, Northern Premier League Division One South, Southern League Division One Central, Southern League Division One South & West, Isthmian League Division One North, Isthmian League Division One South

Steps 5/6 — Steps 5/6 Leagues

Step 7 — Step 7 Leagues

The 2004 Pyramid of Football

With the Western League placed at Step 5/6

On the field, Bideford Town began where they had left off a few months earlier, beating all in their path, but while that was the case in the League, it was not the same in the FA Cup, where they lost in the second qualifying-round after holding Tiverton Town, 0-0, at Ladysmead.

It was Hallen who carried the hopes of the Western League in the competition, by progressing through to a fourth-qualifying round game. However, in front of a huge and vocal crowd in Essex against Canvey Island, they came up against a seasoned professional set-up, who had experienced it all before, and the Bristol club went out, 4-1.

As the season progressed, Bideford did not have it all their own way in the League competition either, and were challenged by Frome Town and Corsham Town, who were both in exceptional form. Frome's progress was only tempered by a long run in the FA Vase, which saw them reach the quarter-finals, away in the North against Jarrow Roofing Bolden Community Association FC, at Bolden Colliery, near Sunderland. When the game resulted in a defeat, 3-0, a quick return to the more 'bread and butter' matter of the League did not afford them the possibility of catching up on results.

The final Screwfix Western League season saw Bideford again crowned Champions, but they again failed to apply to move on. The surprise runners-up were Corsham Town, who had showed great form under manager Colin Bush. With a strong squad signed-up, and a vast amount of work, led by Chairman Colin Hudd, achieved off the pitch with ground improvements. With a confident air, the club declared that come the time they would be aiming to move-on to the Southern League, and after such a season few would doubt they would achieved the aim.

In Division One, Willand Rovers topped the table nine points clear of second placed Calne Town. Both were promoted to the Premier Division, with their places taken by relegated Bridport Town and troubled Devon club, Clyst Rovers. There were no relegations, despite both Biddestone and Shepton Mallet struggling all season, and they were joined by successful new applicant clubs, Bradford Town, Portishead and Longwell Green Sports.

CALNE TOWN FC

Portishead had won the Premier Division of the Somerset County League four times in five years between 1993 and 1998, with recent seasons yielding four successive runners-up positions. The same was also true of Longwell Green Sports, who had finished in the same position in the Gloucestershire County League. Both clubs had worked hard to improve facilities, and with playing strength no issue, they were valuable additions to the League; especially as they pledged to continue upgrading facilities to carry on with the improvements.

With those additions, the League was increased to a total of forty-two clubs, competing over an area of the West Country that covered Bristol to Cornwall, Devon, Somerset, Dorset and Wiltshire. It was both something that the Directors were proud of, and something that did not escape the notice of our new league sponsor, Toolstation.

The summer of 2005 could not have emphasised more graphically the changing face of football in the UK. While close to home the new arrangements that had been put in place were generally welcomed, giving a statistical possibility that, in the right circumstances, a club could progress through to the National League. At the top the football pyramid was attracting the attention of international business that was continuing its stranglehold on 'the peoples game'.

Manchester United, a club that had been in the hands of the local Edwards family for 30 years, was sold to the USA based speculator, the Glazier family, who took control with 70% of the shares, using money from International Trade and Marketing, rather than from their own pocket.

Days later, the FA Cup Final was decided on penalties for the first time in its history, when the game between Glazier's new club and Arsenal had resulted in a goalless draw, with the London club successful on the day.

Until that date, the game would have attracted a replay, but with International games attracting huge amounts of money, the importance of the once premier competition in the UK, had been downgraded. That same day Liverpool won their fifth European Cup Final, when they beat A C Milan in Istanbul.

Football had, indeed, moved a long way from its roots.

Although the game was now not just a national obsession, but an international one, it was the draw of local football that new League Sponsors, Toolstation, were interested in. From previous experience, it had been apparent that the attraction Western League football held to its portfolio of customers made the new association both desirable, and viable; and the savvy company was about to begin an association that would span the years to the benefit of all concerned.

In the FA Cup, only Bitton progressed into the second-qualifying round, but they were then on the wrong end of a 3-0 score-line at Bishops Cleeve. In the FA Vase, it was a similar story, with a third-round exit for the remaining three clubs; Devizes Town, 3-0, at Needham Market; Bideford Town, 2-1, at Hillingdon Borough; and Willand Rovers, 1-0, at Newmarket.

Alongside the concern expressed about the lack of Western League representation at national level, there were also problems with one of the existing member clubs. Exmouth Town were in deep trouble, and eventually had no choice but to withdraw during the year due to financial problems. The club had been members since 1973, but sadly went out of existence until August 2006, when they were reformed as Exmouth Town (2006) AFC, and took over their reserve sides' position in the Devon & Exeter League.

In contrast, Corsham Town once again pushed for the Championship, but were beaten by an unstoppable Bideford Town, who only lost two games all year, and who won the title for the fourth time in five seasons. Newly promoted Calne Town, who had managed to put the problems of previous seasons well and truly behind them, were in fourth place, just two points behind Welton Rovers. At the foot of the Premier Division, Backwell United were relegated, but Torrington Town escaped due to the demise of Exmouth Town.

In Division One, Dawlish Town had bounced back from the relegation of two seasons before, and were crowned Champions, after clocking up 115 goals, and conceding just 33. Chard Town were promoted as runners-up alongside third placed Street; which was a promotion that took the Somerset club to the highest level they had attained in their 126-year history.

Saltash United, who had been unable to repeat their success of the 1980s, left at the end of the season having completed just two years. With the League losing both the Cornish club and Exmouth, no-one was relegated out of the league, which gave an unexpected reprieve to Elmore, who had only won four games all year, and to bottom placed Clyst Rovers.

The heat of summer was oppressive, with July the hottest on record, which did not aid the work on pitches throughout the League. While that caused some problems, most football fans were in front of their TV screens following the World Cup that was taking place in Germany. Once again England were knocked-out on penalties, this time at the quarter-final stage, to Portugal. The Press, however, did not dwell on the loss, but highlighted the progress they discerned the game had made over the past twenty years.

A positive press is not something that has been written about much in this book, despite the history scanning countless years, but Richard Scudamore, Chief Executive of the Premier League, who was brought up in Bristol and is an ardent Bristol City fan, said of the games progress; *'From 1986 to now, it has been an unbelievable evolution. There hasn't been anything to match it since the founding two decades ago of the Premier League'*.

He also talked of technological divergence, pointing out that; *'back in 1986 it was 'violence, poor stadia, Heysel and Bradford, Margaret Thatcher's membership schemes and ID cards, and you couldn't sell football, it was a low point'*.

Although he added that the past twenty years had been revolutionary on the back of technological developments, he also added; *'since the 1880s the fundamentals of the sport have changed very little, and that is the beauty of football'*.

It was, perhaps, an exaggeration of the facts, but the Western Football League and its clubs had lived life throughout all those years, adjusting to the changes, and ensuring that the basic ethos of the League always remains the same, with hospitality and sporting aims at its centre.

As the new season came closer, it was revealed that there was to be another move of significance in the Pyramid of Football, when, from the 2007/08 season, the South-Western League and the Devon County League were to merge to form the 'South West Peninsula League'. The new league was to have a Premier Division, which would sit parallel with Division One of the Western League; which in theory would allow its clubs then to feed directly into our Premier Division.

One of the rationales behind the move was to negate some of the mileage that clubs in the extreme areas of Devon and Cornwall would need to travel if they wanted to move forward, and to encourage movement through the Pyramid without having to directly jump from the local Cornwall and Devon Leagues into one that could entail a journey of up to 200 miles each way.

The implication of such an initiative was viewed with a certain amount of scepticism, which despite much discussion was not allayed.

And there was, of course, the rise, and rise, of one Cornish club who were not about to wait for convention, or for the men of football to dictate their fate.

Truro City had been stirred by the ambition and enthusiasm of a local property developer, Kevin Heaney, who despite a recession beginning to bite throughout the country, was still exhibiting extremely deep pockets. As people of the west would soon see, all the tinkering in the world with 'Pathways of Football' would have little influence on such ambitions, no matter how unsustainable it might be, and could certainly not temper personal agendas in the name of '*the spirit of the game*'.

Truro City FC supporters

The 2006/07 season began, with Truro City joined by Hengrove Athletic and Sherborne Town, affording clubs 42 games in each division. While competition in the Premier Division for honours was led to an even contest with no outstanding winner until the later stages, in Division One, the Cornish men were odds-on favourites before a ball was even kicked.

In the FA Cup, only Bideford Town and Willand Rovers were left in the competition by the second round, and both Devon clubs bowed out to Newport County and Clevedon Town respectively. The FA Vase, however, was a different matter.

While Calne Town were toppled by Slimbridge, 4-1, at home in the third round, Sherborne Town, Truro City and Bideford Town, all went through. As the New Year of 2007 came in, Sherborne also went out, 2-1, away at Mildenhall Town, but Bideford Town made light of their task, beating Barwell, 7-0, to progress through, while Truro City, also at home, dispatched Newcastle Benfield, 3-1.

In the last round before the quarter-finals, interest was further enhanced when Truro came out of the bag with an away game at Slimbridge; a club that had already boasted getting through the competition by beating Southern League Chippenham Town, and then Calne Town.

The Cornish side, however, was another matter altogether for the Hellenic club, who were well beaten by the pretenders, 3-0, and when Bideford Town managed to record a victory, 3-2, away at VCD Athletic, most West Country non-league fans looked for both clubs to be drawn apart to keep alive, once again, the dream of an all-Western League Final at Wembley; a wish that was granted.

While Truro City then managed to sneak a win, 1-0, at Whitehawk FC, who play near Brighton on the South coast, Bideford Town were defeated by the same score-line after travelling to Stockton-on-Tees, to play Northern League club, Billingham Synthonia.

There really did not seem any way of stopping the Cornish club, and even when they came away from the first of the two-legged Vase semi-final a goal down, few would have bet against them not reversing that score-line at Treyew Road; and they would not have been disappointed.

In front of a massive crowd of partisan spectators, Truro City achieved entry into the non-league Hall of Fame, when they became the first Cornish club to progress to an FA Vase Final, winning the game, 3-1, and then, in true style, went on to augment that record, by picking up the magnificent Trophy at the new Wembley Stadium, with a win, 3-1, over AFC Totton.

Truro City FC Winners of the FA Vase 2006/07

While all the action was centered during the season around the Division One club, Corsham Town were quietly creating a record of their own, winning the Les Phillips Cup with a victory, 1-0, over Willand Rovers, and becoming League Champions for the first time in their history, two points ahead of Bridgwater Town.

Corsham players are introduced to Mrs Phillips, Chairman Cliff Ashton and President Rod Webber

CORSHAM TOWN FOOTBALL CLUB

Champions of the Western Football League 2006/07 season.

It was an amazing achievement for the club that had come so far in such a short time thanks to the dedication and work of its back-room boys and girls, committee and playing staff. It was, therefore, extremely sad to find that they were unable to claim a place in the Southern League due to the vagaries of their ground ownership; a decision that was even more unfortunate because they had already installed floodlights and seating in anticipation of progressing.

Their loss was to the advantage of runners-up, Bridgwater Town, who moved into the Southern League, the fifth club to do so in seven years.

In Division One, second placed, Portishead, also saw their progress halted because, without floodlights they too were unable to claim the promotion that their on-field strength had merited. In their place, and just one point behind, Ilfracombe Town qualified, replacing relegated Keynsham Town.

Truro City were, of course, clear Division One Champions, losing just one game, scoring a record 185 goals, conceding 23, and twenty-two points clear of the nearest contender. They had, indeed, set the Western League alight, and after breaking League records, and winning the FA Vase, the bookies had no doubt about who would win the 2007/08 Championship; already offering very low odds on further progression for the ambitious Cornish club, despite rumours that all was not well with Kevin Heaney's development business.

The summer saw an increase in the financial meltdown that was both a national and an international phenomenon, amid news that America was suffering a 'Great Recession'. Reports stated that this was the official start of the worst global downturn since World War Two, and although that was obvious, the effects had already been felt 'on the ground' by some of the League's less financially stable clubs.

And worse was to come.

Plucky village club, Biddestone, who had been improving their performances during the three years they had been in membership, found that they could not sustain football at Western League standard, and left. Such was their meltdown that they also withdrew their reserve side from the Wiltshire League, and are sadly currently only competing in youth and junior football.

Clyst Rovers, who had finished the term second from bottom in Division One, also withdrew and were accepted into the new South West Peninsula League Premier Division; a move that only lasted until 2009/10, when they resigned from that league during the season and their record was deleted.

With new clubs Oldland Abbotonians and Roman Glass St George both replacing the departing clubs, all looked set for the new season with no indication of problems to come. In mid-June, however, the League was informed that Torrington were also withdrawing due to financial difficulties, and would be returning to the North Devon League alongside their reserves.

Life was indeed getting more difficult for those attempting to run non-league clubs in an economic climate that was becoming worse by the day. Throughout the country people were finding the material aspects of life challenging, with banks, who had been so willing to lend money and extend credit on a whim previously, altering course and often threatening foreclosure – in some instances almost at the drop of a hat. The good-will and support of local businesses, which had become such a life-line to many clubs, also dried-up. The new climate was dictating, not just a dearth of companies who were willing to engage commercially, but also a complete clampdown by the financial institutions who were, in reality, 'running scared' of the economic conditions and predictions.

While that was true for most clubs in Western League membership, it did not apply, on the surface, to Truro City, whose property developer Chairman was still pursuing the dream of putting houses on Treyew Road, and then attracting external finance to build a National Stadium for Cornwall. While there were already indications that, as with many millionaires in football, his pockets were filled with complex deals and dreams, the club continued to press for yet another promotion up the Pyramid with more of an eye to the moment, than to the future.

While the aspiration for promotion to the Southern League was realised when they won the Western League Championship at the end of the season, a clear 17 points ahead of second-placed, Dawlish Town and almost twenty points clear of Willand in third place, it was not such an all-round season of success that their spending had predicted.

In the FA Cup, Truro City, Hallen and Corsham Town all went through to the second qualifying-round, but none succeeded in progressing. All three clubs were drawn against Southern League Premier Division opposition, but they did not let the League down, and Hallen put up a characterful fight at Hardenhuish Park against Chippenham Town, but went down, 2-0. Down the road, Corsham Town also put on a superb display, only to lose, 2-1, to Bashley.

The final Western League survivor, Truro City, had been handed a home-tie, which was seen by many to hold a huge advantage for the 'Tigers' against Bath City, but they failed to put the ball in the net and went down to the only goal of the game. Their FA Vase journey was also a short one, losing, 3-0, at home to Whitley Bay in the fifth round, and with Bitton losing out in the fourth round away at St Ives Town, 3-2, the League's interest in the competition was ended early for another year.

Odd Down came in bottom of the Premier Division, and were relegated, to be replaced by Division One Champions Wellington and the runners-up, Sherborne Town, while Larkhall Athletic were unlucky to be pushed into third place on goal difference.

Weston St Johns, who had struggled since joining the League in 2000/01 as Worle St Johns, (changing their name the following year), came in bottom place and left to replace their reserves in the Somerset League. Nine points above them, Almondsbury ended the term a point ahead of Backwell, but were not relegated. Backwell, however, chose to return to County football, because they had failed to recoup lost ground after a change of manager had seen an exodus of experienced players a couple of seasons previously, and opted to rebuild in the face of the growing financial problems that were being experienced by many.

Nationally there seemed to be bad news around almost every corner, and when the government took the unprecedented step of nationalising the ailing Northern Rock Bank and the Royal Bank of Scotland, it became clear that the economic situation was extremely grim. It was reflected with football experiencing a huge amount of bankruptcies of clubs outside the English Premier League.

The demise of Halifax Town, who were expelled from the Conference National with multi-million pounds worth of debt, went out of business a month later, after 97 years in existence. It was not an isolated incident and they were joined by Gretna FC, who were relegated from the Scottish Premier League with debts of £4 million.

It all contributed to a very difficult close season for our clubs, who would normally be busy raising sponsorship from local businesses and hopefully improving their grounds; a task made almost impossible with companies under severe pressure themselves.

Although the economic situation had not improved by the time the 2008/09 season kicked-off, new clubs, Gillingham Town and Wells City, came into the League full of optimism and with plans to progress still further. Gillingham moved up from the Dorset Premier League where they had been runners-up, and had never spread their wings before to embrace a higher standard of football, whereas Wells City had been successful members of the Western League during the early half of the 20th Century, before opting for Somerset County football.

It was a credit to the League, and to its Sponsors, Toolstation, that despite the grim national and international financial situation, football went on as usual. There were twenty-one clubs in the Premier Division and twenty in Division One, representing the counties of Bristol, Devon, Dorset, Gloucester, Somerset and Wiltshire. And contrary to the general condition of the economy, some clubs were about to have a very good season indeed.

As usual, Cup competitions occupied most clubs early in the season, and as the FA Vase reached the fourth-round there were still three Western League names in the hat. Although Larkhall Athletic were knocked-out at home to Norfolk side, Dereham Town, 4-2, both Bitton and Bideford Town went through beating Cogenhoe United, 2-1, and Scarborough Athletic, 1-0, respectively. With both clubs then handed home draws, expectations were high, but in the end Glossop North End were too strong for Bitton, who lost the encounter, 2-0, leaving Bideford, once again, to fly the West Country flag with a victory, 2-0, over Spennymore Athletic.

The quarter-finals saw a difficult game for Bideford with a long trip to the East coast against Lowestoft Town, whose home advantage is always worthy of a goal start, thanks to their vociferous supporters. It unfortunately proved to be a journey too far for the North Devon club, who left empty handed after a one-sided, 4-0, defeat.

In the FA Cup, Bitton were narrowly defeated at Paulton Rovers, 1-0, in the second qualifying-round, leaving Frome Town the only Western League side in the hat after they carved out a 3-1 win, against the odds, away at Poole Town. They then went on to upset the form book again, holding Team

Bath to a decent 2-2 draw, with the reward, a trip to Bath. That led to a huge Frome contingent descending on Twerton Park, outnumbering the home crowd by two to one, but despite putting on a resilient display, the students slotted in four goals without reply to progress through, leaving Frome with a keen eye on the League title, and with promotion as their aim.

The quest for the Championship and promotion was not, however, an easy ambition to realise. Bitton challenged throughout, with Willand Rovers, Dawlish Town, Bristol Manor Farm and Bideford Town, all in contention. In the final months of the season, however, Bitton pulled away to win the honours eight points clear. Due to the demands of the Southern League Ground Grading the new title holders were not able to go for promotion and so, once again, it was the Western League runners-up who progressed through, affording Frome Town the opportunity to realise their ambitions despite ending the year eight points adrift.

At the foot of the Premier Division, Devizes Town were experiencing all sorts of problems, ending the term a clear nine points adrift. They were relegated along with Chard Town and Corsham Town. For Corsham the journey from being Champions, just two years earlier, was something of a tragedy. The inability to progress had resulted in turmoil at the club, as they lost their Chairman, the hard-working Colin Hudd, their charismatic manager, Colin 'Nobby' Bush and many other key people and players, leaving a void that they were unable to fill.

Larkhall Athletic FC

In contrast, Larkhall Athletic, who became members of the League in 1976, experienced one of the most memorable periods in their long history, winning Division One ten points clear of Longwell Green Sports, with a huge goal-difference of +100. They knew all about the problems of success on the pitch not matching the set grading standards, when they were denied promotion to the Premier Division in 1988/89, due to a lack of floodlights, and made no such mistake this time.

As the 2009/10 season began, Bideford Town made it quite clear that they would, at last, not just be aiming for the Championship, but were ready to move on if their target was achieved.

In contrast to that, many clubs were lowering their ambition and tightening their financial belts, to meet the expectations of their Business Bank Manager. Alongside that, there was also another black cloud hanging over some league members, with a new 'tough' Inland Revenue campaign that was targeting even the smallest of clubs to ensure that every penny due would be paid in full. A previously relaxed policy, introduced by Gordon Brown, that had almost encouraged people and organisations into lax accounting was virtually reversed overnight, in the hope of righting the mishandled fiscal policies which threatened a deeper national recession than had been previously predicted.

On the pitch, the FA Vase brought limited Western League success, with Bristol Manor Farm going out, 3-1, at home, to the up-and-coming Brighton side, Whitehawk, while Dawlish Town were putting on a sterling display in Devon against the highly-fancied, Gresley FC, drawing, 4-4. In the return game, they performed equally well, and were unfortunate to bow out of the competition, 7-6, on penalties; ending the League's interest for another year.

The same was true in the FA Cup, where three clubs progressed into the second qualifying round, but it was not to be. Almondsbury Town lost, 4-1, at home to AFC Totton, while Willand Rovers, who were also at home, lost to Bath City, 5-0, and Hallen made the short journey to Bridgwater Town and were narrowly beaten by the only goal of the game.

It was, indeed, a very difficult season for many of the clubs and reflected the general recession that was being faced throughout the country. However, at seasons end Bideford again won the Championship, four points clear of Willand Rovers. After achieving that feat for the fifth time since the turn of the century, they fulfilled the undertaking they made at the beginning of the season and moved on to test their strength, once more, in the Southern League.

The move was made more sustainable by the Devon Link Road that was opened in 1989. The previous time the club had ventured into the Southern League, in the words of Ian King, a Times journalist, it would have been a very different journey. He wrote; *'Reaching the north coast of Devon was a painful process that involved leaving the M5 at the village of Sampford Peverell, braving traffic jams in nearby Tiverton, and grinding up the A361, a twisting, pot-holed two lane main road, on which tractors, heavy lorries and caravans caused frequent tailbacks. From there it was into Barnstaple, for more traffic jams. The 100-mile drive from Bristol alone, took half a day. Interestingly, in July 2016, Devon County Council began a public consultation on possible improvements, but unfortunately the most obvious improvement of all, to upgrade the entire road into a dual carriageway, was rejected on cost grounds, just as it was in the early 1980's'.*

The promotion of Bideford brought the number of teams that had moved on in the Pyramid from the Western League to nine, with six of that number in the previous eight years. The Pyramid System of Football seemed, indeed, to be working well, despite the tendency for clubs to choose promotion at their own pace, rather than have it thrust upon them.

At the other end of the division, neighbours Calne Town and Melksham Town were both relegated to Division One, and were replaced by Wells City, who had taken the title a clear ten points ahead of runners-up, Odd Down, who were also promoted. In contrast to the progress that Wells had achieved in their first year of membership, Minehead, who had struggled for many seasons, ended the year in bottom place, and went out of the League, along with Clevedon United.

The summer of 2010 was taken up for many football fans watching the spectacle of the World Cup staged in South Africa. It was an entertaining distraction for the hard-working men and women of the League, who were endeavoring to keep football alive in their towns and villages at a time when to do so called on every drop of dedication and determination that could be mustered. Over all the years that the League had been in existence little seemed to have changed, with the main secret to football not the advances in technology and wealth, but the dedication and community that embodies the clubs of the League.

With economic uncertainty around every corner, it was the enduring sponsorship of Toolstation that gave assurance all was well. They had not faltered in their sponsorship and were one business that was thriving, despite the economic ambiguity. History was about to show, that when the going gets tough......

CHAPTER 22

Toward 125 years and Counting…

With all that was happening, both nationally, and internationally, the expectation and excitement of ten years past, when the prospects of a new century had promised so much, seemed a long time ago.

Those earlier years of 2000 had seen a huge increase in international terrorism, with the atrocities in America and London still present in people's minds, and now joined by memories of fresh acts of terrorism. There had also been the effects of the far reaching Global recession still ever present, and of course, the rise (and rise) of big money football, which was changing the face of the game. But, as it has throughout history, the game must go on; and go on it did.

A new entry to the Western League for 2010/11 was the Welsh club, Merthyr Town, who had only recently been reformed from their previous successful existence as Merthyr Tydfil FC. They were no strangers to the vagaries of the 21st Century. Like many other clubs, had risen from the ashes after being put into administration, and then out of existence, following severe financial problems.

When they reformed, the FA accepted them as a new club, but insisted they drop from the Southern Premier League to begin life at Step 6, and after much consideration they started their new life in Division One of the Western Football League.

While it was known that Merthyr saw the League as a stepping-stone to a higher level, their membership was welcomed. This was a new club, with a new approach, run by a Supporters Trust who made it clear they would not tolerate the old reputation Merthyr had attracted, where they had a section of fans that gave the sport a bad image.

Symbolic of Merthyr's plight, their locked-out ground

As the season began the member clubs didn't fare well in the national competitions, with only Bristol Manor Farm progressing through to the second qualifying round of the FA Cup, holding Basingstoke, 2-2, at home, but failing to win through, losing the return encounter, 1-0.

The same was true in the fourth round of the FA Vase, where Bitton and Cadbury Heath were drawn at home, while Willand travelled. All three failed to progress: Bitton losing, 3-2, to Coalville Town, Cadbury Heath going out, 5-1, to Spennymore Town, and Willand losing, 2-0, to Dunstable.

The New Year came in after the heavy snow and freezing conditions in December had decimated the programme of games, with the weather so extreme in some areas that schools had to be closed. It caused a heavy backlog of fixtures, which resulted in some clubs committed to two or more games a week. With a good deal of co-operation, the season was surprisingly completed on time, and Larkhall Athletic were crowned Champions, nine points clear of runners-up, Bitton, and twelve points clear of Ilfracombe Town.

It was both a sweet and a bitter victory for Larkhall who, with five games left, had been sitting seven points clear at the top only to be told their Plain Ham ground did not meet the standard required for Southern League football. With an estimated £15,000 of work needed to achieve the Category E standard under the FA's National Ground Grading requirements, there was not enough time to implement the improvements, even if the money could have been raised.

The ambitious club then thought they had found a solution to the problem when an agreement was reached to play at Twerton Park, but they were told that, contrary to a few years previous when Team Bath took up that option to progress, ground sharing to gaining promotion was now not allowed.

While there was very little that the 'Larks' could do about the situation in hand, they embarked on a project of improvements to be sure that when the time came, they would not fall foul of the rules again.

Merthyr Town won Division One, fourteen points clear of runners-up, Oldland Abbotonians, with just four defeats all year. They were promoted alongside Bridport, who had ended the term in third place and were picking up their first promotion since suffering relegation in 2003/04.

Bridport progressed even though they were four points behind Abbotonians, because the Bristol club did not have floodlights, and so were denied the chance to advance. Wellington and Welton Rovers were relegated, with both clubs having struggled in all areas and fighting for survival.

Shortly after the season ended, adjusted figures published by the Government showed unemployment at 2.5 million, indicating no end to the austerity conditions, and when Chester City announced bankruptcy after 125 years of continued existence - just a year after losing Football League membership - it seemed that the news could not get any grimmer; but it did.

The growing reports of football clubs going into administration continued, and when National League Rushden and Diamonds went out burdened with huge debts, it brought home, once again, that life was far from normal within the game. Nevertheless, it was not unique to the time, as life shadowed events in the early 20th century with alarming similarities.

In response to the economic news, the long hot summer of 2011 produced an Emergency Budget from Chancellor, George Osbourne, which in turn was greeted by riots in many major cities against the conditions that were being imposed by the collapsing economy, and the austere measures that were being imposed on both the working and non-working population. It was reminiscent of times past that had been lived through before. This time, however, the League was in a far better position with the wonderful support of our sponsors, Toolstation, ever present to steady the ship.

The violent response by sections of the public was not easily quelled, and in early August both Bristol City and Bristol Rovers, along with other clubs in major cities, had their games postponed at the behest of the police, due to the intimidating mood that prevailed. As a result, a Friendly match that had been planned between the national teams of England and Holland at Wembley was called off, and then David Cameron was recalled from his holiday to Chair an Emergency Meeting of COBRA, the Crisis Committee of the Government, with a view to address the situation.

With that as a backdrop, the weather then contributed to the heated and highly charged atmosphere, with October recording the highest temperature on record of +86`F, but football had to go on, and with a steely determination to normalise conditions, Western League clubs did just that, and carried on regardless.

Once again, interest in the FA Cup was short-lived for our League clubs with Division One side, Cadbury Heath, becoming the only one in the Second-Qualifying round, then unfortunately losing at home to Poole Town, 4-0.

In the FA Vase, Bitton went through to the Fourth Round, but were then defeated, 3-1, by the strong Northern League side, West Auckland Town, and Willand Rovers also succumbed at home to the muscle and talent of the Northern Counties East side, Staveley Miners Welfare, 3-1.

The only other Western League club still in the competition at that stage was Larkhall Athletic, who had been handed a difficult away trip to Reading Town. Although the home side were favourites to progress, the 'Larks' went through, 3-2; demonstrating that it's sometimes easier to play a Cup Match away from the expectations of your home town support, as 'under-dogs'. It was, however, as far as Larkhall went, losing to Herne Bay in a replay, 1-0, in the following round.

Merthyr Town, who during their troubled times had been forced to move from their home ground, Penydarren Park to play at Rhiw Dda'r, home of Taff's Well

A.F.C., continued to attract a good following both home and away. General reports back from clubs about Merthyr were positive, with most loving the additional income their visits generated. Attracting so much support, combined with their rich football history, they were odds-on to win the League, but they were pushed all the way by Bitton. At seasons end, Merthyr's progress continued as planned, and Bitton were beaten to the Championship by just two points, six points clear of third placed, Larkhall Athletic.

Merthyr were promoted back into the Southern League, debt free and with the promise of European funding to move back to their spiritual home at Penydarren Park, complete with a 3G artificial playing surface in the heart of their town. It would not be an exaggeration to say that many of the clubs they had played in their time in the Western League looked with a certain amount of envy at the good fortune that fate had dealt them.

Cadbury Heath and Melksham Town both fought the season out for the Championship of Division One, with the Bristol side eventually triumphing by six points, and while they were both promoted, they were also joined by third placed Gillingham Town, to maintain the Premier Division's numerical strength and replacing the promoted Welsh club.

While football fans watched England reach the quarter-finals of the European Cup during the summer break, when they went out on penalties to Italy in Kiev, the Olympic Games held in London was, undoubtedly the highlight for most sports fans.

There was, of course, an irony in the fact that the last time the Games came to London, in 1948, the occasion were dubbed the 'Austerity Olympics', due to the conditions our population was living under in post-war England. While in the 21st century the standard of living was extremely good for most of the population compared with those far-off days, there were still parallels to be drawn.

Before the new season kicked-off, it was announced that the League had been awarded the FA Charter Standard; a title that denotes a kitemark setting to ensure consistent and high standards of administration. The base criteria on which that was achieved was:

- 60% of all teams in both Leagues were FA Charter Standard Clubs, with the prospect of achieving 100% within two years of attaining the award. New teams joining the Western League would become an FA Charter Standard Club within a year of membership.

- A development plan to reflect the needs of the member clubs.

- A web-based system showing results, fixtures and League tables in operation.

- That each member club would act within the criteria set down in 'Respect'.

- Each member club would have a qualified first aider.

The Development plan included reference to:

- A league referee development programme which would ensure that all league games would have a qualified referee.
- A programme of first aid courses to ensure every team had a player/coach or manager who understands basic first aid.
- A Fair Play Awards system to reward clubs with the best disciplinary record.
- The adoption of FULL-TIME, to reduce the administrative burden on league volunteers.
- A programme of coaching education opportunities for all coaches within the League.
- New manager's evenings providing mentoring around the administration requirements of the League.

With the pathway and administration of football clearly working, the Western League was about to expand again, welcoming five new clubs in membership for the start of the 2012/13 season. Cribbs Friendly Life FC, had just claimed their first Gloucestershire County League title, and earned their promotion along with Cheddar FC, who had achieved the runners-up position in the Somerset League.

While both clubs progressed directly into Division One, Warminster Town moved sideways to join them, returning for the first time since being relegated in 2001/02, despite ending the previous season sixteenth in the Wessex League, Division One. Winterbourne United also moved side-ways after coming third in the Hellenic League, gaining promotion straight into the Premier Division.

The final new entry for the year was Buckland Athletic, who had been a Founder Member of the South West Peninsula League in 2007. The club had experienced considerable success since that time, and after finishing third in 2008/09, won the title twice in the following two seasons. They too progressed directly into the Premier Division, after finishing as runners-up to Champions, Bodmin Town, and were the first club to enjoy the arrangement agreed between the two Step 5 leagues.

In their first season, Buckland proved just how strong they were, when they became the only Western League club to get through to the second qualifying-round of the FA Cup, after beating Plymouth Parkway in a replay at home, 5-1. The following game saw them drawn at home at their Homers Heath ground to Conference South, Bath City, and although they were beaten, 2-1, they held their own for most of the game, showing just how far the club had come.

The FA Vase held more success for clubs, with Bitton, who were by then a well-travelled club in terms of Vase success, drawn at home to Shildon FC in the fourth round, alongside Larkhall Athletic, who also enjoyed home advantage, entertaining Peacehaven and Telscombe FC.

Both games looked to be winnable, but while Bitton failed to step up to the mark on the day and went down, 2-0, Larkhall made no mistake, and progressed through, 2-1. That was, however, as far as the Western League interest in the competition went for another year, with the 'Larks' losing the home game in front of a huge crowd, 4-3, to Tunbridge Wells.

Bishop Sutton, who had finished in the top six in the previous three seasons, took the League Championship, six points clear of Brislington, and nine points ahead of Gillingham Town. After much discussion, they did not apply for promotion, both because they would not have met the Southern League's stringent entry conditions, and because as a small club, it appeared on paper both an unrealistic aim, and a huge financial demand with the rewards not proportional to the investment.

In direct contrast to the form shown by the 'Bishops', Barnstaple Town, had not been out of the bottom six all season with their defence conceding a massive 123 goals, countered only by 23 goals being scored at the other end, and were relegated. They were joined in Division One by Wells City, with both clubs replaced by Champions, Sherborne Town, and runners-up, Hengrove Athletic.

Once again, Devizes Town were at the foot of the league, but survived relegation from the League due to second from bottom place club, Shrewton United, returning to the Wiltshire League after finding life at this level unsustainable.

Elmore also left and transferred to the SW Peninsula League; a move that did not solve their problems, and in 2015/16 their senior team took the place of their reserves in the Devon & Exeter Football League Premier Division, where they still play.

The ultimate game of the season saw Willand Rovers take their place in the Final of the Les Phillips Cup, after Larkhall Athletic had been found to have fielded an ineligible player in the semi-final clash between the sides, which they had gone on to win on penalties.

WILLAND ROVERS

Les Phillip Challenge Cup Winner 2012/13

The game at Cribbs Friends Life ground, saw Hallen contradict their final League position of fourth from bottom, and put on a dogged display in the first 45 minutes. The deadlock was broken ten minutes into the second-half, with Willand firing past the Hallen goalkeeper to score the only goal of the game.

Although the League had lost some clubs, it was still proving to be attractive to those who were looking to progress, and applications were accepted from Slimbridge, Wincanton Town, Chippenham Park and Ashton and Backwell; an eclectic mix if ever there was one!

SHREWTON UNITED

2012/13

In the past Slimbridge had been successful in the Hellenic League, winning promotion to the Southern League after clinching the Championship in May 2007. However, just a few weeks later, on the 10th July, they had crisis talks and resigned without a ball being kicked.

Their First team then took the reserves place in the Gloucestershire Northern Senior League, and won promotion back into the Hellenic League just a couple of seasons later. They then re-established their club in the Hellenic Premier Division, before applying for a place directly into the Premier Division of the Western League in a side-ways move.

In Division One, Ashton and Backwell were accepted into membership having achieved a runners-up spot in the Somerset League, finishing on the same points as Minehead and four behind Champions, Nailsea United, while Wincanton Town gained their promotion, having ended the season in third place in the Dorset Premier Football League. By far the most controversial of the new clubs, however, was Chippenham Park, who were set to play their games at the home of Southern League Premier Division club, Chippenham Town.

Chippenham Park had been formed in 2012 in a move to encourage the thousands of children who play football in the locality a pathway into the English League System. They had already established a link, with the Under 18s team, feeding directly into the Park side. With Western League experience, it was envisaged that the more talented players could move on into Southern League football with Chippenham Town, and beyond. A Chippenham Park reserves side was also formed, and they were accepted into Wiltshire Football League Division One as FC Chippenham Youth, a further step in the pathway links.

It was a totally new, but tested way of looking at the progression of football through the Pyramid system. While using the existing system for players to progress, the club existed as a totally autonomous entity from CTFC, with its own self-governing structure and committee, and had proved successful at Wiltshire Football League Premier Division level, where they ended the year in third place.

It was, indeed, a time to rethink the game, and a proposal was put forward by the Western League at an FA meeting in 2013 which was intended to readjust the system by creating an additional division, thus reducing travelling distance and costs to clubs. It was not a new proposal, as the idea had been submitted in the past, but hopes were high that it would be accepted. Unlike in those days of old, however, when a League decided its own structure and functioning, the decision now lay completely with the FA, who dismissed it. In many people's minds, it was an opportunity missed.

As League Chairman, John Pool, explained, 'With colleagues in the South West Peninsula League acknowledging that the clubs that have the finances to submit to playing budgets are always likely to create a continuing 'roadblock' in the promotion/relegation system, there appears at present no real solution to the problem. A real shame because I will always believe that football in the South West is equally important, and can be as strong as it is in the North of England, if a structure is put in place to satisfy all clubs with aspirations to move forward in the pyramid'.

And so, the scene was set. With the League stretching from Gloucester to Somerset, Devon, Dorset and Wiltshire, and an easing of the fears nationally that the country may go into a 'double-ditch recession', conditions were generally more favourable as the 2013/14 season kicked-off, with twenty-one clubs in the Premier Division and twenty-two in Division One.

Larkhall Athletic, who had been progressing over recent years to consistently meet their growing supporter's expectations, began the season with the avowed intend of putting all those 'nearly' seasons behind them, to progress in both the National Competitions, and move on to the Southern League. While those ambitious aims were kept on track for some time, however, the New Year proved yet again, just how difficult the search for silverware can be.

In the FA Vase, the 'Larks' again moved through into the fourth round, along with Bitton, and when both achieved victories at home, to Blackford & Langley, 3-0, and Arlesford Town, 2-0, respectively, expectation began to grow, once again. The fifth-round draw, however, saw both clubs on the road, and while Larkhall lost at Sholing,1-0, Bitton likewise lost, 2-0 at West Auckland.

The draw had, indeed, been a difficult one and such was the form of Sholing and West Auckland, that they both reached the Final at Wembley a couple of months later, with Sholing the eventual FA Vase winners for 2014 by the only goal of the game. It was West Auckland's third Final and their third defeat.

In the FA Cup Brislington and Bristol Manor Farm flew the Western League flag. 'Farm' put nine goals past Oldland Abbotonians, and then seven past Lymington Town. The following tie against Corsham Town then ended in a 4-4 draw, with the resulting replay won, 1-0, to give a testing game against Bridgwater Town. Scoring all those goals in the FA Cup run brought the club to the attention of The Sun newspaper, who sent a photographer to take photos of the team with the FA Cup. However, despite going three goals up against Bridgwater Town they were pulled back to yet another 4-4 draw, and the replay was lost, 2-1.

Brislington went one better and progressed all the way through to the Fourth Round, beating Truro City, and Weston-super- Mare by the same score-line, 3-2, on both occasions. In that vital last game before the competition proper, with the lure of a possible big money tie just one game away, it was a single goal that saw Welling United walk away with the prize, breaking many hearts in the process.

Despite the disappointment that Larkhall experienced in the Cup competitions, they achieved their number one aim, and gained promotion to the Southern League at seasons end, after picking up the Western League Championship a clear nineteen points ahead of runners-up, Bristol Manor Farm. The table demonstrated just how two-sided the competition had been, with Gillingham a full ten points adrift in third place. Larkhall also completed the double by winning the Les Phillips Cup.

In contrast to the success of previous seasons, Hengrove Athletic had found life in the Premier Division a step too far, and returned to Division One having won just eight games. They were joined by Radstock Town whose relegation battle was not made any easier when they had three points deducted for fielding an ineligible player, leaving them a point below Bishop Sutton. They were also two points behind Ilfracombe Town, who had been experiencing a torrid time, and withdrew at season's end due to their financial problems.

LARKHALL ATHLETIC FC

Premier Division Champions 2013/14

At the AGM, which was held at Wells City ground on the 18th June 2014, our Chairman, John Pool, thanked both new Director, Mark Rogers who had taken-up his role six weeks into the season, and Tony Salvidge for battling with the unpredictable weather to make sure all the fixtures were played. He also extended grateful thanks to Pat Clarke, for all the work done behind the scenes, supporting her husband, Ken, and to Denise Joyce, his sister, who had toiled away over the years ensuring that the results service was updated promptly, waiting by the phone every Saturday and weekday evenings for the past thirteen seasons. Ken was presented with a personalised number plate in appreciation of his dedication. After congratulations were extended to the various seasons winners, the Annual Accounts were presented by Tony Stone, which indicated that the League was in a robust financial state, in no small thanks to our continued sponsorship gratefully received from our friends from Toolstation.

At the same meeting, Mark Edmonds was appointed as Secretary to take over from Ken Clarke, who remained as Company Secretary. Mark was used to the vagaries of football administration having spent his years as both a player and referee, together with fulfilling the onerous role of Discipline Secretary on the Wiltshire County Football Association. He was completely at home behind a computer and totally dedicated to the game he loved, despite having to live with the specter of ill-health at times.

Hon Secretary Mark Edmonds

Mark Blessing filled the vacant Directors position that had been left by the resignation of genial George Fowler. On retiring, George was asked about his long and interesting career both as referee and with the League, to which he wrote; '*Some 40 years ago I wasn't a great person for keeping records of my career. My first appointment as an Assistant Referee was at Teignmouth Road, home of Clevedon Town, who I believe were playing Mangotsfield. The referee was Brian Champion, there was always a debate who was the shortest on the League between him and our past Chairman, Cliff Ashton. There was a joke later about referees leaving the field of play five minutes early at this ground, just so that we could have a shower and not get our feet washed in Persil!*

I also recollect going to Devizes Town as linesman to Cliff Ashton, and as we walked onto the pitch, me one side and the other assistant, Roger, who was built like a rhinoceros both ways and thick skinned on the other, lifted him by both elbows so his feet didn't touch the ground walking to the centre circle. Could you see this happening these days? The game was played in torrential rain, and after it finished we found there was more water on the floor than was there was in the bath, so we all got dressed in the bath due to the rain coming through the ceiling from the Grandstand.

At another game at Radstock I was the assistant to another rather large referee by the name of Don Welch, who later emigrated to USA, who then told both managers at the pre-match instruction that no jewellery was to be worn by any players, but that wedding rings had to be taped up. The problem was that he did not apply the rule to himself, and there he was in front of the dugouts running backwards with a great big silver ingot bouncing off his large stomach and coming up towards his chin. I believe the manager at the time shouted something like (and I am being polite here) 'How about the ******* jewellery, Ref'.

In those days, you could have quite a banter with players, and later at the same ground when I was promoted to the middle a Radstock player said to me 'That was never out Ref',' to which I replied, I saw it, and my Assistant saw it, so two of us can't be wrong'. To which the reply came; 'That's what they said about the Titanic and look what happened to that'. I didn't reply!!

We gradually went farther and farther afield to officiate rather than in the early days when we didn't venture more than 20 or 25 miles outside our area, which was good for us, or should I say it was good for all of us referees and clubs and we started to bring teams of officials to go farther afield. I remember being teamed up with Graham Knight, the referee, and Alan Townsend, the fellow assistant.

Graham had the style of hair in a fuzzy curly style of the day and was shaped like roly-poly with spindly legs. He could move over a short distance and always ran on his toes, which reminded me of an overweight ballet dancer. I remain friends with him to this day. Things were different then and once when I travelled to Torquay United with him there were no cups of tea or sandwiches afterwards – how things have changed for the good of the game. Out of my fee of 30/- it cost me 7/6d for a pie.

Also in my kit bag, I always carried a screwdriver so that I could remove the inner of the shower head to get the lime scale out so I could cover my body in water and not a dribble. I also instructed my assistants to dry themselves off in the shower so we didn't have water all over the dressing room floor because in those days you couldn't swing a cat around because you would have different things stored in the dressing rooms - like paint pots and other accessories. It is pleasing now for officials to have a dressing room of an appropriate size and <u>warmth</u>. Not like after coming off at Clandown on a freezing cold night, switching on the light to get some heat. Remember that Mr Chairman, John Pool - who was the Secretary of Clandown at the time.

The author of this book, Sandie Webb, and her husband Doug, used to play a trick on us assistants at Chippenham, by tethering their dog, Gyp, to the upright of the safety barrier on the assistants' side. I am sure that both trained him that every time an assistant gave a bad decision against Chippenham he would try to take a piece from their leg.

It is pleasing to note that the banter with the players and my decisions on the field of play, which may have sometimes gone against the clubs I officiated at, that no animosity has been held against me and to this day I have been treated with respect from both players and clubs alike - except from Sandie Webb (joke), who has never forgiven me for playing too much extra time against Barry Town in the FA Cup, after which they lost the replay. It wasn't my fault, Sandie, that the minute hand on my Gene Autry watch had fallen off and stopped the watch. What a cowboy!!!

It has been my pleasure and honour to serve this League for some 40 years, both as an assistant and referee, to start the assessment scheme for the referees and my appointment as the Referees Appointments Secretary for the First Division and on the Management Committee. It has also been a privilege to have been honoured as a Life-Member to this wonderful League'.

George sums up perfectly what a lifetime of memories being involved in football can reward you with; as the saying goes, you get out of life what you put into it.

The only other change at the meeting was to appoint a new Vice-President to fill the vacancy that had been sadly left by the death during the season, of Don Milverton. Ken Clarke was elected to fill the vacancy, joining Doug Webb and Maurice Washer. After which the Western League Directors turned their minds to the 125th Anniversary of the League, which was just a few years hence, and began to discuss how it should be celebrated. Although there had been great changes, both in the game and society over those years, it was certainly true that Western League clubs had continued promoting the game as a community team sport, played with passion, and within a League that had been able to adapt to whatever conditions and constrictions life turned up.

A few days later, Toolstation announced a three-year sponsorship agreement with the Northern Counties East League, which is of a similar size to the Western League, and commenting on the move, Toolstation's Marketing Director, John Meaden, said *'We recognise how tough it is for clubs to secure the financial support they need to continue their role within the local community. It was clear to us that the Northern Counties East is a very well-run league and has great local support so we are honoured to be able to assist and extend our support of grass roots football in the UK'.*

BRISTOL MANOR FARM FC

The first Interleague Toolstation Charity Cup winners 2014

With the move evoking memories of those good years in the distant past when Rothmans had taken up the mantle of a national non-league sponsor, the news was greeted with optimism as a move which was welcomed by all non-league football supporters.To cement the new relationship between North and South a Charity Cup match was played in July 2014, between the Toolstation sponsored Leagues, with Bristol Manor Farm travelling to Inkersall Road, the home of Staveley Miners Welfare FC, to take on Knaresborough Town.

The game was played in great spirit, with Bristol Manor Farm coming away winners by the only goal of the game. President of the Northern Counties East League and World Cup referee, Howard Webb MBE, presented the new Trophy, assisted by Neil Carroll, who had been in control of Toolstation since its inception.

The new 2014/15 season saw the usual flurry of clubs taking part in the national competitions, with Willand Rovers progressing through into the second qualifying round of the FA Cup where they were drawn to play away at Blackford and Langley. That day there were just 95 supporters watching the game; a game in which neither side could find the net. The replay, which attracted a good partisan crowd of 221 creating a lively atmosphere, was a similar affair with the deadlock broken by the only goal of the game putting the Devon side through.

Willand Rovers v Gosport County FA Cup Fourth Qualifying Round 2014/15

A home draw then followed against Aveley, where 298 saw Willand progress through, 3-2, earning the 'Devon All-Whites' another home game in the final qualifying round.

The visitors that day were high flying opposition, Gosport Borough, and although Rovers went down, 3-1, the large crowd of over 900 was treated to

284

a match which had all the thrills and spills that the competition is well-known for. Willand did the league proud both by their application on the pitch and the hospitality offered to both supporters and officials.

In the FA Vase, Bradford Town reached the fifth round of the competition, beating Melksham Town in an all Wiltshire game. With Melksham in tremendous form throughout the year, the resulting, 3-1, win for Bradford didn't go by the form book. The following round was also an all Wiltshire affair, but saw the club miss out on a quarter-final place, losing 2-0 at home to Highworth Town, and ended the League's interest in the competition for another year.

MELKSHAM TOWN FC

Premier Division Champions 2014/15`

MELKSHAM TOWN'S DAVE PHILLIP

Proudly holds the League Cup 2014/15

The Premier Division title went down to the wire with Melksham travelling to Willand in the knowledge that a win was needed, and at half-time they were, 2-0, ahead. That lead was then pulled back when the home-side scored twenty minutes into the second-half, and from then on, Melksham players threw their bodies on the line to defend the lead. At the whistle, they had achieved the result they needed, unaware of the fact that Buckland Athletic had lost their game, thus handing them the Championship regardless of their own efforts.

It was Melksham's first ever League Championship title, which they eventually won by five points clear of Buckland Athletic. However, because of ground restrictions due to their impending, but not time-planned, move to a new purpose-built stadium, they were unable to progress.

While that came as devastating news for everyone concerned, third placed Slimbridge, who were ten points behind the Champions, went for the promotion place and were nonetheless accepted by the Southern League.

Barnstaple Town, who had been relegated only a couple of seasons before, had been able to overcome their problems both on and off the pitch, and performed well throughout the season. Ironically, they fell to their first league defeat since the second game of the season, in April, with two games remaining, after Oldland put paid to their 37-game unbeaten run with a goal on the counter-attack in the 65th minute. Despite that result and a little bruised pride, with Welton Rovers and Cribbs sharing a draw, 1-1, they were uncatchable at the top of the table, and the Oldland players applauded them off the pitch in a display of great sportsmanship.

They had won Division One with 100 points, scoring 128 goals and conceding just 27, and were seven points clear of a rejuvenated, Welton Rovers, who also achieved promotion. They were replaced by the bottom two, Winterbourne United and Bishop Sutton.

WILLAND ROVERS

Les Phillips Cup Winners 2014/15

In May, the Final of the Les Phillips Cup concluded the competition for another year, with Willand Rovers again picking up the Trophy after a decisive trouncing of Barnstaple Town, 3-0. It was the third time that Willand had won the Trophy since entering the League in 2001, and highlighted the ambition that they still held.

The second Toolstation Cup took place on Saturday 25th July 2015 at Bitton's ground, with Willand Rovers flying the Western League flag, pitting their skills against a very strong Cleethorpes Town from the Northern Counties East League.

Neil Carroll presenting the Cup to Danny Trott

The nine-goal thriller, proved to be an excellent advertisement for non-league football with some entertaining goals, proficient defending, and good skills on display. It was also played in what was described as, the superb spirit of sportsmanship. After the game, Neil Carroll, the Director of Toolstation, presented the Cup to Cleethorpes, and later, Bitton demonstrated the traditional character that the Western League is renowened for, and put on a tremedous show of hospitality.

Over the years, the concept of football 'Ground Hoppers' has become a familiar term when referring to those football supporters who prefer to visit a variety of grounds rather than pin their allegiance to one club. Although it is a concept that has grown since the widespread use of social media, which began way back in the early 1990s, it is not a new concept. In fact, old Tom wrote an account in 'A View from the Terraces' of visiting four grounds in one day at the end of a season, completely unaware of that he was actually 'Ground Hopping' at his advanced age!

Communications between 'hoppers' in the last twenty-five years has, of course, been facilitated by the widespread use of the internet, and through accessing a Facebook page dedicated to the practice. It was through the work of computer savvy Mark Edmonds, that the idea of a Western League 'Ground-Hop Weekend' came to fruition and resulted in a series of games scheduled for the weekend of 16th to 18th October 2015, when there were no Premier League matches on TV due to the International break. It was not an idea that was hard to sell to the football mad folk of the Western League and it soon inspired a great response.

On the Friday evening a sizable crowd enjoyed the local game between Corsham Town and Calne Town, which was then followed by a crowded agenda the following day with a stream of cars and coaches visiting: Bitton v Street (10.45am); Oldland Abbotonians v Ashton and Backwell United (1.45pm); Cadbury Heath v Cribbs (4.45pm) and Keynsham Town v Westbury United (7.45pm). For those still on the mission, Sunday morning saw Chipping Sodbury Town welcome Bishop Sutton (11am) and then the final game was held at The Conigre, between Melksham Town and Gillingham, kicking-off at 2.30pm.

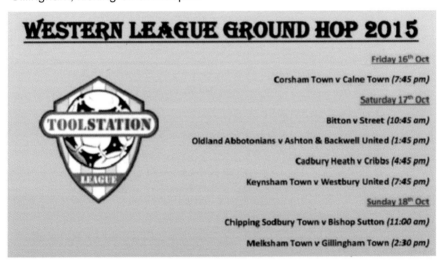

WESTERN LEAGUE GROUND HOP 2015

At the end of the exhausting three-days, those who had attended the games talked glowingly of the experience, and plans began almost immediately to ensure that the Toolstation Western League Ground Hop would become an annual event.

The usual anticipation greeted early games in the national competitions, but not one Western League club got further than the Second Qualifying round in the FA Cup. The most notable performance was put on by Bradford Town who lost, 3-2, in front of 393 supporters, to Southern League Premier Division side, Chippenham Town.

The FA Vase was a different matter, however, with Bristol Manor Farm flying the Western League flag all the way through to the quarter final stage. In the process, the draw wasn't kind to the club, with a trip to Portsmouth to play Wessex League, Premier Division side, Moneyfields FC in the fourth round.

After playing their 2,5000th Western League game (away at Hengrove)

Manor Farm progressed that day, 2-0, which then led to a journey up the M5 to play Northern League side, Sunderland RCA. Against predictions, their game was also won, 3-2, which led to another long trip in the New Year to Morpeth Town FC in the all-important quarter final game. That was one journey too far, however, and the 2-0 score-line was an accurate reflection of the ninety minutes; leaving 'Farm' to concentrate on their dream of promotion, which was still within their grasp.

In the League, there were early indications that while several clubs could aim to progress like Bristol Manor Farm, there were also those who were finding life difficult: a fact that was sadly demonstrated when an official League statement was issued in mid-December announcing the resignation of Winterbourne United FC, which read; *'It is with deep regret that we have to inform you all of the resignation of Winterbourne United from the Toolstation Western League with immediate effect. The club entered the League for season 2012/13 after joining from the Hellenic League. In their inaugural season, they finished in a creditable 12th position in the Premier Division which was to be their highest position as members. The league table has now been updated to reflect the clubs' withdrawal'.*

The League Board, and member clubs all attended a meeting in February at which concerns over the future of the Western League were put forward following discussions to review the Step 5/6 National League System. It was frustrating to learn that, after all the speculation and subsequent disruption that such uncertainties create, the review had been put on hold until a final decision was reached over the introduction of a new 5th Division of the Football League, and all its implications further down the pyramid.

Although there had been significant changes within both the FA, and to the League's administration, it was concluded that Toolstation Western League matters would be addressed at the first available opportunity. In the meantime, clubs were told that promotion and relegation would continue according to existing criteria.

As the season came to an end, playing form at the top of the Premier Division proved unpredictable, leading to an exciting last few games, with both Bristol Manor Farm and Buckland Athletic eventually falling away to end the term in third and fourth place respectively.

ODD DOWN FC

Premier Division Champions 2015/16

Odd Down and Barnstaple Town, however, continued the run-in neck to neck, right up to the final whistle. In the end, it was goal-difference that separated the two contenders, and Odd Down picked-up the magnificent Western League Premier Division Championship Trophy on a goal difference of +53, just eight ahead of the North Devon club.

While the Trophy went their way, however, promotion was a different matter. Odd Down were not able to progress due to ground grading criteria, which left Barnstaple Town with a tense wait while the FA decided if they would progress as runners-up. Eventually, the directive came through, and the club received the news that for the first time in their history, Barnstaple Town would be playing in the Southern League.

BARNSTAPLE TOWN

Premier Division runners-up 2015/16

It was a huge achievement for the club, and for Jasmine Chambers, who became Chairman of the North Devon club just a short time before, when the team was, undoubtedly, in the doldrums. In response, their manager,

Barry Yeo, said, 'We were almost certain it was going to happen, but it's good to finally get the confirmation, so of course we're delighted. The phone hasn't stopped ringing from other clubs congratulating us and wishing us well for next season'.

It was the second promotion for Barnstaple in consecutive seasons, and with the achievement came the prospects of playing many ex-Western League clubs and neighbours, with Bideford Town, Tiverton Town and Taunton Town, offering exciting local derby games in the seasons to come.

For Odd Down, the Championship was a tremendous accolade to the determination of their band of volunteers and workers, who had steered the club from relegation in 2008, to promotion back into the Premier Division two seasons later. Since that time, mid-table positions and two seasons in the top five, has enabled them to build a solid base.

The Les Phillips Cup Final was held at Welton Rovers West Clewes ground, on 14th May 2016, between Hengrove Athletic and Willand Rovers. As with most of these occasions, it's often a time to meet up with old friends, in this case Paul Durkin was watching his son, James, on his journey, hopefully, to the top; while in the club-house was the ex-Chairman of Welton and ex-member of the Western League Management Committee, Maurice Down, enjoying a few bevvies before returning home to Canada.

HENGROVE ATHLECTIC FC

Les Phillips Challenge Cup winners 2014/15

Willand Rovers had reached the Final stage by beating Buckland Athletic at home by the only goal of the game, while First Division side, Hengrove Athletic, did it the hard way having been draw at the same stage against in-form Melksham Town at the Conigre.

That game had ebbed and flowed without a clear result after 90 minutes, but the plucky 'underdogs' made no mistake about it in extra time, scoring the vital goal to make it 2-1; and the Final was equally action-packed. Just one goal separating the two sides, which saw the colours of Hengrove Athletic adorning the historic Trophy.

The summer saw little respite in the pace at Combe Hay Lane, with work on the Odd Down ground and a series of pre-season friendly games, only interrupted by a visit to the Windsor Food Service Stadium in Worksop Town FC, one of the World's oldest football clubs, on Saturday 23rd July, for the third annual Toolstation Cup match. The opposition that day was Handsworth Parramore FC of Sheffield, who had finished second in the NCEL Premier Division. They took the place of a Tadcaster Albion FC at the game because the club had won the League and gained promotion.

Two charities benefited from the proceeds of the match; the RNLI Flood Rescue Team, as the Toolstation official charity partner, and the Weston Park Cancer Charity in Sheffield, which had been selected by the NCEL in memory of Dave Wragg, who was Club Secretary of Handsworth Parramore FC and who had recently passed away.

Ray Johnston, manager of Odd Down AFC said of the game: *'I'm anticipating an extremely tough game against Handsworth Parramore. It involves a hotel stay, and an inevitable night out to follow, but far from being a 'jolly' we'll be taking this game very seriously. The last thing we want is to go back down south with a bad defeat! Usually with our team, goals are guaranteed, albeit we have no idea which end, so that should bode well for the crowd'.*

Neil Carroll, Commercial Development Director at Toolstation, said: *'Congratulations to Odd Down AFC and Handsworth Parramore FC for contesting this years' Toolstation Cup, we're looking forward to what will be a great match. Through our work with grass roots football we're able to both connect with our customers at a local level, and support one of the activities that is close to their hearts and often at the heart of the community itself. May the best team win on the day!'*

As is often the case in pre-season, both sides were missing a few familiar faces due to holiday commitments, and despite some good play by Odd Down, the game was a one-sided affair. A penalty on 12 minutes was converted, then the NCEL clubs' lead was then doubled ten minutes later.

With half chances then being spurned, the humid conditions really kicked-in, and three minutes into the second half 'Down' had a man sent off. Despite the resulting penalty being wasted, the final score-line, 4-0, accurately reflected the 'Ambers' impressive and clinical display.

The 2016/17 season kicked-off with a very early start In the FA Cup competition; a new move by the FA which was met with consternation by most clubs. Cadbury Heath set the standard with a win, 7-0, over Wessex League, Folland Sports FC. Brislington made the journey over the Solent to the Isle of Wight and came away with a win, 3-0, over Cowes Sports, while Newport IOW made the same journey in reverse to play Oldland Abbotonians, who were taking part in their first ever FA Cup match at Castle Road. The Western League hosts rounded off the historic occasion, going through to the next round by the only goal of the game.

That set the season up well, but by the time the second qualifying-round came along, there were only two Western League clubs remaining. While Cadbury Heath won their game, 3-1, away at Alresford Town, Brislington went out, 2-1, to Hellenic Premier League, Brimscombe and Thrupp, despite having home advantage. Cadbury Heath then travelled to rural Sussex to play Burgess Hill Town, who play two leagues higher in the Isthmian Premier Division, and succumbed to a defeat, 6-1, in a tough encounter at Leylands Park.

At the beginning of September, it was announced that former Somerset FA Chairman and friend of the Western League, Alan Hobbs, had died. Alan was Chairman for 29 years, serving from 1984 until he stood down in 2013 on reaching his 80th birthday. During his tenure, the Somerset FA evolved from an Association into a Limited Company. Prior to becoming Chairman, Alan had already served on the Council of Somerset FA as a divisional representative for 12 years, having first been elected in 1972; he became a Life Member of the Association in 1993, and at the time of his passing, was the equal longest serving member of council with a remarkable 44 years of service. Alan also served for over 30 years on the Council of the Football Association. Many of the directors and members of the League attended his funeral at a packed St John the Baptist Church in Midsomer Norton.

While the Leagues' last interest in the FA Cup came to an end, the road to Wembley via the FA Vase was in full swing, as the season progressed. It was a competition that involved most Western League sides, and the initial results were good. By the third round, however, there were just four clubs left and that number was soon reduced still further when Bradford Town were knocked out at home to Southall FC, 4-2, after the game had been taken into extra time, but Buckland Athletic eased through, 3-1, away at Chichester City FC.

Undoubtedly the match of the round saw League leaders, Bristol Manor Farm take on contenders, Melksham Town at the Creek, and when the game failed to separate the two, with a 1-1, score-line, the replay happened to coincide with the Wiltshire clubs' first competitive game at their long awaited and magnificent new Oakfield Stadium on Eastern Way.

The replay attracted a record crowd at that stage of the competition, with 1,215 packing into the stadium. As many know in football, however, the better the quality of stadium the more a visiting team lifts their game, and the thrilling stalemate in normal time soon turned into disappointment for the home club faithful, with a 5-3 score-line after extra-time ensuring that Manor Farm went into the hat for the fifth round.

The following draw was not kind to the two remaining Western League clubs, and it proved the end of the dream for the Bristol side who narrowly went out to Bromsgrove Sporting, 2-1. That left Buckland Athletic to fly the flag, as the lone West Country team in the 6th round draw, after beating Hinkley United, 4-3, after extra-time, which won them the Sunday Independent Team of the Day award.

Their reward for that memorable victory was a trip to the same club that had beaten Bristol Manor Farm, and on the day, in front of a massive 2,984 spectators at the imposing Victoria Ground they went out by two goals without reply.

The second Toolstation Western League Ground Hop took place over the weekend of the 7th to the 9th October 2016, amid lovely weather.

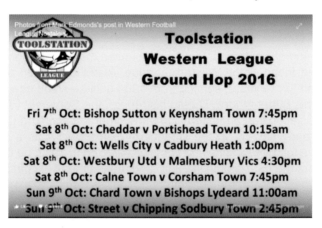

Toolstation
Western League
Ground Hop 2016

Fri 7th Oct: Bishop Sutton v Keynsham Town 7:45pm
Sat 8th Oct: Cheddar v Portishead Town 10:15am
Sat 8th Oct: Wells City v Cadbury Heath 1:00pm
Sat 8th Oct: Westbury Utd v Malmesbury Vics 4:30pm
Sat 8th Oct: Calne Town v Corsham Town 7:45pm
Sun 9th Oct: Chard Town v Bishops Lydeard 11:00am
Sun 9th Oct: Street v Chipping Sodbury Town 2:45pm

Starting the event off in Division One at Lakeview on the Friday evening in front of 247 spectators saw Keynsham Town take all the points with a 1-0 win against Bishop Sutton. Saturday morning then started off at Bowden's Park which saw many of the Hoppers in the crowd of 222 enjoy their full English breakfast laid on by the home club, Cheddar, who won, 2-1, against a battling Portishead Town. The Hop then moved on to the Athletic Ground for a Premier Division match which saw Wells City succumb to a 5-2 defeat against Cadbury Heath in front of 219 spectators. The fourth match back in Division One, moved on to Meadow Lane where a crowd of 233 saw a single goal win for visiting Malmesbury Victoria over hosts, Westbury United. The action then moved on to the evening match to Bremhill View which drew 257 spectators and saw Calne Town defeat visiting Corsham Town, 3-2.

The final two matches on the Sunday, saw an excellent 'Hoppers' breakfast laid on before the morning kick-off against Bishops Lydeard at Chard Town's Denning Sports Field. Eggs and bacon with all the trimmings, were washed down with tea and coffee, (as well as, rumour has it Bushmills, Tyrconnell, Connemara, Lockes, Teeling, Paddy, Glendalough, West Cork, Jameson, Jura Origin and Writers Tears, all courtesy of hospitable League President, Brian Beer). After a rousing speech over the PA by our League President to the 240 spectators, the match eventually got underway with a win for the visitors, 3-2.

The last match in the Premier Division saw the largest attendance with 291 enjoying the final Hop at the Tannery, to watch an entertaining game that Street went on to win, 4-2, over Chipping Sodbury Town. It had been an extremely enjoyable weekend for all concerned, showing just how much the non-league game is supported, and guaranteed the continuation of this most enjoyable annual event.

In November, some tragic news circulated around the non-league scene with the rumour that League Secretary and football nut, Mark Edmonds, was seriously ill. Few could believe the prognosis, and some weeks later, on 13th December 2016, we learned of his death after his brave battle against cancer. As the football family mourned, his widow, Sarah, son Jordon and daughter Aimee prepared to face Christmas without him.

Mark Edmonds

The Directors of the Toolstation Western League are deeply saddened to report the passing of Mark Edmonds, League Secretary, on Tuesday 13th December following a brave battle against cancer. Mark's football commitments included many years as a referee, officiating on the Western League for a considerable time.

He joined Wiltshire County FA as the Discipline Secretary before being appointed as General Secretary of the Toolstation Western League at the start of the 2014-15 season. Mark leaves a wife Sarah, son Jordon and daughter Aimee. Details of his funeral will be circulated when known.

Brian Moore, in his 'Western Beat' Column in the Sunday Independent, who had known Mark for years, wrote this fitting tribute; '*West Country football has been shocked to learn of the death of Toolstation Western League General Secretary Mark Edmonds. The directors of the League said that they were deeply saddened to hear that Mark had died on Tuesday, following a brave fight against cancer. Ken Clarke, the League's Company Secretary, who resumed the general secretary's duties when Mark fell ill, said that his football commitments included many years as a referee, officiating on the Western League for a considerable time. He joined the Wiltshire County FA as the discipline secretary, before being appointed as general secretary of the Toolstation League at the start of the 2014-15 season*'.

'*Social media was also awash with tributes with players and clubs expressing their condolences to Sarah and his family. Justin Carpenter, the secretary of Chipping Sodbury said: 'A true gentleman and nothing was too much trouble, a massive loss to family, friends and football*'.

'*GroundhopUK Organiser, Laurence Reade added: 'Dreadful news this morning. Two years ago, if you'd have said we would be doing a 'Western Hop' Chris Berezai and I would have laughed at you. The fact that it is happening is down to Mark and his backing was what made the two 'Hops' so far, thrive. Mark will not be forgotten*'.

'*All clubs from the Toolstation League, the West Country and beyond have also expressed their sadness at the news, with Evo-Stik Southern League One (Central) side Aylesbury United tweeting: Sad news tonight of the passing of long-standing supporter Mark Edmonds. Despite being 'a distance' fan of late, Mark's devotion to the club was unswerving, running the Aylesbury United Nostalgia groups on Facebook and Twitter. RIP Mark*'...The Western Beat, Sunday Independent.

BRIAN MOORE

WESTERN BEAT
by Bryan Moore

As the New Year came in, the push for Premier Division honours was intensified with the rumoured anticipation that a new FA League system would be introduced at the end of the season, affording more than one promotion from the Western to the Southern League. Bristol Manor Farm, Street, Melksham Town and Buckland Athletic, all expressed their intention to move on.

At the beginning of April, it came as a shock for most people to learn that Gillingham Town was withdrawing from the League. A statement from the club read: *'It's with great regret that Gillingham Town Football Club are today announcing that they have decided to take the very important, strategic decision to withdraw from the Toolstation Western League at the end of this season. Temporarily we will return to the Dorset Premier League until we are ready to push on again'.*

'The reasons for taking this radical decision are to concentrate all our resources on ensuring our new ground is completed as quickly as possible and, even more importantly, to build our financial hub/community centre, which we do not currently have'.

'Once built it will help fund and secure football in Gillingham for generations and then we will be looking for Western League/Southern League football again'.

'We hope that the local community will continue to support us as you have in the past seasons; indeed, we hope this decision will help inspire others to get involved with the Club and assist with its future development. Currently there are too few of us doing too much and, like any club, we need more support behind the scenes'.

'We have built up a reputation for looking after our players over the years and we hope that some players will stay with us during this temporary transition'.

And that was not the only surprise. A short time later many non-league followers in the west were puzzled when the Sunday Independent, which was launched during the Napoleonic Wars in 1808, failed to hit the mat on Sunday 9th April 2017. It was a publication that most of us had grown up with, and so it was with deep regret that news came through reporting its closure during the previous week.

Happily, a while later, the Chairman of Truro City Football Club, Peter Masters, stepped up and took over the publication ensuring its future. Ken Clarke, who had returned as the Western League General Secretary following the death of Mark, said *'It is great news because all the people I met over the past few weeks were very upset that the paper had ceased. I know the news that the Indy has been saved will be welcomed by all. It left a great hole for so many people who enjoyed a good read on a Sunday morning'.*

The season was certainly ending at a pace, in terms of both changing times and in quest for honours. By mid-April the Division One Championship looked to be ending after the season had seen a battle between Wellington, Hengrove Athletic and Cheddar. On Easter Monday, however, Wellington ensured that they would be promoted to the Premier Division, once again, with a win, 3-1, at Chard Town. Even then, the other promotion place was still undecided with Hengrove needing to win both of their final games to ensure that Cheddar would not pip them to the final promotion place.

In the Premier Division, March had seen the question of whether more than one club would be granted promotion by the FA laid to rest with a deferment of any changes to Steps 5 and 6 until the following year.

Bristol Manor Farm, who had topped the table for most of the season, had pledged to make no mistake with their promotion push, and their 32nd league win of the season, 4-1, away at Willand Rovers ensured them Southern League football after they had passed the ground grading test earlier.

They then completed their tremendous year with a win, 5-0, over Sherborne Town in front of 400 fans at the Creek, ending the term a full ten points clear of runners-up, Street, and 17 points clear of third-placed, Melksham Town.

In the First Division, Wellington took the title with an impressive win, 2-0, away at Radstock, after heading into the final game knowing that three points would be enough to realise promotion. Four points behind, runners-up Hengrove Athletic were also promoted

The final game of the season at the Tannery Ground, Street, was an equal affair between Melksham Town and Cribbs FC, in the Les Phillips Challenge Cup Final 2017. Street had just fallen short of the top spot on the pitch, but were in the process of upgrading their ground in anticipation of success in the season to come. They therefore enjoyed the day, showcasing the improvements they had made to the ground to the best advantage, and were perfect hosts.

The game itself was an even affair with both sides missing chances that would have been easier to score, but the subsequent penalty shoot-out saw Melksham hold their nerve and pick-up the Trophy, scoring a 5-4 victory.

MELKSHAM TOWN

Les Phillips Cup Winners 2016/17

The season had seen Cheddar celebrate its 125th year in February; a milestone that the League was to commemorate a few months later in October at the Bristol Marriot City Center hotel. Plans were well underway during the summer for those celebrations, but were also combined with a search for another venue to hold the Convention Weekend in 2018, because the Palace Hotel, Torquay had been sold.

While those activities occupied Directors during those months, the fourth Toolstation Charity Cup took place at Cribbs FC, Bristol on 22nd July. With

Bristol Manor Farm promoted, it lay with Street to battled it out against AFC Mansfield in a close competitive game which went the Northern Counties East League's way for the third season in a row, by the odd goal in three. All the proceeds from the game, including a raffle, were split between the RNLI Flood Rescue Team and The Countess of Brecknock Hospice, which had been nominated by Mark Edmond's widow, Sarah.

AFC MANSFIELD

Winners of the Toolstation Charity Cup 2017

Dave Morrall, Chairman of Toolstation Northern Counties East League, and Brian Gould, who was Secretary and is now, Treasurer, together with their respective wives, Stephanie and Jill, have, become part of the Western League family through their friendship with Ken and Pat Clarke; attending the Convention Weekend for many years, and becoming highly respected guests.

 The summer break is always an active one, where the long round of painting and maintenance too soon gives way to pre-season training. Friendlies then begin, which signals the start of another nine months of hard wear and tear on the pitch and the volunteers alike.

It was, therefore, heartbreaking for the officials at Portishead to find a group of five travellers caravans on the pitch one Friday in mid-July, and by the time bailiffs and police moved them on four days later, the group had caused thousands of pounds worth of damage. Walls and doors had been kicked in, several holes around a foot deep had been dug into the pitch and there had been a general trashing of the site with rubbish strewn around the whole area. It was heart breaking.

Club bosses faced a major clean-up, and a huge repair bill with the specter of the first game due to take place just a few weeks away. As usual, the men and women of football are nothing if not resilient, and in response they declared to do all they could to get everything back to normal for their first scheduled league game on 12th August against Chard Town; and just got on with the job!

While they faced the prospects of a long and difficult process with their insurance company to put their club back together again, the travelers simply moved onto another site just down the road, and by the time the bailiffs got back to Bristol, they were called to deal with them again.

Just some of the damage that Portishead officials faced

Another aspect, on the same theme, happened in the same month at one of the Western Leagues' former clubs, Coleford Athletic, when the club wrote on their Facebook page; *'This is a little message to whoever cut the locks off the football club sheds. We are trying to make the club bigger and better by doing the work we are doing. We have a kids' team and two adult teams and doing **** like this, well it's just taking money away from us supplying the village with the best we can. So, if you want an adrenaline rush, we train on Tuesdays at 6.30. Pop down and see who you are upsetting......'We send best wishes to Coleford Athletic FC.*

As the League moved toward celebrating its 125th Anniversary, our Director and new General Secretary, Andy Radford, put pen to paper to document the changes that have occurred in the way that the modern world communicates. (With a few additions from the author). Andy wrote; *'The last 25 years has seen big changes in the way the world communicates. The World Wide Web is now a part of everyday life, as are smart phones and social media (and in some cases unsocial media). If we go back to 1992, mobile phones and the internet were in their infancy. Although the first mobile phone was introduced in 1973 by Motorola it was not until 1997 that the technology had evolved into something for everyone, with Nokia and Motorola leading the way'.*

'On Tuesday 9th January 2007 in the Moscone Centre in San Francisco, the late Steve Jobs introduced the Apple iPhone to the unsuspecting world, starting the smartphone market. Nokia were unperturbed but RIM, the makers of the wonderful BlackBerry, stirred uneasily in their beds when their shares dropped eleven dollars on that day'.

300

'Six months later, on June 29ᵗʰ the first iPhones went on sale, and ten years on Apple has sold over a billion units. The iPad followed in 2010, a remarkable piece of equipment, selling 360 million to date, making Apple the world's most valuable company'.

'Surfing the web on the move: Facebook, Twitter, WhatsApp, YouTube Instagram and Snapchat, all by the touch of a finger. It is rumoured that the inside of the little finger of the right or left hand might show a clear indentation that is caused by propping a phone in the palm of the hand for hours on end - have a look!'

'In many ways football in general tends to be a little slow on the uptake. As people went about their business using the new technology, football still used pieces of paper to run the game, with most communication by letter or phone-calls'.

'In 2006 the Western League posted their first website, with John Cuthbertson as webmaster, and in 2010 I took over. In those past eleven years the website has been a source of news and not just a place to check-out the latest scores and league tables. The Gallery page has grown and the League now presents a 'Photo of the Year' award, this last year won by the 'man of many talents', the above-mentioned John Cuthbertson.

It is the dedication of the photographers and newsgatherers who are all unpaid that keeps the website vibrant and up to date'.

'The 'Podcast', courtesy of Ian Nockolds and Tom Hiscott has an average audience of some 6500 listeners' per episode. The Bulletin is now emailed to almost 1000 people per week, while an 'app' displays up to date results and tables. For the coming season, the League will be using an on-line Registration and Transfer System for players'.

'And so, the technological revolution continues at pace. From the 'Peasedown Pigeons' to today's 'immediate' news, what will evolve in the future, and the more distant future of the next 125 years, is unfathomable. But we can be sure that the League will endeavor to be at the forefront of technology, and will continue to use whatever is available for the best interests of our clubs and our supporters'.

PHOTO OF THE SEASON 2016/17

John Cuthbertson: www.johncuppy.co.uk

It really has been a whirlwind of change over the generations of non-league football in the West Country, with technology in recent years shaping our lives enormously. As Anthony Scaramucci, who was the US Government Communications chief for just over one brief week said; '*We now walk around with a radio, a television and a movie studio in our pocket, and, in fact, the whole world has transformed'*.

However, as Mr Scaramucci found, nothing is certain in the world we find ourselves in today. Throughout the time of change and technological advances, predictions of the new age taking over communications has been rife; but as you can see reading this, the written word has not been superceded by a paperless society; it lives and flourishes in parallel.

A remarkable period of 125 years has passed, a time that was harsh in places, and which called on all the tenacity and drive that runs through the veins of non-league clubs. It has been one in which the Western Football League has survived, reflecting life as we live it, with the men and women of today being replaced by those yet to come, who will in turn give way for the next generation to pass on another view from the terraces......

THE WESTERN
FOOTBALL LEAGUE

AWARD WINNERS

PREMIER DIVISION CHAMPIONS

1892-93	Warmley		1925-26	Bristol City
1893-94	Warmley		1926-27	Bristol City
1894-95	Hereford Thistle		1927-28	Plymouth Argyle
1895-96	Warmley		1928-29	Bristol Rovers
1896-97	Warmley		1929-30	Yeovil and Petters Utd
1897-98	Bristol City		1930-31	Exeter City
1898-99	Swindon Town		1931-32	Plymouth Argyle
1899-00	Bristol Rovers		1932-33	Exeter City
1900-01	Portsmouth		1933-34	Bath City
1901-02	Portsmouth		1934-35	Yeovil and Petters Utd
1902-03	Portsmouth		1935-36	Bristol Rovers
1903-04	Tottenham Hotspur		1936-37	Bristol Rovers
1904-05	Plymouth Argyle		1937-38	Bristol City
1905-06	Queens Park Rangers		1938-39	Lovells Athletic
1906-07	West Ham United		1939-40	Trowbridge Town
1907-08	Millwall		1940-45	No Competition
1908-09	Millwall		1945-46	Bristol Rovers
1909-10	Treharris		1946-47	Trowbridge Town
1910-11	Bristol City		1947-48	Trowbridge Town
1911-12	Welton Rovers		1948-49	Glastonbury
1912-13	Bristol Rovers		1949-50	Wells City
1913-14	Cardiff City		1950-51	Glastonbury
1914-19	No Competition		1951-52	Chippenham Town
1919-20	Douglas		1952-53	Barnstaple Town
1920-21	Bristol City		1953-54	Weymouth
1921-22	Yeovil and Petters Utd		1954-55	Dorchester Town
1922-23	Weymouth		1955-56	Trowbridge Town
1923-24	Lovells Athletic		1956-57	Poole Town
1924-25	Yeovil and Petters Utd		1957-58	Salisbury City

1958-59	Yeovil Town	1988-89	Saltash United
1959-60	Torquay United	1989-90	Taunton Town
1960-61	Salisbury City	1990-91	Mangotsfield United
1961-62	Bristol City	1991-92	Weston-Super-Mare
1962-63	Bristol City	1992-93	Clevedon Town
1963-64	Bideford	1993-94	Tiverton Town
1964-65	Welton Rovers	1994-95	Tiverton Town
1965-66	Welton Rovers	1995-96	Taunton Town
1966-67	Welton Rovers	1996-97	Tiverton Town
1967-68	Bridgwater Town	1997-98	Tiverton Town
1968-69	Taunton Town	1998-99	Taunton Town
1969-70	Glastonbury	1999-00	Taunton Town
1970-71	Bideford	2000-01	Taunton Town
1971-72	Bideford	2001-02	Bideford
1972-73	Devizes Town	2002-03	Team Bath
1973-74	Welton Rovers	2003-04	Bideford
1974-75	Falmouth Town	2004-05	Bideford
1975-76	Falmouth Town	2005-06	Bideford
1976-77	Falmouth Town	2006-07	Corsham Town
1977-78	Falmouth Town	2007-08	Truro City
1978-79	Frome Town	2008-09	Bitton
1979-80	Barnstaple Town	2009-10	Bideford
1980-81	Bridgwater Town	2010-11	Larkhall Athletic
1981-82	Bideford	2011-12	Merthyr Town
1982-83	Bideford	2012-13	Bishop Sutton
1983-84	Exmouth Town	2013-14	Larkhall Athletic
1984-85	Saltash United	2014-15	Melksham Town
1985-86	Exmouth Town	2015-16	Odd Down (Bath)
1986-87	Saltash United	2016-17	Bristol Manor Farm
1987-88	Liskeard Athletic		

FIRST DIVISION CHAMPIONS

1893-94	Warmley Reserves	1935-36	Swindon Town
1894-95	Warmley Reserves	1936-37	Weymouth
1895-96	Barton Hill	1937-38	Weymouth
1896-97	Eastville Wanderers	1938-39	Trowbridge Town
1897-98	Bedminster	1939-46	No Competition
1898-99	Staple Hill	1946-47	Clandown
1899-00	Bristol East	1947-48	Salisbury City
1900-01	Bristol East	1948-49	Chippenham United
1901-02	Bristol East	1949-50	Barnstaple Town
1902-03	Bristol Rovers	1950-51	Stonehouse
1903-04	Bristol City	1951-52	Bideford
1904-05	Bristol Rovers	1952-53	Chippenham Town Reserves
1905-06	Bristol Rovers	1953-54	Bristol Rovers Colt
1906-07	Staple Hill	1954-55	Yeovil Town
1907-08	Bristol City	1955-56	Torquay United
1909-19	No Competition	1956-57	Cinderford Town
1919-20	Frome Town	1957-58	Poole Town
1920-21	Peasedown St John	1958-59	Bath City
1921-22	Clandown	1959-60	Welton Rovers
1922-25	Single Division	1960-76	Single Division
1925-26	Poole Town	1976-77	Saltash United
1926-27	Poole Town	1977-78	Keynsham Town
1927-28	Trowbridge Town	1978-79	AFC Bournemouth Reserves
1928-29	Bath City	1979-80	Melksham Town
1929-30	Trowbridge Town	1980-81	Chippenham Town
1930-31	Portland United	1981-82	Shepton Mallet
1931-32	Portland United	1982-83	Bristol Manor Farm
1932-33	Swindon Town	1983-84	Bristol City Reserves
1933-34	Weymouth	1984-85	Portway-Bristol
1934-35	Swindon Town		

1985-86	Portway-Bristol	

1985-86	Portway-Bristol
1986-87	Swanage Town & Herston
1987-88	Welton Rovers
1988-89	Larkhall Athletic
1989-90	Ottery St Mary
1990-91	Minehead
1991-92	Westbury United
1992-93	Odd Down
1993-94	Barnstaple Town
1994-95	Brislington
1995-96	Bridgwater Town
1996-97	Melksham Town
1997-98	Bishop Sutton
1998-99	Minehead
1999-00	Devizes Town
2000-01	Team Bath
2001-02	Frome Town
2002-03	Torrington
2003-04	Hallen
2004-05	Willand Rovers
2005-06	Dawlish Town
2006-07	Truro City
2007-08	Wellington
2008-09	Larkhall Athletic
2009-10	Wells City
2010-11	Merthyr Town
2011-12	Cadbury Heath
2012-13	Sherborne Town
2013-14	Bradford Town
2014-15	Barnstaple Town
2015-16	Chipping Sodbury Town
2016-17	Wellington

CHALLENGE CUP

1954-55	Poole Town
1955-56	Salisbury City
1956-57	Trowbridge Town
1957-58	Bridgwater Town
1958-59	Yeovil Town
1959-60	Torquay United
1960-61	Exeter City
1961-62	Bristol City
1965-66	Glastonbury
1970-71	Bridport
1971-72	Bideford
1972-73	Bridport
1973-74	Mangotsfield United
1974-75	Falmouth Town
1976-77	Weston-Super-Mare
1977-78	Bridport
1979-80	Frome Town
1980-81	Dawlish Town
1981-82	Bridgwater Town
1982-83	Frome Town
1983-84	Dawlish Town
1984-85	Bideford
1985-86	Portway Bristol
1986-87	Saltash United
1987-88	Saltash United

LES PHILLIPS CHALLENGE CUP

1988-89 Exmouth Town

1989-90 Plymouth Argyle

1990-91 Elmore

1991-92 Plymouth Argyle Reserves

1992-93 Tiverton Town

1993-94 Tiverton Town

1994-95 Elmore

1995-96 Tiverton Town

1996-97 Tiverton Town

1997-98 Tiverton Town

1998-99 Yeovil Town Reserves

1999-00 Chippenham Town

2000-01 Chippenham Town

2001-02 Bideford

2002-03 Bridgwater Town

2003-04 Bideford

2004-05 Bridgwater Town

2005-06 Corsham Town

2006-07 Willand Rovers

2007-08 Dawlish Town

2008-09 Oldland Abbotonians

2009-10 Hallen

2010-11 Ilfracombe Town

2011-12 Bristol Manor Farm

2012-13 Willand Rovers

2013-14 Larkhall Athletic

2014-15 Willand Rovers

2015-16 Hengrove Athletic

2016-17 Melksham Town

ALAN YOUNG CUP
PREMIER DIVISION HOSPITALITY

2003-04 Keynsham Town

2004-05 Corsham Town

2005-06 Hallen

2006-07 Bridgwater Town

2007-08 Truro City

2008-09 Willand Rovers

2009-10 Willand Rovers

2010-11 Bristol Manor Farm

2011-12 Street

2012-13 Buckland Athletic

2013-14 Willand Rovers

2014-15 Willand Rovers

2015-16 Cribbs

2016-17 Buckland Athletic

WILF ESCOTT CUP
FIRST DIVISION HOSPITALITY

2003-04 Willand Rovers

2004-05 Larkhall Athletic

2005-06 Larkhall Athletic

2006-07 Hengrove Athletic

2007-08 Shepton Mallet

2008-09 Shepton Mallet

2009-10 Wells City

2010-11 Shepton Mallet

2011-12 Chard Town

2012-13 Warminster Town

2013-14 Shepton Mallet

2014-15 Warminster Town

2015-16 Warminster Town

2016-17 Warminster Town

MANAGER OF THE SEASON

1983-84 Frome Town

1984-85 Bideford

1985-86 Exmouth Town

1986-87 Saltash United

1987-88 Saltash United

1988-89 Exmouth Town

1989-90 Taunton Town

1990-91 Mangotsfield United

1991-92 Tiverton Town

1992-93 Clevedon Town

1993-94 Tiverton Town

1994-95 Not Awarded

1995-96 Mangotsfield United

PREMIER DIVISION

1996-97 Tiverton Town

1997-98 Tiverton Town

1998-99 Taunton Town

1999-00 Taunton Town

2000-01 Chippenham Town

2001-02 Bideford

2002-03 Team Bath

2003-04 Bideford

2004-05 Frome Town

2005-06 Bideford

2006-07 Corsham Town

2007-08 Truro City

2008-09 Bitton

2009-10 Willand Rovers

2010-11 Larkhill Athletic

2011-12 Merthyr Town

2012-13 Bishop Sutton

2013-14 Larkhall Athletic

2014-15 Melksham Town

2015-16 Barnstaple Town

2016-17 Bristol Manor Farm

FIRST DIVISION

1996-97 Melksham Town

1997-98 Bishop Sutton

1998-99 Minehead

1999-00 Devizes Town

2000-01 Keynsham Town

2001-02 Frome Town

2002-03 Torrington

2003-04 Bitton

2004-05 Willand Rovers

2005-06 Dawlish Town

2006-07 Truro City

2007-08 Sherborne Town

2008-09 Larkhall Athletic

2009-10 Wells City

2010-11 Merthyr Town

2011-12 Cadbury Heath

2012-13 Sherborne Town

2013-14 Bradford Town

2014-15 Barnstaple Town

2015-16 Chipping Sodbury

2016-17 Wellington

SPORTSMANSHIP

MERIT CUP WINNERS

1967-68 St Lukes College

1968-69 Bideford

1969-70 Bridport

1970-71 St Lukes College

1971-72 Bridport

1972-73 Torquay United

1973-74 Bridport

1974-75 Barnstaple Town

1975-76 Devizes Town

1976-77 Weston-Super-Mare

1977-78 Weston-Super-Mare

1978-79 Swanage & Herston

1979-80 Saltash United

1980-81 Liskeard Athletic

1981-82 Larkhall Athletic

PREMIER DIVISION

1982-83 Frome Town

1983-84 Barnstaple Town

1984-85 Barnstaple Town

1985-86 Plymouth Argyle

1986-87 Exmouth Town

1987-88 Saltash United

1988-89 Plymouth Argyle

1989-90 Plymouth Argyle

1990-91 Dawlish Town/
         Plymouth Argyle

1991-92 Torrington

1992-93 Exmouth Town

1993-94 Torrington

1994-95 Barnstaple Town

1995-96 Taunton Town/Torrington

1996-97 Bridgwater Town

1997-98 Tiverton Town

1998-99 Paulton Rovers

1999-00 Yeovil Town

2000-01 Bristol Manor Farm

2001-02 Team Bath

2002-03 Dawlish Town

2003-04 Exmouth Town

2004-05 Odd Down

2005-06 Devizes Town

2006-07 Willand Rovers

2007-08 Ilfracombe Town

2008-09 Not Awarded

2009-10 Not Awarded

2010-11 Ilfracombe Town

2011-12 Ilfracombe Town

2012-13 Cadbury Heath

2013-14 Bridport

2014-15 Melksham Town

2015-16 Gillingham Town

2016-17 Wincanton Town

FIRST DIVISION

1982-83 Chard Town

1983-84 Larkhall Athletic

1984-85 Larkhall Athletic

1985-86 Larkhall Athletic

1986-87 Elmore

1987-88 Larkhall Athletic
/Yeovil Town

1988-89 Westbury United

1989-90 Elmore

1990-91 Elmore

1991-92 Wellington AFC

1992-93 Clyst Rovers

1993-94 Larkhall Athletic

1994-95 Clyst Rovers/
Larkhall Athletic

1995-96 Wellington AFC

1996-97 Yeovil Town

1997-98 Heavitree United

1998-99 Ilfracombe Town

1999-00 Ilfracombe Town

2000-01 Wellington AFC

2001-02 Hallen

2002-03 Willand Rovers

2003-04 Minehead

2004-05 Cadbury Heath

2005-06 Longwell Green Sports

2006-07 Ilfracombe Town

2007-08 Keynsham Town

2008-09 Not Awarded

2009-10 Not Awarded

2010-11 Shrewton United

2011-12 Almondsbury UWE

2012-13 Hengrove Athletic

2013-14 Calne Town

2014-15 Almondsbury UWE

2015-16 Cheddar

2016-17 Wincanton Town

SUBSIDIARY COMPETITIONS WINNERS

1959-60 Frome Town

1971-72 Bideford Town

1972-73 Devizes Town

CUPRINOL SIX-A-SIDE COMPETITION

1988-84 Chippenham Town

1984-85 Saltash United 'B'

1985-86 Devizes Town

THE WESTERN
FOOTBALL LEAGUE

LEAGUE TABLES

BRISTOL & DISTRICT LEAGUE

1892-93

	P	W	D	L	F	A	PTS
Warmley	16	11	3	2	72	19	25
Trowbridge Town	16	10	4	2	66	17	24
St George	16	9	5	2	36	22	23
Bedminster	16	6	5	5	30	34	17
Clevedon	16	6	4	6	25	36	16
Eastville Rovers	16	6	3	7	36	40	15
Clifton Association	16	4	2	10	27	61	10
Mangotsfield	16	3	2	11	19	45	8
Wells	16	1	4	11	14	51	6

1893-94

Division One	P	W	D	L	F	A	PTS
Warmley	18	12	5	1	32	13	27*
St George	18	10	6	2	39	23	26
Trowbridge Town	18	9	4	5	54	33	22
Bedminster	18	9	2	7	41	36	20
Clevedon	18	7	5	6	34	40	19
Clifton	18	6	4	8	37	30	16
Staple Hill	18	5	5	8	23	33	15
Gloucester	18	6	1	11	32	45	13
Eastvill Rovers	18	5	2	11	30	39	12
Mangotsfield	18	2	4	12	19	48	8
Division Two							
Warmley Res	18	16	1	1	66	12	33
St George Res	18	15	0	3	50	22	30
Trowbridge Town Res	18	11	1	6	47	22	23
St Paul's	18	9	3	6	44	51	21
Barton Hill	18	7	4	7	40	32	18
Bedminster Res	18	6	3	9	35	42	15
Mangotsfield Res	18	6	1	11	26	41	13
Clifton Reserves	18	5	2	11	29	59	12
Eastville Rovers Res	18	4	2	12	23	45	10
Waverley	18	2	4	12	22	53	8

*Warmley had two points deducted

1894-95

Division One	P	W	D	L	F	A	PTS
Hereford Thistle	22	18	3	1	93	21	39
St George	22	18	3	1	76	21	39
Warmley	22	14	2	6	74	30	30
Staple Hill	22	11	4	7	56	38	26
Gloucester	22	10	4	8	65	54	24
Eastville Rovers	22	10	4	8	46	40	24
Trowbridge Town	22	9	4	9	68	48	22
Clifton	22	8	2	12	47	55	18
Bedminster	22	7	0	15	39	73	14
Swindon Wanderers	22	5	3	14	40	63	13
Mangostfield	22	5	2	15	22	68	12
Clevedon	22	1	1	20	23	136	3
Division Two							
Warmley Res	20	17	0	3	75	20	34
St Paul's	20	16	0	4	79	31	32
Willsbridge	20	15	1	4	48	21	31
St George Res	20	14	1	5	69	33	29
Barton Hill	20	11	1	8	57	31	23
Bedminster Res	20	8	1	11	36	30	17
Eastville Res	20	8	0	12	45	45	16
Clifton Res	20	7	0	13	40	68	14
Mangostfield Res	20	4	2	14	30	84	10
Staple Hill Res	20	4	1	15	32	79	9
Waverley	20	2	1	17	15	74	5

WESTERN LEAGUE

1895-96

Division One	P	W	D	L	F	A	PTS
Warmley	20	16	3	1	65	13	35
Eastville Rovers	20	14	1	5	57	22	29
Staple Hill	20	13	3	4	48	19	29
Trowbridge Town	20	13	1	6	50	31	27
St George	20	10	4	6	47	38	24
Clifton	20	8	3	9	44	50	17*
Gloucester	20	6	4	10	29	42	16
Bedminster	20	6	2	12	36	41	14
Swindon Wanderers	20	4	4	12	22	57	12
Mangotsfield	20	3	3	14	17	54	9
St Pauls	20	2	2	16	12	60	6

Division Two	P	W	D	L	F	A	PTS
Barton Hill	18	15	2	1	45	16	32
Fishponds	18	11	4	3	33	14	26
St George Res	18	11	3	4	52	22	25
Eastville Wanderers	18	10	2	6	34	23	22
Eastville Rovers Res	18	8	4	6	43	31	20
Cumberland	18	7	3	8	47	35	17
Staple Hill Res	18	7	2	9	34	58	16
Bedminster Res	18	6	1	11	35	38	13
Warmley Res	18	4	1	13	23	29	9
Clifton Res	18	0	0	18	10	84	0

*Clifton had two points deducted

1896-97

Division One	P	W	D	L	F	A	PTS
Warmley	16	13	2	1	42	9	28
Bristol South End	16	11	0	5	28	22	22
Bedminster	16	8	2	6	32	16	18
St George	16	8	1	7	27	23	17
Eastville Rovers	16	7	2	7	25	23	14*
Trowbridge Town	16	5	3	8	21	30	13
St Pauls	16	3	5	8	29	31	11
Staple Hill	16	5	0	11	18	39	10
Clifton	16	4	1	11	19	48	9
Division Two							
Eastville Wanderers	12	7	4	1	25	9	18
Barton Hill	12	7	3	2	28	7	17
Mangotsfield	12	6	3	3	23	14	15
Fishponds	12	4	5	3	17	16	13
Bedminster Res	12	6	1	5	19	20	13
Eastville Rovers Res	12	1	3	8	7	33	5
Staple Hill Res	12	1	1	10	8	34	3

*Eastville Rovers had two points deducted

1897-98

Professional Division	P	W	D	L	F	A	PTS
Bristol City	14	11	1	2	51	16	23
Swindon Town	14	9	1	4	32	15	19
Reading	14	7	2	5	29	25	16
Bristol St George	14	6	3	5	25	27	15
Eastville Rovers	14	6	2	6	38	25	14
Warmley	14	5	3	6	36	27	13
Eastleigh Athletic	14	3	2	9	22	55	8
Trowbridge Town	14	2	0	12	15	58	4
Amateur Division One							
Bedminster	16	13	0	1	65	11	30
Staple Hill	16	11	1	4	38	15	23
Fishponds	16	8	2	6	26	30	18
Midsomer Norton	16	7	2	7	23	33	16
Barton Hill	16	6	2	8	25	25	14
Radstock	16	5	4	7	17	28	14
St Pauls	16	4	3	9	15	28	11
Eastville Wanderers	16	4	1	11	15	16	9
Mangotsfield	16	1	7	8	5	29	9
Amateur Division Two							
Hanham	10	9	1	0	32	8	19
Cotham	10	8	0	2	16	2	16
Barton Hill Res	10	4	2	4	20	14	10
St Pauls Res	10	2	2	6	19	26	6
Fishponds Res	10	1	1	8	10	25	3
Bedminster Res	10	1	0	9	10	34	2

1898-99

Division One	P	W	D	L	F	A	PTS
Swindon Town	8	5	1	2	16	10	11
Bristol St George	8	4	1	3	18	15	9
Southampton	8	4	0	4	18	15	8
Bristol Easville Rovers	8	2	2	4	14	18	6
Bedminster	8	2	2	4	9	16	6
Division Two							
Staple Hill	14	11	1	2	55	15	23
Fishponds	14	10	2	2	42	15	22
Mount Hill Enterprise	14	5	3	6	31	28	13
Midsomer Norton	14	6	3	5	20	32	13*
Bristol Amateurs	14	5	2	7	31	32	12
Hanham	14	4	3	7	16	28	11
Barton Hill	14	4	1	9	14	31	9
Cotham	14	2	3	9	22	41	7

*Midsomer Norton had two points deducted

1899-1900

Division One	P	W	D	L	F	A	PTS
Bristol Rovers	6	3	1	2	8	6	7
Bedminster	6	3	1	2	10	12	7
Swindon Town	6	3	0	3	7	7	6
Bristol City	6	2	0	4	12	12	4
Division Two							
Bristol East	8	6	2	0	31	3	14
Staple Hill	8	4	4	0	22	3	12
Fishponds	8	3	1	4	16	29	7
Weston (Bath)	8	1	1	6	7	19	3
Cotham	8	1	0	7	8	26	2

1900-01

Division One	P	W	D	L	F	A	PTS
PORTSMOUTH	16	11	2	3	36	23	24
MILLWALL ATHLETIC	16	9	5	2	33	14	23
TOTTENHAM HOTSPUR	16	8	5	3	37	19	21
QUEENS PARK RANGERS	16	7	4	5	39	24	18
BRISTOL CITY	16	6	4	6	27	24	16
READING	16	5	5	6	23	31	15
SOUTHAMPTON	16	5	2	9	19	29	12
BRISTOL ROVERS	16	4	1	11	18	42	9
SWINDON TOWN	16	2	2	12	9	35	6
Division Two							
BRISTOL EAST	12	11	0	1	41	8	22
PAULTON ROVERS	9	6	2	1	32	12	14
STAPLE HILL	10	6	1	3	34	17	13
COTHAM	11	3	2	6	20	49	8
BEDMINSTER ST FRANCIS	6	3	1	2	16	13	7
Weston-super-Mare	10	2	0	8	18	22	4
FISHPONDS	12	1	0	11	6	40	0*

*Fishponds had two points deducted

1901-02

Division One

Division One	P	W	D	L	F	A	PTS
Portsmouth	16	13	1	2	53	16	27
Tottenham Hotspur	16	11	3	2	42	17	25
Reading	16	7	3	6	29	22	17
Millwall Athletic	16	8	1	7	25	29	17
Bristol Rovers	16	8	0	8	25	31	16
Southampton	16	7	1	8	30	28	15
West Ham United	16	6	2	8	30	20	14
Queens Park Rangers	16	5	1	10	17	43	11
Swindon Town	16	0	2	14	8	53	2

Division Two

Division Two	P	W	D	L	F	A	PTS
Bristol East	16	13	1	2	55	11	27
Bristol Rovers Res	16	10	3	3	54	18	23
Paulton Rovers	16	9	3	4	51	29	21
Staple Hill	16	9	3	4	30	24	21
Swindon Town Res	16	7	2	7	44	35	16
Trowbridge Town	16	6	3	7	30	43	15
St George	16	6	2	8	29	36	14
Weston-super-Mare	16	1	2	13	19	68	4
Cotham Amateurs	16	1	1	14	23	71	3

1902-03

Division One

Division One	P	W	D	L	F	A	PTS
Portsmouth	16	10	4	2	34	14	24
Bristol Rovers	16	9	2	5	36	22	20
Southamption	16	7	6	3	32	20	20
Tottenham Hotspur	16	6	7	3	20	14	19
Millwall Athletic	16	6	3	7	23	29	15
Reading	16	7	0	9	20	21	14
Queens Park Rangers	16	6	2	8	18	31	14
Brentford	16	3	4	9	16	34	10
West Ham United	16	2	4	10	15	29	8

Division Two

Division Two	P	W	D	L	F	A	PTS
Bristol Rovers Res	14	10	2	2	45	10	22
St George	14	9	1	4	37	25	19
Swindon Town Res	14	8	0	6	59	24	16
Bristol East	14	6	3	5	23	27	15
Staple Hill	14	5	3	6	27	20	13
Paulton Rovers	14	6	1	7	27	27	13
Trowbridge Town	14	5	1	8	20	48	11
Cotham Amateurs	14	1	1	12	14	71	3

1903-04

Division One	P	W	D	L	F	A	PTS
Tottenham Hotspur	16	11	3	2	32	12	25
Southampton	16	9	3	4	30	18	21
Plymouth Argyle	16	8	4	4	23	19	20
Portsmouth	16	7	2	7	24	22	16
Brentford	16	6	4	6	19	23	16
Queens Park Rangers	16	5	5	6	15	21	15
Reading	16	4	4	8	16	26	12
Bristol Rovers	16	4	3	9	29	29	11
West Ham United	16	2	4	10	13	31	8
Division Two							
Bristol City Res	18	15	2	1	64	17	32
Staple Hill	18	13	1	4	53	19	27
Swindon Town Res	18	10	3	5	50	30	23
Bristol Rovers Res	18	9	2	7	50	30	20
Bristol East	18	9	1	8	30	27	19
Paulton Rovers	18	9	1	8	37	46	19
Trowbridge Town	18	6	2	10	22	57	14
Warmley	18	3	3	12	32	52	9
Welton Rovers	18	3	3	12	32	67	9
Radstock Town	18	3	2	13	26	54	8

1904-05

Division One	P	W	D	L	F	A	PTS
Plymouth Argyle	20	13	4	3	52	18	30
Brentford	20	11	6	3	30	22	28
Southampton	20	11	2	7	45	22	24
Portsmouth	20	10	3	7	29	30	23
West Ham United	20	8	4	8	37	42	20
Fulham	20	7	3	10	29	32	17
Millwall	20	7	3	10	32	40	17
Tottenham Hotspur	20	5	6	9	20	28	16
Reading	20	6	3	11	27	37	15
Bristol Rovers	20	7	1	12	32	44	15
Queens Park Rangers	20	6	3	11	27	45	15
Division Two							
Bristol Rovers Res	16	13	3	0	76	5	29
Bristol City Res	16	14	1	1	46	8	29
Swindon Town Res	16	11	2	3	53	21	24
Staple Hill	16	7	3	6	27	23	17
Bristol East	16	7	1	8	38	27	15
Welton Rovers	16	5	1	10	27	58	11
Radstock Town	16	4	1	11	21	57	9
Trowbridge Town	16	2	2	12	25	64	6
Chippenham Town	16	2	0	14	24	74	4

1905-06

Division One	P	W	D	L	F	A	PTS
Queens Park Rangers	20	11	4	5	33	27	26
Southampton	20	10	5	5	41	35	25
Plymouth Argyle	20	8	8	4	34	23	24
Tottenham Hotspur	20	7	7	6	28	17	21
Bristol Rovers	20	8	3	9	34	34	19
Millwall	20	7	5	8	28	29	19
Portsmouth	20	6	7	7	26	29	19
West Ham United	20	7	5	8	32	35	19
Reading	20	6	6	8	28	35	18
Fulham	20	5	5	10	23	32	15
Brentford	20	6	3	11	25	36	15
Division Two							
Bristol Rovers Res	18	16	1	1	90	19	33
Bristol City Res	18	14	2	2	79	13	30
Welton Rovers	18	10	1	7	40	45	21
Radstock Town	18	8	2	8	37	31	18
Salisbury City	18	8	2	8	29	34	18
Staple Hill	18	8	1	9	32	38	17
Paulton Rovers	18	7	2	9	26	41	16
Chippenham Town	18	5	2	11	23	47	12
Bristol East	17	3	1	13	14	41	7
Trowbridge Town	17	2	2	13	13	73	6

1906-07

Division One Section A	P	W	D	L	F	A	PTS
Fulham	10	7	1	2	16	9	15
Queens Park Rangers	10	5	1	4	17	11	11
Brentford	10	5	1	4	19	19	11
Reading	10	4	1	5	12	18	9
Bristol Rovers	10	3	1	6	17	17	7
Chelsea	10	2	3	5	7	14	7
Division One Section B							
West Ham United	10	7	1	2	25	14	15
Plymouth Argyle	10	5	3	2	16	10	13
Portsmouuth	10	4	2	4	16	19	10
Tottenham Hotspur	10	3	3	4	13	15	9
Southampton	10	4	0	6	14	16	8
Millwall	10	1	3	6	5	15	5
Division Two							
Staple Hill	18	12	2	4	44	28	26
Newport	18	11	3	4	52	38	25
Bristol City Res	18	11	2	5	54	19	24
Treharris	18	12	0	6	62	24	24
Bristol Rovers Res	18	11	1	6	60	27	23
Radstock Town	18	7	3	8	37	41	17
Welton Rovers	18	7	1	10	33	54	15
Paulton Rovers	18	4	4	10	36	53	12
121st R. F. A	18	5	2	11	27	53	12
Trowbridge Town	18	1	0	17	18	86	2

1907-08

Division One Section A	P	W	D	L	F	A	PTS
Southampton	12	8	1	3	30	12	17
Portsmouth	12	7	1	4	25	18	15
Brighton & Hove Albion	12	6	2	4	19	19	14
Plymouth Argyle	12	5	2	5	14	14	12
Queens Park Rangers	12	5	1	6	20	23	11
Brentford	12	2	5	5	13	21	9
Leyton	12	2	2	8	11	27	6
Division One Section B							
Millwall	12	9	2	1	31	13	20
Tottenham Hotspur	12	7	0	5	26	15	14
Bristol Rovers	12	6	2	4	26	29	14
Luton Town	12	4	4	4	16	21	12
Reading	12	4	3	5	20	25	11
Crystal Palace	12	3	4	5	16	17	10
West Ham United	12	1	1	10	16	27	3
Division Two							
Bristol City Res	16	12	1	3	55	13	25
Bristol Rovers Res	16	11	3	2	44	15	25
Treharris	16	11	1	4	53	19	23
Kingswood Rovers	16	7	1	8	27	33	15
Paulton Rovers	16	7	1	8	34	46	15
Welton Rovers	16	4	4	8	23	46	12
Weymouth	16	5	2	9	25	23	12
Radstock Town	16	4	3	9	25	39	11
Staple Hill	16	3	0	13	18	40	6

1908-09

Division One Section A	P	W	D	L	F	A	PTS
Brighton & Hove Albion	12	7	2	3	23	13	16
Queens Park Rangers	12	6	1	5	28	24	13
Crystal Palace	12	5	2	5	23	22	12
Luton Town	12	5	2	5	24	24	12
Croydon Common	12	5	2	5	16	24	12
Reading	12	4	2	6	19	21	10
Leyton	12	4	1	7	16	21	9
Division One Section B							
Millwall	12	8	2	2	24	11	18
Southampton	12	7	0	5	20	20	14
Plymouth Argyle	12	6	1	5	12	13	13
Portsmouth	12	5	2	5	21	21	12
West Ham United	12	5	0	7	21	21	10
Bristol Rovers	12	4	1	7	16	23	9
Brentford	12	3	2	7	10	13	8
Division Two							
Bristol City Res	22	15	4	3	59	16	34
Bristol Rovers Res	22	16	0	6	81	29	32
Aberdare	22	12	5	5	56	30	29
Treharris	22	12	2	8	57	45	26
Staple Hill	22	9	4	9	41	60	22
Radstock Town	22	8	5	9	37	60	21
Weymouth	22	8	4	10	47	64	20
Bath City	22	6	7	9	39	45	19
Barry District	22	8	3	11	42	50	19
Welton Rovers	22	7	3	12	41	54	17
Kingswood Rovers	22	5	3	14	24	55	13
Paulton Rovers	22	5	2	15	39	55	12

1909-10

	P	W	D	L	F	A	PTS
Treharris	24	20	2	2	84	21	42
Bristol City Res	24	18	3	3	86	23	39
Bristol Rovers Res	24	15	3	6	79	25	33
Ton Pentre	24	14	4	6	68	26	32
Merthyr Town	24	14	3	7	57	24	31
Welton Rovers	24	13	5	6	51	46	31
Aberdare Town	23	13	2	8	57	30	28
Barry District	23	11	1	11	57	57	23
Bath City	24	5	6	13	31	66	15*
Kingswood Rovers	23	4	2	17	28	80	10
Radstock Town	24	4	1	19	24	88	9
Weymouth	23	3	2	18	25	93	8
Paulton Rovers	24	2	2	20	28	96	6

*Bath City were deducted one point.

1910-11

	P	W	D	L	F	A	PTS
Bristol City Res	18	15	3	0	58	14	33
Bristol Rovers Res	18	9	6	3	45	26	24
Bath City	18	9	4	5	38	30	22
Barry District	18	8	4	6	49	37	20
Welton Rovers	18	7	3	8	34	35	17
Weymouth	18	7	1	10	42	45	15
Weston-super-Mare	18	5	5	8	32	36	15
Camerton	18	3	7	8	31	42	13
Clevedon	18	4	3	11	22	54	11
Paulton Rovers	18	4	2	12	20	52	10

1911-12

	P	W	D	L	F	A	PTS
Welton Rovers	20	15	2	3	52	19	32
Barry District	20	13	2	5	56	28	28
Weymouth	20	12	3	5	58	29	27
Bristol Rovers Res	20	12	1	7	53	39	25
Bath City	20	10	2	8	31	27	22
Camerton	20	8	1	11	30	35	17
Weston-super-Mare	20	7	3	10	24	30	17
Street	20	7	1	12	32	42	15
Peasedown St John	20	6	2	12	22	37	14
Paulton Rovers	20	5	2	13	28	70	12
Clevedon	20	5	1	14	21	46	11

1912-13

	P	W	D	L	F	A	PTS
Bristol Rovers Res	22	17	3	2	85	23	37
Cardiff City Res	22	17	1	4	72	24	35
Welton Rovers	22	14	5	3	56	16	33
Bath City	22	13	1	8	52	35	27
Barry District	22	10	4	8	48	40	24
Peasedown St John	22	9	3	10	33	35	21
Street	22	10	1	11	44	58	21
Weymouth	22	6	4	12	35	55	16
Weston-super-Mare	22	6	3	13	37	55	15
Camerton	22	6	3	13	27	48	15
Paulton Rovers	22	4	2	16	29	79	10
Clevedon	22	2	6	14	15	68	10

1913-14

	P	W	D	L	F	A	PTS
Cardiff City Res	22	18	3	1	88	10	39
Bath City	22	17	2	3	67	34	36
Bristol Rovers Res	22	16	3	3	72	18	35
Weymouth	22	13	2	7	51	35	28
Peasedown St John	22	12	4	6	33	35	28
Welton Rovers	22	12	2	8	55	33	26
Street	22	7	6	9	37	48	20
Trowbridge Town	22	7	2	13	33	43	16
Camerton	22	5	2	15	33	72	12
Paulton Rovers	22	4	2	16	24	73	10
Clevedon	22	3	3	16	19	60	9
Weston-super-Mare	22	2	1	19	21	72	5

On 18th September 1914, the Western League made the following statement;
"The Western Football League has decided to cancel all matches until December 19th. If the European situation should then still be of a serious character, it is probable that all matches for the season will be abandoned"

1919-20

	P	W	D	L	F	A	PTS
Division One							
Douglas	18	12	4	2	58	18	28
Swansea Town Res	18	13	2	3	39	15	28
Bristolcity Res	18	12	1	5	41	17	25
Swindon Town Res	18	11	3	4	30	21	25
Bath City	18	8	2	8	48	29	18
Welton Rovers	18	6	1	11	29	47	13
Barry Res	18	6	0	12	27	37	12
Bristol Rovers Res	18	4	4	10	28	51	12
Newport County Res	18	5	1	12	25	57	11
Horfield United	18	1	4	13	21	54	6
Division Two							
Frome Town	14	10	2	2	33	20	22
Trowbridge Town	14	8	2	4	36	18	18
Peasedown St John	14	8	2	4	22	14	18
Paulton Rovers	14	6	4	4	26	21	16
Yeovil & Petters United	14	7	2	5	41	34	16
Timbury Athletic	14	4	1	9	19	32	9
Street	14	2	3	9	18	29	7
Glastonbury	14	2	2	10	8	35	6

1920-21

	P	W	D	L	F	A	PTS
Division One							
Bristol City Res	30	18	5	7	58	27	41
Cardiff City Res	30	20	1	9	64	42	41
Abertillery Town	30	16	7	7	61	35	39
Swansea Town Res	30	15	8	7	60	29	38
Douglas	30	15	8	7	52	32	38
Pontypridd	30	15	6	9	60	40	36
Yeovil & Petters United	30	13	6	11	52	46	32
Bath City	30	12	7	11	45	45	31
Swindon Town Res	30	12	6	12	62	50	30
Exeter City Res	30	10	9	11	48	53	29
Bristol Rovers Res	30	10	5	15	46	53	25
Ton Pentre	30	10	5	15	43	60	25
Welton Rovers	30	9	6	15	39	67	24
Mid Rhondda	30	8	6	16	23	57	22
Barry Reserves	30	6	5	19	33	72	17
Cardiff Corinthians	30	4	4	22	24	62	15
Division Two							
Peasedown St John	18	13	2	3	34	12	29
Radstock Town	18	10	4	4	31	23	24
Trowbridge Town	18	10	3	5	36	18	23
Paulton Rovers	18	9	4	5	33	26	22
Timsbury Athletic	18	6	4	8	22	27	16
Street	18	7	2	9	21	35	16
Frome Town	18	5	3	10	26	30	13
Glastonbury	18	5	3	10	17	28	13
Clandown	18	5	3	10	13	24	13
Welton Amateurs	18	2	7	9	20	30	11

1921-22

Division One

	P	W	D	L	F	A	PTS
Yeovil & Petters United	14	10	2	2	26	9	22
Trowbrige Town	14	8	1	5	18	15	17
Welton Rovers	14	7	2	5	31	27	16
Cardiff Corintians	14	7	1	6	30	22	15
Torquay United	14	6	2	6	25	17	14
Peasedown St John	14	5	3	6	21	19	13
Weymouth	14	5	1	8	15	25	11
Horfield United	14	1	2	11	10	42	4

Division Two

	P	W	D	L	F	A	PTS
Clandown	16	10	5	1	22	5	25
Coleford Athletic	16	11	1	4	35	19	23
Radstock Town	16	7	4	5	23	14	18
Timbury Athletic	16	7	2	7	23	22	16
Welton Amateurs	16	8	0	8	22	22	16
Glastonbury	16	6	2	8	21	36	14
Paulton Rovers	16	4	5	7	26	22	13
Frome Town	16	5	2	9	21	29	12
Street	16	2	3	11	25	49	7

1922-23

	P	W	D	L	F	A	PTS
Weymouth	16	10	2	4	35	14	22
Welton Rovers	16	9	2	5	27	14	20
Yeovil & Petters United	16	7	5	4	28	19	19
Trowbridge Town	16	6	6	4	14	22	18
Peasedown St John	16	5	5	6	29	22	15
Radstock Town	16	4	7	5	14	19	15
Hanham Athletic	16	5	3	8	18	31	13
Bath City	16	4	3	9	15	19	11
Cardifff Corinthians	16	3	5	8	14	25	11

1923-24

	P	W	D	L	F	A	PTS
Lovells Athletic	20	16	3	1	43	10	35
Radstock Town	20	13	3	4	43	12	29
Weymouth	20	10	5	5	38	24	25
Cardiff Corinthians	20	11	3	6	32	26	25
Poole	20	8	6	6	37	35	22
Yeovil & Petters United	20	9	2	9	35	42	20
Trowbridge Town	20	6	2	12	29	42	14
Peasedown St John	20	6	2	12	23	42	14
Minehead	20	5	3	12	32	44	13
Bath City	20	5	2	13	21	38	12
Paulton Rovers	20	3	5	12	20	38	11

1924-25

	P	W	D	L	F	A	PT
Yeovil & Petters United	24	19	3	2	65	20	41
Weymouth	24	18	3	3	74	17	39
Swindon Victoria	24	14	3	7	51	48	31
Welton Rovers	24	9	10	5	50	28	28
Poole	24	11	6	7	50	38	28
Radstock Town	24	9	9	6	35	31	27
Frome Town	24	10	6	8	50	44	26
Trowbridge Town	24	9	6	9	46	37	24
Paulton Rovers	24	6	7	11	39	54	19
Minehead	24	7	1	16	47	74	15
Bath City	24	4	5	15	26	58	13
Peasedown St John	24	4	5	15	19	65	13
Lovells Athletic	24	1	6	17	25	63	8

1925-26

	P	W	D	L	F	A	PTS
Division One							
Bristol City Res	18	10	7	1	58	19	27
Bristol Rovers Res	18	11	2	5	53	36	24
Torquay United	18	9	4	5	28	22	22
Yeovil & Petters United	18	7	7	4	33	27	21
Swindon Town Res	18	6	8	4	32	33	20
Weymouth	18	7	4	7	37	45	18
Plymouth Argyle Res	18	6	5	7	31	25	17
Exeter City Res	18	6	4	8	33	41	16
Taunton United	18	3	3	12	18	45	9
Bath City	18	1	4	13	20	50	6
Division Two							
Poole	24	17	3	4	76	30	37
Welton Rovers	24	16	4	4	62	37	36
Weymouth Res	24	12	4	8	69	47	28
Lovells Athletic	24	8	8	8	52	46	24
Radstock Town	24	9	6	9	31	28	24
Minehead	24	10	4	10	42	53	24
Portland United	24	8	7	9	49	56	23
Trowbridge Town	24	8	6	10	56	68	22
Swindon Victoria	24	9	3	12	55	71	21
Paulton Rovers	24	7	6	11	48	68	20
Bath City Res	24	7	5	12	50	53	19
Yeovil & Petters United	24	7	4	13	48	57	18
Frome Town	24	5	6	13	40	64	16

1926-27

	P	W	D	L	F	A	PTS
Division One							
Bristol City Res	22	16	2	4	59	32	34
Torquay United	22	14	4	4	47	27	32
Plymouth Argyle Res	22	13	1	8	63	37	27
Lovells Athletic	22	11	5	6	47	36	27
Bristol Rovers Res	22	12	3	7	49	41	27
Exeter City Res	22	10	3	9	61	53	23
Yeovil & Petters United	22	10	1	11	48	44	21
Swindon Town Res	22	9	2	11	41	47	20
Bath City	22	8	3	11	35	50	19
Poole	22	6	2	14	40	69	14
Taunton United	22	4	3	15	28	55	11
Weymouth	22	3	3	16	30	57	9
Division Two							
Poole Town Res	18	14	2	2	68	19	30
Radstock Town	18	12	1	5	43	29	25
Portland United	18	12	0	6	62	31	24
Welton Rovers	18	9	2	7	61	39	20
Yeovil & Petters United Res	18	8	3	7	44	40	19
Lovells Athletic Res	18	8	0	10	48	48	16
Trowbridge Town	18	5	2	11	44	52	12
Frome Town	18	5	2	11	28	62	12
Weymouth Res	18	4	4	10	25	60	12
Minehead	18	5	0	13	24	67	10

1927-28

	P	W	D	L	F	A	PTS
Division One							
Plymouth Argyle Res	20	13	5	2	76	32	31
Exeter City Res	20	13	4	3	50	24	30
Yeovil & Petters United	20	12	2	6	56	44	26
Bristol City Res	20	10	4	6	71	40	24
Bristol Rovers Res	20	11	2	7	61	39	24
Taunton Town	20	9	5	6	36	33	23
Lovells Athletic	20	7	2	11	40	49	16
Torquay United Res	20	5	6	9	34	52	16
Bath City	20	5	3	12	36	54	13
Weymouth	20	3	3	14	16	60	9
Salisbury City	20	3	2	15	23	72	8
Division Two							
Trowbridge Town	14	12	0	2	43	16	24
Yeovil & Petters United Res	14	10	2	2	56	21	22
Portland United	14	7	1	6	35	30	15
Welton Rovers	14	7	0	7	44	26	14
Radstock Town	14	6	1	7	48	41	13
Weymouth Res	14	4	1	9	22	52	9
Poole Res	14	4	1	9	25	54	9
Minehead	14	3	0	11	17	50	6

1928-29

Division One

	P	W	D	L	F	A	PTS
Bristol Rovers Res	14	10	0	4	39	21	20
Plymouth Argyle Res	14	6	4	4	31	19	16
Bath City	14	6	4	4	33	30	16
Taunton Town	14	7	2	5	32	30	16
Bristol City Res	14	7	1	6	34	31	15
Exeter City Res	14	4	4	6	36	42	12
Torquay United Res	14	3	3	8	21	30	9
Yeovil & Petters United	14	2	4	8	19	42	8

Division Two

	P	W	D	L	F	A	PTS
Bath City Res	16	12	0	4	44	28	24
Portland United	16	10	3	3	44	26	23
Trowbridge Town	16	8	3	5	31	33	19
Yeovil & Petters United Res	16	8	1	7	51	33	17
Welton Rovers	16	5	5	6	30	32	15
Weymouth	16	4	6	6	35	41	14
Salsibury City	16	5	3	8	28	36	13
Bristol St George	16	4	3	9	41	56	11
Radstock Town	16	3	2	11	27	46	8

1929-30

Division One

	P	W	D	L	F	A	PTS
Yeovil & Petters United	14	10	2	2	32	13	22
Exeter City Res	14	5	5	4	26	17	15
Bristol City Res	14	5	5	4	28	27	15
Plymouth Argyle Res	14	6	2	6	23	20	14
Taunton Town	14	6	2	6	17	30	14
Bath City	14	4	5	5	35	33	13
Torquay United Res	14	4	3	7	27	32	11
Bristol Rovers Res	14	3	2	9	18	34	8

Division Two

	P	W	D	L	F	A	PTS
Trowbridge Town	18	12	2	4	50	28	26
Portland United	18	11	3	4	50	27	25
Wells City	18	10	3	5	52	31	23
Bristol City A	18	9	3	6	54	41	21
Welton Rovers	18	9	3	6	50	48	21
Bath City Res	18	6	6	6	43	39	18
Paulton Rovers	18	4	5	9	26	50	13
Bristol St George	18	5	1	12	41	51	11
Radstock Town	18	5	1	12	32	57	11
Weymouth	18	4	3	11	28	52	11

1930-31

	P	W	D	L	F	A	PTS
Division One							
Exeter City Res	12	9	1	2	34	24	19
Yeovil & Petters United	12	7	2	3	43	27	16
Bristol Rovers Res	12	6	3	3	28	19	15
Bristol City Res	12	4	2	6	34	28	10
Taunton Town	12	5	0	7	20	34	10
Plymouth Argyle Res	12	3	1	8	23	33	7
Torquay United Res	12	1	5	6	18	35	7
Division Two							
Portland United	32	24	3	5	111	47	51
Salisbury City	32	22	4	6	93	50	48
Welton Rovers	32	20	6	6	106	64	46
Wells City	32	21	2	9	92	61	44
Bristol City A	32	19	5	8	111	72	43
Bath City Res	32	18	3	11	102	56	39
Warminster Town	32	15	5	12	94	77	35
Radstock Town	32	15	5	12	63	85	35
Poole	32	14	4	14	76	72	32
Chippenham Town	32	10	8	14	82	68	28
Trowbridge Town	32	9	9	14	58	60	27
Paulton Rovers	32	8	10	14	45	67	26
Petters Westland	32	10	2	20	76	101	22
Bristol St George	32	10	1	21	80	135	21
Weymouth	32	9	1	22	81	128	19
Street	32	6	4	22	52	96	16
Coleford Athletic	32	6	0	26	60	143	12

1931-32

	P	W	D	L	F	A	PTS
Division One							
Plymouth Argyle Res	14	10	1	3	41	15	21
Yeovil & Petters Res	14	8	3	3	42	26	19
Lovells Athletic	14	7	3	4	33	25	17
Bristol Rovers Res	14	8	0	6	32	28	16
Torquay United Res	14	5	4	5	29	35	14
Bristol City Res	14	4	3	7	26	37	11
Exeter City Res	14	4	1	9	23	37	9
Taunton Town	14	2	1	11	18	41	5
Division Two							
Portland United	34	27	1	6	122	55	55
Salsibury City	34	23	5	6	122	50	51
Bath City Res	34	23	4	7	104	53	50
Trowbridge Town	34	19	5	10	103	68	43
Bristol City A	34	19	2	13	124	89	40
Street	34	17	4	13	100	84	38
Paulton Rovers	34	17	3	14	78	59	37
Frome Town	34	18	1	15	86	105	37
Poole	34	16	4	14	81	82	36
Wells City	34	15	5	14	119	89	35
Weymouth	34	13	4	17	86	103	30
Chippenham Town	34	11	6	17	99	105	28
Bristol St George	34	12	4	18	74	110	28
Welton Rovers	34	10	7	17	72	90	27
Glastonbury	34	12	2	20	86	113	26
Radstock Town	34	9	5	20	64	101	26
Warminster	34	8	6	20	68	119	22
Coleford Athletic	34	1	4	29	43	156	6

1932-33

	P	W	D	L	F	A	PTS
Division One							
Exeter City Res	16	11	2	3	59	29	24
Torquay United Res	16	11	1	4	55	29	23
Yeovil & Petters United	16	10	0	6	51	31	20
Bath City	16	8	1	7	39	39	17
Bristol City Res	16	6	4	6	54	42	17
Bristol Rovers Res	16	7	2	7	34	34	16
Lovells Athletic	16	6	3	7	36	35	15
Cardifff City Res	16	3	1	12	31	66	7
Taunton Town	16	2	2	12	13	67	6
Division Two							
Swindon Town Res	34	28	1	5	124	51	57
Street	34	20	9	5	105	60	49
Bristol City A	34	18	6	10	91	64	42
Bath City Res	34	16	6	12	100	68	38
Bristol St George	34	17	4	13	92	86	38
Salsibury City	34	16	4	14	92	70	36
Portland United	34	15	5	14	95	72	35
Radstock Town	34	15	5	14	71	65	35
Frome Town	34	16	2	16	92	112	34
Weymouth	34	15	3	16	109	92	33
Wells City	34	11	8	15	82	83	30
Glastonbury	34	13	4	17	67	92	30
Welton Rovers	34	13	3	18	72	91	29
Poole	34	13	3	18	75	97	29
Trowbridge Town	34	11	5	18	66	106	27
Warminster Town	34	10	4	20	68	125	24
Chippenham Town	34	9	5	20	71	99	23
Paulton Rovers	34	9	5	20	50	89	23

1933-34

	P	W	D	L	F	A	PTS
Division One							
Bath City	12	8	2	2	33	14	18
Torquay United Res	12	6	3	3	31	17	15
Bristol Rovers Res	12	7	1	4	40	22	15
Yeovil & Petters United	12	5	3	4	22	21	13
Lovells Athletic	12	5	2	5	21	20	12
Exeter City Res	12	5	1	6	25	31	11
Taunton Town	12	0	0	12	10	57	0
Division Two							
Weymouth	34	20	7	7	101	54	47
Bath City Res	34	20	7	7	101	53	47
Swindon Town Res	34	20	6	8	99	61	46
Salisbury City	34	18	7	9	71	37	43
Portland United	34	17	6	11	99	73	40
Glastonbury	34	17	5	12	99	70	39
Street	34	16	5	13	98	89	37
Poole	34	14	8	12	83	66	36
Welton Rovers	34	15	5	14	77	82	35
Paulton Rovers	34	14	5	15	73	75	33
Radstock Town	34	13	6	15	67	70	32
Trowbridge Town	34	12	8	14	62	86	32
Wells City	34	11	9	14	69	85	31
Bristol City A	34	10	8	16	60	79	28
Frome Town	34	10	8	16	74	96	28
Chippenham Town	34	11	3	20	73	95	25
Warminster Town	34	6	5	23	46	95	17
Bristol St George	34	7	2	25	62	145	16

334

1934-35

	P	W	D	L	F	A	PTS
Division One							
Yeovil & Petters United	12	9	1	2	38	21	19
Bath City	12	7	2	3	32	16	16
Bristol Rovers Res	12	6	3	3	34	21	15
Torquay United Res	12	4	2	6	25	25	10
Cardiff City Res	12	3	3	6	19	30	9
Exeter City Res	12	2	4	6	18	26	8
Lovells Athletic	12	3	1	8	15	42	7
Division Two							
Swindon Town Res	34	25	5	4	108	33	55
Salisbury City	34	21	6	7	86	41	48
Portland United	34	22	3	9	105	65	47
Weymouth	34	19	8	7	107	39	46
Frome Town	34	19	7	8	113	67	45
Bath City Res	34	18	5	11	85	52	41
Glastonbury	34	19	5	10	91	68	39
Street	34	14	8	12	83	65	36
Trowbridge Town	34	14	7	13	79	84	35
Bristol City A	34	15	4	15	87	69	34
Paulton Rovers	34	13	7	14	60	70	33
Bristol Rovers A	34	15	0	19	68	88	30
Welton Rovers	34	10	8	16	71	84	28
Warminster Town	34	11	4	19	63	112	26
Wells City	34	10	5	19	70	83	25
Radstock Town	34	6	7	21	48	101	19
Chippenham Town	34	7	3	24	48	101	19
Bristol St George	34	2	4	28	43	173	8

1935-36

	P	W	D	L	F	A	PTS
Division One							
Bristol Rovers Res	10	5	4	2	29	22	14
Lovells Athletic	10	4	4	2	17	18	12
Torquay United Res	10	4	3	3	28	20	11
Bath City	10	3	3	4	15	16	9
Cardiff City Res	10	3	3	4	13	18	9
Yeovil & Petters United Res	10	1	3	6	22	30	5
Division Two							
Swindon Town Res	34	28	4	2	140	40	60
Weymouth	34	22	4	8	116	54	48
Street	34	21	5	8	106	54	47
Frome Town	34	17	5	12	92	86	39
Bath City Res	34	14	10	10	93	78	38
Portland United	34	16	6	12	95	82	38
Glastonbury	34	15	7	12	97	72	37
Poole Town	34	16	5	13	77	89	37
Paulton Rovers	34	14	8	12	69	77	36
Radstock Town	34	15	5	14	77	80	35
Salisbury City	34	13	8	13	60	65	34
Bristol City A	34	14	3	17	71	76	31
Wells City	34	12	7	15	61	72	31
Trowbridge Town	34	12	6	16	87	91	30
Warminster Town	34	9	4	21	58	103	22
Bristol Rovers A	34	8	5	21	57	78	21
Welton Rovers	34	5	5	24	49	125	15
Chippenham Town	34	6	1	27	64	147	13

1936-37

	P	W	D	L	F	A	PTS
Division One							
Bristol Rovers Res	8	6	0	2	26	15	12
Yeovil & Petters United	8	5	1	2	23	12	11
Bristol City Res	8	4	2	2	18	15	10
Torquay United Res	8	2	0	6	13	24	4
Lovells Athletic	8	1	1	6	11	25	3
Division Two							
Weymouth	34	27	4	3	144	38	58
Swindon Town Res	34	27	4	3	139	49	58
Salisbury City	34	20	9	5	97	45	49
Trowbridge Town	34	22	3	9	89	62	47
Portland United	34	21	3	10	115	60	45
Street	34	18	4	12	90	73	40
Wells City	34	14	9	11	65	60	37
Radstock Town	34	15	7	12	91	92	37
Warminster Town	34	14	7	13	64	69	35
Glastonbury	34	14	3	17	92	98	31
Frome Town	34	9	7	18	68	94	25
Chippenham Town	34	11	3	20	71	98	25
Bristol City A	34	11	2	21	62	90	24
Bristol Rovers A	34	8	7	19	84	112	23
Yeovil & Petters United Res	34	9	5	20	80	131	23
Welton Rovers	34	11	0	23	60	116	22
Poole Town	34	8	3	23	51	95	19
Paulton Rovers	34	5	4	25	46	126	14

1937-38

	P	W	D	L	F	A	PTS
Division One							
Bristol City Res	8	6	1	1	21	7	13
Yeovil & Petters United	8	5	1	2	20	16	11
Bristol Rovers Res	8	4	0	4	15	14	8
Torquay United Res	8	3	1	4	12	15	7
Lovells Athletic	8	0	1	7	9	25	1
Division Two							
Weymouth	34	27	4	3	121	34	58
Street	34	21	4	9	113	53	46
Portland United	34	17	6	11	109	57	40
Yeovil & Peters United Res	34	15	10	9	99	61	40
Salisbury City	34	18	4	12	94	76	40
Chippenham Town	34	18	4	12	91	90	40
Radstock Town	34	18	4	12	79	80	40
Trowbridge Town	34	16	7	11	102	76	39
Glastonbury	34	18	2	14	85	67	38
Poole Town	34	14	7	13	79	67	35
Wells City	34	13	8	13	75	87	34
Bristol City A	34	13	1	18	86	100	31
Warminster Town	34	10	9	15	66	92	29
Frome Town	34	9	7	18	66	94	25
Bristol Rovers A	34	9	6	19	63	89	24
Paulton Rovers	34	9	6	19	61	124	34
Welton Rovers	34	5	7	22	52	142	17
Bath City Res	34	3	6	25	51	103	12

1938-39

	P	W	D	L	F	A	PTS
Division One							
Lovells Athletic	10	7	2	1	27	14	16
Yeovil & Petters United	10	6	2	2	32	20	14
Bristol City Res	10	4	1	5	24	24	9
Bath City	10	2	5	3	16	22	9
Torquay United Res	10	2	4	4	14	17	8
Bristol Rovers Res	10	1	2	7	9	25	4
Division Two							
Trowbridge Town	34	27	3	4	166	49	57
Yeovil & Petters United Res	34	22	4	8	112	66	48
Street	34	21	5	8	93	57	47
Poole Town	34	21	4	9	106	67	46
Weymouth	34	19	5	10	105	51	43
Radstock Town	34	19	5	10	97	64	43
Portland United	34	18	4	12	107	64	40
Bristol City A	34	17	6	11	87	58	40
Welton Rovers	34	14	4	16	64	118	32
Glastonbury	34	13	5	16	76	89	31
Frome Town	34	11	9	14	76	104	31
Bath City Res	34	8	8	18	64	100	24
Wells City	34	10	3	21	63	104	23
Warminster Town	34	8	7	19	49	105	23
Bristol Rovers A	34	9	4	21	58	92	22
Paulton Rovers	34	8	6	20	57	117	22
Salisbury City	34	7	7	20	50	93	21
Chippenham Town	34	8	3	23	56	87	19

1939-40

	P	W	D	L	F	A	PTS
Trowbridge Town	20	18	0	2	87	31	36
Bristol Aeroplane Company	20	13	4	3	78	33	30
Radstock Town	20	12	1	7	68	54	25
Peasedown Miners Welfare	20	9	5	6	45	36	23
Glastonbury	20	9	5	6	49	43	23
Bristol City Res	20	9	2	9	54	43	20
Chippenham Town	20	7	2	11	51	78	16
Welton Rovers	20	6	1	13	44	65	13
Wells City	20	6	1	13	37	66	13
Bath City Res	20	4	3	13	35	69	11
Paulton Rovers	20	3	4	13	34	64	10

At the end of the 1939-40 season the League was suspended throughout the duration of the Second World War.

1945-46

	P	W	D	L	F	A	PTS
Bristol Rovers Res	26	17	6	3	120	46	40
Chippenham Town	26	15	4	7	84	41	34
Trowbridge Town	26	16	2	8	114	62	34
Peasedown Miners Welfare	26	13	8	5	75	44	34
Yeovil Town Res	26	12	5	9	66	58	29
Douglas	26	12	3	11	82	84	27
Bristol City Res	26	10	6	10	90	68	26
Clevedon	26	11	2	13	80	102	24
Bristol Aeroplane Company	26	10	4	12	62	81	24
Paulton Rovers	26	10	3	13	67	93	23
Clandown	26	10	2	14	58	66	22
Radstock Town	26	9	2	15	65	82	20
Soundwell	26	6	3	17	67	132	15
Welton Rovers	26	4	4	18	44	115	12

1946-47

	P	W	D	L	F	A	PTS
Division One							
Trowbridge Town	31	27	1	3	123	42	55
Poole Town	31	21	5	5	96	32	47
Bristol Rovers Res	31	19	4	8	96	53	42
Chippenham Town	33	21	2	13	121	78	44
Yeovil Town Res	30	16	4	10	85	56	36
Clevedon	32	16	5	11	91	68	37
Portland United	33	15	5	13	95	71	35
Street	32	13	5	14	75	80	31
Paulton Rovers	32	14	3	15	83	110	31
Glastonbury	30	13	3	14	64	69	29
Bristol Aeroplane Company	31	12	3	16	72	94	27
Wells City	31	8	9	14	52	78	25
Radstock Town	29	9	3	17	66	92	21
Peasedown Miners Welfare	23	8	6	9	50	52	22
Bristol City Res	24	7	1	16	50	92	15
Bath City Res	27	5	4	18	35	80	14
Frome Town	30	4	4	22	46	130	12
Welton Rovers	20	2	3	15	40	72	7
Division Two							
Clandown	23	20	2	1	13	33	42
Soundwell	24	17	3	4	11	44	37
Douglas	23	14	2	7	107	77	30
Trowbridge Town Res	22	13	3	6	82	50	29
Swindon Town Res	24	11	3	10	91	77	25
Hoffman Athletic	20	11	2	7	62	37	24
Raf Locking	21	11	1	9	83	69	23
Raf Melksham	23	7	4	12	58	83	18
Cinderford Town	21	7	3	11	58	60	17
Bac Res	23	6	3	14	50	76	15
Chippenham Town Res	20	4	3	13	47	86	11
Raf Colerne	20	2	5	13	48	99	9
Thorney Pitts	18	1	0	17	24	158	2

*** The season was not completed but this table is up to and including June 13th 1947 in accordance with research by John Powel. The official table that was published in 'A View from the Terraces' was compiled up to and including the 5th June 1947. The extra games did not affect the final placings.*

1947-48

	P	W	D	L	F	A	PTS
Division One							
Trowbridge Town	34	29	3	2	131	33	61
Glastonbury	34	26	3	5	119	40	55
Street	34	23	7	4	98	40	53
Bristol Rovers Res	34	21	6	7	121	60	48
Clevedon	34	20	4	10	117	66	44
Clandown	34	16	5	13	84	80	37
Poole Town	33	14	6	13	73	72	34
Yeovil Town Res	34	14	4	16	70	79	32
Paulton Rovers	34	13	5	16	78	93	31
Portland United	34	11	7	16	64	72	29
Bristol City Res	34	11	7	16	69	104	29
Bath City Res	34	10	8	16	56	82	28
Wells City	34	11	5	18	58	71	27
Peasedown Miners Welfare	34	11	5	18	74	96	27
Soundwell	32	8	7	17	64	103	23
Chippenham Town	33	8	6	19	65	97	22
Radstock Town	34	8	3	23	64	108	19
Bristol Aeorplane Company	34	4	1	29	56	165	9
Division Two							
Salisbury	34	29	1	4	145	33	59
Weymouth	34	26	4	4	148	37	56
Cheltenham Town Res	34	25	3	6	142	42	53
Welton Rovers	34	21	3	10	85	49	45
Frome Town	33	22	0	11	114	76	44
Hoffman Athletic	34	19	5	10	79	50	43
Trowbridge Town Res	33	17	5	11	92	59	39
Swindon Town Res	34	17	4	13	95	76	38
Douglas	34	18	2	14	104	88	38
Dorchester Town	34	13	6	15	64	79	32
Cinderford Town	34	12	7	15	87	103	31
National Smelting Company	34	13	5	16	80	102	31
Stonehouse	34	7	7	20	64	113	21
Chippenham Town Res	34	8	4	22	63	117	20
Raf Locking	33	9	1	23	52	126	19
Raf Melksham	34	7	4	23	63	136	18
Raf Colerne	33	6	4	23	64	146	16
Bristol Aeroplane Co Res	34	2	1	31	48	157	5

1948-49

	P	W	D	L	F	A	PTS
Division One							
Glastonbury	34	24	6	4	93	50	54
Trowbridge Town	34	22	6	6	109	44	50
Weymouth	34	22	4	8	100	44	48
Chippenham Town	34	19	5	10	94	50	43
Street	34	18	4	12	90	58	40
Salisbury	34	17	5	12	78	51	39
Bristol Rovers Colts	34	12	12	10	65	63	36
Paulton Rovers	34	13	6	15	57	64	32
Wells City	34	14	4	16	51	67	32
Bath City Res	34	14	4	16	63	92	32
Poole Town	34	13	5	16	59	65	31
Soundwell	34	13	5	16	76	100	31
Peasedown Miners Welfare	34	12	3	19	54	81	27
Clandown	34	12	3	19	55	102	27
Portland United	34	11	4	19	51	70	26
Yeovil Town Res	34	7	12	15	61	81	26
Clevedon	34	5	10	19	48	74	20
Bristol City Colts	34	7	4	23	57	105	18
Division Two							
Chippenham United	34	29	3	2	145	35	61
Cheltenham Town Res	34	26	3	5	133	48	55
Welton Rovers	34	23	4	7	139	68	50
Radstock Town	34	21	5	8	107	64	47
Weston-super-Mare	34	21	5	8	101	63	47
Hoffman Athletic	34	20	2	12	88	41	42
Trowbridge Town Res	34	178	5	12	124	75	39
Frome Town	34	16	4	14	85	73	36
Ciderford Town	34	13	6	15	82	103	32
Dorchester Town	34	13	5	16	78	96	31
Barnstaple Town	34	13	3	18	94	88	29
Douglas	34	14	1	19	77	112	29
Chippenham Town Res	34	11	4	19	81	89	26
Swindon Town Res	34	10	6	18	78	107	26
Stonehouse	34	11	2	21	71	102	24
Bristol Aeroplane Company	34	9	5	20	74	109	23
Raf Melksham	34	5	0	29	50	167	10
National Smelting Company	34	2	1	31	42	209	5

1949-50

	P	W	D	L	F	A	PTS
Division One							
Wells City	34	22	7	5	87	43	51
Poole Town	34	22	7	5	88	45	51
Glastonbury	34	23	4	7	78	38	50
Trowbridge Town	34	22	5	7	104	40	49
Cheltenham Town Res	34	21	4	9	91	58	46
Chippenham United	34	16	8	10	57	49	40
Bristol Rovers Colts	34	15	7	12	54	50	37
Chippenham Town	34	13	7	14	77	70	33
Street	34	12	9	13	71	75	33
Weymouth Res	34	13	5	16	67	49	31
Salisbury	34	14	3	17	64	66	31
Yeovil Town Res	34	13	5	16	55	102	31
Paulton Rovers	34	12	3	19	60	76	27
Peasedown Miners Welfare	34	8	9	17	56	82	25
Portland United	34	8	6	20	44	74	22
Clandown	34	8	5	21	46	80	21
Soundwell	34	6	6	22	61	116	18
Bath City Res	34	5	6	23	45	103	16
Division Two							
Barnstaple Town	34	23	7	4	102	41	53
Dorchester Town	34	21	8	5	96	51	50
Welton Rovers	34	20	7	7	87	63	47
Stonehouse	34	19	6	9	83	63	44
Bridgwater Town	34	17	8	9	86	49	42
Trowbridge Town Res	34	17	8	9	81	53	42
Clevedon	34	18	6	10	92	61	42
Weston-super-Mare	34	16	9	9	86	73	41
Bristol City Colts	34	14	8	12	89	60	36
Cinderford Town	34	13	9	12	82	80	35
Chippenham Town Res	34	14	4	16	74	73	32
Frome Town	34	12	7	15	72	74	31
Radstock Town	34	10	7	17	72	98	27
National Smelting Company	34	8	9	17	69	99	25
Swindon Town Colts	34	9	3	22	58	89	21
Hoffman Athletic	34	4	16	17	33	69	21
Bristol Aeroplane Company	34	3	6	25	43	138	12
Douglas	34	3	5	26	49	114	11
Division Three							
Bideford Town	20	19	1	0	103	20	39
Ilfracombe Town	20	16	0	4	745	37	32
Minehead	20	11	5	4	49	30	27
Clevedon Res	20	9	7	4	50	41	25
Chippenham United Res	20	8	2	10	45	48	18
Weston-super-Mare Res	20	7	3	10	44	64	17
Bristol Rovers A	20	56	6	9	36	43	16
Barnstaple Town Res	20	5	5	10	31	45	15
Welton Rovers Res	20	5	2	13	36	64	12
Bridgwater Town Res	20	5	1	14	38	62	11
Stonehouse Res	20	2	4	14	19	69	8

1950-51

Division One	P	W	D	L	F	A	PTS
Glastonbury	34	26	6	2	102	27	58
Wells City	34	22	9	3	83	39	53
Chippenham Town	34	18	8	8	86	48	44
Chippenham United	34	18	6	10	72	44	42
Trowbridge Town	34	17	7	10	83	49	41
Barnstaple Town	34	18	4	12	71	62	40
Poole Town	34	18	3	13	71	71	39
Salisbury	34	14	7	13	65	55	35
Dorchester Town	34	13	8	13	64	58	34
Street	34	13	8	13	74	69	34
Weymouth Res	34	13	6	15	54	56	32
Cheltenham Town Res	34	12	7	15	56	46	31
Brsitol Rovers Colts	34	11	8	15	60	85	30
Clandown	34	10	9	15	49	58	29
Paulton Rovers	34	9	9	16	62	75	27
Portland United	34	6	7	21	56	112	19
Yeovil Town Res	34	8	3	23	38	79	19
Peasedown Miners Welfare	34	1	3	30	25	123	5
Division Two							
Stonehouse	38	29	7	2	133	36	65
Bath City Res	38	28	5	5	114	44	61
Bideford Town	38	27	6	5	158	54	60
Cinderford Town	38	21	12	5	112	51	54
Bridgwater Town	38	24	5	9	124	50	53
Ilfracombe Town	38	23	5	10	105	68	51
Clevedon	38	18	6	14	95	81	42
Welton Rovers	38	18	5	15	103	95	41
Minehead	38	16	8	14	73	74	40
Hoffman Athletic	38	16	4	18	74	66	36
Frome Town	38	12	10	16	81	102	34
Bristol City Colts	38	14	5	19	75	84	33
Radstock Town	38	11	9	18	85	112	31
Chippenham Town Res	38	12	6	20	83	115	30
Swindon Town Colts	38	10	9	19	88	95	29
Trowbridge Town Res	38	11	6	21	69	100	28
Chipping Sodbury	38	10	3	25	75	113	28
Weston-super-Mare	38	8	7	23	46	100	23
Soundwell	38	6	3	29	46	164	15
National Smelting Company	38	3	2	33	50	184	8

1951-52

First Division	P	W	D	L	F	A	PTS
Chippenham Town	34	23	4	7	103	41	50
Glastonbury	34	20	6	8	87	64	46
Barnstaple Town	34	18	6	10	87	62	42
Weymouth Res.	34	18	5	11	84	54	41
Trowbridge Town	34	19	3	12	85	58	41
Stonehouse	34	15	7	12	82	61	37
Wells City	34	12	13	9	65	60	37
Bath City Reserves	34	14	8	12	53	51	36
Cheltenham Town Res.	34	13	8	13	58	55	34
Street	34	14	6	14	65	71	34
Clandown	34	11	10	13	63	75	32
Salisbury	34	10	9	15	62	68	29
Dorchester Town	34	11	7	16	61	81	29
Chippenham United	34	10	8	16	59	70	28
Portland United	34	9	8	17	49	73	26
Paulton Rovers	34	10	5	19	64	96	25
Bristol Rovers Colts	34	6	11	17	46	75	23
Poole Town	34	8	6	20	50	106	22

Second Division	P	W	D	L	F	A	PTS
Bideford Town	36	29	3	4	179	55	61
Bridgwater Town	36	28	1	7	126	38	57
Ilfracombe Town	36	25	4	7	106	50	54
Minehead	36	24	2	10	80	60	50
Gloucester City Res	36	19	5	12	107	73	43
Cinderford Town	36	18	6	12	95	69	42
Peasedown M.W.	36	17	8	11	80	72	42
Bristol City Colts	36	17	7	12	87	58	41
Yeovil Town Res.	36	18	4	14	94	102	40
Frome Town	36	15	7	14	89	76	37
Clevedon	36	16	5	15	98	89	37
Radstock Town	36	17	2	17	108	103	36
Chippenham Town Res	36	12	5	19	63	89	29
Hoffman Athletic	36	13	3	20	66	101	29
Welton Rovers	36	11	2	23	73	116	24
Weston-super-Mare	36	7	5	24	42	115	19
Swindon Town Colts	36	7	4	25	54	120	18
Trowbridge Town Res	36	5	4	27	56	117	14
Chipping Sodbury	36	3	5	28	43	127	11

1952-53

First Division	P	W	D	L	F	A	PTS
Barnstaple Town	32	18	8	6	77	37	44
Street	32	19	6	7	89	43	44
Trowbridge Town	32	17	7	8	76	48	41
Bideford	32	13	13	6	79	52	39
Chippenham Town	32	17	3	12	84	58	37
Weymouth Res.	32	16	5	11	75	58	37
Chippenham United	32	15	5	12	62	62	35
Salisbury	32	11	10	11	60	65	32
Glastonbury	32	15	1	16	61	49	31
Bath City Reserves	32	10	11	11	64	63	31
Stonehouse	32	11	8	13	57	58	30
Portland United	32	11	8	13	66	77	30
Bridgwater Town	32	12	4	16	58	73	28
Wells City	32	9	6	17	52	71	24
Clandown	32	7	9	16	40	74	23
Dorchester Town	32	8	5	19	46	74	21
Paulton Rovers	32	6	5	21	42	125	17

Second Division	P	W	D	L	F	A	PTS
Chippenham Town Res	34	24	4	6	99	51	52
Ilfracombe Town	34	20	11	3	67	28	51
Poole Town	34	21	7	6	97	42	49
Peasedown M.W.	34	19	3	12	76	63	41
Minehead	34	15	8	11	81	53	38
Clevedon	34	17	3	14	82	92	37
Cinderford Town	34	15	6	13	77	50	36
Bristol City Colts	34	14	6	14	75	56	34
Bristol Rovers Colts	34	12	9	13	74	54	33
Frome Town	34	13	6	15	66	66	32
Yeovil Town Res.	34	13	5	16	83	78	31
Gloucester City Res	34	11	6	17	81	97	28
Radstock Town	34	11	6	17	74	102	28
Trowbridge Town Res	34	11	4	19	70	89	26
Stonehouse Res.	34	10	6	18	68	107	26
Welton Rovers	34	10	6	18	53	98	26
Weston-super-Mare	34	10	4	20	66	113	24
Hoffman Athletic	34	8	4	22	60	109	20

1953-54

First Division	P	W	D	L	F	A	PTS
Weymouth Res.	34	21	4	9	102	53	46
Poole Town	34	18	8	8	73	49	44
Trowbridge Town	34	19	5	10	78	62	43
Barnstaple Town	34	17	7	10	74	42	41
Chippenham Town	34	18	5	11	79	49	41
Salisbury	34	17	6	11	74	60	40
Portland United	34	18	3	13	71	63	39
Wells City	34	15	7	12	63	68	37
Bridgwater Town	34	15	6	13	72	76	36
Bideford Town	34	13	8	13	70	66	34
Dorchester Town	34	14	5	15	79	69	33
Chippenham United	34	13	6	15	60	63	32
Glastonbury	34	12	8	14	59	70	32
Street	34	12	8	14	55	69	32
Bath City Reserves	34	10	6	18	40	66	26
Ilfracombe Town	34	9	5	20	40	77	23
Stonehouse	34	7	6	21	51	80	20
Clandown	34	4	5	25	29	87	13

Second Division	P	W	D	L	F	A	PTS
Bristol Rovers Colts	34	24	6	4	89	43	54
Bristol City Colts	34	22	6	6	87	39	50
Frome Town	34	21	7	6	99	50	49
Chippenham Town Res	34	18	9	7	87	58	45
Welton Rovers	34	16	6	12	54	53	38
Cinderford Town	34	15	7	12	82	72	37
Poole Town Res.	34	15	5	14	79	61	35
Weston-super-Mare	34	14	7	13	89	70	35
Trowbridge Town Res	34	12	9	13	90	88	33
Gloucester City Res	34	13	7	14	89	96	33
Hoffman Athletic	34	13	5	16	74	61	31
Yeovil Town Res.	34	12	7	15	90	89	31
Paulton Rovers	34	12	7	15	69	84	31
Minehead	34	11	6	17	62	78	28
Clevedon	34	11	4	19	77	101	26
Radstock Town	34	10	4	20	71	107	24
Peasedown M.W.	34	8	5	21	56	127	21
Stonehouse Res.	34	4	3	27	45	102	11

1954-55

First Division	P	W	D	L	F	A	PTS
Dorchester Town	34	23	5	6	103	46	51
Chippenham Town	34	21	7	6	83	39	49
Bath City Reserves	34	22	4	8	87	52	48
Salisbury	34	17	8	9	71	50	42
Portland United	34	18	6	10	89	70	42
Bideford	34	18	6	10	69	56	42
Bridgwater Town	34	18	5	11	91	69	41
Poole Town	34	13	12	9	80	62	38
Bristol Rovers Colts	34	16	5	13	73	55	37
Barnstaple Town	34	13	8	13	69	66	34
Trowbridge Town	34	14	5	15	65	55	33
Bristol City Colts	34	11	4	19	53	62	26
Weymouth Res.	34	10	6	18	49	67	26
Chippenham United	34	10	5	19	57	97	25
Glastonbury	34	8	9	17	51	89	25
Wells City	34	5	9	20	49	90	19
Street	34	7	4	23	51	100	19
Ilfracombe	34	5	6	23	35	100	16

Second Division	P	W	D	L	F	A	PTS
Yeovil Town Res.	34	23	5	6	115	49	51
Frome Town	34	24	3	7	106	49	51
Weston-super-Mare	34	22	4	8	122	58	48
Chippenham Town Res	34	18	8	8	102	60	44
Taunton Town	34	20	3	11	95	57	43
Gloucester City Res	34	16	8	10	80	61	40
Minehead	34	15	6	13	104	65	36
Cinderford Town	34	12	12	10	85	79	36
Stonehouse	34	15	5	14	87	83	35
Poole Town Res.	34	15	4	15	82	71	34
Welton Rovers	34	13	6	15	70	77	32
Peasedown M.W.	34	12	6	16	79	102	30
Clandown	34	12	6	16	45	75	30
Clevedon	34	12	4	18	82	90	28
Hoffman Athletic	34	11	3	20	53	97	25
Trowbridge Town Res	34	10	3	21	43	86	23
Radstock Town	34	5	6	23	54	127	16
Paulton Rovers	34	5	0	29	47	127	10

1955-56

First Division	P	W	D	L	F	A	PTS
Trowbridge Town	32	24	2	6	100	36	50
Poole Town	32	20	7	5	79	33	47
Dorchester Town	32	21	4	7	106	57	46
Chippenham Town	32	20	4	8	70	50	44
Salisbury	32	17	7	8	64	31	41
Bideford	32	14	10	8	58	50	38
Portland United	32	16	3	13	87	76	35
Barnstaple Town	32	15	4	13	61	66	34
Weymouth Res.	32	10	12	10	63	70	32
Frome Town	32	10	7	15	69	64	27
Yeovil Town Res.	32	11	5	16	57	86	27
Bristol Rovers Colts	32	10	4	18	49	65	24
Bristol City Colts	32	8	7	17	43	63	23
Wells City	32	8	7	17	53	92	23
Bridgwater Town	32	7	5	20	59	98	19
Chippenham United	32	7	5	20	54	90	19
Glastonbury	32	3	9	20	47	92	15

Second Division	P	W	D	L	F	A	PTS
Torquay United Res.	38	27	6	5	135	38	60
Taunton Town	38	26	3	9	115	46	55
Gloucester City Res	38	24	5	9	104	56	53
Weston-super-Mare	38	21	9	8	126	59	51
Stonehouse	38	21	7	10	92	55	49
Trowbridge Town Res	38	20	7	11	98	74	47
Minehead	38	20	6	12	104	69	46
Clevedon	38	19	8	11	99	71	46
Frome Town Res.	38	20	6	12	101	76	46
Ilfracombe Town	38	18	5	11	82	70	41
Poole Town Res.	38	14	8	16	86	71	36
Chippenham Town Res	38	13	7	18	80	97	33
Clandown	38	13	6	19	87	105	32
Cinderford Town	38	13	5	20	85	82	31
Welton Rovers	38	12	6	20	73	95	30
Street	38	11	4	23	70	112	26
Peasedown M.W.	38	8	9	21	57	127	25
Hoffman Athletic	38	7	6	25	46	109	20
Radstock Town	38	7	3	28	52	127	17
Paulton Rovers	38	6	4	28	56	127	16

1956-57

First Division	P	W	D	L	F	A	PTS
Poole Town	36	26	4	6	115	48	56
Trowbridge Town	36	21	5	10	83	55	47
Salisbury	36	20	5	11	98	60	45
Torquay United Res.	36	18	8	10	91	55	44
Portland United	36	18	8	10	84	64	44
Bridgwater Town	36	17	7	12	58	54	41
Dorchester Town	36	16	7	13	83	70	39
Chippenham Town	36	16	7	13	77	67	39
Yeovil Town Res.	36	18	2	16	79	73	38
Glastonbury	36	16	3	17	82	102	35
Bristol Rovers Colts	36	14	6	16	67	90	34
Weymouth Res.	36	16	1	19	87	94	33
Barnstaple Town	36	14	4	18	76	70	32
Bideford	36	12	8	16	70	71	32
Taunton Town	36	11	9	16	59	71	31
Chippenham United	36	12	6	18	80	97	30
Bristol City Colts	36	13	4	19	58	74	30
Frome Town	36	10	2	24	46	91	22
Wells City	36	4	4	28	46	127	12

Second Division	P	W	D	L	F	A	PTS
Cinderford Town	34	28	2	4	114	31	58
Trowbridge Town Res	34	25	4	5	112	35	54
Poole Town Res.	34	23	6	5	87	39	52
Minehead	34	20	5	9	83	52	45
Dorchester Town Res	34	18	6	10	113	69	42
Gloucester City Res	34	17	7	10	81	50	41
Welton Rovers	34	18	3	13	87	74	39
Stonehouse	34	14	10	10	98	70	38
Bath City Reserves	34	16	6	12	91	82	38
Weston-super-Mare	34	11	7	16	68	80	29
Peasedown M.W.	34	10	6	18	69	99	26
Hoffman Athletic	34	8	10	16	52	92	26
Street	34	9	7	18	48	68	25
Clevedon	34	10	4	20	64	85	24
Ilfracombe Town	34	7	8	19	43	82	22
Radstock Town	34	9	3	22	65	127	21
Paulton Rovers	34	7	3	24	50	111	17
Clandown	34	6	3	25	49	114	15

1957-58

First Division	P	W	D	L	F	A	PTS
Salisbury	36	18	11	7	55	30	47
Bridgwater Town	36	20	5	11	78	53	45
Dorchester Town	36	19	6	11	87	57	44
Barnstaple Town	36	17	7	12	83	48	41
Trowbridge Town	36	15	11	10	80	61	41
Bristol Rovers Colts	36	16	8	12	80	74	40
Torquay United Res.	36	15	9	12	70	56	39
Bristol City Colts	36	16	7	13	70	59	39
Minehead	36	16	5	15	68	76	37
Frome Town	36	16	5	15	66	77	37
Cinderford Town	36	17	2	17	72	70	36
Taunton	36	11	13	12	48	55	35
Bideford	36	14	5	17	62	55	33
Weymouth Res.	36	13	7	16	89	85	33
Chippenham Town	36	13	7	16	71	74	33
Glastonbury	36	12	7	17	50	79	31
Yeovil Town Res.	36	13	4	19	66	92	30
Portland United	36	12	3	21	58	80	27
Chippenham United	36	5	6	25	51	123	16

Second Division	P	W	D	L	F	A	PTS
Poole Town Res.	34	26	3	5	141	48	55
Gloucester City Res	34	24	5	5	109	40	53
Weston-super-Mare	34	22	9	3	102	46	53
Dorchester Town Res	34	19	6	9	73	41	44
Welton Rovers	34	18	6	10	87	64	42
Trowbridge Town Res	34	19	3	12	88	69	41
Wells City	34	16	6	12	82	68	38
Street	34	13	7	14	60	73	33
Bath City Reserves	34	12	8	14	76	64	32
Peasedown M.W.	34	13	6	15	75	98	32
Ilfracombe Town	34	13	3	18	84	99	29
Radstock Town	34	11	5	18	78	114	27
Clandown	34	10	7	17	52	78	27
Hoffman Athletic	34	9	5	20	55	85	23
Taunton Town Res.	34	9	4	21	51	89	22
Paulton Rovers	34	7	7	20	59	98	21
Clevedon	34	9	2	23	67	112	20
Stonehouse	34	8	4	22	62	115	20

1958-59

First Division	P	W	D	L	F	A	PTS
Yeovil Town Res.	36	26	3	7	115	54	55
Salisbury	36	24	3	9	91	53	51
Dorchester Town	36	23	2	11	110	61	48
Bridgwater Town	36	21	6	9	81	57	48
Barnstaple Town	36	20	5	11	85	68	45
Chippenham Town	36	20	3	13	104	66	43
Bideford	36	15	11	10	83	60	41
Torquay United Res.	36	18	3	15	70	70	39
Weymouth Res.	36	18	2	16	84	63	38
Cinderford Town	36	15	4	17	60	63	34
Bristol Rovers Colts	36	14	6	16	73	77	34
Glastonbury	36	15	3	18	63	81	33
Taunton	36	15	2	19	53	68	32
Bristol City Colts	36	12	7	17	75	88	31
Portland United	36	13	5	18	68	82	31
Poole Town Res.	36	10	7	19	63	91	27
Gloucester City Res	36	9	5	22	64	91	23
Minehead	36	6	7	23	50	111	19
Frome Town	36	4	4	28	52	127	12

Second Division	P	W	D	L	F	A	PTS
Bath City Reserves	32	20	7	5	95	39	47
Trowbridge Town Res	32	20	5	7	88	56	45
Street	32	18	5	9	73	56	41
Bridgwater Town Res	32	16	8	8	81	55	40
Welton Rovers	32	18	3	11	80	53	39
Dorchester Town Res	32	16	6	10	73	52	38
Weston-super-Mare	32	16	5	11	80	59	37
Paulton Rovers	32	16	5	11	87	71	37
Stonehouse	32	16	4	12	85	47	36
Chippenham United	32	14	7	11	65	54	35
Taunton Town Res.	32	11	6	15	58	81	28
Peasedown M.W.	32	9	9	14	64	89	27
Clandown	32	10	6	16	58	74	26
Radstock	32	10	5	17	61	76	25
Ilfracombe Town	32	7	5	20	48	108	19
Hoffman Athletic	32	4	4	24	49	107	12
Wells City	32	5	2	25	44	112	12

1959-60

First Division	P	W	D	L	F	A	PTS
Torquay United Res.	36	29	5	2	132	40	63
Salisbury	36	20	7	9	85	43	47
Chippenham Town	36	18	6	12	70	56	42
Bridgwater Town	36	18	5	13	79	62	41
Weymouth Res.	36	18	4	14	72	58	40
Portland United	36	17	6	13	61	68	40
Bideford	36	15	8	13	61	62	38
Bath City Reserves	36	15	7	14	63	61	37
Yeovil Town Res.	36	17	3	16	74	77	37
Poole Town Res.	36	15	6	15	73	66	36
Dorchester Town	36	17	2	17	87	88	36
Minehead	36	12	11	13	68	72	35
Bristol Rovers Colts	36	13	8	15	79	80	34
Glastonbury	36	11	10	15	66	78	32
Barnstaple Town	36	13	5	18	50	65	31
Taunton Town	36	11	7	18	67	96	29
Bristol City Colts	36	12	4	20	65	82	28
Gloucester City Res	36	9	4	23	49	92	22
Trowbridge Town Res	36	5	6	25	36	91	16

Second Division	P	W	D	L	F	A	PTS
Welton Rovers	26	20	2	4	95	40	42
Stonehouse	26	17	4	5	78	43	38
Weston-super-Mare	26	15	6	5	100	42	36
Frome Town	26	14	5	7	63	38	33
Chippenham United	26	14	2	10	64	52	30
Clandown	26	9	9	8	48	43	27
Paulton Rovers	26	11	5	10	58	64	27
Radstock Town	26	12	3	11	48	62	27
Street	26	10	5	11	48	53	25
Wells City	26	8	5	13	46	73	21
Bridgwater Town Res	26	8	4	14	58	64	20
Taunton Town Res.	26	5	7	14	43	59	17
Dorchester Town Res	26	5	5	16	43	82	15
Peasedown M.W.	26	1	4	21	38	114	6

354

1960-61

First Division	P	W	D	L	F	A	PTS
Salisbury	40	31	4	5	135	42	66
Dorchester Town	40	26	6	8	115	63	58
Minehead	40	24	8	8	100	62	56
Torquay United Res.	40	23	6	11	122	70	52
Bridgwater Town	40	18	12	10	88	71	48
Exeter City Res.	40	21	5	14	99	68	47
Weymouth Res.	40	19	9	12	91	79	47
Bristol City Colts	40	18	10	12	94	70	46
Welton Rovers	40	20	5	15	119	110	45
Portland United	40	16	10	14	93	87	42
Yeovil Town Res.	40	18	5	17	73	73	41
Chippenham Town	40	18	5	17	79	81	41
Bristol Rovers Colts	40	12	12	16	80	74	36
Bath City Reserves	40	11	11	18	75	79	33
Weston-super-Mare	40	13	7	20	76	98	33
Bideford	40	12	9	19	76	99	33
Glastonbury	40	13	4	23	66	114	30
Poole Town Res.	40	8	9	23	57	87	25
Trowbridge Town Res	40	9	7	24	62	122	25
Barnstaple Town	40	8	4	28	55	111	20
Taunton Town	40	5	6	29	59	127	16

1961-62

First Division	P	W	D	L	F	A	PTS
Bristol City Res.	38	28	7	3	132	36	63
Salisbury	38	27	2	9	105	41	56
Bideford	38	21	11	6	84	49	53
Torquay United Res.	38	20	5	13	95	78	45
Poole Town Res.	38	19	5	14	115	85	43
Dorchester Town	38	19	5	14	102	85	43
Bridgwater Town	38	17	8	13	89	69	42
Minehead	38	17	8	13	80	68	42
Chippenham Town	38	17	6	15	79	71	40
Portland United	38	16	8	14	92	85	40
Weston-super-Mare	38	14	11	13	63	68	39
Weymouth Res.	38	16	6	16	85	71	38
Bath City Reserves	38	13	9	16	74	80	35
Bridport	38	11	8	19	72	93	30
Yeovil Town Res.	38	13	3	22	74	99	29
Welton Rovers	38	11	7	20	61	104	29
Taunton Town	38	11	4	23	59	114	26
Bristol Rovers Colts	38	6	13	19	59	93	25
Barnstaple Town	38	8	7	23	52	120	23
Glastonbury	38	7	5	26	44	107	19

1962-63

First Division	P	W	D	L	F	A	PTS
Bristol City Res.	42	31	5	6	120	56	67
Bideford	42	29	7	6	115	51	65
Minehead	42	25	6	11	102	62	56
Andover	42	25	5	12	106	59	55
Bridgwater Town	42	23	8	11	77	48	54
Salisbury	42	21	9	12	89	56	51
Portland United	42	23	5	14	80	66	51
Weymouth Res.	42	20	5	17	104	78	45
Yeovil Town Res.	42	18	9	15	67	72	45
Barnstaple Town	42	19	6	17	81	75	44
Dorchester Town	42	17	9	16	92	79	43
Chippenham Town	42	15	12	15	92	60	42
Poole Town Res.	42	17	7	18	82	77	41
Exeter City Res.	42	15	10	17	55	74	40
Bath City Reserves	42	14	6	22	82	96	34
Weston-super-Mare	42	11	9	22	72	108	31
Welton Rovers	42	11	8	23	71	107	30
Glastonbury	42	13	4	25	56	114	30
Torquay United Res.	42	10	8	24	48	78	28
Bridport	42	9	8	25	66	111	26
Taunton Town	42	11	4	27	56	112	26
Bristol Rovers Colts	42	6	8	28	56	120	20

1963-64

First Division	P	W	D	L	F	A	PTS
Bideford	42	30	6	6	113	36	66
Bristol City Res.	42	24	15	3	122	43	63
Bridgwater Town	42	25	10	7	82	32	60
Welton Rovers	42	24	6	12	84	54	54
Dorchester Town	42	19	14	9	94	56	52
Salisbury	42	21	8	13	80	61	50
Barnstaple Town	42	20	9	13	92	69	49
Minehead	42	20	8	14	96	85	48
Weymouth Res.	42	16	12	14	94	74	44
Andover	42	17	10	15	89	78	44
Torquay United Res.	42	18	7	17	81	73	43
Yeovil Town Res.	42	17	9	16	73	99	43
Chippenham Town	42	15	8	19	75	62	38
Bath City Reserves	42	12	12	18	77	92	36
Frome Town	42	11	11	20	69	97	33
Weston-super-Mare	42	11	11	20	58	86	33
Glastonbury	42	11	9	22	70	91	31
Exeter City Res.	42	8	15	19	73	100	31
Poole Town Res.	42	11	6	25	56	98	28
Bridport	42	7	14	21	40	100	28
Portland United	42	10	5	27	63	127	25
Taunton Town	42	8	9	25	37	105	25

1964-65

First Division	P	W	D	L	F	A	PTS
Welton Rovers	42	35	3	4	148	36	73
Bideford	42	32	6	4	120	29	70
Minehead	42	27	7	8	88	42	61
Dorchester Town	42	26	4	12	89	53	56
Weston-super-Mare	42	22	9	11	89	58	53
Weymouth Res.	42	24	4	14	96	46	52
Bridgwater Town	42	20	9	13	74	59	49
Torquay United Res.	42	21	5	16	74	59	47
Bristol City Res.	42	21	4	17	96	82	46
Salisbury	42	17	9	16	80	67	43
Frome Town	42	17	8	17	66	71	42
Exeter City Res.	42	18	5	19	92	84	41
Chippenham Town	42	16	8	18	75	82	40
Glastonbury	42	15	6	21	69	109	36
Yeovil Town Res.	42	15	5	22	65	99	35
Andover	42	13	8	21	74	66	34
Bath City Reserves	42	12	6	24	54	98	30
Bridport	42	11	7	24	60	99	29
Taunton Town	42	10	8	24	54	104	28
Barnstaple Town	42	11	5	26	51	89	27
Portland United	42	6	8	28	40	122	20
Poole Town Res.	42	5	2	35	49	127	12

1965-66

First Division	P	W	D	L	F	A	PTS
Welton Rovers	34	25	9	0	105	28	59
Portland United	34	23	2	9	75	50	48
Bideford	34	19	8	7	90	49	46
Andover	34	16	8	10	74	57	40
Minehead	34	13	12	9	46	44	38
Frome Town	34	14	9	11	53	53	37
Glastonbury	34	12	11	11	61	46	35
Taunton Town	34	15	5	14	73	69	35
Bridgwater Town	34	12	10	12	63	62	34
Salisbury	34	12	8	14	62	57	32
Torquay United Res.	34	11	10	13	56	56	32
Exeter City Res.	34	13	4	17	63	70	30
Weymouth Res.	34	11	8	15	65	76	30
Weston-super-Mare	34	12	5	17	48	61	29
Bridport	34	12	5	17	57	90	29
Dorchester Town	34	9	5	20	41	79	23
Barnstaple Town	34	7	8	19	35	59	22
Bristol City Colts	34	4	5	25	33	94	13

1966-67

First Division	P	W	D	L	F	A	PTS
Welton Rovers	40	29	7	4	102	37	65
Minehead	40	25	10	5	98	42	60
Bridgwater Town	40	25	7	8	93	47	57
Salisbury	40	22	9	9	83	54	53
Dorchester Town	40	22	8	10	89	48	52
Bideford	40	23	6	11	76	47	52
Glastonbury	40	20	9	11	71	54	49
Exeter City Res.	40	17	7	16	54	63	41
Torquay United Res.	40	15	9	16	66	56	39
Andover	40	13	13	14	69	60	39
Portland United	40	15	7	18	61	76	37
Frome Town	40	17	1	22	60	82	35
Bristol City Colts	40	13	8	19	63	64	34
Weston-super-Mare	40	12	9	19	52	69	33
Taunton Town	40	11	10	19	67	77	32
Plymouth Argyle Colts	40	12	8	20	66	97	32
Bridport	40	11	8	21	50	80	30
Weymouth Res.	40	12	4	24	39	75	28
St Lukes College	40	10	7	23	61	90	27
Barnstaple Town	40	8	8	24	50	92	24
Yeovil Town Res.	40	8	5	27	52	111	21

1967-68

First Division	P	W	D	L	F	A	PTS
Bridgwater Town	40	27	8	5	92	41	62
Salisbury	40	28	3	9	105	35	59
Glastonbury	40	24	7	9	103	64	55
Bath City Reserves	40	21	9	10	81	63	51
Frome Town	40	22	6	12	98	72	50
Minehead	40	18	13	9	72	49	49
Dorchester Town	40	17	14	9	81	50	48
Welton Rovers	40	20	6	14	74	55	46
Plymouth Argyle Colts	40	18	7	15	76	72	43
Bridport	40	18	5	17	68	58	41
Torquay United Res.	40	17	7	16	58	55	41
Andover	40	17	5	18	61	66	39
Taunton Town	40	11	15	14	76	68	37
Bideford	40	13	9	18	52	63	35
St Lukes College	40	12	9	19	60	78	33
Portland United	40	10	12	18	39	80	32
Bristol City Colts	40	9	10	21	33	59	28
Weston-super-Mare	40	9	10	21	40	79	28
Barnstaple Town	40	8	6	26	48	91	22
Devizes Town	40	7	7	26	56	113	21
Yeovil Town Res.	40	5	10	25	36	98	20

1968-69

First Division	P	W	D	L	F	A	PTS
Taunton Town	36	24	5	7	96	53	53
Bideford	36	21	7	8	77	44	49
Bridgwater Town	36	18	12	6	72	30	48
Glastonbury	36	22	4	10	85	49	48
Frome Town	36	18	11	7	57	38	47
Andover	36	16	9	11	63	43	41
Minehead	36	16	9	11	57	43	41
Welton Rovers	36	14	9	13	51	51	37
Dorchester Town	36	15	6	15	63	53	36
Bath City Reserves	36	15	6	15	58	49	36
Barnstaple Town	36	14	7	15	58	67	35
Devizes Town	36	14	7	15	56	77	35
Torquay United Res.	36	15	3	18	51	60	33
Bristol City Colts	36	13	6	17	64	68	32
Bridport	36	8	11	17	34	54	27
Weston-super-Mare	36	7	11	18	29	54	25
St Lukes College	36	9	5	22	44	74	23
Portland United	36	7	8	21	36	80	22
Yeovil Town Res.	36	4	8	24	41	105	16

1969-70

First Division	P	W	D	L	F	A	PTS
Glastonbury	38	29	5	4	100	37	63
Andover	38	26	6	6	76	20	58
Bridgwater Town	38	23	7	8	97	41	53
Minehead	38	21	10	7	70	37	52
Taunton Town	38	21	8	9	84	56	50
Bideford	38	20	7	11	84	58	47
Dorchester Town	38	18	8	12	78	69	44
Torquay United Res.	38	15	10	13	70	54	40
Bath City Reserves	38	16	7	15	71	67	39
Welton Rovers	38	17	3	18	72	62	37
Weston-super-Mare	38	14	8	16	53	72	36
Frome Town	38	12	10	16	62	73	34
Portland United	38	14	6	18	63	94	34
Bristol City Colts	38	13	7	18	58	76	33
Devizes Town	38	10	9	19	44	70	29
Barnstaple Town	38	11	6	21	58	73	28
Yeovil Town Res.	38	9	6	23	38	78	24
Weymouth Res.	38	10	4	24	34	74	24
Bridport	38	6	9	23	43	86	21
St Lukes College	38	4	6	28	35	93	14

1970-71

First Division	P	W	D	L	F	A	PTS
Bideford	34	26	4	4	96	39	56
Andover	34	21	8	5	65	24	50
Bridgwater Town	34	20	9	5	63	38	49
Glastonbury	34	18	8	8	78	52	44
Minehead	34	18	5	11	66	40	41
Taunton Town	34	17	7	10	66	42	41
Plymouth City	34	17	6	11	67	41	40
Welton Rovers	34	17	6	11	60	56	40
Dorchester Town	34	16	6	12	58	50	38
Devizes Town	34	12	11	11	53	50	35
Barnstaple Town	34	13	7	14	60	61	33
Bridport	34	11	8	15	43	49	30
Weston-super-Mare	34	9	6	19	36	73	24
Torquay United Res.	34	8	6	20	43	54	22
Bristol City Colts	34	7	8	19	40	78	22
Frome Town	34	8	3	23	50	91	19
Bath City Reserves	34	7	5	22	33	77	19
St Lukes College	34	2	5	27	21	83	9

1971-72

First Division	P	W	D	L	F	A	PTS
Bideford	26	19	4	3	63	21	42
Minehead	26	18	5	3	59	22	41
Glastonbury	26	16	5	5	58	26	37
Devizes Town	26	11	9	6	44	33	31
Welton Rovers	26	10	7	9	38	37	27
Frome Town	26	9	7	10	33	45	25
Dorchester Town	26	9	6	11	39	38	24
Weston-super-Mare	26	9	5	12	39	45	23
Bridport	26	9	5	12	32	47	23
Bridgwater Town	26	7	9	10	28	42	23
Taunton Town	26	7	7	12	50	54	21
Torquay United Res.	26	5	9	12	29	55	19
Barnstaple Town	26	6	6	14	40	46	18
St Lukes College	26	3	4	19	25	66	10

1972-73

First Division	P	W	D	L	F	A	PTS
Devizes Town	30	21	5	4	68	27	47
Taunton Town	30	19	7	4	69	26	45
Mangotsfield United	30	21	3	6	69	35	45
Bridgwater Town	30	17	7	6	65	24	41
Weston-super-Mare	30	13	9	8	42	36	35
Glastonbury	30	14	6	10	45	44	34
Barnstaple Town	30	13	7	10	57	52	33
Bridport	30	10	10	10	40	30	30
Torquay United Res.	30	11	6	13	53	47	28
Frome Town	30	9	9	12	30	44	27
Welton Rovers	30	9	8	13	35	41	26
Exeter City Res.	30	7	11	12	39	47	25
St Lukes College	30	9	3	18	33	73	21
Avon (Bradford)	30	6	3	21	27	68	15
Bristol City Colts	30	5	4	21	35	76	14
Ashtonians United	30	4	6	20	26	63	14

1973-74

First Division	P	W	D	L	F	A	PTS
Welton Rovers	36	27	5	4	80	32	59
Taunton Town	36	25	8	3	86	19	58
Bridgwater Town	36	23	6	7	71	34	52
Exeter City Res.	36	21	7	8	61	33	49
Devizes Town	36	18	9	9	73	44	45
Glastonbury	36	18	7	11	69	46	43
Frome Town	36	16	9	11	64	43	41
Barnstaple Town	36	17	7	12	76	60	41
Mangotsfield United	36	17	7	12	57	52	41
Dawlish	36	17	6	13	53	67	40
St Lukes College	36	14	5	17	48	48	33
Weston-super-Mare	36	13	7	16	44	50	33
Keynsham Town	36	11	5	20	39	65	27
Tiverton Town	36	7	11	18	42	67	25
Bridport	36	10	5	21	41	67	25
Exmouth Town	36	6	11	19	31	70	23
Ashtonians United	36	8	5	23	43	75	21
Avon (Bradford)	36	5	6	25	36	85	16
Chippenham Town	36	3	6	27	25	82	12

1974-75

Premier Division	P	W	D	L	F	A	PTS
Falmouth Town	40	31	9	0	122	26	102
Taunton Town	40	30	9	1	136	24	99
Bridgwater Town	40	27	8	5	92	38	89
Mangotsfield United	40	24	6	10	88	44	78
Barnstaple Town	40	17	11	12	79	66	62
Frome Town	40	17	10	13	65	59	61
Glastonbury	40	17	10	13	62	57	61
Westland Yeovil	40	17	7	16	66	60	58
Welton Rovers	40	15	11	14	63	59	56
Dawlish	40	16	7	17	69	72	55
Keynsham Town	40	15	10	15	63	67	55
Paulton Rovers	40	13	11	16	63	59	50
Devizes Town	40	11	11	18	39	59	44
Weston-super-Mare	40	11	10	19	39	52	43
Chippenham Town	40	10	12	18	55	85	42
St Lukes College	40	11	7	22	44	83	40
Tiverton Town	40	9	12	19	45	79	39
Bridport	40	9	7	24	71	110	34
Melksham Town	40	7	12	21	39	82	33
Clevedon	40	8	8	24	52	94	32
Exmouth Town	40	8	6	26	39	96	30

1975-76

Premier Division	P	W	D	L	F	A	PTS
Falmouth Town	44	35	5	4	134	43	110
Taunton Town	44	27	8	9	86	43	89
Clevedon	44	27	6	11	77	51	87
Bridgwater Town	44	25	10	9	81	44	85
Glastonbury	44	23	10	11	84	49	79
Barnstaple Town	44	21	9	14	95	66	72
Tiverton Town	44	20	12	12	73	70	72
Paulton Rovers	44	19	12	13	60	58	69
Mangotsfield United	44	18	10	16	63	63	64
Bideford	44	17	12	15	60	56	63
Frome Town	44	17	10	17	76	61	61
Exeter City Res.	44	16	10	18	64	69	57
St Lukes College	44	16	7	21	60	70	55
Weston-super-Mare	44	13	15	16	52	57	54
Westland Yeovil	44	14	11	19	66	82	53
Welton Rovers	44	14	9	21	57	71	51
Bridport	44	13	11	20	49	72	50
Dawlish	44	13	10	21	51	69	49
Devizes Town	44	10	15	19	45	59	45
Chippenham Town	44	12	7	25	66	94	43
Melksham Town	44	12	7	25	66	106	43
Keynsham Town	44	8	6	30	50	86	30
Exmouth Town	44	5	10	29	38	114	25

362

1976-77

Premier Division	P	W	D	L	F	A	PTS
Falmouth Town	34	26	2	6	69	24	80
Weston-super-Mare	34	18	12	4	57	31	66
Clevedon	34	18	10	6	58	31	64
Bridgwater Town	34	17	10	7	51	36	61
Barnstaple Town	34	16	9	9	64	48	57
Bideford	34	15	11	8	70	38	56
Bridport	34	16	8	10	53	35	56
Paulton Rovers	34	13	10	11	52	46	49
Taunton Town	34	14	6	14	49	46	48
Dawlish	34	11	10	13	36	41	43
Glastonbury	34	11	8	15	56	58	41
Frome Town	34	10	11	13	45	52	41
Tiverton Town	34	11	7	16	35	61	40
Welton Rovers	34	9	9	16	35	46	36
Mangotsfield United	34	10	4	20	36	66	34
St Lukes College	34	7	6	21	32	61	27
Exeter City Res.	34	7	3	24	36	76	23
Westland Yeovil	34	4	10	20	31	69	22

First Division	P	W	D	L	F	A	PTS
Saltash United	34	24	6	4	81	29	78
Shepton Mallet Town	34	23	7	4	84	39	76
Keynsham Town	34	23	2	9	87	38	71
Melksham Town	34	20	7	7	69	30	67
Chippenham Town	34	17	6	11	53	43	57
Devizes Town	34	15	8	11	58	44	52
Torquay United Res.	34	15	3	16	61	59	48
Portway Bristol	34	13	9	12	57	58	48
Larkhall Athletic	34	13	7	14	59	69	46
Clandown	34	10	12	12	54	58	42
Yeovil Town Res.	34	11	7	16	52	55	40
Brixham United	34	9	8	17	45	77	35
Ottery St Mary	34	8	10	16	41	61	34
Exmouth Town	34	9	7	18	40	68	34
Chard Town	34	8	9	17	43	63	33
Swanage T & Herston	34	8	9	17	48	72	33
Ilminster Town	34	8	9	17	39	69	33
Heavitree United	34	4	10	20	23	56	22

1977-78

Premier Division	P	W	D	L	F	A	PTS
Falmouth Town	34	26	5	3	98	30	83
Bideford	34	25	8	1	86	25	83
Barnstaple Town	34	18	10	6	75	37	64
Saltash United	34	17	7	10	66	53	58
Bridport	34	14	13	7	44	21	55
Clevedon Town	34	16	9	9	62	41	55
Frome Town	34	14	8	12	43	39	50
Paulton Rovers	34	15	5	14	55	52	50
Weston-super-Mare	34	14	8	12	44	48	50
Exeter City	34	11	13	10	48	41	46
Bridgwater Town	34	12	9	13	52	56	45
Tiverton Town	34	8	10	16	47	61	34
Shepton Mallet Town	34	9	6	19	52	93	33
Glastonbury	34	9	5	20	46	77	32
Mangotsfield United	34	7	10	17	50	75	31
Welton Rovers	34	8	6	20	34	68	30
Dawlish	34	6	10	18	39	67	28
St Lukes College	34	1	10	23	20	78	13

First Division	P	W	D	L	F	A	PTS
Keynsham Town	36	23	10	3	77	22	79
Clandown	36	22	4	10	77	36	70
Ilminster Town	36	21	6	9	69	47	69
Bristol Manor Farm	36	20	5	11	67	38	65
Devizes Town	36	20	5	11	73	52	65
Torquay United Res.	36	18	5	13	69	53	59
Portway Bristol	36	17	8	11	57	42	59
Melksham Town	36	17	7	12	76	60	58
Ottery St Mary	36	16	7	13	55	55	55
Larkhall Athletic	36	15	8	13	58	66	53
Exmouth Town	36	13	7	16	41	55	46
Brixham United	36	11	9	16	61	79	41
Chard Town	36	12	5	19	56	81	41
Westland Yeovil	36	8	12	16	40	52	36
Odd Down	36	9	9	18	52	75	36
Yeovil Town Res.	36	9	8	19	52	65	35
Heavitree United	36	9	5	22	32	64	32
Swanage T & Herston	36	6	11	19	48	85	29
Chippenham Town	36	8	4	24	40	74	28

1978-79

Premier Division	P	W	D	L	F	A	PTS
Frome Town	38	21	12	5	60	29	75
Bideford	38	22	8	8	76	39	74
Saltash United	38	19	10	9	65	39	67
Barnstaple Town	38	18	10	10	65	35	64
Tiverton Town	38	17	9	12	71	60	60
Clandown	38	16	11	11	58	49	59
Weston-super-Mare	38	14	15	9	65	48	57
Falmouth Town	38	15	9	14	51	47	54
Paulton Rovers	38	15	9	14	40	48	54
Bridport	38	13	13	12	54	50	52
Bridgwater Town	38	14	9	15	57	53	51
Keynsham Town	38	13	12	13	47	57	51
Mangotsfield Pf	38	15	2	21	53	64	47
Ilminster Town	38	11	12	15	45	55	45
Welton Rovers	38	11	8	19	44	59	41
Exeter City Res.	38	12	5	21	48	75	41
Clevedon Town	38	11	7	20	50	64	40
Dawlish	38	10	10	18	43	61	40
Shepton Mallet	38	10	10	18	48	74	40
Glastonbury	38	8	9	21	42	76	33

First Division	P	W	D	L	F	A	PTS
AFC Bournemouth Res	36	25	6	5	101	41	81
Portway Bristol	36	23	5	8	81	43	74
Bristol Manor Farm	36	20	5	11	59	47	65
Chippenham Town	36	19	7	10	56	43	64
Torquay United Res.	36	20	4	12	82	47	62
Melksham Town	36	18	4	14	58	57	58
Devizes Town	36	16	9	11	71	54	57
Wellington	36	18	3	15	48	46	57
Chard Town	36	15	6	15	57	58	51
Brixham United	36	15	5	16	55	61	50
Elmore	36	15	3	18	48	65	48
Ottery St Mary	36	13	5	18	51	60	43
Larkhall Athletic	36	12	6	18	52	56	42
Westland Yeovil	36	11	9	16	43	53	42
Heavitree United	36	12	5	19	39	61	41
Swanage Town & Herston	36	11	6	19	51	60	39
Odd Down	36	10	5	21	38	71	35
Exmouth Town	36	8	9	19	41	72	33
Yeovil Town Res.	36	5	10	21	30	65	24

1979-80

Premier Division	P	W	D	L	F	A	PTS
Barnstaple Town	38	23	10	5	67	31	56
AFC Bournemouth Res	38	24	7	7	100	26	55
Weston-super-Mare	38	22	11	5	81	45	55
Frome Town	38	19	10	9	57	38	48
Bridgwater Town	38	17	12	9	64	43	46
Exeter City Res.	38	16	11	11	71	59	43
Clevedon Town	38	16	10	12	74	58	42
Portway Bristol	38	16	10	12	66	53	42
Saltash United	38	14	14	10	64	51	42
Bideford	38	16	10	12	61	51	42
Keynsham Town	38	16	10	12	56	53	42
Falmouth Town	38	14	10	14	58	53	38
Dawlish	38	10	11	17	39	67	31
Clandown	38	12	6	20	53	76	30
Tiverton Town	38	8	14	16	36	65	30
Welton Rovers	38	10	9	19	59	84	29
Paulton Rovers	38	11	6	21	50	68	28
Mangotsfield United	38	7	10	21	37	80	24
Bridport	38	4	14	20	31	67	21
Ilminster Town	38	2	11	25	31	87	15

First Division	P	W	D	L	F	A	PTS
Melksham Town	42	27	8	7	78	27	62
Devizes Town	42	25	9	8	91	42	59
Liskeard Athletic	42	23	10	9	70	31	56
Bath City Reserves	42	22	8	12	89	62	52
Exmouth Town	42	22	8	12	67	43	52
Torquay United Res.	42	21	10	11	84	61	52
Elmore	42	20	9	13	63	45	49
Bristol Manor Farm	42	20	9	13	70	58	49
Ottery St Mary	42	16	12	14	64	52	44
Glastonbury	42	16	11	15	60	68	43
Chippenham Town	42	16	10	16	58	62	42
Radstock Town	42	15	10	17	63	75	40
Shepton Mallet Town	42	15	9	18	75	78	39
Chard Town	42	14	11	17	51	59	39
Yeovil Town	42	14	10	18	71	85	38
Brixham Town	42	14	9	19	60	70	37
Heavitree United	42	11	14	17	57	69	36
Larkhall Athletic	42	11	10	21	48	85	32
Odd Down	42	9	12	21	46	76	30
Wellington	42	8	13	21	38	59	29
Swanage Town & Herston	42	6	13	23	45	91	24
Westland Yeovil	42	5	9	28	31	81	19

1980-81

Premier Division	P	W	D	L	F	A	PTS
Bridgwater Town	38	25	6	7	54	25	56
Barnstaple Town	38	22	6	10	58	40	50
Frome Town	38	21	6	11	74	51	48
Falmouth Town	38	18	9	11	71	53	45
Bideford	38	18	8	12	58	42	44
Saltash United	38	17	9	12	73	47	43
Portway Bristol	38	16	11	11	55	45	43
Clevedon Town	38	15	11	12	65	52	41
Clandown	38	16	9	13	60	53	41
Devizes Town	38	14	13	11	61	56	41
Bridport	38	12	15	11	56	52	39
Keynsham Town	38	12	15	11	33	34	39
Melksham Town	38	13	11	14	45	49	37
Liskeard Athletic	38	11	11	16	58	70	33
Mangotsfield United	38	8	15	15	43	66	31
Dawlish Town	38	7	16	15	40	50	30
Welton Rovers	38	9	11	18	50	69	29
Weston-super-Mare	38	11	7	20	42	61	29
Paulton Rovers	38	9	11	18	45	72	29
Tiverton Town	38	1	10	27	23	77	12

First Division	P	W	D	L	F	A	PTS
Chippenham Town	36	25	8	3	76	24	58
Wellington	36	22	8	6	80	36	52
Exmouth Town	36	22	7	7	74	37	51
Bath City Reserves	36	19	11	6	79	44	49
Odd Down	36	20	8	8	59	41	47
Yeovil Town Res.	36	18	9	9	58	38	45
Torquay United Res.	36	16	11	9	60	35	43
Swanage Town & Herston	36	13	11	12	58	55	37
Chard Town	36	11	14	11	42	38	36
Bristol Manor Farm	36	14	8	14	53	57	36
Shepton Mallet Town	36	13	8	15	68	75	34
Elmore	36	12	10	14	44	53	34
Glastonbury	36	9	10	17	44	60	28
Brixham United	36	11	5	20	50	70	27
Larkhall Athletic	36	5	12	19	44	76	22
Ottery St Mary	36	7	8	21	37	77	22
Heavitree United	36	7	8	21	40	86	22
Ilminster Town	36	7	6	23	39	70	20
Radstock Town	36	8	4	24	47	80	20

1981-82

Premier Division	P	W	D	L	F	A	PTS
Bideford	38	26	10	2	88	20	62
Barnstaple Town	38	26	8	4	78	31	59
Bridgwater Town	38	16	16	6	70	46	48
Clandown	38	17	12	9	49	37	46
Melksham Town	38	17	11	10	58	50	45
Frome Town	38	16	9	13	67	58	41
Weston-super-Mare	38	15	11	12	47	42	41
Saltash United	38	15	7	16	47	53	37
Devizes Town	38	14	7	17	53	60	35
Dawlish	38	11	13	14	45	53	35
Liskeard Athletic	38	11	12	15	39	48	34
Bridport	38	12	10	16	43	54	34
Clevedon Town	38	11	12	15	58	60	33
Chippenham Town	38	12	9	17	33	39	33
Falmouth Town	38	12	9	17	46	55	33
Portway Bristol	38	9	13	16	40	47	31
Wellington	38	10	11	17	50	62	31
Keynsham Town	38	9	13	16	39	55	31
Mangotsfield United	38	11	6	21	30	59	28
Welton Rovers	38	7	7	24	37	88	21
Bideford	38	26	10	2	88	20	62

First Division	P	W	D	L	F	A	PTS
Shepton Mallet	36	25	8	3	88	30	58
Exmouth Town	36	24	8	4	74	31	56
Swanage Town & Herston	36	21	5	10	90	47	47
Wimborne Town	36	19	9	8	67	35	47
Bath City Reserves	36	19	6	11	72	46	44
Elmore	36	19	6	11	58	45	44
Paulton Rovers	36	17	6	13	54	48	40
Bristol Manor Farm	36	15	9	12	58	50	39
Torquay United Res.	36	15	9	12	50	44	39
Tiverton Town	36	13	8	15	62	63	34
Chard Town	36	12	10	14	43	55	34
Odd Down	36	14	5	17	51	57	33
Radstock Town	36	10	11	15	44	67	31
Glastonbury	36	12	6	18	63	69	30
Heavitree United	36	11	7	18	39	69	29
Yeovil Town Res.	36	10	8	18	40	53	28
Larkhall Athletic	36	10	5	21	42	84	25
Ottery St Mary	36	6	3	27	28	79	15
Ilminster Town	36	3	5	28	20	70	11

1982-83

Premier Division	P	W	D	L	F	A	PTS
Bideford	38	26	9	3	67	32	61
Frome Town	38	23	10	5	75	34	56
Dawlish	38	20	8	10	68	47	48
Clandown	38	19	9	10	54	39	47
Saltash United	38	14	18	6	50	39	46
Falmouth Town	38	16	13	9	63	57	45
Plymouth Argyle Res.	38	15	14	9	67	41	44
Barnstaple Town	38	18	6	14	67	57	42
Liskeard Athletic	38	16	9	13	69	47	41
Weston-super-Mare	38	15	11	12	57	46	41
Shepton Mallet	38	15	4	19	50	55	34
Devizes Town	38	12	9	17	50	58	33
Chippenham Town	38	12	8	18	40	54	32
Clevedon Town	38	9	12	17	36	56	30
Bridport	38	8	13	17	49	60	29
Exmouth Town	38	10	9	19	40	59	29
Melksham Town	38	8	13	17	43	63	29
Wellington	38	8	12	18	46	74	28
Keynsham Town	38	7	11	20	32	68	25
Portway Bristol	38	8	4	26	35	72	20

First Division	P	W	D	L	F	A	PTS
Bristol Manor Farm	36	26	7	3	85	31	59
Mangotsfield United	36	24	8	4	75	32	56
Paulton Rovers	36	20	12	4	75	37	52
Odd Down	36	19	9	8	56	41	47
Glastonbury	36	15	15	6	69	47	45
Swanage Town & Herston	36	21	1	14	83	54	43
Wimborne Town	36	17	9	10	74	51	43
Bath City Reserves	36	14	9	13	64	49	37
Chard Town	36	15	5	16	54	50	35
Weymouth Res.	36	12	8	16	43	56	32
Welton Rovers	36	12	8	16	46	61	32
Yeovil Town Res.	36	14	3	19	49	55	31
Bristol City Res.	36	9	11	16	57	77	29
Elmore	36	12	4	20	48	65	28
Heavitree United	36	11	5	20	40	66	27
Larkhall Athletic	36	9	8	19	40	64	26
Radstock Town	36	9	6	21	50	79	24
Tiverton Town	36	8	5	23	42	85	21
Ottery St Mary	36	8	1	27	35	85	17

1983-84

Premier Division	P	W	D	L	F	A	PTS
Exmouth Town	38	21	11	6	59	35	53
Saltash United	38	22	7	9	72	39	51
Barnstaple Town	38	21	9	8	68	40	51
Frome Town	38	20	10	8	78	35	50
Liskeard Athletic	38	18	9	11	64	38	45
Bideford	38	16	10	12	71	49	42
Clevedon Town	38	16	8	14	55	56	40
Bristol Manor Farm	38	14	11	13	54	42	39
Plymouth Argyle Res.	38	16	8	14	68	58	38
Minehead	38	15	7	16	55	68	37
Shepton Mallet	38	14	9	15	55	74	37
Taunton Town	38	10	15	13	46	52	35
Mangotsfield United	38	12	10	16	47	48	34
Dawlish Town	38	13	8	17	38	43	34
Weston-super-Mare	38	13	8	17	46	56	34
Chippenham Town	38	13	8	17	44	56	34
Clandown	38	12	10	16	34	51	34
Melksham Town	38	9	11	18	49	66	29
Devizes Town	38	7	11	20	41	74	25
Wellington	38	4	8	26	29	95	16

First Division	P	W	D	L	F	A	PTS
Bristol City Res.	40	26	8	6	96	36	60
Chard Town	40	22	8	10	82	44	52
Paulton Rovers	40	20	12	8	74	46	52
Swanage Town & Herston	40	19	12	9	89	61	50
Keynsham Town	40	19	11	10	50	36	49
Backwell United	40	18	13	9	47	42	49
Glastonbury	40	15	9	16	68	61	39
Welton Rovers	40	13	13	14	49	56	39
Portway Bristol	40	13	12	15	57	49	38
Wimborne Town	40	14	10	16	51	60	38
Bath City Reserves	40	13	11	16	61	57	37
Warminster Town	40	15	7	18	61	67	37
Odd Down	40	12	13	15	60	66	37
Larkhall Athletic	40	12	12	16	50	55	36
Radstock Town	40	13	10	17	51	63	36
Heavitree United	40	14	8	18	66	80	36
Yeovil Town Res.	40	11	13	16	65	72	35
Ottery St Mary	40	14	7	19	42	58	35
Elmore	40	11	12	17	47	78	34
Weymouth Res.	40	12	7	21	43	64	31
Tiverton Town	40	5	10	25	37	95	20

370

1984-85

Premier Division	P	W	D	L	F	A	PTS
Saltash United	42	26	12	4	88	43	64
Bideford Town	42	26	8	8	78	29	60
Bristol City Res.	42	21	14	7	69	49	56
Exmouth Town	42	22	8	12	83	51	52
Paulton Rovers	42	20	11	11	61	45	51
Bristol Manor Farm	42	21	7	14	70	55	49
Chippenham Town	42	16	14	12	62	49	46
Mangotsfield United	42	17	11	14	63	56	45
Melksham Town	42	17	11	14	57	59	45
Liskeard Athletic	42	17	10	15	69	54	44
Chard Town	42	15	13	14	58	57	43
Minehead	42	16	9	17	55	54	41
Barnstaple Town	42	18	5	19	65	65	41
Clandown	42	14	12	16	50	52	40
Plymouth Argyle Res.	42	12	14	16	58	62	38
Dawlish Town	42	12	13	17	44	54	37
Clevedon Town	42	12	12	18	45	56	35
Frome Town	42	10	14	18	56	63	34
Weston-super-Mare	42	11	11	20	58	78	33
Taunton Town	42	11	11	20	53	74	33
Shepton Mallet	42	4	15	23	35	86	22
Devizes Town	42	2	9	31	34	121	13

First Division	P	W	D	L	F	A	PTS
Portway Bristol	42	30	3	9	97	42	63
Torrington	42	27	8	7	83	35	62
Wimborne Town	42	26	7	9	81	37	59
Swanage Town & Herston	42	23	13	6	86	50	59
Wellington	42	20	12	10	78	57	52
Radstock Town	42	23	5	14	79	47	51
Backwell United	42	21	9	12	59	42	51
Keynsham Town	42	20	9	13	70	54	49
Ottery St Mary	42	17	14	11	58	51	48
Larkhall Athletic	42	18	7	17	51	46	43
Heavitree United	42	14	11	17	81	84	39
Glastonbury	42	14	11	17	55	63	39
Bath City Reserves	42	16	7	19	60	69	39
Elmore	42	16	6	20	69	95	38
Yeovil Town Res.	42	14	10	18	63	63	37
Welton Rovers	42	14	9	19	61	72	37
Tiverton Town	42	11	12	19	61	66	34
Weymouth Res.	42	14	3	25	67	96	31
Warminster Town	42	8	13	21	54	93	29
Westbury United	42	10	7	25	57	99	27
Ilfracombe Town	42	6	7	29	47	101	19
Odd Down	42	5	7	30	38	83	17

1985-86

Premier Division	P	W	D	L	F	A	PTS
Exmouth Town	42	30	9	3	95	31	69
Liskeard Athletic	42	31	6	5	103	34	68
Bideford Town	42	27	8	7	97	27	62
Saltash United	42	21	13	8	81	44	55
Chippenham Town	42	21	10	11	60	44	52
Mangotsfield United	42	18	13	11	86	58	49
Taunton Town	42	19	9	14	59	54	47
Dawlish Town	42	19	8	15	53	49	45
Bristol City Res.	42	18	6	18	74	61	42
Clevedon Town	42	12	18	12	55	47	42
Bristol Manor Farm	42	16	9	17	71	72	41
Minehead	42	16	9	17	55	70	41
Frome Town	42	14	12	16	49	62	41
Clandown	42	15	8	19	46	57	38
Torrington	42	13	11	18	51	62	37
Melksham Town	42	11	13	18	50	77	35
Barnstaple Town	42	13	7	22	46	68	35
Weston-super-Mare	42	12	8	22	69	93	32
Paulton Rovers	42	9	12	21	50	82	30
Plymouth Argyle Res.	42	9	11	22	60	67	29
Chard Town	42	8	4	30	33	112	20
Shepton Mallet	42	4	8	30	36	110	13

First Division	P	W	D	L	F	A	PTS
Portway Bristol	42	27	9	6	100	42	63
Radstock Town	42	26	9	7	116	54	61
Yeovil Town Res.	42	25	7	10	79	36	56
Wimborne Town	42	18	13	11	77	51	49
Larkhall Athletic	42	18	11	13	72	56	47
Backwell United	42	19	9	14	63	47	47
Ottery St Mary	42	18	11	13	61	46	47
Swanage Town & Herston	42	18	9	15	91	79	45
Weymouth Res.	42	18	8	16	84	78	44
Heavitree United	42	17	10	15	60	69	44
Bath City Reserves	42	16	10	16	74	86	42
Wellington	42	14	12	16	70	70	40
Tiverton Town	42	16	7	19	68	74	39
Devizes Town	42	10	18	14	43	58	38
Elmore	42	12	13	17	56	78	37
Keynsham Town	42	9	18	15	37	53	36
Welton Rovers	42	13	9	20	61	84	35
Glastonbury	42	12	11	19	52	79	35
Ilfracombe Town	42	10	14	18	55	69	34
Westbury United	42	10	10	22	55	82	30
Odd Down	42	9	12	21	57	90	30
Warminster	42	9	6	27	40	93	24

1986-87

Premier Division	P	W	D	L	F	A	PTS
Saltash United	42	31	8	3	101	40	70
Exmouth Town	42	22	10	10	82	62	54
Bristol City Res.	42	23	5	14	94	57	51
Liskeard Athletic	42	20	9	13	68	46	49
Bristol Manor Farm	42	19	10	13	58	46	48
Bideford	42	21	4	17	59	57	46
Plymouth Argyle Res.	42	21	4	17	92	56	45
Taunton Town	42	17	9	16	61	64	43
Chippenham Town	42	14	14	14	52	50	42
Mangotsfield United	42	17	8	17	71	71	42
Barnstaple Town	42	15	12	15	56	66	42
Clevedon Town	42	14	13	15	58	60	41
Weston-super-Mare	42	13	13	16	66	69	39
Dawlish Town	42	14	10	18	63	62	38
Torrington	42	14	10	18	61	69	38
Paulton Rovers	42	14	8	20	56	72	36
Radstock Town	42	11	13	18	55	73	35
Melksham Town	42	10	15	17	39	62	35
Frome Town	42	12	10	20	50	65	34
Clandown	42	12	10	20	40	59	34
Minehead	42	10	12	20	54	87	32
Chard Town	42	11	7	24	49	89	29

First Division	P	W	D	L	F	A	PTS
Swanage Town & Herston	42	25	12	5	93	52	62
Portway Bristol	42	25	8	9	103	51	58
Bath City Reserves	42	25	6	11	85	58	56
Yeovil Town Res.	42	21	10	11	85	53	52
Wimborne Town	42	23	6	13	96	58	51
Devizes Town	42	21	10	11	62	43	51
Larkhall Athletic	42	21	8	13	71	53	50
Welton Rovers	42	20	6	16	66	53	46
Backwell United	42	15	15	12	55	53	45
Warminster Town	42	18	10	14	72	71	44
Ottery St Mary	42	17	6	19	66	68	40
Odd Down	42	13	13	16	57	65	39
Keynsham Town	42	16	7	19	57	69	39
Elmore	42	14	10	18	60	69	38
Tiverton Town	42	12	12	18	66	79	36
Weymouth Res.	42	12	12	18	75	87	35
Wellington	42	14	7	21	55	67	35
Westbury United	42	12	10	20	78	87	34
Calne Town	42	11	12	19	54	73	34
Ilfracombe Town	42	11	8	23	40	68	30
Heavitree United	42	9	9	24	48	96	26
Glastonbury	42	5	7	30	38	109	17

1987-88

Premier Division	P	W	D	L	F	A	PTS
Liskeard Athletic	42	29	10	3	98	33	68
Saltash United	42	27	6	9	116	41	60
Mangotsfield United	42	25	10	7	99	38	60
Plymouth Argyle Res.	42	26	8	8	105	46	60
Weston-super-Mare	42	21	8	13	81	62	50
Exmouth Town	42	19	10	13	61	55	48
Bristol City Res.	42	16	15	11	76	53	47
Bristol Manor Farm	42	17	14	11	66	52	47
Taunton Town	42	15	15	12	49	48	45
Bideford	42	17	9	16	60	61	43
Swanage Town & Herston	42	16	10	16	73	63	42
Barnstaple Town	42	17	6	19	62	72	40
Clevedon Town	42	13	12	17	42	56	38
Paulton Rovers	42	13	10	19	46	72	36
Dawlish Town	42	14	6	22	49	77	34
Radstock Town	42	13	9	20	44	57	33
Torrington Town	42	12	7	23	49	83	31
Frome Town	42	9	13	20	36	69	30
Minehead	42	10	10	22	47	87	30
Chippenham Town	42	10	8	24	35	62	28
Melksham Town	42	7	14	21	45	84	28
Clandown	42	5	12	25	33	102	22

First Division	P	W	D	L	F	A	PTS
Welton Rovers	36	21	12	3	74	36	54
Chard Town	36	21	11	4	75	41	53
Tiverton Town	36	21	7	8	82	46	49
Bath City Reserves	36	18	11	7	61	46	47
Larkhall Athletic	36	17	8	11	72	49	42
Devizes Town	36	15	9	12	44	38	39
Keynsham Town	36	16	7	13	53	54	39
Westbury United	36	15	7	14	61	56	37
Ottery St Mary	36	16	5	15	43	41	37
Backwell United	36	11	13	12	49	52	35
Warminster Town	36	15	5	16	46	55	35
Wellington	36	14	6	16	60	67	34
Calne Town	36	11	10	15	45	59	32
Odd Down	36	10	11	15	51	62	31
Ilfracombe Town	36	11	7	18	45	59	29
Heavitree United	36	11	6	19	49	62	28
Yeovil Town Res.	36	7	11	18	39	57	25
Elmore	36	7	6	23	46	81	20
Glastonbury	36	5	8	23	39	73	18

1988-89

Premier Division	P	W	D	L	F	A	PTS
Saltash United	40	26	10	4	90	35	62
Exmouth Town	40	29	4	7	79	43	62
Taunton Town	40	23	10	7	95	41	56
Liskeard Athletic	40	20	12	8	46	25	52
Plymouth Argyle	40	19	13	8	84	39	51
Bristol Manor Farm	40	20	7	13	72	49	47
Weston-super-Mare	40	17	8	15	73	52	42
Paulton Rovers	40	14	14	12	60	53	42
Barnstaple Town	40	17	7	16	61	54	41
Swanage Town & Herston	40	15	10	15	71	73	40
Clevedon Town	40	16	7	17	63	70	39
Chippenham Town	40	11	14	15	48	52	36
Welton Rovers	40	13	10	17	50	57	36
Radstock Town	40	9	18	13	38	65	36
Chard Town	40	12	11	17	49	78	35
Bideford Town	40	12	9	19	49	72	33
Frome Town	40	11	10	19	54	80	32
Mangotsfield United	40	10	9	21	53	74	29
Dawlish Town	40	11	7	22	48	69	29
Torrington Town	40	7	12	21	46	84	26
Minehead	40	5	4	31	30	94	14
Saltash United	40	26	10	4	90	35	62

First Division	P	W	D	L	F	A	PTS
Larkhall Athletic	38	25	11	2	88	40	61
Tiverton Town	38	27	6	5	108	33	60
Bridport	38	24	7	7	90	35	55
Calne Town	38	17	14	7	58	34	48
Devizes Town	38	19	9	10	55	39	47
Odd Down	38	17	12	9	57	45	46
Wellington	38	17	11	10	72	56	45
Ilfracombe Town	38	16	13	9	59	47	45
Backwell United	38	15	8	15	49	46	38
Keynsham Town	38	11	13	14	55	55	35
Heavitree United	38	13	9	16	54	58	35
Melksham Town	38	11	13	14	43	49	35
Ottery St Mary	38	12	8	18	46	71	32
Clandown	38	10	11	17	47	63	31
Bath City Reserves	38	11	7	20	60	67	29
Westbury United	38	10	9	19	59	66	29
Yeovil Town Res.	38	10	9	19	42	49	29
Warminster Town	38	5	11	22	34	84	21
Glastonbury	38	6	9	23	38	97	21
Elmore	38	8	2	28	38	118	18

1989-90

Premier Division	P	W	D	L	F	A	PTS
Taunton Town	40	28	8	4	80	41	92
Liskeard Athletic	40	28	7	5	91	30	91
Mangotsfield United	40	27	7	6	96	42	88
Tiverton Town	40	26	6	8	92	51	84
Exmouth Town	40	24	5	11	74	37	77
Weston-super-Mare	40	20	8	12	86	56	68
Plymouth Argyle Res.	40	19	10	11	75	47	67
Saltash United	40	19	9	12	62	41	66
Swanage Town & Herston	40	18	7	15	77	67	61
Clevedon Town	40	16	8	16	58	60	56
Paulton Rovers	40	16	7	17	51	52	55
Bristol Manor Farm	40	13	12	15	49	59	51
Chippenham Town	40	14	7	19	36	46	49
Dawlish Town	40	12	7	21	55	78	43
Chard Town	40	8	14	18	50	74	38
Bideford	40	8	14	18	37	76	38
Torrington	40	8	11	21	48	74	35
Barnstaple Town	40	8	10	22	38	75	34
Radstock Town	40	7	12	21	43	82	33
Frome Town	40	4	14	22	43	77	26
Welton Rovers	40	3	5	32	30	106	14

First Division	P	W	D	L	F	A	PTS
Ottery St Mary	38	27	4	7	72	36	85
Backwell United	38	21	10	7	63	32	73
Ilfracombe Town	38	20	11	7	67	38	71
Bridport	38	20	8	10	69	46	68
Odd Down	38	20	6	12	53	44	66
Larkhall Athletic	38	19	8	11	73	57	65
Westbury United	38	17	8	13	66	55	59
Keynsham Town	38	15	11	12	57	46	56
Melksham Town	38	16	7	15	46	41	55
Devizes Town	38	14	12	12	38	44	54
Heavitree United	38	15	8	15	53	44	53
Calne Town	38	14	11	13	52	45	53
Clandown	38	14	8	16	45	45	50
Elmore	38	14	5	19	46	60	47
Warminster Town	38	10	12	16	43	54	42
Yeovil Town Res.	38	9	9	20	46	67	36
Wellington	38	7	13	18	40	60	34
Bath City Reserves	38	9	4	25	37	82	31
Glastonbury	38	7	7	24	35	72	28
Minehead	38	5	12	21	29	62	27

1990-91

Premier Division	P	W	D	L	F	A	PTS
Mangotsfield United	40	28	8	4	113	39	92
Torrington	40	25	7	8	91	41	82
Plymouth Argyle	40	25	8	7	100	28	79
Tiverton Town	40	22	11	7	85	45	77
Weston-super-Mare	40	20	10	10	74	57	70
Saltash United	40	20	6	14	67	46	66
Taunton Town	40	18	9	13	62	49	63
Liskeard Athletic	40	18	7	15	85	69	61
Dawlish Town	40	15	16	9	58	49	61
Paulton Rovers	40	16	11	13	74	60	59
Clevedon Town	40	16	10	14	52	55	58
Bideford	40	13	10	17	61	76	49
Frome Town	40	14	6	20	56	78	48
Bristol Manor Farm	40	12	9	19	52	66	45
Welton Rovers	40	11	11	18	40	61	44
Chard Town	40	11	10	19	48	86	43
Chippenham Town	40	10	12	19	42	64	42
Ottery St Mary	40	11	4	25	43	88	37
Exmouth Town	40	9	8	23	59	93	35
Barnstaple Town	40	8	10	22	44	86	34
Radstock Town	40	4	5	31	46	116	17

First Division	P	W	D	L	F	A	PTS
Minehead	40	28	9	3	102	42	93
Elmore	40	24	6	10	89	47	78
Calne Town	40	25	2	13	85	55	77
Odd Down	40	22	10	8	59	36	76
Westbury United	40	21	9	10	60	44	72
Bridport	40	18	11	11	65	48	65
Torquay United	40	17	10	13	62	52	61
Devizes Town	40	17	10	13	68	66	61
Ilfracombe Town	40	15	12	13	62	54	57
Crediton United	40	14	13	13	55	48	55
Wellington	40	15	10	15	58	55	55
Bath City	40	14	11	15	67	64	53
Keynsham Town	40	14	9	17	59	58	51
Clandown	40	14	8	18	43	71	50
Melksham Town	40	13	10	17	54	60	49
Backwell United	40	11	9	20	56	70	42
Yeovil Town	40	10	6	24	59	91	36
Warminster Town	40	9	9	22	39	74	36
Larkhall Athletic	40	9	8	23	38	74	35
Heavitree United	40	6	12	22	32	81	30
Glastonbury	40	5	14	21	39	65	29

1991-92

Premier Division	P	W	D	L	F	A	PTS
Weston-super-Mare	40	12	2	6	110	44	98
Clevedon Town	40	28	5	7	90	28	89
Tiverton Town	40	27	5	8	106	48	85
Bideford	40	25	9	6	102	49	84
Saltash United	40	24	5	11	89	51	77
Plymouth Argyle	40	24	4	12	89	52	76
Taunton Town	40	17	11	12	88	56	62
Mangotsfield United	40	16	13	11	53	39	61
Elmore	40	17	10	13	76	72	61
Paulton Rovers	40	16	11	13	71	60	59
Minehead	40	16	10	14	65	74	58
Liskeard Athletic	40	14	10	16	68	69	52
Dawlish Town	40	15	5	20	77	75	50
Chippenham Town	40	13	7	20	58	95	46
Torrington	40	11	10	19	48	62	43
Bristol Manor Farm	40	10	10	20	42	66	40
Exmouth Town	40	10	8	22	56	97	38
Chard Town	40	8	8	24	48	76	32
Frome Town	40	9	5	25	44	91	32
Welton Rovers	40	8	6	26	32	78	30
Ottery St Mary	40	2	2	36	26	127	8

First Division	P	W	D	L	F	A	PTS
Westbury United	42	27	10	5	80	39	91
Torquay United	42	26	11	5	96	32	89
Crediton United	42	20	12	10	57	32	72
Bath City	42	22	6	14	91	68	72
Warminster Town	42	19	13	10	80	49	70
Keynsham Town	42	19	13	10	80	69	70
Calne Town	42	20	9	13	73	49	69
Brislington	42	21	6	15	70	51	69
Bridport	42	17	16	9	61	50	67
Ilfracombe Town	42	17	14	11	76	44	65
Odd Down	42	20	5	17	58	46	65
Backwell United	42	17	10	15	64	49	61
Bishop Sutton	42	17	10	15	58	50	61
Glastonbury	42	14	8	20	52	61	50
Larkhall Athletic	42	12	12	18	58	65	48
Radstock Town	42	11	14	17	65	68	47
Barnstaple Town	42	12	8	22	42	55	44
Clandown	42	10	13	19	56	72	43
Wellington	42	9	11	22	42	70	38
Devizes Town	42	8	13	21	57	84	37
Melksham Town	42	8	12	22	44	77	36
Heavitree United	42	2	2	38	26	127	8

1992-93

Premier Division	P	W	D	L	F	A	PTS
Clevedon Town	38	34	4	0	137	23	106
Tiverton Town	38	28	8	2	134	30	92
Saltash United	38	22	8	8	98	51	74
Taunton Town	38	22	8	8	62	37	74
Mangotsfield United	38	20	8	10	89	47	68
Torrington	38	17	10	11	69	44	61
Westbury United	38	18	7	13	50	45	61
Paulton Rovers	38	15	10	13	76	51	55
Torquay United	38	16	7	15	58	62	55
Plymouth Argyle	38	15	9	14	72	64	54
Exmouth Town	38	14	9	15	47	59	51
Elmore	38	14	5	19	54	71	47
Bristol Manor Farm	38	19	13	15	49	59	43
Bideford	38	11	8	19	59	66	41
Frome Town	38	9	12	17	57	75	39
Chippenham Town	38	8	14	16	65	86	38
Minehead	38	10	8	20	59	88	38
Liskeard Athletic	38	8	9	21	61	87	33
Chard Town	38	6	3	29	37	119	21
Dawlish Town	38	2	2	34	17	127	8

First Division	P	W	D	L	F	A	PTS
Odd Down	40	27	10	3	87	26	91
Calne Town	40	23	12	5	97	47	81
Crediton United	40	23	11	6	79	43	80
Brislington	40	22	8	10	77	41	74
Warminster Town	40	22	7	11	70	50	73
Clyst Rovers	40	18	13	9	75	48	67
Keynsham Town	40	19	10	11	66	50	67
Backwell United	40	16	14	10	68	52	62
Barnstaple Town	40	15	10	15	62	58	55
Bridport	40	14	13	13	67	66	55
Heavitree United	40	14	9	17	64	69	51
Devizes Town	40	15	6	19	61	84	51
Bishop Sutton	40	14	8	18	55	55	50
Welton Rovers	40	12	11	17	69	65	47
Wellington	40	11	14	15	53	65	47
Glastonbury	40	13	5	22	52	70	44
Larkhall Athletic	40	11	5	24	59	81	38
Ilfracombe Town	40	8	9	23	47	94	33
Ottery St Mary	40	9	5	26	53	116	32
Radstock Town	40	7	10	23	38	60	31
Melksham Town	40	6	12	22	39	98	30

1993-94

Premier Division	P	W	D	L	F	A	PTS
Tiverton Town	34	31	3	0	125	22	96
Taunton Town	34	26	2	6	98	38	80
Mangotsfield United	34	19	6	9	75	40	63
Paulton Rovers	34	18	7	9	55	42	61
Saltash United	34	18	6	10	67	36	60
Torrington	34	16	10	8	66	46	58
Liskeard Athletic	34	16	5	13	66	46	53
Chippenham Town	34	14	7	13	58	51	49
Bideford	34	13	8	13	60	69	44
Odd Down	34	10	12	12	59	58	42
Crediton United	34	10	8	16	42	65	38
Westbury United	34	9	9	16	40	61	36
Bristol Manor Farm	34	11	3	20	51	77	36
Calne Town	34	8	9	17	50	76	33
Frome Town	34	9	6	19	33	61	33
Elmore	34	8	8	18	51	83	32
Exmouth Town	34	6	4	24	35	93	22
Minehead	34	6	3	25	38	105	15

First Division	P	W	D	L	F	A	PTS
Barnstaple Town	38	27	8	3	107	39	89
Bridport	38	24	7	7	90	46	79
Brislington	38	23	8	7	73	35	77
Pewsey Vale	38	20	11	7	84	47	71
Keynsham Town	38	21	7	10	80	50	70
Clyst Rovers	38	16	15	7	68	50	63
Backwell United	38	18	8	12	64	45	62
Welton Rovers	38	16	10	12	73	53	58
Devizes Town	38	16	10	12	64	61	58
Chard Town	38	16	9	13	48	51	57
Ilfracombe Town	38	16	8	14	70	42	56
Bishop Sutton	38	12	14	12	58	48	50
Glastonbury	38	14	8	16	68	66	50
Larkhall Athletic	38	12	7	19	52	69	43
Warminster Town	38	8	11	19	47	57	35
Wellington	38	9	6	23	51	92	33
Dawlish Town	38	9	5	24	46	125	32
Heavitree United	38	8	7	23	47	90	31
Radstock Town	38	8	6	24	44	73	30
Ottery St Mary	38	2	5	31	37	127	11

1994-95

Premier Division	P	W	D	L	F	A	PTS
Tiverton Town	34	28	3	3	128	23	87
Elmore	34	27	5	2	94	39	86
Taunton Town	34	15	12	7	59	28	57
Barnstaple Town	34	16	8	10	58	48	56
Westbury United	34	16	6	12	71	53	54
Mangotsfield United	34	16	6	12	51	50	54
Paulton Rovers	34	15	7	12	62	71	52
Chippenham Town	34	14	9	11	54	54	51
Bristol Manor Farm	34	14	6	14	51	48	48
Liskeard	34	12	9	13	59	55	45
Saltash	34	12	9	13	38	43	45
Odd Down	34	11	9	14	47	53	42
Bridport	34	11	6	17	44	59	39
Calne Town	34	11	3	20	36	68	36
Bideford	34	10	5	19	48	69	35
Crediton	34	8	6	20	43	77	30
Torrington	34	6	10	18	49	89	28
Frome Town	34	3	3	28	36	101	12

First Division	P	W	D	L	F	A	PTS
Brislington	40	30	7	3	113	25	97
Glastonbury	40	26	8	6	91	35	86
Backwell United	40	26	8	6	75	33	86
Warminster Town	40	26	7	7	93	42	85
Chard Town	40	25	10	5	74	35	85
Bridgwater Town	40	18	13	9	62	47	67
Keynsham Town	40	17	11	12	73	62	62
Bishop Sutton	40	17	7	16	61	61	58
Exmouth Town	40	16	6	18	55	63	54
Melksham Town	40	14	10	16	62	61	52
Clyst Rovers	40	15	5	20	60	84	50
Amesbury Town	40	14	7	19	67	61	49
Wellington	40	14	7	19	55	59	49
Ilfracombe Town	40	13	8	19	64	58	47
Heavitree United	40	12	7	21	52	94	43
Welton Rovers	40	11	9	20	50	62	42
Devizes Town	40	11	7	22	57	82	40
Pewsey Vale	40	10	8	22	52	77	38
Larkhall Athletic	40	8	8	24	39	89	32
Dawlish Town	40	8	8	24	41	92	32
Minehead	40	5	7	28	24	98	22

1995-96

Premier Division	P	W	D	L	F	A	PTS
Taunton Town	34	25	7	2	84	20	82
Tiverton Town	34	25	4	5	101	34	79
Mangotsfield United	34	22	7	5	88	23	73
Torrington	34	23	4	7	65	37	73
Brislington	34	17	4	13	60	41	55
Bideford	34	16	7	11	63	47	55
Backwell United	34	15	7	12	54	46	52
Paulton	34	14	10	10	59	53	52
Calne Town	34	14	9	11	41	40	51
Chippenham Town	34	11	12	0	53	41	45
Bridport	34	13	5	16	51	60	44
Bristol Manor Farm	34	11	6	17	55	69	39
Westbury United	34	9	9	16	39	54	36
Barnstaple Town	34	10	6	18	61	78	36
Odd Down	34	6	6	22	39	77	24
Elmore	34	6	6	22	30	91	24
Frome Town	34	5	7	22	31	85	22
Crediton United	34	3	6	25	18	96	15

First Division	P	W	D	L	F	A	PTS
Bridgwater Town	36	29	3	4	93	29	90
Chard Town	36	28	6	2	65	17	90
Keynsham Town	36	22	7	7	67	35	73
Clyst Rovers	36	18	7	11	74	52	61
Bishop Sutton	36	18	9	10	48	36	60
Welton Rovers	36	15	11	10	52	44	56
Devizes Town	36	15	10	11	61	50	55
Dawlish Town	36	14	9	13	56	53	51
Melksham Town	36	13	11	12	59	54	50
Warminster Town	36	14	6	16	51	57	48
Glastonbury	36	12	10	14	45	54	46
Wellington	36	12	8	16	47	52	44
Pewsey Vale	36	10	6	20	35	69	36
Heavitree United	36	9	8	19	64	81	35
Larkhall Athletic	36	10	4	22	50	78	34
Amesbury Town	36	7	10	19	37	67	31
Minehead	36	8	7	21	41	73	31
Exmouth Town	36	9	3	24	44	67	30
Ilfracombe Town	36	6	11	19	43	64	29

1996-97

Premier Division	P	W	D	L	F	A	PTS
Tiverton Town	34	31	1	2	108	20	94
Taunton Town	34	24	6	4	99	28	78
Mangotsfield United	34	19	8	7	5	44	65
Paulton Rovers	34	17	10	7	86	42	61
Chippenham Town	34	12	12	10	58	52	48
Odd Down	34	11	15	8	42	46	48
Brislington	34	12	9	13	53	48	45
Calne Town	34	13	6	15	55	42	45
Torrington	34	11	11	12	54	54	44
Bridgwater	34	12	8	14	53	55	44
Bridport	34	11	10	13	41	50	43
Bideford	34	11	6	17	51	84	39
Barnstaple Town	34	10	8	16	54	62	38
Bristol Manor Farm	34	9	10	15	40	60	37
Backwell United	34	9	9	16	42	55	36
Chard Town	34	9	7	18	45	67	34
Westbury	34	8	6	20	40	70	30
Elmore	34	4	4	26	30	127	16

First Division	P	W	D	L	F	A	PTS
Melksham Town	38	27	8	3	82	20	89
Keynsham Town	38	27	7	4	77	21	88
Exmouth Town	38	23	7	8	77	42	76
Clyst Rovers	38	23	6	9	92	48	75
Bishop Sutton	38	21	7	10	96	52	70
Wellington FC	38	21	5	12	82	62	68
Devizes Town	38	18	11	9	75	39	65
Dawlish Town	38	18	9	11	66	36	63
Ilfracombe Town	38	15	12	11	62	44	57
Welton Rovers	38	15	7	16	68	59	52
Minehead	38	16	4	18	61	56	52
Frome Town	38	12	11	15	45	60	47
Yeovil Town II	38	12	8	18	66	77	44
Glastonbury	38	12	7	19	54	72	43
Crediton United	38	12	4	22	58	91	40
Warminster Town	38	9	8	21	44	75	35
Larkhall Athletic	38	7	13	18	51	92	34
Heavitree United	38	7	11	20	44	95	32
Pewsey Vale	38	5	4	29	26	105	19
Amesbury Town	38	1	9	28	27	107	12

1997-98

Premier Division	P	W	D	L	F	A	PTS
Tiverton Town	38	36	2	0	154	20	110
Taunton Town	38	31	3	4	107	28	96
Melksham Town	38	22	7	9	75	37	73
Bridgwater	38	22	6	10	73	43	72
Paulton Rovers	38	19	6	13	76	69	63
Mangotsfield United	38	18	8	12	76	50	62
Barnstaple Town	38	18	5	15	79	64	59
Brislington	38	17	8	13	62	55	59
Calne Town	38	16	9	13	68	67	57
Backwell United	38	15	7	16	70	68	52
Bridport	38	16	4	18	62	72	52
Chippenham Town	38	13	11	14	53	57	50
Bideford	38	14	6	18	68	90	48
Elmore	38	10	8	20	54	100	38
Westbury United	38	9	8	21	39	65	35
Bristol Manor Farm	38	8	10	20	37	73	34
Keynsham Town	38	10	4	24	46	94	34
Odd Down	38	9	6	23	33	80	33
Chard Town	38	8	8	22	44	77	32
Torrington	38	2	8	28	21	88	14
Tiverton Town	38	36	2	0	154	20	110
Taunton Town	38	31	3	4	107	28	96

First Division	P	W	D	L	F	A	PTS
Bishop Sutton	36	26	8	2	86	25	86
Yeovil Town II	36	24	6	6	95	47	78
Devizes Town	36	22	7	7	83	38	73
Street	36	21	7	8	61	32	70
Clyst Rovers	36	20	10	6	89	39	67
Minehead	36	16	14	6	60	39	62
Dawlish Town	36	17	10	9	78	48	58
Crediton United	36	15	8	13	65	67	53
Exmouth Town	36	15	6	15	68	60	51
Bitton	36	14	8	14	55	53	50
Wellington FC	36	13	10	13	72	54	49
Ilfracombe Town	36	14	7	15	75	67	49
Larkhall Athletic	36	12	7	17	45	58	43
Welton Rovers	36	9	6	21	51	78	33
Warminster Town	36	9	5	22	40	83	32
Glastonbury	36	9	4	23	41	86	31
Frome Town	36	8	6	22	47	74	30
Heavitree United	36	3	7	26	34	135	16
Pewsey Vale	36	3	8	25	40	102	14

1998-99

Premier Division	P	W	D	L	F	A	PTS
Taunton Town	38	33	3	2	133	32	102
Tiverton Town	38	29	4	5	118	27	91
Chippenham Town	38	25	7	6	93	41	82
Melksham Town	38	20	10	8	73	44	70
Paulton Rovers	38	18	12	8	70	42	66
Brislington	38	18	10	10	74	44	64
Yeovil Town Res.	38	18	4	16	70	66	58
Bridport	38	16	7	15	61	68	55
Bridgwater Town	38	15	9	14	68	51	54
Backwell United	38	15	7	16	56	48	52
Mangotsfield United	38	14	9	15	60	58	51
Barnstaple Town	38	14	8	16	71	55	50
Bristol Manor Farm	38	15	4	19	61	57	49
Elmore	38	14	6	18	67	80	48
Bishop Sutton	38	12	7	19	65	81	43
Westbury United	38	9	8	21	42	103	35
Bideford	38	10	1	27	40	108	31
Odd Down	38	5	15	18	44	86	30
Keynsham Town	38	6	7	25	33	99	25
Calne Town	38	3	4	31	34	127	13

First Division	P	W	D	L	F	A	PTS
Minehead	36	31	4	1	124	25	97
Dawlish Town	36	27	6	3	83	28	87
Street	36	27	4	5	85	36	85
Devizes Town	36	20	7	9	79	43	67
Clyst Rovers	36	21	4	11	76	51	67
Wellington	36	20	6	10	71	42	66
Exmouth Town	36	20	4	12	80	49	64
Pewsey Vale	36	17	4	15	71	47	55
Corsham Town	36	15	10	11	47	58	55
Welton Rovers	36	13	7	16	61	58	46
Bitton	36	12	9	15	67	59	45
Larkhall Athletic	36	13	5	18	51	65	44
Ilfracombe Town	36	12	7	17	61	71	43
Torrington	36	13	0	23	56	79	39
Warminster Town	36	10	3	23	41	78	33
Chard Town	36	9	2	25	49	102	29
Frome Town	36	7	5	24	44	102	26
Glastonbury	36	3	6	27	47	111	15
Heavitree United	36	4	3	29	31	120	15

385

1999-2000

Premier Division	P	W	D	L	F	A	PTS
Taunton Town	36	30	4	2	116	37	94
Mangotsfield United	36	23	9	4	95	31	78
Brislington	36	20	5	11	64	43	65
Chippenham Town	36	18	9	9	69	41	63
Paulton Rovers	36	16	11	9	53	34	59
Melksham Town	36	15	11	10	50	46	56
Backwell United	36	15	9	12	50	44	54
Bridport	36	12	13	11	56	56	49
Dawlish Town	36	12	11	13	51	45	47
Yeovil Town Reserves	36	11	14	11	64	63	47
Elmore	36	13	8	15	51	63	47
Bishop Sutton	36	13	4	19	51	73	43
Bideford	36	10	10	16	46	68	40
Bridgwater Town	36	10	8	18	42	53	38
Barnstaple Town	36	9	7	20	35	51	34
Westbury United	36	9	7	20	39	67	34
Bristol Manor Farm	36	8	9	19	48	78	33
Odd Down	36	9	6	21	36	82	33
Minehead Town	36	9	5	22	60	101	32

First Division	P	W	D	L	F	A	PTS
Devizes Town	32	23	9	0	88	30	78
Welton Rovers	32	22	4	6	74	19	70
Clyst Rovers	32	19	5	8	83	39	62
Exmouth Town	32	16	9	7	67	43	57
Keynsham Town	32	16	9	7	48	34	57
Bitton	32	16	6	10	60	47	54
Torrington	32	16	6	10	62	50	54
Street	32	13	10	9	56	40	49
Larkhall Athletic	32	11	8	13	45	55	41
Wellington	32	11	7	14	46	44	40
Ilfracombe Town	32	12	2	18	59	65	38
Warminster Town	32	10	6	16	40	77	36
Calne Town	32	10	5	17	48	70	35
Pewsey Vale	32	10	2	20	50	88	32
Chard Town	32	8	7	17	31	52	31
Corsham Town	32	5	5	22	36	86	20
Frome Town	32	3	2	27	30	84	11

2000-2001

Premier Division	P	W	D	L	F	A	PTS
Taunton Town	38	31	4	3	133	41	97
Chippenham Town	38	30	5	3	109	27	95
Paulton Rovers	38	23	10	5	92	44	79
Yeovil Town	38	21	8	9	84	46	71
Bideford	38	19	10	9	71	45	67
Backwell United	38	19	7	12	59	37	64
Devizes Town	38	19	5	14	88	62	62
Brislington	38	17	10	11	67	48	61
Melksham Town	38	17	6	15	58	54	57
Welton Rovers	38	15	8	15	63	53	53
Dawlish Town	38	14	6	18	50	68	48
Elmore	38	14	4	20	67	80	46
Bridport	38	10	13	15	51	63	43
Barnstaple Town	38	12	7	19	45	79	43
Bridgwater Town	38	11	11	16	45	58	41
Odd Down	38	10	8	20	34	57	38
Bishop Sutton	38	9	11	18	57	86	38
Bristol Manor Farm	38	8	8	22	37	66	32
Westbury United	38	3	5	30	27	101	14
Minehead Town	38	5	0	33	34	127	12

First Division	P	W	D	L	F	A	PTS
Team Bath	36	26	6	4	108	22	84
Keynsham Town	36	25	7	4	79	35	82
Frome Town	36	21	4	11	77	45	67
Hallen	36	20	6	10	81	52	66
Bitton	36	19	7	10	66	49	64
Bath City Reserves	36	17	6	13	74	70	57
Exmouth Town	36	15	7	14	76	54	52
Warminster Town	36	14	10	12	48	53	52
Corsham Town	36	16	4	16	60	67	52
Torrington	36	14	8	14	69	72	50
Chard Town	36	11	9	16	52	75	42
Pewsey Vale	36	12	6	18	48	79	42
Street	36	10	9	17	40	63	39
Wellington	36	11	5	20	40	63	38
Larkhall Athletic	36	11	5	20	46	73	38
Ilfracombe	36	9	10	17	48	64	37
Cadbury Heath	36	10	5	21	48	68	35
Worle St Johns	36	10	5	21	64	87	35
Calne Town	36	8	7	21	35	68	31

387

2001-2002

Premier Division	P	W	D	L	F	A	PTS
Bideford	38	28	7	3	105	37	91
Taunton Town	38	26	5	7	104	43	83
Brislington	38	24	11	3	72	32	83
Team Bath	38	22	7	9	74	36	73
Devizes Town	38	22	4	12	72	51	70
Dawlish Town	38	21	6	11	86	56	69
Paulton Rovers	38	18	11	9	77	54	65
Bridgwater Town	38	17	9	12	53	45	60
Backwell United	38	16	9	13	56	41	57
Melksham Town	38	15	9	14	47	46	54
Odd Down	38	13	11	14	49	45	50
Barnstaple Town	38	12	8	18	57	66	44
Keynsham Town	38	11	9	18	47	71	42
Elmore	38	10	7	21	47	96	37
Bishop Sutton	38	9	8	21	53	89	35
Yeovil Town Res.	38	10	4	24	57	86	34
Bridport	38	9	6	23	51	86	33
Welton Rovers	38	7	9	22	46	67	30
Bristol Manor Farm	38	7	8	23	30	80	29
Westbury United	38	7	4	27	35	91	25

First Division	P	W	D	L	F	A	PTS
Frome Town	38	29	5	4	103	22	92
Bath City Reserves	38	24	12	2	79	22	81
Exmouth Town	38	23	11	4	84	39	80
Torrington	38	23	5	10	87	49	74
Clyst Rovers	38	18	11	9	73	53	65
Bitton	38	18	9	11	66	55	63
Shepton Mallet	38	18	8	12	59	47	62
Street	38	17	10	11	76	58	61
Corsham Town	38	14	13	11	55	48	55
Hallen	38	16	6	16	69	60	54
Chard Town	38	14	8	16	66	59	50
Larkhall Athletic	38	13	8	17	55	71	47
Weston St Johns	38	13	7	18	71	77	46
Ilfracombe	38	14	4	20	59	84	46
Willand Rovers	38	9	15	14	59	58	42
Cadbury Heath	38	10	7	21	55	84	37
Wellington	38	9	8	21	48	89	35
Minehead Town	38	9	5	24	52	90	32
Calne Town	38	6	7	25	40	86	25

388

2002-03

Premier Division	P	W	D	L	F	A	PTS
Team Bath	34	27	3	4	109	28	84
Brislington	34	22	7	5	71	28	73
Bideford	34	21	7	6	105	35	70
Backwell United	34	21	4	9	70	33	67
Paulton Rovers	34	18	9	7	68	35	63
Bridgwater Town	34	17	8	9	71	43	59
Bath City	34	14	5	15	66	57	47
Melksham Town	34	12	7	15	65	68	43
Odd Down	34	12	6	16	49	67	42
Keynsham Town	34	11	7	16	55	65	40
Frome Town	34	11	7	16	49	62	40
Bishop Sutton	34	11	5	18	57	83	38
Dawlish Town	34	11	5	18	47	107	38
Bridport	34	9	8	17	40	54	35
Barnstaple Town	34	8	8	18	41	68	32
Welton Rovers	34	9	5	20	40	99	32
Elmore	34	8	7	19	45	81	31
Devizes Town	34	6	8	20	40	75	26

First Division	P	W	D	L	F	A	PTS
Torrington	36	27	5	4	113	47	86
Exmouth Town	36	26	7	3	83	29	85
Westbury United	36	20	8	8	92	65	68
Hallen	36	19	6	11	70	56	63
Calne Town	36	16	9	11	62	43	57
Clyst Rovers	36	17	5	14	67	55	56
Willand Rovers	36	16	6	14	63	53	54
Bitton	36	13	10	13	50	48	49
Shepton Mallet	36	13	10	13	53	55	49
Chard Town	36	12	10	14	59	60	46
Bristol Manor Farm	36	14	4	18	56	71	46
Wellington	36	12	8	16	49	57	44
Larkhall Athletic	36	13	4	19	48	73	43
Cadbury Heath	36	10	11	15	49	61	41
Street	36	13	7	16	59	81	40
Corsham Town	36	8	12	16	44	51	36
Weston St Johns	36	9	4	23	54	76	31
Ilfracombe Town	36	7	9	20	47	85	30
Minehead	36	7	5	24	34	86	26

2003-04

Premier Division	P	W	D	L	F	A	PTS
Bideford	34	25	7	2	110	30	82
Paulton Rovers	34	25	2	7	85	28	77
Frome Town	34	21	5	8	84	43	68
Backwell United	34	20	5	9	67	35	65
Exmouth Town	34	19	7	8	70	34	64
Bridgwater Town	34	19	3	12	67	47	60
Brislington	34	18	4	12	57	40	58
Welton Rovers	34	14	7	13	62	54	49
Odd Down	34	13	10	11	48	44	49
Barnstaple Town	34	12	11	11	47	42	47
Torrington	34	12	10	12	69	74	46
Bridport	34	12	6	16	52	52	42
Devizes Town	34	11	2	21	55	69	35
Melksham Town	34	9	6	19	38	61	33
Keynsham Town	34	8	5	21	45	84	29
Bishop Sutton	34	8	4	22	42	77	28
Dawlish Town	34	6	5	23	30	103	23
Elmore	34	4	1	29	26	127	13

First Division	P	W	D	L	F	A	PTS
Hallen	36	24	7	5	75	26	79
Bitton	36	23	7	6	84	37	76
Bristol Manor Farm	36	20	14	2	74	38	74
Clyst Rovers	36	21	9	6	74	41	72
Corsham Town	36	19	9	8	70	41	66
Willand Rovers	36	17	8	11	72	50	59
Shrewton United	36	17	4	15	87	70	55
Larkhall Athletic	36	15	10	11	65	54	55
Calne Town	36	13	10	13	49	45	49
Wellington	36	14	7	15	54	55	49
Westbury United	36	14	6	16	52	56	48
Street	36	11	10	15	54	51	43
Clevedon United	36	11	9	16	60	75	42
Weston St Johns	36	11	9	16	72	95	42
Cadbury Heath	36	9	10	17	50	64	37
Ilfracombe Town	36	7	6	23	43	106	27
Chard Town	36	7	5	24	48	87	26
Shepton Mallet	36	5	9	22	49	82	24
Minehead	36	5	9	22	35	94	24

2004-05

Premier Division	P	W	D	L	F	A	PTS
Bideford	38	28	4	6	105	26	88
Corsham Town	38	25	8	5	79	33	83
Frome Town	38	23	7	8	78	35	76
Hallen	38	23	6	9	81	38	75
Exmouth Town	38	21	8	9	64	39	71
Bridgwater Town	38	22	4	12	66	46	70
Bristol Manor Farm	38	17	7	14	56	59	58
Bitton	38	15	12	11	64	66	57
Backwell United	38	14	13	11	58	46	55
Brislington	38	14	8	16	50	51	50
Keynsham Town	38	14	7	17	39	62	49
Barnstaple Town	38	15	3	20	51	68	48
Odd Down	38	12	9	17	47	57	45
Melksham Town	38	10	9	19	57	70	39
Devizes Town	38	10	8	20	37	63	38
Torrington	38	11	5	22	50	83	38
Welton Rovers	38	8	12	18	59	80	36
Bishop Sutton	38	9	9	20	44	71	36
Bridport	38	10	4	24	52	75	34
Clyst Rovers	38	2	9	26	44	113	18

First Division	P	W	D	L	F	A	PTS
Willand Rovers	38	27	7	4	88	31	88
Calne Town	38	23	10	5	91	30	79
Radstock Town	38	24	7	7	67	38	79
Dawlish Town	38	20	12	6	81	42	72
Larkhall Athletic	38	21	8	9	65	35	71
Shrewton United	38	22	3	13	83	56	69
Street	38	17	12	9	68	46	63
Ilfracombe Town	38	16	11	11	72	76	59
Clevedon United	38	15	7	16	61	64	52
Elmore	38	14	7	17	59	67	49
Weston St Johns	38	14	7	17	62	88	49
Almondsbury	38	11	10	17	55	79	43
Cadbury Heath	38	10	12	16	46	58	42
Wellington	38	11	9	18	58	76	42
Chard Town	38	11	8	19	43	63	41
Westbury United	38	8	14	16	57	75	38
Saltash United	38	8	11	19	61	77	35
Minehead	38	8	10	20	41	64	34
Biddestone	38	3	14	21	40	81	23
Shepton Mallet	38	3	9	26	38	90	18

2005-06

Premier Division	P	W	D	L	F	A	PTS
Bideford	38	29	7	2	93	25	94
Corsham Town	38	24	10	4	78	30	82
Bristol Manor Farm	38	24	4	10	86	43	76
Welton Rovers	38	19	12	7	61	39	69
Calne Town	38	19	10	9	70	41	67
Willand Rovers	38	18	11	9	63	42	65
Frome Town	38	18	10	10	61	45	64
Bitton	38	18	9	11	63	41	63
Hallen	38	15	12	11	71	54	57
Brislington	38	15	8	15	55	53	53
Bridgwater Town	38	15	7	16	66	54	52
Radstock Town	38	14	5	19	62	73	47
Barnstaple Town	38	12	9	17	54	62	45
Melksham Town	38	12	8	18	43	68	44
Odd Down	38	11	10	17	34	44	43
Bishop Sutton	38	7	13	18	36	52	34
Keynsham Town	38	5	11	22	34	78	26
Devizes Town	38	7	5	26	27	94	26
Torrington	38	6	7	25	33	89	25
Backwell United	38	3	10	25	30	93	19

First Division	P	W	D	L	F	A	PTS
Dawlish Town	42	33	6	3	115	33	105
Chard Town	42	29	10	3	87	27	97
Street	42	24	11	7	80	39	83
Ilfracombe Town	42	23	9	10	82	50	78
Westbury United	42	22	10	10	95	50	76
Bridport	42	22	6	14	81	60	72
Larkhall Athletic	42	19	11	12	93	56	68
Portishead	42	18	12	12	59	49	66
Shrewton United	42	18	7	17	88	79	61
Bradford Town	42	15	13	14	71	81	58
Clevedon United	42	15	12	15	62	67	57
Longwell Green Sports	42	15	9	18	49	52	54
Weston St Johns	42	18	3	21	63	81	54
Cadbury Heath	42	15	8	19	70	62	53
Saltash United	42	15	7	20	71	84	52
Biddestone	42	13	11	18	54	59	50
Wellington	42	14	8	20	69	81	50
Almondsbury	42	10	11	21	46	70	41
Minehead	42	9	9	24	47	100	36
Shepton Mallet	42	10	4	28	34	85	34
Clyst Rovers	42	7	7	28	47	92	28
Elmore	42	4	4	34	42	127	16

2006-07

Premier Division	P	W	D	L	F	A	PTS
Corsham Town	42	29	9	4	81	30	96
Bridgwater Town	42	29	7	6	91	34	94
Frome Town	42	28	7	7	86	41	91
Bideford	42	23	8	11	88	48	77
Melksham Town	42	21	10	11	84	48	73
Willand Rovers	42	21	10	11	69	46	73
Barnstaple Town	42	21	9	12	72	71	72
Bitton	42	19	10	13	66	49	67
Hallen	42	20	7	15	72	60	67
Dawlish Town	42	17	8	17	73	66	59
Odd Down	42	17	7	18	50	53	58
Bristol Manor Farm	42	14	12	16	50	51	54
Calne Town	42	15	7	20	57	58	52
Devizes Town	42	14	10	18	58	70	52
Welton Rovers	42	12	15	15	54	47	51
Radstock Town	42	14	5	23	58	78	47
Brislington	42	11	13	18	44	61	46
Chard Town	42	9	11	22	51	78	38
Street	42	9	11	22	50	83	38
Torrington	42	9	6	27	46	105	33
Bishop Sutton	42	9	4	29	38	89	31
Keynsham Town	42	4	8	30	35	107	20

First Division	P	W	D	L	F	A	PTS
Truro City	42	37	4	1	185	23	115
Portishead	42	29	6	7	88	33	93
Ilfracombe Town	42	29	5	8	98	51	92
Sherborne Town	42	25	8	9	87	44	83
Larkhall Athletic	42	24	8	10	88	41	80
Westbury United	42	19	10	13	71	57	67
Wellington	42	18	9	15	63	60	63
Longwell Green Sports	42	17	11	14	51	44	62
Cadbury Heath	42	17	9	16	78	69	60
Hengrove Athletic	42	17	7	18	58	64	58
Bridport	42	17	6	19	84	81	57
Shrewton United	42	15	11	16	65	71	56
Biddestone	42	15	9	18	69	73	54
Clevedon United	42	14	12	16	54	69	54
Almondsbury	42	11	11	20	47	73	44
Elmore	42	10	14	18	62	94	44
Bradford Town	42	12	4	26	42	86	40
Backwell United	42	10	8	24	48	105	38
Weston St Johns	42	8	10	24	47	93	34
Shepton Mallet	42	8	10	24	34	83	34
Clyst Rovers	42	8	9	25	61	108	33
Minehead	42	7	9	26	42	100	30

2007-08

Premier Division	P	W	D	L	F	A	PTS
Truro City	40	33	4	3	132	39	103
Dawlish Town	40	25	11	4	103	45	86
Willand Rovers	40	22	10	8	78	48	76
Frome Town	40	21	11	8	86	41	74
Corsham Town	40	20	11	9	71	63	71
Bideford	40	17	17	6	85	46	68
Bitton	40	19	7	14	71	46	64
Ilfracombe Town	40	19	7	14	76	69	64
Welton Rovers	40	17	10	13	44	35	61
Devizes Town	40	16	12	12	68	70	60
Melksham Town	40	13	12	15	51	57	51
Barnstaple Town	40	14	8	18	71	67	50
Brislington	40	12	13	15	55	61	49
Calne Town	40	15	4	21	57	70	49
Hallen	40	13	10	17	64	81	49
Bristol Manor Farm	40	10	9	21	64	84	39
Radstock Town	40	10	8	22	60	83	38
Street	40	8	9	23	36	80	33
Bishop Sutton	40	7	8	25	41	99	29
Chard Town	40	8	4	28	53	104	28
Odd Down (Bath)	40	5	7	28	30	108	22

First Division	P	W	D	L	F	A	PTS
Wellington	40	27	8	5	124	45	89
Sherborne Town	40	26	7	7	111	41	85
Larkhall Athletic	40	26	7	7	87	43	85
Shrewton United	40	23	5	12	82	71	74
Cadbury Heath	40	22	7	11	82	59	73
Hengrove Athletic	40	20	9	11	83	61	69
Westbury United	40	20	8	12	92	62	68
Longwell Green Sports	40	19	11	10	71	47	68
Portishead	40	17	12	11	81	59	63
Roman Glass St George	40	15	10	15	70	55	55
Shepton Mallet	40	16	5	19	71	79	53
Oldland Abbotonians	40	13	11	16	80	77	50
Bradford Town	40	14	8	18	62	84	50
Keynsham Town	40	14	7	19	51	67	49
Clevedon United	40	12	8	20	50	75	44
Elmore	40	11	7	22	73	106	40
Minehead	40	10	10	20	55	96	40
Bridport	40	10	6	24	64	77	36
Backwell United	40	7	10	23	48	101	31
Almondsbury	40	6	12	22	44	82	30
Weston St Johns	40	5	6	29	54	127	21

2008-09

Premier Division	P	W	D	L	F	A	PTS
Bitton	40	26	6	8	85	32	84
Frome Town	40	23	7	10	74	44	76
Willand Rovers	40	20	13	7	72	49	73
Dawlish Town	40	23	3	14	93	52	72
Bristol Manor Farm	40	22	6	12	75	53	72
Bideford	40	20	9	11	68	43	69
Wellington	40	20	7	13	87	53	67
Welton Rovers	40	19	9	12	64	52	66
Hallen	40	19	8	13	57	40	65
Brislington	40	18	6	16	62	54	60
Melksham Town	40	15	14	11	59	53	59
Sherborne Town	40	17	8	15	55	59	59
Street	40	13	7	20	55	65	46
Ilfracombe Town	40	11	11	18	48	70	44
Bishop Sutton	40	9	16	15	48	48	43
Calne Town	40	11	10	19	70	78	43
Radstock Town	40	12	6	22	56	95	42
Barnstaple Town	40	10	9	21	49	82	39
Corsham Town	40	10	8	22	37	80	38
Chard Town	40	9	5	26	30	77	32
Devizes Town	40	5	8	27	41	106	23

First Division	P	W	D	L	F	A	PTS
Larkhall Athletic	38	30	5	3	127	27	95
Longwell Green Sports	38	27	4	7	78	40	85
Bradford Town	38	22	6	10	106	55	72
Cadbury Heath	38	21	8	9	84	54	68
Keynsham Town	38	19	9	10	62	46	66
Hengrove Athletic	38	19	4	15	57	52	61
Oldland Abbotonians	38	17	8	13	65	60	59
Shrewton United	38	18	4	16	73	66	57
Westbury United	38	16	8	14	71	50	55
Wells City	38	14	10	14	54	70	52
Portishead Town	38	14	9	15	56	59	51
Gillingham Town	38	14	8	16	71	72	50
Bridport	38	14	7	17	51	65	49
Elmore	38	12	7	19	72	104	43
Clevedon United	38	11	7	20	60	78	40
Roman Glass St George	38	8	15	15	58	77	39
Shepton Mallet	38	10	6	22	51	88	36
Almondsbury	38	8	11	19	70	91	35
Odd Down (Bath)	38	7	9	22	51	80	30
Minehead	38	5	3	30	33	116	18

2009-10

Premier Division	P	W	D	L	F	A	PTS
Bideford	38	27	6	5	93	37	87
Willand Rovers	38	24	11	3	79	30	83
Ilfracombe Town	38	21	10	7	64	45	73
Bishop Sutton	38	19	6	13	69	55	63
Welton Rovers	38	16	13	9	66	52	61
Street	38	19	4	15	65	62	61
Bristol Manor Farm	38	16	11	11	70	55	59
Bitton	38	16	8	14	58	55	56
Brislington	38	14	9	15	44	48	51
Dawlish Town	38	14	9	15	57	63	51
Longwell Green Sports	38	13	10	15	50	63	49
Hallen	38	13	8	17	52	55	47
Wellington	38	13	7	18	63	72	46
Larkhall Athletic	38	12	10	16	61	72	46
Barnstaple Town	38	13	6	19	67	76	45
Radstock Town	38	12	5	21	44	63	41
Corsham Town	38	11	5	22	51	64	38
Sherborne Town	38	9	9	20	63	80	36
Melksham Town	38	10	5	23	41	84	35
Calne Town	38	8	8	22	51	77	32

First Division	P	W	D	L	F	A	PTS
Wells City	38	29	4	5	76	33	91
Odd Down (Bath)	38	25	6	7	75	43	81
Gillingham Town	38	23	8	7	95	51	77
Bradford Town	38	21	10	7	82	50	73
Westbury United	38	22	5	11	81	49	71
Oldland Abbotonians	38	20	10	8	82	42	70
Hengrove Athletic	38	20	8	10	75	43	68
Keynsham Town	38	22	5	11	68	45	68
Shrewton United	38	18	5	15	76	67	59
Bridport	38	16	6	16	65	66	54
Cadbury Heath	38	15	8	15	62	64	53
Portishead Town	38	14	6	18	53	59	48
Almondsbury UWE	38	13	4	21	79	84	43
Elmore	38	13	4	21	66	93	43
Clevedon United	38	12	6	20	58	72	42
Chard Town	38	7	11	20	40	74	32
Shepton Mallet	38	8	6	24	33	78	30
Roman Glass St George	38	5	11	22	38	72	26
Devizes Town	38	8	2	28	40	104	26
Minehead	38	3	7	28	39	94	16

2010-11

Premier Division	P	W	D	L	F	A	PTS
Larkhall Athletic	36	25	4	7	83	46	79
Bitton	36	21	7	8	71	37	70
Ilfracombe Town	36	20	7	9	59	37	67
Willand Rovers	36	18	11	7	69	40	65
Bishop Sutton	36	18	9	9	66	38	63
Dawlish Town	36	17	10	9	78	65	61
Bristol Manor Farm	36	18	7	11	73	63	61
Odd Down (Bath)	36	17	8	11	60	47	59
Wells City	36	16	7	13	67	55	55
Corsham Town	36	14	9	13	48	49	51
Barnstaple Town	36	15	6	15	65	74	51
Radstock Town	36	15	3	18	59	56	48
Street	36	12	9	15	50	61	45
Sherborne Town	36	13	4	19	58	70	43
Brislington	36	9	11	16	36	56	38
Hallen	36	10	6	20	56	79	36
Longwell Green Sports	36	7	5	24	35	79	26
Wellington	36	5	6	25	48	87	21
Welton Rovers	36	4	7	25	38	80	19

First Division	P	W	D	L	F	A	PTS
Merthyr Town	36	29	3	4	118	33	90
Oldland Abbotonians	36	22	10	4	93	46	76
Bridport	36	23	3	10	74	44	72
Cadbury Heath	36	20	9	7	88	49	68
Devizes Town	36	21	2	13	63	65	65
Bradford Town	36	18	7	11	84	62	61
Gillingham Town	36	18	6	12	73	57	60
Melksham Town	36	14	13	9	63	51	55
Shrewton United	36	15	6	15	71	79	51
Hengrove Athletic	36	13	7	16	52	58	46
Calne Town	36	14	6	16	72	56	44
Almondsbury UWE	36	11	11	14	55	64	44
Chard Town	36	11	8	17	57	68	41
Shepton Mallet	36	11	5	20	47	76	38
Roman Glass St George	36	10	6	20	43	76	36
Keynsham Town	36	9	8	19	45	61	35
Westbury United	36	9	3	24	45	82	30
Portishead Town	36	6	11	19	48	84	29
Elmore	36	5	2	29	47	127	17

2011-12

Premier Division	P	W	D	L	F	A	PTS
Merthyr Town	34	22	9	3	96	32	75
Bitton	34	23	4	7	74	35	73
Larkhall Athletic	34	21	4	9	67	29	67
Hallen	34	19	8	7	59	41	65
Willand Rovers	34	18	7	9	62	37	61
Bishop Sutton	34	16	10	8	60	37	58
Brislington	34	14	11	9	49	34	53
Bristol Manor Farm	34	13	8	13	63	57	47
Odd Down (Bath)	34	13	9	12	54	48	47
Street	34	14	4	16	56	58	46
Ilfracombe Town	34	12	8	14	52	52	44
Wells City	34	13	5	16	54	66	44
Longwell Green Sports	34	10	8	16	30	47	38
Bridport	34	10	4	20	42	81	34
Barnstaple Town	34	9	5	20	45	66	32
Radstock Town	34	8	3	23	33	74	27
Sherborne Town	34	8	3	23	36	91	27
Corsham Town	34	6	4	24	21	68	22

First Division	P	W	D	L	F	A	PTS
Cadbury Heath	36	25	9	2	88	32	84
Melksham Town	36	24	6	6	77	42	78
Gillingham Town	36	22	6	8	94	52	72
Calne Town	36	21	7	8	60	34	70
Bradford Town	36	16	10	10	72	44	58
Chard Town	36	15	7	14	62	54	52
Welton Rovers	36	14	8	14	61	57	49
Roman Glass St George	36	13	10	13	48	51	49
Almondsbury UWE	36	14	6	16	70	67	48
Hengrove Athletic	36	12	10	14	53	59	46
Oldland Abbotonians	36	11	11	14	52	53	44
Portishead Town	36	12	8	16	48	61	44
Keynsham Town	36	11	13	12	52	59	43
Elmore	36	12	6	18	51	64	42
Shrewton United	36	10	9	17	63	88	39
Shepton Mallet	36	9	10	17	59	84	37
Westbury United	36	10	5	21	48	65	35
Wellington	36	9	5	22	40	84	32
Devizes Town	36	5	8	23	34	82	23

2012-13

Premier Division	P	W	D	L	F	A	PTS
Bishop Sutton	38	24	10	4	94	34	82
Brislington	38	22	10	6	73	42	76
Gillingham Town	38	23	4	11	93	59	73
Cadbury Heath	38	22	4	12	85	53	70
Larkhall Athletic	38	21	6	11	77	50	69
Street	38	18	6	14	74	62	60
Bitton	38	17	8	13	60	63	59
Odd Down (Bath)	38	16	10	12	84	58	58
Hallen	38	17	6	15	78	68	57
Buckland Athletic	38	15	10	13	77	59	55
Willand Rovers	38	15	10	13	52	53	55
Winterbourne Utd	38	15	4	19	66	84	49
Melksham Town	38	14	6	18	62	74	48
Bridport	38	11	14	13	55	63	47
Longwell Green Sports	38	12	9	17	49	64	45
Ilfracombe Town	38	13	5	20	52	70	44
Radstock Town	38	10	10	18	60	85	40
Bristol Manor Farm	38	11	6	21	55	72	39
Wells City	38	7	6	25	57	90	27
Barnstaple Town	38	3	4	31	23	123	13

First Division	P	W	D	L	F	A	PTS
Sherborne Town	40	28	9	3	116	53	93
Hengrove Athletic	40	29	4	7	93	34	91
Bradford Town	40	26	5	9	103	48	83
Corsham Town	40	24	8	8	92	55	80
Oldland Abbotonians	40	24	7	9	77	37	79
Chard Town	40	24	5	11	94	58	77
Shepton Mallet	40	21	7	12	85	63	70
Cribbs Friends Life	40	19	8	13	79	55	65
Calne Town	40	16	11	13	67	59	59
Almondsbury UWE	40	15	8	17	67	65	53
Cheddar	40	15	3	22	76	85	48
Elmore	40	14	7	19	88	100	48
Keynsham Town	40	15	6	19	59	73	48
Portishead Town	40	15	3	22	63	82	48
Warminster Town	40	10	11	19	60	82	41
Welton Rovers	40	11	7	22	54	88	40
Roman Glass St George	40	9	10	21	49	76	37
Wellington	40	9	6	25	61	99	33
Westbury United	40	8	8	24	46	82	32
Shrewton United	40	8	6	26	43	105	30
Devizes Town	40	8	5	27	65	127	29

2013-14

Premier Division	P	W	D	L	F	A	PTS
Larkhall Athletic	40	34	5	1	114	33	107
Bristol Manor Farm	40	26	8	6	104	32	86
Gillingham Town	40	23	7	10	87	47	76
Odd Down (Bath)	40	22	8	10	76	45	74
Street	40	21	5	14	75	65	68
Bitton	40	19	8	13	75	58	65
Melksham Town	40	20	5	15	74	67	65
Willand Rovers	40	18	6	16	69	63	60
Sherborne Town	40	18	5	17	74	70	59
Brislington	40	16	11	13	61	59	59
Buckland Athletic	40	16	10	14	72	51	58
Bridport	40	15	8	17	78	81	53
Cadbury Heath	40	15	5	20	77	80	50
Longwell Green Sports	40	11	14	15	52	69	47
Slimbridge	40	12	7	21	53	70	43
Winterbourne United	40	13	6	21	77	104	42
Hallen	40	11	11	18	55	75	34
Ilfracombe Town	40	10	3	27	47	93	33
Bishop Sutton	40	8	8	24	47	92	32
Radstock Town	40	10	4	26	51	110	31
Hengrove Athletic	40	8	4	28	33	87	28

First Division	P	W	D	L	F	A	PTS
Bradford Town	42	32	6	4	143	43	102
Shepton Mallet	42	26	11	5	113	52	89
Barnstaple Town	42	26	5	11	102	62	83
Wincanton Town	42	23	8	11	116	70	77
Cribbs	42	23	8	11	89	61	77
Welton Rovers	42	21	11	10	82	56	74
Corsham Town	42	20	10	12	62	71	70
Wellington	42	18	10	14	65	64	64
Almondsbury UWE	42	19	7	16	77	77	64
Chippenham Park	42	19	6	17	64	72	63
Devizes Town	42	19	7	16	71	72	60
Roman Glass St George	42	16	5	21	78	91	53
Calne Town	42	14	10	18	74	70	52
Ashton & Backwell United	42	15	7	20	49	63	52
Chard Town	42	14	9	19	56	58	51
Wells City	42	14	8	20	63	75	50
Cheddar	42	12	9	21	66	92	45
Warminster Town	42	11	9	22	54	88	42
Keynsham Town	42	12	6	24	56	94	42
Westbury United	42	11	8	23	50	75	41
Oldland Abbotonians	42	5	10	27	54	104	25
Portishead Town	42	5	4	33	34	108	19

400

2014-15

Premier Division	P	W	D	L	F	A	PTS
Melksham Town	36	23	7	6	89	41	76
Buckland Athletic	36	23	2	11	90	41	71
Slimbridge	36	20	6	10	55	36	66
Bristol Manor Farm	36	18	9	9	67	40	63
Odd Down (Bath)	36	18	8	10	78	56	62
Willand Rovers	36	18	7	11	78	60	61
Bitton	36	17	7	12	67	52	58
Bradford Town	36	17	6	13	71	61	57
Shepton Mallet	36	16	7	13	70	70	55
Brislington	36	14	10	12	64	45	52
Sherborne Town	36	13	11	12	62	53	50
Cadbury Heath	36	15	5	16	71	83	50
Street	36	12	8	16	64	64	44
Bridport	36	13	5	18	44	66	44
Gillingham Town	36	13	4	19	66	68	43
Longwell Green Sports	36	12	5	19	49	67	41
Hallen	36	8	7	21	41	70	31
Winterbourne United	36	8	4	24	49	93	28
Bishop Sutton	36	4	2	30	30	139	14

First Division	P	W	D	L	F	A	PTS
Barnstaple Town	42	30	10	2	128	27	100
Welton Rovers	42	28	9	5	85	41	93
Cribbs	42	26	12	4	88	43	90
Wincanton Town	42	24	4	14	101	77	76
Chard Town	42	21	7	14	74	68	70
Almondsbury UWE	42	21	6	15	77	67	69
Wellington	42	20	8	14	70	62	68
Ashton & Backwell United	42	19	10	13	81	62	67
Corsham Town	42	19	7	16	79	67	64
Cheddar	42	19	9	14	92	85	63
Chippenham Park	42	15	10	17	68	62	55
Hengrove Athletic	42	15	10	17	75	75	55
Radstock Town	42	15	10	17	73	73	55
Oldland Abbotonians	42	15	10	17	58	70	55
Calne Town	42	13	12	17	63	85	51
Warminster Town	42	12	9	21	63	74	45
Keynsham Town	42	11	9	22	62	109	42
Devizes Town	42	11	6	25	59	83	39
Wells City	42	9	10	23	62	84	37
Roman Glass St George	42	7	15	20	39	74	36
Portishead Town	42	8	5	29	39	88	29
Westbury United	42	6	8	28	52	112	26

2015-16

Premier Division	P	W	D	L	F	A	PTS
Odd Down (Bath)	38	28	4	6	98	45	88
Barnstaple Town	38	27	4	7	78	33	85
Bristol Manor Farm	38	25	5	8	109	44	80
Buckland Athletic	38	24	6	8	91	34	78
Melksham Town	38	22	7	9	65	38	73
Willand Rovers	38	21	7	10	72	52	70
Street	38	20	5	13	82	63	65
Bradford Town	38	19	5	14	91	58	62
Gillingham Town	38	16	8	14	75	65	56
Shepton Mallet	38	18	7	13	61	52	52
Brislington	38	14	5	19	44	64	47
Cadbury Heath	38	11	10	17	66	77	43
Sherborne Town	38	10	10	18	50	70	40
Bitton	38	11	6	21	55	73	39
Cribbs	38	10	7	21	55	72	37
Bridport	38	10	6	22	51	90	36
Hallen	38	11	3	24	49	94	36
Longwell Green Sports	38	10	7	21	45	90	36
Clevedon Town	38	6	6	26	33	100	24
Welton Rovers	38	4	8	26	42	98	20

First Division	P	W	D	L	F	A	PTS
Chipping Sodbury Town	40	23	7	10	84	52	76
Wells City	40	23	7	10	91	61	76
Chard Town	40	22	8	10	70	49	74
Oldland Abbotonians	40	22	6	12	81	54	72
Cheddar	40	21	9	10	81	57	72
Portishead Town	40	20	10	10	83	52	70
Hengrove Athletic	40	21	7	12	57	37	70
Ashton & Backwell United	40	20	9	11	86	56	66
Keynsham Town	40	20	6	14	84	65	66
Corsham Town	40	17	9	14	81	61	60
Almondsbury UWE	40	16	8	16	75	56	56
Wellington	40	15	10	15	71	56	55
Radstock Town	40	16	6	18	67	71	54
Chippenham Park	40	14	11	15	51	52	53
Calne Town	40	15	7	18	60	76	52
Wincanton Town	40	13	7	20	75	90	46
Warminster Town	40	13	7	20	52	75	46
Roman Glass St George	40	11	7	22	71	95	40
Devizes Town	40	11	5	24	55	107	38
Westbury United	40	8	6	26	50	98	30
Bishop Sutton	40	2	2	36	29	134	8

2016-17

Premier Division	P	W	D	L	F	A	PTS
Bristol Manor Farm	38	33	3	2	118	33	102
Street	38	29	5	4	112	46	92
Melksham Town	38	26	7	5	105	43	85
Buckland Athletic	38	26	5	7	98	49	83
Bradford Town	38	20	8	10	90	56	68
Willand Rovers	38	20	7	11	69	52	67
Odd Down (Bath)	38	19	7	12	89	64	64
Cribbs	38	18	7	13	77	54	61
Gillingham Town	38	18	6	14	80	54	60
Brislington	38	16	5	17	78	74	53
Cadbury Heath	38	16	5	17	75	75	53
Shepton Mallet	38	13	9	16	67	71	48
Chipping Sodbury Town	38	12	6	20	55	83	42
Clevedon Town	38	12	4	22	70	87	40
Wells City	38	10	10	18	67	90	40
Bridport	38	10	7	21	63	86	37
Longwell Green Sports	38	11	1	26	40	113	34
Hallen	38	6	4	28	39	97	22
Bitton	38	5	4	29	41	97	19
Sherborne Town	38	3	4	31	41	150	13

First Division	P	W	D	L	F	A	PTS
Wellington	42	27	11	4	92	36	92
Hengrove Athletic	42	27	7	8	105	37	88
Cheddar	42	24	10	8	92	52	82
Keynsham Town	42	26	3	13	82	50	81
Radstock Town	42	21	11	10	85	47	74
Bishops Lydeard	42	20	8	14	77	67	68
Ashton & Backwell United	42	19	7	16	71	69	64
Chippenham Park	42	19	9	14	74	78	63*
Malmesbury Victoria	42	18	7	17	82	82	61
Chard Town	42	16	11	15	74	74	59
Devizes Town	42	16	10	16	72	81	58
Westbury United	42	18	4	20	60	73	58
Wincanton Town	42	16	8	18	83	79	56
Portishead Town	42	16	7	19	48	58	55
Roman Glass St George	42	16	4	22	72	96	52
Bishop Sutton	42	15	6	21	60	63	51
Oldland Abbotonians	42	15	5	22	60	85	50
Warminster Town	42	12	11	19	68	75	47
Corsham Town	42	11	9	22	61	83	42
Welton Rovers	42	10	7	25	54	95	37
Calne Town	42	10	4	28	50	99	34
Almondsbury UWE	42	7	7	28	67	110	28

*Points Deducted

THE WESTERN
FOOTBALL LEAGUE

CLUB HISTORIES

121ˢᵗ RFA

HISTORY

The Royal Field Artillery (RFA) of the <u>British Army</u> provided close artillery support for the infantry. It came into being when created as a separate entity from the <u>Royal Artillery</u> on 1 July 1899, and was re-amalgamated in 1924. They first played in the Wiltshire League in 1905/06 and won it by three points from Wootton Bassett. 1906/07 they joined the Western League where they came one from bottom of Division Two, ten points clear of bottom club Trowbridge Town.

1906-07 Division Two

AFC BOURNEMOUTH Reserves

'The Cherries' Est 1890 as Boscombe St John's. Reformed 1899 as Boscombe FC

HISTORY

Although the exact date of the club's foundation is not known, there is proof that it was formed in the autumn of 1899 out of the remains of the older Boscombe St. John's Lads' Institute. In 1910, the club was granted a long lease on some wasteland which was developed into a stadium named Dean Court after the benefactor. Around 1910 the club obtained their nickname 'The Cherries', either because of their cherry-red striped shirts or, perhaps less plausibly, because Dean Court was built adjacent to numerous cherry orchards

After playing in the Southern League, the club, who had changed its name to Bournemouth and Boscombe Athletic Football Club, were promoted to the Football League in 1923 and after a shaky start eventually established themselves as a Third Division club, remaining as the longest continuous members of the Third Division. There was another change of name in 1972 where they became known as the more familiar AFC Bournemouth, and in 1978 entered the Western League for the first time with a reserve team, winning Division One at the first attempt. The following season the club was pipped to the Championship on a single point by Barnstaple Town, scoring a hundred goals in the process. Much to the annoyance of the Western League Chairman, Les Phillips, the club then withdrew from the League.

Under Harry Redknapp, Bournemouth gained promotion to the second tier of the English league for the first time in their history as Third Division Champions in 1987 and made a challenge for the top-flight. The following years saw Championship challenges fall short and mounting financial problems which eventually culminated in administration in 2008 with debts in the region of £4 million. Since that date, Bournemouth have achieved promotion to the Premier Division and the reserves play in the Central League against fellow reserve teams from West Country League clubs.

GROUND BH7 7AF

Bournemouth play at (The Vitality Stadium), Dean Court, Kings Park, Bournemouth at a ground with a capacity of 11,647.

1978-79 Division One; 1979-80 Premier Division

ABERDARE FC

HISTORY
Founded in 1893, Aberdare were Welsh Cup runners-up, in 1903/04 1904/05 and 1922/23. They took part in the Western League from 1908/10. Aberdare spent six seasons in the Southern League, with their best season being 1921/22, when they finished 8th. That same year, 1926, Aberdare merged with nearby Aberaman Athletic; the first team continued to compete in the Football League under the name Aberdare Athletic, however, in the next season they finished bottom of the Third Division South, and failed to gain re-election to the League; Torquay United took their place.

After World War II a reformed Aberdare and Aberaman Athletic was formed, but this side also split into two in 1947; Aberdare Town FC club continue to this day, and play in the Welsh Football League.

GROUND CF44 7RP

Athletic Ground, Aberdare, the Sobell Sports Centre is located on the same site. The artificial pitch almost directly overlays the pitch of the old stadium.

1908-1909 Division Two; 1909-1910 Division One as Aberdare Town

ABERTILLERY TOWN F.C.

HISTORY

The club were formed prior to 1910, and initially played in the South Wales League until being elected to Division Two of the Southern League in 1913/14. In 1920/21 they played in both the Welsh section of the Southern League and the Western League, finishing sixth in the Southern League and third in the Western League.

The club then withdrew from the Western League, but continued to play in the Southern League, finishing eighth (out of nine) in 1921/22.

They disbanded in the late 1950s. The club was reformed in 1982, and existed until 2000 when they merged with Cwmtillery AFC to form Abertillery Excelsior.

1920-21 Division One

ALMONDSBURY UWE

'The Almonds' established 1969

HISTORY

Founded in 1969 as Patchway North End, the club changed their name to Patchway Old Boys in 1971, when they were playing in the Bristol Suburban League. They moved the short distance from Patchway to Almondsbury in 1989 and changed their name to Almondsbury and were promoted to the Gloucestershire County League two years later, after winning the Bristol Suburban League title.

Almondsbury were Champions of the Gloucestershire League in 2004 and won promotion to Western League Division One. A tie-in with the University of the West of England (UWE) was announced in 2009, resulting in the club changing its name to Almondsbury UWE.

GROUND BS32 4AA

The club play at The Field, Almondsbury Sports and Social Centre.

2004-2009 Division One as Almondsbury; 2009 – Division One as Almondsbury UWE

AMESBURY TOWN F.C.

'The Blues' Established 1904

HISTORY

Amesbury Town Football Club was founded in 1904 and first played in the Salisbury & District League near the historic monument of Stonehenge.

They moved into the County League and won the Wiltshire League Division One title in 1959/60, the Hospital Cup in 1959/60 and the Wiltshire Subsidiary Cup in 1960/61. In 1974/75 they won the Wiltshire Combination League, repeating the feat in 1979/80. In season 1983/84 they lifted the Wiltshire Senior Cup for the first time beating Penhill YC in the Final.

In the early 90s they won the Wiltshire County title twice, in 1990/91 and 1991/92 and finished runners-up on three occasions, as well as lifting the Wiltshire Senior Cup in 1993/94 for the second time. They joined the Western League in 1994/95 season finishing 14th.

In 1996/97 the club finished bottom and decided to regroup and run just one senior side in the Salisbury & District League Premier Division.

The 1999/2000 season saw Amesbury meet the criteria to gain entry into the newly formed Hampshire League Premier Division, winning the title in its inaugural season. They now play in the Wessex League, Division One.

GROUND SP4 7BB

Amesbury Town play their home games at Bonnymead Park, Recreation Road, Amesbury, Wiltshire

1994-1997 Division One

409

ANDOVER F.C.

'The Lions' Established 1883

HISTORY

Andover Football Club was formed in 1883 and played their first game on 27 October at Stride's Field, against Basingstoke Mechanical Engineers. Three years later they moved to the Walled Meadow, where they played their home matches for the next 96 years until it was sold for re-development.

The following years were mainly enjoyed in the Hampshire League which they won in 1934/35, and again in 1944/45 having remained active during the Second World War. Two further Championships and the Hampshire Senior Cup were won between 1948/51.

In 1962, they stepped up to the Western League, and reached the First Round Proper of the FA Cup for the only time in their history after defeating Hendon 5–4 in a Fourth Qualifying Round replay. In that game Fourth Division side, Gillingham, won at the Walled Meadow 1-0, in front of a record 3484 spectators. In the league Andover finished fourth, but that was their highest placing until 1969/70 when they finished as runners-up.

They then alternated between the Wessex League and Southern League, winning the Wessex League Championship in 2000/01, together with the Hampshire Senior Cup for the fifth time and retaining the North Hampshire Senior Cup to complete the treble. Times were, however, tough, and the club was then only saved when twelve supporters secured its future by purchasing the lease for the Portway Stadium from the outgoing chairman, and the 2003/04 season then brought success in the FA Vase competition, reaching the Quarter Finals.

The club was formally wound up and resigned from the Southern League in July 2011. A new club named Andover Lions F.C. was formed two weeks later. After gaining clearance from the Football Association and the Hampshire F.A., the club was accepted into the Hampshire League 2004 (where the original club's reserve side had been playing) in time for the start of the 2011/12 season, with home games played at the Charlton Sports Centre.

GROUND SP10 3LF

Portway Stadium, Portway Industrial Estate, Andover. Capacity 3,000

1962-1971 Division One

ASHTON AND BACKWELL UNITED F.C.

'The Stags' Established 1911

HISTORY

The club was established in 1911 as Backwell United and played in various local leagues, although activities were suspended during both World Wars. They moved to their current home in 1947, the Backwell Recreation Ground, on land given by local benefactor Theodore Robinson for the benefit of residents, although this is now leased from the local Recreation Ground Trust, whose land was given to the community by the Robinson family in the 1920s.

At this time they played in the Bristol Church of England League, progressing to the Bristol and Suburban League in the 1950s. The Club's true senior football aspirations got under way with their promotion to the Somerset Senior Football League in 1970 when that League formed a First Division, the club finishing in third position. It was in the late 1970s that the club really progressed, ending up League Champions for the 1977/78 season and again League Champions from 1979 to 1983, equaling a record set by Paulton Rovers, and then setting a new League record of five Championships in six years.

The 1983/84 season saw the first team elected to the Western League Division One, where steady progress was made with the club gaining the runners-up position for the 1989/90 season which entitled them to promotion to the Premier Division. That was denied, however, owing to the local authority's refusal to grant planning permission for floodlights to be erected. The club went to appeal, led by Secretary Bill Coggins and with help from Stan Priddle, which they won, and floodlights were in place for the 1993/94 season, allowing the club to progress to Premier Division football.

Performance has been steady over the years and the first team reached the 5th round of the FA Vase in the 2004/05 season. For the 2005/06 season a change of manager and an exodus of experienced players resulted in a last-place finish and thus the club was relegated to Division One.

Ashton & Backwell United F.C. was formed in 2010 and originally called Backwell United before merging with one of Bristol's largest youth clubs Ashton Boys FC, a football club based in Backwell.

GROUND BS48 3HQ

Ashton & Backwell United play their home games at The Lancer Scott Stadium, West Town Road, Backwell, Somerset. Capacity 1,000 with 150 seated

As Backwell 1983-1995 Division One; 1995-2006 Premier Division; 2006-2008 Division One

As Ashton and Backwell United 2013 – Division One

ASHTONIANS UNITED

HISTORY

Bristol team, Ashtonians United, were managed by 32-year-old Jimmy Rogers, who had played for several non-league clubs before emigrating to Australia where he managed Merton Rovers in Queensland Division One. After returning to England he spent four years changing Ashtonians from a highly successful youth team, into a Western League side; albeit coming in bottom in their first season in 1972/73 with just 4 wins from 30 games played.

The following season the manager left to join Chippenham Town, and with his appointment it was agreed to let Ashtonians play their Western League home games at Hardenhuish Park, because they had lost their own ground. Ironically, Chippenham Town came bottom that year, with Ashtonians two places ahead. The ground-sharing arrangement did not continue, as the club then merged with Clevedon, who took their place in the Western League.

GROUND BS9 2HS

The club formerly played their games at The Creek, Bristol where Manor Farm now play, and for one season at Hardenhuish Park, Chippenham.

1972-1974 Division One

AVON BRADFORD

HISTORY

Originally called Spencer Moulton FC and playing on the same ground that Bradford Town now occupy, the works team were based at Kingston Mill and played a significant role in the Wiltshire League pre-war. After the company merged with the Avon Rubber Company, Avon Bradford tried their hand in the Western League for a couple of years before joining the Premier Division of the Hellenic League in 1983/84, only to be relegated the same year.

GROUND B15 1EE

The club played their games at Bradford on Avon Sports and Social Club, Trowbridge Road, Bradford on Avon

1972-74 Division One

412

BARNSTAPLE TOWN

'Barum' Established 1904

HISTORY

The club was established in 1904 as Pilton Yeo Vale, and were founder members of the North Devon League in the same year. They played in the league's first match, hosting Ilfracombe on 1 October; the visitors won 4–2 with several hundred in attendance. However, that was to be the only defeat all season and the club went on to win the inaugural title. At the end of the season they adopted their current name.

After winning a second North Devon League title in 1908/09, they switched to the Devon & Exeter League, where they remained until World War I. After the war they returned to the North Devon League, before rejoining the Devon & Exeter League, winning the title in 1946/47.

They joined Division Two of the Western League in 1948 and the following year won promotion to Division One. In 1951/52 they reached the First Round of the FA Cup for the first time, losing 5–2 to Folkestone in a replay. The club were Western League Champions in 1952/53, and reached the first round of the FA Cup again in 1954/55, losing 4–1 at home to Bournemouth & Boscombe Athletic in front of a record crowd of 6,200. They reached the First Round of the FA Cup for a third time in 1959/60, losing 4–0 at Exeter City, and again in 1972/73, before losing 2–0 at home to Bilston.

The Western League expanded back to two divisions in 1976, with Barnstaple placed in the Premier Division. In 1979/80 they won their second Western League title, and finished as runners-up in the following two seasons. After finishing second-from bottom in 1990/91, Barnstaple were relegated to Division One, earning promotion back to the Premier Division three seasons later.

They remained in the Premier Division until being relegated again at the end of the 2012/13 season, which saw them finish bottom of the Premier Division. However, they made an immediate return to the top division after winning Division One in 2014/15. The following season saw the club finish as runners-up in the Premier Division, earning promotion to Division One South & West of the Southern League.

GROUND EX31 1JQ

The club play their home games at Mill Road in Barnstaple. It has a capacity of 5,000, of which 250 are seated and 1,000 covered.

1948-50 Division Two; 1950-1976 Division One; 1976-1991 Premier Division; 1991-1994 Division One; 1994-2013 Premier Division; 2012 – 2015 Division One; 2015-2016 Premier Division

BARRY DISTRICT FC

'Town' Established 1892

HISTORY

1892, a team named Barry & Cadoxton District was formed, beginning a decade of football under various names at numerous grounds in the town.

In November 1912, a meeting at The Windsor Hotel in Holton Road saw townsfolk choose to pursue membership of the Southern League, as Barry AFC. On returning after the First World War, the 1920/21 season ranks as one of the finest in Barry's history, as they surprised many by becoming Champions of the Southern League's Welsh section. The achievement was more impressive when considering the small Barry squad played over 100 matches in all competitions during the season. Competing simultaneously in both the Welsh and the Western League, the Board gave priority to Southern League fixtures, swayed by the hopes this would act as a springboard to Football League membership, but Charlton Athletic and Aberdare Athletic were elected instead.

Barry then concentrated on membership of the Southern League set-up until the creation of the League of Wales in 1992 prompted a decree that Barry would no longer be able to compete in the English Pyramid from their Jenner Park base, but after a season of playing at the Worcester City St. George's Lane ground, they were accepted into the Welsh League Division One for the 1993/94 campaign.

After a turbulent period in 2013 the supporters, who had been operating the football club for several seasons, outlined their will to continue in the Welsh League, and a court granted them entry to Division Three of the Welsh League - ensuring that the club's colourful story would continue. Having added the United suffix months earlier, the team hit the ground running and won consecutive promotion to Division One. They now go under the name of Barry Town United as a non-profit community football club, owned by their supporters.

GROUND CF62 9BG

The club play at Jenner Park Stadium, Gladstone Road, Barry which was named after the family who gifted the land. The grounds capacity is 2,000.

1908-1909 Division Two; 1909-1913 Division One.
Barry reserves 1919-1921

BARTON HILL FC

Established 1888

HISTORY

Barton Hill were founder members of the Bristol and District League, Division Two, in 1893. They were Champions of that division in the 1895/96 season when the League was renamed the Western League, and were runners-up the following year. They left after the 1898/99 season when just five clubs remained, to join the Bristol and District League.

1895-1898 Amateur Division Two

BATH CITY F.C.

The 'Romans' Established 1889

HISTORY

In 1889 Bath City were formed as Bath AFC and began to play at the Belvoir ground. In1908 they started playing competitive league format football, joining the Western League Division Two. For the 1921/22 season they moved into the Southern League, English Section, where they remained until the Second World War, when they were by chance accepted to join the temporary Division Two Northern Division, finishing the eventual Champions, thereby becoming the only semi-professional side ever to win a Football League Trophy.

After the War, they were forced to resume playing in the Southern League which they won in the 1959/60 season. A year later they were runners-up in the same league, and over the next thirteen years were relegated and promoted three times. In 1977/78, they won the Southern League title for a second time.

Bath City then became founder members of the Alliance Premier League, now the National League, finishing runners-up in 1985, but Champions Wealdstone did not meet Football League stadium capacity requirements, so the club were allowed to apply for election to the Football League Fourth Division, narrowly missing out on election to the Football League.

In1989 they were relegated to the Southern League, gaining promotion the next season, where they remained until they were relegated once more to the Southern League in 1997, gaining promotion to Conference South in 2006/07.

GROUND BA2 1DB

Bath City play their home games at Twerton Park, Twerton, Bath, Somerset, a stadium with capacity of 8,840, seating for 1,006.

1908-09 Division Two; 1909-14 Division One; 1919-21 Division One;
1922-30 Division One; 1932-36 Division One; 1939-39 Division One

Reserves. 1925-26 Division Two; 1928-36 Division Two;
1937-39 Division Two; 1939-40 Division One; 1946-50 Division One;
1950-50 Division Two; 1951-55 Division One; 1957-59 Division Two;
1959-65 Division One; 1967-71 Division One; 1979-92 Division One;
2000-2003 Division One; 2002-2003 Premier Division

BEDMINSTER FC

Established 1887

HISTORY

Originally formed as Southville FC, they merged with the cricket club in 1889, which saw a change of name to Bedminster FC. The club were founder members of the Bristol and District League in 1892, prior to the change of name to the Western Football League. They won Division Two in 1893 and then introduced a reserve team, with both competing until the 1989/99 season when the depleted League ran with just eleven teams in two divisions. In 1900 Bedminster, who were also playing in the Southern League, merged with Bristol City in what was little less than the co-existence that it was billed to be, and more of an absorption. Although five Bedminster members joined the Board, and the badge of City was placed onto Bedminster's maroon and old gold colours, the club, in reality, had been totally incorporated and ceased to exist.

GROUND BS3 1JA

The club originally played at Greenway, Bush Lane (now the site of Aldi supermarket) and moved to Ashton Gate at the start of the 1896-97 season.

1892-97 Division One; 1897-98 Amateur Division One;
1898-1900 Division One

Reserves. 1893-1898 Division Two

BEDMINSTER ST FRANCIS FC

Established 1897

HISTORY

Originally playing in the Bristol and District Alliance and the East Bristol League, they joined the Western League just as Bristol City began their expansion and played just six of the scheduled twelve games, winning three and drawing one in the process.

GROUND BS3 1JA

The club played at Ashton Gate, a ground just across from the St Francis Church.

1900-1901 Division Two

416

BIDDESTONE F.C.

Established 1976

HISTORY

Based in the village of Biddestone, near Corsham, Biddestone Football Club has been in existence since the 1920s and the modern-day team was established in 1976 as a social team, competing in the Chippenham & District Sunday League.

Biddestone also played in the Wiltshire Junior League until 1990, when they entered the Wiltshire Football League. Progressing through the County League, the club eventually won promotion to the Western League in 2004, where they remained until the 2006/07 season, after which the club withdrew from the League. They also withdrew their reserve side from the Wiltshire League, and are currently only competing in youth and junior football.

GROUND SN14 7BZ

Biddestone play at The Sports Ground, Yatton Road, Biddestone

2004-2007 Division One

BIDEFORD AFC

'The Robins' Established 1946

HISTORY

Founded in 1946, Bideford A.F.C. played their first three seasons in the Exeter & East Devon League before joining the Western League in 1949. Bideford had requested to the Western League to be elected to the Second Division, but this was denied and they had to start in Division Three instead. This was the only season the Western League ran a Third Division, and Bideford won it without losing a game. In the 1951/52 season, they then won Division Two.

Bideford won the Western League three times before joining the Southern League in 1972. The club spent three seasons in the Southern League before the extra expense involved and increased travelling took its toll, forcing them to drop down back to the Western League.

Two more Western League titles followed in the early 1980s, before a financial crisis hit the club. A re-formation took place in 1987, leading the club to the current setup under the revised company name of Bideford AFC (1987) Ltd.

Despite winning the Western League four times under Manager Sean Joyce between 2000 and 2006, the club elected not to apply for promotion to the Southern League, however, after winning the Western League again for the 10th time in the 2009/10 season they applied for and were accepted into the Southern League in May 2010.

GROUND EX39 2NG

The Sports Ground, Kingsley Road, Bideford, a stadium with a capacity of 6,000, 375 seated

As Bideford Town, 1949-50 Division Three; 1950-52 Division Two; 1952-63 Division One. As Bideford, 1963-72 Division One; 1975-76 Division One; 1976-1987 Premier Division. As Bideford AFC (1987) Ltd, 1987-2010 Premier Division

BISHOP SUTTON FC

Established 1977

HISTORY

Bishop Sutton are a reformed version of the club that date from the early 1900s, joining the Western Football League in 1991 after playing in the Somerset County League and prior to that the Bristol and Avon League. They reached the Third-round of the FA Vase in the 1995/96 season for the first time, losing to AFC Lymington, and two years later won the Division One title, gaining promotion to the Premier Division.

In 2012/13 the club became Champions of the Western League Premier Division for the first time in their history, winning the League by a six-point margin. However, with the loss of their manager and most their players the club has struggled, finishing bottom of the Premier Division in season 2014/15.

GROUND BS39 5XN

Bishop Sutton play their home games at Lakeview, Wick Road, Bishop Sutton and has a capacity of 1,500

1991-1998: 2015 - Division One; 2016-17 1998-2015 Premier Division

BITTON AFC

'The Ton' Established 1892

HISTORY

Although founded in 1892, little is known of the club's history before the Second World War. From 1945 until the late 1980s Bitton played in the Bristol & District League without notable achievement. However, the club was promoted to the Bristol Premier Combination in 1990, and quickly moved to that league's top division. Runners-up in the 1994/95 season allowed promotion to the Gloucestershire County League, where a second-place finish two years later allowed them to advance to Western League football.

Bitton played in Division One for several seasons before another second-place finish earned them promotion to the Premier Division; winning that division in the 2008–09 with three games left to play, and were runners up in the 2010–11 season. Bitton were unable to gain promotion as the Recreation Ground did not satisfy Southern League standards. With this in mind, Chairman John Langdon invested heavily in the facilities at the ground, and the wooden clubhouse was replaced by a brand-new facility, ready for promotion in the future.

In national competitions, Bitton reached the 4th round in the FA Vase, losing out to Bedlington Terriers of the Northern League.

GROUND BS30 6HX

Bitton play their home games at The Recreation Ground, Bath Road, Bitton, a stadium that has a capacity of 1,000 with 50 seated.

1997-2004 Division One; 2004- Premier Division

BRADFORD TOWN FC

'Bobcats' Established 1992

HISTORY

Bradford Town FC was formed by Les and Pat Stevens in 1992, playing in the Wiltshire County League at St. Laurence School, where the pitch had to be roped off before every home game, and the half-time tea was made in the boot of a car.

In the 1993/94 season they gained promotion to the Wiltshire County Premier League, and in 1996 moved to their present ground in Bradford on Avon.

They gained promotion to the Western League in the 2005/06, and during the 2008/09 season turned on floodlights for the first time. The following year seating for 100 was installed; the same year that the club reached the Second-round proper of the FA Vase losing out to Wellington in a very close fought game.

They won the Division One title in 2013/2014 by a clear 13 points, with top goal scorer, Sammy Jordan, netting 77 goals and winning the League's 'Top Goal Scorer' Award, and Manager Paul Shanley the 'Manager of the Year' award.

The following season saw the club progress to the Third-Qualifying round of the FA Cup, and progressed through six rounds of the FA Vase, before missing out in the Quarter-Finals losing 2-1 to Highworth Town.

In 2015/16 season saw Bradford go one stage more in the FA Vase winning 2-1 away at Buckland, giving them a trip to Hartley Witney, where Bradford unfortunately lost 3-1.

GROUND BA15 1EE

Bradford on Avon Sports and Social Club, Trowbridge Road, Bradford on Avon.

Division One 2005-2014; Premier Division 2015 -

BRENTFORD FC

'The Bees' Established 1889

HISTORY

On 10th October 1889, at the Oxford and Cambridge Hotel public house in Brentford, next to Kew Bridge, a meeting between members of the Brentford Rowing Club decided by 8 votes to 5 to form an Association Football Club (as opposed to adopting rugby union rules), to serve as a winter pursuit for the rowing club and its members.

After several changes of ground, a 21-year lease was agreed in January 1904 on an orchard, once owned by Chiswick brewers Fuller, Smith and Turner, which became their home. The first competitive match was a reserve team game in the Western League against eventual Champions, Plymouth Argyle, on 7th September 1904, which was lost despite the first ever goal being scored at the new park, leaving them in runners-up place at seasons end by those two points. That game was followed by the First team turning out for a Southern League First Division match against West Ham United which resulted in a 0–0 draw. Their reserves continued in the League until it disbanded its professional sections in 1909; albeit having lost seven of its twelve games during the previous season and ending bottom of Section B of Division One.

GROUND TW8 0NT

Brentford played at Boston Park Cricket Ground, York Road, Brentford before moving to Griffin Park in 1904

1902-1906 Division One; 1906-1908 Division One Section A; 1908-1909 Division One Section B

BRIDGWATER TOWN F.C.

'The Robins' Established 1984

HISTORY

The first club to bear the name of the town was formed in 1898 and played in the grounds of Sydenham House off Bath Road, winning the Somerset Senior Cup in its first season by beating Yeovil Casuals in the final, played at Wells. They were finalists once more the following season, but ended as runners-up, and later they were forced to disband due to lack of support and financial difficulties.

In 1903 a second attempt was made to establish senior football in the town, a club playing in local leagues until the outbreak of World War One.

In 1919, local works side, Wills Athletic, was formed, changing their name to Bridgwater Town FC two years later, but that club eventually went into junior football and faded away during the early 1930s.

Local side Crown Dynamos FC was formed in 1946, changing its name to Bridgwater Town AFC Ltd two years later and moving to a new ground at Castle Field. Originally playing in the Somerset Senior League, they soon successfully applied for promotion to the Western Football League and reached the top division after three seasons. They remained at that level for the next 30 years, winning the title in 1967/68 and 1980/81. After a 3rd-place finish in 1981/82, they were accepted into the Southern League, but increased costs, plus a large debt incurred in enlarging the Robins Social Club, forced them into liquidation after only two years at the higher level.

In 1984, *Bridgwater Town (1984) FC* was formed and joined the Somerset Senior League. The club advanced to the Premier Division and finished in the top three for six years in a row from 1988-1994, including a hat-trick of successive League titles, culminating in a promotion to the Western League. The second season in the League ended with the Championship and promotion to the Premier Division, where Bridgwater remained until a second-place finish in 2006/07 was enough to see the club promoted, once more, to the Southern League after a 23-year absence.

In the 2009/10 season Bridgwater recorded the most successful season in the club's history, reaching runners-up in the Southern League Division One South and West Play-offs, and a runners-up position in the Somerset Premier Cup.

GROUND TA6 4YQ.

Bridgwater Town play their home games at Fairfax Park, College Way, Bridgwater, Somerset. It has a capacity of 2,500 and seating for 318.

As Bridgwater Town AFC. 1949-52 Division Two; 1952-76 Division One; 1976-82 Premier Division; As Bridgwater Town (1984) FC 1994-96 Division One; 1996-2007 Premier Division.

Reserves; 1949-50 Division Three; 1958-60 Division Two

BRIDPORT FC

'The Bees' Established 1885

HISTORY

Bridport FC was established on 7 October 1885 and, in their early years, played in a variety of leagues, including the Dorset, South Dorset, West Dorset, and Perry Street Leagues. They were also not adverse to adapting to prevailing conditions; as was the case at the start of 1895 when no matches were played for ten weeks due to a frozen pitch, and so they played ice-hockey instead!

The club was among the founding members of the Dorset Combination in 1957 and joined the Western Football League in 1961 where they played until the 1983/84 season when they resigned and their record was expunged. Taking their reserve side's place in the Dorset Combination, the club finished third in 1984/85 and then went on to win the League three times in a row. Following the third title, Bridport was accepted back into the Western League, this time playing in Division One. A runners-up performance in 1993/94 allowed the club to return to the Premier Division, but an 11-year run in the top flight came to an end with relegation following the 2004/05 season, but were promoted back to the Premier Division in 2010/11 after finishing in third place.

They have reached the Fourth Round of the FA Vase twice and the Fifth Round once in their history. All three Vase runs came within a four-year period from the 1987/88 season to the 1990/91 season. In FA Cup, they reached the Third Qualifying Round in season 1957/58.

GROUND DT6 5LA.

Bridport play at St Mary's Field, Skilling Hill Road, Bridport, Dorset

1961-76 Division One; 1976-83 Premier Division; 1988-94 Division One;
1994-2005 Premier Division; 2005-2011 Division One;
2011- Premier Division.

BRIGHTON & HOVE ALBION FC

'The Seagulls' Established 1901

HISTORY
Brighton were founded in 1901 and played First team games in the Southern League, where they won their only national honour to date, the FA Charity Shield, by defeating Football League Champions Aston Villa in 1910. Their reserve team took part in the Professional sections of the Western League as a subsidiary competition, winning Section A in 1908-09 ahead of QPR by 3 points.

GROUND BN3 7BB
Whilst in the Western League the club played at Goldstone Ground, which is now a retail park, where the pitch was situated under the Toys-R-Us store.
1907-1909 Division One Section A

BRISLINGTON FC

'Bris'/'Foxes' Established 1956

HISTORY

The club was established in 1956 as an under-16 team, and initially played in the Bristol Church of England League. They won the Somerset Intermediate Cup in 1961/62 and 1962/63, and the Somerset Junior Cup in 1963/64.

By the mid-1960s they were playing in the Senior Division of the Bristol and Suburban Association Football League, and during the 1970s the club moved up to the Somerset County League They won the League Cup in 1976/77 and finished as runners-up in the Premier Division in 1979/80 and 1984/85. They won the title and the Somerset Senior Cup in 1988/89, and after finishing as runners-up again in 1990/91, were promoted to Division One of the Western League.

After a third-place finish in 1993/94, the club won Division One in 1994/95 by a clear 11 points, earning promotion to the Premier Division and repeating the success of the previous year in the Senior Cup Final, overcoming Bridgwater Town on penalties.

The installation of floodlights and the construction of the 'Park Pets' Stand enabled promotion to the Premier Division of the Western League and a new era. In 2013/14, the club reached the 4th Qualifying Round of the FA Cup before bowing out to Conference, Welling United, 1-0, in front of a home crowd of 600.

GROUND BS4 5RS

Brislington play at Ironmould Lane, Brislington, with a capacity of 2,000 which includes144 seats and 1,500 covered standing places.

1991-95 Division One; 1995 – Premier Division

BRISTOL AEROPLANE COMPANY FC

'The Fighters' Established 1930s

HISTORY

Joining the Western League in time for the final season of football before World War Two, Bristol Aeroplane Company F.C. had a successful season, finishing as runners-up to Champions Trowbridge Town. After the war they fared less well, gradually dropping down the division before finishing bottom and being relegated to Division Two in 1947/48. Life in Division Two was equally tough, with the club finishing third from bottom and second from bottom in their final two seasons, leaving the League at the end of the 1949/50 season.

The club fielded a reserve side in Division Two of the Western League for two seasons, the second year being particularly unsuccessful. When the first team was relegated, the reserves were dropped.

BAC entered the FA Cup for three consecutive seasons during the late 1940s, without scoring any goals. In their first Cup tie in 1947/48 they were defeated in the Preliminary Round 2–0 at Western League rivals Soundwell. They lost to local rivals again the following season, 1948/49, this time 4–0 at home to Hoffman Athletic in the Extra Preliminary Round. Their final attempt in 1949/50 resulted in a 3–0 Preliminary Round defeat at Troedyrhiw of the Welsh League.

GROUND BS34 7RG

Whilst in the Western League the club played at the BAC Ground, Southmead, which is now known as the BAWA Sports Ground

1939-40 Division One; 1945-48 Division One; 1948-1950 Division Two.

Reserves 1946-48 Division Two

BEDMINSTER/BRISTOL AMATEURS FC

Established 1898

HISTORY

Formed by some disgruntled supporters of amateurism, on the back of Bedminster turning professional. It was time when a huge number of clubs were forming in the City, and while they joined the Western League that year, they only lasted for one season, winning seven of their twelve games played.

GROUND BS3 2EJ

The club played at Bedminster Athletic, now Ashton Gate

1898-99 Division Two Amateur

BRISTOL CITY FC/BRISTOL SOUTH END

The 'Reds/Robins' Established 1894

HISTORY

The club was founded in 1894 as Bristol South End and changed their name to Bristol City on adopting professionalism three years later, when they were admitted into the Southern League after competing in the Western League, where they had finished as runners-up in three of their first four seasons.

As South End, they were runners-up to Warmley in their final year under that name, and then won the Professional Section the following season, beating Swindon Town to the title by four points.

In 1900 the club amalgamated with local rivals Bedminster, who had been founded as Southville in 1887. City joined the Football League in 1901 when they followed in the footsteps of Woolwich Arsenal and Luton Town to become only the third club South of Birmingham to be accepted into the competition.

City reserves took part in the Western League at various times throughout history and were later replaced by an 'A' team, and eventually the City Colts. The reserve's won Division Two in 1903/04, the same year that saw a team from Tottenham Hotspur pick up the Division One title. City and Rovers reserves then went on to dominate for honours during those early years.

When they re-entered the League in the 1960s, the reserves won the Championship twice, only being denied a third consecutive success by Bideford.

With the League in a strong position in the beginning of the 1980s the City second eleven picked up the challenge, and were promoted to the Premier Division after winning Division One in 1983/84 by eight points from Chard Town.

Various notable men attached to City have been instrumental in keeping the League going throughout its long history, and were instrumental in the introduction of the Charities Cup to the Competition. Terry Cooper, whilst manager, introduced his son, Mark to the rigours of Western League fooball, when the poor lad was coming up to his sixteenth birthday.

GROUND BS3 2EJ

The club initially played at St John's Lane until 1896, and then moved to their present home at Ashton Gate.

As Bristol, South End; 1896-1897. As Bristol City 1897-1898 Professional Section; 1889-1901 Division One; Bristol City Reserves 1903-09 Division

Two; 1909-11 Division One; 1919-21 Division One; 1925-33 Division One; 1936-40 Division One; 1945-48 Division One; 1961-65 Division One; 1982-84 First Division; 1984-88 Premier Division. Bristol City 'A' team 1929-39 Division Two. As Bristol City Colts 1948-49 Division One; 1949-54 Division Two; 1956-61 Division One; 1965-71 Division One; 1972-73 Division One.

BRISTOL EAST FC

Established 1899

HISTORY

Joined the Western League in 1899 and won the small Second Division for the first three years. They left at the end of 1905/06, having failed to complete their fixtures, with their game at Trowbridge Town on 17th March 1906, left unplayed because they could not raise a side.

GROUND BS15 1TE

The club played at the Chequers Ground, Kingswood, now the site of the Britton Gardens Housing Estate.

1899-1906 Division Two

BRISTOL ROVERS FC/BRISTOL EASTVILLE ROVERS/ EASTVILLE ROVERS

The 'Pirates'/'Gas': Established 1893 as the Black Arabs FC

HISTORY

1892 was a major landmark in the history of the club, with Eastville Rovers joining an organised league for the first time. Rovers became a founding member of the Bristol & District League, which was later to become the Western Football League, and their first league game was played on 1st October 1892 against Mangotsfield F.C. Although it was officially a home game for Rovers, the match was played at Mangotsfield, with Rovers defeated, 3 -1.

The 1893/94 season was a poor one, with Rovers finishing 11th out of 12 teams, with only Mangotsfield below them in the League. Things improved in 1894/95, however, with a 6th-place finish. That season saw Rovers move to their fifth home, locating themselves at Ridgeway in the Fishponds area of the City.

On 22nd September 1894, the first meeting of the two teams that went on to become Bristol Rovers and Bristol City took place, when Bristol South End beat Eastville Rovers, 2–1, at St. John's Lane, Bedminster.

For the 1895/96 season the Bristol & District League renamed itself the Western League, and expanded to two divisions. Eastville Rovers were allocated two places in the League, one in the Division One for the First Team and one in Division Two for the Second XI. Rovers' first game in the Western League, like their first game in the Bristol & District League three years earlier, was against Mangotsfield. This time, however, the result was a win to Rovers, with the game finishing 4–0. Rovers ended the season tied for second place in the League with Staple Hill, and after a play-off game between them ended in a 2–2 draw, the teams were declared joint runners-up.

The 5th October 1895 saw their first appearance in the FA Cup, although this ended in a 2–0 defeat at the hands of Warmley, and on 25th January 1896 the first competitive match between Eastville Rovers and Bristol South End took place, with Rovers winning, 4–0, in the Gloucestershire Cup.

In the 1896/97 FA Cup, after having beaten Newbury and Bristol St. George, Rovers were drawn away to Royal Artillery Portsmouth. Rovers decided though that they had no hope of winning the game, and decided to save the travel expenses by withdrawing from the competition. During the 1896/97 season, Rovers purchased the Eastville ground from Bristol Harlequins Rugby club on 26th March 1897, and on 3rd April played their first game at the new ground against Aston Villa. That would remain their home for almost 100 years.

During the last few years of the 19th century, Eastville Rovers had gradually become known as Bristol Eastville Rovers, and on 7 February 1899 the club officially changed its name to Bristol Rovers.

When the newly renamed Bristol Rovers FC, joined the Southern League in 1899/00 they continued to put a First team in the Professional Sections of the League until it ceased after the 1908/09 season. In the meantime, a reserve team had played under the name of Eastville Rovers reserves from 1893 until 1898 and were then replaced by a Bristol Rovers reserve team in the 1898 season, coming in second place to Bristol East.

Such was the rivalry that spurred the club on, and for the next three seasons Rovers second string won their Western League Division on three consecutive occasions, only to be denied a fourth victory by City who ended on the same points but with a better goals average.

The Rovers Reserve's also won the Championship in 1928/9, 1935/36, 1936/37and 1945/46, before the club replaced the reserves with a Colts side.

GROUND BS3 2EJ

From 1898 to 1894 they played on Durdham Downs open pitch at BS9 1PG and then moved to Ridgeway, Fishponds, which was probably close to where Dominion Road meets Ridgeway Road. They then moved in 1897 to Eastville

Stadium, BS5 6XX known then at the Black Swan Ground, on Stapleton Road. The Black Swan pub was used as Rovers club office until 1920.

As Eastville Rovers 1892-97 Division One; 1897-98 Professional Section. As Bristol Eastville Rovers 1898-99. As Bristol Rovers 1899-1906 Division One; 1906-07 Division One Section A; 1907-09 Division One Section B. Eastville Rovers Reserves 1893-96. Bristol Rovers Reserves 1901-14 Division One; 1919-21 Division One; 1925-39 Division One; 1945-48 Division One. Bristol Rovers A 1934-39 Division Two; 1949-50 Division Three. Bristol Rovers Colts 1948-52 Division One; 1952-54 Division Two.

BRISTOL MANOR FARM FC

'The Farm' Established 1960

HISTORY

Bristol Manor Farm Football Club was formed in 1960 and joined the Western Football League Division One in 1977. In 1982/83 they won the First Division, three points clear of second placed Mangotsfield United, gaining promotion to the Premier Division. In the same year, the club entered the FA Cup for the first time and reached the Second Qualifying Round. The following season they reached the Fifth Round of the FA Vase. Farm were relegated in 2001, but soon returned after finishing third in 2003/04.

The 2011/12 season was the most successful in the history of the club, winning the GFA Challenge Trophy after beating Shortwood United 5-0 in a thrilling final. That was followed three days later with another Cup triumph, beating Willand Rovers in extra-time to lift the Toolstation League Les Phillips Cup.

The 2013/14 season saw an FA Cup run as the highlight of the season, putting nine goals past Oldland Abbotonians, and then seven past Lymington Town. The Corsham Town tie then ended in a 4-4 draw, winning the hard-fought replay, 1-0. Although that is as far as they went, scoring all those goals in the FA Cup brought the club to the attention of The Sun newspaper who had sent a photographer to take photos of the team with the FA Cup.

The club then continued to fight for top spot in the League and applied for promotion, but as runners-up were unsuccessful when Champions, Larkhall Athletic, were accepted into the Southern League instead. The second placed finish was the best in the club's history, and it also saw the team break the club record for the most goals scored in a season and the least goals conceded.

Season 2014/2015 was a season that the Farm targeted to gain promotion into the Southern league, but it was not to be again, finishing in a respectable fourth position and were only able to watch as Slimbridge gained that promotion place. They did, however, win the GFA County Challenge Trophy with a 2-0 win over local club Shirehampton.

In 2015/16, they got to the Quarter-Final of the FA Vase narrowly going out away at Morpeth Town after winning the previous round, again away, at Sunderland RCA. A third-place finish in the Western League, however, saw them just miss out on promotion to the Southern League again, but the GFA County Challenge Trophy was picked-up for the second time in succession with a record 9-2 win over Lydney Town.

GROUND BS9 2HS

Their current home at The Creek used to be the site of the Port of Bristol Authority Sports & Social Club, but Manor Farm took it over in 1965 when they moved to new premises, with a capacity of 2,000 spectators; 100 seated. The pitch at the Creek has always been notorious for its sloping surface but work has been undertaken in recent years to eliminate the slope. This caused the club many problems initially, but they now appear to have achieved their aim. With seating and floodlights added since 1980, the club now boasts excellent facilities alongside a spacious clubhouse.

1977-83 Division One; 1983-202 Premier Division;
2002-2004 Division One; 2004- Premier Division.

BRIXHAM UNITED FC

Established 1899

HISTORY
Brixham were an established local club when they took the big step of applying for the expanding Western League at a time when the Rothman's sponsorship had made it a very exciting place to be. It was, however, a very tough League in which they could not match the strength of the more established clubs. After five seasons of mid to low table positions in Division One, they left. The club was them reformed in June 2012, when Brixham United and Brixham Villa merged, two very successful football clubs with over 100 years of history combined, in the South Devon League. They now play in the South Western Peninsular League, Division One East.

GROUND TQ5 9UL

The club played at Wall Park Road, Brixham.

1976-81 Division One

BUCKLAND ATHLETIC F.C.

'The Bucks' Established 1977

HISTORY

Buckland started playing in the Torbay Pioneer League at Sandringham Park, before moving to the Senior Division Three of the Devon and Exeter Football League for the 1987/88 season. That year they moved to Coach Road and immediately gained promotion as Champions of Division Three. The club then moved grounds again to Decoy Park for the 1990/91 season, but two seasons later moved to Homers Lane in Kingsteignton, which later was renamed Homers Heath in honour of two faithful supporters who had passed-on. The move proved successful as they gained promotion to the Premier Division of the Devon and Exeter League, which they won in 1994/95, and went on to win the title in 1990/2000, allowing the club to gain promotion to the Devon County League.

They maintained membership of the Devon County League, with a best position of second in their debut season, until 2007 when they became Founder Members of the South West Peninsula League.

After finishing third in the 2008/09 season, they then went on to win the title twice in a row in the following two seasons. During their first Championship winning season the club also made their debut in the FA Cup, losing in a replay to Hamworthy United 3-2 at the County Ground.

After finishing as runners-up in the Peninsula, the club gained promotion straight into the Premier Division of the Western Football League, a successful move that saw Buckland knocking on the door of the Championship as runners-up in 2014/15, and fourth in both 2015/16 and 2016/17

GROUND TQ12 5JU

Buckland Athletic play at Homers Heath, Kingskerswell Road, Newton Abbot. Capacity 1,000

2013- Premier Division

CADBURY HEATH F.C.

'The Heathens' Established 1894

HISTORY

Cadbury Heath Football Club was formed in 1894. The club joined the Gloucestershire County League in 1968 as Founder Members. Between 1970 and 1974 they won the League on four successive occasions. After finishing runners-up in 1974/75, the 'Heathens' joined Midland Combination Division One, and reached the Quarter Finals of the FA Vase.

They rejoined the Gloucestershire County League in 1980/81, and after finishing runners-up in 1999/2000, joined Western League Division One, where they remained until the end of the 2011/12 season when they were promoted to the Premier Division as Champions. In the same year the club entered the FA Cup for the first time and reached the Second Qualifying Round.

GROUND BS30 8BX

Springfield, Cadbury Heath Road, Bristol. Capacity 2,000

2000-2012 Division One; 2012- Premier Division

The Lilywhites

CALNE TOWN F.C.

'The Lilywhites': Established 1886

HISTORY

Calne Town was founded in 1886. For the first few years they played friendlies, entering the Wiltshire Cup for the first time in 1891/92. Their first game in the Wiltshire League was in September 1884, when they beat Bradford Town 9-0.

At that time, Calne played in the centre of the town at the Recreation Ground, and amalgamated with Harris F.C. in 1920, to become Calne and Harris United F.C. The Harris in the name came from the bacon factory that dominated the skyline in the middle of Calne.

The name remained the same until the early 1960s when the original name of Calne Town was re-adopted, and the club relocated to Bremhill View, a

432

ground that is still home today.

Throughout the first hundred years of its existence Calne played in local Wiltshire leagues and enjoyed limited success, winning the Wiltshire Senior Cup in 1912/13 and 1984/85, Wiltshire County Division Two in 1979/80, and the League Senior KO Cup in 1984/85.

In 1985/86 a new committee was formed with the objective of bringing a higher standard of football to Bremhill View, and in 1986/87, the club's Centenary Year, their application to join the Western League was accepted.

With entry to the League a series of ground improvements were undertaken and further development work at the ground in 1991/92 saw the expansion of the social club to provide lounge as well as bar facilities.

Those further improvements were opportune as promotion to the Premier Division was earned after achieving runners-up spot in 1992/93, but there was a return to Division One some years later after a last place finish in 1998/99.

In 2005 Calne were promoted again, also becoming the First Division One club to reach the Les Phillips Cup Final; an achievement that was realised again in 2009, where they lost 2–1 to a late goal against Oldland Abbotonians.

They were relegated to Division One again at the end of the 2009/10 season, the same year that they won the Wiltshire FA Senior Cup by defeating Laverstock and Ford FC at Salisbury's RayMac Stadium. The Cup was won again in the season 2011/12, defeating holders Bemerton Heath Harlequins, 2–1, at Hardenhuish Park, Chippenham. The best season in the FA Cup was in 1997/98 reaching the Third-Qualifying round only to lose narrowly to Isthmian League side, Basingstoke Town.

GROUND SN11 9EE

Calne Town play their home games at Bremhill View, Calne, which has a capacity of 2,500 with seating for 150.

1986-96 Division One; 1993-99 Premier Division; 1999-2005 Division One; 2005-2010 Premier Division; 2010- Division One.

CAMERTON UNITED FC

Established pre-1891

HISTORY

The club played at Meadgate Recreation Ground, Camerton. The Camerton Inn, the HQ for the club, is now, we are told, an Indian restaurant. A ballot took place in 1909/10 for three places in the League. Clevedon, Weston-super-Mare and Camerton were successful, whilst Mardy, Gwn Albion, Tredegar and Combe Park were the unsuccessful clubs. For a small village, with even now a population in the region of 600, the village experienced some incredible matches. Cardiff City reserves were in contention with Bristol Rovers reserves all season to win the League, when they visited Camerton for an evening kick-off late in the season, with two matches remaining. Somerset passion won the evening, winning 3-1, leaving Cardiff as runners-up by two points. The next season Cardiff took their revenge by well and truly beating the plucky villagers.

1910-1914 Division One

GROUND BA2 0NQ

CARDIFF CITY FC Reserves

'The Bluebirds' Established 1899

HISTORY

A club called Cardiff FC played in the Western League during the 1895/96 season at Grange Athletic Ground, Ferry Road, Grangetown, Cardiff, a stadium that was demolished in 1927. They failed to pay fines and were expelled from the League that season; their record was expunged.

In 1912, Cardiff reserves, who had begun life as Riverside AFC changing their name in 1908, entered the League. They came in as runners-up that first year to Bristol Rovers reserves, and then won the title the following season by three points from Bath City. They then came as runners-up again after the war in 1920/21, on level points with Bristol City reserves, but with an inferior goal-average. Although they entered again for a couple of years in the 1930s, the same form could not be replicated, and they left to play in Wales after the 1935/36 season.

GROUND CF11 8SX

The club now play at Ninian Park, Cardiff

1912-1914 Division One; 1920-21 Division Two; 1932-33 Division One; 1934-36 Division One

CARDIFF CORINTHIANS FC

'Corries' Established 1898

HISTORY

Formed in 1898 after players from the Alpha Cricket Club decided to form a football team to keep in touch during the winter months, they had their base at Sophia Gardens, Cardiff, for the first six years and only played friendlies, but then joined the Rhymney Valley League. It was in Cup Competitions that the team made its mark, and in 1914 won the Welsh Amateur Cup, beating Holywell 1-0 at Newtown.

After WW1, the Corinthians played a series of friendly matches, the first British club to do so, against FC Barcelona, losing 4-0, 2-1 and 2-1, at the Plaza de Armas del Parque de la Cuidadela, where the Catalan Parliament now stands. The Club also took the bold step of joining the Professional Section of the Western League, but because travelling expenses were so high, left after the 1923/24 season to join the Welsh League. In1985 they won both the Welsh Premier Division and the Welsh Intermediate Cup. They now play in Welsh League Division Three

GROUND CF24 2RZ

Corinthians play at The Riverside Drive, County Road, Cardiff, formerly of Pengram Farm, Tremorfa; a ground that was built over in the 1930s to house an engineering works. The site is now an indoor climbing centre.

1920-1922 Division Two; 1922-24 Division One

CHARD TOWN

'The Robins', Est. 1920

HISTORY

Formed in 1920, the club originally played at Bonfire Close where they built a stand which they took with them a few years later when they moved to Zembard Lane; a ground that is well known for its slope from end to end of some 12ft. which was even greater in the early years, but a concerted effort saw earth transported from top to bottom to help alleviate the problem.

The club had a brief spell in the Somerset Senior League before joining the local Perry Street League where they played until 1949. From there they re-joined the Somerset Senior League and won the Championship at the first attempt in 1949/50; going on to win the title a further four times in 1953/54, 1959/60, 1967/68, and 1969/70. Chard also gained success in the Somerset Senior Cup during that period, which they won in 1952/53 and 1966/67.

The Somerset Senior League Cup was won in 1962, 1972 & 1976 when they were elected to join the Western League. After playing for seven years in Division One they gained promotion to the Premier Division as runners-up in season 1983/84. They spent three seasons in the higher flight before being relegated in 1987, when they immediately re-gained promotion again the following year. Further success came in the 1988/89 season when they were winners of the South West Counties Cup.

Chard then played at Premier Division level until being relegated in 1993, regaining their Premier Division status in 1995/96 by finishing runners-up to Bridgwater Town, only losing out on the title on goal difference. They were relegated at the end of the 1997/98 season by the narrow margin of one point, where they continued to play until gaining promotion, once again, in 2005/2006. After coming second from bottom in the 2008/2009 season, relegation followed.

GROUND TA20 1JL

Chard play at Zembard Lane with a present capacity of 1000 with seating for 50 and hardstanding on three sides. It is within the complex including the Tennis and Cricket Clubs and the entire area is known as Dening Sports Field. The whole area has been used for sport since the mid-1800s and is owned by the successors of Bass Brewery. At present, there is a long lease on the ground which will hopefully give the club the opportunity to move to a purpose-built ground at some time in the future.

1976-84 Division One; 1984-87 Premier Division; 1987-88 Division One; 1988-93 Premier Division; 1993-96 Division One; 1996-98 Premier Division; 1998-2006 Division One; 2006-2009 Premier Division; 2009-Division One

CHEDDAR A.F.C.

The 'Cheesemen' Established 1892

HISTORY

The club was established in 1892 and became Founder Members of the Cheddar Valley League in the early 1900s. They won the League in 1911 and after fifteen years joined the Weston and District League. Cheddar rejoined the Cheddar Valley League after the Second World War and won every competition they entered in 1948. This was repeated in 1950.

They later joined the Somerset County League. Finishing third in Division Two in 1988/89, they were promoted. However, relegation followed again at the end of the1992/93 season. In 1997/98, they again returned to Division One after another third-place finish, and after winning Division One in 2003/04, were promoted to the Premier Division. In 2011/12, they finished second in the Premier Division, and were promoted to the Western League.

GROUND BS27 3RL

Cheddar play their home games at Bowdens Park, Draycott Road, Cheddar

2012 – Division One

CHELSEA FC

'The Blues/Pensioners' Established 1905

HISTORY
Chelsea entered the Western League for just one year as a Subsidiary Competition in their first year of formation. They pitted their newly found team against Fulham, QPR, Brentford, Reading and Bristol Rovers, ending bottom of the small division, having won just two of their games.

GROUND SW6 1HS

The club play at Stamford Bridge, London

1906-07 Division One Section A

CHELTENHAM TOWN FC RESERVES

'The Rubies/Robins' Established 1887

HISTORY
Cheltenham was founded in 1887 by Albert Close White, a local teacher, and spent the first three decades in local football. In the early 1930s the club turned professional and joined the Birmingham Combination before joining the Southern League in 1935.

Their reserve team joined the Western League for two seasons after the Second World War, and competed in Division Two against reserve sides from Chippenham Town and Trowbridge Town. They came in third during the first season below Weymouth and Salisbury, who were both promoted. In their second, and last, season of competing they were runners-up to Chippenham United, who were six points ahead.

GROUND GL52 5NA

The club play at Whaddon Road, Cheltenham

1947-49 Division Two

CHIPPENHAM PARK F.C.

'Park' Established 2012

HISTORY

Formed in 2012 with the intention of following the guidelines based on the FA Pyramid of Football which aims to give youths a pathway in which to progress through to the English League System. Starting in a youth set-up that was already in place, the players could then progress to Under 18 level, then into a Western League standard team, with a view that the most talented could progress into Southern League football with Chippenham Town FC and beyond.

A Chippenham Park reserves side was also formed that year, and accepted into Wiltshire Football League Division One. They are known as FC Chippenham Youth.

The senior side began in the Wiltshire Football League Premier Division with a very solid first season, spending several week on' top of the League, but ultimately finished in third place. A top-five finish enabled the club's application for admission to the Western League to be considered, and on Friday 24th May 2013, the application was approved for Division One.

The 2013/14 season saw the club play in the FA Vase for the first time and ended their first year in the League in 10th place. This last season their finishing position was 8th.

GROUND SN14 6LR.

Chippenham Park play their home games at Hardenhuish Park, Bristol Road, Chippenham. The stadium has a capacity of 2,815 with seating for 260

2013- Division One

CHIPPENHAM TOWN FC

'The Bluebirds' Established 1873

HISTORY

The club was established in 1873. They joined the new Wiltshire League in 1901, and finished joint top of the table with Warminster Town, but lost the Championship play-off replay 1–0, following a 1–1 draw in the first match. They joined Division Two of the Western League in 1904, but also continued to play in the Wiltshire League. The 1904/05 season saw them finish bottom of the Western League and second in the Wiltshire League. At the end of the 1905/06 season the club withdrew from the Western League, and went on to win the Wiltshire League in 1907/08 and 1908/09, before finishing as runners-up in 1909/10. They were runners-up again in 1912/13, 1921/22 and 1922/23, before winning the League and every competition they entered in 1928/29.

In 1930 Chippenham rejoined Division Two of the Western League. The League was reduced to a single division in 1939, and the club were runners-up when the League resumed its programme in 1945/46 season. The 1951/52 season saw them win the Western League for the first and only time, and they also reached the First Round of the FA Cup for the first time, losing 3–0 at Leyton. They were Western League runners-up again in 1954/55. However, they left the Western League at the end of the 1964/65 season, dropping back into the Wiltshire League. In 1968 the club joined the Premier Division of the Hellenic League, where they played until rejoining the Western League in 1973.

When the League gained a second division in 1976, the club was relegated to the new Division One. They were Division One Champions in 1980/81, earning promotion to the Premier Division.

In 1999/2000 the club reached the Final of the FA Vase, eventually losing 1–0 to Deal Town in one of the last games to be held at the old Wembley Stadium.

After finishing as runners-up in 2000/01, Chippenham were promoted to Division One West of the Southern League. Their first season in the division saw them finish as runners-up, resulting in promotion to the Southern League Premier Division. In 2004/05 they were Premier Division runners-up, qualifying for the promotion play-offs. However, after beating Bedford Town 5–4 on penalties following a 2–2 draw in the semi-finals, they lost the final 1–0 to Hednesford Town to the only goal of the game with just nine minutes remaining.

The following season saw them reach the First Round Proper of the FA Cup for a second time, eventually losing 1–0 at Worcester City in a replay. They also qualified for the promotion play-offs again, after finishing fourth, beating King's Lynn 3–1 in the semi-finals before losing 3–2 to Bedford Town in the Final game. Another fourth-place finish in 2007/08 led to another play-off campaign, this time ending with a 2–1 defeat to Halesowen Town in the semi-finals. In 2009/10 the club finished third, and after beating Hednesford Town 2–0 in the play-off semi-finals, lost for the fourth year in the final game, 2–1 to Nuneaton Town.

GROUND SN14 6LR

The club play at Hardenhuish Park, Bristol Road, Chippenham in a stadium with seating for 250, and a capacity of 2,750

1904-06 Division Two; 1930-39 Division Two; 1939-40 Division One; 1945-65 Division One; 1973-76 Division One; 1976-81 First Division; 1981-2001 Premier Division. **Reserves** *1946-57 Division Two*

CHIPPENHAM UNITED F.C.

'The Firs' Established 1947

HISTORY

There was a club called Chippenham United that existed in the Town from 1895 until 1910 and who, ironically, were the first club to occupy Hardenhuish Park, that has been the home to Chippenham Town FC since 1919.

The United club who played in the Western League, however, was formed in July 1947, after an acrimonious split between officials at Chippenham Town over whether the club should turn professional. They were immediately accepted into the Wiltshire League for the 1947/48 season, and moved on to join Western League Division Two for the 1948/49 season, winning that Division at the first attempt, gaining promotion to join Chippenham Town Reserves in Division One.

The following season, they finished above their local rivals for what was to be the only time in the club's history. United's best Western League finish was in 1950/51, when they finished fourth, with Town one place above. The following seasons they were less successful, and they only escaped relegation in 1955/56 due to the expansion of Division One. However, the club was relegated in 1957/58 after finishing bottom. The club dropped out of the Western League at the end of the 1959/60 season when the Western League reverted to just one Division. The club disbanded a couple of years later.

Chippenham United entered the FA Cup throughout the late 1940s and 1950s. During their first Cup run in 1948/49 they defeated Radstock Town before losing 2-1 at home to Trowbridge Town in the Preliminary Round. The following season they reached the First Qualifying Round, losing 3–0 at Clandown. Their best efforts in The FA Cup were in 1953/54, when they reached the Fourth Qualifying Round, losing 3–1 at Newport (IOW); and 1955/56, when they defeated four clubs before losing 6–2 to Salisbury, again in the Fourth Qualifying Round. The club's last attempt in the competition was during the 1961/62 season just before they disbanded.

GROUND SN14 0EU.

Chippenham United played their games at The Firs, Hungerdown Lane, Chippenham. It is now a part of the Queens Crescent housing estate, with just a street name to remember them by.

1948-49 Division Two; 1949-58 Division One; 1958-60 Division Two. **Reserves** *1949-50 Division Three.*

CHIPPING SODBURY TOWN
FOOTBALL CLUB
FOUNDED 1885

CHIPPING SODBURY TOWN F.C.

'The Sods' Established 1885

HISTORY
The oldest printed record of the club can be found in an old GFA Handbook, on the same page as Bristol City, Bristol Rovers and Cheltenham Town. The club began playing in the Western League at a semi-pro level until they disbanded in 1954. A few years later, in 1959, a retired police officer by the name of Cliff Phelps started a local junior side in the Dursley and Wotton League, and as the team grew up they entered the Bristol and District League, in Division Three.

The early 90s saw the new clubhouse and changing rooms built by the committee and players. The first team climbed the league's, reaching the Bristol Combination, Division One in 1991, and in 1999 gained promotion to the Premier League, but were relegated in 2004, but were promoted back in 2006.

Sadly, John Bee passed away in 2007, after giving over 30 years of his life to the club, as player, manager and Chairman and is remembered by the Clubman of the Year Award being named in his honour.

The Gloucester County League beckoned in 2008, where successful seasons continued, and after finishing third in the Gloucestershire County League Premier Division in 2015, the club was promoted to the Western League, winning the 1st Division at the first attempt. The club currently have five teams competing; three men's, one women's and one under 18s Development squad.

GROUND BS37 6GA

The Ridings, Wickwar Road, Chipping Sodbury

1950-52 Division Two; 2015-16 Division One; Premier Division 2016-

CINDERFORD TOWN F.C.

'The Foresters' Established 1922

HISTORY

The modern club was formed in 1922, and joined the Gloucestershire Northern Senior League. They were runners-up in 1935/36 and 1937/38, before winning the League in 1938/39, subsequently joining the Bristol Charity League. After the war the club joined Division Two of the Western League, winning Division Two in 1956/57, however, they left at the end of the 1958/59 season to rejoin the Gloucestershire Northern Senior League where they were Champions in 1960/61 and runners-up for the following two seasons.

They joined the Western Division of the Warwickshire Combination in 1963, and were both League Cup winners and Western Division Champions in 1964/65, after which they moved to the Premier Division of the West Midlands (Regional) League. In 1968/69 the club reached the League Cup Final, drawing 1–1 with Kidderminster Harriers, with the League then declaring them joint winners. In 1969 the club transferred to the Gloucestershire County League, finishing as runners-up in their first season, and again in 1971/72 and 1973/74. In 1974 they joined Division One of the Midland Combination, which became the Premier Division in 1983. They won the League Cup in 1982/83, and then returned to the Gloucestershire County League at the end of the 1983/84 season.

In 1990 the club joined Division One of the Hellenic League, which they won at the first attempt, earning promotion to the Premier Division. After winning the Premier Division, the Premier Division Cup and the Floodlit Cup in 1994/95, the club were promoted to Division One South of the Southern League.

They were then transferred to the Division One Midlands in 1998, and back to the renamed Division One Western in 1999, moving back to the Division One Midlands in 2006, before returning to Division One South & West in two years later. In 2015/16 they won the division and were promoted to the Premier Division.

GROUND GL14 2QH

The Causeway Ground, Cinderford has a capacity for 3,500 with 250 seated.

1945-57 Division Two; 1957-59 Division One

CLANDOWN F.C.

'The Down' Established 1875

HISTORY

Clandown were formed in 1875 and joined Division Two of the Western League in 1920/21, leaving after winning the division the following year. They rejoined immediately after the Second World War and remained in the League until 1959/60. They were Division Two Champions in 1946/47 and were promoted to Division One, but little success followed, and they were relegated in 1954; remaining in Division Two until 1959/60, when they joined the Wiltshire Premier League.

They rejoined the Western League in 1976/77 and won promotion to the Premier Division the following season. Their best seasons were 1981/82 and 1982/83, with fourth-place finishes. However, in 1987/88 they finished bottom and were relegated to Division One, where they remained for a further four seasons before resigning in 1992, when they replaced their reserve team in the Somerset Senior League. After 12 seasons with little success, the club folded at the end of 2003/04.

GROUND BA3 3DR

The club played at Tynne Field, Clandown, north east of the village. It still exists in outline, although all the structures have been demolished and it lies derelict.

1920-22 Division Two; 1945-46 Division One; 1946-47 Division Two; 1947-60 Division One; 1976-78 Division One; 1978-88 Premier Division; 1988-92 Division One

CLEVEDON TOWN FC

'The Seasiders', Established 1880

HISTORY

Clevedon Town FC are one of the oldest clubs in the West Country. They were Founder Members of the Western League in 1892, although their stay only lasted three seasons. After dropping back into local football, they re-joined the Western League in the 1910/11 season. They initially played at Dial Hill, still the home of the local cricket club, but moved to a new site at Old Street, which was later renamed Teignmouth Road in 1895, where they remained until 1992.

After the First World War, they played in both the Bristol & District League and the Bristol & Suburban League, before a switch to the Somerset Senior

League in the early 1930s, where they remained until World War Two. After the War the club again returned to the Western League and also made their debut in the FA Cup for the 1945/46 season.

The club became better known for their runs in the FA Amateur Cup, reaching the rounds proper no less than eight times in 13 years. That Cup success, however, was not matched in the League, and Clevedon spent several years in Division Two before resigning for financial reasons at the end of 1957/58.

For the next fifteen years the club once again played in the Bristol & District League, before finally rejoining the Western League in 1973/74 after a merger with Ashtonians United, who were already members of that League.

The building of a new clubhouse and the installation of floodlights in the early 1980s nearly bankrupted the club, but things began to change when the club decided to sell their Teignmouth Road ground and move to a new site at Davis Lane on the edge of the town.

It was through the dedication of the Hand family over generations, that stretched back to the 1890s when Herbie Hand became Secretary just 15 years after the club was formed, that the move was possible. Bill Hand followed in his father's footsteps when he too became Secretary, and it was he who negotiated the purchase of the Teignmouth Road ground for £450 back in 1949, using his own house as security. His foresight enabled them to sell off the ground, pay off their remaining debts, and build a purpose-built stadium from the proceeds, much to the delight of Doug Hand, the club President until 1995, who had served the club for 50 years; Doug sadly passed away in November 2013 at the grand old age of 92.

In their first season at their new home in 1992/93, the club gained promotion to the Southern League for the first time. Promotion to the Premier Division followed in 1998, and although Town were relegated again in 2000/01, the 2005/06 season saw them win Division One West to return to the top flight. In 2006 they reached the first round proper of the FA Cup but went down 4–1 to Football League opposition Chester City.

GROUND BS21 6TG

Clevedon Town play at the Everyone Active Stadium, (The Hand Stadium), Davis Lane, Clevedon, which has a capacity of 3,900 with seating for 1,900.

As Clevedon, 1892-95 Division One; 1910-14 Division Two; 1945-49 Division One; 1949-58 Division Two; 1974-76 Division One. 1976-77 Premier Division; As Clevedon Town, 1977-93 Premier Division. Clevedon Reserves, 1949-50 Division Three

CLEVEDON UNITED F.C.

Established 1974

HISTORY

Clevedon United was formed in the early 1970s as a merger between Clevedon Sports AFC and Tickenham United. After years in the Somerset County League, they achieved promotion to the Western Football League Division One after a 3rd place finish in the 2002/03 season. They remained members of Division One until 2010.

Playing at the Hand Stadium enabled them to enter National Competitions, with their best progressions, the Second Round Qualifying of the FA Cup in 2003/04 and the Second Round Proper of the FA Vase in 2000/01. They left the Hand Stadium in 2010 to play at Colderidge Vale and left the Western League.

GROUND BS21 6NS

The club play at Colderidge Vale, Clevedon.

2003-2010 Division One

CLIFTON (ASSOCIATION) F.C.

Established 1883

HISTORY

Clifton Association Football Club, later known as Clifton Football Club, was based in the Clifton area of Bristol and was a Founder Member of the Western League (then called the Bristol and District League) in 1892. The club was also instrumental in the creation of the Gloucestershire Cup competition in 1888.

In 1893 the word *Association* was dropped from their name, which became Clifton. The club resigned from the League shortly after the start of the 1897/98 season, and its record was expunged. They folded in 1914.

GROUND BS15 1TF

The club initially played at the County Ground at Neville Road before moving to the Chequers, Kingswood at the start of 1892/93, which is now Britton Gardens housing estate. They moved to Westbury-on-Trym in 1897

1892-97 Division One; 1897-98 Amateur Division One

CLYST ROVERS F.C.
'The Rovers' Established 1951

HISTORY

The club joined the South Western League in 1981, and played there until the 1991/92 season, after which they joined the Western League. They were forced to resign from the League near the end of the 2000/01 season, but successfully re-applied for their spot in Division One the following season. Promotion to the Premier Division was finally achieved following a 4th-place finish in 2003/04, but the club went straight back down after finishing bottom. They remained members of Division One of the Western League until 2007, when they left to join the new South West Peninsula League Premier Division. They resigned from that League in 2009/10 and their record was expunged.

GROUND EX5 2DS

Waterslade Park, Clyst Honiton; a now derelict ground that is situated between Cyst Honiton by-pass and Exeter Airport.

1992-2004 Division One; 2004-2005 Premier Division; 2005-2007 Division One

COLEFORD ATHLETIC F.C.
Established 1890

HISTORY

Coleford Athletic Football Club was formed in 1890. They participated in the Western League for three seasons, coming runners-up to Clandown in 1921/22, but came bottom in the both years they re-joined as members in 1930/31 and 1931/32. In the FA Cup the team won away in the Extra Preliminary Round to Somerton Amateurs, 4-0, in 1948/49, but lost at home to Clandown 1-4 in the Prelim Round. In 1949/50, in the Extra Prelim, they lost at home to Swindon Victoria 2-5, and in 1950/51 they lost 6-0 at the Firs, home of Chippenham United in the Extra Prelim Round.

The club now plays in the Mid Somerset Football League and is run by an enthusiastic set of local supporters.

GROUND BA3 5NT

The club play at Highbury Playing Fields Highbury Street, Coleford, Radstock, behind the Eagle Inn.

1921-22 Division Two; 1930-32 Division Two

CORSHAM TOWN FC

'The Peacocks' Established 1884

HISTORY

Corsham Town was founded in 1884 and affiliated to the Football Association in 1893. The club had to wait just over sixty years before its first success; the Wilts Junior Cup in 1946/47. Four seasons later they entered the FA Cup for the first time making it to the First Qualifying Round that season. In the 1960/61 season, they won their second honour, winning Wiltshire League Division Two.

In 1976 Corsham became Founding Members of the Wiltshire Football League, when the Wiltshire Combination and Wiltshire Leagues were amalgamated, starting in Division Two. During their first season, they won the Wiltshire Senior Cup, and were promoted to the top division in the League.

The club then spent time being relegated and promoted between the top two divisions, and did not achieve any more silverware until winning the Addkey Senior Cup in 1995/96. The first Championship followed in 1997/98, also winning the Addkey Senior Cup again, along with the Wilts Senior Cup. The following season they were accepted into the Western League, and then entered the FA Vase in 2001/02 season for the first time, and a season afterwards entered the FA Cup, after a gap of 49 years since they last played in the competition in the 1950s.

After spending six years in Western League Division One, they were promoted to the Premier Division in 2004 after finishing fifth. That season also saw ground improvement with floodlights being installed and a stand built. They finished runners-up to Bideford in their first two seasons in the Western League's top division, and were crowned as Champions for the 2006/07 season, winning the division by two points from Bridgwater Town. For financial reasons Corsham were unable to gain promotion to the Southern League, and they then remained in the Premier Division until 2011/12 season where, on finishing 18th, they were relegated back into Division One.

GROUND SN13 9HS.

Corsham Town play their home games at Southbank Ground, Lacock Road, Corsham, which has a capacity of 1,200 with seating for 112.

1998-2004 Division One; 2004-2012 Premier Division. 2012- Division One.

COTHAM/COTHAM AMATEURS F.C.

Established 1890

HISTORY

Cotham joined the League when it changed its format and split into a Professional Section and two Amateur Division's. In their first year, they came in as runners-up to Hanham, winning eight games in a division with just six clubs. When the Amateur Divisions were amalgamated the following season, they found the challenge too great, winning just two of the fourteen games played. Between 1899-1903 they came bottom on four of the five occasions, winning just six games in total with three of those in 1900/01 season, enabling a mid-table finish, below Bristol East, Rovers Reserves, Paulton Rovers and Staple Hill.

GROUND BS7 0BW

The club played at Horfield Court Farm, now an ATS Tyre Centre, and moved to the Chequers Field, behind the Chequers Public House, in 1899/00.

*As **Cotham**, 1897-98 Amateur Division Two; 1898-99 Division Two (Amateur); 1898-99 Division Two. **As Cotham Amateurs**, 1899-1901 Division Two.*

CREDITON UNITED A.F.C.

'The Kryton/Creddy' Established 1910

HISTORY

After spending eighty-years in local football, latterly the Devon & Exeter League, Crediton United joined the Western League in 1990. After two successive third-place finishes in Division One, they were promoted to the Premier Division, which was the highest level they had reached.

After six seasons, Crediton were relegated back into Division One, and two years later the club voluntarily dropped down another level into the Devon County League, where they remained until 2007, when they joined the South West Peninsula League Division One East.

During their period in the Western League, the club entered the FA Vase on seven occasions, with the best performances coming in the first two seasons, 1991/92 and 1992/93, when on each occasion they reached the First Round Proper. The team failed to win a tie on each of their last four appearances in the Competition.

GROUND EX17 1ER

Crediton United play their home games at Lords Meadow Sports Centre, Crediton

1990-93 Division One; 1993-96 Premier Division; 1996-98 Division One

CRIBBS FRIENDS LIFE/CRIBBS FC

'Cribbs' Established 1958

HISTORY

Cribbs Football Club was established in 1976 when Sun Life first relocated to Bristol from London. Initially, two teams were run, participating in the Bristol and Avon League, playing at Dundridge Farm. However, when the Cribbs Causeway ground was opened in 1978, the first team were promoted straight into the Avon Premier Combination League, which was later renamed the Bristol Premier Combination, where they stayed for 20 years until they eventually won promotion to the County League in 1999/2000.

In the summer of 2011, the club changed from AXA to its new name of Cribbs Friends Life FC ready for the 2011/12 season, which was to be the clubs most successful season to date, when they claimed their first Gloucestershire County League title. They also completed a League and Cup double, later adding the Les James League Cup to the League Championship. As well as winning the double, the club was promotion to the Western League Division One for the 2012/13 season as League Champions. To add further to their success their Reserve and 'A' sides also gained promotion.

In 2013, Cribbs Friends Life F.C. changed their name to Cribbs F.C. after losing the backing of their sponsors.

GROUND BS10 7TB

Cribbs play their home matches at The Lawns, Station Road, Henbury, Bristol. It has capacity for 1,000 spectators with 50 seated.

2012- Division One

CROYDON COMMON F.C.

'The Robins' Established 1897

HISTORY

Croydon Common was formed in 1897 as an amateur church team competing in local leagues. They turned professional in 1907, joining the Southern League Second Division. A final place of third was achieved despite the stand at the Crescent being burnt down.

A move was made to the Nest (future home of Crystal Palace) in 1908, where promotion to the Southern League First Division was achieved, and they also played in the Western League to supplement those games. In the FA Cup, Football League members, Bradford Park Avenue were beaten, and Woolwich Arsenal were taken to a replay before their final defeat.

An immediate return was made to the Second Division after finishing second from bottom. In 1917 the club was finally wound up.

GROUND SE25 6LJ

The club played at The Nest, which was to be the future home of Crystal Palace FC. It is now under the railway depot at Selhurst.

1908-09 Division One Section A

CRYSTAL PALACE FC

'The Eagles/Glaziers' Established 1905

HISTORY

In 1895, the Football Association had found a new permanent home for the FA Cup Final at the site of the famous Crystal Palace Exhibition building. Some years later the owners of the attraction, who were reliant on tourist activity for their income, sought fresh attractions for the venue, and decided to form their own football team to play at the Palace stadium. There had been an amateur Crystal Palace team as early as 1861, which was formed by workers from the exhibition building, but they had disappeared from historical records around 1876. The owners of the venue wanted a professional club to play there, to tap into the vast crowd potential of the area.

Crystal Palace Football Club, originally nicknamed 'The Glaziers', was formed on 10th September 1905, under the guidance of Aston Villa assistant secretary Edmund Goodman. The club applied to enter the Football League alongside Chelsea and Southampton, but was the only unsuccessful club. Instead, the club found itself in the Southern League, Second Division, for the 1905/06 season. That inaugural season was successful and they were promoted to the First Division as Champions. In their first season Crystal Palace also played in the mid-week United Counties League, and later played in the Professional Section of the Western League before it was disbanded.

GROUND SE19 6LJ

The club played at The Crystal Palace Sports Arena, London

1907-08 Division One Section B; 1908-09 Division One Section A

CUMBERLAND F.C.

Established 1883

HISTORY

The club was formed as a section of the existing cricket club to provide sport in the winter months, and played one season in the Western League, coming in just below mid-table, having won seven of their eighteen games played.

GROUND BS3 2JT

The club played at Bower Ashton, Bristol, an area now used by Bedminster Cricket Club.

1895-96 Division Two

DAWLISH TOWN FC

'The Seasiders' Established 1889

HISTORY

The club was formed in 1889 as Dawlish Argyle, but the Argyle was dropped many years ago, and the name 'Town' was added in recent years to distinguish the club from other local teams. In the early years, they played at two different locations before moving to Sandy Lane midway through the 20th century. Originally, there was only one team, but the club added another side around the same time, and in 1950, Dawlish introduced a third team into junior football. One of the earliest recorded honours was in season 1931/32 when the club lifted the East Devon Senior Cup. In 1960, Dawlish became East Devon Champions, but the best season at that level was in 1972/73, when they won every competition they entered; a total of seven trophies in all.

The club joined the Western League in 1973, installed floodlights in 1987, and new changing rooms were added in 1989/90.

In May 1996, Dawlish won the inaugural Carlsberg Pub Cup Competition Final at Wembley Stadium 4-2, on penalties, and a second visit to Wembley followed, on the 22nd September 1996, when they played Dutch Carlsberg Champions, Brigade Bodega, in the first Carlsberg European Pub Cup Championship; losing the encounter after conceding the only goal of the game late on.

In season 1998/99 Dawlish regained their Premier Division place after finishing as runners-up in the First Division, but were again relegated in 2003/4 only to bounce back two seasons later as First Division Champions, eight points ahead of Chard Town. Two seasons later they picked up both the Les Phillips Cup and the Devon St. Luke's Bowl, and finished in their highest ever League position as Premier Division runners-up behind big-spending, Truro City.

Season 2008/09 saw the 1st team have an unbeaten start to the season, eventually finishing the year in third place, and a year later they reached the FA Vase Fifth round, being defeated by Gresley Town in a replay at the Moat Ground after two battling legs of football. The club left the Western League on July 23, 2011.

GROUND EX7 0AF

Sandy Lane, Dawlish

As Dawlish 1973-76 Division One; 1976-80 Premier Division. As Dawlish Town 1980-83 Premier Division; 1993-99 Division One; 199-2004 Premier Division; 2004-06 Division One; 2006-2011 Premier Division

DEVIZES TOWN

'The Town' Established 1884

HISTORY

Devizes Town FC was formed by the members of Southbroom Cricket Club as a winter activity in 1884, as Southbroom Football Club. In 1898 Southbroom and other smaller clubs amalgamated to form Devizes Town Football Club. The new club leased a playing field in Quakers Walk, and in their first season won the Wiltshire League as well as reaching the First-Round Proper of the FA Amateur Cup, and the Wiltshire Cup Final.

After the Second World War the club moved to Nursteed Road, having been offered a free 21-year lease on the ground.

In the 1961/62 season the club won the County Senior Cup, the Premier League Championship and the League Subsidiary Cup.

In 1965 the club purchased the Nursteed Road Ground, and in 1967 joined the Western League. In the 1972/73 the club won both the Western League Championship and the Subsidiary Cup. They stayed in the top division for a further three years, but were then relegated to Division One. For four season's the club remained in that division, but returned to Western League Premier as Division One runners-up, in 1979/80.

The 1980/81 season saw the club reach the Quarter-Finals of the FA Vase, losing to the eventual winners Wickham, 3-0. With the resignation of their manager in 1984, the club was relegated back to the First Division, but then regained Premier membership in 1999/00 as Division One title winners; only to be relegated, once again, in 2008/09, where they have since remained.

GROUND SN10 3DX

Nursteed Road, Devizes

1967-76 Division One; 1976-80 Division One; 1980-1985 Premier Division; 1985-2000 Division One; 2000-09 Premier Division; 2009- Division One

DORCHESTER TOWN F.C.

'The Magpies' Established 1880

HISTORY

Founded in 1880, Dorchester Town were Dorset Senior Cup finalists in 1888 and 1890, before joining the Dorset League in 1896. Despite being Founder Members of the League, the club had little success before winning the Championship in 1937/38.

The club joined the Western League in 1947, winning promotion from Division Two in 1950, and going on to take the League Championship in 1954/55. The fifties proved to be a successful decade for the Magpies, winning the Dorset Senior Cup for the first time, and having several good runs in the FA Cup, facing the likes of Norwich City, Queens Park Rangers, Port Vale and Plymouth Argyle. In 1954, Dorchester reached the 2nd Round before eventually losing out to York City in front of 5,500 fans at the old Avenue ground, in the season where York went on to reach the semi-finals.

Following four more victories in the Dorset Senior Cup, the club entered the Southern League, Division One South, in 1972. The formation of the Alliance League (now the Vanarama National League) unfortunately meant the Magpies ended up back in the reformed Southern Division a year later, but the club celebrated its Centenary by winning the Southern Division in 1979/80 by a one-point margin over Aylesbury

Relegated at the end of the 1983/84 season following a severe financial crisis, the club only just avoided dropping out of the League altogether the following year. The Club then returned to the Premier Division as Champions at the end of the 1986/87 season.

The following years saw a see-saw of promotion and relegations and today the community-run club is competing in the Southern League.

GROUND DT1 2RY

The club play at The Avenue Ground, Weymouth Road, Dorchester which has a capacity of 5,229 with 710 seated. This is the third ground they have occupied in the area with the original one now the site of a retail park.

1947-50 Division Two; 1950-72 Division One.
***Dorchester Reserves**, 1957-60 Division Two*

DOUGLAS F.C.

Established 1903

HISTORY

Douglas F.C. were a works team from the Douglas Motorcycle Factory, Kingswood, which later produced the Vespa scooter under license. The club was formed in 1903, and joined the Western Football League Division One in 1919–20, winning the title in their first season. However, they left the League soon after, and did not rejoin until the 1945/46 season, by which time they had been taken over by BAC (1935), a company that already had both a senior and reserve team in the Western League. After finishing bottom of Division Two in 1949/50, the club, which was affiliated to the Gloucestershire County FA, left the League, but still exist today as Bendix FC, members of the Bristol and District Football League.

GROUND BS15 8JN

The club played at Wood Road, Kingswood; a ground that was later used by both Bristol City and Bristol Rovers Colts sides in the Western League. The ground is now covered by the houses in Barter Road.

1919-21 Division One; 1945-50 Division One

EASTLEIGH ATHLETIC F.C.

Established 1885

HISTORY

The club was formed by the London and South-Western Railway works that were situated in Eastleigh and played in the Western League in 1897/98. They continued playing in various guises, which included Southern Railway Eastleigh Athletic, Eastleigh Athletic, and the British Rail Staff Association, until 1977.

GROUND SO50 6AB

They played at Dutton Lane, but the site is now a railway siding at the north end of Eastleigh Yard. It was 200 yards further down than the end of Dutton Lane today.

1897-98 Professional Section

EASTVILLE WANDERERS F.C.

Established 1894

HISTORY

Eastville Rovers played at the old Rovers Ground near Eastville Park at a time when football was generating numerous clubs in the area. They joined the League in 1895 but eventually withdrew during the 1897/98 season and their record was erased.

GROUND

The club played at Mr Lait's field near Eastville Park; a ground sometimes referred to as Bristol Rovers old ground.

1895-97 Division Two; 1897-98 Amateur Division One. Eastville Reserves 1897-98 Amateur Division Two.

ELMORE F.C.

'The Eagles' Established 1947

HISTORY

The club was founded in 1947 as the Elmore Sports Club to provide sporting and social facilities for the people of Tiverton. In its early years, it was forced to continually move premises, and in 1958 a major decision to purchase land was made. The raising of funds for such a project was an immense undertaking by the membership, and resulted in the purchase of a piece of land called Slaughterhouse Field.

Now renamed Horsdon Park, this remains today the cornerstone of the club, and the firm base for their football and social club sections.

Since moving to Horsdon, the members have continued to improve the facilities, with a purpose-built grandstand incorporating changing facilities fitted to the highest standard in 1983, the refurbishment of clubhouse in 1994 and new floodlights in 2012.

Elmore joined the South Western League in 1974, playing there for four years before gaining admittance to the Western League. The club spent more than a decade languishing near the bottom of Division One, but finally a runners-up performance in 1990/91 enabled promotion to the top flight of the League. In the 1994/95 season, they reached the 4th round of the FA Vase, as well as claiming a runner-up spot in the Premier Division. However, the club's fortunes declined following that successful season, and Elmore returned to Division One after a last-place finish in 2003/04.

Elmore transferred to the SW Peninsula League after the 2012/13 season, but resigned early in the 2014/15 season. The first team then took the reserves' place in the Devon & Exeter Football League Premier Division.

STADIUM EX16 4DB

The club play at Horsdon Park, Heathcoat Way, Tiverton, with a stadium capacity of 2,000.

1978-91 Division One; 1991-2004 Premier Division;
2004 - 2013 Division One.

EXETER CITY Reserves FC

'The Grecians' Established 1904

HISTORY
Exeter City was formed from two clubs, Exeter United F.C. and St Sidwell's United. Exeter United was a football club from Exeter, Devon, that played between 1890 and 1904. In 1904, Exeter United lost 3–1 to local rivals St Sidwell's United and after the match it was agreed that the two clubs should become one. The new team took the name 'Exeter City' and continued to play at Exeter United's ground, St James Park, where Exeter City still play today. They turned professional in 1908 and first entered a reserve team in the Western League after the First World War in 1920.

GROUND EX4 6PX

Exeter play at St James Park, Exeter, which has a capacity of 8,541 with 3,000 seated.

1920-21 Division One; 1925-35 Division One; 1960-61 Division One; 1962-67 Division One; 1972-74 Division One; 1975-76 Division One; 1976-80 Premier Division.

EXMOUTH TOWN F.C.

'The Town' Established 1933

HISTORY
The club was formed in 1933, and played their first forty years of existence in local football, primarily in the Devon and Exeter Football League.

In 1954 the club moved from their original home of the Maer Cricket Field, to their current home at Southern Road.

They joined the Western League in 1973. At the end of their second season they finished bottom and were relegated to the newly formed Division One for the 1976/77 season. Six seasons later the club achieved promotion into the Premier Division where they finished as runners-up in 1981/82. Two seasons later they won the League title, and then repeated that success in the 1985/86 campaign.

In between their two League title successes, the club made it to the FA Vase semi-finals, where they missed out on a trip to Wembley Stadium, losing to Fleetwood Town 4–3 on aggregate.

Exmouth Town remained in the Premier Division until the 1993/94 season, when finishing second from bottom, they were relegated to Division One. The club gained promotion back into the Premier Division in 2002/03 after finishing as runners-up to Torrington.

In January 2006, the club withdrew from the League due to financial problems, and seven months later was reformed as Exmouth Town (2006) AFC; taking over the reserve teams place in the Devon & Exeter League.

In 2007, the club became one of the Founder Members of the South West Peninsula League, joining Division One East.

The 2012-13 season then saw the club win the Division One East title and the Devon Premier Cup.

GROUND EX8 3EE

Exmouth Town play their home games at King George V Ground, Southern Road, Exmouth, Devon. Capacity of 2,500 with 100 seated

1973-82 Division One; 1982-94 Premier Division; 1994-2003 Division One; 2003-06 Premier Division.

FALMOUTH TOWN FC

'The Ambers' Established 1949

HISTORY

Falmouth Town joined the Cornwall Senior League in 1950, and became a Founder Member of the South-Western League in 1951/52. After an interim two seasons playing at Union Corner, the opening game at Bickland Park, which had been purchased by Shell Mex & BP, was played against Cornwall in 1957, and the club won its first piece of silverware, the South-Western League Cup, without conceding a goal during the competition.

The Cup was retained the following year, beating Truro City 6–3 in the Final, and in 1961/62 they picked up their first South Western League title, as well as the League Cup and the Cornwall Senior Cup. The next season they reached the First-Round Proper of the FA Cup, losing 2-1, in front of 8,000 to Oxford United.

In 1967/68, a second domestic treble was achieved, which was then repeated in 1970/71, without losing a single match in all three competitions. The club then went on to dominate the League, winning the treble again at the end of the 1973/74 season, before joining the Western League. In their first season in they completed the League and Cup double without losing a match, and three more consecutive Western League titles were then won, making it eight Championships in a row.

After spending nine seasons in the Western League they withdrew to join the Cornwall Combination Football League after their application to rejoin the South-Western League had been refused by member clubs. They then won the Combination League, and rejoined the South-Western League for the start of the 1984/85 season, picking up the Championship for the eighth time, with further Championship titles then added in 1986/87, 1988/89 and 1989/90. The 1999/00 season saw Falmouth win the title for the fourteenth time; also, winning the Durning Lawrence Cornwall Charity Cup.

The club then spent the next few years in the Premier Division of the South-Western League, before becoming Founder Members of South West Peninsula League Premier Division, where they still compete.

GROUND TR11 4PB

The club plays at Bickland Park, Bickland Water Road, Falmouth, Cornwall. It has a capacity of 3,572, with 500 seats

1974-76 Division One; 1976-1983 Premier Division.

FISHPONDS F.C.

Established 1889

HISTORY

A team from the Fishponds area of Bristol joined the League the first season that it changed its name from that of the Bristol and District League to the Western League, and initially came in as runners-up in Division Two below Barton Hill. They were competing in a section of the League with all competing clubs from other areas of the City.

Two seasons later the League, faced by competition from the many other leagues that were springing up, introduced a Professional section and two Amateur divisions, encouraging the smaller clubs to put in a reserve side alongside a senior team. That only happened for the one season in 1897/98, after which time Fishponds continued to compete in the new streamlined Division Two, coming in as runners-up, just a point behind Staple Hill in,1898/99. Two seasons later, however, they won just one of the twelve games played, and then had those two points deducted for fielding an ineligible player. Without one single point to their credit, they then left to join the Bristol and District League.

GROUND BS16 3BA

The club played at the rear of the Golden Lion Pub, Fishponds; a ground that is now covered by the extension to Alexandra Park.

1895-97 Division Two; 1897-98 Amateur Division One; 1898-99 Division Two (Amateur); 1899-1901 Division Two. Fishpond Reserves,1897-98 Amateur Division Two.

458

FRENCHAY F.C.

Established around 1889

HISTORY

The club took part in the League in the first year that the League had changed its name to the Western League, but failed to complete the season and their record was deleted.

GROUND

The club played at Dees Field, Frenchay, and held their functions at Frenchay School.

1895-96 Division Two.

FROME TOWN F.C.

'The Robins' Established 1904

HISTORY

The club was founded in 1904, and started playing in the Wiltshire Premier League at their home ground of Badgers Hill. In seasons 1906/07, 1908/09 and 1910/11, they won the Somerset Senior League Championship, and won the Wiltshire League title in the 1909/10 season. After the league successes, the club made its debut in the FA Cup in 1911/12, reaching the Fifth-Qualifying Round before losing, 4–1, to Southport Central.

Joining Division Two of the Western League in the 1919/20, they won the division at their first attempt, and continued in and out of the League until the Second World War, while also competing in the Somerset Senior Cup, winning that in 1932/22 and 1933/34.

After the war, the club rejoined the Western League at the beginning of the 1946/47 season and played its first FA cup game for 35 years. The 1953/54 season saw the club reach the First round of the FA Cup, where they were defeated by Football League club, Leyton Orient, in front of a record crowd of 8,000.

The club once again joined the Western League in 1963/64, and spent the next 32 seasons in the top division, during which time they went on to become Champions once, in 1978/79. They also experienced Cup success during that time, winning the Somerset Premier Cup three times in 1966/67, 1968/69 and 1982/83, as well as winning the Western League Cup twice, and the Western Counties Floodlit Cup once.

At the end of 1999/2000, the club finished bottom of Division One, but were spared relegation, and two seasons later Frome were Division One Champions, and were promoted back to the Premier Division.

At the end of the 2008/09 season the club finished as runners-up in the Premier Division, and secured promotion to the Southern Football League, Division One-South & West, The club also achieved Cup success that season when they beat Paulton Rovers, 3–1, to win the Somerset Premier Cup. Since that time Frome have been members of the Premier Division of the Southern League.

GROUND

The club play at Badgers Hill, now known as the 'Special Effects' Stadium, Frome. It has a capacity for 3,000 with seating for 500.

1921-22 Division Two; 1924-25 Division One; 1925-27 Division Two; 1931-39 Division Two; 1946-47 Division One; 1947-55 Division Two; 1955-59 Division One; 1959-60 Division Two; 1963-76 Division One; 1976-1996 Premier Division; 1996-2002 Division One; 2002-2009 Premier Division.

FULHAM F.C.

The Cottagers; Established 1897

HISTORY

Fulham were formed in 1879 as Fulham St Andrew's Church Sunday School FC, founded by worshipers who were mostly adept at cricket. They won the West London Amateur Cup in 1887, and having shortened the name from Fulham Excelsior to its present form in 1888, won the West London League in 1893 at the first attempt.

Fulham started playing at their current ground at Craven Cottage in 1896, and gained professional status on 12 December 1898, the same year that they were admitted into the Southern League's Second Division. They were the second club from London to turn professional, following Arsenal, then named Royal Arsenal 1891. In 1902/03, the club won promotion to the Southern League First Division, winning it twice, in 1905/06 and 1906/07.

The club initially took part in the Western League during this time, and played against ten other professional clubs from London and the West of England, who used the League as a Subsidiary Competition. In 1906/07 Fulham won their section by four points over QPR, but lost the play-off Final to West Ham United by the only goal of the game.

GROUND SW6 6HH

The club play at Craven Cottage, London with a capacity for 27,500.

1904-06 Division One; 1906-07 Division One Section A

GILLINGHAM TOWN F.C.

'The Gills' Established 1879

HISTORY

Founded on 14 November 1879, the club is the oldest in Dorset, and joined the Dorset Combination in 1970. The League was later renamed the Dorset Premier, and Gillingham finished runners-up in 2002/03. They repeated that in 2007/08 and gained promotion to the Western Football League Division One. They won the Dorset Senior Cup in 2009/10, beating Wimborne Town, 2–1, after extra-time in the Final, which was held on 13 April 2010. The club was promoted to the Premier Division in 2011/12 after finishing third behind Melksham Town and Cadbury Heath. In their first two years of Premier Division membership they achieved third place each season.

During the 2016/17 season, the club announced its intention to concentrate resources on ensuring that their new ground was completed as quickly as possible and to build a financial hub/community centre, that, once built, would help fund and secure football in Gillingham for generations to come. Their eye was to the future with both Western League and then Southern League Membership their aim.

GROUND SP8 4HX

Gillingham Town play at Hadings Lane, Gillingham which has a capacity of 1,500.

2008-12 Division One; 2012-2017 Premier Division

GLASTONBURY F.C.

'The Dollies' Established 1890

HISTORY

The club was founded in 1890, and was originally called Glastonbury Avalon Rovers. They entered the FA Cup for the first time in the 1902/03 season, by which time they had changed their name to Glastonbury, and won the Somerset Football League in 1904/05 and 1912/13. They also won the Somerset Junior Cup 1912/13, and retained it the following season.

After the First World War, the club joined Division Two of the Western League for the 1919/20 season, and stayed in that division for three seasons until the League decided to disband it. The club then played in the Bristol & District and Bristol Suburban Leagues, until rejoining Division Two of the Western League again for the 1931/32 campaign. Four seasons later, they won the Somerset Senior Cup.

When football returned after the Second World War, the club joined Division One of the Western League for the 1946/47 season, and two seasons later won the League title, and completed a double by winning the Somerset Premier Cup. The club then won the League again two seasons later, but would have to wait 15 more years for silverware when they picked up the Western League Challenge Cup in the 1965/66 season. Four seasons later they were League Champions again for the third time.

The club remained in the top division until the end of the 1978/79 campaign when they finished bottom and were relegated to Division One. They remained in that division until the end of the 1998/99 campaign, with their best season during that time being 1994/95, when they finished as runners-up, but were denied promotion as their new ground did not meet the standard required for the Premier Division.

The 1998/99 campaign saw the club finish eighteenth out of 19 teams, and they were relegated to the Somerset County Football League Premier Division, where they still play today.

GROUND BA6 9AF

Glastonbury Town have played their home games at the Abbey Moor Stadium, Glastonbury, Somerset since 1982. The club previously played at The Abbey Stadium, owned by the Church of England, and therefore were not allowed to provide a licensed clubhouse.

1919-22 Division Two; 1931-39 Division Two; 1939-40 Division One; 1946-76 Division One; 1976-79 Premier Division; 1979-99 Division One.

GLOUCESTER CITY FC/Reserves

'The Tigers' Established 1883

HISTORY

The club was established in 1883 as Gloucester FC, but during that era was written as 'The Gloucestrians' and 'The Citizens' in local media They became members of the Bristol and District League a year after its formation, and left at the end of 1895/96 due to financial difficulties.

Gloucester City reserves entered Division Two of the Western League in 1951/52, and after taking time to settle in, ended in their best position to date

462

in 1955/56, when they achieved third place, behind Trowbridge reserves and Taunton Town. Promotion to Division One was gained in 1957/58 when they ended the term runners-up to Poole Town reserves, but the transition to the stronger division was not successful, and after finishing the 1958/59 season one place off the bottom, the League's decision to run with just one division for the following year, prompted their resignation.

In July 2007, the club was considerably affected by the Gloucestershire floods with their Meadow Park stadium under eight feet of water. The floods have meant the club has been in exile away from Gloucester since 2007.

GROUND GL52 5NA

In 2013 the club received full planning permission from Gloucester City Council to build a new 3,060 capacity stadium, raised by several feet, on the site of their former home of Meadow Park with plans to expand to over 4,000.

Senior Team 1893-96 Division One. Reserve Team 1951-58 Division Two; 1958-1960 Division One

HALLEN F.C.

'The Armadillos' Established 1949

HISTORY

The club was established in 1949 as Lawrence Weston Athletic, playing their early years in the Bristol and District League, and then the Bristol Premier Combination.

In 1979, the club moved to Hallen, changing its name to Lawrence Weston Hallen. The facilities available at the new base enabled them to move up to the Gloucestershire County League in 1987, and three years later, they changed their name again, to simply Hallen.

In 1992 they gained a further promotion, joining the Hellenic League Division One, and after further improvements to the facilities, particularly the erection of floodlights and an all-seater stand, a runners-up position in 1996/97 facilitated Hellenic League Premier Division football.

After three seasons in the Premier, they were granted permission to switch to the Western League, but had to take an effective demotion to Division One, where they became Champions in 2003/04, thereby gaining promotion to the Premier Division, where they remain today.

Hallen have been entering the FA Vase since 1983, with the best run coming in 2000/01 when they reached the Fifth Round (last 16).

Their FA Cup history only dates back to 2002/03, but in 2004/05 they came close to making the competition proper, losing in the Fourth Qualifying Round, to Football Conference side Canvey Island.

In 2009/10, they were winners of the Western League Les Phillips League Cup, defeating Bishop Sutton 1–0 in the final, and in 2014 they won the Gloucestershire Challenge Trophy for the third time.

GROUND BS10 7RU

The club play at The Hallen Centre, Moorhouse Lane. It has a capacity of 2,000. In the summer of 2015 the club fought a well publicised battle with the Parish Council who own the land on which the ground sits and who wanted the club to leave. The club were successful in keeping their ground, and in the process, saw a petition signed by nearly 6000 people help their cause, along with many famous sportsmen showing their support.

2000-2004 Division One; 2004- Premier Division.

HANHAM F.C.

Established 1896

HISTORY

In the 19th century Hanham was a small mining village bordering the South East of Bristol, where the players were almost certainly local to the area, many of them coming straight from a shift down the pits to play for the club. Between the years of 1891 and 1893, fixtures were played by Hanham Victoria FC (1st & 2nd XI) and Hanham Rovers FC.

In 1895, they played in the South and Bristol District League Division One, and in 1897/8 won their first honours, the Gloucestershire Junior Cup, as well the Western League Amateur Division Two title, and runners-up in the Bristol & District Alliance League.

Hanham moved from the Western League after the 1898/99 season, and in 1907 experienced one of the most successful periods in the club's history, cut short only by the outbreak of the First World War in 1914. During that period, they won four Bristol & District League titles, finished as runner-up once, won the Gloucestershire Senior Amateur Cup three years in succession, and finished runner-up in the same Cup twice, losing out to Dominicans in 1908/9 and St. Michaels in 1912/13.

In 1919 after the end of World War One, the club changed its name to Hanham Athletic AFC and continued where it left off by winning honours on a regular basis. In 1968 the club were Founder Members of the Gloucestershire County League, and in their first season finished in a respectable 3rd position. The League consisted of many clubs that have gone on to achieve a higher standard of football, with clubs like Yate Town, Forest Green Rovers, Bristol Rovers 'A', and arch rivals Bristol St George FC.

In 1982 the club took control of Mount Hill Enterprise FC, another Hanham club who themselves were formed in 1889. Mount Hill Enterprise became the 'reserves' and because of the amalgamation, the club again underwent a name change, becoming Hanham Mount Hill Athletic FC. The club reverted to the name of Hanham Athletic FC in 1984, to avoid confusion with another local club Hanham Mount FC, and now play in Gloucester County Football League.

GROUND BS15 3AP

The club played on the Swan Ground, which is now known as Vicarage Road. Recently they have signed a lease with South Gloucestershire Council at Vicarage Road, to secure its future.

1897-89 Amateur Division Two; 1898-99 Division Two (Amateur); 1922-23 Division One.

HEAVITREE UNITED F.C.

Established 1885

HISTORY

Formed in 1885, Heavitree United played at various locations in and around Heavitree Park until World War Two. Around 1950, they moved to Wingfield Park.

Until 1976/77, they played in local leagues, but that season they moved from the Devon and Exeter League, to the new First Division of the Western League.

That move was encouraged by David Henson, who was a representative on the Devon FA, and Chairman of the club. He became a Vice-Chairman of the FA, and is now fully involved in the FA's Futsal Cup, and serves on the FA Small-side Football Committee.

Heavitree never managed to gain promotion to the Premier Division during their time with the League; their best finish being 10th in 1985/86. They finished bottom in their first season, and then again in 1991/92, and 1998/99, after which they went into the Devon County League.

The club found little success at that level, although they finished fourth in 2000/01, and went down a further level in 2004 when they left the Devon County League and merged with Heavitree Social Club F.C. in the Devon and Exeter League. Since that time, they have formed a youth team with the intention of bringing on local young talent.

GROUND EX1 3BS

Heavitree United, Wingfield Park, East Wonford Park, Exeter

1976-1999 Division One.

HENGROVE ATHLETIC F.C.

'The Grove/Hens' Established 1948

HISTORY

Hengrove was founded in 1948 by ex-members of Christchurch Hengrove Boys Club, and played at school pitches until moving to their current base at Norton Lane in 1964.

The club played in the Bristol & Suburban League before progressing to the Somerset County League in 1974. In 2005/06, they were the Somerset County League Premier Division, Champions, and successfully applied for promotion to Western League Division One, finishing 10th and 6th in their first two seasons at the higher level.

The 2012/13 season saw the club gain promotion to the Premier Division of the Western League when they finished as runners-up behind Sherborne Town in Division One. They were relegated back to Division One at the end of the 2013/14 season, after finishing in bottom spot.

GROUND BS14 0BT

Hengrove Athletic play their home games at Norton Lane, Whitchurch, Bristol

2006-13 Division One; 2013-2014 Premier Division; 2014- Division One.

HEREFORD THISTLE F.C.

Established 1885

HISTORY

Hereford Thistle won the Western League title in the only year that they took part, beating St George to the Championship on goal average, after both clubs had ended the year on thirty-nine points. They left the League after that to join the Birmingham and District League.

GROUND HR1 2QX

The club played at The Barrack Ground, Hereford, which is still an open area next to the Army Cadet Corps building.

1894-95 Division One.

HOFFMAN ATHLETIC F.C.

Established 1938

HISTORY

The club was formed as the works team of the Hoffman Bearings Company, who relocated from Chelmsford to Stonehouse in 1938, and played in the Western League for thirteen seasons after World War II.

They joined the Western League Division Two for the start of the1946/47 season; the clubs best years being the first three, which saw the club finish in sixth position each season.

Athletic then dropped down the division and finished bottom in 1952/53. They won the Gloucestershire Senior Amateur Challenge Cup (North) in 1951/52 and 1953/54, and a recovery in the First Division meant they finished eleventh the following season. They never again managed to achieve a top ten finish and dropped out of the Western League at the end of the 1958/59 season.

They were managed by their Production Manager and former RAF Bomber Command radio operator, Bill Clark, and participated in the FA Cup for five consecutive seasons during the late 1940s and early 1950s. During their first Cup run in 1946/47 they defeated Frome Town, Paulton Rovers, Clandown and Melksham before losing, 4–3, at home to Trowbridge Town in the Third Qualifying Round. That was their best effort in the FA Cup, as they subsequently never managed to reach further than the First Qualifying Round, which they achieved in 1950/51, when they lost 7–0 at Merthyr Tydfil.

When they left the Western League, Hoffman's joined Division Two of the Gloucestershire Northern Senior League, which they won at the first attempt.

GROUND GL10 3RQ

The club played at Stonehouse, Gloucestershire on the Sports Ground adjoining the Hoffman factory. The area is now beneath the Customade UK premises on the Stonedale Road Industrial Estate.

1946-1959 Division Two.

HORFIELD UNITED F.C.

Established 1885

HISTORY

Horfield were elected to the Western League after World War One in 1919. At that time, the League was made up without seven of the pre-war clubs, but such was the large number of applications for entry, that a second division was then added. Horfield were not added to that new division, but included alongside the likes of reserve teams from Swindon Town, Bristol City, Swansea, Newport and Bristol Rovers, which indicates either the influence of a local cabal, or the emergence of a club which enjoyed a pedigree from previous football associations.

After coming in bottom that year, with just one win to their name, they withdrew, but were then given another chance just a year later. The 1921/22 season also proved difficult for the club, ending in bottom place, once again, with just one win and two draws. It was to be the last time that they would take part.

GROUND BS7 0AD

Horfield played adjacent to the Memorial Ground which is now used by Bristol Rovers FC. The football ground continued in use until around the mid-1950s but is now covered by housing in Trubshaw Close.

1894-95 Division One.

IFRACOMBE TOWN FC

'The Bluebirds' Established 1902

HISTORY

The club was founded in 1902 as Ilfracombe FC, and became a founder member of the North Devon League in 1904. In 1920, the 'Town' suffix was added to the club's title. In 1922, the club switched to the East Devon League, and a year later acquired its present ground of Marlborough Park, laying out the pitch ready to start in the 1924/25 season.

After the Second World War in 1949, they were the Founding Members of the Western Football League, Division Three, and progressed through until reaching the Western League top flight in 1953. After only two seasons, they were relegated, and after four more seasons in Division Two, they left the Western League to join the North Devon League. With that they also stopped playing in the FA Cup, which they first took part in during the 1949/50 season - having to wait until 1989 before entering again.

After a quarter of a century back in local football in the North Devon League, they re-joined the Western League, Division One, in 1984; a status they had retained until promotion to the Premier Division in 2007.

In 2010/11 the club then went on to win the Les Phillips Cup by beating Cadbury Heath 3–1 in the Final.

With mounting problems, however, they resigned from the League at the end of the 2013/14 season, replacing their reserves in the North Devon Premier League.

GROUND EX34 8PD

Ilfracombe Town play their games at Marlborough Park, Ilfracombe. The ground has 1500 seats in two covered stands.

1949-50 Division Three; 1950-53 Division Two; 1953-55 Division One; 1955-59 Division Two;1984-2007 Division One; 2007-2014 Premier Division.

ILMINSTER TOWN F.C.

'The Blues' Established 1920

HISTORY

Ilminster was formed in 1920, but did not entered the FA Cup until 1948/49. They continued to play regularly in the Cup throughout the 1950s with their best performance reaching the Second Qualifying Round.

The club joined the Western League in the newly reformed Division One for the 1976/77 season, and were promoted to the Premier Division the following year after finishing in third spot. They lasted two seasons in that division, during which time they reached the Third Round of the FA Vase, before being relegated back to Division One; leaving the Western League altogether two seasons later.

Ilminster Town then joined the Somerset Senior League, Division One, in 1985/86, but were relegated to Division Two in 1988. The following season they were crowned Champions, and then remained in Division One until being relegated in 1995. Again, they bounced back the following season by winning Division Two, only to be relegated, once again in 1999.

After finishing runners-up in 2002/03 they returned to Division One where they were crowned Champions, enabling them to reach the Premier Division for the first time. In 2008, the club was relegated back to Division One, but returned to the Premier Division in 2012 after again winning the League title.

GROUND TA19 0EY

Ilminster Town play their home games at The Recreation Ground, Ilminster, Somerset

1976-78 Division One; 1978-80 Premier Division; 1980-82 Division One.

KEYNSHAM TOWN F.C.

'The Canaries/Ks' Established 1895

HISTORY

Keynsham Town Football Club was formed in 1896. In the early days, the club played at the 'Hams' and then moved to 'Gaston' in 1910. 1n 1925 the club played in Park Road, and then moved again in 1930, to a pitch on Charlton Road. All those grounds have now been built on, and there is no evidence of them remaining.

In 1939 Keynsham FC was disbanded for the duration of the Second World War and was reformed in 1945, when they found a new home at Crown Fields, where they have played ever since. It was due to the foresight of Roy Neal and Ken Dowling and the Committee at that time that the ground is left in trust ensuring that football can be played for the generations to come. The main clubhouse was built in the 1970s with new dressing rooms added in 1984, floodlights in 1989, and most recently, the seats have been replaced, courtesy of the old Williams Stand at Ashton Gate, home of Bristol City Football Club.

The club first played in the Bristol & District League, progressed to the Bristol Premier Combination, and then into the Somerset County League, before joining the Western League, First Division, in 1974. In 1977/78, they won the Champions title, nine points clear of Clandown.

After five years at the higher level they were relegated to Division One for the start of season 1983/84, along with Portway-Bristol, and then returned to the top flight in 1997, as runners-up to Melksham Town.

The yo-yo effect then kicked-in again two seasons later, when the Town returned to Division One, only to gain promotion again in 2000/01, after finishing runners-up to Team Bath. After brief flirtations with the Premier Division in the mid-2000s, the Ks have been in Division One for several seasons now.

The club were awarded 'Community Development Club' status, the highest level of the FA's Charter Standard initiative, and now operates under the ethos of the Charter.

GROUND BS31 2BE

The club play at Crown Fields, Keynsham

1973-76 Premier Division; 1976-78 Division One; 1978-83 Premier Division; 1983-97 Division One; 1997-99 Premier Division; 1999-2001 Division One; 2001-2007 Premier Division; 2007- Division One

KINGSWOOD ROVERS F.C.

Established 1905

HISTORY

The club joined the Western League in 1907 and played in the same division as Bristol Rovers and City reserve sides, Treharris from Wales, Paulton, Welton, Radstock, Weymouth and Staple Hill, which must have involved some very interesting journeys. Barry District and Aberdare also joined the following season, increasing the journey's across the Bristol Channel.

The increase in membership stretched the division to twenty-two games, which contributed to six resignations at the end of the 1909/10 season, including Kingswood Rovers. They did not return to the League again.

GROUND BS15 1TF

The club played at the Chequers Ground, Kingswood, which is now Britton Gardens housing estate. It was previously the ground of Clifton Association FC, until they moved to Westbury-on-Trym in 1897.

1907-09 Division Two; 1909-10 Division One

LARKHALL ATHLETIC F.C.

'The Larks' Established 1914

HISTORY

The club was founded in 1914, and played local football until joining the Western League after its expansion to two divisions in 1976.

They won promotion to the Western Football League Premier Division as Champions for the first time in 2008/09.

They had previously won the Division One title in the 1988/89 season, but failure to comply with ground grading standards, denied them promotion.

In 2010/11, in only their second ever season at Premier level, Larkhall won the Western League Premier Division for the first time by nine clear points from Bitton. They remained in the Premier Division for the 2011/12 season however, once again, due to their ground grading they were denied promotion.

In 2013/14, they won the Western League double, the League title and the Les Phillips Cup, and were promoted to the Southern League, having improved their Plain Ham ground.

The Larks' best FA Vase runs before 2008/09 saw them reach the Second Round on three occasions, but that season they beat Gillingham Town and Plymouth Parkway in the Qualifying Rounds, then beat Portleven away in the First Round, and Lymington Town of the Wessex League Premier Division 4–1, on the way to the Third Round. That was, however, as far as they went.

In the 2011/12 season, the club reached the Fifth Round, but lost to Herne Bay, and equaled that feat in 2012/13, losing in the Fifth Round to the eventual Finalists, Tunbridge Wells.

They now play in Division One, South and West, Southern League

GROUND BA1 8DJ

Larkhall Athletic play their home games at Plain Ham, Charlcombe Lane, Larkhall, Bath. Capacity of 1,000.

1976-2009 Division One; 2009-2014 Premier Division.

LEYTON F.C.

'The Lilywhites/Swifts' Established 1868 reformed 1997

HISTORY

Leyton Football Club was based in the London Borough of Waltham Forest. They were the first team to go by that name, and were founded in 1868, but then disbanded several times in their history - late 1890s, 1911, 1914 and 2011.

Leyton entered the Western League in 1907/0/8 and played in the professional Division One, entering at the same time as Brighton and Hove Albion, Crystal Palace and Luton Town. They ended both years in the League in bottom spot, scoring just 27 goals in those two years and losing 15 of the 24 games played.

In 1975 the club merged with Wingate F.C. to become Leyton-Wingate F.C., but in 1992 the two clubs parted company and the name reverted to Leyton. In 1995 the club merged with Walthamstow Pennant and moved away from Leyton Stadium to become Leyton Pennant FC, now known as Waltham Forest.

The new Leyton Football Club that had been set-up in 1997, won the right to be recognised as a continuation of the original club following a High Court case in 2002, making it the second oldest existing club in Greater London, after Cray Wanderers.

In October 2009, following an investigation by HMRC, the club's Chairman and a former director pleaded guilty to their part in a VAT fraud. New men

472

were then voted in, but in January 2011 after a short suspension from the Isthmian League for not paying its subscription, the Club was forced to withdraw from the League due to debt. Following this, the Chairman, Secretary, management and players all left the club, effectively ending its existence.

GROUND E10 5NF

Leyton F.C. played at the Leyton Stadium, previously known as the Hare and Hounds, and prior to that at the Wingate-Leyton Stadium.

1907-09 Division One section A.

LISKEARD ATHLETIC F.C.

'The Blues' Established 1946

HISTORY

Until 1912, Lux Park, which has always been the present Liskeard Athletics home, facilitated both the cricket club and football club for a nominal rent of a shilling a year. The owner, Viscount Clifton, then agreed to sell it for £300, providing the ground was used for sports.

In the spring of 1922 a field adjoining the cricket ground was purchased for £500, after deals were struck with a local man who had a Slaughter House in one corner. The dividing hedge was removed and the first game of football was played by Liskeard FC on 9th September 1922 against Woodland Villa.

Unfortunately, the club folded in 1935 with heavy debts, and the local Rugby Club took up residence until the current Liskeard Athletic FC was formed in 1946.

The club joined the South Western League in 1966, which they won twice, and then elected to join the Western League in 1979; winning promotion from the First Division a year later. They won the Western League title once, and finished as runners-up twice, before returning to the South Western League in 1995, and became a Founder Member of the South West Peninsula League in 2007, where they compete today.

GROUND PL14 2HZ.

Liskeard Athletic play their home games at Lux Park Sports Association, Coldstyle Road, Lux Park, Liskeard, Cornwall. It has a capacity of 2000 with seating for 50

1979-80 Division One; 1980-95 Premier Division

LONGWELL GREEN SPORTS F.C.

'The Green/Sports' Established 1966

HISTORY

The club was formed by workers from Longwell Green Coachworks, whose name was adopted for the team in 1966 after the great upsurge of interest in football following England's World Cup success against West Germany. The team started in the old regional Bristol Saturday League, and then moved to the Bristol & District League in the mid-1970s, gaining promotion at regular intervals until winning their first major Championship in 1983 when lifting the Division Four crown.

Between 1984 and 1990 they gained promotion five times in nine seasons, which included becoming Bristol & District League Senior Division Champions in 1990.

Further success was achieved when they became Bristol Combination Division One runners-up resulting in election to the Premier Division. The team remained in the Premier Division for nine seasons, often pushing for promotion but never reaching the top spot.

At the end of the 2003/04 season, the team finished runners-up in the Bristol Premier Combination, and carried out the necessary work to step up to the Gloucestershire County League.

The following season Longwell Green Sports finished as runners-up in the Gloucestershire County League, and were promoted to Division One of the Western League for the first time.

Because of the promotion, they made further improvements to their home ground at Shellards Road, and in the 2008/09 they were promoted to the Premier Division of the Western League after finishing as Division One runners-up.

GROUND

Longwell Green Community Stadium, Shellards Road, Longwell Green. Capacity 1,000 with seating for 75.

2005-09 Division One; 2009 – Premier Division

LOVELL'S ATHLETIC F.C.

'The Toffee Men'; Established 1918

HISTORY

Lovell's Athletic F.C. was the works team for Lovell's sweet factory in Newport, Monmouthshire, South Wales, and played both semi-professional and professional football from 1918 until 1969. They joined the Western Football League in 1923 and won the title in their inaugural season. Although there were only eleven teams taking part at the time, by February, after only one defeat and a single draw, they were three points clear at the top, a position that they maintained to win, ten points ahead of Weymouth and six points clear of Radstock. They then ended the following season in bottom spot, and moved to play in the Southern League in 1928.

Lovell's rejoined the Western League in 1931, and won their second title in 1938/39.

In the 1945/46 FA Cup, they reached the Third Round, losing 12–3 on aggregate in a two-legged match against Wolves. Lovell's returned to the Southern League in 1947. Following the 1947/48 season the club applied for election to the Football League, along with nine other non-league clubs. However the two Third Division South teams seeking re-election, Norwich City and Brighton and Hove Albion, were both re-elected.

Lovell's left the Southern League in 1959, after finishing in the relegation zone of the North-West Division, and continued to play in the Welsh League until disbandment in 1969.

GROUND NP20 5NR

The Old Rexville Ground, Albany Road, Newport, which is now a housing estate, constructed in the 1980s, named 'The Turnstiles'.

1924-25 Division One; 1925-26 Division Two; 1926-28 Division One; 1931-39 Division One. Reserves. 1926-27 Division Two

LUTON TOWN F.C.

'The Hatters' Established 1885

HISTORY

Luton Town Football Club was formed on 11 April 1885, the product of a merger of the two leading local teams, Luton Town Wanderers and Excelsior. Initially based at Excelsior's Dallow Lane ground, the club began making payments to certain individual players in 1890. The following year, Luton became the first club in Southern England to be fully professional. The club was a founder member of the Southern Football League in the 1894/95 season and finished as runners-up in its first two seasons. It then left to help form the United League and came second in that league's inaugural season, before joining the Football League, which was then based mostly in northern and central England, and moved to a new ground at Dunstable Road. The club continued to enter a team to the United League for two more seasons, and won the title in 1897/98. Poor attendance, high wages and the high travel and accommodation costs that resulted from Luton's distance from the northern heartlands of the Football League crippled the club financially, and made it too expensive to compete in that league. A return to the Southern League was therefore arranged for the 1900/01 season.

Eight years after arriving at Dunstable Road, Luton moved again, settling at their current ground, Kenilworth Road, in 1905. Captain and left winger Bob Hawkes became Luton's first international player when he was picked to play for England against Ireland on 16 February 1907, the same year that they joined the Western League to supplement the number of games needed to bring income into the club.

They played for two seasons against fellow Southern clubs such as Millwall, Spurs, West Ham, QPR and Crystal Palace, before all fourteen clubs in Division One resigned.

GROUND LU4 8AW

The club play at Kenilworth Road, Luton.

1907-08 Division One, section B; 1908-09 Division One, section A

MANGOTSFIELD UNITED F.C.

'The Field/Mangos' Established 1951

HISTORY

Mangotsfield United Football Club's roots lay in the original football club that was formed following a meeting in The Crown Hotel, St. James Street, 127 years ago, as Mangotsfield FC. At the time their ground was situated on St. James Street, Mangotsfield, which is currently a council playing field. They later moved to some land on Pomphrey Hill near Shortwood and Mangotsfield North Railway station. From that location, they were given the nickname of 'The Railway Men' by the local press. In 1892, Mangotsfield F.C. was one of the founding members of the Bristol & District League, which three years later became the Western League, but the club folded after finishing bottom of the Western League Amateur Division One in season 1897/1898.

Numerous attempts were made to reform the club, but due to financial difficulties it eventually went out of existence in 1950, leaving many men without a team to play in, and so the ex-players decided to form a club of their own, which they did, Mangotsfield United F.C.

Entering the Bristol & District League, Division VII, they only lost one game that year, whilst amassing 144 goals and conceding 21 in the 34 games played. They also won the Bristol & District League VI the following year, scoring a club record 172 goals, then entering the newly formed, Bristol & District League Premier Combination, Division One, where they continued their success, gaining promotion to the Bristol & District League Premier Combination, Division One in 1957/58.

476

Mangotsfield remained in the forefront of the local Bristol football scene, and applied for membership of the Western Football League in 1972, which was subsequently accepted by the League's Management Committee.

The club's first match was at Avon (Bradford) and at the end of the season they finished in a creditable third spot, missing out on the runners-up place on goal-difference to Taunton Town. The following season the club went on to win the Western League Challenge Cup and installed floodlights at Cossham Street.

Mangotsfield went on to win the Premier Division Championship in 1990/91 and were, unjustly in many people's minds, refused entry to the Southern League. It did not deter the well supported club and in 1995/96 they were FA Vase Semi-Finalists, losing the second-leg game to Clitheroe, 2-0, in extra-time, having gone into the game a goal-up from the first-leg. In 2000/2001, they eventually realised the ambition of promotion, and went into the Southern League, Western Division, which they won in 2004/2005. 'The Mangos' has almost superseded 'The Field' as the nickname of the Club, given to them by Geoff Twentyman, the Bristol Rovers defender and Radio Bristol presenter, who is our guest speaker tonight.

GROUND BS16 9NF and BS16 9EN

As Mangotsfield, the club played at Pomphrey Hill, the field next to what is the A4174 where it crosses by the B4465. Since reforming they have played at Cossham Street, Mangotsfield, which has a capacity of 2,500

As Mangotsfield, 1892-96 Division One; 1896-97 Division Two; 1897-98 Amateur Division One. As Mangotsfield United,1972-76 Division One; 1976-78 Premier Division; 1979-82 Premier Division; 1982-83 Division One; 1983-2000 Premier Division. As Mangotsfield PF (Park Furnishers) 1978-79

MELKSHAM TOWN F.C.

'Town' Established 1876

HISTORY
The club was formed as Melksham F.C. in 1876 and in 1894 became founding members of the Wiltshire League. They then spent the next eighty years in the Wiltshire League, during which time they won the League once in the 1903/04 season, and, also completed a League and Cup double when they took the Wilts Senior Cup as well. They entered the FA Cup for the first time in 1946. In 1951 the club changed their name to their current one.

They joined the Western Football League in 1974 and won Division One in 1979/80, gaining promotion to the Premier Division. They stayed in the division until they were relegated in 1988. The club left the Western League in 1993, when they were relegated to the Wiltshire County League after finishing in bottom position. However, they returned to the Western League just one season later, when under manager Mel Gingell, they won the Wiltshire County League.

Three seasons later in the 1996/97 campaign they were promoted to the Premier Division, as Champions of Division One.

The club then spent the next thirteen seasons in the top division of the Western League before being relegated, once again, at the end of the 2009/10 campaign. At the end of the 2011/12 season they gained promotion back to the Premier Division when they finished as runners-up to Cadbury Heath.

In the 2014/15 season Melksham won the Western Football League Premier Division, but could not be promoted to the Southern League due to not being able to meet ground standards on time.

GROUND SN12 7GU

Melksham Town played their games at The Conigre, Market Place, Melksham from 1926 until 2017, when they moved to the purpose built ground and first-rate facilities at The Oakfield Stadium, Eastern Way, Melksham

1974-80 Division One; 1980-88 Premier Division; 1988-93 Division One; 1994-97 Division One; 1997-2010 Premier Division; 2010-2012 Division One; 2012 – Premier Division.

MERTHYR TOWN F.C.

'The Martyrs' Established 1909 – Reformed 2010

HISTORY

From 1909 Merthyr played in the Southern League until the creation of a new English Third Division, when they became Members of the Football League. They were then voted out in 1930 when they dropped back into the Southern League for four seasons, before ceasing to play in 1934. They then reformed and played over time in various leagues.

In 2010, Merthyr Tydfil F.C. played in the Southern Football League Premier Division, were put into administration with severe financial problems, but after being liquidated, were reformed under the name of Merthyr Town. As a part of the bankruptcy procedures they were required to drop three divisions, and began the 2010/11 season in the Western Football League Division One.

The club was also forced to switch grounds, and left Penydarren Park to take Rhiw Dda'r, the home of Taff's Well AFC. as their temporary home ground.

In their first season with the League, they won Division One and were promoted to the Premier Division.

The newly promoted club once again called Penydarren Park home, and went on to secure a second consecutive Championship.

On 6 April 2015, Merthyr Town were promoted back to the Southern League and are now owned by the Supporters' Trust.

GROUND CF47 8RF

Merthyr Town now play at Pendarren Park, Merthyr, which has a capacity for 10,000 with seating for 1,500 and a 3G playing surface.

1909-10 Division One; 2010-2011 Division One; 2011-2012 Premier Division.

MID RHONDDA F.C.

'The Mush/Mushrooms' Established 1912

HISTORY

Early attempts to form a football club were unsuccessful when industrial unrest spread through the Rhondda during 1910 and 1911. In 1912, with the strikes and riots of previous years settled, the Mid Rhondda Football Club was set up, with a Board of Directors from the Tonypandy area who represented a cross section of tradesmen and workers. Amongst the shareholders was D.A. Thomas, the owner of the Cambrian Combine of Collieries, which had been at the heart of the strike just a year prior.

The club applied to join the Southern League, and was accepted even though they had yet to select a team. With a fortnight to go before the start of the 1912/13 season they were facing closure due to lack of funds, but good press coverage encouraged the promoters to carry on. Their first season in the Second Division of the Southern League saw them face the first teams of Cardiff City, Swansea Town, Croydon Common and Luton Town. Over the next few seasons the team was often supported by crowds of over 10,000.

The club and supporters expected continued success for the 1920/21 season in the First Division of the Southern League. A new stand was built, and other ground improvements added, including a press box and a gymnasium. Then ready for the new season, the Southern League was invited to form a Third Division of the Football League. The current First Division of the Southern League then became the new Third Division, and no promotions were accepted. Mid Rhondda remained in the Second Division.

At that stage, Mid Rhondda joined the Western League and played in a strong Division One, which included reserve teams from Bristol City and

Rovers, Cardiff City, Swansea Town and Swindon Town as well as fellow Welsh clubs, Abertillery Town, Pontypridd, Ton Pentre, Barry and Cardiff Corinthians. However, players left the club for a higher standard of football and that, combined with the national coal strike in 1921, which crippled the South Wales valley's, saw the Club in trouble, and were suspended by the Football Association of Wales for non-payment of debts.

The club reformed in 1922, mainly thanks to voluntary donations from local miners, but the economic depression of the 1920s worsened, and there was real poverty in the Rhondda with little money for leisure. The club continued until March 1928 when, with debts of £1,400, Mid Rhondda was forced to close when the banks called in its overdraft.

GROUND CF40 1DB

The club played at the Mid Rhondda Athletic Ground, Tonypandy where a sports field still exists. The capacity was in the region of 10,000

1920-21 Division One.

MIDSOMER NORTON F.C.

Established 1889

HISTORY

Midsomer Norton FC became a member of the Somerset Senior League which was formed in 1890. They continued in membership of that League when they joined the Western League in 1897, and as such, gained direct membership into Amateur Division One; a division that featured clubs mainly from mining districts of Bristol with neighbours, Radstock, the exception. They remained in the League for two years until membership declined rapidly.

GROUND

The club played at Rackfurnel, Midsomer Norton, possibly close to the Wesleyan School.

1897-98 Amateur Division One; 1898-99 Division Two (Amateur).

MILLWALL ATHLETIC F.C.

'The Lions' Established 1885

HISTORY

Millwall Rovers were formed by the workers of J.T. Morton's Canning and Preserve factory in the Millwall area of the Isle of Dogs in London's East End, in 1885. In April 1889, Millwall dropped Rovers from their name in favour of the name Millwall Athletic, inspired by their move to their new home at the Athletic Ground. They were founding members of the Southern Football League which they won for the first two years of its existence, and were runners-up in its third.

They joined the Western League in 1900/01, when the Professional Section was introduced, but resigned at the end of 1902/03 to be replaced by Brentford. Just a season later they re-joined with Fulham, and won the League in 1907/08, in the sectional play-off with Southampton, by the only goal of the game. They repeated that feat the following year, when they beat Brighton, 2-1, in a replay after the first game resulted in a 1-1 draw.

Milwall left the Western League at the end of 1908/09 when the Professional Section was disbanded, and in 1920 entered the English League where they have competed ever since.

GROUND

The club last played in the Millwall area of the Isle of Dogs in 1910. From then until 1993, the club moved to a new stadium, named The Den, in New Cross, South London in 1910, which cost and estimated £10,000. Their current home is a stadium nearby, also called The Den.

1897-98 Amateur Division One; 1898-99 Division Two (Amateur).

MINEHEAD FC

Established 1889

HISTORY

The club was established in 1889, and initially played in local leagues until joining the Western League in 1923. After finishing in tenth place in 1924/25, they were relegated to the newly established Division Two. However, after finishing bottom in both 1926/27 and 1927/28, the club withdrew from the League.

Minehead returned to the Western League in 1949, joining Division Three. After finishing third in their first season back, they were promoted to Division Two. A fourth-place finish in 1956/59 saw the club promoted to Division One, with both clubs directly ahead of them unable to accept promotions because they were reserve teams of existing League members.

In 1970/71 they reached the first round proper of the FA Cup for the first time, but lost 2–1 at home to Shrewsbury Town, and after finishing as runners-up in 1971/72, were elected to Division One South of the Southern League.

They won promotion to the Premier Division of that League in 1975/76, and the following year finished as runners-up in the Premier Division, which at the time, was just one below the Football League. They also reached the first round of the FA Cup again, where they beat Swansea City 1–0 at the Vetch Field, before losing 2–1 at Portsmouth.

In 1982/83 they finished second bottom in the Midland Division, dropping back into the Premier Division of the Western League, and in 1988/89 were relegated to Division One. Although they then finished bottom of Division One the following season, they were not relegated and went on to quickly earn promotion back to the Premier Division.

In 1993/94 the club finished bottom of the Premier Division again, and returned to Division One, where they again finished bottom the following season. In 1998 the club changed its name to Minehead Town and won Division One in the season that followed, losing only one match all year.

However, the club finished bottom of the Premier Division for two consecutive seasons and were relegated to Division One, where they finished bottom in 2009/10 and were relegated to the Somerset County League, where they still play.

GROUND TA24 5DP

Minehead play their home games at The Recreation Ground, Irnham Road, Minehead, Somerset.

1923-25 Division One; 1925-28 Division Two; 1949-50 Division Three; 1950-57 Division Two; 1957-72 Division One; 1983-89 Premier Division; 1989-91 Division One; 1991-94 Premier Division; 1994-98 Division One; As Minehead Town, 1998-99 Division One; 1999-2001 Premier Division; 2001-2010 Division One.

MOUNT HILL ENTERPRISE F.C.

Established 1890s

HISTORY
The club played in the Western League for just one year during the 1898/99 season in a division comprised almost exclusively of Bristol clubs. It was a time when the League had been losing member clubs and at the end of the season, Midsomer Norton, Barton Hill, Bristol Amateurs, Hanham and Mount Hill all resigned.

They continued in existence, and in both 1949/50 and 1950/51 took part in the FA Cup where they travel to Lovells Athletic in the First Qualifying Round only to go out 4-1. The following year a Preliminary Round game with Hoffman Athletic was lost away in Wales, 2-1, on a replay after drawing the first game at home 1-1.

GROUND BS15 9JA

The club played at the Tennis Courts, Warmley, behind the Tennis Court Inn where there are still playing fields that are used for rugby.

1898-99 Division Two (Amateur).

NATIONAL SMELTING COMPANY F.C.

Established 1935

HISTORY

The club played in the Bristol and District League from 1935, joining the Western League after the Second World War in Division Two for the 1947/48 season. They never came in the top ten, in a division that sported eighteen strong clubs, including sides from the RAF stations in the area. After coming bottom in 1950/51, winning only three of the 38 games played and letting in 184 goals, they left the League, continuing in existence until folding in 2005.

GROUND BS9 1TZ

The club played at the National Smelting Company works ground in Shirehampton Road, Bristol. It is now the Queens Gate housing estate.

1947-51 Division Two

NEWPORT ATHLETIC F.C.

Established

HISTORY

The club played in Division Two of the Western League in the 1906/07 season travelling across the bridge from Wales with Treharris. At the time, it was a reasonably strong League, with both Bristol City reserves and Bristol Rovers reserves in membership, and the club managed to pick up a very respectable runners-up position, just one point behind Staple Hill. Despite that show of strength, however, they disbanded at the end of that season.

GROUND NP19 0AP

The club played on a complex which, at the time included an arena and a rugby ground. It was a large area which was eventually converted to accommodate bowling greens and tennis courts, together with a cricket field. There is now a school on the site.

1906-07 Division Two

NEWPORT COUNTY F.C. Reserves

'The Exiles' Established 1912

HISTORY

Newport were originally nicknamed 'The Ironsides' due to Newport being home to Lysaght Orb steel works. They started out in the Southern League in 1912 at Somerton Park. The official name of the club was The Newport &

Monmouth County Association Football Club, although the shorter Newport County was soon adopted.

The club was reformed in 1919, and entered a reserve team into the Western League to play alongside reserve teams from Swansea, Bristol Rovers and Swindon Town. Although they did not compete well that year, finishing one place from bottom in the First Division, they were elected to the Football League in 1920 and withdrew from the League.

The club played in the Football League from that date until they went out of existence, before then reforming in 1989.

GROUND NP19 0GD

The club played at Somerton Park, Cromwell Road, Newport. It is now the site of the Somerton Park housing estate.

1919-21 Division One.

ODD DOWN A.F.C.

The 'Downs' established 1901

HISTORY

The club was founded in 1901 by Fred Weaver and the brothers Walt and Stan Noad. Odd Down, then a self-contained village on the outskirts of Bath, played in the Bath and District Football League. In 1920, they won the Bath City Knockout Cup.

Odd Down FC spent their formative years on pitches at both Stirtingale Farm, and at the Quarr Ground, before moving to Combe Hay Lane in the 1930s. The club was finally able to purchase the ground in 1952, when it was renamed in memory of former President Lew Hill.

During the 1920s the club played in the Wiltshire Football League, but prior to World War Two had graduated to playing in the Somerset Senior League.

Re-grouping after the war, the club started off again in the Somerset Senior League and in the 1946/47 season finished as runners-up to Somerton. They also won the Mid-Somerset Football League that season, a league formed to make up for the shortage of Somerset Senior League fixtures at that time.

Following a bad report into the facilities at Odd Down, the club were expelled from the Somerset Senior League, whereupon an application to join the Wiltshire Football League was accepted. A few years later the Wiltshire League voiced disapproval of Somerset-based teams competing in their league, and Odd Down found themselves re-admitted to the Somerset Senior League.

From 1967 to 1972 the club formed a steering committee which worked hard to provide a social club, eventually opening one on April 5, 1972. The hard work paid off as Odd Down gained admittance to the Western Football League for the start of the 1977/78 season.

It was to be season 1991/92 before the club won its first major honour, lifting the Somerset Senior Cup, and further success followed when the club won promotion to the Western League Premier Division, finishing as the 1992/93 Division One Champions.

In their Centenary Year, Odd Down reached the final of the Somerset Premier Cup for the first time, losing 1–0 to Southern League side Clevedon Town. The feat was repeated in 2004, this time going down 5–0 to Yeovil Town at the clubs' Huish Park home.

They remained in the Premier Division until relegation to Division One in 2008, but were promoted back to the Premier Division in 2010. In season 2015/16 Odd Down picked up the League Championship title on goal difference from Barnstaple Town, who took promotion to the Southern League in their place.

GROUND BA2 8AP

Odd Down play their home games at the Lew Hill Memorial Ground, Combe Hay Lane, Odd Down, Bath, Somerset, which has a capacity of 1,000 with seating for 160.

1977-93 Division One; 1993-2008 Premier Division; 2008-10 Division One; 2010- Premier Division.

OLDLAND ABBOTONAINS F.C.

'The Os' Established 1910

HISTORY

The club was founded as St. Anne's Oldland, in 1910, but the current incarnation of the club was formed from a merger between Oldland and Longwell Green Abbotonians in 1998. Oldland had played in the Gloucestershire County League on-and-off from 1974, while Longwell Green Abbotonians had been playing in the Somerset Senior League since 1985, winning Division One in 1993/94.

The newly formed Oldland Abbotonians started out in the Somerset Senior League Premier Division, but were relegated to Division One in 2000. The club returned to the Premier Division after winning the League in 2004/05, and in the 2006/07 season, finished third, gaining promotion to the Western Football League Division One.

In 2010/11, Oldland finished as runners-up in Division One, but were denied promotion to the Premier Division after their facilities failed to meet the necessary ground grading standards.

GROUND BS30 9SZ

Abbotonians play at Atkinson Playing Fields, Oldland, Bristol.

2007- Division One.

OTTERY ST MARY A.F.C.

'The Otters' Established 1911

HISTORY

The club was established in 1911 and after the Second World War joined the Exeter and Devon League, which in 1972 was renamed the Devon and Exeter League. After coming in as League Champions in 1974, they joined the South Western Football League.

After two seasons, Ottery moved on to the Western League's newly created Division One.

The 1989/90 season saw the club earn a further upward move, after winning the First Division title, eight points clear of Backwell United. That was, however, one promotion too many, and after two years of struggling in the Premier Division, relegation then saw another two seasons of struggle in Division One.

At the end of 1993/94, the club finished bottom of Division One and joined the Devon County League, and then joined the newly formed South West Peninsula League Division One East in 2007/08.

During 2011/12, the club resigned from the South West Peninsula League at the end of the season after finishing bottom with just five points, and joined the Devon and Exeter League in Division Three.

GROUND EX11 1EL

Ottery St Mary play their home games at Washbrook Meadows, Butts Road, Ottery St. Mary, Devon

1976-90 Division One; 1990-95 Premier Division; 1992-94 Division One.

PAULTON ROVERS F.C.

'The Rovers' Established 1881

HISTORY

Paulton Rovers first played competitive football in the Western League between 1900 and 1904, then rejoined the League in 1905, competed until the First World War and then competed intermittently in the 1920s.

After World War Two, Rovers were placed in Division One, but were relegated to Division Two in 1953. In the 1960/61 season Division Two was scrapped, and for the next fourteen years the team played in the Somerset County Football League, eventually rejoining the Western League in 1974.

When the League expanded back to two divisions in 1976, Paulton Rovers were placed in the Premier Division, but were relegated in 1981, only to bounce back three years later.

A series of strong finishes in the late 1990s and early 2000s eventually saw them promoted to the Southern League, Division One South and West, in 2003/2004, after finishing the year as runners-up to Bideford Town. In 2013/14, they won a play-off semi-final at Tiverton Town, 3–1, and then surprised Methyr Town in front of a 2,201 crowd, winning, 2–0, and gained promotion to the Southern League Premier Division.

They were relegated to Division One in 2015/16, where they still play.

GROUND BS39 7RF

Paulton Rovers play their home games at The Athletic Ground, Winterfield Road, Paulton, Bristol, where they have played for over 50 years. Previous grounds include Chapel Field, the Cricket Ground, and the Recreation Ground.

1900-04 Division Two; 1905-09 Division Two; 1909-14 Division One; 1919-22 Division Two; 1923-25 Division One; 1925-26 Division Two; 1929-39 Division Two; 1939-40 Division One 1945-53 Division One; 1953-60 Division Two; 1974-76 Division One; 1976-81 Premier Division; 1981-84 Division One; 1984-2004 Premier Division.

PEASEDOWN ST JOHN/MINERS WELFARE

Established 1890s

HISTORY

As Peasedown St John, the club played at its highest level when it joined the Western League in 1911, and stayed for three seasons, finishing fifth in 1913/14, the last season before the war disrupted regular football in England.

After the war, Peasedown resumed in Division Two of a restructured Western League, winning promotion to Division One in 1920/21. They managed fifth place in Division One again in 1922/23, but left two years later after a poor season.

The club returned to the Western League in 1939/40 as Peasedown Miners Welfare, securing the highest finish in their history of fourth, but football was again disrupted, this time by World War Two.

After the resumption of football in 1945/46 they equaled their best finish of fourth place before a run of poor form resulted in relegation to Division Two in 1950/51. They gradually dropped down the division, and left the League in 1960.

During the post-war period, Peasedown competed in the FA Cup, reaching the Fourth Qualifying Round in 1945/46. They missed out on the First-Round Proper after losing a replay 1–0 at home to Cheltenham Town.

Dropping into the Bath and District League during the 1960s and 1970s, the club eventually graduated to the Somerset County League as Peasedown Athletic, finishing runners-up in the Premier Division twice in the mid-1990s. Relegated to Division One in 1999, they achieved promotion in 2001, but were again relegated in 2003, and subsequently dropped to Division Two in 2005. They are now members of Division One East.

GROUND BA2 8AA

The club play at The Miners Welfare Recreation Ground, Church Road, Peasedown, and previously played at a field near the Red Post Inn, and at the cricket ground.

As Peasedown St John 1911-14 Division One; 1919-21 Division Two; 1921-25 Division One. As Peasedown Miners Welfare 1939-40 Division One; 1945-51 Division One; 1951-60 Division Two.

PETTERS WESTLAND WORKS FC

Established 1920s

HISTORY
In 1915 the Westland Aircraft Works was formed as a division of Petters Ltd in response to the government orders for aircraft for the war effort. The earliest record of the football club was in season 1925/26 when they won the Yeovil and District League under the name 'Westland Aircraft', a feat that was repeated in season 1928/29. Around that time another team 'Westland Engine Works' was also playing in the league.

Season 1929/30 saw Yeovil and Petters FC, who later became Yeovil FC, fold their reserve team, most of whom then went to play for Westland's, and so in season 1930/31, boosted by that influx of talent, the club entered the Western League under the name of 'Petters-Westland', and won the Crewkerne Charity Cup. The club soon returned to junior football, and in 1935 re-entered the Yeovil and District League.

The club are still in existence and play in the Dorset Premier League.

GROUND BA20 2AU

The club used to play at the Westland Aircraft Works Athletic ground that is now under a factory extension immediately behind MacDonald's in Lysander Road.

1930-31 Division Two

PEWSEY VALE F.C.

'The Vale' Established 1945

HISTORY

The club was formed in 1945 as Pewsey YM, but changed its name to Pewsey Vale FC in 1948. There is also evidence that there was a six-a-side group that played under the name of Pewsey Boys in 1921.

Promoted to the Great Mills League as Champions of the Wiltshire League in 1993/94, Pewsey were one of the first clubs to benefit from the Pyramid System, moving sideways into Hellenic League Division One, West, in 2001.

The club immediately won promotion to the Premier League after finishing runners-up to Hook Norton, before being relegated back to Division One West. After three seasons in the Premier Division the club was relegated, and after a further year of struggling, at the end of 2008/09 they took the step to drop down to rebuild.

The following season they won the Wiltshire Premier League Cup, and successfully applied to join the Wessex League, Division One, where they are still members today.

GROUND SN9 5BS

The Club play their home games at the Recreation Ground, Kings Corner, Ball Road, Pewsey.

1993-2001 Division One.

PLYMOUTH ARGYLE FC

'The Pilgrims/Green Army' Established 1886

HISTORY

The club was founded in 1886 as Argyle Football Club, with the first match taking place on 16th October 1886, losing 2-0, to Caxton, a team from Cornwall. They played several friendlies against Plymouth United, but poor performances on the pitch led to the club going out of existence in 1894, before being resurrected in 1897 as one part of the Argyle Athletic Club.

The club adopted its current name when it became fully professional in 1903 and joined the Southern League. Their first home game as a fully professional club was on 5th September 1903, when they beat Northampton Town 2–0 in front of a crowd of 4,438.

Since becoming professional, the club has won five Football League titles (one Division Two and two Division Three), five Southern League titles and one Western League title.

The club joined the Western League in 1903/04 where they came in third behind Spurs and Southampton. The following season they won the title, two points clear of Brentford, and six ahead of Southampton. In 1906/07, they were unlucky to be pipped by West Ham for the play-off game against Fulham, by just two points. Argyle then continued in membership until the Professional section was disbanded in 1910.

The reserve team from Plymouth have had a longer association with the League and won many honours in their time: the League Championship in 1927/28 and again in 1931/32, and the Les Phillips Cup in both 1989/90 and 1991/92.

The greatest accolade to the professional club, however, must be in the Merit Cup, that acknowledges the good running and hospitality of the Western League members, with Argyle winning that in 1985/86, 1988/89, 1989/90 and 1990/91. For those who were fortunate enough to go to Home Park when they were in membership, the accolades were, indeed, well deserved in the way that they treated all visiting teams, officials and supporters.

GROUND PL2 3DQ

Argyle play at Home Park which has a capacity of 17,441

1903-06 Division One; 1906-07 Division One Section B; 1907-08 Division One Section A; 1908-09 Division One Section B. Plymouth Argyle reserves, 1925-32 Division One; 1982-93 Premier Division. Plymouth Argyle colts, 1966-68 Division One.

PLYMOUTH CITY FC

Established 1970

HISTORY

The club lasted just one season from its formation, entering the Western League that ran just one division. For such a new club, they did not fare too badly with 17 wins from the 36 games played. They now play in Division Three of the Plymouth and West Devon Football League.

GROUND PL2 3EF

The new club played at the Pennycross Stadium which has now been demolished in favour of housing.

1970-71 Division One

PONTYPRIDD FC

'The Dragons' Established 1911

HISTORY

A team from Pontypridd joined the Southern League in 1911, and after the war transferred to the Western League for just one season, in 1920/21, where they played in a very strong and competitive Division One alongside fellow Welsh clubs, Barry, Cardiff, Swansea reserves, Abertillery Town, Ton Pentre, Mid Rhondda and Cardiff Corinthians. Except for Cardiff Corinthians, all the other Welsh teams pulled out at the end of the season with an economic recession biting and near poverty conditions prevailing in many areas.

They then merged with Ynysybwl and played in the Welsh League.

GROUND CF37 1BE

The club played at Taff Vale Park, Treforest, Pontypridd. The ground remains as a playing field behind Parc Lewis Primary School, Treforest.

1920-21 Division One

POOLE/POOLE TOWN FC

'The Dolphins' Established 1890

HISTORY

Poole Town was formed when two local teams, Poole Hornets and Poole Rovers, merged in 1890. Both teams had been in existence since 1880. They then joined the Dorset League in 1896, before moving to the Hampshire League in 1903, where the club enjoyed success in the Dorset Senior Cup in their early years, winning it five times.

After several seasons without football because of the First World War, the club began playing again in the 1919/20 season under the name Poole & St. Mary's. They changed their name back to Poole FC after one season, and joined the Western League in 1923.

Poole won the Dorset Senior Cup again in 1926, turned professional, and joined the Southern Football League, Eastern Division.

The 1926/27 season saw the best FA Cup run in its history, reaching the Third Round, playing Everton, losing 3–1 at Goodison Park. They won the Dorset Senior Cup again in 1927, and reached the First Round of the FA Cup three seasons in a row. Poole rejoined the Western League in 1930 and competed each season, except for the 1934/35 season, until 1957.The senior team was then replaced by their reserve side in Division One until leaving in 1965.

GROUND BH

The club now play at Tatnam Ground, School Lane, Poole in a stadium that has a capacity for 2,500.

1923-25 Division One; 1925-26 Division Two; 1926-27 Division One; 1930-34 Division Two. As Poole Town, 1935-39 Division Two; 1946-52 Division One;1953-53 Division Two; 1953-57 Division One. Poole reserves, 1926-28 Division Two. Poole Town reserves, 1953-58 Division Two; 1958-65 Division One.

PORTISHEAD TOWN F.C.

'Possets' Established 1912

HISTORY

Originally known as St. Peter's Portishead until a name change in 1948, the club played in small regional leagues for years until joining the Somerset

County League in 1975. They won the Premier Division title four times in five years between 1993/94 and 1997/98.

After their fourth successive runner-up campaign in 2004/05, Portishead successfully applied for promotion to the Western League, where they finished in the top half of the table in that initial season.

In 2006/07 Portishead achieved their highest ever finish in the history of the club, finishing runners-up to Truro City, but were unable to be promoted to the Premier Division because their ground did not have floodlights at the time.

GROUND BS20 6QG

Portishead Town play their home games at Bristol Road, Portishead, Bristol. The ground has a capacity of 1,200 standing and 197 seated

2008- Division One.

PORTLAND UNITED FC

'The Blues' Established 1921

HISTORY

The club was established in 1921, and joined the Western League Division Two in 1925; winning the division twice before the Second World War.

During that time, the club made its debut in the FA Cup in the 1928/29 season and won the Dorset Senior Cup on four occasions.

After the Second World War Portland rejoined the Western League Division One in 1946/47, and spent the next 24 seasons in that division, during which time they finished as runners-up once, and won six more Dorset Senior Cup Finals.

Portland then left the Western League to join the Dorset Football Combination League for the start of the 1970/71 season, winning the League at their first attempt. Twenty-eight years later they achieved the double by winning the League and League Cup, and repeated that success the following season.

In 1994, the club moved from their original home of Grove Corner to New Grove Corner, and after finishing as League runners-up, joined the Wessex Football League for the start of 2001/02, dropping back into the Dorset Premier Football League four seasons later.

In the 2013/14 season the club won the Dorset Premier League for the seventh time in their history and were promoted to the Wessex League in 2015/16 season after achieving a runners-up finish.

GROUND DT5 1DP.

Portland United play their home games at New Grove Corner, Grove Road, Portland which has a capacity for 2,000 supporters.

1925-1939 Division Two; 1946-70 Division One.

493

PORTSMOUTH F.C.

'Pompey' Established 1898

HISTORY

The club was founded in 1898 and joined the Southern League in 1899, with their first League match played at Chatham Town on 2nd September 1899, a 1–0 victory, followed three days later by the first match at Fratton Park; a friendly against local rivals Southampton, which was won, 2–0.

They joined the Western League as a subsidiary competition to be played alongside their Southern League commitments in 1900/01, and won the League title at the first time of trying a point clear of Milwall Athletic and three points ahead of Spurs.

They repeated the feat the following year, ending the term two points clear of Spurs who came in runners-up, eight points ahead of Reading. There were different levels of commitment shown to games in the Western League, with Portsmouth showing their 100% backing by winning the title for a third time in 1902/3, four points clear of Bristol Rovers and eighteen clear of bottom placed newcomers, West Ham United. Their success spurred on the entry of Plymouth Argyle, who emulated their success a couple of seasons later.

GROUND PO4 8RA.

Portsmouth play at Fratton Park, Portsmouth which has a capacity of 21,178.

1900-06 Division One; 1906-07 Division One Section B; 1907-08 Division One Section A; 1908-09 Division One Section B

PORTWAY BRISTOL FC

Established 1970s

HISTORY

Portway joined the First Division of the Western League in 1976, and after two mid-table finishes, were League runners-up at the end of the 1978/79 season and won promotion to the Premier Division, where they remained for four years.

After finishing bottom of the Premier Division in 1983, they had another mid-table finish in Division One, followed by two successive Division One titles, but as they failed to meet the minimum ground requirements, they were denied promotion's in successive years.

They were runners-up again in 1987, but after again failing to be promoted, withdrew from the League that summer.

GROUND BS11 0EA

Portway played at the Shirehampton Recreation Ground, Penpole Lane, Bristol. The ground is across the road from the cricket club.

1976-79 Division One; 1979-83 Premier Division; 1983-87 Division One.

QUEENS PARK RANGERS F.C.

'The Hoop/The Rs' Established 1882

HISTORY

The club was formed in 1886, when a team known as St Jude's (formed in 1884) merged with Christchurch Rangers (formed in 1882). The resulting club was called Queen's Park Rangers, because most of the players came from the Queen's Park area of north-west London.

QPR became a professional club in 1889, and played their home games in nearly twenty different stadia before permanently settling at Loftus Road in 1917.

Like many other professional clubs, QPR joined the Western League Professional Section to increase the number of competitive games on offer from the Southern League, and played mid-week.

They came bottom of their division in 1904/05, having won only six of their twenty games, but the following year won the title a point clear of Southampton. They were also runners-up in Section A in both 1906/07 and 1908/09, to Fulham and Brighton and Hove Albion respectively.

GROUND

The club play at Loftus Road, which has a capacity of 18,439.

1900-96 Division One; 1906-09 Division One Section A.

RAF COLERNE FC

HISTORY

The club was formed after RAF Colerne became home in the Second World War to The Fighter Command and Bomber Command. Playing in Division Two of the Western League, in 1946/47 and 1947/48, they finished second from bottom, gaining just 27 points from the fifty-four games played; conceding 245 goals and scoring just 112.

GROUND SN14 8QE

The team played at a pitch located between Doncombe Lane and Popular Road, close to Cherry Road, Colerne.

1946-48 Division Two

RAF LOCKING FC

HISTORY

The club was formed after the Number 1 Training School for Radio, Radar and Missile Technicians was established at Locking, near Weston-super-Mare in 1937. Playing in Division Two of the Western League, in both years that they were member, 1946/47 and 1947/48, they finished above the other two RAF teams, but still ended in the bottom five. The club continued until the 1970s competing in Service football.

GROUND BS24 8PJ

The ground, that included a stadium for athletics, was situated at the RAF base, which was some way from the airfield, and was adjacent to the A371. Until a few years ago, it was still visible from the road.

1946-48 Division Two

RAF MELKSHAM FC

HISTORY

The club was formed after the RAF created The Number 12 School of Technical Training for Ground Technicians in July 1940. They played in Division Two of the Western League for three years, 1946/1947, 1947/48, and finishing second from bottom at the end of the 1948/49 season, having lost 29 of their 34 games played. The station was closed in 1965.

GROUND SN12 6TR

The ground was situated in the Bowerhill area of Melksham and is now the site of housing and a thriving industrial estate.

1946-49 Division Two.

RADSTOCK TOWN FC

'The Miners' Established 1895

HISTORY

Believed to be one of the oldest clubs in the County of Somerset, Radstock Town was formed in1895; although there is evidence that appears to show a Radstock team playing as early as the 1860s.

After playing in the Western League in 1897/98 as Radstock, they rejoined the League as Radstock Town in 1903/04, along with near neighbours Welton Rovers, but resigned in 1910/11.

They rejoined the League after the First World War, and the 1920s were to see several top six finishes. Indeed, 1923/24 was the club's most successful season, finishing as runners-up to Lovell's Athletic.

In the early days, the club played home games at Roundhill, where the 'A' team and some youth section sides still play, before moving to South Hill Park for several years, where their stay was enforced because of an American Tank Division being billeted at Southfields during the Second World War.

The original move to Southfields took place in 1927 when, as a First World War Memorial, the miners purchased the field through an issue of £5 shares. Unfortunately, it appears that the issue was not totally successful, and therefore the control of the ground was gifted to the Urban District Council and the Miners Welfare, who remain ultimately responsible for the area to this day.

The club's lengthy spell in the League came to an end after the 1959/60 season, when they, along with several other Somerset clubs, left to join a County League. Radstock, Frome Town and Clandown, all chose to compete in the Wiltshire League, and they won the Championship in 1965/66 and 1966/67; then switched to the Somerset County League which they won in 1976/77 and again in 1978/79.

Radstock rejoined the Western League for the 1979/80 season, where they spent the next few years either in Division One or at the foot of the Premier Division.

At the end of the 1993/94 season the club was relegated to the Somerset County League, where they remained for ten seasons before gaining promotion after finishing in third place in 2003/04.

The following season, a third place in Division One was achieved, and that was sufficient to ensure promotion to the Premier Division of the Western League. After ending below half-way for a few years, however, they were relegated back into Division One, where they remain today.

GROUND BA3 3NZ.

Radstock Town play their home games at Southfields Recreation Ground, Southfields, Radstock, with a capacity for 1,250

1903-09 Division Two; 1909-10 Division One; 1920-22 Division Two; 1922-25 Division One; 1925-39 Division Two; 1939-40 Division One; 1945-48 Division One;1948-60 Division Two; 1979-86 Division One; 1986-91 Premier Division; 1991-94 Division One; 2004-2005 Division One; 2005-2014 Premier Division; 2014- Division One.

READING F.C.

'The Royals' Established 1871

HISTORY

Reading are nicknamed 'The Royals' because of the town's location in the Royal County of Berkshire, though they were previously known as 'The Biscuitmen', due to the their association with Huntley and Palmers.

Reading FC was formed on 25th December 1871, following a public meeting at the Bridge Street Rooms, organised by the future club secretary, Joseph Edward Sydenham. The early matches were played at Reading Recreation Ground, and later the club held fixtures at Reading Cricket Ground, Coley Park and Caversham Cricket Ground. The switch to professionalism in 1895 resulted in the need for a bigger ground and, to this end, they moved again, to the purpose-built Elm Park on 5th, September 1896.

Reading was one of the clubs involved with the evolution of a Professional Section in the first season that the Western League incorporated the concept in 1897/98. Although they then left briefly to try their luck in the United League, the idea was dropped and they returned in time for the 1900/01 season.

At a special committee meeting in June 1900, the rules for a new Division One were drawn up with all meetings to be held at Reading FC. Mr Sawyer, an official from Reading, was also appointed as the Division's Press Secretary; a version of our modern-day spin-doctors.

Although they never managed to gain any honours in the Western League competition, they continued in membership until joining all the other professional sides in 1909/10 in leaving.

Reading joined the Third Division South of the Football League in 1920 and have been members since that date.

GROUND RG30 2TP

The club played at Elm Park, Reading, which is now a housing estate. They now play at the Madejski Stadium, Green Park, Reading, which has a capacity of 24,161.

1897-98 Professional Section; 1900-06 Division One; 1906-07 Division One Section A' 1907-08 Division One Section B; 1908-09 Division One Section A.

ROMAN GLASS ST GEORGE F.C.

Formerly ST GEORGE and BRISTOL ST GEORGE

'The Glass' Established 1872

HISTORY

The club was formed in 1872 as St George and became Bristol St George when they adopted professionalism in 1897. They were among the Founder Members of the League. They left between 1899 and 1901, but then returned in 1903, after which time they folded with debts of £340. During that period, the team also played in the Birmingham and District League, and won the Gloucestershire FA Senior Challenge Cup on two occasions, in 1894 and 1895.

After dropping back to local football, they did not re-appear in the Western League until 1928, competing for a seven-season period in Division Two, where they only finished in the top-half of the table once. After finishing bottom in 1934/35, they once again left the Western League for the Bristol and District League. They won the Division One in 1949/50 and became Founder Members of the Bristol Premier Combination League in 1957; winning the Division One title five seasons in a row, from 1963 to 1968.

In 1968, the Gloucestershire County League was formed, with St George among the Founder Members. They were runners-up in the first season, winning the title in 1969/70 and finishing as runners-up again in 1972/73. Despite staying in the League for a further fourteen seasons (including three when known as Immediate Bristol St George), they did not finish in the top two again until being expelled from the League in 1987 due to substandard facilities.

The club then played in the County of Avon Premier Combination, winning Division One in 1988/90, finishing as Premier Division runners-up in 1990/91, eventually winning the Premier Division two years later. However, despite winning, the club was not promoted, and over the next few seasons were in danger of folding.

In 1995 the club amalgamated with local side Roman Glass, forming Roman Glass St George F.C.

Roman Glass originated as a street team called Wyndham Wanderers in 1960, and played in the Bristol Church of England League, joining the Bristol & District League in 1974. The club enjoyed moderate success, gradually climbing the leagues, and in 1980 changed its name to Roman Glass. Although the Division 4 title and successive promotions, until the amalgamation with Bristol St George, little progress was made.

The amalgamation enjoyed instant success with the club achieving promotion back to the Premier Division in the 1995/96 season. They then joined the Gloucestershire County League in 1999, and within three season's had won that League as well. Another County League triumph followed in 2006/07, earning them a further promotion to the Western League Division One for 2007/08, where they still play today.

GROUND BS32 4AG.

Roman Glass St George play their home games at Oakland's Park, Gloucester Road, Almondsbury, Bristol, which has capacity for 1,000.

Bristol St George and St George played at the Athletic Ground behind the Lord Rodney Pub which is now a pharmacy. From 1895 they played at the New Athletic Ground, St George, BS5 7RW.

1892-1897 Division One; 1897-98 Professional Section; 1898-99 Division One; 1901-03 Division Two; 1928-35 Division Two. As Roman Glass St George, 2007- Division One. As St George reserves, 1893-96 Division Two.

ROYAL ARTILLERY (HORFIELD) F.C.

HISTORY

The title 'Royal Artillery' (RA) can be traced back to 1720, and on the 1st July 1899, it was divided into three groups: The Royal Horse Artillery and Royal Field Artillery comprised one group, while the Coastal Defence, Mountain, Siege and Heavy Artillery were split off into another group, namely, the Royal Garrison Artillery.

The third group continued to be titled simply, Royal Artillery, and was based at Horfield Barracks, Bristol, entering a team into the Western League in 1897. It was to be a short-lived membership as it was interrupted when most of the players were posted to the North-West Frontier of India during that year. The season was not completed and their record was expunged from the table.

GROUND BS7 0QA

The club played at the Horfield Barracks, Bristol in an area that is now Bartholomew's Square housing estate.

1897-98 Amateur Division Two.

ST LUKE'S COLLEGE FC

'The Scholars' Established 1866

HISTORY

St Luke's College FC was one of the first football clubs in the country in 1866. Exactly one hundred years later they joined the Western League, and to commemorate their Centenary, a new initiative was introduced when

500

Mr W.O. Rice from the College, presented a Merit Cup to the League. The Cup was engraved with the words 'Western Football League Merit Cup, Presented by WO Rice Esq. 1967', and is still in use today, presented annually to the Sportsmanship Winners.

The most famous student was Sir Stanley Rous who attended the college in the 1920s, where he gained his qualification as a football referee. In 1934, he refereed the FA Cup Final in 1938 helped rewrite the laws of the game. He was also a Founder Member of FIFA.

Although St Luke's struggled in the League during their membership, their most successful season was in 1975/76 when they finished just below half-way, entitling them to membership of the new Premiership Division. For the next two seasons, they struggled, and ended 1977/78 in bottom place with just one win.

They disbanded after the college became the School of Education, within the University of Exeter.

GROUND EX4 6QB

The club had played at the Cat and Fiddle, and at other sports areas around Exeter, but then moved to St James Park, Exeter. The Cat and Fiddle site is still used by Exeter City reserves.

1893-94 Division Two; 1895-97 Division One; 1897-98 Amateur Division One.

ST PAUL'S FC

'The Saints' Established 1887

HISTORY

In the 1870s, the Brooks Dye Works opened in St Werburghs, on the edge of the St Paul's area of Bristol, and became a major local employer. That, together with migration to the City from overseas and from within Britain, led to St Paul's becoming a densely-populated area.

A local football team was formed in 1887 who were members of the Western League from 1983 until 1898; leaving to join the Bristol and District League.

GROUND BS3 2JT

The club played on a simple field with few facilities at Long Ashton, before moving to Bower Ashton, immediately north of the area now used by Bedminster Cricket Club.

1893-94 Division Two; 1895-97 Division One; 1897-98 Amateur Division One.

SALISBURY F.C.

'The Whites' Established 1947

HISTORY

The club was founded as Salisbury F.C. in 1947. A previous Salisbury City Football Club existed during the late 19th century, and played in the

Southern League Second Division between 1906 and 1911, but the later club did not consider itself to be related.

Salisbury immediately entered the Western League, and won the Second Division title at the first attempt. An attendance of 8,902, a figure never beaten, saw the Championship decider, a 1–1 draw against Weymouth.

Salisbury remained Members of the Western League until 1968, winning the Championship in 1957/58 and 1960/61, as well as finishing second on four occasions. They also reached the FA Cup First-Round proper on four occasions, and the Second-Round proper, once. In 1968 the club was elected to the Southern League.

In 1992 the club's name was officially changed to Salisbury City FC., and competing in the Nationwide Conference South followed in 2006/07, then the Blue Square Conference Premier in 2008/09, only for the club to be removed from the Football Conference after failing to pay their debts. The club reformed as Salisbury FC for the 2015/16 season.

GROUND SP1 3JH

The club played at Victoria Park in the middle of the City of Salisbury and in 1997 moved to the RayMac Stadium, a wonderful tribute to Raymond McEnhill, their Chairman and benefactor of the club for many a year.

1947-48 Division Two; 1948-68 Division One.

SALISBURY CITY F.C.

Established 1889

HISTORY

A club that holds no claims to the later Salisbury City F.C. or the current Salisbury F.C., joined the Western Football League in 1905/06, having previously played in the Hampshire League.

The following season they moved up to the Southern League, where they stayed until 1911.

The club resurfaced in the Western League in 1927, and then left again in 1929, returning a season later.

They remained in Division Two of the Western League throughout the 1930s, finishing as runners-up three times.

The original Salisbury City club folded during the Second World War, and a new club, named Salisbury, was formed in 1947. City were also regular entrants in the FA Cup, reaching the Fourth Qualifying Round twice in 1928/29 and 1931/32.

GROUND SP1 3JH

The club played at Victoria Park in the middle of the City of Salisbury.

1905-06 Division Two; 1927-28 Division One; 1928-29 Division Two; 1930-39 Division Two.

SALTASH UNITED F.C.

'The Ashes' Established 1946

HISTORY

Football in Saltash was first played as long ago as 1893. Teams played under several names – Essa, Saltash Stars and Saltash Town among them. The Saltash team disbanded with the onset of the Second World War, but a new club, Saltash United, was formed for the 1946/47 season, playing in the Cornwall Senior League Eastern Section.

In the 1950/51 season the Ashes won the 'Triple Crown' taking all three Cornish Senior Trophies: the Cornwall Senior Cup, the Durning Lawrence Charity Cup and the Herald Cup.

Two seasons later, they won the title in the 1953/54 campaign. The club stayed in the South-Western League until the end of the 1976 season, except for a four-season period when they left the League at the end of the 1958/59 campaign and rejoined again for the 1962/63 season. In their last season in the South-Western League, 1975/76, they won the League for a second time.

On gaining promotion from the South-Western League to the Western League in 1976, Saltash won the First Division Championship in their first season. The Ashes performed well in the Western League Premier Division during the 80s, in which barely a season went by without the team securing at least one piece of silverware.

Saltash fell agonisingly close to reaching the FA Cup First-Round in 1987 when they were beaten by Farnborough FC, then of the Isthmian League Premier Division, in the Fourth-Round Qualifying tie.

At the end of the 1994/95 season the club returned to the South-Western League as the high travelling expense of competing in the Western League took its toll.

Despite rejoining the Western League First Division for two seasons in 2004/05 and 2005/06, the club have since been unable to repeat the success of the 1980s.

In 2007, they joined the newly formed South West Peninsula League, finishing the inaugural season as runners-up, and where they still play today.

GROUND PL12 6DX.

Saltash United play their home games at the Kimberley Stadium, Callington Road, Saltash, Cornwall, with a capacity of 3,000.

1976-77 Division One; 1978-1995 Premier Division; 2004-06 Division One

SHEPTON MALLET F.C.

'The Mallet' Establishes 1986

HISTORY

Established in 1986 after Shepton Mallet Town's demise, the club is affiliated to the Somerset County FA.

The old Shepton Mallet Town had spent 10 years in the Western League, enjoying six of those years in the Premier Division. The club, however, go into financial difficulties and became bankrupt.

The new Shepton Mallet F.C. then took the place of the old club's reserves in the Somerset Senior League Division Two, playing at their West Shepton ground.

In 1989, they gained promotion to the Premier Division of the County League, and played there until winning the title in the 2000/01 season, when they were accepted into the Western League, and in 2013/14 came in as runners-up to Bradford Town and were promoted to the Premier Division, where they are still members.

GROUND BA4 5XN

Shepton Mallet play their home games at Playing Fields, Old Wells Road, West Shepton, Shepton Mallet. Capacity 2,500 with 120 seated.

As Shepton Mallet Town, 1976-77 Division One; 1978-79 Premier Division; 1979-82 Division One; 1982-86 Premier Division. As Shepton Mallet FC 2001-2014 Division One; 2014- Premier Division.

SHERBORNE TOWN F.C.

The Bourne' Established 1894

HISTORY

The club initially played their matches at Marston Road, before moving to the Terrace Playing Fields, just before the Second World War. They then moved grounds again in 1985 to their present home of Raleigh Grove; a name that pays reference to Sir Walter Raleigh's historical connection with the town.

504

In 1962, they joined the Dorset Combination, and in 1986/87 entered the FA Vase for the first time, competing every year until the end of the 1996/97 season, when their ground was deemed not fit for the competition as it had no floodlights.

In the season 2003/04, the club completed facility improvements, with floodlights and a 150-seater stand installed. They also finished fourth in the League that season, and won the Dorset Senior County Cup.

An application was then made to join the Western League, but the Dorset Premier League refused to grant consent.

In 2005/06 Sherborne re-entered the FA Vase, and at the end of that year, finished second in the Dorset Premier Football League and this time gained promotion to the Western League Division One.

After finishing 4th in 2006/07, they finished runners-up in 2007/08, gaining promotion to the Premier Division. That season saw the club make its debut in the FA Cup, however it was very short-lived, a 4–1 loss away to Liskeard Athletic ensued in the Extra Preliminary Round.

The club remained in the Premier Division until the end of 2011/12, when they finished second from bottom, forcing them to be relegated back to Division One, but bounced back to the Premier Division at the first attempt when finishing as Champions of Division One in 2012/13.

GROUND DT9 5NS.

Sherborne Town play their home games at Raleigh Grove, Terrace Playing Fields, Sherborne,

2006-08 Division One; 2008-12 Premier Division; 2012-13 Division One; 2013- Premier Division.

SHREWTON UNITED F.C.

'The Shrews' Established 1946

HISTORY

The club was formed in 1946. They entered the Wiltshire Football League and won Division Three in 1977/78, 1978/79 and 1980/81.

After finishing runners-up in Division One in 1990/91 and 1992/93, the club won the League in 1996/97. The division was renamed the Premier Division in 1998, and in the following seasons they finished runners-up twice. They won the Wiltshire Football League Premier Division in 2001/02 and 2002/03, and after the second title, were accepted into the Western League Division One.

505

After a couple of poor seasons, they returned to the Wiltshire League at the end of the 2012/13 season, where they play today.

GROUND SP3 4JY.

Shrewton United play their home games at the Recreation Ground, Mill Lane, Shrewton

2003 –13 Division One.

SLIMBRIDGE A.F.C.

'Swans' Established 1902

HISTORY

Slimbridge Football Club's history can be traced back to the 1899/1900 season when they played local football at various venues in and around the village, but as they do not appear to have played matches every season initially, the club officially dates its foundation to 1902.

In 1951 the club moved to their current ground at Wisloe Road after former player, Evi Thornhill, bequeathed the land to the club in his will. From then until the 1990s the club mainly competed in the Stroud and District League, except for a spell in the Gloucestershire Northern Senior League in the 1960s.

In the late 1980s, after a period of severe financial difficulties had been overcome, the club was finally able to upgrade its facilities, and step up to the Gloucestershire County League, where they finished runners-up in their first season, and were promoted to the Hellenic League Division One West.

The success continued with the Division One West title at the first attempt, and with it came promotion to the Premier Division, where three top-five finishes were achieved in the first three seasons, before clinching the Championship in 2006/07.

This earned promotion to the Southern League, but a few months later, on 10 July 2007, the club resigned, and as a result, the first team took the reserves' place in the Gloucestershire Northern Senior League. They won that League at the first attempt, and were promoted to the Gloucestershire County League, where the club maintained back to back promotions; winning promotion back to the Hellenic League.

The club re-established itself in the Hellenic League Premier Division, and achieved sixth place in the 2010/11 season, and fifth place the following year.

In 2013 they transferred to the Western League Premier Division, and after securing a 3rd-place finish at the end of the 2014/15 season, it was confirmed that the club had earned promotion back into the Southern League, where they still play today.

GROUND GL2 7AF

Thornhill Park, Slimbridge, Gloucestershire. Capacity 1,500

2012 –2015 Premier Division

SOUNDWELL F.C.

Established 1926

HISTORY

Soundwell Football Club was formed in 1926, and played in the Western League and the FA Cup in the 1940s and 1950s. Their best season was as runners-up in Division Two in 1946/47, when they scored 111 goals and conceded 44.

In the late eighties Soundwell United merged with Victoria Park, resulting in the name change to Soundwell Victoria. The club now play in the Bristol and District Division One.

GROUND BS16 4RH

While in the Western League, the club played at the Star Ground, Soundwell, Bristol.

1945-47 Division Two; 1947-50 Division One; 1950-51 Division Two.

SOUTHAMPTON F.C.

'The Saints' Established 1885

HISTORY

The club was nicknamed 'The Saints' because of its connection to a church football team. It was founded on 21st November 1885, by members of the St Mary's Church of England Young Men's Association (St Mary's Y.M.A), and played most of their early games on Southampton Common, where games were frequently interrupted by pedestrians insistent on exercising their right to roam.

More important matches, such as Cup games, were played either at the County Cricket Ground in Northlands Road, or the Antelope Cricket Ground in St Mary's Road.

They became simply St Mary's F.C. in 1887/88, before adopting the name Southampton St Mary's when the club joined the Southern League in 1894. After winning the Southern League title in 1896/97, the club was renamed Southampton F.C.

Southampton joined the Western League in 1898 to play games alongside their Southern League commitments, during which time they won the League for three years running between 1897 and 1899, and again in 1901, 1903 and 1904. During that time, they also moved to a newly built £10,000 stadium, The Dell, in 1898.

In their initial year with the Western League, they were in a very small division with just five other professional teams, and for that reason they withdrew, returning in 1900, when neighbours and rivals, Portsmouth, was one of the new clubs in an expanding league.

Portsmouth went on to win the division for three years, prompting Southampton to give the mid-week competition a real shot; after which they ended in runners-up place, four points behind Spurs.

They repeated the feat two years later, losing the title that time to QPR by just one point. With the Professional Section in two divisions, in 1907/08, they won Section A, two points clear of Portsmouth, but lost the play-off final to Milwall by the only goal of the game.

In their final year of competing they, once again, came in as runners-up, this time in Section B, four points adrift of Millwall.

They withdrew along with every other professional club in 1909.

GROUND SO15 2BU

While in the Western League, the club played at The Dell in Milton Road, a site now forming a housing estate of the same name. After 2001 they have played at St Mary's Stadium which has a capacity of 37,505.

1898-99 Division One; 1900-06 Division One; 1906-07 Division One Section B; 1907-08 Division One Section A; 1908-09 Division One Section B.

STAPLE HILL F.C.

'The Hillians' Established 1887

HISTORY

Staple Hill F.C. was based in Staple Hill, Bristol. The club joined the Bristol & District League in 1893/94, the League's second season, before it was renamed the Western Football League in 1895.

They were joint runners-up of Division One in 1895/96, but were placed in Division Two of the League after the new Professional Section was formed in 1897.

They won their division twice, in 1898/99 and 1906/07, and were runners-up on two other occasions, but there was no promotion at the time with simply the amateur/professional divide establishing membership credentials.

Staple Hill were regular entrants in the FA Cup, and reached the First Round Proper in 1905/06, when they travelled to Manchester United's Bank Street ground, where they lost 7–2 in front of 7,560 spectators.

After finishing as the winners' the previous season, Staple Hill finished bottom of the Western League Division Two in 1907/08, and dropped out of the League at the end of the following season.

GROUND BS16 5QW and BS15 1TE

Initially the club played at Staple Park, now a part of Page Park, but in 1898 moved to Soundwell Road, possibly the Chequers Ground, Kingswood, returning to Staple Park in 1902.

1893-97 Division One; 1897-98 Amateur Division One; 1898-99 Division Two (Amateur); 1899-1909 Division Two.

STONEHOUSE F.C.

'Magpies' Established 1889

HISTORY

Stonehouse joined the Western League after the War in 1947, and won the Division Two title in 1950/51.

Between the 1950s and 1970s, they were regularly attracting crowds of over 2000 to their games and during that time took part in the Western League, Wiltshire Premier League, and Gloucestershire County League. They won their first ever League title while members of the Gloucestershire County League.

Stonehouse FC entered the FA Cup every season between 1947 and 1975, reaching the Second Qualifying Round on seven occasions.

The club left the Western League in 1960.

GROUND GL10 2DG

The club played at Oldends Lane until 1949, and then moved to the Magpies Stadium, Recreation Ground, next to Wycliffe Prep school.

1949-50 Division Three; 1952-54 Division Two

STREET F.C.

'The Cobblers' Established 1880

HISTORY

Founded in 1880, Street FC is one of the oldest clubs in Somerset. Nicknamed 'The Cobblers', due to the large shoe making industry, namely Clarks, in the village. The early years were extremely successful, and Street won the Somerset Senior League four times before the end of the century, the first occasion being the 1882/83 season.

They joined the Western League in 1911, where they stayed until 1922, then rejoined again in 1931. The 1930s marked a successful period in the club's history, twice finishing runners-up in the League, Second Division. In 1938 Street reached the First Round of the FA Cup, only to lose away to Ipswich Town, 7-0.

After the resumption of regular football activities following the end of the Second World War, Street rejoined the Western League for a fourth stint in 1946, this time in the First Division.

The 1946/47 season saw the team achieve a steady eighth-place finish out of eighteen teams, which they bettered the following campaign when finishing third behind Trowbridge Town and Salisbury. The following season was also noteworthy for the Club with two Cup encounters against Southern League, Yeovil Town.

The first was when 5,000 spectators turned out at Street's 'Victoria Ground' to witness their 'famous', 2-1, FA Cup Fourth Qualifying Round victory over Yeovil. The 'Glovers' manager, Alec Stock, was so upset with his team's performance that day, he refused to let them shower after the game, and put them straight back on the coach. The club then lost away from home in the First-Round Proper against another Southern League side, Cheltenham Town.

Yeovil got their revenge later in the season when they beat Street in the Final of the Somerset Professional Cup, to pick-up their first silverware post war… or it would have done, but the Somerset FA had not gotten around to commissioning a Trophy!

The 1952/53 season saw Street achieve a second-place finish in the First Division, marking their highest ever position in the Football Pyramid. However, two relegations in six seasons resulted in them rejoining the Somerset League in 1960.

Street won the League title in 1996, enabling the club to return to the Western League for the season 1996/97, and nine years later they were promoted to the Premier Division, where they play today.

GROUND BA16 0TA.

Street play their home games at The Tannery Ground, Middlebrooks, Street, Somerset

1911-14 Division One; 1919-22 Division Two; 1930-39 Division Two; 1946-55 Division One; 1955-60 Division Two; 1997-2006 Division One; 2006- Premier Division

SWANAGE TOWN AND HERSTON FC

'Swans' Established 1898

HISTORY

The club was formed in 1898 as Swanage Albion Football Club, winning the Dorset Junior Cup in their first season. They then made it to the Dorset Senior League during the 1920s.

In the 1957/58 season the club became one of the Founder Members of the Dorset Combination League, winning the title at the first attempt.

After a certain amount of success, Swanage Town merged with local side Herston Rovers F.C. in 1966, and was renamed Swanage Town and Herston FC. In 1975/76, they joined the newly reformed Division One of the Western Football League.

After eleven seasons in Division One, the club gained promotion to the Premier Division after finishing as Champions in the Division. The 1989/90 campaign saw the 'Swans' play their last season in the Western League, and they moved side-ways to join the Wessex Football League. The last season in the Western league saw the club clinch the Dorset Senior Cup for the first and only time, when they beat Weymouth, 1–0, in the Final.

Swanage Town and Herston now play in the Dorset Premier Football League.

GROUND BH19 1NN.

Swanage Town and Herston play their home games at Days Park, Swanage, Dorset.

1976-87 Division One; 1987-1990 Premier Division

SWANSEA CITY FC reserves

'Swans' Established 1912

HISTORY

Swansea was always a rugby area in the early years, and despite previous attempts by a football club named Swansea Villa, there were no notable football clubs until the establishment of Swansea City AFC in the summer of 1912, with the club joining the Second Division of the Southern League the following season.

Following the First World War, the Swans reserves entered the Western League, where they came in as runners-up to Douglas on goal average; both clubs having finished the year on 28 points.

GROUND SA1 3RB

The reserves played at The Vetch Field, Swansea.

1919-1921 Division One.

SWINDON TOWN F.C.

'The Robins/Railwaymen/Moonrakers' Established 1879

HISTORY

Swindon Town Football Club was founded by Reverend William Pitt in 1879. The team turned professional in 1894 and joined the Southern League in its inaugural year.

Three years later they joined the new Professional Section of the Western League alongside their membership of the Southern League, coming in as runners-up to Bristol City by four points, and ahead of Reading by three. They won Division One the following year, two points ahead of Bristol St George, but for the following three seasons were at the foot of the division.

Their reserve team joined in 1901, but withdrew four seasons later, returning for periods in the 1920s. In 1932, they began another period in membership that saw them lift the Championship in both 1934/35 and 1935/36, but they failed to make it three in a row when they achieved the same number of points as Weymouth in 1937, but recorded a lower goal-average.

The War Department took over the County Ground in 1940 at the outbreak of the war, and for a while POWs (Prisoners of War) were housed in huts placed on the pitch. For this the club received compensation of £4,570 in 1945.

After the War a reserve side was entered into the Western League, and then for three season, a Colts side, but they failed to register success, and since the early 1950s no Swindon Town team has been entered.

GROUND SN1 2ED

Swindon play at the County Ground, a stadium with a capacity of 15005.

1897-98 Professional Section; 1898-1902 Division One. Swindon Town reserves, 1901-05 Division Two; 1919-21 Division One; 1925-27 Division One; 1932-37 Division Two; 1946-49 Division Two. Swindon Colts, 1949-52 Division Two.

SWINDON VICTORIA F.C.

Established around 1900

HISTORY

Swindon Victoria spent most of their existence in Wiltshire League football, and experienced probably their most successful Cup run in 1920/21. reaching the Final of the FA Amateur Cup after beating Bromely, 1-0, Willington, 2-1, and Leynstone, 3-1, only to lose 4-2 to Bishop Auckland in the Final at Middlesbrough.

In 1924/26, they joined the Western League, achieving third place in their first year, a good ten points behind the League Champions, Yeovil and Petters United. They failed to make the standard the following year when the League expanded, ending in the bottom-half of the Second Division.

In 1975, they merged with Malmesbury Town FC, who in effect took over the local Swindon club, and adopted the name Malmesbury Victoria.

GROUND

While in the Western League, the club played at the Croft Ground.

1924-25 Division One; 1925-26 Division Two.

SWINDON WANDERERS F.C.

Established pre-1894

HISTORY

Swindon Wanderers shared the Croft ground with Swindon Town, and were elected to the Western League at the AGM in May 1894. They withdrew before the start of the season with many of their players defecting to the Town side, and were in serious financial difficulty. They did, however, manage to get a team together, and played in Division One from October 1894 until the end of the 1895/96 season; ending third from bottom each year.

GROUND SN1 2ED

While in the Western League, the club played at Croft, Swindon, Wiltshire

1894-96 Division One.

TAUNTON UNITED/TAUNTON TOWN F.C.

Established 1920

HISTORY

Taunton United entered the League in 1925, and changed their name to Taunton Town in 1927. They finished at the foot of the Professional Division One for the last three years of membership. They have no link to the present-day club of the same name.

GROUND TA1 1PX

While in the Western League, the club played at Priory Park, Taunton, which is now a housing estate of the same name.

Taunton United 1925-27 Division One. Taunton Town 1927-1934 Division One

TAUNTON TOWN F.C.

'The Peacocks' established 1947

HISTORY

In December 1947, a group of businessmen founded Taunton Football Club, and the club played its first match at Easter the following year. They joined the Somerset Senior League, in which they played until 1953, then gained admission to the Western League. In the same year, the club moved into their present ground on Wordsworth Drive, which they leased from Taunton Borough Council. During those early years they battled with financial problems, and very much relied on their Supporters Club.

In 1968/69, the club enjoyed success for the first time, winning the Western League, and continued to do well; finishing as Western League runners-up in four consecutive seasons from 1973 until 1976. During that time, the club bought their Wordsworth Drive ground from the local council, with some conditions, and installed floodlights.

In 1977 they were promoted into the Southern League, but after becoming a Limited Company in 1981, they decided that competing in the Southern League was too much of a financial burden and returned to the Western League for the 1983/84 season.

The club finished as League Champions for the second time in 1989/90 and followed that with further success, winning the League again in 1995/96, 1998/99, 1999/2000 and 2000/01 both won the Championship and the FA Vase. They also finished as runners-up on four occasions; 1993/94, 1996/97, 1997/98 and 2001/02.

Following their runners-up position in 2001/02, and the improved financial position of the club compared to twenty years earlier, the club re-entered the Southern League.

GROUND TA1 2HG

Taunton Town play their home games at The Viridor Stadium, Wordsworth Drive, Taunton, Somerset.

1954-56 Division Two; 1956-75 Division One; 1976-77 Premier Division; 1983-2002 Premier Division.

TEAM BATH F.C.

'The Scholars' Established 1999

HISTORY

In 1999, the Sports Department at the University of Bath, who called themselves, TeamBath, set out to establish a football club that played within the English professional league structure, but also allowed the players to continue their education with studies at the University.

In the 2000/01 season, they entered the Western League, gaining access to the English Football League system.

The team won promotion from Division One to the Premier Division of the League in their first season, and continued to be successful in their second year, but missed out on back-to-back promotions, finishing fourth in their first season in the Premier Division.

In their third season, Team Bath entered the FA Cup for the first time, getting to the First-Round Proper, beating Horsham in a replay, 4–2 on penalties after a 1–1 draw. They were the first University side to reach that stage since Oxford University, who won the competition in 1880. TeamBath were drawn to play Mansfield Town, who won the game at the University, 4-2, in front of 5,469.

In the League, they won 27 of their 34 matches that season, and were unbeaten at home to finish top of the Western League Premier Division and gain promotion to the Southern League.

For the 2008/09 season, Team Bath played at their highest level, two promotions away from The Football League. Towards the end of the season, however, the FA notified them that, as they were not a Limited Company, they would be ineligible for further promotion, and would no longer be allowed to compete in the FA Cup. The club then opted to resign from the Conference at the end of the season rather than restructure.

Team Bath discussed the possibility of a merger with Bath City, with the aim of getting the merged team into the Football League, but questions were being asked about just how many of the team were full-blooded students, and although the 'nucleus' of the side were, it was found that those players were supported by many semi-professional players.

A further problem was that the team was supported financially by the University of Bath, and in the 2005/6 season £48,510 was paid to players on sports scholarships, although no figures have been released for the amount paid to those not on scholarships.

With mounting problems, the club folded in 2009.

GROUND BA2 7AY

While in the Western League, the club played at the Bath University Sports Ground, Combe Down, Bath.

2000-2001 Division One; 2001-2003 Premier Division.

THORNEY PITTS HOSTEL F.C.

Established 1945

HISTORY

Thorney Pitts was almost a small village situated on the Bradford Road near Corsham, Wiltshire. The prefabricated units, with a communal canteen dining area was built for Displaced Persons. One unit is still standing, and is lived in, and proudly flies the Union Flag, close to the entrance to the Wadswick Country Store. Residents from Latvia, Estonia and Lithuania fled their countries in the build-up to WW2, and was used to bring in workers to the wartime munitions plants underground. Spring Quarry Shaft-Goods Lift GL1 (alternative name: Thorney Pitts Air Shaft 1) was close by.

They entered and played in Division Two for just one season, winning only one game and losing seventeen, with 158 goals conceded, and just 24 scored. They left at the end of the season, and the hostel was later used to house Polish, Indian and numerous citizens from Europe and beyond. In 1956 Hungarian refugees were housed after their uprising against Russian control caused them to flee to the UK. Joe Bugner is reputed to have spent his formative years at Thorney Pitts before moving to Cambridgeshire with his parents.

GROUND SN13 0NR

It is believed that Thorney Pitts played on the Recreation Ground at the corner of Leafy Lane and Boxfields, which is still used for football today, under the guise of AFC Corsham Youth, providing football opportunities, including artificial surfaces, for children of all ages.

1946-47 Division Two

TIMSBURY ATHLETIC F.C.

Established 1920

HISTORY

Timsbury evolved from a team called Timsbury Ramblers, who were playing football in the village during the early 1880s. They entered the Western League for three years after World War One, and ended each season around half-way. When the League reduced to just one division of nine clubs with varying ability, they opted to joined a local league.

GROUND BA2 0JQ

When competing in the Western League, Timsbury played at North Road, a recreation ground that is still used by Timsbury Athletic FC today, playing in the Somerset County League.

1919-22 Division Two.

TIVERTON TOWN F.C.

'The Gold Army/Tivvy/Yellows' Established 1913

HISTORY

The summer of 1913 saw the birth of what is now Tiverton Town Football Club from the ashes of the recently demised rugby club as Tiverton Athletic FC. In 1921, it was decided that a merger between Athletic and Uffculme St. Peters would take place, having been rejected the previous year. The newly formed club, known as Tiverton AFC, moved from the Tiverton & District League to the East Devon League and finally grabbed their first piece of major silverware by pipping Exminster to the title. It was a Championship they would retain for the following three years.

When action got underway again in 1946 after the War, the club, now with the familiar Tiverton Town moniker, relocated to their current home at Ladysmead, changing in a pub ten minutes away. They then won consecutive League Championships in 1965 and 1966.

In the early 1970s, they join the Western League, achieving a Premier Division place when the new structure was formed. The 1980/81 season, however, yielded just 23 goals and relegation to the First Division and in 1984 ended bottom of the table.

Town clinched promotion back to the Premier Division at the end of the 1988/89 season, and were then to embark on an unprecedented twenty years of success.

The 1992/93 season saw them both in runners-up spot, and FA Vase Finalists at Wembley, where they were defeated 1-0 by Bridlington. The Western League Championship then finally arrived at Ladysmead in 1994, and stayed at Ladysmead the following year; by which time they had made three appearances in the First-Round Proper of the FA Cup, playing host to Leyton Orient and having the cheek to take an early lead on the most recent occasion.

The 1997/98 season then saw a second FA Vase Final appearance where this time a single Peter Varley goal in May 1998 clinched the ancient Trophy. Not satisfied with just one trip up the 39 steps to lift the Cup, Tiverton did it again the following year, this time getting the better of a very highly fancied Bedlington Terriers side thanks to Scott Rogers late, late strike.

They also came in as runners-up in the League and were accepted into the Southern League, where they have played ever since.

GROUND EX16 6SG

The club currently play at Ladysmead, Bolham Road, Tiverton, Devon, which was opened in 1946, and has a capacity of 3,500, of which 520 is seated·

1973-76 Division One; 1976-81 Premier Division; 1981-89 Division One; 1989-99 Premier Division.

517

TON PENTRE F.C.

'Rhonddas Bulldogs' Established 1896

HISTORY

The present club was founded in 1935, but there were at least two earlier Ton Pentre FC's, dating back to 1896, when Ton Pentre was a soccer-playing island in the Rugby Union sea of South Wales valleys.

A team from Ton Pentre entered the Western League in the year that it re-formed as a single division in 1909. They joined fellow clubs, Merthyr Town, Aberdare Town and Treharris. Although they fared well, coming in fourth, ahead of Merthyr by a point, all the Welsh clubs withdrew the following season to concentrate on the Welsh League.

They then rejoined in 1920, alongside six other Welsh clubs, but again their tenure only extended to that one season.

The following year they reached the Welsh Cup Final in 1922, but lost, 2-0, to Cardiff City at Tonypandy.

GROUND CF41 7AF

The club played at Ynys Park, Ton Pentre, which they still use today.

1909-10 Division One; 1920-21 Division One

TORQUAY UNITED

'The Gulls' Established 1899

HISTORY

Torquay United was formed in 1899 by a group of school-leavers under the guidance of Sergeant-Major Edward Tomney. After a season of friendlies, the club joined the East Devon League and moved into the Recreation Ground, their home for the next four years,

In 1904, Torquay Athletic RFC secured the lease on the Recreation Ground, leaving United to a nomadic existence; Teignmouth Road, Cricketfield Road (now the home of Upton Athletic FC) and won their first honour, the Torquay and District League title in 1909.

The club merged with local rivals Ellacombe in 1910, adopted the name Torquay United, and finally moved into Plainmoor. Torquay United then won the Plymouth and District League in 1911/12.

They joined a reduced Western League in the 1921/22 season after thirteen clubs had chosen to leave, but then left. With the loss of more clubs the following year the League was reduced to just a single division of nine club. Following a recruitment drive by the League in 1924/25, Torquay rejoined and came in as runners-up in their second season, two points adrift of Bristol City reserves.

The 1927/28 season saw the Club promoted to the Football League and their reserves replaced them in the League, continuing in membership until the start of the Second World War.

After the war, they re-entered a reserve side, and between 1955 and 1973, they won Division Two in their inaugural year back, and were then the Champions in 1959/60, sixteen points clear of runners-up, Salisbury.

They withdrew from the League for a short time between 1973 and 1976 but took up membership again when the League became sponsored by Rothmans, until again leaving in 1982.

When they returned to the League, in their second season, they came in as runners-up to Westbury United and were promoted, but their time in the Premier Division was cut short in 1993 when the midweek league that they had been playing in, was absorbed into the Combination League, forming a Second Division. The reserves then played in that league for the following four years.

GROUND TQ1 3PS

Plainmoor, Torquay with a capacity of 6,500, 2,950 seated

1921-22 Division One; 1925-27 Division One. Reserves, 1927-39 Division One; 1955-56 Division Two; 1956-73 Division One; 1976-82 Division One; 1990-92 Division One; 1992-93 Premier Division

TORRINGTON F.C.

'Torrie/Super Greens' Established 1908

HISTORY

Torrington Football Club was founded in 1908, and was originally a church side with clerics playing for the club as late as 1914. The team quickly established themselves as consistent contenders in the Senior Division of the North Devon Football League, winning the League title for the first time in the 1912/13 season, and in the first season after the war, they were crowned Champions for the second time.

In the 1948/49 season, the club won their third North Devon League Senior Division title, and also broke a number of club records. Torrington also briefly played in the Devon and Exeter League, winning the Senior Division title in 1973, and the Premier Division title in 1974.

At the beginning of the 1978/79 season, Torrington moved into the South Western Football League, struggling in their first two seasons, but in both 1980/81 and 1982/83 they were crowned runners-up of the division, and won the South Western League Cup.

Torrington joined the Western League, Division One, in 1984/85 and were promoted to the Premier Division that year after finishing as runners-up, just one point behind Champions Portway Bristol. They also achieved their furthest progression in the FA Vase, reaching the Fifth Round before being knocked out by Steyning Town. For their first few seasons in the Premier Division, Torrington struggled to move out of the bottom half, but in 1990/91 they finished second in the League.

They remained in the Premier Division until 1998, usually finishing in the top eight, before being relegated.

In 2002/03, they won their first Western League Division One Championship, but at the end of the 2006/07 season, were forced to withdraw from the League due to financial difficulties.

GROUND EX38 7AJ

Torrington play their home games at Vicarage Field, School Lane, Great Torrington

1984-85 Division One; 1985-98 Premier Division; 1998-2003 Division One; 2003-2007 Premier Division.

TOTTENHAM HOTSPUR F.C.

'The Spurs' Established 1882

HISTORY
The club was formed in 1882, as Hotspur F.C., and played in the Southern League from 1896/1908, and the Western League from 1900/1908, when they were elected to the Football League Second Division. Before that promotion Tottenham had won the FA Cup in 1901, making them the only non-League club to (or likely to), do so since the formation of the Football League in 1888.

That same year they came third in the Western League, having won eight of their sixteen games, just three points adrift of the Champions, Portsmouth.

The following season they ended the year again three points behind, and runners-up to, the same club. The 1903/04 season saw the Championship go to North London, with Spurs four points clear of Southampton, having won eleven of their sixteen games,

Spurs left the League at the end of 1907/08.

GROUND N17 0AP

White Hart Lane, Seven Sisters Road, Tottenham with a capacity of 36,284

1900-1906 Division One; 1906-08 Division One, Section B

TREHARRIS FC

Established 1889

HISTORY

The village and the club were born because of the sinking of a coal mine in 1873, which was known as the 'Harris Navigation Colliery'. Football was brought to the area by the men who arrived to work in the mine from the North of England.

Treharris Football Club was formed in 1889, and is the oldest in South Wales. In 1902/1903, they were the Founder Members of the Welsh Football League, and joined the Western League in 1906 to play in Division Two.

At that time, they pitted their skills against the reserve sides of Bristol City and Bristol Rovers, and won the Championship in 1910 ahead of both clubs by four and nine points respectively.

They left the League after that season, and in subsequent years could attract players from all over Wales; hosting many Amateur Internationals in its teams.

During the latter 19th and early 20th century, Treharris became the centre of the surrounding villages, which today constitutes an area of over 15,000 people. However, the closure of the deep navigation Colliery, once the deepest pit in the country, as well as the nearby Taff Merthyr and Trelewis Drift, had a detrimental effect on what were once thriving towns. The club still competes in the Welsh Football League.

GROUND CF46 5PY

Athletic Ground, Treharris

1906-09 Division Two; 1909-10 Division One.

TROWBRIDGE TOWN F.C.

'The Bees' Established 1880

HISTORY

Trowbridge Town was originally formed in 1880, and became one of the Founding Members of the Bristol & District League (Western League) in 1892, finishing as runners-up in that first season. They stayed in the Western League until 1958, apart from two occasions; between 1898/1901, when they went into abeyance, and from 1907/1913.

Trowbridge Town FC were successful competitors in the League winning Division One in 1939/40, 1946/47, 1947/48, 1955/56 and coming in as runners-up in 1921/22, 1948/49, 1956/57. They also had success in Division Two as winners in 1927/28, 1929/30, 1938/39 and runners-up in the 1919/20 season.

After success in the Western League, they won promotion to the Southern League in 1958, and in 1981 won promotion to the Football Conference, which was then known as the Alliance Premier League, where they played for three seasons, before being relegated back to the Southern League where they remained until they went out of existence in 1998. The name of the Club is still used, and the team play in the Wiltshire League.

GROUND BA14 9AP, BA14 8JN and BA14 NA

Until 1923, Trowbridge played at The Flower Show Field which is now the Stallards Recreation Ground adjacent to the town's railway station. They then played at Bythesea Road, which is now the site of County Hall. In 1934, they moved to Frome Road; a ground that they continued to play at until their demise in 1998. It is now a housing estate. The re-formed club play at Woodmarsh, North Bradley, Trowbridge BA14 0SA

1892-97 Division One; 1897-98 Professional Section; 1898-99 Division One – resigned during the season and their record expunged; 1901-07 Division Two; 1913-14 Division One; 1919-21 Division Two; 1921-25 Division One; 1925-39 Division Two; 1939-40 Division One; 1945-46 Division Two; 1946-58 Division One. Reserve Team, 1893-94 Division Two; 1946-59 Division Two; 1959-61 Division One.

TRURO CITY F.C.

'The Tinners/White Tigers' Established 1889

HISTORY

In 1889 Truro City became one of the Founder Members of the Cornwall County Football Association (CCFA). Later in 1889, they played their first game at Truro School, against Penzance, winning 7–1. They moved to Tolgarrick, and in 1895 won their first Trophy, the Cornwall Senior Cup, beating Launceston 5–0.

In the 1930s Truro left Cornish football for a time, joining the Plymouth and District League, which they went on to win in 1936/37.

They were Founder Members of the South-Western League in 1951, but stumbled in the initial years, requiring re-election in both of their first two seasons. However, they won the Championship five times since, and were only out of the division for three seasons, when they lost their ground due to road widening.

In the 2005/06 season, they finished runners-up in the South-Western League, and were promoted to the Western League Division One, becoming Champions at the first attempt. They also won the 2006/07 FA Vase, beating AFC Totton, 3–1, at the new Wembley Stadium, becoming the first Cornish football club to win a National Trophy.

In their first season in the Western League Premier Division, Truro gained promotion to the Southern League, and became the first Cornish side ever to play in the Southern League, and on 23 April 2011, Truro were promoted as Champions to the Conference South for 2011/12.

On 25 August 2011, HM Revenue and Customs presented a winding-up petition to the club due to unpaid taxes of over £100,000. Chairman Kevin Heaney stepped down on 24 August 2012 after being declared bankrupt, and the club went into administration on 18th September of that year. Ten points were deducted from Truro's total, leaving them bottom of the Conference South table. Truro were relegated at the end of the season, but lucky to be alive and kicking after the club's very survival was in doubt until the last-minute intervention of two local businessmen.

The club gained promotion to the newly re-named Vanarama National League South in 2014/15 via the play-offs, where they still play.

GROUND TR1 2TH

Truro City currently play their home games at Treyew Road, Truro. It has a capacity of approximately 3,000 with 1685 seated.

2006-07 Division One; 2007-8 Premier Division.

WARMINSTER TOWN F.C.

'The Red and Blacks' Established 1885

HISTORY

Warminster Town FC can be traced back to 1878, and with a short two-year break between 1883–85 it has been in existence ever since. They started playing friendly games at Holly Lodge, Boreham Road, before joining the Wiltshire County League, winning the Wilts Senior Cup in 1900/01, and then on an irregular basis up to 1933. They joined the Western League for the first time in 1930 to1939, and following the end of WW2 reverted back to the Wiltshire County League.

Having performed well in that league, they were accepted into the Western League in 1983, and in the 1994/95 season, finished in their highest position of 4th.

The club was relegated from the Western League in the 2001/02 season, and returned to the Wiltshire League, playing in the Premier Division. In most seasons, Warminster then finished in the top half of the Premier Division, until the 2005/06 season when they finished third and applied to join the Wessex League, an application that was accepted. In their first season, they finished 8th and their best season has been a 5th place in

2008/09. That same season they won through to the final of the Wiltshire Senior Cup for the first time in 50 years, but lost in extra-time to Highworth Town from the Hellenic Football League.

In June 2012, the club was accepted back into Western League, Division One, where they still play today.

GROUND BA12 9NS

Home games are played at Weymouth Street, Warminster.

1930-39 Division Two; 1983-02 Division One; 2012- Division One

WARMLEY F.C.

Established 1882

HISTORY

Warmley F.C. was a football club based near Kingswood, Bristol. They were formed in 1882, and played the first organised football match in the Bristol region against St George on the opening day of the Bristol and District League (renamed the Western Football League later).

Alongside Clifton, St George and Eastville Rovers, they were also Founder Members of the Gloucestershire FA and won the Western League title four times in their history, 1893, 1894, 1896, and 1897.

In 1896, Warmley joined the Second Division of the Southern League, before either Bristol City or Bristol Rovers, where the 1897/ 98 season saw the club finishing in second place to the Royal Artillery, who were forerunners to Portsmouth. In the process, they became the first team in the Southern League to score 100 goals in a season.

Only seventeen matches were completed before the club folded in February 1899. A new club was then formed and entered the Western League in 1903, but resigned when they disbanded during the 1904/05 season, and their record was expunged.

GROUND

Warmley played at the Tennis Court Ground, Warmley, before moving to the Chequers, the former ground of Clifton FC.

1892-97 Division One; 1897-98 Professional Section; 1898-99 Division One; 1903-5 Division Two. Reserves, 1893-96 Division Two.

WAVERLEY F.C.

Established 1889

HISTORY

Waverley F.C. was formed as the football section of the Waverley Cricket Club to provide all year-round sport. They played for just one season in Western League Division Two, winning two games and conceding 53 goals in the eighteen games played.

GROUND BS4 2QG

Waverley played at the rear of the Talbot Public House, at 304 Wells Road, Knowle, Bristol. The pub is now called Charlies Bar, and there is still green space between Redcatch Road and Broad Walk.

1893-95 Division Two.

WELLINGTON A.F.C.

'The Tangerines' Established 1896

HISTORY

Founded in 1896, Wellington have played at the Playing Fields in North Street since 1954. The club is affiliated to the Somerset County FA.

After joining the Western League for the 1978/1979 season, Wellington have played at Premier Division level twice, between 1981/82 and 1984/85, and more recently from 2008/09 to 2010/11, all other seasons have been at Division One level.

The club entered the FA Cup for four seasons in the early 1980s, twice winning a Preliminary Round tie, but never progressing past the First Qualifying round. Their best FA Vase run to date was in 1990/91, when they reached the Third Round (last 64).

Although officially named simply Wellington AFC, the county in which they play is often appended to their name to differentiate them from Wellington F.C. based in Herefordshire. They are also sometimes erroneously listed as Wellington Town.

GROUND TA21 8NE

Wellington play at the Playing Fields, Wellington.

1978-81 Division One; 1981-84 Premier Division; 1984-2008 Division One; 2008-11 Premier Division; 2011- Division One.

WELLS CITY F.C.

'City' Established 1890

HISTORY

Wells City joined Western League Division Two in 1929, and won the Western League title in 1950, but were relegated to Division Two after finishing the 1956/57 season in bottom place with just twelve points. Three seasons later the Western League disbanded Division Two, and Wells City rejoined the Somerset Senior League, finishing sixth in their first season back, with their reserves competing in the Mid-Somerset Football League. Mid-table positions then followed until 1965/66 when they were third behind Street and Welton Rovers reserves. They were runners-up behind Paulton Rovers in 1971/72.

Relegation from the Premier Division to Division One occurred at the end of the 1977/78 season, with promotion back to the top section being gained at the end of 1979/80.

The 1981/82 saw another relegation, and promotion was then a long time in arriving. It was not until 1994 that Wells City graced the top flight of Somerset football again and soon the yo-yo effect happened, once more, with relegation at the end of 1997/98 followed by bouncing straight back up in 1998/99.

The club maintained their Premier Division status, and reclaimed the Somerset Senior Cup in 2006/07. They were then accepted back into the Western League, Division One, in 2008/2009, and in their first season back finished in 10th place. The following season, their form improved and on 24th April 2010, they earned promotion to the Premier Division, after finishing as Champions, ten points clear of runners-up, Odd Down. After three seasons, however, they were relegated back to Division One.

Promotion was, once again, gained in coming in as runners-up to Chipping Sodbury Town in 2016.

GROUND BA5 1TU

Wells City play their home games at the Athletic Ground, Rowdens Road, Wells and has a capacity for 1,500 supporters.

1929-39 Division Two; 1939-40 Division One; 1946-57 Division One; 1957-60 Division Two; 2008-10 Division One; 2010-13; 2016- Premier Division; 2013-15 Division One.

WELTON AMATEURS F.C.

Established - unknown

Welton Amateurs FC was formed at a time when there were many football clubs springing up in the mining communities of Midsomer Norton and Radstock.

They shared a ground with Welton Rovers, and were members of the Somerset League. As an offshoot of Rovers, they shared the same Secretary, and joined Rovers after the First World War in petitioning for the League to accept professional clubs, and when that failed, joined the Western League for the 1920/21 and 1921/22 seasons.

GROUND BA3 2QD

The Amateurs played at West Clewes, Midsomer Norton.

1920-22 Division Two

WELTON ROVERS F.C.

'Rovers' Established 1887

HISTORY

Welton Rovers FC was formed to provide the opportunity for the mining communities of Midsomer Norton and Radstock to play, and watch, football. One of several long-established clubs in the North Somerset coalfields, their ground is the oldest in the area.

They joined the Western League in 1903, and in the 1911/12 season won the title for the first time; only losing two games and finishing 4 points ahead of Barry District. The Somerset Senior Cup was also won that season and for three consecutive seasons both pre-and post-war.

At the end of the 1922/23 season, Welton finished as runners-up to Weymouth, by two points. Troubled times, however, lead to the ground at West Clewes being sold to the Miners Welfare, but the generosity of local miners' contributions enabled the club to stay in existence. After going into abeyance for just one year, the club then rejoined the Western League, and won the Somerset Senior Cup again.

They then continued in Division One until the outbreak of the Second World War, and when they rejoined in 1945/46 they finished bottom of the single division League. The following season was notable for bad weather and severe petrol shortages, and although they managed to complete only twenty of the thirty-four games, they were still relegated.

Things gradually improved and after finishing as League Champions in 1959/60, four points ahead of Stonehouse, they then won the Somerset Senior Cup on two occasions and, in 1964/65 reached the First Round Proper of the FA Cup, losing to Weymouth after a replay. They also won the League Championship, three points ahead of Bideford Town.

The following season they were unbeaten for the entire year, and finished eleven points clear of Portland United; winning the Championship for the second year running, which was a feat they also matched for a third consecutive time in 1966/67.

With the decline of the local coal industry, the Miners Welfare donated the ground to the local authority in 1971 and since then, Welton Rovers have leased West Clewes from the local council. The 1970s, however, saw a decline in playing standards, which culminated in Welton's relegation at the end of the 1980/81 season.

There was a return to form in 1987/1988, and the First Division Championship was achieved by a single point ahead of Chard Town. That hard-earned Premier Division status, however, was lost at the end of the 1991/92 season and for most of the 1990s they continued in Division One, until securing the runners-up place in 1999/2000.

Welton again lost their Premier Division status ten seasons later, but bounced back in 2015/16 only to once again lose their Premier Division status after finishing the year in bottom spot.

GROUND BA3 2QD

Welton Rovers have played at West Clewes, Midsomer Norton, from Victorian times. The stadium holds 2,400 spectators and has seating for 300.

1903-09 Division Two; 1909-10 Division One; 1919-23 Division One; 1924-40 Division One;1945-47 Division One; 1947-60 Division Two; 1960-76 Division One; 1976-82 Premier Division; 1982-88 Division One; 1988-1992 Premier Division; 1992-00 Division One; 2000-11 Premier Division; 2011-15 Division One; 2015-16 – Premier Division; 2016- Division One. Welton reserves, 1949-50 Division Three.

WESTBURY UNITED F.C.

'Green Army/White Horse Men' Established 1920

HISTORY

The club started in 1920 with the amalgamation of two local sides; Westbury Old Comrades FC, who had just won promotion to the First Division of the Wiltshire County League and local junior side, Westbury Great Western Railway XI. Together they became Westbury United Football Club. In their first year the club finished third from bottom of the County League, and struggled throughout the 1920s, but in the 1930s Westbury won everything possible in Wiltshire football, as well as reaching the First-Round proper of the FA Cup in 1936. The club then purchased, and moved to, its present ground in Meadow Lane, at a cost of £475 for the four-acre site. The very first game played on what was then the Jubilee Playing Field, was against Bristol City and a crowd of around 4000 attended.

Westbury joined the Western League in 1984, and initially struggled. In 1988 floodlights were erected, with Southampton FC the visitors for the official switch on. Season 1988/89 saw the club win its first honour in the League, winning the Sportsmanship Trophy, and in 1991, they won the First Division title to gain promotion to the Premier Division.

The highest League placing to date came in the 1994/95 season where they finished fifth. They were relegated back into the First Division in 2001/02, when a top five position was achieved in season 2009/2010.

GROUND BA13 3AF.

Westbury United play their home matches at Meadow Lane, Westbury, Wiltshire,

1984-92 Division One; 1992-02 Premier Division; 2002- Division One.

WEST HAM UNITED FC

'The Irons/The Hammers' Established 1895

HISTORY

West Ham United was founded 1895 as the Thames Ironworks team by foreman and local league referee, Dave Taylor, and owner Arnold Hills. Its formation was announced in the Thames Ironworks Gazette of June 1895.

The team played on a strictly amateur basis for the 1895/96 season, with a group featuring several works employees. They turned professional in 1898 when they entered the Southern League Second Division, and were promoted to the First Division at the first attempt. The following year they came second from bottom, but had established themselves as a fully-fledged competitive team. They comfortably fended off the challenge of local rivals, Fulham, in a relegation play-off, winning, 5–1, in late April 1900, and retained their First Division status. Following growing disputes over the running and financing of the club, Thames Ironworks F.C. was disbanded in June 1900, then almost immediately relaunched on 5 July 1900, as West Ham United F.C.

West Ham United joined the Western League for the 1901/02 season while also continuing to play in the Southern Division One. In 1907, they were crowned the Western League Division One Section 'B' Champions, and then defeated Division One Section 'A' Champions, Fulham, 1–0, in a play-off game, to become the Western League Champions. They left in 1909 alongside all the other professional clubs.

GROUND E13 9AZ

The Club initially play their games at the Memorial Grounds, Canning Town in Plaistow, but moved to a pitch in the Upton Park area in the guise of the Boleyn Ground stadium in 1904. They now play at the London Stadium (originally known as the Olympic Stadium).

1901-06 Division One; 1906-09 Division One Section B

WESTON (BATH) A.F.C.

Established 1899

HISTORY

Weston was a village on the north-west edge of Bath, and the football club originated as All Saints FC, changing its name in 1899/1900, when they entered a team into Western League Division Two.

At that time, there were just five clubs competing, and of the eight games played, Weston won one game and drew one. They then entered the Competition the following season, but withdrew without playing a game.

GROUND BA1 3BL

Higher Court Mead, opposite the gasworks in Lower Weston, Bath

1899-1901 Division Two

WESTON-SUPER-MARE A.F.C.

'The Seagulls' Established 1948

HISTORY

Weston-super-Mare A.F.C. was formed in 1887. The team's first record of a competitive match was against near-neighbours, Clevedon Town, in a 'Medal Competition' organised by the Somerset FA. In 1900, they joined Division Two of the Western League, but left after two years; rejoining in 1910/11 until the outbreak of World War One.

Between the wars, the club played in the local Bristol and District Football League, and then the Somerset County League, and disbanded on the outbreak of hostilities in 1939.

The club reformed in 1948, and immediately rejoined the Western League, initially in Division Two. At that time, the club played at the Great Ground in Locking Road, where initially there was no cover for spectators and the players had to change in a marquee. They remained in the Second Division until the League consolidated to a single division in 1960. During that time, they moved to the Langford Road.

In 1976, they were placed in the Western League Premier Division on the creation of a second tier, meaning that by the time of their Centenary in 1987, they had never been promoted or relegated in their history. Under the Chairmanship of Paul Bliss the club moved to Woodspring Park in 1983, and moved just down the road to the Woodspring Stadium in 2004.

The club finally won the Western League Championship in 1991/92 and gained promotion to the Southern League Midland Division. They now play in the Vanarama National League South.

GROUND BS24 9AA

Woodspring Park, (Woodspring Stadium), Winterstoke Road, Weston-super-Mare, with a capacity of 3,500, with 350 seated.

1900-02 Division Two; 1910-14 Division One; 1948-60 Division Two; 1960-76 Division One; 1976-92 Premier Division. Reserves, 1949-50 Division Three

WEYMOUTH F.C.

'The Terras' Established 1890

HISTORY

Weymouth Football Club were founded in 1890, and played their first game on 24th September that year.

Nicknamed 'The Terras' due to their terracotta strip, the team won the Dorset Junior Cup for the first three seasons, becoming a senior club as they began to progress.

Founder members of the Dorset League, Weymouth joined the Western League in 1907/08. The club embraced full-time professionalism in 1923 after winning the Western League, joining the Southern League in the process. By 1928/29 with debts mounting, the club withdrew from the Southern League, to become amateur once again.

The Second World War saw an end to football in Weymouth as the Recreation Ground was requisitioned for the War effort in 1939. The club reformed in 1947 on a semi-professional basis, and soon achieved promotion back into the Southern League. Their reserves were then involved in the Western League on-and-off for many years until withdrawing in 1987.

GROUND

Bob Lucas Stadium, Weymouth with a capacity of 6,600 and seating for 900 spectators.

1907-09 Division Two; 1909-14 Division One; 1921-28 Division One; 1928-39 Division Two; 1947-48 Division Two; 1948-49 Division One. Weymouth Reserves, 1925-28 Division Two; 1949-67 Division One; 1969-70 Division One; 1982-87 First Division.

WILLAND ROVERS F.C

'Rovers/Devon All-Whites' Established 1946.

HISTORY

Willand Rovers Football Club was formed in 1946, after the financial collapse of Willand Wanderers FC during the Second World War, which had been formed in 1907.

The club moved to their present home of 'The Stan Robinson Stadium', in the 1950s, and played in the Devon and Exeter Football League. In 1990 Willand were relegated to the Senior Division of the Devon and Exeter Football League, because their ground was not considered to be up to the standard of the Premier Division. However, they went back to that division in 1991/92, after work both on and off the pitch.

For the start of the 1992/93 season they were among the Founder Members of the Devon League, and went on to win the league twice, before gaining promotion to the Western League Division One in 2001. They won the Western League Division One title in 2004/05, earning promotion to the Premier Division, where they have finished in the top six during each of their seasons at that level.

Willand Rovers made it to the Les Phillips Cup Final in 2006, losing to Corsham Town, but went one better in 2007, winning the Cup after a Final against Welton Rovers. They reached the Fifth Round of the FA Vase in 2009/10.

GROUND EX15 2RG

Willand Rovers play their home games at The Stan Robinson Stadium, Silver Street, Willand.

2001-05 Division One; 2005 – Premier Division.

WILLSBRIDGE F.C.

Established 1891

HISTORY

Willsbridge joined the Western League after taking part in the South Bristol and District League in its inaugural season. They performed well in a division made-up exclusively of local Bristol clubs, winning fifteen of their twenty matches and drawing one. They were just three points behind the eventual Champions, Warmley reserves. Willsbridge resigned at the end of that year, and returned to the South Bristol League, along with Mangotsfield reserves and Waverley.

The club played somewhere between Longwell Green, Oldland Common and Bitton but the exact location is not known.

1894-95 Division Two

WIMBORNE TOWN F.C.

'The Magpies' Established 1878

HISTORY

Wimborne Town Football Club was formed in 1878 and originally catered for both football and rugby. In 1884, Wimborne Town were one of the Founder Members of the South Hampshire and Dorset Football Association. In 1887, the club became a Founder Member of the Dorset County Football Association.

Wimborne Town's first senior honour came in 1937, winning the Dorset Senior Amateur Cup, and they repeated that success in 1964. In 1957, Wimborne became Founder Members of the Dorset Combination (now the Dorset Premier League), but returned to the Dorset League after just a season, where they remained until 1973, when they returned for another spell, this time lasting three seasons.

The club's fortunes dramatically took off when they won the Dorset League Division One title in 1980/81 without losing a match. In 1981, following the installation of floodlights and the construction of a perimeter fence and new changing rooms at their Cuthbury ground, Wimborne Town were admitted to the First Division of the Western League.

The club entered both the FA Cup & FA Vase for the first time in 1982/83. That season brought them their best run to date in the FA Cup when defeats of Bridport, Falmouth Town, St Blazey, Bath City and Merthyr Tydfil earned them a visit to Aldershot, in the First Round Proper where they lost 4-0. The 1984/85 season was Wimborne Town's most successful in the Western League when they finished in third place, ahead of Swanage on goal difference.

In 1987, Wimborne Town moved sideways to join the Wessex League, won the FA Vase in 1992, and were promoted to the Southern League Division One in 2010.

GROUND BH21 4EL

The Cuthbury/W+S Stadium, Cowgrove Road, Wimborne Minster. Capacity estimated at 2,800 with 275 seated.

1981-87 Division One

WINCANTON TOWN F.C.

'Winky' Established 1890

HISTORY

Established in 1890, and originally based at Dancing Lane on West Hill, the club played most of its football in the Yeovil and District League in its early years.

They won Division Two of the Yeovil League in the 1988/89 campaign, followed by two more years of league success, when they won Division One the following season, and were crowned League Champions just a season later.

Sometime after that in the 1990s, the club sold its ground at Dancing Lane and moved to its current home at Moor Lane.

At the end of the 2002/03 campaign, the club was promoted to Division Three of the Somerset County League when they finished as runners-up in the Yeovil League. Their first season in the new league saw them gain promotion to Division Two where they again finished as runners-up.

They played for two seasons in that division, before deciding to swap to the Dorset Football League, winning the Senior league at the first attempt and gaining promotion to the Dorset Premier Football League.

The club stayed in the Dorset Premier League until the end of 2012/13, when they finishing as runners-up and gained promotion to Division One of the Western Football League, and on October 15, 2013, the club hosted Yeovil Town F.C. to celebrate the opening of Moor Lane's new floodlights.

GROUND BA9 9EJ.

Wincanton Town play their home games at Wincanton Sports Ground, Moor Lane, Wincanton, Somerset with a capacity of 1,500 and seating for 150.

2013- Division One

WINTERBOURNE UNITED F.C.

'The Bourne' Established 1911

HISTORY

Winterbourne United Football Club was formed in 1911 and were initially known as Winterbourne Wasps until after the First World War.

The club then entered the Bristol and Suburban League, and enjoyed one of the most successful periods in their history, finishing as runners-up four times during the 1930s.

In the 1933/34 season, they reached the semi-finals of the G.F A Senior Amateur Cup, losing to Victoria Albion at the Douglas Ground, Kingswood. In the home-leg of the Quarter-Final, against Dockland Settlement, over 2000 paid to watch the game.

Season 1967/68, saw the club move into senior football, winning the Bristol & District League Division One Championship, the GFA Intermediate Cup, and the Berkeley Hospital Senior Cup.

Their success brought promotion to the Bristol Premier Combination, and three years later in 1970/71, they won the Second Division Championship, and the Cossham Hospital Premier Cup.

Winterbourne continued in membership of the County of Avon Premier Combination, until their most successful season, and in 1991/92, they won the Premier Combination Cup, and finished runners-up to Highridge United in the Premier Division; gaining promotion to the Gloucestershire County League for the first time.

A poor season in 1995/96 saw the club relegated from the Gloucester County League back to the Bristol Premier Combination, despite reaching the G.F.A. Challenge Trophy semi-finals for the first time.

The slump did not last long, however, and a year later they were promoted back into the County League after winning the 'double' - beating Highridge United, 2–1, in the Final of the G.F.A. Senior Amateur Cup, and the Premier Combination Championship by 7 clear points from their nearest rivals, Hambrook.

In season 1998/99, the reserves won the Bristol & District League Senior Division to gain promotion to the Premier Combination, and two years later in 2000/01 the First Team finished as Champions of the Gloucestershire County League, and promotion to the Hellenic League.

In season 2012/13 they successfully applied for a side-ways move to the Western League Premier Division, where they found playing standards different and ended the year in what was to be their highest position of twelfth.

They resigned three months into the season in December 2015 and their record was deleted from the tables.

GROUND

Winterbourne played at Oakland's Park, Almondsbury, Gloucestershire (Ground share)

2012 – 2015 Premier Division.

WORLE ST JOHN/WESTON ST JOHNS F.C.

Established 2000

HISTORY

Worle St John joined the Western League in 2000/01, and changed their name to Weston St Johns after a merger with that club the following year.

They continued in membership until 2007/08, but struggled at that level. After coming bottom of Division One that season, winning just five of their forty games played, and conceding 127 goals in the process, they went out of the League into the Somerset League and now play in the Second Division, West.

GROUND BS23 3UP

The club played at Coleridge Road, Weston.

2000-2001 Division One; As Weston St John, 2001-2008 Division One.

YEOVIL AND PETTERS UNITED/ YEOVIL TOWN F.C.

'The Glovers' Established 1895

HISTORY

Yeovil Football Club was founded in 1890 after reforming from Yeovil Casuals FC who were formed in 1895. In 1907, the name Yeovil Town was adopted which, on amalgamation with Petters United, became Yeovil and Petters United. The name reverted to Yeovil Town prior to the 1946/47 season.

They joined the Western League after the First World War in 1919 in the amateur Division Two, but the following year opted to join Division One, which offered thirty games with professional teams from the West Country and Wales. Thirteen of those clubs resigned before the start of the following season, but Yeovil remained to pick-up the Championship five points clear of runners-up, Trowbridge Town.

They remained members of the League up until the Second World War, picking up another Championship in 1924/25, 1929/30 and 1934/35, as well as runners-up on five other occasions.

After the War Yeovil changed the Petters part of the name to Town, and their reserve side entered the League; taking a while to settle and finishing most years in the bottom half, until the 1954/55 season when they ended the term joint-top on 51 points with Frome Town, wining Division Two on goal difference. They then went on to win the Western League Championship in 1958/59, in a strong division, four points clear of Salisbury.

A decade later, however, after finishing in the bottom four in consecutive seasons, and bottom in 1968/69, they left the League, only to return when the League expanded in 1976. They then spent the following seasons making little headway to gain Premier Division football, which prompted another exit in 1991 to join the extended Combination League.

After a five-season break, they returned to the League, and in 1997/98 came in as runners-up to Bishop Sutton, thereby gaining promotion. Having faired reasonably well at the higher level, they left at the end of 2001/202 to again play in the Combination League.

GROUND BS23 3UP

The club play at Huish Park, Lufton Way, Yeovil which has a capacity of 9,565

Yeovil and Petters United, 1919-20 Division Two; 1920-21 Division One. Yeovil and Petters reserves, 1925-29 Division Two; 1936-39 Division Two. Yeovil Town reserves, 1945-51 Division One; 1951-55 Division Two; 1955-65 Division One; 1966-70 Division One; 1976-91 Division One; 1996-98 Division One; 1998-2002 Premier Division.

THE WESTERN FOOTBALL LEAGUE

DIRECTORS

BRIAN BEER

League Management Committee 2003-08, President 2011 -

I joined the Committee of Chard Town in 1957 before which I played in the second and third teams of the club in junior football. At the time of my joining the club there were more than enough people seeking to serve on the committee and elections were necessary; unlike today when you have got to beg or drive them off the streets to get involved in a voluntary capacity.

My first post was that of team Secretary when each Monday evening a Selection Committee would deliberate on the teams for the coming matches. Players would be informed by post of their selection together with the teams posted on the notice board outside the George Hotel; no emails, text messages or mobiles in those days!

In 1963 Colin Dunford joined the club and for ten years he was the First Aid Trainer and Treasurer, prior to which I had been elevated to Secretary of the club. In 1973, I became Chairman and Colin took up the role of joint Secretary/Treasurer, and together we served the club for twenty-one years until Colin resigned due to his commitments as a Director of a company in Devon, and stood down in 1994. Both Colin and myself are vice-Presidents of the Somerset Football Association.

Colin will recall the best of times where, in the mid-60s, Chard were a strong Somerset Senior team with many of the clubs in membership now playing in the Western and Southern leagues.

In Chard Town's early days in the Western League, officers like Jack Veale, Maurice Washer and Don Milverton became personal friends, as did many club officers such as Tom Harris of Taunton Town and Les Heal of Glastonbury, and even at County FA level, with Doug Cummins and Lew Webb. Much of this was due to the personal contact via the telephone; not impersonal emails as it is today.

Colin and myself often remark on past referees who were Western League Officials, with perhaps the likes of Roger Milford uppermost, who we first saw at Chippenham when Chard lost 2-0. He always had a smile on his face and, despite the result, Colin gave him 10/10. Then there was Paul Durkin, Don Morgan (my drinking partner), and Micky Gale; along with many others who had great personalities.

During my term as President of the League, my wife, Eileen, and I have made many friends, and working alongside John Pool, Chairman, his fellow officers and the Board members, is a great pleasure.

Member clubs extend their great hospitality when I can visit them even if they don't always have the right brand available!

JOHN POOL

League Management Committee in 1995, Vice-Chairman 2001-2010; Chairman 2010 -

I was born no more than 500yds from Welton Rovers West Clewes ground and it was without doubt that which defined my involvement and long association with the Western League. With a father and grandfather who supported Welton Rovers for many years, whose loyalty was rewarded during the mid-sixties by witnessing the Club's most successful years under the Arnold Rogers reign, the Western League became a huge part of my football life.

After a playing career that lasted into the mid-70s with Radstock Town, Clandown and Paulton Rovers I was persuaded in 1977 by Terry Gillard, the Manager of Clandown, to join him and take up what was my first role in the Western League, as trainer.

It is Terry Gillard who I will always be grateful to for giving me the opportunity to have an active involvement in the Western League, which started as a Committee member at Clandown in 1977, before taking on the Secretaries role in 1981. It was, therefore, with great sadness that we learned of his death at the end of July 2017. He will be sadly missed by, players, officials and family alike. He was a friend to many.

Clandown provided some terrific times for those involved. The 'club on the hill', which no one ever wanted to visit (especially in the winter), but who always departed with memories of what a good time could be had with very limited resources, but with an awful lot of enthusiasm in the company of honest football people.

Among the many highlights were 'the double headers' where we would travel on Saturday to play teams such as Falmouth Town or Plymouth Argyle Res. followed by either Saltash United or Liskeard Athletic on the Sunday (after Saturday night out on the town in Plymouth and trying to get players in a fit state to perform the following day). The enjoyable times continued with Cup runs at places like Maidenhead United, drawing 0-0 at home but losing 0-1 in the replay.

In the FA Trophy, Waterlooville away, when the fog came down and sitting in the stand where you could see very little but could hear the booming voice of League Chairman Les Phillips cheering on Clandown. The excitement of the FA Cup visiting Forest Green Rovers, Llanelli, St Blazey, Basingstoke, Haverfordwest County, Dorchester Town and RS Southampton. Two consecutive years of finishing 4th in the Western League Premier Division in what was an extremely strong League was a tremendous achievement for what was pretty much the smallest club in the League. My involvement ended in 1989 when I stepped down from the Secretarial role and sadly left the Club.

My next opportunity to get involved came with again joining Terry Gillard, who after a short sabbatical had joined Paulton Rovers, and again invited me to join him. Taking on the role again on the bench (as trainer) my administrative role didn't commence until the then long serving secretary Keith Simmons, who had been Football Secretary of the Club for a considerable number of years, took up the role of Social Club Secretary. Having been given the opportunity to go back into football administration again it seemed an opportunity too good to miss. This then brought about in 1995 my election to the Western League Management Committee.

In 2001, after stepping down from the secretary role at Paulton I became Vice Chairman of the Western League, which had become available when Doug Webb (Chippenham Town) wished to dedicate more of his time to the Club he had been associated with for many years, when Chippenham achieved promotion to the Southern League.

It was during this period that a major change came about in the structure of the Western League and its geographical boundaries. In 2008, a proposal came forward and was accepted that the Devon County League be amalgamated with the South-Western League; this resulted in football in the South West being totally transformed.

From a Western League perspective, it has meant that the Devon County League was lost as a feeder League to the Western League, and the strength and financial support within Cornish football has left the Devon clubs finding themselves with limited opportunities to seek promotion; not good for football in the South West.

A proposal put forward by the Western League at a meeting in 2013 to readjust the system by creating an additional division (reducing travelling distances), was dismissed by the FA. This was an opportunity sadly missed.

With colleagues in the SWPL acknowledging that the clubs that have the finances to increase playing budgets are always likely to create this continuing 'roadblock', there appears at present, no real solution to the problem. A real shame because I will always believe that football in the South West is as equally important and can be as strong as it is the North of England if a structure is put in place to satisfy all clubs with aspirations to move forward in the pyramid.

My role as Vice Chairman came with the added involvement of being responsible for carrying out ground grading which continued up until the time when I became Chairman in 2010. To follow in the footsteps of the numerous Chairmen who had gone before me was without doubt a real learning curve. To look back at the personalities of Stan Priddle, with Maurice Washer as his General Secretary, with their 'measured approach', compared to that of Les Phillips who's 'passion and commitment' showed all of us that once you were involved in the Western League, even after you left, you would never forget the experiences and friendships you would create along the way.

To be part of a League which has always been blessed with excellent sponsorship going back to Rothmans, Great Mills, Screwfix and our present sponsors Toolstation, they have all offered so much to the standing of the League throughout the Country, to all those past and present whether in administration or playing, my wife, Helen and I will be eternally grateful for all the memories.

ALLAN SKUSE

League Management Committee in 2008; Vice-Chairman 2011 -

My earliest experience of football is playing in the Bristol Downs League with college friends. I can admit to standing outside the changing rooms with my boots on, waiting for a game with teams that were short of players playing under the name of Billy Boots or Sammy Sub.

My main sport was basketball and I played at a very high level for a team in Exeter playing in the National League all over England, (Sunderland on a Sunday night and working the next day) so don't talk to me about travelling to games as my home games were in Exeter on a Saturday night and I lived in Bristol!

My son, Paul was the reason I got into the Western League.

Paul played for the county and reps teams and was asked to go to Southampton in goal for their under-13/14s, a year below Matt Huxley.

Like so many, he was released and joined Keynsham Town under my mate Malcolm Trainer in the under-18s team. Paul Hirons and Nigel| Lee were first team and reserve team manager respectively, and were always keen to give the young lads a chance. Paul made a couple of first team appearances but played mostly in the reserves with Nigel Lee and in the under-18s with Malcolm Trainer.

I joined the committee with my wife Jean, who worked in the tea-hut, and I helped with the 3rd team and the under-18s, as well as working on the pitch. Football seemed to take over our weekends. Keynsham had a very strong committee with Phil Gane as Chairman, but as with all clubs, money was very tight. The managers were both very committed to the club and we could not have asked more of them. The first team was promoted to the Premier Division, second to Team Bath, in 2000/1.

My son left Keynsham for Longwell Green Sports under Matt Hale, and as the Chairman, Chris Wyrill, was a very close friend, I joined them.
Longwell Green Sports were playing in the Premier Combination League, and were working very hard to get the work around the ground/changing rooms ready to enable them to gain County League status. This was achieved by a very hard-working committee.

Longwell Green Sports came in as runners-up that season, but were promoted because Highridge FC did not have the grading required.

At Longwell Green Sports, I asked about becoming a club representative on the Western League Board, and the following season applied and was voted on by the clubs in 2008. When John Pool became Chairman in 2010, he asked me to stand for Vice-Chairman. I was proud to accept, and my wife, Jean and I have really enjoyed the last seven years in that role.

KEN CLARKE

Honoury Secretary 2000-2014; Company Secretary 2001-

It was via Maurice Washer that I first made official contact with the Western League, when I was still operating in referee mode. One Saturday morning back in the early 80s, Tony Knee, the secretary of Chippenham Town called on me to carry out a pitch inspection. The pitch was hard with frost, but not dangerous in my opinion. I passed the pitch fit for play and proceeded to Swindon to take charge of a Wilts Senior Cup quarter final. There was

544

some doubt expressed by Swindon Supermarine, the home club, as to the suitability of the pitch, but we played and at the end of the game both sides agreed that I had made the correct call. When I returned home, my wife said that I had received a call from Maurice Washer, Secretary of the Western League, who wanted me to call him. I rang Mr Washer who, after establishing who I was, asked me very curtly why I had sanctioned play at Hardenhuish Park earlier. I told him that the pitch was fit, he said that it couldn't have been due to the almost skating rink conditions down one wing. He then replaced his 'phone, forcibly. A couple of weeks later I found out that members of the club had rolled ice into the pitch to make sure that it would not pass the referee's inspection, perhaps they didn't have a full side!

Fast forward 15 odd years and, having spent all those years as secretary of Chippenham and District Sunday Football League and variously as a Wiltshire FA Councillor, Secretary and Chairman of Chippenham Referees' Society, Referee Instructor and Referee Assessor, I applied for the soon to be vacant role of General Secretary of the Western Football League. The management committee called me to meet them in a hotel conference room in Taunton, and I was surprised to be confronted by eight or nine officers and management committee members in the room, but that assembly fired questions at me and then decided that I should be able to succeed Maurice Washer, who was a member of that interview panel. I assume he didn't remember our previous encounter.

At the 1999 AGM, I was elected General Secretary and it was all systems go. My first task was to assist in compiling the fixtures for the coming season and my eyes were opened to one of the big differences between Non-League Football and local football; less teams but many more complications; but with the help of League Committee members and club secretaries my inauguration commenced.

As I found my feet as General Secretary, I was fortunate to be able to represent the League on a committee at the FA, at that time situated in their offices in Soho Square. The meetings worked well. A Focus Group was then formed and we adopted the responsibility to enhance football at our level, I was appointed chairman of the Focus Group and the six of us met in the magnificent surroundings of Wembley Stadium, the new headquarters of the FA, and attempted to enhance our level of football. The meetings at the new Wembley were interesting but it's the FA Vase Finals that I have attended, at the old and new Wembley as well as Villa Park, that I experienced some of the best times I've had with the League, especially when it involved Western League Clubs.

Just over a season into the League secretary's role I received a registered letter one Saturday morning advising me that legal action was being taken against me, and others, which could have cost me my house such was the size of the claim. Telephone lines (pre-easy mobile access) were red hot that morning and following consultation on the following Monday the FA employed their lawyers to defend a complicated case against five League and FA personnel. There was a satisfactory conclusion on our part but the

League was advised to incorporate as a limited company to modulate claims against any future League administrators. The Western Football League Limited was the outcome of that recommendation, and I was appointed Company Secretary.

During my tenure as Western League Secretary the management didn't get easier, but then it was no more difficult than I had expected, and I continued to gain satisfaction from the day to day administration of an organisation involving so many good people. For quite a few years I spent a week in June compiling the fixtures for the coming season, always taking my wife, Pat, on holiday so that I could spend the mornings working on the fixtures whilst she explored wherever we had travelled to. That wasn't her only contact with League administration, she very kindly took on the tedious roles connected with player registrations, while my sister, Denise, became adept in her role as my assistant, both girls on a purely voluntarily basis, relieving me of those tasks.

Politics aside, and with some of the strong characters involved it is not always easy to put politics aside, I had loads of enjoyable times with the League and met some good and interesting people. I have been welcomed by club officials all over the Western League area and most of those club officials ensure that their clubs continue to thrive, or maybe just get by such are these difficult times, but more importantly it's their involvement that keeps their clubs functioning. These are the people that operate mostly without thanks and are sometimes not as appreciated as they should be.

SPONSORSHIP

Sponsorship of the Western League played a big part in my time with the League, which is why I decided to dedicate an entire section to the subject. Elsewhere the Rothman's sponsorship is referred to and as it was over forty years before my involvement I knew little of its inner working. In my refereeing times, I knew the League as the Great Mills Western League, but again the worth was of little concern to me.

When I moved to the League it was already operating as the Screwfix Direct Western League with Derek Skeavington as the main company contact, and he made dealings with the company very easy. Screwfix Direct Ltd lent its' name to the League boosting its coffers quite substantially, as well as offering other benefits.

In 2001 Screwfix, Direct Ltd gave several season's notice of their intention to discontinue their support of the League. At the end of that season Taunton Town reached the final of The FA Vase and I took a friend to the final, and he had a chat with Derek Skeavington. Sometime later my friend, having got a feel for what was happening, called me to say that he had read that the Goddard-Watts family, who had launched Screwfix Direct Ltd, had unveiled a new company dealing in similar products, and the company was called Toolstation Ltd.

We wondered if the Western League had created a good enough impression with the Goddard-Watts family for them to align their new company with us.

A call to the new offices led to an invitation to meet Neil Carroll and Adam Keates. They offered to put together a sponsorship package which proved to be the best deal at our level of football, so the offer was snapped up for the start of the 2005/06 season. What a sponsorship that has proven to be - it is better than anything that has gone before - it has given clubs support with lower affiliation fees – it has enabled the League to distribute free match balls – it has meant the League can operate at the best level for member clubs, and hopefully we can look forward to an ongoing relationship with Toolstation Ltd.

MARK EDMONDS

League Management Committee; Honoury Secretary 2014 -2016

I think we can easily say right from the word go, Mark was a football fanatic, plain and simple. Mark's devotion to his home team Aylesbury Utd was unwavering. In the earlier years, he travelled far and wide to watch the 'Ducks'. However, in the most recent years he had to be content with being a long-distance fan, but always tried to get to at least a couple of games during the season. He continued his lifelong love of the club with setting up an Aylesbury United nostalgia page on Facebook which relives memories of 'Duck's games over the years.

During his army career, he took up refereeing and was very honoured in 1992-93 to be awarded The Dobson's Trophy. This trophy is awarded in April every year in the season about to end to the Referee considered by the Members of the Army FA Referees' Committee to have made the most significant contribution to Army Football.

Whilst stationed at Larkhill, around 92/93 he joined the local referee's society and started officiating in the Salisbury and District League; following promotions he then officiated on the Wiltshire Football League, Hellenic League, Wessex League and for many years on the Toolstation Western League, before finally retiring from refereeing in 2003 on the National Conference League.

In 2004, he proudly took on the role as Discipline Secretary for Wiltshire County FA and for 10 years loved dealing with the bad boys of football. Following this position, for a very short period he took over as secretary of Salisbury City FC.

At the start of season 2014/15 he was delighted to take on the role as League Secretary for the Toolstation Western Football League, and this was where he hoped to achieve many more aspirations in his football career. He set up the first and second Western League groundhops, which were a huge success.

Mark was involved over many years with numerous football leagues/ associations and throughout the years undertook many committee roles. He served on the Wiltshire FA, Salisbury and District League, Nadder Valley League, South Wiltshire Referees Association, Western League Referees Association and the Toolstation Western Football League to name a few.

His work-horse attitude, energy, enthusiasm and passion for grass roots football will be remembered by everyone who knew him.

Mark died way too early, on 13th December 2016, following a short illness. RIP

ANDY RADFORD

Company Director 2015-; Fixtures Secretary 2015-16; Honoury Secretary 2017-

I am not someone who has been involved in Western League football for years. I have never played the game or been a referee. I came to the game in what many would consider 'late on'. In fact, my involvement with the Western League and therefore grassroots football only dates to 2007. It was a twist of fate. That 'right time and the right place' moment that only seems to happen in movies.

I had a job but outside work the only thing that occupied my time was my family and they were growing up. For many years, my wife, Sally, was a governor at the local school. Evening meetings for her left me home alone at times. I needed a hobby. I needed something to do with all this time and wasted energy. The Bristol Evening Post carried an advert for Bristol Manor Farm who were looking for a club secretary. I knew the club only from the point of view that years past we had celebrated New Year's Eve there with friends on a couple of occasions. I telephoned the number given and spoke with club chairman Geoff Sellek. It was a hot day one weekend when I met him at his shop in Downend. I had no idea what was involved in being the club secretary. Geoff had notes. Small pieces of paper he kept handing to me; each one carrying some vital information. I started to think this was not for me. I assumed that other people had applied to be the club secretary and that this was an interview to judge my suitability. But Geoff soon put me right – I was the only one who had contacted him.

And so, it began.

I had no idea what I had let myself in for. I had no idea just how much work was involved. But I was excited at the prospect. I went home and immediately talked to my eldest son about developing a website for the club. At the time, he must have been only fifteen but he had been writing and developing websites for a couple of years (he now runs his own development company). Before the season kicked off we had a website up and running and I had a stack of handbooks, team sheet books and old paperwork. I binned the old paperwork. I had met the new manager, John Black. I had met the team who one by one moved to other clubs before the season even kicked off. The club was rebuilding both on and off the pitch.

On holiday in July of 2007 I received a phone call from Geoff; there had been a fire and the function room had been burned to the ground. Was this an omen? The opening match saw a 5-0 thrashing of 'The Farm' by Barnstaple Town. Not one win was recorded in the month of August and we were knocked out of the FA Cup by Odd Down. The first game in September at home to Street finally saw us record our first win of the season. The sun shone. The drinks flowed. And all was well with the world. With the team slowly being rebuilt, we finished sixth from bottom. At one time, it looked as though we would be relegated.

But there were better times ahead in the seasons that followed. My youngest son came with me to every game. Home and away we travelled the South West enjoying our football. Being the club secretary necessitated being at the game early so we would take packed lunches and drinks and each Saturday away at a new venue was a new adventure. Bristol Manor Farm was now our club.

It was a steep learning curve but after that first season things settled down. I knew what I was doing and I enjoyed it. Travelling around the Western League it soon struck me that clubs only survived because of the willingness of their volunteers to put in the time and effort. There was always a friendly welcome from every club and it was a pleasure meeting new people with the same passion for our level of football.

In 2010, I applied to join the Board of the Western League but was not successful. In 2011, I was approached by the league to take over their website and I have been the webmaster since then. In that time, the website has been changed several times with new features and additions and I became a Board member at that time.

During the 2014/15 season I took the decision to stand down as club secretary of Bristol Manor Farm. It was not an easy decision but I felt I had 'done my bit' and that it was time for someone else to continue taking the club forward. Nearing the end of that season I was asked if I would be interested in becoming the Fixtures Director for the league. I thought about it for a while before taking the plunge!

The Western League now celebrates 125 years. Over those years, every club, each volunteer, all the Board members and League Officers have made the league what it is today - one of the oldest and most respected and I am proud to have been just a small part of that history…

DAVE BRAMMER

League Management Committee 2015; Finance Director 2016-

I began as an Assistant Referee (Linesman) in 1981, where my first game was Mangotsfield United v Barnstaple Town. Three years later I was promoted to the Referees list with the first game in the middle Welton Rovers v Larkhall Athletic

On reaching retirement age in 2001, I began assessing, operating at Steps 3, 4 and 5 and alongside that I was the Match Officials Assessment Officer for three seasons.

I re-joined the Western League Board in 2015 as Finance Director, a role I still perform today alongside my time assessing.

Whilst on the officials list I acted as an Assistant Referee on the Premiership and Football League; the latter from 1989 to 2001.

I was Assistant Referee in the 1993 FA Youth Cup Final between Manchester United and Leeds United at Old Trafford, when the referee was another ex-Western League official, Paul Durkin. It was more enjoyable because that was the year which saw David Beckham, Paul Scholes, Nicky Butt, the Neville brothers and Robbie Savage all part of the Manchester United squad.

Other notable games that I have refereed include the Somerset Premier Cup Final between Yeovil Town v Bristol City, the Gloucestershire Senior Cup Final, between Mangotsfield United v Patchway, and the Somerset Senior Cup Final between Brislington v Saltford.

I am currently a referee coach for Somerset FA and both a Trustee and coach for Refsupport UK, the first registered charity to be involved in refereeing. This is work which I find very rewarding and gives me a break from looking at numbers, invoices and bank statements.

I feel proud and privileged to have been associated with the Western League for so long. I have no doubt that in terms of hospitality and friendliness the League has always set a very high standard across all its member clubs, which my wife, Teresa and I have enjoyed, to have achieved this so consistently for all 36 years of my involvement is a fantastic testament to all the club volunteers.

GEORGE McCAFFERY

Fixtures Secretary & Director 2017-

George is a retired Royal Navy Officer, who has lived in Corsham with his wife Janice since 1993, having served for 32 years in the Royal Navy where he was an Aeronautical Engineer Officer, mainly working with the Sea Harrier.

They are both actively involved with the Guide Dogs, as Puppy Walkers, you have probably seen them at the League Convention with one of their pups over the last few years.

His experience in football has been mainly as an official, he qualified as a referee in 1976 and as he moved around the Country due to his service, was involved with the Western League as early as 1980.

Since retiring he has been involved with the Football Association as a referee tutor, coach and assessor. He introduced the referee coaching scheme as the initial coordinator of the FA's South West Referee Development Group, and as the Support Officer for the South West Supply Leagues Observers. As a result, he is well known around the clubs, attending many Western League games every season.

He also was the Chippenham Town Football Club Secretary for three seasons in 2006 in the Southern Premier League.

TONY STONE

Financial Director 2003-2015; Grading Officer 2011-

I was Promoted to the Football League as a linesman (1980-1991) and a Referee on the Football Combination. However, following the re-organisation of the system and introduction of the Panel League system for Referee's I officiated as a Referee on the Alliance League, a league that has had many changes in names since then, but now known as the National League, and Football Combination.

At that time, I also refereed on the Western League, joining such erstwhile characters as Don Morgan, Micky Gale, Paul Durkin, Roy Osborne, Steve Dunn and many, many, others during that time. On retirement from the Football League due to age restrictions I refereed my last game in the League at Weston-s-Mare v Liskeard.

I particularly remember officiating at both Les Phillips Cup Semi-Finals in the 1984/85 season, the first at Exmouth Town and the more memorable one at Bideford Town who were entertaining Melksham Town. I remember the after-match hospitality most vividly from that day where I met up with the then Melksham Chairman, the late Jack Goodenough who really knew how to enjoy the after-match entertainment!

I also had the honour that year of being appointed by the FA to referee what was an annual fixture; the FAXI v Western League.

I then undertook referee assessments for the following season, but called it a day due to other commitments in the football world. During that time, I worked with both Maurice Washer at first, and then Cliff Ashton, in their roles as Referee Secretary, and when Malcolm Taylor indicated he was to stand down as the Western League Treasurer, Cliff Ashton, who was by then League Chairman, contacted me to suggest I might consider making an application.

I had also known Cliff for many years through the GFA, and his connection with two local Bristol leagues where I have been Treasurer since 1979, and so I applied and was called for an interview at Bridgwater Town FC, by what seemed the whole Committee. Despite the nerves, it went well and I was successful in being appointed.

I became involved in ground grading due to my personal interest in

Stadiums, and have really enjoyed it over the past few years. Out in the open air assisting clubs in meeting the FA requirements is invigorating and indeed satisfying when clubs improve their facilities either to be accepted to join the League or indeed to move onto higher levels at Step 4. There have been many successes during the last few years where I have worked in an advisory role with clubs on the grading front, with such examples as Barnstaple Town, Buckland Athletic, Bristol Manor Farm, Slimbridge and most recently Chipping Sodbury.

My success in the role has also seen me being employed by the FA as a Ground Inspector where I am also involved with Southern league clubs at Steps 3 & 4 as well as in other reviews at Steps 5 & 6. I feel this is also a feather in the league's cap with the relationship maintained with the FA.

Since that time there have been many changes to the administration of the League with the introduction of IT and increased Sponsorship. Both myself and my wife, Karen have enjoyed the very good relationship I had with the Secretary, Ken and Pat Clarke. I handed over the reins of Finance Director to Dave Brammer in 2015.

MARK ROGERS

Match Officials Officer

RICHARD MELLIN

Match Officials Assessors Officer

MIKE BLESSING

Director

GEOFF ENDICOTT

League Director 2015-

My interest in football began as a schoolboy and since then I have been a player, referee, club administrator, league management committee member, Gloucestershire County Football Association Councillor and a Board Member of the Western League.

Whilst at school I played for Bath City reserves in the Western League when Arnold Rodgers was manager, along with his son David, who later played for Bristol City. I was a member of the Bristol Rovers Youth Team and played alongside such distinguished players as Phil Roberts, Larry Lloyd, Frankie Prince, Bobby Brown and Wayne Jones, all of whom had distinguished playing careers, Sadly I never made it. As a player, I played for Shaftesbury Crusade, St James YC, Lockleaze Community Association, Winterbourne Utd, and Old Georgians, finishing playing in 1982.

In 1975, I became Secretary of Winterbourne United who were at that time in the Bristol Premier Combination and was with them throughout their progression through the Gloucestershire County League, the Hellenic League through to the Toolstation Western League. I was the Secretary of their first team until their withdrawal from that league in December 2015.

When finished playing I took up refereeing in the Bristol and District League and the Bristol Premier Combination and was promoted through the Gloucestershire County League, then the Western League and onto the

Football Combination and FA Conference. I finished refereeing at this level in 1993 when the upper age limit was forty-three, a limit which was at the time enforceable but which is now no longer acceptable in terms of equality. I remember it being very contentious at the time as well.

My time on the Western League as a linesman and then as a referee was a very enjoyable time and visits to Plymouth Argyle, Exmouth, Dawlish, Falmouth, Bideford, Saltash, Liskeard, Torrington and Barnstaple were pleasant excursions especially on Bank Holidays when the M5 was often a car park. We also enjoyed the shorter journeys Taunton, Weston, and Tiverton, ironic that none of the clubs are still with the Western League.

As a Panel League official, I was fortunate enough to visit Highbury, Upton Park, Stamford Bridge and of course The Den where in a Football Combination match the only spectator on one side of the ground wanted to dispute every decision given by our own George Fowler, who was acting as Linesman.

At an FA Cup match in Merthyr Tydfil the crowd showed just how much they appreciated English officials when referee Steve Dunn quite rightly dismissed a Merthyr player whilst he was being stretchered off. Hostility is an understatement. We were taken to the local pub by the clubs' Liaison Officer rather than risk a visit upstairs to the Boardroom.

Another interesting experience was in the Conference at Wycombe Wanderers, managed by Martin O'Neill, with Macclesfield Town, managed by Sammy McIlroy. Wycombe were unbeaten at the time. By the final whistle their unbeaten record had been surrendered, two Wycombe players dismissed and both Martin O'Neill and Director Alan Parry received sanctions from the FA for post-match remarks to the referee. On this occasion, we had a police motor cycle escort us to the M4.

In 2006, I was elected to the Gloucestershire Football Association as a Councillor to represent the Challenge Trophy clubs and since then have been actively involved with Cups, Discipline and Rules Revision.

In 2015, I became a Director of the Toolstation Western League, a role in which I play a leading part in the management and continuing success of the league.

In January 2016, I joined Chipping Sodbury Town mainly to enable me to continue my work on both the GFA and the Western League Board. However, I have enjoyed being with the club so much that I have decided to take on the role of Secretary of their Western League side for the 2017/18 season. The club also has teams in the Bristol Premier Combination and the Bristol and District Leagues and I will be actively involved in the running of these leagues as a member of their management committees'.

JULIAN FRENCH

Director 2015-

SUE MERRILL

League Management Committee in 1996; Company Director 2002 -

Sue was born just down the road from Badgers Hill, home to Frome Town FC, and in her early years was a regular supporter of the club. She met and married Kelvin, who lived next to the club, and became the Frome Town Football Secretary from 1987 until 2000.

Sue joined the Western League Board at the start of the 1996/97 season and has been an active member ever since that time, with a huge amount of work each season devoted to the organisation of the Annual League Convention, alongside being the League Charter Standard and Respect Coordinator, organiser of the Long Service awards, and in her words – various other jobs that nobody else wants to take on!

During her long service with the League she has also represented Larkhall Athletic and is now been a member of Bradford Town for the past three years.

MARTIN PAINTER

League Management Committee 2011-

I played local football until I was 25, then retired from playing after breaking both my legs in a car accident.

I then returned to football at the age of 35 years to become a referee, progressing to the old Level One, refereeing and assisting on the Gloucestershire County League, Western League, local leagues and the Avon Youth League.

At 45 years old, I moved on from refereeing to manage an Under16 boys team at Cadbury Heath FC. Two years later became Secretary and Treasurer of Cadbury Heath who at that time had just joined the Western League. Joined the Western League Board of Directors in 2011 as club representative. At present, still Secretary and Treasurer at Cadbury Heath FC, and still on the Board of Directors of the Western League.

MALCOLM PRICE

League Director 2014 -

I first become involved with Welton Rovers in the early 1970s when I relocated from London for business. Prior to moving I supported amateur football, as it was then called, supporting the local club of Wealdstone who won the F. A. Amateur Cup in 1966.

At Welton Rovers I assisted in match day requirements and become involved in day to day running of the club and was appointed a Director in October

1975 and appointed Financial Director the following year, a position I held for over forty years before stepping down.

During my involvement with Welton Rovers, I have held every position within the club from Chairman, Company Secretary and to assisting with ground repairs and cleaning the changing rooms.

In June and July 2007 parts of the main stand were damaged by fire on two occasions due to arson. Following negotiations with the ground trustees and part funding from The Football Stadia Improvement Fund we could complete the installation of two new grandstands in May 2015.

In September 2006, I was invited to join the board of the Western League as Club Director. Representing clubs within the league at board level. It is a role that I have enjoyed enormously together with my wife, Carol.

The pinnacle of my involvement with Welton Rovers was the success of winning the Somerset Premier Cup in May 2010 beating Bridgwater Town in the final.

I am currently Chairman, and have been Football Secretary for the last 14 years.

ROD WEBBER

Vice Chairman 1988-1996; Chairman 1996-2000; President 2000-2010; Immediate Past President 2010 -

I have always thought of my time with the Western League as a sort of fairy tale!

It started one Saturday in 1976 when the then vice Chairman of Exmouth Town called to me in our shop doorway and asked if I liked gardening; it turned out that they needed a groundsman! My immediate thought was that our shop was open on a Saturday, but then thought - well I have got Heather; everyone needs a 'Heather' – and that was the start of my love affair with the Western League.

I will not use too many names for fear of missing some, Ray Clements was my Chairman and I became Vice-Chairman; Geoff Morris was Secretary. In 1984, I became Chairman and we won the Premier Division. In 1988, I resigned from Exmouth and within two days, Stan Priddle rang me to ask if I would be co-opted onto the League Management Committee as Vice-Chairman, which was a very proud moment.

We both agreed totally on policy and beside Stan, those people who made my Chairmanship possible are my wife, Heather, Maurice Washer, Joan Ellis, Mike Crichton, Brian Beer, Cliff Ashton and Doug Webb.

My love for the Western League has increased each year and I am proud of my part in making the League as good as it is.

I wish the present Board of Directors all the luck and best wishes for the future.

ACKNOWLEDGEMENTS

Our thanks go to all who contributed to *'A View from the Terraces'* in 1992, and to those who contributed to this book, especially....

John Pool, Chairman and Director of the Western Football League

Ken Clarke, Company Secretary and Director of the Western Football League

Andy Radford, General Secretary and Director of the Western Football League

Ian Nockolds, Western League Podcast

John Cuthbertson, photographer - www.johncuppy.co.uk

Keith Fussell, photographer

Mike Hall, photographer

Rob Mitchell, front cover picture

Chris Perry of Corsham Print

Ron Low and Kevin Ford

Steve Small, Clevedon Town Historian

Mark and Sarah Edmonds

Denise Joyce and Pat Clarke

Ian Madge

Mel Barnett, Curator at Chippenham Museum and all her wonderful staff and volunteers

The Wiltshire and Swindon History Centre

All Member Clubs who have contribute

BIBLIOGRAPHY

'A View from the Terraces' by Sandie and Doug Webb 1992

Western Football League Handbooks, 1991-2017

Richard Rundle at the Football Club History Data Base

The British Newspaper Archives online

Western League Almanac 1892-2015 by Mike Blackstone

Wikipedia: the free Encyclopaedia

Soccer Statistics Foundation

'The Boys on the Hill', the official history of Frome Town FC by Kerry Miller

'Western Beat' by Brian Moore, Sunday Independent Newspaper

'Hammond has Golden Chance' By Ian King

The Times Newspaper 2016